T0180756

Lecture Notes in Computer Science 14475

Founding Editors

Gerhard Goos
Juris Hartmanis

The series Lecture Notes in Computer Science (LNCS), including its subseries Lecture Notes in Artificial Intelligence (LNAI) and Lecture Notes in Bioinformatics (LNBI), has established itself as a medium for the publication of new developments in computer science and information technology research, teaching, and education.

LNCS enjoys close cooperation with the computer science R & D community, the series counts many renowned academics among its volume editors and paper authors, and collaborates with prestigious societies. Its mission is to serve this international community by providing an invaluable service, mainly focused on the publication of conference and workshop proceedings and postproceedings. LNCS commenced publication in 1973.

Pierpaolo Dondio · Mariana Rocha ·
Attracta Brennan · Avo Schönbohm ·
Francesca de Rosa · Antti Koskinen ·
Francesco Bellotti
Editors

Games and Learning Alliance

12th International Conference, GALA 2023
Dublin, Ireland, November 29 – December 1, 2023
Proceedings

Springer

Editors
Pierpaolo Dondio 🆔
Technological University Dublin
Dublin, Ireland

Attracta Brennan
University of Galway
Galway, Ireland

Francesca de Rosa 🆔
CAPTRS
Austin, TX, USA

Francesco Bellotti 🆔
University of Genova
Genoa, Italy

Mariana Rocha
Technological University Dublin
Dublin, Ireland

Avo Schönbohm
Berlin School of Economics and Law
Berlin, Germany

Antti Koskinen 🆔
Tampere University
Tampere, Finland

ISSN 0302-9743   ISSN 1611-3349 (electronic)
Lecture Notes in Computer Science
ISBN 978-3-031-49064-4   ISBN 978-3-031-49065-1 (eBook)
https://doi.org/10.1007/978-3-031-49065-1

This Springer imprint is published by the registered company Springer Nature Switzerland AG
The registered company address is: Gewerbestrasse 11, 6330 Cham, Switzerland

Paper in this product is recyclable.

Preface

This volume includes contributions from the Games and Learning Alliance (GALA) conference, which is dedicated to the advancement of research into serious games. The twelfth edition of the GALA conference was held in Dublin, Ireland, November 29th – December 1st, 2023. This edition was organized by the Serious Games Society (SGS) and Technological University Dublin.

The 'rich' three-day event provided an international discussion forum to advance the theories, technologies, and knowledge that support the design, development, and deployment of serious games. GALA 2023 received 88 paper submissions from academic researchers and practitioners from 25 countries. Each paper was reviewed by three Program Committee members. The accepted papers, covering various aspects of serious game theories and applications, were presented in nine paper sessions (36 full papers) and a poster session (13 short papers).

The papers contained in this book have been organized into six categories, reflecting the variety of theoretical approaches and application domains of research into serious games.

The *Serious Games and Game Design* section presents novel design methodologies for serious games, game element classification frameworks, and the design of new control devices, such as a sensor-filled hat for controlling the game using brain waves.

The *User Experience, User Evaluation and User Analysis in Serious Games* section presents research which investigates the complex relationship between player traits, game elements, and user experience in serious games, in particular the engagement, motivation, and performance of players. It also contains papers on user analytics and user assessment strategies for serious games.

The *Serious Games for Instruction* section includes papers that consider the use of games in a variety of learning contexts in formal and informal education, including games for chemistry, biology, economy, healthcare, cybersecurity, and cultural heritage.

The *Serious Games for Health, Wellbeing and Social Change* section includes games aimed at encouraging a healthier lifestyle addressing and promoting pro-social behaviors and the wellbeing of players. This section includes serious games to address cyberbullying, promote equality in remote areas, and improve stakeholder decision-making processes during a pandemic. It also includes games to promote physical activity for elderly people, help autistic adolescents express their emotions, and motivate children engaged in speech training therapy.

The *Evaluating and Assessing Serious Games Elements* section includes papers which focus on the evaluation of serious game elements such as design choices, different input modalities, game mechanics, and computer-generated dialogue.

Finally, the *Poster* section addresses various topics, ranging from game feedback system taxonomy, to serious games for astronomy, leadership, and blended learning, and novel applications of serious games in the fields of cognitive load measurement, exam anxiety mitigation, and personality assessment.

We were delighted to have three prominent keynote speakers, Luca Chittaro (University of Udine, Italy), Alf Wang (Norwegian University of Science and Technology, Norway), and the BAFTA-winner game designer Brenda Romero.

Prof. Chittaro discussed immersive games for training in dangerous and hazardous situations, Ms. Romero delivered a talk on the expressive power of games for education, and Prof. Wang, the inventor of *Kahoot!*, talked about the evaluation of serious games for formal education.

The conference featured a Game Exhibition and a *"Games for a better world"* game competition with the aim of rewarding games that positively impact society, community, and well-being. The game competition received 34 submissions in the following three categories: business, academic, and student. Twelve shortlisted games were invited to demo their games at the conference.

As in previous years, the authors of the selected best papers presented at the GALA conference will be invited to submit an extended version of their paper for a dedicated special issue of the International Journal of Serious Games, the scientific journal managed by the Serious Games Society, indexed by the Emerging Sources Citation Index (ESCI), in the Web of Science Core Collection since 2015, and by Scopus since 2020.

We thank the authors for submitting many interesting papers and the international Program Committee for their careful and timely review of these papers. We are also thankful to our conference sponsors for their financial support: the Science Foundation Ireland *Happy Maths* project, the TU Dublin School of Computer Science, and CAPTRS, the Center for Advanced Preparedness and Threat Response Simulation. Finally, we gratefully acknowledge the Serious Games Society and Technological University Dublin for organizing the conference.

November 2023

Pierpaolo Dondio
Mariana Rocha
Attracta Brennan
Francesca de Rosa
Antti Koskinen
Avo Schönbohm
Francesco Bellotti

Organization

General Chair

Pierpaolo Dondio Technological University Dublin, Ireland

Program Chairs

Mariana Rocha Technological University Dublin, Ireland
Attracta Brennan University of Galway, Ireland
Antti Koskinen Tampere University, Finland
Francesca de Rosa Center for Advanced Preparedness and Threat
  Response Simulation, USA
Avo Schönbohm Berlin School of Economics and Law, Germany

Competition Chairs

Kristina Risley University of Southampton, UK
Vanissa Wanick University of Southampton, UK

Exhibition Chair

Bryan Duggan Technological University Dublin, Ireland

Publication Chair

Riccardo Berta University of Genoa, Italy

Local Arrangements Chair and Support

Ciarán O'Leary Technological University Dublin, Ireland
Ilaria Furlan Technological University Dublin, Ireland

Administrative and Financial Chair

Francesco Bellotti   University of Genoa, Italy

Program Committee

Alessandra Tesei	NATO Science and Technology Organization, CMRE, Italy
André Almo	Technological University Dublin, Ireland
Angel Torres-Toukoumidis	Universidad Politécnica Salesiana, Ecuador
Bryan Duggan	Technological University Dublin, Ireland
Carolina Islas Sedano	University of Turku, Finland
Chiara Catalano	Italian National Research Council (CNR), Italy
Ciaran O'Leary	Technological University Dublin, Ireland
Dirk Ifenthaler	Universität Mannheim, Germany
Dominique Jaccard	University of Applied Science of Western Switzerland, Switzerland
Elena Camossi	NATO Science and Technology Organization, CMRE, Italy
Elena Novak	Kent State University, USA
Francesco Bellotti	Università degli Studi di Genova, Italy
Francesco Zanichelli	University of Parma, Italy
George Kritikos	University of the Aegean, Greece
George Lepouras	University of Peloponnese, Greece
Georgios Fesakis	University of the Aegean, Greece
Giuseppe Città	Italian National Research Council (CNR), Italy
Heinrich Söbke	Bauhaus-Universität Weimar, Germany
Herre Van Oostendorp	Utrecht University, The Netherlands
Ioana Andreea Stefan	Advanced Technology Systems, Romania
Iza Marfisi-Schottman	Le Mans Université, France
Jake McMullen	University of Turku, Finland
Jannicke Baalsrud Hauge	KTH Royal Institute of Technology, Sweden
Johan Jerung	Utrecht University, The Netherlands
Kevin Korner	Eberhard Karls Universität Tübingen, Germany
Kostas Karpouzis	Panteion University of Social and Political Sciences, Greece
Lahcen Oubahssi	Le Mans Université, France
Luca Botturi	Scuola Universitaria professionale della Svizzera italiana, Swizterland
Luca Lazzaroni	University of Genova, Italy
Ludovic Hamon	Le Mans Université, France
Maira Amaral	Technological University Dublin, Ireland

Manuel Gentile	Italian National Research Council (CNR), Italy
Manuel Ninaus	TU Graz, Austria
Marco Temperini	Sapienza University of Rome, Italy
Margarida Romero	Université Côte d'Azur, France
Maria B. Carvalho	Tilburg University, The Netherlands
Maria Popescu	Carol I National Defence University, Romania
Marianna Cossu	Università degli Studi di Genova, Italy
Marius Preda	Institut Polytechnique de Paris, France
Matheus Cezarotto	New Mexico State University, USA
Mathieu Murat	LIP6 Sorbonne University, France
Matthias Teine	University Paderborn, Germany
Michael Kickmeier Rust	St. Gallen University of Teacher Education, Switzerland
Michael Saiger	University of York, UK
Michela Mortara	Italian National Research Council (CNR), Italy
Nour El Mawas	Université de Lille, France
Pedro A. Santos	INESC-ID, University of Lisbon, Portugal
Phuong Bui	University of Turku, Finland
Pierre Laforcade	Le Mans Université, France
Rafael Bidarra	Delft University of Technology, The Netherlands
Ramesh Gorantla	Arizona State University, USA
René Röpke	RWTH Aachen University, Germany
Riccardo Berta	Università degli Studi di Genova, Italy
Riikka Aurava	University of Tampere, Finland
Rob Nadolski	Open University of the Netherlands, The Netherlands
Roger Azevedo	University of Central Florida, USA
Sam Redfern	University of Galway, Ireland
Sari Merilampi	Satakunta University of Applied Sciences, Finland
Simon Hoermann	University of Canterbury, New Zealand
Sinead Impey	Trinity College Dublin, Ireland
Stefanie Vanbecelaere	KU Leuven, Belgium
Stelios Xinogalos	University of Macedonia, Greece
Thierry Nabeth	P-Val Conseil, France
Timothy Gallagher	Utrecht University, The Netherlands
Toby Best	Queen Mary University of London, UK
Varvara Garneli	Ionian University, Greece
Ville Kankainen	Aalto University, Finland
Vipin Verma	Arizona State University, USA
Vlasios Kasapakis	University of the Aegean, Greece
Yoones Sekhavat	Tabriz Art University, Iran
Yunjo An	University of North Texas, USA

Contents

Serious Games and Game Design

Posters

Serious Games for Instruction

An Engaging Serious Game that Strengthens High School Students' Understanding of the Periodic Table

Thomas Bjørner$^{(\boxtimes)}$![ORCID], Nick B. Blume, Nicolaj J. D. Frederiksen, Victor S. Hjort, Amalie F. H. Mørck, and Martin Ø. Petersen

Department of Architecture, Design and Media Technology, Aalborg University, A.C. Meyersvænge 15, 2450 Copenhagen, SV, Denmark
tbj@create.aau.dk

Abstract. This study aimed to strengthen Danish high school students' understanding of the periodic table by designing a serious game. The study included 46 students from two classes in chemistry. One class with 24 students was included in the experimental study, which employed game-based learning as part of understanding the periodic table. One class with 22 students served as the control group and engaged only in an analog reading of the periodic table. The evaluation consisted of data logging, a knowledge test, a questionnaire with items from the user engagement scale, and interviews with 12 students. The findings revealed the game engaged the students. Students in the experimental gaming group reported significantly higher positive engagement than the control group did. The knowledge test revealed, that in four out of six questions, the gaming group answered more correctly than the control group did. Interestingly, the highest percentage of correct answers was a question linked to a game-designed surprise with an alarm.

Keywords: Serious games · Game-based learning · chemistry · knowledge test · surprise · engagement

1 Introduction

Many high school students struggle to learn chemistry concepts [1–4], including the periodic table, as part of the mandatory curriculum. Even though chemistry grades have improved over the past 10 years, chemistry is still among the lowest scoring subjects for Danish high school students [5]. These difficulties might underpin their entire experience with chemistry [1–4] or even disciplines related to science, technology, engineering, and mathematics (STEM) disciplines in general [4, 6]. Previous studies have addressed some of the reasons why chemistry is a difficult subject for many students [1–4, 6]. Scholars have especially emphasized the gap between abstract, difficult chemistry concepts and the world in which they live; this also includes language and syntax difficulties related to misunderstandings of the connections between models, symbols, and the microscopic and macroscopic levels [6, 7]. Given these difficulties and the imagination required to connect concepts to real-life situations [3], various attempts to use gamification and

P. Dondio et al. (Eds.): GALA 2023, LNCS 14475, pp. 3–12, 2024.
https://doi.org/10.1007/978-3-031-49065-1_1

serious gaming to increase learning motivation in chemistry and to fill the gap between the abstract level and the real world have been presented [2, 3, 6, 8–10]. However, there is still a need to direct serious gaming to address specific learning objectives in chemistry [3]. The background of using serious gaming in chemistry is based on the idea that games, because of their ability to engage and excite [2, 3, 6, 9, 10], can provide a level of learning engagement. However, there is currently a lack of games that focus on specific learning objectives for understanding the periodic table and that follow the curriculum for chemistry in Danish high schools. The periodic table is an important foundation in chemistry, and subsequent learning assumes an understanding [11] of it. This study is based on the following research question: What is the impact in terms of engagement and knowledge acquisition of a serious game to understand the periodic table?

2 Previous Research

Previous research on serious games focused on teaching chemistry has shown positive effects on especially students' engagement and motivation [12–15]. Studies investigating whether the periodic table can be taught through serious games have focused on both physical and digital games [16, 17]. Studies have already investigated the effects of digital games when teaching the periodic table [17, 21–23]. Previous studies have presented some empirical short-term evidence that serious games can have a positive effect on student learning achievement and learning attitudes in chemistry [2, 3]. However, there is still a need for serious chemistry games that act as an interface for presenting specific chemistry concepts, and games that can be used both in class and at home as part of the students' homework. Previous research has described multiple principles for serious games in a learning context, including the important aspects of motivation, learning goals, engagement, realism, feedback, discovery, repetition, guidance, flow, storytelling, social interaction, briefing, and debriefing [24–27]. However, an important aspect of a successful serious game that strengthens high school students' understanding of the periodic table is to include the teacher. Scholars have argued that teachers are key to the success of serious games for educational purposes [27–29] as a tool to motivate students and promote deep learning. In this study, we provided the teacher with the necessary gaming knowledge and skills to allow her to integrate game-based learning effectively and efficiently [28, 29]. The teacher provided the learning objectives and made the calibration of the difficulty and the content of the game. The teacher also provided important instructions for the game in a pedagogical approach [11] and included supplementary learning materials in the teaching progression.

3 Methods

3.1 Participants

This study is made in cooperation with a Danish high school. The high school has 750 students, 80 teachers, and two study lines including basic chemistry. This study included two classes consisting of 46 students in chemistry. Class A consisted of 24 students (Age mean: 16.86. Interested in Chemistry, mean: 3.71, 5-point Likert scale). Class

A functioned as the experimental group that used the serious game about the periodic table. Class B consisted of 22 students (Age mean: 16.91. Interested in Chemistry, mean: 3.73, 5-point Likert scale). Class B functioned as a control group for the evaluation, provided with the same reading and evaluation criteria, but without playing the game (analog reading about the periodic table). The teacher in chemistry selected which of the classes would be in the experimental group and which would be the control group. All participants gave informed consent and were informed they could withdraw from the study at any time and their participation did not influence their grade. In addition, all participants were provided with anonymous ID numbers, and all data were labeled with these IDs. We applied special considerations when recruiting teenagers (ages 16–18) in accordance with Danish data law, the international code of conduct, and ethical approval from the high school.

3.2 Procedure and Data Analysis

Students in the experimental group were seated individually in a quiet space in front of a laptop made ready for playing the game. The students were provided with a short briefing on the procedure. Then the students individually played the game, and after the game, they filled out a questionnaire including six knowledge test questions corresponding to the learning objectives. Further, included in the questionnaire were eight items from the User Engagement Scale – Short Form (UES-SF) [30], presented on a 5-point Likert scale. The data logging that was used included speed, number of hints provided, and score/points. After filling in the questionnaires, students were selected for interviews. Twelve students were interviewed, grouped in pairs of two, giving six interviews in total. The students were also interviewed in pairs of two to facilitate a comfortable environment and bring spontaneity to the interviews [31].

Students in the control group were provided with the same briefing and had the same learning objectives but with an analog text read. The control group was provided the same knowledge test and questionnaire (UES-SF items) as the experimental group. However, we did not conduct interviews with students in the control group.

A Shapiro–Wilk test was used to assess the normality of data collected from the knowledge test and the UES-SF. Because the data was non-parametric, a Mann–Whitney U test was conducted. The interview data was coded using Nvivo 12 and was deductively coded. Two coders independently coded the verbatim transcribed interviews. An intercoder reliability test (ICR) was performed to determine the degree of agreement between the coders in selecting coded statements [32]. The test resulted in a Cohen's Kappa value of $\kappa \approx 0.7832$, which determined the level of agreement to be substantial.

4   Design and Implementation

The game was developed in Unity version 2022.2.5f1, where the programming language C# is used. The game takes place in a warehouse, where the boxes for delivery are situated as in the periodic table (Fig. 1). The game was designed based on the principles of player enjoyment that Sweetser and Wyeth suggested [33]. The implementation of each principle from Sweetser and Wyeth is shown in Table 1. We supplemented Sweetser and

Wyeth's principles with the principle of surprise [26, 34]. Included surprises in the game design can be used to facilitate reasoning skills and improve the learning effect [20, 34]. By that, surprising events should be considered to reveal the potential of serious games, where learners might obtain significantly more knowledge structures and foster more in-depth learning than those without surprising events [19]. The game can be watched with much further details on YouTube [35].

Table 1. The game design principles and the applied game design.

Concentration: To help concentration, the game used integrated text-based prompts (Fig. 1, top center) and strategically positioned visual cues (e.g., color/table explanation) within the game environment to facilitate task-solving and information retrieval (Fig. 1)
Challenge: To match the right level of challenge, the difficulty was set according to the students' educational material (textbook) and in collaboration with the teacher. Further, helpful hints were included if some of the learning tasks were too challenging. Examples of included tasks in the game were "I need an element from group 17", "I need all the alkali metals", and "What is the atomic mass of Lithium"
Player skills: All students, regardless of game experience, should be able to play the game easily. Therefore, the game was designed as a simple point-and-click game. A display showing the controls was also added to the game to ensure students would not get stuck in the game (Fig. 1)
Controls and clear goals: The controls were presented clearly to the student upon starting the game. To ensure everyone understood the controls, they were presented both visually and with text. The points were integrated to give the students a clear goal
Feedback: The students received feedback by acknowledging their completion of a task, such as "thanks" (Tak), "you made it," "very good," etc. (Fig. 2). This was followed by further information about the collected chemical elements. The accumulated points gathered in each task were displayed in the upper right corner of the game (Fig. 1)
Immersion: The game imitated a warehouse with chemical elements, containers, and barrels (Fig. 1, Fig. 2). Further, non-playable stereotyped scientists (Fig. 2) came into the warehouse and ordered various tasks/boxes from the periodic table. The scientists were made as stereotyped characters including an Albert Einstein looking. Male and female scientists were equally represented
Surprise: A surprise was placed in the game because it is considered essential to a serious game's effectiveness [26, 34]. The surprise was placed at specific spots in the game to support essential information presented in the game. The surprise was a spinning red light (Fig. 2), and a scientist was coming into the warehouse with an emergency task

5   Findings

5.1   Knowledge Test and Log Data

The knowledge test revealed that in four out of six questions, the experimental group (EXP) scored higher than the control group (CON) (Table 2). LG3 has the largest gap between the two groups, 19 students (79%) in the EXP answered correctly and only 8

Fig. 1. The warehouse with the periodic table

Fig. 2. The included surprise (red alarm), and the scientist ordering different tasks

students (36%) in the CON did. Interestingly, it was also for LG3 that we implemented the in-game surprise with the alarm. The lower scores for the EXP in LG1 and LG2 were a bit unexpected, and they did not correspond with the set learning goals from the teacher. Comparing the results to the success criteria of the learning goals, three out of six learning goals (LG4, LG5, and LG6) were met. LG3 was almost met with 79% correct answers. The results from the knowledge test revealed no significant difference between the EXP and the CON, with a p-value of 0.38 (z-test: − 0.88).

In total, 14 tasks needed to be solved in the game. The log data revealed that most hints were given at later stages in the game, with task 11 and task 13 needing 21 and 19 hints, respectively. Tasks 1–6 are all tasks related to the groups and periods in the periodic table, and participants only needed 13 hints (in total) during this part of the

Table 2. Findings from the knowledge test. EXP = Gaming group (n = 24) and CON = Analogue reading group (n = 22).

Learning goals (LG) and success criteria (in % of the students), set by the teacher		No. With correct answers	% Correct answers	Difference
LG1: 80% know that the columns in the periodic table are called groups	EXP	16	67	28%
	CON	21	95	
LG2: 80% know that the rows in the periodic table are called periods	EXP	17	71	20%
	CON	20	91	
LG3: 80% can identify which elements are alkali metals	EXP	19	79	43%
	CON	8	36	
LG4: 70% can identify sodium (Na) from the atomic structure and the periodic table	EXP	24	100	5%
	CON	21	95	
LG5: 70% can identify the average atomic mass of iodine (I) based on the periodic table	EXP	23	96	14%
	CON	18	82	
LG6: 70% can identify the number of electrons (outer shell) based on the periodic table	EXP	24	100	14%
	CON	19	86	

game. On average, the students played the game for 8 min and 28 s (range: 13 min and 7 s to 6 min and 9 s). The maximum score (points) was 7,000, and two students completed the game without using any hints and they gathered the max score. One of these students was also the one who completed the game fastest. The lowest score received was 5,100 (needed all hints possible), but the average score was 6,325 points.

5.2 Engagement

We found a significant difference in all themes for the user engagement scale (Table 3); accordingly focused attention (SD difference: 0.07. $p = 0.027$), perceived usability (SD difference: 0.38. $p = 0.007$), aesthetic appeal (SD difference: 0.35. $p = 0.037$), and reward (SD difference: 0.04. $p = 0.015$). These findings suggest that using game-based learning can positively supplement teaching chemistry among high school students. These results reflect those from previous research based on the UES-SF [18, 26], which also revealed an increased engagement in a learning context due to gaming. For all items, except Q7, there is a higher score in favor of the EXP. The three highest mean differences are found in Q1 (Mean difference: 0.77), Q8 (Mean difference: 0.71), and Q4 (Mean difference: 0.69). The items from the UES that yielded the highest mean scores were in Q4 (M = 4.17), Q5 (M = 4.08), and Q8 (M = 4.04), all in favor of the gaming group. The only item that scored higher in the CON was in Q7 (Learning about the periodic table was fun). However, we do not have any data (neither from the interviews nor any contextual information) that can explain this difference in favor of the CON.

Table 3. Engagement findings. The P-value is generated by a Mann–Whitney U test, * =< 0.05.

	EXP/CON	1	2	3	4	5	Total	Mean	Mean Diff	SD Con	SD Exp	SD Diff	p-value
Focused Attention										0.51	0.58	0.07	0.027*
Q1: The time slipped away while learning about the periodic table	EXP	0	4	12	6	2	24	3.25	0.77				
	CON	1	10	9	1	0	21	2.48					
Q2: I was absorbed in learning about the periodic table	EXP	0	5	8	10	1	24	3.29	0.19				
	CON	0	4	#	4	1	21	3.10					
Q3: I was concentrated on learning about the periodic table	EXP	0	1	5	17	1	24	3.75	0.37				
	CON	0	4	5	12	0	21	3.38					
Percieved Usability										0.59	0.94	0.38	0.007*
Q4: The periodic table was easy to read	EXP	0	2	3	8	11	24	4.17	0.69				
	CON	0	0	12	8	1	21	3.48					
Aesthetic Appeal										0.56	0.91	0.35	0.037*
Q5: Learning about the periodic table was conveyed visually well	EXP	1	0	3	12	8	24	4.08	0.41				
	CON	0	0	8	12	1	21	3.67					
Reward										0.55	0.51	0.04	0.015*
Q6: Learning about the periodic table was worthwhile	EXP	0	1	4	17	2	24	3.83	0.31				
	CON	0	2	6	13	0	21	3.52					
Q7: Learning about the periodic table was fun	EXP	1	4	5	11	3	24	3.46	0.11				
	CON	0	1	8	11	1	21	3.57					
Q8: Learning about the periodic table was interesting	EXP	0	0	4	15	5	24	4.04	0.71				
	CON	1	1	9	10	0	21	3.33					

5.3 Qualitative Findings

The interviews were coded into five themes with positive (P) and negative (N) statements (Table 4). We coded 125 positive statements in contrast to 46 negative statements. Most positive comments are within the educational value with engaging and immersive positive remarks toward the game. Most critiques regarded the functionality, and several students mentioned it was confusing to enter numbers instead of continuing to use the mouse. Several students mentioned that the tasks were too easy and the level could be increased. The included alarm (the surprise) had mixed opinions in the interviews, where some students felt it was included randomly and/or did not understand the alarm's purpose.

Table 4. Coded interviews in five themes. Number of positive (P) and negative (N) statements.

Themes	P or N	Quote examples
Challenge	P: 19	"It gave you a lot of hints, which was nice" (B: Female). "I liked it. It was an effective way of learning the periodic system" (J: Female)
	N: 11	"It could be more challenging. It was too easy to just turn and click" (H: Female). "The questions need to be harder" (F: Male)
Educational Value	P: 55	"It caught me. It was quite interesting" (D: Female). "It didn't feel long, boring and chemistry-like" (I: Female). "answering incorrectly was not that embarrassing" (A: Female)
	N: 8	"It was almost too easy" (A: Female). "You could make it in VR?" (D: Female). "I doubt that relying solely on a game would be adequate" (J: Female). "There were 18 groups in the game, but usually there are only 8, right?" (G: Male)
Func-tionality	P: 19	"I liked that you were able to zoom in" (A: Female). "It seemed pretty stable…There were no technical issues" (F: Male)
	N: 13	"…entering some numbers. That was confusing" (J: Female)
Visual Appearance	P: 18	"I liked the color-coding of the periodic table" (J: Female). "It was so cute when the scientists jubilated afterwards" (I: Female)
	N: 5	"Improve the visual quality" (A: Female). "…more realistic" (F: Male)
Surprise Element	P: 14	"There was a feeling of urgency…find it quickly" (G: Male)
	N: 9	"I didn't understand it" (C: Female). "It felt a bit random, didn't it?" (E: Male)

6   Conclusion

Students in the experimental gaming group reported significantly higher positive engagement than the control group. However, there were no significant differences in the knowledge test regarding the periodic table, but four of six questions in the knowledge test showed a higher percentage of correct answers in favor of the experimental group. The interviews revealed positive feedback toward the game as a supplement to the existing teaching. However, some students expressed a desire for other gameplay mechanics or platforms (e.g., VR) to increase the immersion. Further, the specific tasks in the game seemed a bit too easy. We conclude the most important element in developing educational games may be engagement. A successful educational game engages students and teachers, and an interplay among game play, students, and teachers can create some dynamic learning opportunities. However, a core foundation for making these learning opportunities possible is having the right balance of skills and challenges for the participants, both within specific learning objectives and for controlling gameplay. A further direction for the game design could be to increase the game's competitiveness and personalization by including the students' knowledge and motivation. The game could also be improved by having groups of students play the game and solving the various tasks jointly.

References

1. Brecher, J.: Name=struct: a practical approach to the sorry state of real-life chemical nomenclature. J. Chem. Inf. Comput. Sci. **39**(6), 943–950 (1999)
2. Wood, J., Donnelly-Hermosillo, D.F.: Learning chemistry nomenclature: comparing the use of an electronic game versus a study guide approach. Comput. Educ. **141**, 103615 (2019)
3. Srisawasdi, N., Panjaburee, P.: Implementation of game-transformed inquiry-based learning to promote the understanding of and motivation to learn chemistry. J. Sci. Educ. Technol. **28**(2), 152–164 (2018)
4. Lamb, R., Akmal, T., Petrie, K.: Development of a cognition priming model describing learning in a STEM classroom. J. Res. Sci. Teach. **52**(3), 410–437 (2015)
5. Educational statistics. https://uddannelsesstatistik.dk/Pages/Reports/1694.aspx. Accessed 01 Sept 2023
6. Suits, J.P., Srisawasdi, N.: Use of an interactive computer-simulated experiment to enhance students' mental models of hydrogen bonding phenomena. In: ACS Symposium Series, pp. 241–271 (2013)
7. Taskin, V., Bernholt, S.: Students' understanding of chemical formulae: a review of empirical research. Int. J. Sci. Educ. **36**(1), 157–185 (2014)
8. Ferrer, V., Perdomo, A., Rashed-Ali, H., Fies, C., Quarles, J.: How does usability impact motivation in augmented reality serious games for education? In: 5th International Conference on Games and Virtual Worlds for Serious Applications (VS-GAMES), pp. 1–8 (2013)
9. Garneli, V., Patiniotis, K., Chorianopoulos, K.: Designing multiplayer serious games with science content. Multimodal Technol. Interact. **5**(3), 1–17 (2021)
10. Baalsrud Hauge, J., Stefan, I.: Improving learning outcome by re-using and modifying gamified lessons paths. In: Ma, M., Fletcher, B., Göbel, S., Baalsrud Hauge, J., Marsh, T. (eds.) JCSG 2020. LNCS, vol. 12434, pp. 150–163. Springer, Cham (2020). https://doi.org/10.1007/978-3-030-61814-8_12
11. Krathwohl, D.R.: A revision of Bloom's taxonomy: an overview. Theory Pract. **41**(4), 212–218 (2002)
12. Bjørner, T., Hansen, L. G., Valimaa, M., Sørensen, J. U., Dobre, M.: Design and evaluation of a serious game to supplement pupils' understanding of molecular structures in chemistry. In: 7th Proceedings of Serious Games: Joint International Conference, pp. 263–275 (2021)
13. Filippas, A., Xinogalos, S.: Elementium: design and pilot evaluation of a serious game for familiarizing players with basic chemistry. Educ. Inf. Technol. 1–26 (2023)
14. Lay, A.-N., Osman, K.: Developing 21st century chemistry learning through designing digital games. J. Educ. Sci. Environ. Health **4**(1), 81–92 (2018)
15. Belova, N., Zowada, C.: Innovating higher education via game-based learning on misconceptions. Educ. Sci. **10**(9), 221 (2020)
16. Montejo Bernardo, J.M., Fernández González, A.: Chemical battleship: discovering and learning the periodic table playing a didactic and strategic board game. J. Chem. Educ. **98**(3), 907–914 (2021)
17. Plungsombat, K., Jearapan, P., Pittayanukit, T., Wongsawang, D.: Pelement: a periodic table game for elements learning. In: 2017 6th ICT International Student Project Conference (ICT-ISPC), pp. 1–4 (2017)
18. Bjørner, T., Sum, A.J., Ludvigsen, R.K., Bouquin, N.L., Larsen, F.D., Kampel, U.: Making homework fun: the effect of game-based learning on reading engagement. In: Proceedings of Information Technology for Social Good, pp. 353–359 (2022)

19. van der Spek, E.D., van Oostendorp, H.C., Meyer, J.-J.: Introducing surprising events can stimulate deep learning in a serious game. Brit. J. Educ. Technol. **44**(1), 156–169 (2012)

20. Wouters, P., van Oostendorp, H., ter Vrugte, J., vanderCruysse, S., de Jong, T., Elen, J.: The effect of surprising events in a serious game on learning mathematics. Brit. J. Educ. Technol. **48**(3), 860–877 (2016)

21. Traver, V.J., Leiva, L.A., Martí-Centelles, V., Rubio-Magnieto, J.: Educational videogame to learn the periodic table: design rationale and lessons learned. J. Chem. Educ. **98**(7), 2298–2306 (2021)

22. Birchall, J., Gatzidis, C.: The periodic table of elements via an XNA-powered serious game. Trans. Edutainment **IX**, 1–28 (2013)

23. Boletsis, C., McCallum, S.: The table mystery: an augmented reality collaborative game for chemistry education. In: 4th International Conference, SGDA, Trondheim, Norway, 25–27 September 2013, pp. 86–95 (2013)

24. Moizer, J., et al.: An approach to evaluating the user experience of serious games. Comput. Educ. **136**, 141–151 (2019)

25. Adams, E., Rollings, A.: Fundamentals of Game Design. Prentice Hall, Upper Saddle River (2007)

26. Bjørner, T., Petersen, M.S., Hansen, N.L.S., Jakobsen, G., Hendriksen, D.: How can a foundation be outlined for a successful serious game to increase reading engagement. Int. J. Serious Games **10**(1), 81–95 (2023)

27. Gros, B.: Digital games in education: the design of games-based learning environments. J. Res. Technol. Educ. **40**(1), 23–38 (2007)

28. Hansen, C.B.S., Bjørner, T.: Designing an educational game: design principles from a holistic perspective. Int. J. Learn. **17**(10), 279–290 (2011)

29. Molin, G.: The role of the teacher in game-based learning: a review and outlook. Serious Games Edutainment Appl. **2**, 649–674 (2017)

30. O'Brien, H.L., Cairns, P., Hall, M.: A practical approach to measuring user engagement with the refined user engagement scale (UES) and new UES short form. Int. J. Hum. Comput. Stud. **112**, 28–39 (2018)

31. Bjørner, T.: Data collection. In: Bjørner, T. (ed.) Qualitative Methods for Consumer Research, pp. 57–94. Hans Reitzels, Copenhagen (2015)

32. MacPhail, C., Khoza, N., Abler, L., Ranganathan, M.: Process guidelines for establishing intercoder reliability in qualitative studies. Qual. Res. **16**(2), 198–212 (2016)

33. Sweetser, P., Wyeth, P.: Gameflow: a model for evaluating player enjoyment in games. Comput. Entertain. (CIE) **3**(3), 1–24 (2005)

34. Zhonggen, Y.: A meta-analysis of use of serious games in education over a decade. Int. J. Comput. Games Technol. **2019**, 1–8 (2019)

35. Media Innovation & Game Research. https://www.youtube.com/@MEdiainnovation-GAm eresearch. Accessed 19 Nov 2023

EscapeCell: Serious Game Integration to a University Biology Course on an E-Learning Platform

Ying-Dong Liu[1]([⊠]) [ID], Bertrand Marne[2] [ID], Iza Marfisi-Schottman[2] [ID],
Tiphaine Galpin[2], and Aurore Caruso[2] [ID]

[1] University of Strasbourg, LISEC, 67000 Strasbourg, France
`yingdong.liu@etu.unistra.fr`
[2] Le Mans Université, LIUM, PRN and BIOSSE, 72085 Le Mans, France
`{bertrand.marne,iza.marfisi,tiphaine.galpin,`
`aurore.caruso}@univ-lemans.fr`

Abstract. This paper presents *EscapeCell*, a Serious Game to help undergraduate students understand plant cellular biology. Each course chapter is enriched with one mini-game, a gamification module integrated into the e-learning platform and several reminders of the game in the course material. We conducted a study on 117 students to compare their exam results with a control group from last year. We also correlated the collected feedback from the students and usage tracks. This helped us measure the usefulness of specific game elements such as a non-player character that provides help and bonus information modules hidden throughout the mini-games. The preliminary results indicate that the integration of *EscapeCell* improves students' learning outcomes in the final exam and that Blob, the virtual tutor, facilitates the usage of the mini-games. Although the bonus information modules do not directly correlate with the final exam result, they show a positive correlation with the scores of the intermediate tests - the multiple-choice questions (MCQs) - taken by the students just after playing the mini-games.

Keywords: Serious Games · cellular biology · university · e-learning platform · gamification

1 Introduction

The context of this paper is a plant cell biology course, part of the undergraduate curriculum of first-year students (approx. 120) at the Biology Faculty in Le Mans (France). The teacher in charge of this course noticed that its content was often challenging for students. They have difficulties staying motivated and grasping concepts, vocabulary and phenomena. Gamification and Serious Games (SGs) have proven to be efficient tools to engage students and enhance learning [1, 2]. Hence, we present an attempt to overcome the challenges identified by the teacher by using both dedicated serious mini-games and a specific gamification module for the e-learning platform used by students. Together, they form a whole called *EscapeCell*.

P. Dondio et al. (Eds.): GALA 2023, LNCS 14475, pp. 13–22, 2024.
https://doi.org/10.1007/978-3-031-49065-1_2

EscapeCell's design and usage are the opportunity for a study that aims to address two key research questions. The first question is: Does the use of SGs improve students' learning outcomes? This question aims to understand if *EscapeCell* is effective in this learning context. The second question is related to the effectiveness of two game elements of *EscapeCell*: a non-player character, called "Blob", and bonus information modules. Our objective is to understand the influence of Blob and the bonus information modules on the student's game experience and learning outcome.

To this end, Sect. 2 begins with a brief review of SGs and gamification in higher education and biology courses. Section 3 elaborates on the context surrounding the creation of *EscapeCell*, along with some game design elements. The experiment and data collection method will be described in Sect. 4. The results gathered will be presented and discussed in Sect. 5. Finally, Sect. 6 will conclude our research.

2   State of the Art and Scientific Positioning

Literature provides many examples of SGs on biology and cell biology for secondary school. Kara and Cheng propose two systematic reviews that show that most of them are adventure games, simulations or sport-type games [3, 4]. Authors also highlight the importance of a strong integration of the SGs in the courses and the learning environment. Nonetheless, there are few publications about SGs in (cell) biology for higher education, and the studies are not thorough enough to explore learning outcomes [5, 6].

Recent work on biology provides additional design principles [7]: SGs must help explore concepts and mechanisms that teachers cannot provide, teachers should accompany the learners during the play, and SGs must be very interactive and their design must include the teachers.

Following our cell biology teacher needs and Kara's findings [3] about the importance of SGs' integration to courses, we also explored results about e-learning platforms gamification. Recent systematic research shows few articles have addressed motivation and gamification in higher education [8]. However, recent research by Reyssier et al. [9] suggests that gamification is more suitable for our target group, which consists of less motivated learners. The most efficient approach to gamification would be one that is specifically tailored to the learner. Nevertheless, as detailed in Sect. 3, we cannot alter every aspect of the course and design a fully adaptable SG. Therefore, we focused on the findings from Reyssier et al. that can be generalized to most of our targeted learners: avatars, badges, and progress bars are harmless gamification mechanics for most player types and can be used safely to enhance motivation.

As we wanted to go further to engage learners, we wanted to explore bonuses and secondary objective mechanics. Indeed, in a wide study ($n = 27000$), Andersen et al. show that secondary objectives that support the primary goal of the game are consistently useful and very positive on the learning outcomes and motivation [10].

3   Serious Game *EscapeCell*

3.1   Objectives and Challenges of the Cell Biology Course

During the cell biology course, the lecturer introduces a large number of new terminology and complex phenomena that are not easy to grasp such as operation photosynthesis, respiration and cell concentration. Yet, these are very important to understand since they set the foundations for the following classes. The course is led in a fairly classic way, with 16 h of lectures, followed by several lab sessions. All the course material is available on a *Moodle* e-learning platform and the teacher even added extra self-evaluation MCQ. However, students do not seem to find much interest in them. At the end of the course, the students take a final test. The large number of students and the limited number of teaching hours make it difficult to change this structure or even provide a personalized follow-up. The challenge is therefore to find a way to motivate students to work on their own, beyond classroom hours, and help them remember the terminology and better understand the biological phenomena.

3.2   EscapeCell

EscapeCell is composed of three elements: a set of mini-games to review the terminology and concepts for each chapter, a gamification module integrated into the e-learning platform that encourages the students to complete the mini-games and several references to the games in the course material and during the lecture. Let us describe each of these in detail.

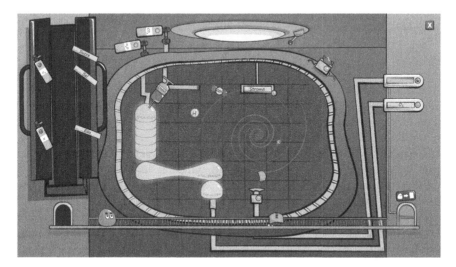

Fig. 1. Mini-game 1 - Operation photosynthesis

The course is comprised of an introductory chapter followed by five other chapters. One mini-game has been designed for each of these five chapters. Thus, *EscapeCell* includes five mini-games, three of which have been developed so far. For example, the concepts in the chloroplast and plastids chapter were used to create the *mini-game 1: Operation Photosynthesis* (Fig. 1). It is a **puzzle-type game** in which the students need to select the objects in the toolbox (left of the screen), that represent the elements in the chloroplast and correctly place them in the middle of the scene, to recreate the photosynthesis process. If the object is not positioned correctly, it flies back to its initial position in the toolbox. **A non-player character, called "Blob", provides explanations** to help the students throughout their mission (e.g., "it is too dark in here" to encourage students to switch on the light button that is necessary for photosynthesis). As students complete the scene, Blob moves forward on the bridge to materialize their progression. When the scene is complete, an animation shows the photosynthesis process which converts light into chemical energy that is then stored in organic compounds and releases gas. **Three bonus information modules are hidden in the game**. They provide extra information about the photosynthesis process. These modules can be unlocked by clicking on specific parts of the scene (e.g., lever and battery on the top right of Fig. 1). Two similar mini-games were created for chapters 2 and 3 (Fig. 2). The mini-games for the last two chapters were designed but are not yet fully developed.

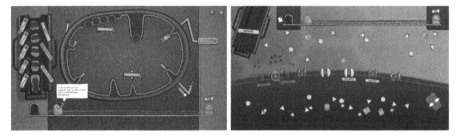

Fig. 2. Mini-game 2 - Mission respiration and Mini-game 3 - Vacuole commando

The look of the course space on the e-learning platform was completely transformed. Figure 3 shows how the artwork from the mini-games was used to illustrate the different sections of the course. When students click on the chapter related to chloroplasts and plastids (illustrated by a green Blob) for example, they have access to the slides used by the teacher during the lecture, the first mini-game in Fig. 1 and the MCQ related to this chapter. We also developed a custom gamification module for the platform that shows if the students have completed the mini-games and the MCQs. This **completion meter is presented in the form of a plant** that gradually develops. A new branch grows each time the student completes a mini-game. On each branch, **a small flower appears for each bonus** information module the student has discovered, **and a leaf will sprout if the student completes the MCQ** related to the chapter. Students see this completion meter, as a progress bar, an avatar and a set of badges, at all times, on the top right of their course space.

Finally, the teacher modified her course to integrate the game in three ways. First of all, she completely changed her slides by using the mini-games graphics to illustrate the elements in a plant cell and the biological phenomena. Second, she strongly encouraged the students to complete the mini-games and the MCQs at the beginning of each lecture. While going this, she would show the plant completion meters of the entire promotion of students on the board. Each student could see the plant associated with their name and compare it with others. This was intended to encourage students to work between lectures. Finally, the teacher also programmed a 2-h "autonomous lab session" before the final exam during which the students were asked to play or replay the mini-games and do the MCQs for each chapter.

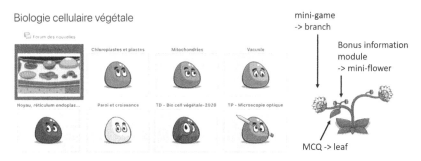

Fig. 3. Integration of EscapeCell to the e-learning platform

3.3 Design Method

The mini-games, the gamification module for the e-learning course and their integration in the lecture were designed during the *Ludifik'action* professional training session, provided by the university [11]. In addition to the two trainers, who specialize in SG design, the teacher was accompanied by a team of two educational engineers, a graphic designer, a multimedia developer and an audiovisual artist who recorded the Blob's voice. The *Moodle* plugin was also developed by a research engineer. Several groups of students were involved in the design process by testing paper prototypes of the mini-games.

4   Experimentation

4.1 Hypothesis

The experimentation aims to measure if *EscapeCell* improved students' learning performances in the final exam. A second objective is to investigate the influence of specific game design elements such as Blob and the bonus information modules. Based on the research objectives, we established the following hypotheses:

- H1: *EscapeCell* enhances students' performance in the final exam.
- H2: The presence of Blob, the non-player character, helps and guides students throughout the mini-games.
- H3: The bonus information modules, hidden in the mini-games, increase students' results in the final exam.

4.2 Experimental Protocol

This study follows the General Data Protection Regulation (GDPR), which serves as the legal reference for personal data protection in Europe. The data registration for this study was submitted to the Data Protection Officer at the University of Strasbourg.

To examine H1, we conducted a comparative study between this year's and last year's results of the final exam. It should be noted that the content of the course, the teacher and the exam were identical both years. The difference is that last year's students (n = 133) only followed the classic course before taking the final exam whereas this year's students (n = 117) also engaged in the *EscapeCell* SG and Gamification. The mini-games could be played individually or in groups on computers or smartphones.

To examine H2 and H3, this year's students were asked to answer a set of questions after completing each mini-game. For each of the five following affirmations, they needed to indicate whether they agreed or not on a 5-point Likert scale:

- A1. The mini-game is easy to use.
- A2. The game design motivated me to play.
- A3. Blob helped and guided me.
- A4. The mini-game helped me better understand the course content.
- A5. The mini-game helped me better understand the biological phenomenon.

At the end of the semester course, the students were also asked to fill in a questionnaire that provided us with information on their profile (age, sex, gaming habits) and specifically measured their learning experience in SGs using a Learner Experience Questionnaire developed by Liu [12]. Besides, several usage tracks were also retrieved from the e-learning platform such as the number of times the students completed a mini-game and the number of bonus information modules they discovered. SPSS (Statistical Package for the Social Sciences) version 27 was used for data processing in this study.

5 Results of the Study

The usage tracks show that 88 out of 117 (around 75%) completed at least one mini-game and 66 (around 56%) completed all three mini-games. 40 students also played the mini-games several times. This is already a positive result given the fact that the mini-games were not mandatory.

5.1 Results for H1: Effect of EscapeCell on the Final Exam Results

Table 1 presents a comparative analysis of the final exam results between the control group and the experimental group that used *EscapeCell*. The control group obtained a mean score of 13.65/20, with a standard deviation of 3.19, denoting a moderate spread of scores around this mean. On the other hand, the experimental group showed a higher mean score of 14.46/20. In addition, this group had a standard deviation of 2.6, indicating smaller differences in scores around the mean as compared to the control group. This lower standard deviation suggests less variability in the performance of the students who used *EscapeCell*.

Table 1. Comparison of students' final exam across the two groups

Group	n	Mean grade	Standard deviation
Control group	133	13.65	3.19
Experimental group	117	14.46	2.6

In order to analyze the significance of this difference, we examine at first the distribution of the data, then select the most suitable comparison test. Figure 4 shows that the scores of the two groups slightly deviate from a normal distribution and the Kolmogorov-Smirnov test shows that the p-value of two groups is less than 0.05, which indicates the observed data didn't follow a normal distribution [13]. We therefore apply the Mann-Whitney test, the result indicates $p = 0.026$, which is less than 0.05, and therefore indicated that the difference between the means of the two groups is statistically significant. Therefore, **we can confirm H1:** *EscapeCell* **has led to an improvement in student performance in the final exam in this study**.

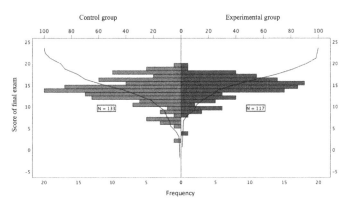

Fig. 4. Kolmogorov-Smirnov test for two independent groups

5.2 Results for H2: Usefulness of Blob

In terms of game design, we are interested in the role Blob plays in the game and if he acts as a facilitator in the students' gaming process. The results from the correlation analysis of the questionnaires indicate a positive correlation between Blob's perceived usefulness (affirmation A3) and the mini-games' perceived ease of use (affirmation A1). **The presence of Blob therefore seems to facilitate the use of the three mini-games**. However, as shown in Table 2, there are some notable differences among the mini-games. Blob seems especially useful and well-designed in the second and third mini-games and, in the third mini-game, Blob's perceived usefulness (affirmation A3) is even correlated to the fact that students understand the course content better (affirmation A4). This suggests that the presence and actions of Blob may have enhanced the usability of the game for students, making the gaming experience more intuitive and enjoyable. As such, Blob could facilitate student interaction with the game and could potentially contribute to improving learning outcomes. These results also provide us with insight on how the mini-game 1 could be improved by taking example on what Blob does in the mini-game 2 and 3.

Table 2. Impact of Blob in three mini-games.

A3. Blob usefulness	Mini-game 1	Mini-game 2	Mini-game 3
A1. Mini-game ease of use	0.349**	0.427**	0.525**
A2. Game design	0.243	0.349**	0.407**
A4. Comprehension course	0.161	0.199	0.290*
A5. Phenomena understanding	0.101	0.169	0.551

** The correlation is statistically significant at a 0.01 level.
* The correlation is statistically significant at a 0.05 level.

5.3   Results for H3: Effects of the Bonus Information Modules on the Exam

The number of bonus information modules discovered by students is positively correlated with the perceived ease of use (affirmation A1) of mini-game 2 ($r_s = 0.297$, $p < 0.05$) and mini-game 3 ($r_s = 0.380$, $p < 0.01$). Interestingly, students who unlocked more bonus information modules also achieved higher scores on the MCQ related to each chapter ($r_s = 0.320$, $p < 0.01$). The results further indicate that the MCQ scores are significantly associated with the student's final exam grade ($r_s = 0.296$, $p < 0.01$). In other words, **the more students discover bonuses, the better they are at the MCQ.** Contrarily, **there is no correlation between the number of bonuses a student receives and their final exam scores.** When we look at the students' profiles, it appears that the frequency with which students play video games (gaming habits) has a positive influence on the number of bonuses they discover. Indeed, students who are casual to hard-core gamers demonstrate a higher propensity to unlock bonus in the mini-games. There is, however, no correlation between the frequency with which students play video games and their MCQ scores. This suggests that, although students may derive additional value from these mini-games, it does not necessarily guarantee a high performance in the final exam (Table 3).

5.4   Limitations

Even though this year's exam results are very encouraging for H1, this could be due to an overall better level of the students, a pre-test is required for further study. The teacher did notice that this year's promotion was "particularly motivated and pleasant". We could argue that their pleasantness and motivation could be due to *EscapeCell* and the fact that the teacher visibly went out of her way to provide a motivating experience

Table 3. Impact of Bonus Information Modules

Impact of bonus	Number of discovered bonuses
Gaming habits	0.220*
MCQ scores	0.320**
Scores of final exam	0.204
Perceived ease of use for Mini-game 1	0.125
Perceived ease of use for Mini-game 2	0.297*
Perceived ease of use for Mini-game 3	0.380**

** The correlation is statistically significant at the 0.01 level.
* The correlation is statistically significant at the 0.05 level.

by setting it up. In addition, only 3 out of the 5 mini-games were finalized this year so the final exam results could be even better with all 5 games. However, this hypothesis remains to be validated next year.

The statistics concerning the effectiveness of the game mechanics (Blob and bonus information modules) are exploratory. They mostly rely on the answers on the Likert scale, provided by the students, to the 5 affirmations right after each game. However, these affirmations could have induced a confirmation bias. In addition, participation in the *EscapeCell* is voluntary, and only 66 out of 117 students answered these question-naires. Further experimentation should be led to confirm those hypotheses by comparing *EscapeCell* with and without these game elements.

6   Conclusion

In this study, the integration of *EscapeCell* (composed of several mini SGs and a gami-fication module) shows that can enhance students' performance in the final exam. This result could be attributed to two circumstances. Firstly, this improvement could be due to the supplementary work undertaken by students in the experimental group (who used *EscapeCell*), compared to those in the control group. Indeed, these students had the opportunity to apply their course knowledge within the game, which further con-solidated their understanding. Secondly, translating course content into a game-based context might have enhanced the students' engagement and interest, leading to a more proactive learning approach. This was the initial objective of the teacher. The engaging and fun nature of the game could have helped students, who may have not been attentive during traditional classroom sessions, to actively participate. Moreover, the non-player character, called Blob, who assists to players, facilitates their procession through the mini-games. The presence of this guide makes the game more accessible and engaging, especially for those who are new to gaming. Besides, the hidden bonus information modules introduce an aspect of rewards (progress bar). They motivate students to dive deeper into the game, thereby increasing their interactions and engagement with it. This could potentially lead to a more comprehensive understanding and internalization of the educational content presented within the game. However, the number of bonuses the students unlocked does not correlate with their final exam scores. *EscapeCell*, therefore serves as a valuable supplement to conventional instruction. It provides a complementary teaching method to enhance understanding of the course material. These inferences are based solely on this study, and further research is needed to confirm them.

Acknowledgements. This project was financed by Le Mans Université, France. We specially want to thank the entire conception and development team: Tiphaine GALPIN, Tiphaine INGUERE, Raphaël LALANNE, Fréderic LABRE, Franck VARET and Mohamed Hamza FALIH.

References

1. Malone, T., Lepper, M.: Making learning fun: a taxonomy of intrinsic motivations for learning, vol. 3 (2005)
2. Gee, J.P.: What Video Games Have to Teach Us About Learning and Literacy. Palgrave Macmillan (2004)
3. Kara, N.: A systematic review of the use of serious games in science education. Contemp. Educ. Technol. **13**, ep295 (2021)
4. Cheng, M.-T., Chen, J.-H., Chu, S.-J., Chen, S.-Y.: The use of serious games in science education: a review of selected empirical research from 2002 to 2013. J. Comput. Educ. **2**, 353–375 (2015)
5. Schneller, W., Campbell, P.J., Bassham, D., Wurtele, E.S.: Meta! Blast computer game: a pipeline from science to 3D art to education. In: The Engineering Reality of Virtual Reality 2012, pp. 36–47. SPIE (2012)
6. Wurtele, E.S., et al.: Meta! Blast: a serious game to explore the complexities of structural and metabolic cell biology. In: ASME World Conference on Innovative Virtual Reality, pp. 237–240 (2010)
7. Hodges, G.W., Oliver, J.S., Jang, Y., Cohen, A., Ducrest, D., Robertson, T.: Pedagogy, partnership, and collaboration: a longitudinal, empirical study of serious educational gameplay in secondary biology classrooms. J. Sci. Educ. Technol. **30**, 331–346 (2021)
8. Khaldi, A., Bouzidi, R., Nader, F.: Gamification of e-learning in higher education: a systematic literature review. Smart Learn. Environ. **10**, 10 (2023)
9. Reyssier, S., Hallifax, S., Serna, A., Marty, J.-C., Simonian, S., Lavoué, E.: The impact of game elements on learner motivation: influence of initial motivation and player profile. IEEE Trans. Learn. Technol. **15**, 42–54 (2022)
10. Andersen, E., Liu, Y.-E., Snider, R., Szeto, R., Cooper, S., Popović, Z.: On the harmfulness of secondary game objectives. In: Proceedings of the 6th International Conference on Foundations of Digital Games, pp. 30–37 (2011)
11. Marfisi-Schottman, I., Longeon, T., Furnon, C., Marne, B.: 10 commandments of the serious game padawan: lessons learned after 4 years of professional training. In: Kiili, K., Antti, K., de Rosa, F., Dindar, M., Kickmeier-Rust, M., Bellotti, F. (eds.) GALA 2022. LNCS, vol. 13647, pp. 63–73. Springer, Cham (2022). https://doi.org/10.1007/978-3-031-22124-8_7
12. Liu, Y.-D.: Évaluer l'expérience d'apprentissage pour un design écologique dans les Serious Games éducatifs sur appareil mobile (in process)
13. Tchibozo, G.: Introduction pratique aux méthodes quantitatives en Sciences de l'éducation et de la formation (2019)

Using Meaningful Choices and Uncertainty to Increase Player Agency in a Cybersecurity Seminar Game

Peadar Callaghan[(✉)] and Mikhail Fiadotau

Tallinn University School of Digital Technologies,
Narva mnt. 29, 10120 Tallinn, Estonia
`peadar@tlu.ee`

Abstract. The paper proposes an approach to improving player engagement and learning outcomes in seminar-style games, based on emphasizing player agency, meaningful choices, and uncertainty. As a case study, it introduces a game focused on trust in cybersecurity, whose design incorporates resource management, hidden agendas for each player, and a shared failure condition.

Keywords: Wargaming · Seminar game · Player agency · Uncertainty

1 Introduction

Seminar games are an intriguing sub-group of learning games. Coming from a long tradition within wargaming, seminar games ask players to engage with complex real-life problems that are presented to the group by an umpire [2,10]. In many regards, they resemble commercial tabletop roleplaying games, except, rather than overcoming dragons, players are tasked with tackling serious societal issues and engaging with possible futures. This utility and relatively low cost of use has seen them used across a wide range of domains [6,8,10,14,18,20].

Sadly, the proliferation of their use has not been accompanied by much evolution of form. These games' mechanics have remained fixed and are often overly simplistic for the ambitious tasks they aim to accomplish. Seminar games have been particularly criticized for being overly subjective, only reinforcing preconceived notions and not providing much by way of player agency. This has led some commentators to refer to them with the derogatory acronym B.O.G.S.A.T. ("bunch of guys sat around a table") [2,21].

This paper examines how to increase the sense of player agency within such games by incorporating resource management and a decision loop into the gameplay, as well as emphasizing meaningful player choices and integrating uncertainty. As its case study, it outlines the design of a cybersecurity-themed seminar

The authors would like to thank the NATO Cooperative Cyber Defence Centre of Excellence for their support in running the game.

P. Dondio et al. (Eds.): GALA 2023, LNCS 14475, pp. 23–32, 2024.
https://doi.org/10.1007/978-3-031-49065-1_3

game that was played during the 2023 CyCon conference. The paper provides a description of traditional seminar games, followed by a description of how the updated game was designed to increase player agency. Initial observations from the first deployment are discussed before the paper concludes with recommendations for the next iteration and future designs.

2   Theoretical Background

2.1   Agency and Meaningful Choice in Games

One of the defining features of games is player agency: the players' ability to influence the flow of the game by their actions. Janet Murray has defined player agency as "the satisfying power to take meaningful action and see the results of our decisions and choices" [12].

Murray's definition highlights two crucial aspects. First, agency is essential to player satisfaction and engagement. The sense of being able to affect the course of the game is both empowering and gives the act of playing meaning and value. This links to the concepts of autonomy and competence in Deci and Ryan's self-determination theory, which (alongside relatedness) are the required elements for a person to experience intrinsic motivation: a state characterized by enjoyment and inherent interest in an activity, which is exactly what game designers seek to achieve [15,16].

Second, agency is intrinsically connected not only to consequences, but to the player's ability to make meaningful decisions and choices. Agency is often viewed as comprising three components: iteration (considering past experience and existing knowledge), projectivity (analyzing future potentialities), and practical evaluation (contextualizing iteration and projectivity within the specifics of the present situation) [4]. All three components are essential to designing meaningful choices: players must be able to rely on their past knowledge and experience, as well as need to reflect on the current state of the game, in order to make assumptions about the consequences of their decisions. Supporting these meaningful choices is a key goal in game design [17].

At the same time, the longer-term consequences of player choices must not be entirely predictable. While the players need to have some notion of what kind of repercussions their actions might entail (otherwise, choices become arbitrary and random), there also needs to be some degree of uncertainty. Greg Costikyan outlined 11 common types of uncertainty in games, including performative (e.g., can I time my action right?), analytic (e.g., how will this complex system respond if I do this?), and narrative (how will the story evolve?) [3]. Incorporating a reasonable degree of uncertainty into learning games has also been found to increase player motivation in learning games [9].

In sum, player agency involves the presence of both tangible consequences and meaningful choices, while at the same time being shaped by various kinds of uncertainty.

2.2   Seminar Games: Use and Design

Seminar Games in Training. In a seminar game, a group of players—each representing a different entity—are presented with a scenario consisting of a set of pre-scripted injects (in-game events) that must be resolved through deliberation, with the process being facilitated by an umpire [2,11]. Traditionally, the learning goals of this type of games have focused on how the group would react in a specific scenario. These decision points can then be used to generate emergency plans in the event of a similar situation occurring in real life. In effect, these games often act as a rehearsal for potential issues or an opportunity to replay previous events to look at how people may come to alternate solutions.

Seminar-style games have particular utility in examining complex fields of study in which the answers are unclear. The dynamic of a group of players collectively working out novel solutions, while supported by a skilled umpire, makes these games suited to a wide range of educational applications, including the creation of heuristics for dealing with possible futures [8].

Seminar games come from a long tradition of umpire-led wargaming, tracing its roots back to the staff rides pioneered by Lt. Helmuth von Moltke of the Prussian Army in the mid-19th century [2]. These were "planned learning events that recreate[d] a significant historical incident," often while incorporating decision-making to facilitate deeper reflection and have since become a common instructional technique in military education [1]. Seminar games also draw on role-playing methods developed by Austrian psychologist Jacob Moreno, initially as a form of group therapy and then as an educational methodology [13]. Another prominent influence on modern seminar games have been the "politico-military desk games" developed by RAND Corporation in the 1950s. Like other Pol-Mil (political-military) games, these combined military and diplomatic considerations in modeling various, mostly Cold War-related scenarios, but particularly emphasized uncertainty and scenario realism [10].

Seminar games have been used in a variety of contexts, ranging from promoting nuclear nonproliferation [20] to teaching environmental issues [6]. They have been noted for their open-endedness and potential for player creativity, but also criticized for their lack of rigor and the fact that player actions often entail few meaningful consequences [14,21].

Traditional Seminar Game Design. In a standard seminar game, the players follow a predetermined path of pre-scripted injects until either the time for play elapses or the game runs out of injects [11]. The simplicity of play can quickly lead to disengagement, as the players may begin to see through the illusion of agency that is being presented to them, realizing that their decisions do not affect the pre-determined chain of events planned by the game designers.

Figure 1 visualizes the core loop of a traditional seminar game. (A core loop is a repeated pattern of play, i.e., interactions between the player and the game system, that is found in any game. Core loops are widely used in both game design and game analysis [19]).

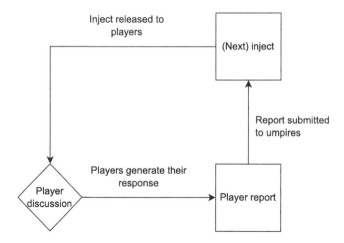

Fig. 1. Core loop of a traditional seminar game: player response does not influence next round.

The primary issue with this type of gaming is that the majority of player answers have little to no impact on the outcome of the game. While seminar games do involve some degree of uncertainty, namely relating to player behavior and to some extent narrative, the players' engagement with the story can disappear once they realize their decisions have little influence on the narrative progression. The fact that subsequent injects are fundamentally unaffected by the players' prior actions renders the decisions players make during the course of the game inconsequential in terms of Fullerton's Decision Scale [7]. This can cause players to feel powerless. A lack of agency reduces the intrinsic motivation of playing the game because it minimizes the sense of autonomy, which is crucial for the act of play to be intrinsically motivating [15].

Having a pre-ordained outcome also opens the games up to a great deal of criticism in that the conclusions to be drawn from the game are largely defined before any player takes action [21]. This limits their utility for one of their main stated purposes: discovering new solutions to complex issues.

These limitations call for an alternative approach to designing seminar games.

3   Game Design

3.1   Context of Use

The learning game discussed in this paper was designed to be played at the 2023 CyCon (International Conference on Cyber Conflict, organized by the NATO Cooperative Cyber Defence Centre of Excellence). The primary goal of the game was to explore the issues of trust in cybersecurity. Trust was a major theme that had been identified at CyCon over three previous years [5]. It is an issue that permeates many of the domains that conflict in cyberspace brings together, including international relations, public policy, and military science, as well as the technical aspects of securing systems. In other words, one of the key issues in cybersecurity (and cyber-defense specifically) is how do the many different stakeholders develop trust not just in the computer system, but in the behavior of their counterparts in other countries or departments.

While the previous workshops had focused on international stage intergovernmental trust, in 2023 the focus shifted to intra-governmental trust. It was decided to see if a seminar game could be used to get the participants to explore trust in a more experimental than theoretical way.

Various games, mainly of the non-learning variety, have explored the issue of trust. Such games typically have key mechanics that allow trust to be created and eroded, often using a voting system to eject players deemed untrustworthy by the group [22]. "Social deduction" games such as Resistance, Mafia (Werewolf), and Among Us use hidden roles and secret information to influence the players' behavior. In each of these games, there is a hidden economy with trust at its core. The decisions the player takes have consequences both for the player themselves and, crucially, for the outcome of the game as a whole.

Unfortunately, the core loop of a standard seminar game does not lend itself equally well to exploring the issue of trust, as the actions of each party at the table have negligible consequences to the outcome of the game. In order to explore trust, there must be a cost to player actions, meaning there is something at stake for each player when they decide whether to trust a fellow player. Furthermore, the actions have to have an impact not just on that player, but on the game state, to render them consequential for the entire group. These considerations informed the game design discussed below.

3.2 Game Premise

The game is set in a fictional country of Gameland, a moderately prosperous parliamentary democracy with free and open elections. Gameland has a modern well-developed infrastructure in terms of both physical and information technology. It also becomes the site of a series of escalating cybersecurity incidents, which serves as the backdrop for the game.

Table 1. Player roles in the game: each player has their own agenda hidden from others.

Role title	Hidden agenda
Office for Information Security	Resolve as many incidents as possible
Office of the Interior	Make sure the Office of Defence is not involved in more than three projects
Office of Defence	Spend all of your budget before the game ends
Intelligence services	Create as many cross-organization solutions as possible
Office of Foreign Affairs	Convince others to pay as much as possible
Gameland Telecom	Finish the game with the most resources of any of the players

The main story starts with the discovery of a potential vulnerability of a key system. Upon investigation (carried out at a fee), further information is revealed about the nature and extent of the threat. If players do not pay for the investigation, they receive a report that the situation is deteriorating. The series of events centers on a vulnerability with several security cameras used in restricted areas of Gameland's military and governmental facilities.

Each player takes responsibility for one role within the country as summarized in Table 1. Drawing on "social deduction" games, each role is accompanied by a hidden agenda unique to the specific player.

3.3   New Core Loop

To address the limitations of the traditional seminar game outlined above, a new design was developed, which built on the base pattern of pre-scripted injects. This design focused on increasing the number of decisions that each player was required to make, and increasing the meaningfulness and consequentiality of these decisions.

To make the player actions feel more consequential, a doom tracker was added as a fail condition. The doom tracker would start at 0 and increase each time the players were unable to reach a consensus or pay the appropriate cost, reflecting the worsening situation in Gameland. If the tracker ever reached level 5, the game would end and all players would have lost. As such, a common goal shared by the players was to prevent the doom tracker from reaching 5 until the injects were exhausted.

In addition, to make the choices available to the players both meaningful and challenging, the player actions were assigned a resource value. These resources, signifying money, created a virtual economy where players would have something to gain or lose through their interactions with the other players around the table. This also created a tension between the common goal shared by the players and their individual priorities. To make this tension more meaningful and relate it to the issue of trust, hidden agendas were added for each player. This mimics the reality of cyber-defense cooperation, whereby, in addition to the common goal, each of the represented agencies has their own priorities which, given the limited resources at their disposal, must be negotiated against the cyber-defense needs they share with their intragovernmental partners.

At the end of each turn, players could be assigned +1 resource each by the umpire of the game. One extra resource would be open to be assigned to one of the players based on the group's collective decision, reinforcing the tension between teamwork and individual agendas and creating a way for the group to reward valuable contributions to problem resolution. This was put in place to make sure teams did not completely exhaust their resources as the game progressed. The updated core loop is presented in Fig. 2.

A prominent type of uncertainty the game relies on (in Costikyan's terms) is hidden information, as each player had an individual victory condition on their card that none of the other players could see. This affected not only the player's

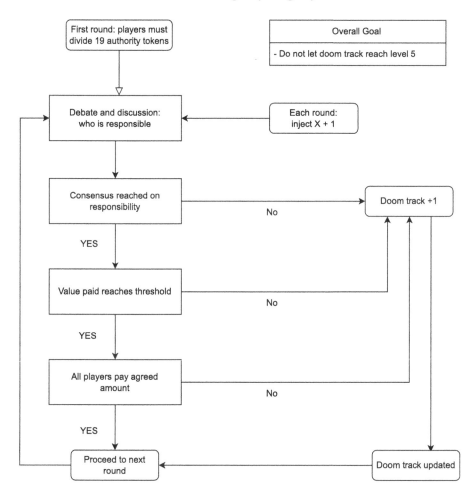

Fig. 2. Updated seminar game core loop: using resources and multiple decision points per round.

own actions, but also those of the other players, as the mere knowledge that a player has a hidden agenda can affect the ways other players act towards them.

Another type of uncertainty found in the game is player uncertainty. When the players have reached a consensus on who is responsible and whether and what to pay, each individual player may pay the agreed amount or not; as such, it is impossible for other players to know if the solution will be successful, speaking to the issue of trust in other players' good-faith behavior.

Additionally, the game contains analytic uncertainty, with players having to anticipate how their decisions, and those of other players, will shape the overall situation. Another prominent type of uncertainty, preserved from the traditional seminar game, is narrative uncertainty. Taken together, these forms of uncertainty mean that player choices are not obvious or trivial but must rely on inference, planning, and teamwork, thus increasing their meaningfulness.

4 Game Evaluation

4.1 Player Experience

30 participants joined the workshop at CyCon 2023 during which the game was played, with the play session lasting around three hours. Player decisions were tracked throughout the session, to be analyzed in a later paper. After the play session concluded, semi-structured interviews of around 15 min were conducted with four volunteering participants in order to gauge to what extent the goals behind the game design had been accomplished. The interview questions covered the following categories: general impression, understanding of subject matter, meaningfulness of decision-making, perceived agency, player engagement, and suggestions for improvement. The full interview guide is available at http://www.tlu.ee/~fiadotau/cycon23_interview_guide.pdf.

All four interviewees found the game engaging, highlighting both the decision-making process and interactions with fellow players as interesting. The players also reported finding the experience to be useful in terms of understanding how trust works in cybersecurity, with one player elaborating: "[Y]ou come about some of the insights naturally by virtue of doing this game, as opposed to sitting down and having a discussion or a lecture." Two of the players mentioned that the game drew attention to the "softer" aspects of cybersecurity, such as cultural differences and empathy towards others. On a more critical note, two players pointed out that the gameplay could have been deeper if more time had been allocated for it to run, and if the play time had been used more efficiently.

The players found the choices offered to them to be meaningful in terms of recognizing a plurality of options available to them and needing to reconcile their hidden agenda with the common goal. The players also reported having a sense of agency in that they felt that their actions had an influence on the course of the game.

4.2 Recommendations for Future Design

Players were also asked to provide suggestions as to how the game could be improved in the future. Together with the facilitator's own observations from running the session and input from a separate questionnaire sent out to workshop participants after the event, these have informed the following initial recommendations, which will be tested and refined during subsequent iterations.

1. Incorporate multiple factors beyond just money to measure success and consider integrating aspects such as public opinion to make the game more comprehensive. This would increase the game's analytic complexity, and the uncertainty associated with it, but would also increase the meaningfulness of player choices.

2. Design more scenarios with varying levels of severity and stress to create a more dynamic and challenging gameplay experience.
3. Experiment with the doom tracker and stress feedback to observe its impact on trust levels and decision-making; adjust the gameplay accordingly.
4. Clarify time limitations for making player decisions and provide warnings to ensure efficient gameplay and time management.
5. Introduce additional learning elements to help players understand correct decision-making for specific roles, enhancing the overall learning experience.

5   Conclusion

This case study offers a way of improving the engagement and learning value of a seminar game by increasing player agency. This is accomplished through considering the importance of meaningful choices and uncertainty to the game experience. In practical terms, the game achieves this by introducing a collective failure condition (doom tracker), incorporating in-game resources and a decision loop, as well as giving each player a hidden agenda in addition to their shared goal. Playtesting results suggest the approach taken is largely effective, leading to high player engagement and a meaningful learning experience.

As of the time of writing, an updated version of the game is scheduled to be played at the Swedish Defence University in fall 2023, as well as by the Ministry of National Defense of Chile in 2024. It is also being adapted into a digitally mediated format.

The aim of the present paper has been to introduce the updated game design. A more empirical study into actual player behavior in the context of trust is planned once data from more game sessions has been collected. Other topics for future research include the role of cultural factors in discussing decisions and navigating trust [11] and the use of additional trust-related game mechanics. The latter could include, for example, a rogue player whose hidden agenda goes against the group's interest, as seen in many "social deduction" games [22].

References

1. Becker, W.S., Burke, M.J.: Instructional staff rides for management learning and education. Acad. Manage. Learn. Educ. **13**(4), 510–524 (2014). https://doi.org/10.5465/amle.2012.0306
2. Caffrey, M.B.: On wargaming: how wargames have shaped history and how they may shape the future. No. 43 in Naval War College Newport papers, Naval War College Press, Newport, RI (2019)
3. Costikyan, G.: Uncertainty in Games. Playful Thinking. MIT Press, Cambridge (2015)
4. Emirbayer, M., Mische, A.: What is agency? Am. J. Sociol. **103**(4), 962–1023 (1998). https://doi.org/10.1086/231294
5. Ertan, A., Buckles, C.R., Lillemets, P., Nordli, G.M., Schauss, L.C.: Trust in cyber exercises: a vision for NATO. Technical report, NATO Cooperative Cyber Defence Centre of Excellence, Tallinn (2022). https://ccdcoe.org/uploads/2022/07/Trust-in-Cyber-Exercises-March-2022.pdf

6. Fiadotau, M., Tramonti, M., Brander, H., Callaghan, P.: BIG GAME: balancing player preferences and design considerations in a serious game about environmental issues. In: Kiili, K., Antti, K., De Rosa, F., Dindar, M., Kickmeier-Rust, M., Bellotti, F. (eds.) GALA 2022: Games and Learning Alliance, pp. 329–334. Springer, Cham (2022). https://doi.org/10.1007/978-3-031-22124-8_34

7. Fullerton, T., Swain, C., Hoffman, S.: Game Design Workshop: A Playcentric Approach to Creating Innovative Games, 2nd edn. Elsevier Morgan Kaufmann, Amsterdam, Boston (2008)

8. Harrigan, P., Kirschenbaum, M.G. (eds.): Zones of Control: Perspectives on Wargaming. MIT Press, Cambridge (2016)

9. Howard-Jones, P.A., Demetriou, S.: Uncertainty and engagement with learning games. Instr. Sci. **37**(6), 519–536 (2009). https://doi.org/10.1007/s11251-008-9073-6

10. Mason, R.C.: Wargaming: its history and future. Int. J. Intell. Secur. Public Affairs **20**(2), 77–101 (2018). https://doi.org/10.1080/23800992.2018.1484238

11. McGrady, M., Trentacoste, C.M.: Serious games with serious players: game play with international decision-makers. Technical report, CNA Corporation, Arlington, VA (2014)

12. Murray, J.H.: Hamlet on the Holodeck, Updated Edition: The Future of Narrative in Cyberspace. MIT Press, Cambridge (2017)

13. Piu, A., Fregola, C.: Simulation and Gaming for Mathematical Education: Epistemology and Teaching Strategies. IGI Global, Hershey (2011)

14. Pournelle, P.E.: Designing wargames for the analytic purpose. Phalanx **50**(2), 48–53 (2017)

15. Reid, G.: Motivation in video games: a literature review. Comput. Games J. **1**(2), 70–81 (2012). https://doi.org/10.1007/BF03395967

16. Ryan, R.M., Rigby, C.S., Przybylski, A.: The motivational pull of video games: a self-determination theory approach. Motiv. Emot. **30**(4), 344–360 (2006). https://doi.org/10.1007/s11031-006-9051-8

17. Salen, K., Zimmerman, E.: Rules of Play: Game Design Fundamentals. MIT Press, Cambridge (2004)

18. Schwarz, J.O.: Business wargaming for teaching strategy making. Futures **51**, 59–66 (2013). https://doi.org/10.1016/j.futures.2013.06.002

19. Sicart, M.: Loops and metagames: understanding game design structures. In: Proceedings of the 10th International Conference on Foundations of Digital Games. Society for the Advancement of the Science of Digital Games, Santa Cruz, CA (2015)

20. Stanbro, W.D.: Seminar war gaming in nonproliferation studies. J. Nucl. Mater. Manag. **34**(2), 10–13 (2006)

21. Weuve, C.A., et al.: Wargame pathologies. Technical report, CNA Corporation, Alexandria, VA, September 2004. https://doi.org/10.21236/ADA596774

22. Zagal, J.P.: Collaborative games redux. In: Brown, D., McCallum-Stewart, E. (eds.) Rerolling Boardgames: Essays on Themes, Systems, Experiences and Ideologies, pp. 29–47. McFarland, Jefferson, NC (2020)

Yabusame!!! - Historical Japanese Cross Scroll Meets VR

Kevin Körner$^{(\boxtimes)}$ (ID), Patrick Muczczek (ID), and Jana Knickrehm (ID)

Digital Humanities Center, University of Tübingen, Keplerstr. 2, 72072 Tübingen,
Germany
kevin.koerner@uni-tuebingen.de,
{patrick.muczczek,jana.knickrehm}@student.uni-tuebingen.de

Abstract. The progressive advancement of digital technologies offers novel prospects for the preservation and exhibition of cultural heritage assets in day-to-day museum operations. Within this framework, contemporary media platforms like virtual reality (VR) still maintain an element of novelty in public perception, thereby serving as a catalyst to engage individuals in cultural knowledge. Drawing on these assumptions, this paper introduces our serious game, *Yabusame!!!* - a collaborative endeavor between our team and the esteemed city museum, *Hornmoldhaus*, developed during the *Coding da Vinci Hackathon for cultural data* (https://codingdavinci.de/en/node). The game, a VR bow shooting experience, creatively imparts the contents of a historical Japanese cross scroll that portrays the eponymous Japanese sport, Yabusame, alongside associated historical and cultural knowledge. The game design encompassed deliberate strategies aimed at optimizing usability and mitigating potential causes of motion sickness, ensuring the practical applicability of the game within the corresponding museum exhibition. This paper unfolds in three parts: firstly, an exposition of the cultural backdrop behind the game; secondly, an exploration of our didactic strategy, game design choices, and our vision for seamlessly integrating the VR game within a museum exhibition; and finally, the presentation of a study we conducted to examine the practical usability of *Yabusame!!!* in this setting.

Keywords: Serious Game Development Report · VR-supported Cultural Asset Presentation · Usability Study

1 Introduction

Cultural institutions, such as museums, bear the primary responsibility of safeguarding the cultural, social, and technological accomplishments of our forebears. Furthermore, they meticulously curate and present these achievements to a wide audience, facilitating the establishment of shared understanding among diverse social groups.

The ever-evolving technological landscape compels museums to incorporate new digital media into their exhibition strategies. This entails digitizing physical artifacts and employing modern presentation media, such as virtual reality, in their showcases. The *Coding da Vinci hackathon for cultural data*[1] addresses this trend by bridging institutions with digitized cultural heritage and teams eager to implement modern media.

In this paper, we introduce the serious game *Yabusame!!!*, which was developed during the *Coding da Vinci* event, held from May to June 2022, in collaboration with the data-providing museum, *Hornmoldhaus*, and the Digital Humanities Center at the University of Tübingen. The game draws inspiration from one of the museum's exhibits, a Japanese cross scroll, and employs a virtual reality bow shooting experience to convey knowledge about the traditional Japanese equestrian sport, Yabusame, and its associated cultural and historical information. Emphasizing user-friendly usability and mitigating potential causes of motion sickness during immersion, we ensured that the application can be seamlessly integrated into the museum exhibition without causing frustration for visitors. To validate the effectiveness of our design decisions, a brief study was conducted following the game's development.

2   Related Work

The significance of virtual reality (VR) in the context of museum exhibitions is evidenced by numerous scholarly articles in recent years. For instance, Kaysers et al. [1] consider VR as a "promising technology for knowledge transfer". Likewise Giannini and Bowen assert in [2] "Increasingly, museums are using their public stage as a space shared with visitors designed for participation and interaction facilitated by digital intermediaries [...]" and list VR in their list of suggested media types. Li et al. [3] also advocate for the use of VR to "enrich the constituent of an interactive museum". In alignment with these viewpoints, our daily work experience confirms that VR, as a medium in exhibitions, enables visitors to actively engage rather than passively observe.

In recent years, notable museums have featured a range of VR exhibitions, as exemplified by Jim Richardson in [4]. For instance, Richardson highlights the immersive experience of *Curious Alice*[2], which was presented by the Victoria and Albert Museum in 2021 and allowed visitors to delve into the timeless novel *Alice in Wonderland* by Lewis Carroll. Another noteworthy example is *Mona Lisa: Beyond the Glass*[3], presented by the Louvre in 2019.

In the realm of presenting cultural heritage, several comprehensive studies have delved into the use of VR and related technologies. Noteworthy contributions include works by Hubert Cecotti [5] and Anastasios Theodoropoulos and Angeliki Antoniou [6]. These studies offered valuable insights and inspiration for

---

[1] https://codingdavinci.de/en/node.
[2] See https://www.vam.ac.uk/articles/curious-alice-the-vr-experience, last accessed 11.06.23.
[3] See   https://www.louvre.fr/en/what-s-on/life-at-the-museum/the-mona-lisa-in-virtual-reality-in-your-own-home, last accessed 11.06.2023.

our own planning. For reasons of space, only two examples from the aforementioned publications are referred to here. For instance, *The dawn of art*[4] serves as a captivating example from which we drew inspiration. This VR experience ingeniously presents the ancient drawings of Chauvet Cave, dating back 36.000 years. Through an atmospheric VR setting, visitors are playfully immersed in the rich history of these remarkable artworks. Another source of inspiration, *The Night Cafe*[5] adopts a different approach, enabling players to fully immerse themselves in the artistic realm of Vincent Van Gogh. By presenting his works as immersive 3D worlds, this VR experience not only provides a visually stunning encounter but also imparts knowledge about the artist, his masterpieces, and relevant background information.

During our research, we discovered two notable examples of VR-based teaching in the realm of Yabusame sports. In their publication [7], Imura et al. introduce a compelling approach to immersing oneself in Yabusame sports. The authors present their system, *Kibakiba Mushamusha*, which differs from traditional head-mounted VR by utilizing a CAVE (Cave Automatic Virtual Environment). This unique approach incorporates a rocking horse to simulate horse movement, enhancing the immersive experience. Additionally, a real-world bow controller is employed for realistic shooting interactions. Adachi et al. [8] present a head-mounted VR application that takes advantage of controllers and additional sensors to provide an archery experience that closely mimics real-world conditions.

However, despite the numerous positive examples of VR implementation in a museum context, it is essential to acknowledge the limitations and challenges associated with it, as highlighted in the review by Shehade and Stylianou-Lambert [9]. According to their study, one of the most significant challenges "relates to staffing and training needs". Specifically, "In many cases visitors are not familiar enough with VR and usually need assistance, [...]". Another problem to be mentioned is the occurrence of motion sickness during the usage of VR applications. As Keshavarz and Golding elaborate in [10] motion sickness "is considered a serious concern that threatens their [the applications] success and acceptance". Armed with this knowledge, we adopted an iterative approach during our architecture process to mitigate potential sources of discomfort and minimize factors that could lead to the rejection of the application.

3   Cultural Background

The *Hornmoldhaus*, the museum for which the game was designed, is situated in the city of Bietigheim-Bissingen, located in southwestern Germany. It occupies

---

[4] Atlas V, Novelab, Google Arts & Culture. The Dawn of Art. Available online: https://store.steampowered.com/app/1236560/The_Dawn_of_Art/ (accessed on 20 June 2023).

[5] Borrowed Light Studios. The Night Cafe: A VR Tribute to Vincent Van Gogh. Available online: https://store.steampowered.com/app/482390/The_Night_Cafe_A_VR_Tribute_to_Vincent_Van_Gogh/ (accessed on 20 June 2023).

the former residence of Erwin Otto Eduard Baelz, a physician who served as the personal physician to the Japanese heir to the throne and later emperor from 1890 to 1905, as noted by the director of the *Hornmoldhaus* Catharina Raible [11]. After retiring from this prestigious role, Baelz brought numerous gifts from the Japanese imperial family back to Germany, which now form part of the *Hornmoldhaus'* exhibition collection. Notable items include a samurai suit of armor, works of art by the Japanese artist Kawanabe Kyosai, and various Japanese cross scrolls portraying historical events and legends. The left side of Fig. 1 provides an illustration of some of these artifacts[6].

In preparation for the Coding da Vinci hackathon held between May and June 2022, several high-resolution photographs were taken to digitize a selection of Japanese cross scrolls[7]. The right side of Fig. 1 displays a segment of one of these, featuring a depiction of Yabusame, the traditional Japanese art of archery on horseback. According to Catharina Raible, this particular cross scroll is likely a copy of a representation owned by the Ana-Hachiman Shrine in Tokyo. In the accompanying text of the scrolls provided in the repository, which is linked in footnote 7, Raible further explains that the scroll was created in honor of the annual ritual Yabusame held at the shrine every October since 1738.

Fig. 1. Left side: Photograph from the Baelz exhibition of the Hornmoldhaus. **Right Side:** Section from the photography of the Yabusame cross scroll, Source: https:// codingdavinci.de/daten/emakimono-japanische-querrollen, CC BY-SA 4.0 Stadtmuseum Hornmoldhaus Bietigheim-Bissingen.

4   *Yabusame!!!* - Game Design

4.1   Didactic Goals

Our primary objective was to present the content of the Yabusame scroll discussed in Sect. 3. This involved offering players visual presentations of both the central graphics of the scroll and its complete representation, considering that

---

[6] The exhibition can also be visited as 360° photography at https:// stadtmuseum.bietigheim-bissingen.de/fileadmin/user_upload_hornmoldhaus/ virtuelle-rundgaenge/baelz/index.html.

[7] See https://codingdavinci.de/daten/emakimono-japanische-querrollen.

the physical scroll is too large to be showcased in its entirety to the public at once. Additionally, we aimed to provide players with an immersive experience of the key element of Yabusame: Archery. Lastly, our intention was to convey interconnected knowledge of Japanese culture and history.

4.2   Game Design

During the planning phase, we diligently followed the guidelines proposed by Caserman et al. [12] to ensure the highest possible quality for our game. For instance, we focused on "achieving the characterizing goal" by integrating both "physical and cognitive training" aspects, as recommended. In our case, this involved combining bow shooting mechanics with audio-based knowledge transfer. Furthermore, we implemented "Appropriate feedback on progress" by providing players with audio and visual cues to acknowledge their successful interactions.

Considering our objective of providing players with an authentic Yabusame sports experience, our initial design decision was to employ VR as the target medium. Figure 2 provides a glimpse into the game, showcasing some impressions. By utilizing VR controllers, we were able to simulate the process of drawing a bow and realistically aiming at targets. However, to mitigate motion sickness, we opted for a stationary position for players instead of simulating horseback riding, which is customary in Yabusame sports. In the vicinity of this fixed position, we placed the core graphics extracted from the digitized scroll, thereby creating an immersive experience that transports players into the scroll itself.

Fig. 2. Left to right: Main Menu, Gameplay, Boss Battle, Cross-Scroll Showcase.

The gameplay centers around the captivating art of Yabusame archery. Players must skillfully perform bow shots, aiming to hit traditional targets with their arrows. To provide an engaging challenge, the game features levels of increasing difficulty and diverse objectives. These objectives range from hitting moving targets to uncovering hidden targets within the room, and even engaging in a climactic boss battle. Each level has a duration of two minutes and consists of three rounds. Upon completing a level, players are rewarded with a one to three star ranging *Measurement Achievement*, as described by Blair [13], based on their performance.

To imbue the game with a lighthearted and creatively entertaining touch, we devised a fictional narrative that, while not strictly adhering to scientific accuracy, adds an enjoyable layer to the overall experience. The story revolves around a young samurai named Sanro, who attends a Yabusame event conducted to beseech the spirits of the Ana Hachiman shrine for the recovery of a young heir to the throne afflicted with smallpox. However, Sanro finds himself facing an inexplicable challenge: despite his usual accuracy, he fails to hit a single target during the preparations. Consequently, he implores the patron deity of the land, whose role the player assumes, for assistance in his Yabusame ride and to vanquish the malevolent Yōkai responsible for the prince's illness.

Building upon the narrative, our game incorporates two primary educational objectives: conveying the story of the scroll and providing cultural and historical insights. In between each level, Sanro rides in the simulated room in front of the player and shares informative details, such as how the original target design is inspired by the weak spots in a traditional samurai armor. To enhance the user experience, all information is presented audibly.

In line with the gameplay mechanics, our focus for user interaction centers around archery. Rather than creating an overlay Head-Up Display (HUD), we devised an intuitive approach where players can interact with various elements by shooting arrows at them, even within the main menu. However, an exception to this is the digital showcase, which allows players to view the entire digitized Yabusame scroll, as well as other selected scrolls from the *Hornmoldhaus* collection, in their true size. For ease of use, players can navigate through the scrolls using the joystick on the controllers. Additionally, an audio guide accompanies the digital showcase, offering further insights into the historical background of the scrolls.

4.3   Exhibition Design

As *Yabusame!!!* was intricately linked to the exhibits contributed by the *Hornmoldhaus*, we devised an exhibition integration that revolves around the game itself. The following outlines this integration:

To begin with, museum visitors are directed to an information area where they can access essential details about Erwin Baelz and his life. Subsequently, they have a look at the physical Yabusame cross-scroll, which can only be partially opened due to material preservation requirements. Motivated by the desire to explore more of the scroll and learn about its contents, thereafter, visitors play the game. After experiencing the interactive gaming aspect of *Yabusame!!!*, visitors can utilize the application's showcase functionality to view the entire cross-scroll digitally.

Upon leaving the virtual world, visitors then enter an exhibition room where they encounter elements featured in the game. For instance, they may find a samurai suit of armor. This integration serves to reactivate the previously acquired knowledge, resulting in a consolidation of understanding and insights among visitors.

5   UserStudy

5.1   Hypothesis

During the development process, a significant design requirement was to ensure practical usability within the permanent Baelz exhibition at the *Hornmold-haus*. To encourage visitor engagement with *Yabusame!!!*, we prioritized two key aspects: intuitive controls and interactions, as well as minimizing the risk of motion sickness. Based on these design considerations, we formulated the following hypotheses: (1) *The interactions are intuitive to use* and (2) *Players do not experience motion sickness after completing a single playthrough.*

From an educational standpoint, our aim was to assess the effectiveness of information retention through the game. Therefore, we posited the following hypothesis: (3) *After playing the game once, visitors are capable of locating information presented in the game within the exhibition.*

5.2   Study Design

The study workflow was based on the exhibition design outlined in Sect. 4.3. The participants were initially provided with an introduction to the topic of Erwin Baelz and his life. Subsequently, the participants were equipped with the Meta Quest 2 VR device and received a verbal explanation of the game controls. Each participant then completed a full playthrough of *Yabusame!!!*. For the second part of the study, the participants were presented with the digital version of the exhibition room linked in footnote 6, which featured various exhibits mentioned in the game.

To investigate the hypotheses (1) and (2), we administered a questionnaire immediately after the gameplay session. The questionnaire incorporated selected questions from the System Usability Scale (SUS) [14], the Usability Metrics for User Experience (UMUX) [15], and the Virtual Reality Sickness Questionnaire (VRSQ), proposed by Hue et. al. [16]. The SUS and UMUX questions utilized a response scale ranging from (1) strongly disagree to (6) strongly agree. In contrast, the VRSQ questions focused on selecting the sickness symptoms experienced from a provided list. The 10-question questionnaire used for the qualitative data collection is presented in Fig. 3.

To examine the hypothesis (3), participants who had seen the exhibition room were asked to identify and record presented exhibits and information that they could associate with elements they recognized in the game.

5.3   Results

Our study involved 15 participants, ranging from 19 to 42 in age [M: 25.5, SD: 6.3]. Among those surveyed, 8 individuals had previous experience with VR applications, while 7 did not. The collected data of the SUS and UMUX questions are depicted in Fig. 4. In terms of usability, we received predominantly positive feedback, with participants perceiving the interaction design as intuitive. The

SUS	UMUX	VRSQ
a) I found Yabusame!!! unneccessarily complex. b) I think that I would need the support of a technical person to be able to use Yabusame!!!. c) I would imagine that most people would learn Yabusame!!! very quickly.	a) Using Yabusame!!! is a frustrating experience. b) Yabusame!!! is easy to use.	· General Discomfort · Eyestrain · Headache · Blurred Vision · Vertigo

Fig. 3. Questionnaire based on the SUS, UMUX, and VRSQ scales.

results for SUS-a) [M: 1.2, SD: 0.4], SUS-c) [M: 4.9, SD: 0.8], and UMUX-a) [M: 1.6, SD: 0.6] indicate that participants encountered minimal difficulties in using the controls of *Yabusame!!!*. This aligns with our observation during the experiment, as no participants requested additional assistance after the verbal briefing. Particularly noteworthy for the daily operations of the *Hornmoldhaus*, SUS-b) [M: 1.4, SD: 0.9] and UMUX-b) [M: 4.8, SD: 0.7] emphasize that the application is easy to learn and that only a few participants indicated the need for technical support to understand the game. It is important to mention that the feedback suggesting difficulties with interaction and a desire for technical support consistently came from participants without prior experience with VR applications, likely due to their limited familiarity with the medium. In our view, these results confirm hypothesis (1).

The findings from the VRSQ assessment indicate that participants did not exhibit significant symptoms of motion sickness after a single playthrough. One participant reported experiencing *General Discomfort* and *Eyestrain*, while two participants mentioned *Blurred Vision*. Additionally, another participant reported *Eyestrain*. These results further support hypothesis (2) and provide reassurance that *Yabusame!!!* can be employed as an interactive medium within the exhibition without concerns about visitors having to interrupt their museum visit due to motion sickness.

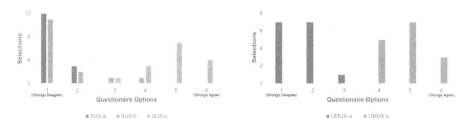

Fig. 4. Results of the questionnaire depicted in Fig. 3. **Left:** System Usability Scale (SUS) questions. **Right:** Results of the Usability Metrics for User Experience (UMUX) questions.

We received various textual feedback from participants, and we have compiled the most noteworthy excerpts here. Out of the participants, twelve mentioned that they would have appreciated an indicator, such as an arrow or a crosshairs, on the bow asset to enhance shooting precision. Two participants highlighted the potential benefits of an additional in-game tutorial, particularly to provide further practice with aiming before engaging in the levels. Two participants expressed their desire for more levels and additional background information. Lastly, one participant suggested the inclusion of a level selection feature to allow players to revisit and attempt levels they had not yet completed with a three-star rating.

In relation to hypothesis (3), almost all participants acknowledged the connection between the art style of the exhibits and the graphics presented in the game; especially that of the picture scrolls exhibited. Nine participants identified the samurai armor on display within the exhibition. However, only two of them were able to draw the connection to the Yabusame targets. Four participants recalled the information about Erwin Baelz when they encountered his likeness in the exhibition. Three participants expressed a sense of absence regarding arrows within the exhibition, as they were referenced by the in-game narrator. Furthermore, one participant speculated that a depicted flying turtle might represent a Yōkai or a Kami, concepts that were described in the game.

6   Conclusion

In this paper, we have presented *Yabusame!!!*, our virtual reality serious game designed to educate players about the traditional Japanese archery on horseback and related content. We discussed the game's design choices, specifically focusing on its integration into a museum exhibition. Through a user study, we ensured the practical usability of *Yabusame!!!* in this context, and the results indicated that the game's interactions were intuitive to use and did not induce motion sickness. Additionally, the study demonstrated that players were able to make connections between the information learned during a single playthrough of *Yabusame!!!* and the exhibition.

Building upon the valuable suggestions provided by study participants, we are currently exploring opportunities for further game development. Specifically, we are actively considering the implementation of the requested crosshairs and an in-game tutorial, both of which have been deemed important by the participants. Additionally, we are interested in assessing the opinions of older players to ensure the game meets their expectations as well. Furthermore, we aim to investigate whether the information learned during a single playthrough remains accessible after an extended period, such as two weeks. These areas pose interesting questions for future exploration and development.

References

1. (Hrsg.) Kaysers, A., Kollar, E., Kunz-Ott, H., Mergen, S., Nettke, T.: Leitfaden Bildung und Vermittlung im Museum gestalten, Deutscher Museumsbund & Bundesverband Museumspädagogik, Berlin (2020). ISBN 978-3-9819866-7-9

2. Giannini, T., Bowen, J.P.: Rethinking museum exhibitions: merging physical and digital culture—past to present. In: Giannini, T., Bowen, J.P. (eds.) Museums and Digital Culture. SSCC, pp. 163–193. Springer, Cham (2019). https://doi.org/10.1007/978-3-319-97457-6_8

3. Li, Y.-C., Liew, A.W.-C., Su, W.-P.: The digital museum: challenges and solution. In: 2012 8th International Conference on Information Science and Digital Content Technology (ICIDT2012), Jeju, pp. 646–649 (2012)

4. Richardson, J.: Virtual Reality is a big trend in museums, but what are the best examples of museums using VR?, museumnext.com, 5 June 2023. https://www.museumnext.com/article/how-museums-are-using-virtual-reality. Accessed 16 June 2023

5. Cecotti, H.: Cultural heritage in fully immersive virtual reality. Virtual Worlds 1, 82–102 (2022). https://doi.org/10.3390/virtualworlds1010006

6. Theodoropoulos, A., Antoniou, A.: VR games in cultural heritage: a systematic review of the emerging fields of virtual reality and culture games. Appl. Sci. 12, 8476 (2022). https://doi.org/10.3390/app12178476

7. Imura, M., Kozuka, J., Minami, K., Tabata, Y., Shuzui, T., Chihara, K.: Virtual Horseback archery. In: Nakatsu, R., Hoshino, J. (eds.) Entertainment Computing. ITIFIP, vol. 112, pp. 141–148. Springer, Boston (2003). https://doi.org/10.1007/978-0-387-35660-0_17

8. Adachi, T., Yamada, M., Kanematsu, A., Miyazaki, S., Naka, T.: Horseback archery VR based on multiple sensors. In: 2020 IEEE 9th Global Conference on Consumer Electronics (GCCE), Kobe, Japan, pp. 648–650 (2020). https://doi.org/10.1109/GCCE50665.2020.9291780

9. Shehade, M., Stylianou-Lambert, T.: Virtual reality in museums: exploring the experiences of museum professionals. Appl. Sci. 10(11), 4031 (2020). https://doi.org/10.3390/app10114031

10. Keshavarz, B., Golding, J.F.: Motion sickness: current concepts and management. Curr. Opin. Neurol. 35(1), 107–112 (2022). https://doi.org/10.1097/WCO.0000000000001018

11. Raible, C.: In Japan hoch verehrt - in Württemberg wenig bekannt: Der Bietigheimer Arzt und Kunstsammler Erwin von Baelz, May 2022, Schwäbische Heimat 2022—2, pp. 33–39 (2022). ISSN 0342-7595

12. Caserman, P., et al.: Quality criteria for serious games: serious part, game part, and balance. JMIR Serious Games 8(3), e19037 (2020). https://doi.org/10.2196/19037. PMID: 32706669; PMCID: PMC7414398

13. Blair, L.: The Cake Is Not a Lie: How to Design Effective Achievements, Gamedeveloper.com, 27 April 2011. https://www.gamedeveloper.com/design/the-cake-is-not-a-lie-how-to-design-effective-achievements. Accessed 14 June 2023

14. Brooke, J.: SUS-A Quick and Dirty Usability Scale. Usability Evaluation in Industry. CRC Press, London (1996). ISBN: 9780748404605

15. Finstad, K.: The usability metric for user experience. Interact. Comput. 22(5), 323–327 (2010). https://doi.org/10.1016/j.intcom.2010.04.004

16. Kim, H.K., Park, J., Choi, Y., Choe, M.: Virtual reality sickness questionnaire (VRSQ): motion sickness measurement index in a virtual reality environment. Appl. Ergon. 69, 66–73 (2018). https://doi.org/10.1016/j.apergo.2017.12.016. Epub 16 January 2018, PMID: 29477332

Astral Body: A Virtual Reality Game for Body Ownership Investigation

Yimin Zhou, Merlijn Mac Gillavry, Pengzhi Yang, Zihao Xu, Baitian Zhang, and Rafael Bidarra(✉) (iD)

Delft University of Technology, Delft, Netherlands
R.Bidarra@tudelft.nl

Abstract. As one of the most disruptive human-computer interaction techniques, Virtual Reality (VR) provides a novel way to examine human movements, e.g. when investigating Body Ownership (BO) in the field of cognitive sciences, especially when the visual output diverges from real-world actions. Previous research in BO uses questionnaires and brain imaging, where the former is a highly subjective metric, and the latter is very costly in time, money, and personnel. To answer the question *How can a VR serious game help overcome current challenges of BO assessment?*, we designed *Astral Body*, a VR game that helps cognitive science researchers assess people's level of BO. In the game, players are asked to grab 'flying collectibles' coming from a portal in space. Researchers can inject different types and levels of asynchrony into the arms of the visualized avatar, thus affecting the players' BO experience and perception. Players, in turn, can also report whenever they perceive possible mismatched avatar behavior. In addition, researchers can analyze player data, including looking for unconscious responses, e.g. small adjustments in physical movements to mitigate injected asynchrony. Preliminary results from playtesting and qualitative analysis of *Astral Body* indicate that a VR game can effectively help researchers investigate BO phenomena.

Keywords: Virtual reality · Body ownership · Control asynchrony

1 Introduction

The study of the self has a deep and far-reaching history in philosophy from Buddhism and Taoism to Ancient Greece and later philosophers such as David Hume and Descartes. Although it has been a widely discussed topic over millennia, no real consensus has been reached on what the self really means and, from a philosophical standpoint, that might not even be achievable. The scientific field of cognitive sciences, however, has tried to link the domains of psychology, philosophy, and neurology together to investigate the subject and the experiences it produces. Gallagher [7] argues that in terms of the 'minimal self' (an idea of the self unbounded by a temporal dimension) a distinction can be made between *self-agency* (the sense of agency over one's actions) and *self-ownership* of one's actions. The latter is also called *Body Ownership* (BO).

© The Author(s), under exclusive license to Springer Nature Switzerland AG 2024
P. Dondio et al. (Eds.): GALA 2023, LNCS 14475, pp. 43–55, 2024.
https://doi.org/10.1007/978-3-031-49065-1_5

Many BO researchers, such as by Ehrsson et al. [6] and Budai et al. [11], study this phenomenon by both using questionnaires and brain imaging techniques. These questionnaires, although easily deployed, are highly subjective and hard to use in the study of covert cognitive phenomena. Brain imaging techniques are scientifically more objective, but cost a lot of resources in terms of money, time and personnel. Additionally, even when doing research by using equipment such as fMRI, investigating BO dynamically is difficult. EEG can be used in a dynamic setting but there is still no good paradigm to map brain signals related to BO. Real-life BO illusions are also more time-consuming to set up and are hard to perform without the participants having an idea about what is being studied with them.

We pose that by employing an immersive Virtual Reality (VR) serious game, the above limitations can be overcome. Therefore, our main research question is: *How can a serious game overcome the current challenges of BO assessment?* To answer this question we created *Astral Body*, a VR serious game in which players move their hands to grab moving objects from the air. The game allows for the controlled stealthy injection of both spatial and temporal asynchrony between the actual player movements and their visualized counterparts. Many parameters of the game can be configured at will by researchers, so that a variety of experiments can be easily designed, reproduced and/or modified. *Astral Body* collects a variety of player movement data, permitting researchers to measure and analyze the behavior of players, including their reactions attempting to mitigate injected asynchrony. Due to *Astral Body*'s immersive gameplay, experiments are more engaging and have fewer confounding variables, particularly regarding players' awareness of its concrete research purposes.

2   Related Work

This section provides an overview of prior research related to BO, using both traditional methods and virtual reality.

2.1   The Self and Body Ownership

Gallagher [7] reviews the concept of the *self* and also differentiates between the sense of self-agency and the sense of self-ownership of one's actions (e.g. the sense of driving or washing) that can also be regarded as BO. If the information received by the body from different sensory modalities such as vision, proprioception, and kinesthetics, all correspond and match with each other, it results in a sense of BO [9]. Previous research proposed various ways to estimate the sense of limb ownership or global body awareness [4], while we are concentrating on the former setting.

BO experiments have been devised in multiple domains, including the study of psychological disorders [17]. The Rubber Hand Illusion (RHI), devised by Botvinick & Cohen [2], is seen as the pioneer and most famous experiment to show the proprioception drift. They describe that mixing experiences from different modalities could be sufficient for a sense of BO in participants, regarding objects that are not physically connected to them. In the platform, one artificial limb would be placed in front of the participants which could be visually observed by the participant, while the real limb was hidden or covered. Then, researchers applied the same stimulus signals on virtual and real limbs. An illusion of BO over the artificial limb would be induced in most cases: participants mislocalized their real limbs to be at the artificial limbs' position.

To further explore the inducements which also lead to BO illusion, various RHI extensions have been conducted. Walsh et al. leveraged a mechanical facility for synchronous finger movement in their platform [18]. As measured by the questionnaires, BO illusions were also reported by a majority of the participants, which demonstrated synchronous body movements as another source for the illusion besides visuotactile stimulus. However, the limited adaptability of the experimental facilities impairs the advancement of experimental methodology within this area of study. Furthermore, the utilization of conventional instruments also leads to issues of inefficiency and reduced data precision.

2.2   Virtual Reality and Body Ownership

Similarly to the RHI, the sense of BO can also be replicated in a VR environment [15,16]. Bourdin et al. investigated the effects of altered visual feedback on unconscious motor and muscular adjustments during limb movement within an immersive virtual reality environment [3]. Participants were instructed to perform a movement of 90°C while their virtual arm movement angles were manipulated. The use of sensors to assess BO in their studies, and having users mechanically repeat the arm movement, may not be ergonomically valid and may amplify users' awareness of the purpose of their research.

Yizhar et al. conducted a study on BO using virtual reality [19]. Participants performed the task of lifting and hitting balls while their virtual hands were either incongruent or congruent with their real-world hands. BO was then assessed through surveys filled out by the participants. In their study, a VR scenario was employed; however, some participants reported experiencing ennui. Moreover, their method cannot determine the moment at which participants become aware of incongruities.

Little research has been conducted on the study of BO in the presence of asynchronous elements. The categorization of asynchronous elements can be differentiated into two types: spatial and temporal asynchrony. This distinction is in accordance with the findings of Chancel et al. [5], who showed that the temporal and spatial congruence principles of multi-sensory stimulation are determinants of BO discrimination. In a study [13], participants were instructed to alternately switch between a virtual body closely resembling themselves, in which they described a personal problem, and a virtual character representing Dr. Sigmund Freud, from which they offered themselves counseling. The study found that when the virtual Freud moved synchronously with the participant, a stronger illusion of ownership over the Freud body was experienced, compared to when it moved asynchronously. They primarily examine the impact of temporal asynchrony on BO; however, the effect of spatial asynchrony would also be worth investigating. Andreasen et al. [1] conducted a study on spatial asynchrony, where participants underwent visuo-tactile stimulation on their arms while viewing an object touching a bat wing at three varying spatial displacements between the virtual touchpoint and the actual arm position. The results indicated that a level of BO could be achieved, but the degree of BO declined as the spatial displacement increased. The study only focused on three mappings and further investigation with a continuous and diverse range of scales was not explored.

González-Franco et al. [8] investigated the BO of an avatar viewed in a virtual mirror. This study incorporated elements of both spatial and temporal asynchrony to some extent, under two conditions: a synchronous condition, where the avatar reflected the participant's upper-body movements in real time, and an asynchronous condition, where the avatar displayed pre-recorded actions similar to the participant's movements. Results showed that participants felt a stronger sense of BO in the synchronous condition. However, the approach of pre-recorded actions was limited in revealing detailed information on asynchrony and suffered from a lack of flexibility as different actions may have resulted in varying effects.

Summarizing, current research has identified the following main challenges for BO assessment: limited adaptability of experimental facilities, laborious and costly experiments, and exposed research goals, leading to participation bias [10].

3   Game Design

To address the deficiencies identified above, and capitalize on the immersiveness of virtual reality, we designed and developed *Astral Body*, a serious game that integrates both spatial and temporal asynchrony into its key game mechanics. *Astral Body* has been designed with the purpose of helping cognitive science researchers identify key predictors of BO with a VR avatar. In addition, the game immerses players in a fictive scenario, keeping their focus away from the researchers' intention of evaluating BO. By adopting this decision, bias stemming from research participation could be potentially eliminated, as suggested by McCambridge et al. [12].

3.1   Synopsis

The player, using VR goggles, is placed in a fictive virtual environment, in which they control the visible hands of their avatar. Objects come sequentially floating towards the player, who has to catch and deposit them, one at a time, in a container. The player wears conventional VR hand controllers, in order to track their arm and hand movements. Players are encouraged to reach a proposed threshold score across several levels. In addition, they are invited to press on the controller main button, if on any occasion they perceive something anomalous with the game's responsiveness.

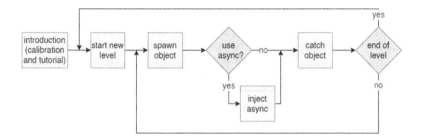

Fig. 1. Main game loop of *Astral Body*, with each level consisting of a series of object catches, possibly affected by asynchrony.

3.2   Main Design Choices

As a game to be played only once by each player, and for research purposes, it is desirable that the gameplay of *Astral Body* is made accessible to a broad range of participants, without presenting a steep learning curve. We therefore chose for simple mechanics of catching and collecting items, as shown in the main game loop of Fig. 1.

Typically, a game level can take up to 90 seconds to complete as, after all, there is physical movement involved, and one should be given some rest periodically. Initially, game levels operate as normally expected. However, after a while, asynchrony will start being introduced at different levels, according to the settings chosen by the researcher, as discussed in the following subsection.

Players are not informed of the real research goals nor, for that matter, ever hear terms like 'asynchrony' or 'body ownership'. Instead, they are simply instructed to press the 'feedback' controller button might they perceive any game anomalies, as if they were e.g. beta-playtesting the game.

Researchers are offered a large flexibility to configure a variety of input parameters, which help customize in detail the injection of asynchrony (e.g. type, amplitude, frequency, duration, etc.). In addition, logging of the above player data is automatically performed, including asynchrony parameters, possible 'feedback' signaled and its timestamp, so that researchers can then use it for further analysis.

3.3   Asynchrony Injection

Our hypothesis is that there will be BO perception as long as the virtual arms closely follow the movements of the physical arms of the player. To assess the extent of this 'closeness', we introduce asynchrony to the movements of the virtual arm. In the context of this game, *asynchrony is defined as a disparity between the movements of the physical arm and of the virtual arm*. This introduction is done incrementally, in a controlled fashion, so that as the asynchrony increases, participants may start experiencing a decline in BO. The expectation is that at some point, the player will feel uncomfortable with the discrepancy between their movements and the respective visualization, and signal the fact pressing the 'feedback' controller button. The game will then record the event, including the timestamp at which the participant reports a loss of control over the virtual body. In this way, we can determine at which point the participants' BO will break due to inconsistency between real arm movements and virtual arm movements.

For the purposes of this research, we consider two types of asynchrony: spatial and temporal. Each type of asynchrony can be configured at each game level, as desired by the researcher. This can possibly include combining the two types in the same game level, whenever desired.

Spatial Asynchrony: consists of inserting a deviation between the virtual arm position and that of the real arm. For this, a target displacement vector is computed which is gradually applied to the position of the virtual arm as the actual movement of the arm progresses. Under this scenario, the virtual hand moves together with the player's hand, but ends up at a shifted location, possibly leading to a sensation of movement inaccuracy.

Temporal Asynchrony: consists of inserting a target latency in the response of the virtual arm visualized. For this, samples of the actual hand trajectory are recorded in a memory buffer, and are used, after a target delay, to reproduce that same movement on the virtual hand. Under this scenario, the virtual hand accurately ends up at the same location of the player's hand, but with a delay, possibly leading to a sensation of movement latency due to the lagged motion visualization.

3.4 Specific Game Mechanics

Game Level Configuration. The implementation of multiple levels in the game serves to mitigate the drawbacks of having a player face exactly the same challenges over and over again, which often arises in many experimental trials. Because *Astral Body* aims at helping cognitive science researchers identify key predictors of BO, the game features fully configurable and directly accessible input parameters, including the object spawning rate, the target level scores, etc. as shown in Appendix A.

By offering various levels with differing settings, the game is able to maintain participants challenged and engaged, as well as distract them from the true research objectives. This is instrumental in ensuring the validity and reliability of the data and results obtained.

Introductory Level. Due to the nature of *Astral Body*, which heavily focuses on arm movements, it is important to avoid disparities associated with the player's diverse height or arm length, to assure that the main player challenge remains the asynchrony mentioned in the previous subsection. Therefore, an introductory level, consisting of calibration and a tutorial, was designed. The *calibration phase* requires players to perform hand-waving actions to record their actual hand positions; see Fig. 2a. This information is relevant to help determine the range from which objects will spawn during the game. Subsequently,

(a) The player calibrates spawning points by mimicking avatar's motions.

(b) The player reaches out the arms to catch an object.

(c) The player catches an object, drops it in the basket, and scores points.

Fig. 2. In-game footage of game mechanics.

in the *tutorial phase*, players will play several rounds of the game under guidance, gaining a basic understanding of the game mechanics and learning how to effectively interact with the virtual environment using the controllers. The tutorial phase serves to suppress possible unfamiliarity factors with VR, which might otherwise hinder the players' performance during the experiments and, therefore, negatively impact the accuracy of the collected data.

Object Catching. Following the introductory level, at each game level, the player is tasked with catching objects of specific shapes and colors and dropping them in the basket in front of them to earn points, as depicted in Figs. 2b and 2c. The action of catching occurs commonly, is brief in duration and is physically light, allowing for a reasonable amount of data to be easily collected. Additionally, as objects fly towards the player from various starting points, this guarantees a sufficient variety in direction and type of movement, thus reducing boredom. When a player's score reaches the required threshold, they progress to the next level, while a high rate of missed objects results in a failure of the current level. The explicit scoring mechanism helps to ensure that participants are focused on the gameplay rather than on other topics, while also maintaining the enjoyment of the game. As the game progresses to higher levels, it will switch from mostly synchronous to increasingly more asynchronous and challenging. Furthermore, the basket is designed such that participants must deposit the objects in close proximity to its opening. This standardizes the movements performed by all participants, enabling the comparison of movement patterns across individuals, which can potentially be used to correlate with questionnaire data collected by other researchers from this game.

3.5   Data Collection

Astral Body logs a variety of data, aimed at providing researchers with insight into the perceptual aspects of BO and the effects of spatial and temporal asynchrony on it. This data includes several key elements, as outlined in Appendix B.

By collecting and analyzing this data in conjunction with research questionnaires, such as the Virtual Embodiment Questionnaire (VEQ) developed by Roth et al. [14], researchers can gain a comprehensive understanding of body ownership at different levels of spatial and temporal asynchrony. Additionally, Confirmatory Factor Analysis (CFA) can be applied to the obtained data to explore the underlying factors and relationships between different aspects of body ownership perception.

3.6   Game Style

The art style used in *Astral Body* is inspired in low-poly games, characterized by stylized and simple characters and environments. This was done to avoid heavy rendering demands on low-end hardware, as well as to maintain focus on measuring BO without being overly realistic and risking the 'uncanny valley' problem. *Astral Body* offers a casual and relaxing atmosphere for the participants.

4   Game Evaluation

A thorough evaluation of the efficacy of *Astral Body* in assessing the influence of asynchrony in perceived BO levels is currently underway, performed by cognitive science researchers. That is an endeavour that takes many months of careful preparation (including ethical approval), execution and data analysis. In due time, its results will be reported elsewhere.

We did a preliminary study, focusing on how players react to different levels of asynchrony. The evaluation session consisted of playtesting three levels of *Astral Body*, and filling in a survey. All participants played the same levels with the same parameters, to eliminate other interfering factors.

4.1   Experimental Settings

The evaluation session was carried out among college students, and no prior VR gaming experience was required. The participants were simply introduced to the VR hardware and instructed to press the feedback button if they perceived anything unusual during gameplay, without disclosing the game's purpose. They then played three levels, one with no asynchrony, one with spatial asynchrony only, and one with temporal asynchrony only. After completing each level, the participants were asked to fill out a survey immediately. The evaluation session had 6 student participants, aged between 19 and 24.

4.2   Results

The results of the survey are summarized in Fig. 3. In the level with no asynchrony, 100% of the students felt they were accurately controlling the virtual movements; see Fig. 3a. In the level with spatial asynchrony, 16.7% of the participants weakly disagreed that they felt like the virtual body was their own body; see Fig. 3b. In the level with temporal asynchrony (Fig. 3c), the participants were split: half of them disagreed that the virtual body was matching their own movements. Lastly, most participants agreed that it was enjoyable to control the virtual body.

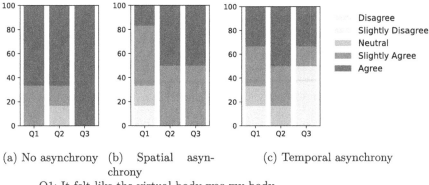

(a) No asynchrony (b) Spatial asyn-   (c) Temporal asynchrony
                    chrony

Q1: It felt like the virtual body was my body
Q2: I enjoyed controlling the virtual body
Q3: The movements of the virtual body matched my own movements

Fig. 3. Survey results for 3 different levels.

During the playtest session, we found that around half of the participants totally forgot to press the user feedback button at any point. For those participants who did remember about it, we analyzed their feedback reaction instant, and concluded that it occurred on average, when a temporal asynchrony of 0.2 s was injected.

4.3   Discussion

The survey results for the 'no asynchrony' level, see Fig. 3a, seem to indicate that all the participants either slightly or completely considered the virtual body was their own body. This is in line with what one could expect for a fully synchronous level, and confirms that in *Astral Body*, BO perception is not affected by factors other than injected asynchrony. The survey also reveals that the majority of the participants enjoyed controlling the virtual body in all levels, including the two levels with asynchrony, indicating that the game is enjoyable to play. Moreover, we confirmed that by increasing temporal asynchrony, players reach a point at which they report feeling uncomfortable with the virtual body response. Although there is a clear need for more experimental data, we can say that *Astral Body* seems to be helpful in assessing the threshold for the acceptable level of asynchrony in BO.

From a comparison of the responses to Q3 between Fig. 3a and Figs. 3b and 3c, we can clearly conclude that incorporating asynchrony into the game response directly led to a break in BO perception. From a comparison between the responses to Q1 and Q3 for levels with asynchrony, in Figs. 3b and 3c, we see there is a larger spreading for the temporal asynchrony level, which was the last level played. This can very well be due to the low n in this evaluation. However, we believe that might also be because after completing the first two levels (no asynchrony and spatial asynchrony), some participants are becoming used to the game and accommodating to its asynchrony.

In short, for this preliminary evaluation, it can be observed that manually injected asynchrony is the sole factor that affects BO perception in the game. This seems to confirm that the *Astral Body* game is a helpful tool for cognitive science researchers to study BO.

5   Conclusions

We presented *Astral Body*, an immersive VR game that helps cognitive science researchers assess the level of body ownership (BO) of its players. To the best of our knowledge, *Astral Body* is the first game combining both spatial and temporal asynchrony, that was developed specifically for such BO research purposes. Another key innovation of this assessment method is that it keeps players focused on the gameplay, rather than exposing them to the actual research goals.

From our preliminary game evaluation, we concluded that the game provides players with an engaging and immersive experience. We also found reasonable evidence that *Astral Body* effectively elicited among its players a sense of BO, which in turn clearly decreased whenever asynchrony elements are introduced in the game mechanics. We can therefore conclude that the *Astral Body* game is a useful tool for researchers to effectively assess BO. Among other reasons for this, the game offers researchers full control over all settings, allowing for a wide range of customization and experimentation, and provides them valuable player data, including asynchrony events and their timestamps.

Despite the game's potential, our evaluation constitutes only a preliminary trial, designed by the developers. Its promising results, therefore, will have to be confirmed by a more comprehensive, rigorous and long evaluation experiment, which is presently underway, lead by cognitive science experts. Its results, involving a much larger and varied sample of participants, should reveal whether the above findings and conclusions can be confirmed and generalized.

In the future, we would like to develop better methods to help effectively explore the collected game data, and possibly expand it with other useful data. A deeper analysis of the in-game statistics, including the identification of new relationships and models, will likely provide a deeper understanding of the factors contributing to the assessment of BO. It might also be interesting to enhance the level of immersion of the game by incorporating haptic feedback to the action of catching objects.

The *Astral Body* game investigates the perception of body ownership with arm movement tasks. We believe that it could serve as a precursor for further research into a variety of disorders, both physiological and psychological. We therefore expect that, in the future, researchers investigate transferring this game concept to other clinical populations, to further understand the causes of their motor impairments.

Acknowledgments. We thank Ineke van der Ham and Julie Hall of Leiden University for their inspiration, expertise and guidance throughout this project.

Appendices

A. Configuration parameters for research experiments

Input	Usage
General settings	
Player name	Identifier of the participant
Calibration	Toggle whether to enable calibration
Debug	Toggle whether to enable debug window (shows e.g. asynchrony data)
Log frequency	How often the player data is recorded
Task description	The instruction on the game's virtual panel guiding the participants to fulfill the tasks
Object value	The score of an object
Difficulty	
Maximum misses	How many times a participant can miss a catch
Spawn rate	How fast the objects spawn
MaxAmountSpawned	The max number of objects to be spawned at each level
Object speed	How fast the objects fly to the player
Asynchrony	
Async chances	Probability of asynchrony injection
Spatial async offset	offset applied to the virtual arms
Temporal async offset	Temporal offsets
Injection time	Time required for asynchrony to reach the set offset
Async streak max	Maximum number of object spawns before decreasing asynchrony
Async streak min	Minimum number of object spawns before decreasing asynchrony
Game level	
Is target	Whether the spawned object is a target which should be grabbed to gain score
Despawn time	Duration before a spawned object disappears (if it is not grabbed)
Object selection	What objects to spawn
Level name	Identifier of the level
Score goal	Required score to finish the level
Max level duration	How long the participants can spend on one specific level

B. Data logged during research experiments

Data	Usage
Item id	serves as a unique identifier for the target object in the game, allowing researchers to track its behavior and interactions
Item position	provides information about the current position of the target object in the game world, which can be useful for analyzing player interactions and spatial relationships
Left item & Right item	indicate the item IDs held by the player's left and right hands, respectively, if they have already been caught
Player feedback	(left and right) records the timestamp when the participant presses the controller feedback button, which can give measurable insights about perceived asynchrony
Left & right controller position	provide the coordinates of each controller. These coordinates can be used to analyze the player's hand movements during the game, which may contribute to the sense of body ownership
Level duration	indicates the time the participant has spent in the level. This overall duration of the gameplay experience helps researchers understand its potential relation to BO
Spatial asynchrony data	records the spatial offset of the virtual arms in x, y, and z coordinates. This information helps researchers investigate the effects of spatial asynchrony on BO perception, including the player's ability to coordinate their movements with the virtual body
Temporal asynchrony data	indicates the delay introduced into the virtual arms movement. This data helps researchers assess the impact of temporal asynchrony on BO perception and the player's sense of agency

References

1. Andreasen, A., Nilsson, N.C., Serafin, S.: Spatial asynchronous Visuo-Tactile stimuli influence ownership of virtual wings. In: 2018 IEEE Conference on Virtual Reality and 3D User Interfaces (VR), pp. 503–504 (2018). https://doi.org/10.1109/VR.2018.8446569
2. Botvinick, M., Cohen, J.: Rubber hands 'feel' touch that eyes see. Nature **391**(6669), 756–756 (1998). https://doi.org/10.1038/35784
3. Bourdin, P., Martini, M., Sanchez-Vives, M.V.: Altered visual feedback from an embodied avatar unconsciously influences movement amplitude and muscle activity. Sci. Rep. **9**(1), 1–9 (2019)
4. Braun, N., et al.: The senses of agency and ownership: a review. Front. Psychol. **9**, 535 (2018)
5. Chancel, M., Ehrsson, H.H.: Which hand is mine? Discriminating body ownership perception in a two-alternative forced-choice task. Atten. Percept. Psychophysics **82**(8), 4058–4083 (2020). https://doi.org/10.3758/s13414-020-02107-x

6. Ehrsson, H.H., Holmes, N.P., Passingham, R.E.: Touching a rubber hand: feeling of body ownership is associated with activity in multisensory brain areas. J. Neurosci. **25**(45), 10564–10573 (2005)
7. Gallagher, S.: Philosophical conceptions of the self: implications for cognitive science. Trends Cogn. Sci. **4**(1), 14–21 (2000)
8. González-Franco, M., Pérez-Marcos, D., Spanlang, B., Slater, M.: The contribution of real-time mirror reflections of motor actions on virtual body ownership in an immersive virtual environment. In: 2010 IEEE Virtual Reality Conference (VR), pp. 111–114 (2010). https://doi.org/10.1109/VR.2010.5444805
9. Kalckert, A., Ehrsson, H.H.: Moving a rubber hand that feels like your own: a dissociation of ownership and agency. Front. Hum. Neurosci. **6**, 40 (2012)
10. Keeble, C., Barber, S., Law, G.R., Baxter, P.D.: Participation bias assessment in three high-impact journals. SAGE Open **3**(4), 2158244013511260 (2013). https://doi.org/10.1177/2158244013511260
11. Matuz-Budai, T., Lábadi, B., Kohn, E., Matuz, A., Zsidó, A.N., Inhóf, O., Kállai, J., Szolcsányi, T., Perlaki, G., Orsi, G., Nagy, S.A., Janszky, J., Darnai, G.: Individual differences in the experience of body ownership are related to cortical thickness. Sci. Rep. **12**(1), 808 (2022)
12. McCambridge, J., Kypri, K., Elbourne, D.: In randomization we trust? there are overlooked problems in experimenting with people in behavioral intervention trials. J. Clin. Epidemiol. **67**(3), 247–253 (2014)
13. Osimo, S.A., Pizarro, R., Spanlang, B., Slater, M.: Conversations between self and 'self as Sigmund Freud' - a virtual body ownership paradigm for self counselling. Sci. Rep. **5**(1), 1–14 (2015)
14. Roth, D., Latoschik, M.E.: Construction of the Virtual Embodiment Questionnaire (VEQ). IEEE Trans. Visual Comput. Graphics **26**(12), 3546–3556 (2020). https://doi.org/10.1109/TVCG.2020.3023603
15. Slater, M., Pérez Marcos, D., Ehrsson, H., Sanchez-Vives, M.V.: Towards a digital body: the virtual arm illusion. Front. Hum. Neurosci. **2**, 6 (2008)
16. Slater, M., Pérez Marcos, D., Ehrsson, H., Sanchez-Vives, M.V.: Inducing illusory ownership of a virtual body. Front. Neurosci. **3**, 29 (2009)
17. Thakkar, K.N., Nichols, H.S., McIntosh, L.G., Park, S.: Disturbances in body ownership in schizophrenia: evidence from the rubber hand illusion and case study of a spontaneous out-of-body experience. PLoS ONE **6**(10), e27089 (2011)
18. Walsh, L.D., Moseley, G.L., Taylor, J.L., Gandevia, S.C.: Proprioceptive signals contribute to the sense of body ownership. J. Physiol. **589**(12), 3009–3021 (2011)
19. Yizhar, O., et al.: Body ownership of anatomically implausible hands in virtual reality. Front. Hum. Neurosci. **15**, 713931 (2021)

Towards a Competitive Two-Player Anti-phishing Learning Game

Rene Roepke$^{(\boxtimes)}$ (iD) and Johannes Ballmann (iD)

Learning Technologies Research Group, RWTH Aachen University, Aachen, Germany
roepke@cs.rwth-aachen.de, johannes.ballmann@rwth-aachen.de

Abstract. This paper explores the design and implementation of a competitive two-player anti-phishing learning game on the topic of phishing emails, aiming to educate users on how to recognize and create phishing emails, leveraging Cialdini's principles of persuasion. By moving towards a competitive environment, the game presents a more constructive learning environment, in which players can compete against each other during the game-based learning process. A preliminary user study investigates the new game mode and evaluates usability and user experience to further improve its implementation.

Keywords: Anti-Phishing Learning Game · Competitive Gameplay

1 Motivation

Phishing poses a large threat to end-users, in which impersonation is used to obtain information from a target [6]. Complementary to technical countermeasures, which fail to stop the ever evolving attack schemes [1], user education is considered in order to train and prepare end-users to recognize phishing attacks, e.g., in emails with suspicious features and characteristics. Over the last decade, game-based anti-phishing education has gained a lot of attention and various game prototypes have been the subject of research [8]. So far, many games have focused on teaching end-users the necessary knowledge to recognize phishing attacks and offer opportunities to practice essential skills in single-player game environments. Games most often present learners with a classification task in which they have to decide whether given emails or URLs are phishing or benign.

In [9], learners not only learn to recognize malicious emails, they are also asked to create their own phishing emails to better understand how persuasion principles are used to trick end-users into trusting the phishing email content and act upon it. This presents the opportunity to take a step towards competitive gameplay for anti-phishing learning games and explore the design of a competitive two-player anti-phishing learning game. As such, this paper describes the design and implementation of a competitive game version of [9], an anti-phishing learning game in which players learn how to recognize phishing emails and create emails using different principles of persuasion. The paper provides details on how competitive gameplay can be designed for anti-phishing education as well as first usability insights on the developed game prototype.

P. Dondio et al. (Eds.): GALA 2023, LNCS 14475, pp. 56–66, 2024.
https://doi.org/10.1007/978-3-031-49065-1_6

2   Theoretical Background and Related Work

When it comes to game-based anti-phishing education, various game prototypes have been developed and studied [8]. Most often, games focus on the detection of phishing URLs or emails, educate learners about classical attack schemes, and allow learners to practice the classification of URLs or emails in a rather limiting binary decision scheme. While this scheme does actually mimic a simplified version of real-world decisions, it limits the potential of learning games as it fails to address higher order cognitive processes (e.g., applying, evaluating [5]) and support learners in gaining a deeper understanding and stronger skills. By enriching anti-phishing learning games with different game mechanics and making gameplay more elaborate, game design aims for creating a more suitable learning environment that motivates and engages learners, is able to capture learners misconceptions and provide more elaborate feedback. Furthermore, by allowing players to apply the learned knowledge and create their own content, we move toward a more constructivistic learning design, in which learners become more active and incorporate new knowledge to construct their own understanding.

To also include a social component (as part of constructivism), collaborative and competitive gameplay can be explored. Here, research shows that "competition has attracted the attention of many researchers" [2], while still not reaching unified results on its role in game-based learning. This is due to its multifaceted nature and possible negative effects, depending on its implementation. Research shows that neither one type of competition is superior to others nor the same type of competition shows the same effects across different contexts. From the perspective of the social interdependence theory, first, competition was viewed as a negative force in the learning environment, but recently its constructive role in learning is explored more and more [4]. Besides its influence on engagement and motivation, competition is also considered influential to flow, as it is immediately linked to feelings of pleasure and satisfaction during gameplay [2].

Overall, the role of competition has not yet been widely explored in anti-phishing learning games. While some game prototypes may have considered leaderboards and scoring systems, none have implemented active competitive gameplay. This presents a research gap that will be addressed with the design and implementation of a first competitive anti-phishing learning game.

3   Game Design Requirements

For the extension of the game presented in [9], first, a use case is outlined and a requirement analysis was performed to determine user needs and required functionality. Both form the basis for guiding game design and implementation.

Use Case: In a competitive two-player game, we consider two primary user roles: (1) the initiator and (2) the competitor. While the initiator sets up a game session for two players to compete against each other, the competitor joins the session to start the game. The game itself may consist of two alternating modes in round-based level system. The two modes can be derived from the implemented creation and decision modes in [9]. Integrating the two user roles and connecting them in a shared game session allows for the following design:

– In the first mode, each player is required to craft a phishing email that will later be shown to the opponent for classification (as part of the second mode). When creating a phishing email, players have to first choose a sender address. Next, they can specify common email content like the subject line and the email body. Alternatively to suggested text fragments of an email as used in [9], free text creation should be considered, so players can creatively write their own phishing emails. After the email is created, players can submit it to continue to the next mode of the game.

– The second mode is based on the decision mode in [9]. Similar to before, players are presented with an email inbox interface with a set of emails, one which is the created email of the competing player. The players can open an email and are then asked to classify the email as either phishing or benign. When players suspect an email to be phishing, they are required to mark potential phishing features, capturing their decision process. After all emails in the inbox are processed, players receive feedback on their decisions and findings. Additionally, they receive feedback on the performance of the competing player, i.e. the decision and possible marking on the own, previously created email. For each correct decision and found phishing feature, as well as for each included element in the own phishing email that the opponent did not find, players obtain reward points.

After both players complete both modes, a level is completed. The game can then continue in a round-based manner depending on its configuration. Collected points are transferred between rounds and summed up to a final score in the end.

Requirements: Based on the outlined use case and the general idea of a competitive game mode, functional and non-functional requirements for the implementation were identified (for reference, see Table 1).

First of all, we consider which functionality can be included, for which the previously outlined use case serves as starting point. As such, a player, as the initiator, must be able to create a shared game session to start a new competitive game against a competitor (**RF1**). Alternatively players must be able to join a created game session in their role as a competitor. For the alternating game mode, in which created emails from one player are classified by the other, both players must be able to compete directly, i.e. they must be able to create potential phishing mails and submit them to the opponent (**RF2**). For competition, they must also be able to classify received emails by the opponents.

In general, players should be guided through the game by explanatory elements and storytelling (**RF3**). This is needed to structure the gameplay and instruct players in the different game modes. While the creation mode in [9] relied on pre-formulated sentences as part of a potential phishing email, players in the competitive mode should be able to write own email content in an

Table 1. Identified functional (RF) and non-functional (RN) requirements.

RF1	Game session management	**RF7**	Round-based level structure
RF2	Direct competition	**RF8**	Display of used text modules
RF3	Textual user guidance	**RF9**	Indirect competition
RF4	Easy-to-use email editor	**RN1**	Intuitive and clear design
RF5	Phishing feature selection	**RN2**	Seamless user interface
RF6	Phishing feature detection	**RN3**	(Near) real-time communication

easy-to-use text editor (**RF4**). To make sure detectable phishing features can be included, players should be given a selection of text fragments representing phishing features (**RF5**). These should be based on the persuasion principles by Cialdini [3], similar to the game in [9]. Next, players should be able to classify emails for a set of emails, where one email is the created email of the opponent (**RF6**). If players decide that a shown mail is phishing, they are prompted to mark all suspicious content, similar to the decision mode in [9].

In order to play multiple sets of emails, a round-based level system is required (**RF7**). This way, players can improve their performance during the game by learning from mistakes in previous rounds. At the end of each round, feedback needs to given to both players regarding their correct and incorrect decisions/markings as well as the opponents performance on the crafted email (**RF8**). Besides the direct competition realized through creation and decision mode per round, indirect competition can increase players' motivation, e.g. by collecting points and presenting both players scores at all times (**RF9**).

Besides the game's functionality, the way in which it should be implemented must also be determined. In particular, care must be taken to ensure the game mode adapts to the other game environment in an integrated way. Players must be able to navigate through the game without problems and need to be able find all controls in an appropriate time and manner (**RN1**). Every design decision must be reasonable and serve a purpose. The game elements in the competitive mode should be designed and integrated seamlessly in the existing game (**RN2**). If similar or equal elements are already used in other modes, these elements should be reused. Furthermore, for a better game flow, the game instances should be communicate in (near) real-time (**RN3**). However, necessary game flow interruptions need to be implemented so players progress equally. While it is important to implement the game mode functionality in an intuitive way and with clear user interface, the flow and UI elements should be similar to the pre-existing creation and decision mode. Thus, the goal is to reuse existing game elements or introduce new components with a fitting design, similar to [9] (Fig. 1).

4 Implementation

This section described the different implemented components of the competitive game mode. The competitive game mode is fully integrated in the pre-

Fig. 1. Screenshot of the editor for email creation showing a crafted email with phishing feature text snippets (as blue highlighted text). (Color figure online)

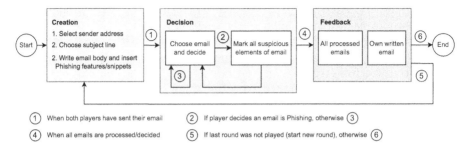

Fig. 2. Gameplay flow chart.

existing anti-phishing learning game "More than meets the eye" [9]. Thus, it is implemented using the Multitouch Learning Game (MTLG) framework[1], a JavaScript-based web framework supporting learning game development using the HTML5 Canvas element. While the framework was initially designed for multitouch interaction (e.g., on large multitouch tabletop displays), it can also support mouse and keyboard interactions in the browser. The game is executed fully client-side and only for the competitive mode, a communication server is implemented to host shared game sessions and connect the two game prototype instances of the initiator and the competitor. The gameflow is outlined in Fig. 2.

Game Mode Integration: To start the competitive game mode, players find a third game mode option as a button added to the start screen of the game. If the competitive game mode was selected, the MTLG level handler loads the corresponding view, in which players can either create a new shared game session as the initiator or join an existing one (cf. **RF1**). To enter a shared game session as the competitor, a 5-digit session code is needed. This code is generated upon

---

[1] https://mtlg-framework.gitlab.io, last accessed 29.06.2023.

creating a shared game session and needs to be shared between players on any communication channel (e.g., sharing it by reading it out loud in a face-to-face setup). When both players have joined the shared game session, the game begins with direct competition (cf. **RF2**), i.e. the creation mode for both players, where they are ask to craft their own email and embed different features (e.g., "within 24 h" for scarcity [3]). Depending on the configuration, a game session can last multiple rounds of creating and classifying emails (cf. **RF7**).

Email Creation: To provide an easy-to-use text editor for email generation (cf. **RF4**), the game prototype was extended by including HTML `form` elements besides the `Canvas`. Since text editing on the `Canvas` is less intuitive, due to text only being recognized as a graphical object, HTML elements like `input` fields and `div` elements were more suitable. As such, the text editor for email creation is built as an overlay modal containing a `select` element displaying a customizable pool of sender addresses as a dropdown, an `input` field for the email subject line and a fixed receiver field since all created emails are addressed to the opponent. For the email body, a `div` element with editable content is used, such that players can type text in it as well as embed `span` elements inside of it. To create a phishing email, a set of selected phishing features in form of text snippets displayed as small clickable rectangular boxes is provided above the `div` element for players to choose from and add them into their text (cf. **RF5**). This way, players can start writing their custom email and pick and choose appropriate phishing features via simple click selection to create a convincing phishing email and trick the opponent. The provided phishing features are based on Cialdinis persuasion principles [3]. They are necessary to enable marking, when the opponent suspects it to be a phishing email. When completing the email creation, the email is sent to the opponent in a JSON representation containing all email fields as well as information on the embedded phishing features for marking.

Email Classification: After email creation, players are presented with the email inbox interface from the decision mode in [9] (cf. **RN2**). The inbox is filled with a set of emails for the players to classify. Hidden among the shown emails is also the created email by the opponent. One after another, players go through all emails and classify them as either phishing or benign (cf. **RF6**). When players suspect an email to be phishing, in a next step, they have to mark all suspicious characteristics with digital stamp. In distinction to the decision mode in [9], there is no instant feedback regarding the player's marking instead the processed email is disappears marked as read and the player continues with the next email until all emails are processed.

Feedback: After players have decided on all emails, they receive feedback on their performance, i.e. their decisions and placed/missed markings (cf. **RF8**). First, the inbox interface is reset and all mails are marked as unread again. Additionally it is visually indicated whether a player's decision for each was correct or not. When clicking on a phishing email, it is opened and all phishing features are shown. Depending whether a stamp was placed on the feature or not, it is indicated and players receive points for correct markings (cf. **RF9**). To continue, all mails must be opened at least once to receive the feedback and collect the points. Afterwards, the players receive feedback on the opponents performance on their created email. Similar to before, all features are marked and it is indicated whether the opponent has marked them successfully. For every feature that was not found by the opponent, the player also receives points.

Communication Server: The communication server is the interface between the different browser sessions and is responsible for exchanging necessary game data between the initiator and the competitor. It is implemented as standalone web server providing low-latency, bidirectional and event-based communication using Socket.IO[2], a ready-to-use web-socket server able to join individual sessions, sending data to all or all other joined members of a shared session (or room) in (near) real-time (cf. **RN3**). As for the competitive game mode, exchanged information includes the generated email, the players' scores, as well as decisions and marking of phishing features of the emails created by the players.

5   User Evaluation

Study Design and Participant Sample: To evaluate the game prototype, a first user study was conducted, in which a group of participants ($n = 14$) played in seven game sessions with two players in each session. Each study session was conducted by one experimenter, instructing and observing the participants. The objective of the study was to collect initial user feedback on the implementation of the competitive game mode and evaluate usability and user experience.

The study design is split into five phases: (1) introductory interview, (2) game exploration, (3) constructive interaction, (4) competitive gameplay and (5) closing survey. First, the participants were interviewed briefly on demographical questions and their experiences with phishing. Next, the participants were introduced to the game were able to first play 10 min of the creation mode presented in [9], before continuing to the competitive game mode. Players were asked to explore the competitive mode together following a constructive interaction approach (also called co-discovery), i.e. a technique where users collaboratively use a system [7]. Compared to a think-aloud approach, users can talk about what they do more naturally and help each other when faced with difficulties. After exploring the competitive mode, the players were then asked to play against each other (without constructive interaction). Lastly, to quantify usability and user experience, a survey was handed out containing the Post-Study System Usability Questionnaire (PSSUQ) and the User Experience Questionnaire (UEQ).

Among the participants (13 males, 1 female), the average age was 23 years and all participants were university students enrolled in different study programs

---

[2] https://socket.io/, last accessed 30.06.2023.

(10× computer science, 1× chemistry, 1× geography, 2× teacher training). Every participant was familiar with the concept of phishing and has reported they have been confronted with phishing in the past. Only three participants took part in a phishing training before and one reported they have previously lost an online account due to a successful phishing attack.

Study Results: During the constructive interaction [7], the participants were tasked to play the first round of the competitive mode together, while also being able to see the opponents screen, unlike in the competitive gameplay phase. Participants were asked to talk to each other about the game to capture their understanding and impressions of the implementation as well as any confusion or misunderstandings. This way, we were able to uncover issues with the creation interface. As such, it was noted that email texts were line-wrapped horizontally, but without vertical scrolling, thus not fully displayable, if players created particularly long emails. Here, scrollable text fields should resolve this issue. Furthermore, a salient aspect was that some players did not understand how they can mark suspicious elements with the stamp functionality in the email classification task. Moreover it was apparent that some participants did not read the instruction texts thoroughly and thus, they needed more time to proceed.

Overall, the results of the closing survey show that the participants like the competitive character of the game and are pleased that they can create their own emails with room for creativity. While they generally liked the creation functionality, they criticized the fixed text snippets for phishing features because they restrict the ways how emails can be written. However, it should be noted, that this is required at this point as defined phishing features need to be available for later marking in the classification task. Further, the quality of auto-generated emails presented in the classification task besides the opponent's custom email were criticized. Here, the auto-generated emails were too similar and rather simple, which calls for a more elaborate generator in the future. Results show mixed responses on the question whether email creation or email classification was more fun: Four groups favor email creation, while three groups favor email classification. Participants also noted that task descriptions and game instructions were understandable and clear, without any misleading navigation elements or controls (cf. **RN1**). The game flow did not contain any surprises for the participants and was perceived as logical and without any technical delays (cf. **RN23**).

Regarding the usability and user experience, results of the PSSUQ show an overall score of 2.65. Compared to investigated mean PSSUQ scores in the literature [10], the game is slightly better (i.e. lower) overall ($2.65 < 2.82$) and also for system usefulness ($2.32 < 2.80$) and information quality ($2.45 < 3.02$). Only the interface quality is above the mean ($3.43 > 2.49$), explainable by reported certain limitations and suggested improvements for the editor interface. Results of the UEQ show only medium values for attractiveness (0.63) and hedonic quality (0.27). While pragmatic quality was good (1.30), the games attractiveness, stimulation and perceived novelty indicate room for improvement.

Suggestions towards game improvements include more variety among emails presented in the classification task and randomized phishing features for email creation. A wider range of features could be implemented when players would be able create own phishing text snippets or adapt them to the email content on the fly. Further, participants suggested that they should be able to write more than one email and can decide themselves whether they write a phishing or legitimate email. The participants also proposed a timer for email creation and/or classification. Since phishing is not only present in emails, it was also mentioned that other forms of phishing channels could be considered for competitive gameplay.

6   Discussion and Future Work

We have to consider certain limitations and open issues for future work. Regarding game design, a reported limitation was the quality of auto-generated emails shown besides the opponents custom email in the email classification task. While the auto-generated email were too similar to each other, they were also rather easy to classify, weakening the competitive gameplay as it was not perceived as a challenge. However, emails written by players bring more variety in the game, which improves the game experience. Here, it should be considered both improving the auto-generated emails (e.g., by using artificial intelligence and natural language processing) and allowing players to create more custom emails per round. Overall, this would increase the possible pool of emails for classification and increase variability. Another issue regarding email creation occurs if players purposely create obvious or silly emails without serious gameplay intentions. While this can be an issue in many games, the competitive gameplay experience is directly linked to the players' level of seriousness.

The current game prototype is implemented using the MTLG framework, and thus, the frameworks limitations may also apply to the game. With the implementation using the HTML Canvas element, there are considerable restrictions regarding the use of text and the handling of user input. Further text scrolling is not implemented and hover events must be implemented manually. To this end, it should be considered to reimplement the game in a different framework, e.g., with full support of the HTML DOM, JavaScript and CSS (e.g., Vue.js[3]). Next, another limitation is due to the game mode integration and underlying storytelling. For the purpose of our study, the game mode was directly integrated as third mode besides the creation and decision modes presented in [9]. However, for proper, meaningful gameplay, it would be reasonable to guide players through the individual game modes first, before getting access to the competitive mode. This way we can ensure that all persuasion principles and phishing features of emails have been introduced and practiced individually, before applying them in email creation in the competitive mode.

Regarding the chosen study design and evaluation setup, it should be noted that generalizability is limited since our participant sample was small and consists of only students. In particular, for CS students, we considered them to have

---

[3] https://vuejs.org/, last accessed 12.07.2023.

prior knowledge of phishing and also might therefore be more critical about the game design and functionality and thus, impacting their user experience. As prior knowledge and knowledge was not focus of the evaluation, it should be investigated in future work. If so, the number of participants should be increased and recruitment should focus on a very diverse sample to avoid strong biases. However, depending on the evaluation goals, the study setup should be adapted. While during development, constructive interaction is very insightful, it is a costly setup, requiring two participants and more time than just gameplay.

For future work, we plan on improving the game prototype by exploring AI-based email generation methods but also allow for more user-generated emails. Here, we argue that the creation process could be improved with more flexible phishing features and this way, more creativity in the creation process. To make customize competitive sessions, we plan on including configuration options (e.g., number of rounds, emails to create, emails to classify). While for now, competitive gameplay is implemented in 1-versus-1 setup, a multiplayer mode could also be explored, e.g., for a classroom activity. To investigate the game's impact on players performance and confidence in classifying phishing emails, we suggest a pre-/post- and re-test design to measure before and after the intervention as well as some time afterwards. Furthermore, qualitative research towards the impact of competition should be explored by comparing it to non-competitive games. Lastly, future games can be explored covering further phishing channels as well as situational awareness when and how phishing attacks may occur.

References

1. Anti-Phishing Working Group: phishing attack trends report, 4th Quarter 2022. Report (2022). https://apwg.org/trendsreports/
2. Chen, C.H., Law, V., Huang, K.: The roles of engagement and competition on learner's performance and motivation in game-based science learning. Educ. Tech. Res. Dev. **67**(4), 1003–1024 (2019)
3. Cialdini, R.B.: Influence: The Psychology of Persuasion, Revised William Morrow, New York (2006)
4. Johnson, D.W., Johnson, R.T.: An educational psychology success story: social interdependence theory and cooperative learning. Educ. Res. **38**(5), 365–379 (2009)
5. Krathwohl, D.R.: A revision of bloom's taxonomy: an overview. Theory Into Pract. **41**(4), 212–218 (2002)
6. Lastdrager, E.E.: Achieving a consensual definition of phishing based on a systematic review of the literature. Crime Sci. **3**(1), 9 (2014)
7. Miyake, N.: Constructive Interaction and the Iterative Process of Understanding. Cogn. Sci. **10**(2), 151–177 (1986)
8. Roepke, R., Koehler, K., Drury, V., Schroeder, U., Wolf, M.R., Meyer, U.: A pond full of phishing games - analysis of learning games for anti-phishing education. In: Hatzivasilis, G., Ioannidis, S. (eds.) MSTEC 2020. LNCS, vol. 12512, pp. 41–60. Springer, Cham (2020). https://doi.org/10.1007/978-3-030-62433-0_3

9. Roepke, R., et al.: More than meets the eye - an anti-phishing learning game with a focus on phishing emails. In: Kiili, K., Antti, K., de Rosa, F., Dindar, M., Kickmeier-Rust, M., Bellotti, F. (eds)Games and Learning Alliance, vol. 13647, pp. 118–126. Springer, Cham (2022). https://doi.org/10.1007/978-3-031-22124-8_12

10. Sauro, J., Lewis, J.R.: Quantifying the User Experience: Practical Statistics for User Research. Morgan Kaufmann (2016)

The Design and Implementation of Biological Evolution as a Video Game Mechanic

Barrie D. Robison[(⊠)] [ID] and Terence Soule

Institute for Interdisciplinary Data Sciences, University of Idaho, Moscow, ID 83844, USA
brobison@uidaho.edu

Abstract. Video games have the potential to help teach evolutionary biology, but most commercial games misrepresent evolutionary principles by allowing player choice to dictate evolutionary trajectories. Our game studio aims to incorporate scientifically accurate evolutionary models into gameplay mechanics. In our previous games Darwin's Demons and Project Hastur, we designed digital genomes and implemented evolutionary models to create enemy populations that adapt to player strategies. However, accurately simulating evolution can sometimes conflict with crafting an enjoyable game. Here we examine balancing scientific realism with fun in the game design process. Using experimental data from Project Hastur, we show enemies evolve increased size and sensory abilities to counter player defenses, demonstrating the game mechanic's adaptive capabilities. We discuss how mutation rates, population sizes, generation times and other parameters can be adjusted to balance accuracy and enjoyment, with the goal of creating engaging games that reinforce and demonstrate, rather than misrepresent, evolutionary principles.

Keywords: Evolution · Video Games · Adaptation · Gamification · STEM

1 Introduction

Biological evolution is an important process that frames much of our understanding of the natural world. Unfortunately, public misconceptions about evolution are common. Acceptance of evolution as a real process is low in many demographic groups, and in the United States educators often face direct opposition to teaching evolution in their classrooms [1]. Evolution is also a concept that can be difficult to present in a formal learning setting but is very understandable when directly observed. Games and simulations could therefore be useful for engaging students, demonstrating evolutionary concepts, and correcting pervasive public misconceptions about the discipline.

Game designers have long recognized the potential of evolution to sell games. Unfortunately, the most successful commercial games that emphasize evolution (for example, Spore™, Evolve™, and Pokemon™ Evolution) aren't evolutionary at all. Most of these games substitute player choice for true evolutionary processes, allowing for example, the player's character to choose whether to "evolve" a beak, or a lightning attack. This approach inadvertently represents intelligent design, a pseudoscientific reskinning of young

© The Author(s), under exclusive license to Springer Nature Switzerland AG 2024
P. Dondio et al. (Eds.): GALA 2023, LNCS 14475, pp. 67–76, 2024.
https://doi.org/10.1007/978-3-031-49065-1_7

earth creationism. These games, which use evolution as a marketing angle, potentially exacerbate the public's confusion about evolution and reinforce existing misconceptions. The question then emerges, can accurate models of biological evolution be incorporated as a game mechanic?

There have been a few games that incorporate reasonably accurate models of evolution. *Intelligent Design: An Evolutionary Sandbox* [2] is an evolutionary game in which players create species that are placed in an evolving ecosystem - once released, the creatures continue to evolve on their own. *Niche* [3] is a turn-based game in which the player breeds members of a species to avoid extinction. Although they have not been released commercially, the game *NeuroEvolving Robotic Operatives* (NERO) and a spin-off, *EvoCommander*, are also examples of games that incorporate evolution.

Incorporating accurate models of biological evolution has interesting implications for game design. Encoding evolution as a game mechanic could create a system that adapts to player strategy, produces unexpected results and emergent properties, and inherently scales difficulty in response to player skill. These features have the potential to increase replayability and decrease development effort on game balancing.

While the gamification of evolution can potentially help expose players to real evolutionary models in an engaging way, there are several tradeoffs between playability and realism that should be considered when developing an evolutionary video game. In this paper, we discuss the lessons learned from developing and releasing games that feature evolution as a core mechanic, and the design decisions inherent to balancing gameplay with scientific realism.

2   Polymorphic Games

Polymorphic Games is an interdisciplinary game studio at the University of Idaho that explicitly focuses on the gamification of evolution. The studio is motivated by the idea that evolution can make games more compelling and more fun because the game adapts to the player. By implementing evolution as a core game mechanic, we seek to make players inherently motivated to learn the underlying evolutionary concepts in order to succeed at the game objectives.

Polymorphic Games has commercially released two games that incorporate evolution as a central game mechanic. Darwin's Demons [4] is an arcade style space shooter in which the player battles an evolving population of aliens. The enemies' traits are encoded by a digital genome, and the fittest enemies reproduce to create the next generation. The enemy population then adapts to the player's strategy. To our knowledge, Darwin's Demons was the first commercially released game to fully feature evolving enemies [5]. Project Hastur [6] is an evolutionary tower defense game that features a 3D game environment with enemies procedurally generated from a digital genome to produce a wide variety of morphologies, behaviors, capabilities, and other game traits. Both games feature experiment mode, in which the evolutionary parameters can be altered, and game data written to a *.csv* file. Experiment mode allows exploration of the model on which the game is built and allows the player to autonomously test "cause and effect" as they adjust parameters. Darwin's Demons and Project Hastur are both available for free on Steam [4, 6]. For the purposes of this paper, we focus primarily on empirical examples using our more recent game, Project Hastur.

Gameplay: In Project Hastur, the player must defend their base against waves of ene-mies called the Protean Swarm. The player places defensive towers with uniqe capa-bilities, strengths, and weaknesses in strategic locations. Enemies appear in "waves", a classic trope of tower defense games in which the developers script the number and type of enemies that appear over the course of the level. Project Hastur replaces scripted waves of enemies with a generational evolutionary model - each new enemy wave is comprised of the offspring of the most successful enemies in the previous wave. This leads to an enemy population adapts to the player defenses as the game progresses.

3   Evolution as a Game Mechanic

Here, we explain our approach to the gamification of evolution using four commonly taught components of the evolutionary process: Variation, Inheritance, Selection, and Time. When these components are present, the evolutionary process leads to Adaptation, which is the foundation of the evolutionary process and the core component of engaging games that feature evolution as a central mechanic.

3.1   Variation

Most video games feature some kind of variation among enemy types. Even the first arcade games, such as Space Invaders, Asteroids, Centipede, and Tempest, used variation among enemies or obstacles to add interest and challenge. In Space Invaders for example, there were three types of aliens in each wave, along with the occasional bonus flying saucer. Centipede and Tempest featured categorically different enemy types that varied in their appearance and capabilities. Variation is a central component of game development and is a big part of what makes video games exciting. The difficulty in video games is often increased over time by introducing new variations of enemies, changing the enemies' capabilities (like speed or fire rate) over time, or increasing enemy number.

When implementing evolution as a game mechanic, we encode variation of enemy traits using a digital representation of a genome. Often, the digital genome is a simple vector of numbers. Each individual has the same structure (e.g. everyone has a vector size of 10), and the variation among individuals is represented in the different numbers contained in the vector. The game engine then uses the values in each individual's genome to calculate game traits, such as speed, hit points, etc.

Genetic variation can be classified into two categories, Standing Genetic Variation [7] and Mutational Variation. Standing genetic variation is the genetic differences among individuals at the start of the game. This can be adjusted as design principles dictate, but a general rule of thumb is that more variation in the initial population corresponds to a faster rate of adaptation in the early phases of the game. Were the game to proceed solely using the standing genetic variation present at the beginning, the combination of selection and random genetic drift would quickly result in a homogeneous population and a rather bored player.

Mutational processes can be used each generation to introduce new genetic variation into the enemy population. During gameplay, selection imposed by the player can act on this new variation. This is akin to adding more "fuel" to the process of adaptation, sustaining the evolutionary game play longer than one would observe with only standing genetic variation. In Darwin's Demons and Project Hastur, we used a mutational step between generations, mutating the digital gametes passed on by the parents to the next generation. It is here that we must acknowledge a tension between designing a game for playability and creating an accurate evolutionary simulation. Mutation rates in biological populations are well studied, and rates range between 1 in 10^6 and 1 in 10^9 per locus [8]. These rates are much too low to make for very compelling game play, as new variation would take much too long to accumulate in the population. In our games, we typically use mutation rates that are much higher than those found in nature, accelerating the infusion of mutational variance into the population.

Another link between the model parameters and playability is related to game difficulty. Increasing genetic variation in the population tends increase game difficulty. In our previous games, we have used the rate and effect size of new mutations as one of the key differentiators between modes of difficulty. If these parameters are too low, the game is boring and takes much too long for evolution to occur. If these parameters are too high, enemies with extreme trait values tend to destroy the player in the early game.

Genetic Variation in Project Hastur: Each member the enemy population is defined by a digital genome of 80 genes encoded as real numbers. Enemies are diploid (they have two copies of each gene, one from each parent), such that its final trait value is calculated as the sum of the genetic values for the given locus on each chromosome. All genes are used by the game engine to render a wide variety of visually distinct game enemies, and a subset of the genes also affect traits that are relevant to game play. When the game begins, trait values are instantiated using starting values modified by mutations from a Gaussian distribution. This creates the standing genetic variation in the initial population upon which selection (imposed by the player) will act. When offspring are created in subsequent generations, additional mutational variance is introduced. In campaign mode, the per locus mutation rate and effect size vary depending on the map's degree of difficulty - more mutational variance causes the game to become much more difficult. In experiment mode, mutation rate and effect size are determined by the user. Mutation Rate (u) is defined as the per locus probability that the genetic value of the locus will be changed by a number drawn from a Gaussian distribution with mean zero and standard deviation defined by the variable Mutation Effect Size (e).

3.2 Inheritance

In most video games there is no relationship between enemies within a wave or between waves. They are instantiated (spawned) with developer defined traits at a specified rate, location, and time. In an evolutionary game, enemy traits are specified by digital genomes which are passed to offspring through a model of reproduction. Reproduction models can be asexual (in which one parent is sufficient to create one or more offspring) or sexual (two parents contribute to the genome of the offspring).

Inheritance in Project Hastur: Each "wave" of enemies in Project Hastur is a discrete generation created from the previous generation using a tournament selection algorithm. Individuals are sexually reproducing hermaphrodites and individuals that are selected as parents each contribute one of their chromosomes, determined randomly, for each locus. Project Hastur uses a free recombination model (each locus acts as its own chromosome), but this can be modified in experiment mode. The chromosomes passed to the offspring are each subjected to the mutation algorithm, and each locus has a chance (specified by u) to receive a mutation of effect size e. Once the new offspring's genome is instantiated, it is passed to the population for the next generation. On game maps that contain human civilians, enemy creatures can also reproduce using an asexual model. In this case, if a creature kills a civilian the creature clones itself. This cloning process produces an offspring that is genetically identical to its parent and the number of clones produced by this process depends on the parent creature's size (smaller creatures produce more clones).

3.3 Selection

Selection occurs when there is a correlation between a trait (such as Health or Speed) and Fitness, which in biological populations is defined as the number of offspring produced by a given individual. We often measure proxy traits in empirical biology that are correlated with fitness, such as seed-set in plants, survivorship, or number of eggs in a nest. In our games, we can make explicit linkages between performance and fitness using Fitness Functions.

In evolutionary games, the selection process should include a stochastic component that favors more fit individuals but leaves opportunities for less fit individuals to be selected to maintain diversity within the population. Two common approaches are roulette wheel selection [9] and tournament selection [10]. Roulette wheel selection is 'fitness proportional' the probability of being selected is proportional to an individual's relative fitness. Tournament selection is a 'rank based' process in which a small (typically 3–5) subset of the population is picked at random and the highest fitness individual in that subset wins the 'tournament' and thus the opportunity to reproduce.

Tournament Selection in Project Hastur: Project Hastur specifies two Fitness Functions that determine the probability that enemies will be selected to reproduce at the end of each generation. The first Fitness Function, called Base Fitness, specifies the closest distance to the player's base that was achieved by a given enemy. Should the individual reach the base (a distance of zero), then Base Fitness includes the Damage the Protean does to the base. Tower Damage is the other fitness function used to calculate whether an individual will reproduce. In this case, the game sums the total Damage done by the individual to any defensive structure. Total Fitness is calculated by combining Tower Damage and Base Fitness.

At the end of each generation, we use tournament selection to identify individuals that will serve as parents. A random sample of individuals from the previous generation is drawn, and the individual with the best value for Total Fitness is selected as a parent. A new tournament is then conducted to select the mate. Reproduction proceeds as described above and a single offspring is passed to the population for the next generation. This process is repeated until the population size for the next generation has been reached.

In Fig. 1, we present an example of how the combination of inherited variation and selection via fitness functions can produce directional selection, in this case for larger

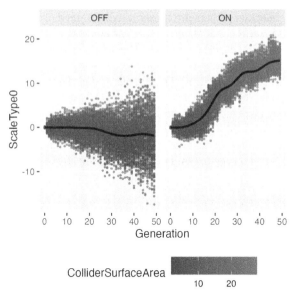

Fig. 1. Values of the *ScaleType0* gene in two replicates of Project Hastur over 50 generations using a standardized defense of only Autocannon Towers. Each point represents an individual enemy, and is colored according to Collider Surface Area, which measures total body size within the game environment. *ScaleType0* controls the size of the main body of the individual. LEFT: Fitness functions are turned OFF, resulting in the accumulation of mutational variance over time, but no change in mean body size (black line) of the population. RIGHT: Fitness functions are turned ON, resulting in directional selection for increased body size.

enemies (which tend to have more Health). Extending this example, we can show that the patterns of trait adaptation in Project Hastur are in response to game conditions and strategies instituted by the player. To demonstrate the effects of the evolutionary model, we used Project Hastur's experiment mode to run replicated instances of the same game play conditions. We therefore simulate the decision of a player in terms of the organization of a fixed number of defensive towers, but then let the game proceed without the ability of the enemies to destroy the player base. We refer to each individual game play session as a replicate.

The data presented in Fig. 1 used a standardized arrangement of Autocannon turrets on the same game map ("Crater Mountain"). The Autocannon turret relies on a ray-cast for targeting, firing numerous projectiles that do not miss. We ran a total of 9 replicates (separate instances of game play) under both conditions (with and without fitness functions) using the Autocannon. We ran additional replicates using the identical arrangement of towers using the Chip Shredder, a turret that fires a single, slower projectile that relies on collision detection. Figure 2 shows the pattern of trait evolution we observed under these conditions. This experiment is intended to show the potential outcomes if players specialize their defenses toward a single tower type.

We can test whether selection causes the observed changes in game traits by calculating the selection gradients within each generation. Selection gradients are standardized measures of the strength of selection, calculated by measuring the slope (Beta) of the relationship between a trait and fitness [11]. An estimate of Beta = 0 indicates no selection. Positive values of Beta indicate directional selection for increased trait values, and negative values the opposite. Combining replicates within each treatment reveals a general pattern of positive directional selection on the ScaleType0 gene by the Autocannons, and negative directional selection on the ScaleType0 gene by the Chip Shredders (Fig. 2).

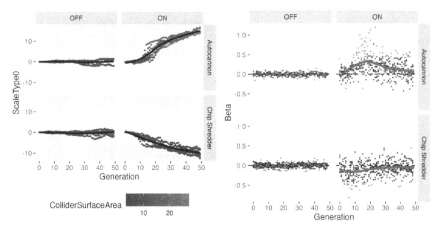

Fig. 2. LEFT: Mean values of the ScaleType0 gene in 9 replicates of Project Hastur under four gameplay conditions (36 total replicates). Each point represents the mean value of a replicate at each generation, and is colored according to Collider Surface Area, which measures body size. When Fitness Functions are inactive (OFF column), mean trait values change randomly because of genetic drift. When Fitness Functions are active (ON column), the Autocannon towers select for larger individuals (which have more Health), while the Chip Shredder towers select for smaller individuals (which are faster and can evade projectiles). RIGHT: Estimates of the selection gradient, Beta, for the ScaleType0 gene in Project Hastur. Red points indicate estimates of Beta that are significantly different from 0 in individual tests, while the blue line indicates the Loess estimate of Beta across the entire experiment.

As Fig. 2 shows, the type of tower chosen by the player has a dramatic effect on the evolutionary trajectory of the game enemies. This example is a simplified experiment intended to isolate a single trait's response to manipulation of a single variable. The enemies in Project Hastur have more than 20 traits, and the defensive combinations available to the player are innumerable. This creates a great deal of potential variation in gameplay.

In project Hastur, we often observe variation in the evolutionary outcomes even when gameplay conditions are identical. In Fig. 3, we show a heatmap of the standardized trait means across 9 replicates of the exact same game conditions. The first two rows of the heatmap (replicates 2 and 3) are a distinct cluster representing an outcome dominated by small and fast enemies with a large sight radius. The remainder of the replicates produced some variation of large, slow "tanks" that evolve to absorb most of the hits from the Autocannons. This variation in evolutionary outcomes is inherent to the stochastic nature of the evolutionary model. New mutations occur randomly, and the rather small population sizes cause random genetic drift. Even within a single game replicate, we can sometimes observe subdivision of the population as evolution drives individuals toward two separate optima in the fitness landscape.

For example, when we plot the individual values of the ScaleType0 gene and color by the Sight Range trait, we observe that replicates 2 and 3 are clearly evolving towards smaller individuals. Further, the individual patterns of evolution among the replicates differ in their temporal dynamics. The most extreme example is replicate 8, in which two sub-populations are clearly present between generation 25 and 40, after which point the larger individuals out-compete the smaller and the mean size of the enemies changes dramatically.

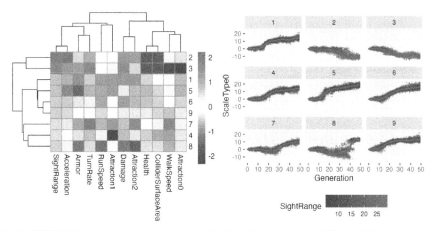

Fig. 3. RIGHT: Heatmap of traits (columns) for 9 replicates (rows) of Project Hastur using the Autocannon conditions from Figs. 1 and 2. Each cell represents the Z-score of that trait, with each unit change representing one standard deviation from the overall mean of zero. LEFT: Temporal pattern of individual values of ScaleType0 over 50 generations, colored by the Sight Range trait.

3.4 Time

The concept of time in video games is often defined in terms of waves or levels that imply a progression toward the game's goal and a corresponding increase in difficulty. In our evolutionary games, time is specified in terms of generations. As the generations (waves) proceed, the enemies with traits that are best able to optimize the fitness functions have more offspring, and the population adapts to the game play conditions. Most of these conditions are created by player choices and playstyle, and thus the enemies adapt to the player. Difficulty increases organically and repeated gameplay often creates novel adaptive solutions to the same play style.

To make an interesting and challenging game, evolution must occur within the rather limited time frame of gameplay. In nature, biological evolution can take thousands to tens of thousands of generations to result in obvious changes. This is much too long for most games, necessitating sacrifices in realism of the model. Potential changes to model parameters include increasing the amount of genetic variance and selection pressure, both of which can speed up the evolutionary process.

4 Limitations

In this paper we have focused on the implementation of accurate evolutionary models as game mechanics, and how those models can be adjusted to accommodate engaging gameplay. A critical un-answered question is whether these types of evolutionary games result in measurable learning gains. We have recently begun formal research projects focusing on this topic, and invite interested educational researchers to contact the authors.

5 Conclusion

Video games present an engaging opportunity to teach core scientific concepts like evolution. However, most commercial games fail to accurately represent evolutionary processes, and some even mislead players. This paper discusses attempts to incorporate scientifically valid evolutionary models into game mechanics using digital genomes, variation, inheritance, selection, and generational time. Balancing realism and playability is challenging, but our data indicate the systems can demonstrate adaptive evolution in response to player actions. With further research into potential learning outcomes, evolution-driven games hold promise to improve public understanding of science while retaining intrinsic motivational appeal. Interactive games that reinforce evolutionary principles could ultimately help counter widespread misconceptions and have significant educational value.

References

1. Miller, J.D., et al.: Public acceptance of evolution in the United States, 1985–2020. Public Underst. Sci. **31**, 223–238 (2022). https://doi.org/10.1177/09636625211035919
2. Intelligent Design: An Evolutionary Sandbox. https://store.steampowered.com/app/627620/Intelligent_Design_An_Evolutionary_Sandbox/
3. Niche. https://store.steampowered.com/app/440650/Niche__a_genetics_survival_game/
4. Wood, N., Soule, T., Heck, S., Wright, L.R., Robison, B.D.: Darwin's demons. https://store.steampowered.com/app/572020/Darwins_Demons/
5. Soule, T., Heck, S., Haynes, T.E., Wood, N., Robison, B.D.: Darwin's demons: does evolution improve the game? In: Squillero, G., Sim, K. (eds.) EvoApplications 2017. LNCS, vol. 10199, pp. 435–451. Springer, Cham (2017). https://doi.org/10.1007/978-3-319-55849-3_29
6. Heck, S., Soule, T., Wright, L.R., Robsion, B.D.: Project Hastur. https://store.steampowered.com/app/800700/Project_Hastur/
7. Matuszewski, S., Hermisson, J., Kopp, M.: Catch me if you can: adaptation from standing genetic variation to a moving phenotypic optimum. Genetics **200**, 1255–1274 (2015). https://doi.org/10.1534/genetics.115.178574
8. Bergeron, L.A., et al.: Evolution of the germline mutation rate across vertebrates. Nature **615**, 285–291 (2023). https://doi.org/10.1038/s41586-023-05752-y
9. Blickle, T., Thiele, L.: A comparison of selection schemes used in evolutionary algorithms. Evol. Comput. **4**, 361–394 (1996). https://doi.org/10.1162/evco.1996.4.4.361

10. Fang, Y., Li, J.: A review of tournament selection in genetic programming BT - advances in computation and intelligence. Presented at the (2010)
11. Stinchcombe, J.R., Agrawal, A.F., Hohenlohe, P.A., Arnold, S.J., Blows, M.W.: Estimating nonlinear selection gradients using quadratic regression coefficients: double or nothing? Evolution (N. Y). **62**, 2435–2440 (2008). https://doi.org/10.1111/j.1558-5646.2008.00449.x

The Nurse's Knowledge Bank: A Serious Knowledge Elicitation and Evaluation Game

Sinead Impey$^{(\boxtimes)}$, Declan O'Sullivan, and Gaye Stephens

ADAPT Centre, School of Computer Science and Statistics, Trinity College Dublin, Dublin, Ireland
impeys@tcd.ie

Abstract. The problem addressed in this research is that not all nursing knowledge is captured in a way that is easy to access outside the border of a community of practice (CoP) or beyond geography or time. As nursing accounts for over half the healthcare professionals globally, the role is broad in scope, performed in various healthcare settings and across the human lifespan; managing this knowledge is important. To address this problem, this research explores to what extent a serious game could elicit and evaluate specialist nursing knowledge so that it can be preserved beyond its initial use. However, no suitable game was found. Using an elaborated action design research (eADR) approach, this research designed, implemented, and evaluated a serious knowledge elicitation and evaluation game – The Nurse's Knowledge Bank. In total, three cycles of the game were played by nurses (n = 18) based in an oncology setting. From the three cycles n = 112 evaluated knowledge submissions were captured. These submissions included concepts such as '*Check patients' temperature on discharge*' or '*Ensure patient has their prescription before discharge*'. These submissions were mapped into two clinical terminologies, providing a means of sharing this knowledge beyond the clinic border and demonstrating that serious games could potentially have a role in knowledge management. This paper presents an overview of the development and design of the game.

Keywords: Serious Game · Nursing Knowledge · Knowledge Management

1 Introduction

1.1 Problem Statement

This section describes the problem domain and provides background to the research. The problem addressed is that not all nursing knowledge is captured in a way that is easy to access outside the border of a community of practice (CoP) or beyond geography or time. A CoP describes a "group of people who share a concern, a set of problems, or a passion about a topic, and who deepen their knowledge and expertise in the area by interacting on an ongoing basis" [1]. To address this problem, the aim of this research was to explore to what extent a serious game could elicit and evaluate specialist nursing knowledge. A serious game is one that is both educational and entertaining [2]. The

© The Author(s), under exclusive license to Springer Nature Switzerland AG 2024
P. Dondio et al. (Eds.): GALA 2023, LNCS 14475, pp. 77–85, 2024.
https://doi.org/10.1007/978-3-031-49065-1_8

serious game used was specially designed for this research. In total n = 112 knowledge submissions were captured by the game. These submissions included '*Check patients' temperature on discharge*' or '*Ensure patient has their prescription before discharge*'. From these n = 112 submissions, n = 107 were represented in a clinical terminology. 5 of the submissions did not have a matching concept in the clinical terminology, such as, "*Remove huber needle from Portacath and flush same before discharge*".

Many definitions of knowledge exist. To avoid confusion, the concepts of data, information, knowledge as core concepts within clinical information systems are adopted in this research. These concepts and their applicability to clinical information systems (CIS) are generally attributed to the work of Blum [3]. Their work presents a way to understand CIS by the objects the system processes – namely data, information, and knowledge. Building on Blum's work, Graves and Corcoran [4], in their seminal paper on nursing informatics, note that data are "discrete entities that are described objectively without interpretation". Information is "data that are interpreted, organised or structured". Knowledge is information that has been "synthesised so that interrelationships are identified and formalised".

The paper is structured as follows: Sect. 1 presents a description of nursing knowledge and how nurses use serious games as learning tools. Section 2, describes the methodology, elaborated action design research (eADR) [5] used to design, develop and evaluate a serious knowledge elicitation and evaluation game for nurses based in a specialist healthcare setting. The participants and study site are also discussed in this section. Section 3 presents the final game and the knowledge elicited and evaluated through playing the game. Section 4 concludes the paper.

1.2 Nursing Knowledge

While all healthcare knowledge is valuable, this research focuses on nurses' knowledge for several reasons. For instance, approximately 59% of the world's health professionals are nurses and worldwide there are nursing shortages (5.9 million in 2018) [6]. Nurses hold a broad knowledge base to perform a variety of clinical, educational and health promotion functions [7]. Even though nurses spend a significant amount of their day completing documentation [8], there is evidence that not all tasks completed, or care given, are documented or documented fully [8–12]. Eliciting nursing knowledge is a 'wicked problem' as it is 'ill-formulated', information is 'confusing', and there are many stakeholders', often holding antagonistic perspectives [13]. Without careful consideration of the problem, solutions to wicked problems risk being 'worse than the symptoms' [13]. To address this wicked problem of eliciting and evaluating nursing knowledge, a serious game was proposed. As no appropriate game was found in the literature, the purpose of this research was to design, implement and evaluate a low-fidelity prototype of a serious game capable of eliciting and evaluating nursing knowledge.

1.3 Serious Games in Nursing

Serious games "have an explicit and carefully thought-out education purpose and are not intended to be played primarily for amusement" [2]. Serious games have been used primarily for learning in healthcare. For instance, clinical education [14, 15], skill development [16] or teaching soft skills [17]. There is a wealth of studies describing how learners positively rate incorporating serious games into nursing education [16, 18–25]. For instance, participants (nursing students) in a study by Aljezawi and Albashtawy [18] preferred the game format for learning compared to traditional lectures. Participants also perceived the training session as more engaging, as reflected by their significantly increased motivation, according to findings by Bayram and Caliskan [16]. However, while serious games are prevalent in healthcare, only a small number of authors describe a potential role for serious games in knowledge management [26–29]. These papers, however, did not discuss nursing.

2 Research Approach

2.1 Methodology

To the authors' knowledge, no papers have previously described the role of serious games as knowledge management tools for nurses. This section introduces the research methodology and describes the study participants used to design a serious knowledge elicitation and evaluation game for nurses – The Nursing Knowledge Bank. The research used an elaborated action design research (eADR) [5] approach. The four stage eADR approach combines action research and design science and is used to produce relevant artefacts and generate knowledge about the artefact [5]. Each stage can be performed in multiple cycles. Movement can be back or forth depending on research needs. Each cycle contains five intervention activities – problem formulation, artefact creation, evaluation, reflection, and formalisation of learning. Three of the four stages were applied in this research and are shown in Fig. 1. The final evolution stage is concerned with understanding an artefact, in the case of this research, the serious game, in the problem environment over time. This was not performed for this research and is considered a limitation that should be addressed in future work.

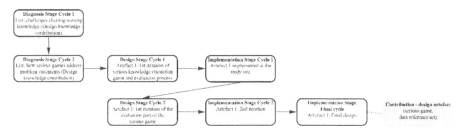

Fig. 1. How the eADR stages were applied in this research and number of cycles of each stage performed.

During the design stage, a game design framework developed by Verschueren et al. [30] was used. This 5-stage framework had been used previously for designing serious games for the healthcare domain [31]. Stages have specific aims: 1–3 are concerned with game development, 4–5 are concerned with evaluation and implementation. In addition, roles and components from a knowledge elicitation method (WICKED method) [32] were incorporated into the design. A full explanation of the game roles and components is provided in Sect. 3.

2.2 Participants

The study site was a specialist Haematology/Oncology department in a large teaching hospital in the Republic of Ireland. This is considered a specialist clinical area. Through this specialisation, a community of practice (CoP) can be formed around the specific area or disease. In total, three participant groups were used in this research – co-inquiry group, knowledge Holders and knowledge Reviewers. The co-inquiry group had n = 11 members. They represented nursing education (n = 2), clinical experts (nurse) (n = 7) and health informatics specialists (n = 2). While the co-inquiry group was concerned with game design, they were not involved in game play. Only Holders and Reviewers participated in the game. The primary purpose of the Holders group was to share their knowledge of oncology with an avatar in the game. This Holder and avatar relationship mimics the preceptor/preceptee model of knowledge sharing that occurs in clinical practice. Preceptorship describes a form of situated learning that occurs through participation monitored in clinical practice of student nurses [33]. In total, n = 10 Holders took part in this research.

The Reviewers role was held by experienced nurses based at the study site. In the clinical setting experienced nurses would oversee the learning needs of new nurses, ensuring that correct lessons were acquired. The primary purpose of the Reviewer group in the game was, therefore, to evaluate the elicited knowledge captured during the game. In total, n = 8 Reviewers took part in this research. Membership of the Holders group was limited to new nurses based at the site for less than 18 months, whereas Reviewers were nurses based at the site for over 18 months. Due to the specialism at the site, the clinical experts in the co-inquiry group identified 18 months as a probable time to become accustomed to the area. It is noted this was based on their experience and was a heuristic rather than a definitive time. A more robust way to identify a 'new nurse' was not found in the literature. Therefore, 18 months was taken as a benchmark for this research. The total research process went from October 2021 to September 2022 and included three game cycles.

3   The Nurse's Knowledge Bank

3.1   Introduction

The final game has two parts. Part 1 is concerned with eliciting knowledge. Part 2 is concerned with evaluating the elicited knowledge. Game flow is shown in Fig. 2.

Part 1: Elicitation. To elicit knowledge, participants referred to as Holders, acted as mentors to knowledge seekers. The Seeker is represented in the game by an avatar. Through their interactions, knowledge is elicited and captured on the evaluation game board. This approach was inspired by Nonaka and Takeuchi [34]. They discuss how to understand the processes used by an expert bread maker and capture them in a way that can be replicated by technology, a team member took on the role of an apprentice. This mirrors how knowledge is shared in the clinical environment, where experienced nurses, who receive training, act as mentors to new nurses and students. In the game, Holders earn a point for each piece of knowledge shared with their avatar. The winner was the Holder with the most points at the end of game play. Roles and game components used in the elicitation part are shown in Tables 1 and 2. These roles and game components (clinical scenario, game sheet and game board) were identified from a knowledge elicitation method by the author [32] and adapted for the game.

Table 1. Roles required for the elicitation part of the game.

Role	Description
Experts based at the study site	*No direct involvement in game. Shares knowledge with Holders as part of their normal work*
Knowledge Holder (KH)	*The role that shares knowledge they have accumulated in practice with an avatar (seeker)*
Knowledge Seeker (KS)	*The role that elicits knowledge from the Holder*
Knowledge Gatekeeper (KG)	*The role that manages the game*

Table 2. Game components required for the elicitation part of the game.

Component (Wicked Method)	Description
Knowledge topic (KT)	*Clinical topic that is explored during the game to manage the scope of the knowledge generated. The KT was a general adult discharge from an oncology setting. This topic was developed into a **clinical scenario** for the game*
Control knowledge base (CKB)	*A pre-existing object used to guide knowledge collection. A patient medication record was used. Along with the KT, this was developed into a **game sheet** for use by Holders*
Knowledge bank (KB)	*A repository containing elicited knowledge. The **game board** acted as a KB. This was a printed poster with space to put the submitted knowledge (in the form of post-it notes)*

Part 2: Evaluation. In the second part of the game, elicited knowledge is evaluated by nurses based at the study site over 18 months. These participants were referred to as Reviewers. The purpose of this part is to evaluate the knowledge elicited so that it can be shared beyond the community where it is generated. The game was designed by the author as a turn taking game based on the traditional format of 'Snakes and Ladders' game. To play the game, three components were developed. These are a game board (evaluation), community knowledge cards and challenge cards. These are described in

Tables 3 and 4. How knowledge is prepared for evaluation is not discussed here due to word count, but a paper is being prepared on the topic.

Table 3. Roles required for the evaluation part of the game.

Role	Description
Knowledge Reviewer (KR)	*The role that evaluates knowledge elicited during the first part of the game*
Knowledge gatekeeper (KG)	*The role that manages the game and arbitrates in case of disputes relating to knowledge*

Table 4. Game components required for the elicitation part of the game.

Component	Description
Evaluation game board	*Evaluation game board contained 100 sequentially numbered squares. Reviewers moved across the board based on points earned by reviewing knowledge (on the community knowledge cards). Winner was the Reviewer who reached the 100th square first or the highest placed individual at the end of game time*
Community knowledge card	*Elicited knowledge was constructed into a set of cards for review. Each card had a number that indicated how many moves a Reviewer could make*
Challenge card	*16 squares on the evaluation game board were allocated 'challenges'. Each related to a challenge associated with managing nursing knowledge. For example, tacit aspects*

3.2 Evaluation of knowledge

A total of n = 112 knowledge submissions were identified from game play. Participants reported enjoying the game, to access its suitability as a knowledge management tool a final evaluation was conducted by a subject expert. Following this review no submissions were removed, deemed irrelevant or had patient safety implications. Demonstrating that the game could potentially be used to help manage nursing knowledge. However, this knowledge remained within the game at the study site. Therefore, to share this knowledge beyond the study site, the evaluated knowledge was mapped to a clinical terminology. Two terminologies were used in this research – Systematized Nomenclature of Medicine Clinical Terms (SNOMED CT) and International Classification for Nursing Practice (ICNP). From this mapping process, knowledge could be considered a match, near match or no match (see Table 5).

This research demonstrated that a serious game could elicit knowledge and that it could be preserved and shared using a data reference set. This indicates that a serious

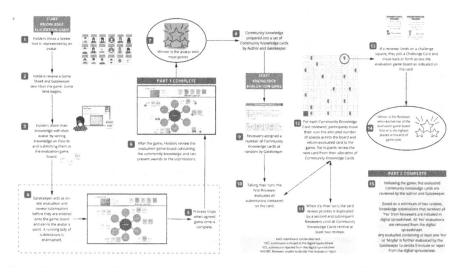

Fig. 2. Numbers 1 to 8 show the flow of game play during the knowledge elicitation part of the serious game, 9 to 15 show the evaluation part.

Table 5. Outcome of mapping evaluated knowledge into two clinical terminologies.

Category	SNOMED CT	ICNP
Match	67	52
Near Match	19	22
No Match	26	38

game could have a role in managing nursing knowledge. However, limitations remain. For instance, the game did not provide guidance on when to move from elicitation to evaluation. For this research, game time took place during an existing education session (approx. 30 min) at the study site. As a result, no comment on the time required can be made. As the goal of the game was to elicit knowledge, it was unclear if all potential knowledge was captured. The game time was limited to a regular education session that occurred at the study site. It was unclear if additional time could capture additional knowledge.

4   Conclusion

The game was designed to mirror knowledge sharing in practice. That is, new nurses learn from their experienced peers through the preceptor/preceptee relationship. The final game design contained two parts - elicitation and evaluation. The aim of this research was to understand to what extent a serious game designed for this research could elicit and evaluate specialist nursing knowledge so that it could be preserved and shared mindful of geography and time. Mapping elicited and evaluated knowledge to a standard terminology demonstrates that serious games could have a role in managing specialist nursing knowledge.

References

1. Wenger, E., McDermott, R.A., Snyder, W.: Cultivating Communities of Practice: A Guide to Managing Knowledge. Harvard Business Press (2002)
2. Abt, C.C.: Serious Games. The Viking Press, New York (1970)
3. Blum, B.I.: Clinical information systems—a review. West. J. Med. **145**(6), 791 (1986)
4. Graves, J.R., Corcoran, S.: The study of nursing informatics. Image J. Nurs. Sch. **21**(4), 227–231 (1989)
5. Mullarkey, M.T., Hevner, A.R.: An elaborated action design research process model. Eur. J. Inf. Syst. **28**(1), 6–20 (2019)
6. WHO. State of the world's nursing 2020: investing in education, jobs and leadership, W.H.O. (WHO), Editor: Geneva (2020)
7. NMBI. Scope of Nursing and Midwifery Practice Framework. Nursing and Midwifery Board of Ireland (NMBI): Dublin, Ireland (2015)
8. Fore, A., Islim, F., Shever, L.: Data collected by the electronic health record is insufficient for estimating nursing costs: an observational study on acute care inpatient nursing units. Int. J. Nurs. Stud. **91**, 101–107 (2019)
9. De Marinis, M.G., et al.: 'If it is not recorded, it has not been done!'? consistency between nursing records and observed nursing care in an Italian hospital. J. Clin. Nurs. **19**(11–12), 1544–1552 (2010)
10. Gunningberg, L., Dahm, M.F., Ehrenberg, A.: Accuracy in the recording of pressure ulcers and prevention after implementing an electronic health record in hospital care. Qual. Saf. Health Care **17**(4), 281–285 (2008)
11. Paans, W., et al.: Prevalence of accurate nursing documentation in patient records. J. Adv. Nurs. **66**(11), 2481–2489 (2010)
12. Thoroddsen, A., et al.: Accuracy, completeness and comprehensiveness of information on pressure ulcers recorded in the patient record. Scand. J. Caring Sci. **27**(1), 84–91 (2013)
13. Churchman, C.W.: Guest editorial: Wicked problems. JSTOR. pp. B141–B142 (1967)
14. Adhikari, R., et al.: A mixed-methods feasibility study to assess the acceptability and applicability of immersive virtual reality sepsis game as an adjunct to nursing education. Nurse Educ. Today **103**, 104944 (2021)
15. Foss, B., et al.: Digital game-based learning: a supplement for medication calculation drills in nurse education. E-learning Digit. Media **11**(4), 342–349 (2014)
16. Bayram, S.B., Caliskan, N.: Effect of a game-based virtual reality phone application on tracheostomy care education for nursing students: a randomized controlled trial. Nurse Educ. Today **79**, 25–31 (2019)
17. Calik, A., Kapucu, S.: The effect of serious games for nursing students in clinical decision-making process: a pilot randomized controlled trial. Games Health J. **11**(1), 30–37 (2022)
18. Aljezawi, M., Albashtawy, M.: Quiz game teaching format versus didactic lectures. Br. J. Nurs. **24**(2), 86–92 (2015)
19. Brull, S., et al.: Using gamification to improve productivity and increase knowledge retention during orientation. J. Nurs. Adm. **47**(9), 448–453 (2017)
20. Chang, C.-Y., et al.: From experiencing to critical thinking: a contextual game-based learning approach to improving nursing students' performance in electrocardiogram training. Educ. Tech. Res. Dev. **68**, 1225–1245 (2020)

21. Chee, E.J.M., et al.: Play and learn with patients—designing and evaluating a serious game to enhance nurses' inhaler teaching techniques: a randomized controlled trial. Games Health J. **8**(3), 187–194 (2019)

22. Cook, N.F., et al.: Impact of a web based interactive simulation game (PULSE) on nursing students' experience and performance in life support training—a pilot study. Nurse Educ. Today **32**(6), 714–720 (2012)

23. Del Blanco, Á., et al.: Using a videogame to facilitate nursing and medical students' first visit to the operating theatre. A randomized controlled trial. Nurse Educ. Today **55**, 45–53 (2017)

24. Hwang, G.-J., Chang, C.-Y.: Facilitating decision-making performances in nursing treatments: a contextual digital game-based flipped learning approach. Interact. Learn. Environ. 1–16 (2020)

25. Soyoof, A., et al.: A mixed-methods study of the incidental acquisition of foreign language vocabulary and healthcare knowledge through serious game play. Comput. Assisted Lang. Learn. (2021)

26. Ahmed, A., Sutton, M.J.: Gamification, serious games, simulations, and immersive learning environments in knowledge management initiatives. World J. Sci. Technol. Sustain. Dev. (2017)

27. Allal-Cherif, O., Bidan, M., Makhlouf, M.: Using serious games to manage knowledge and competencies: the seven-step development process. Inf. Syst. Front. **18**(6), 1153–1163 (2016)

28. Allal-Chérif, O., Makhlouf, M.: Using serious games to manage knowledge: the SECI model perspective. J. Bus. Res. **69**(5), 1539–1543 (2016)

29. Bayart, C., et al.: Serious games: leverage for knowledge management. TQM J. **26**(3), 235–252 (2014)

30. Verschueren, S., et al.: Development of CliniPup, a serious game aimed at reducing perioperative anxiety and pain in children: mixed methods study. JMIR Serious Games **7**(2), e12429 (2019)

31. Suppan, M., et al.: A serious game designed to promote safe behaviors among health care workers during the COVID-19 pandemic: development of "Escape COVID-19." JMIR Serious Games **8**(4), e24986 (2020)

32. Impey, S., et al.: Eliciting and confirming data, information, knowledge and wisdom in a specialist health care setting: the WICKED method. Int. J. Comput. Inf. Eng. (2023)

33. Nielsen, K., et al.: The art of preceptorship. A qualitative study. Nurse Educ. Pract. **26**, 39–45 (2017)

34. Nonaka, I., Takeuchi, H.: The Knowledge-Creating Company: How Japanese Companies Create the Dynamics of Innovation. Oxford University Press, Oxford (1995)

eKinomy: Designing a Serious Game to Promote Economic Decision-Making Skills from Elementary Level

Zhixin Li(✉) and Sharon Jessica

University of Michigan, Ann Arbor, MI 48014, USA
{zhixinli,sharjess}@umich.edu

Abstract. Serious games are designed to provide purposeful and engaging learning experiences, fostering knowledge acquisition and skills development. They hold the potential to simplify complex theories and concepts, making them easily comprehensible for learners. While the versatility and effectiveness of serious games provide immersive experiences in complex subject matter areas, such as STEM subjects, healthcare, environment science, etc., the integration of serious games into K-12 economic education, particularly for enhancing decision-making skills, remains limited. This paper proposes a work-in-progress role-play simulation serious game design with the theme of international trade designed for grades 5–8 to enact roles of producers, importers, and exporters as well as develop economic decision-making strategies. The paper begins by discussing the necessity of serious games in K-12 economic education. Next, the paper elucidates the design process employed in creating the serious game "eKinomy" and embedding the simulation and role-play elements into it. We outline the steps taken to ensure that the game aligns with the learning objectives of economic education while providing an engaging and immersive experience for learners.

Keywords: Game Design · Serious Game · Simulation · Role-Play Games (RPG) · K-12 Education · Economic Education

1 Introduction

Serious games, simulations, and role-playing offer valuable opportunities for learners to apply their knowledge and strategies while assuming specific roles. Michael and Chen [1], as cited in [2], stated that the main purpose of serious gaming is for players to learn while still experiencing fun. Simulations and role-playing activities provide an authentic learning environment without consequences in the real world [3–5]. Given their potential, it is intriguing to consider integrating these approaches together into economic education for elementary and middle students. Often, young students might perceive economics as an

---

Z. Li and S. Jessica—Contributed equally to this paper.

P. Dondio et al. (Eds.): GALA 2023, LNCS 14475, pp. 86–96, 2024.
https://doi.org/10.1007/978-3-031-49065-1_9

abstract or challenging subject, therefore, introducing them to serious games with simulations and role-playing features could possibly provide them with experiential learning opportunities that are close to the real-world economy.

In this paper, we present a role-play simulation serious game design called "eKinomy". The game has a theme of international trade and is designed for grades 5–8, allowing students to enact roles of producers, importers, and exporters while developing economic decision-making strategies.

2   Related Work

Serious games have been employed in various fields to enhance decision-making skills. A serious game on life choice simulation enables learners to engage in decision-making by immersing them in specific roles and prompting them with real-world scenarios through that role [6]. In mathematics, a serious game named Festarola, aims to foster motivation and knowledge in problem-solving by bridging the content with real-world scenarios [7]. Additionally, serious gaming in the field of climate change has demonstrated its ability to prompt reflection, facilitating better decision-making [8]. Another game in the same domain, Climate Adaption Game, emphasizes the uncertainty of complex problems, enabling players to grasp the importance of trade-offs and compromises in decision-making [9].

In the business realm, serious games are frequently utilized for business simulations to enhance decision-making skills, particularly in higher education settings [10]. The prevalence of serious games has grown significantly in primary and secondary education [10]. However, when it comes to economic education in the K-12 setting, most games primarily focus on personal finance, leaving a gap in addressing broader economic education topics (see Subsect. 3.1), the niche that eKinomy seeks to fill. Opportunities arise to apply serious gaming with simulation and role-play concepts, successfully utilized in other subjects and settings, to enhance economic education at the elementary and middle school levels.

3   The Game

In the following, we will address the current gap in economic education, particularly in the United States, and explore economic education curricula, leading to our serious game design with an international trade theme. Furthermore, we will delve into the purpose, description, and gameplay of our serious game.

3.1   Background

The Need for Early Economic Education
The Council for Economic Education (CEE) recognizes the importance of economic understanding as a vital skill, alongside reading, writing, and arithmetic [11]. Economic education is crucial because decisions made based on inaccurate economic systems could lead to disaster [12]. This also highlights

the significance of moving beyond mere economic knowledge and focusing on decision-making skills in economic education. Since economics is an integral part of people's lives, it becomes essential to teach it in schools beginning in the elementary grades [13]. Moreover, it has been pointed out that a significant challenge exists in the gap between the need for social understanding and what is currently taught in elementary classrooms [14]. Therefore, introducing decision-making skills in economics to students at the elementary level holds significant value.

The Gap in Economic Education
While personal finance education in the United States has shown progress, economic education lags behind, possibly due to insufficient course requirements, assessments, and teacher training [15]. Although the CEE collaborates with schools to integrate learning technologies, such as digital games, the focus has primarily been on financial literacy. The integration of learning technology into economic education, specifically to enhance decision-making skills, is still limited.

Exploring Global Economic Education Curricula
To effectively design a serious game that can be seamlessly integrated into classrooms and foster the development of economic decision-making strategies, we adhere to the knowledge base of economic education [16]. Our research initially centered around the social studies curriculum offered in Michigan schools. This encompasses vital economic education concepts, including market economy, national economy, and international economy [17]. Recognizing that we will eventually target global learners, our investigation expanded to curricula from diverse world regions, namely Australia [18], Japan [19], Sweden [20], Singapore [21], Ecuador [22], Uganda [23], and Kuwait [24,25]. These regions similarly address pertinent concepts in grades 5–8, thereby constituting our target audience.

The Possible Solution
In light of this comprehensive exploration, we have made a deliberate choice to devise a serious game with an international trade theme targeted at global young learners, encompassing various economics concepts imparted during these grade levels. By doing so, we aim to create a serious game that effectively merges with existing curricula, providing students with an immersive learning experience that enhances their understanding of economic principles and decision-making skills, preparing them for active participation in an interconnected global economy.

3.2   Game Description

eKinomy is a role-play simulation serious game designed to supplement economic education lessons in the classroom for grades 5–8, with the theme of international trade. It offers learners the opportunity to engage in authentic economic activities, assuming different roles of producers, exporters, and importers (See Fig. 1).

The game is developed with the main goal of enhancing economic decision-making skills by allowing players to understand economic concepts, enact various economic roles, consider economic factors in decision-making, negotiate with other roles, and have the autonomy to exercise and be comfortable with making decisions. By integrating eKinomy into existing economic education frameworks, it serves as an extension of traditional classroom instruction.

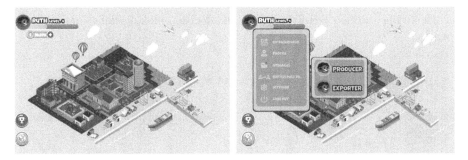

Fig. 1. eKinomy's homepage (Left). Learners can switch different roles of importer, producer, and exporter. (Right).

3.3   Incorporating Learning Theories into the Game

We incorporated learning, motivation, and scaffolding theories into the design of eKinomy. From a learning theory perspective, eKinomy integrates cognitivism by presenting learners with scenarios [26], fostering active engagement and critical thinking. This perspective becomes imperative for eKinomy since critical thinking is important for decision-making skills [27]. An example of these scenarios is when multiple exporters offers various pricing, reviews, and other factors, the importer needs to make selection. Additionally, a constructivist approach allows learners to construct their understanding of economic activities and roles by building a trade enterprise and having simulated firsthand experience on various roles [28], promoting a deeper understanding of economic concepts. Moreover, the social-constructivist aspect promotes interaction and knowledge-sharing among learners, facilitating collaborative learning (e.g., contacting and negotiating with other roles when undertaking trade activities).

Motivationally, eKinomy leverages the inherent motivational aspects of games to stimulate intrinsic motivation [29]. The game design combines elements of autonomy, granting learners the freedom to build and manage a simulated trade enterprise, and external rewards, such as leaderboards, to further motivate and engage them (refer to Fig. 3). Autonomy encourages students to tackle challenges and persist with complex tasks, while external rewards provide additional incentives for active participation and perseverance [30].

Furthermore, scaffolding strategies are employed to support learners in enacting economic activities effectively. This includes the provision of representations to help them apply economic frameworks and the facilitation of articulation and reflection on the activities they undertake [31]. See the example of this in Subsect. 3.4, B2B Page - Discover. To enhance the learning experience further, a teacher character named Nomy has been introduced in the game to support learners in making informed economic decisions. Nomy's role exemplifies the scaffolding strategy of embedding expert guidance within the game environment [31].

By incorporating these learning, motivation, and scaffolding theories, eKinomy aims to create an academically rigorous and engaging learning experience, fostering autonomy, collaboration, and decision-making skills among young learners.

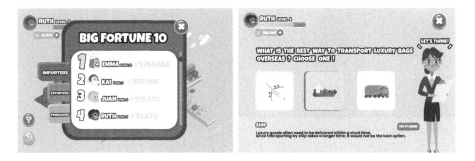

Fig. 2. Leaderboard (left) as an external motivation tool for the learners and Teacher Nomy (right) as the embodiment of the scaffolding strategy of expert guidance.

3.4   Gameplay

We have developed a learner journey accompanied by corresponding screen views (See Fig. 2) to illustrate a potential scenario from the perspective of an importer. This scenario encompasses various economic activities, wherein the importer utilizes key features of the game to engage in tasks such as exploring popular merchandise, evaluating and selecting exporters, negotiating with exporters, managing foreign currency exchange, and finalizing trade agreements. By incorporating these elements, the serious game offers a comprehensive experience that enables learners to actively participate in economic decision-making processes.

B2B Page - Discover
The importer first opens the Business-to-business (B2B) page, where they will be directly led to the Discover tab on the navigation bar. As this is the first step in completing the task, they will be introduced to the concept of economic interdependence as the rationale behind international trade, through a world map showing different natural resources being available in different regions of the world. To assist the learners in deciding which product to import, we provide a ranking chart named Most Popular Today on the right side of the Discover page, displaying the products being sold the most.

Forum - Offers

The importer visits the Forum tab on the B2B page, which includes Posts from all players, along with Comments on the Posts. In the forum, the importer can access different types of Posts in various sub-tabs. For example, they can view the Offers, where other players offer their products. Through this activity, they learn from the social interaction among players, gaining information that could influence their economic decisions. They also have the option to specifically filter the Offers sub-tab to display only Posts from exporters, as exporters are a crucial factor in their decision-making process as an importer.

Find - Search Bar

The importer wants to start the trade activity, so they go to the Find tab and type the product they want to import in the Search Bar. The list of exporters appears, and for each exporter entry, the Avatar, Business Name, Product Price, No. of Items Exported, and Rating are displayed. The importer can consider these elements while making decisions in choosing the exporter. eKinomy provides scaffolding in the form of a comparison between the Product Price of each exporter and the Market Price to assist their decision-making process.

Messaging Platform

They contact some exporters, who are also players of the game, with whom express an interest in doing trade using the eKimail e-mail feature. The communication process includes negotiation with exporters. Similar to real life, whether the deal occurs depends on various factors, such as price negotiation, product

Fig. 3. Screen views from eKinomy game.

availability, and communication style. The importer makes a deal with one of the exporters and sends them the agreed-upon currency with the appropriate amount. Once the exporter receives the payment, they ship the products. After receiving the products, the importer and exporter provide rating for one another.

4   Discussion

4.1   Expected Positive Effects on Learning

eKinomy offers a valuable opportunity for enhanced learning. The interactive nature and role-play feature of eKinomy hint at the potential to foster engagement and active learning, rather than passive content absorption. The ability to choose products and currencies for trade not only imparts an understanding of economics but also fosters decision-making skills. After every task, players are expected to progress in their decision-making skills as the economic factors become more complicated (See Fig. 4). Moreover, eKinomy addresses a critical pedagogical gap in economics, showing the potential of adopting serious gaming in social studies. Additionally, eKinomy has the capacity to reinforce classroom-taught concepts, thereby extending the learning environment beyond school. These suggest that eKinomy provides an interactive learning experience that may resonate with various stakeholders-students, teachers, and parents.

Roles	Grade 5	Grade 6	Grade 7	Grade 8
Producers	Production capacity	Production capacity for different products	Compete with other producers within the same country	Deal with government policies on production
Exporter	Which importers' needs to fulfill first	Composition of different product to export	Compete with other exporters within the same country	Deal with government policies on export
Importer	Fulfill the needs in the country	Importing natural resources vs derivative products	Compete with other importers within the same country	Deal with government policies on import

Fig. 4. Different economic factors to consider in decision-making for different roles in eKinomy as grades progress.

4.2   Challenges and Opportunities

However, the design of eKinomy faces challenges in scalability, adaptability, and assessment of learning gains. Its development requires a flexible, yet uniform framework for diverse educational settings, innovative measurement techniques for an interactive game environment, and ethical and strict data handling protocols, particularly given the young learners.

Ensuring scalability and adaptability has posed a challenge. The game needs to cater to different grade levels, educational contexts, and learner abilities. Designing a flexible framework that allows for customization and adaptation, while ensuring a consistent learning experience across diverse settings, requires careful consideration of instructional design principles and implementation strategies.

Measuring learning gains presents another challenge due to eKinomy's interactive and experiential nature, requiring unique evaluation methods. As there is currently no unified measurement method to assess serious games' effectiveness [32], it is crucial to identify suitable metrics. We are actively exploring strategies to collect meaningful data reflecting learners' progress, such as decision-making patterns, time allocation on various tasks, and post-game assessment.

Maintaining the integrity and privacy of these data is also an additional hurdle. It is crucial to ensure that all data collected is securely stored and handled in a manner consistent with privacy laws and ethical guidelines, especially considering the users are primarily minors. This aspect necessitates careful design and strict controls within the data collection and management system.

These challenges emphasize the necessity of a research-driven, iterative approach to the development and refinement of eKinomy. As a significant stride in enhancing economic education via gamification, eKinomy aims to arm young learners with essential economic knowledge and skills. The continuous refinement of the game through iterative design and evaluation intends to foster an increasingly effective and engaging learning experience.

5   Future Work

eKinomy, presently still a work-in-progress serious game project, has the primary objective of designing and implementing a learner-centered learning experience. Therefore, further collaborations with interdisciplinary researchers in child psychology, serious games, educational science, and human-computer interaction will help enrich our research, providing a more comprehensive understanding of the applications of game-design frameworks and educational and psychological theories in the current phase of developing our serious game - eKinomy. We also plan to incorporate a participatory design approach, actively involving children, social studies educators and economic education researchers to ensure their needs are met. Our next step is to test our executable version of eKinomy with students and teachers in Ann Arbor public schools in Michigan, the United States, and measure learners' performance and gather both students' and teachers' feedback to evaluate our design choices. Subsequently, we plan to create a guide to assist teachers in effectively facilitating students' learning through eKinomy.

6   Conclusion

This paper presents a role-play simulation serious game design project designed with a theme of international trade, aiming to help grades 5–8 students learn economic content and develop economic decision-making strategies. However, the development journey also underlines some challenges such as maintaining data integrity and privacy, ensuring scalability, and innovating unique evaluation methodologies, emphasizing the need for a research-driven, iterative approach. Nevertheless, the potential of eKinomy to enhance economic education through serious games is promising and warrants further development and research.

References

1. Michael, D., Chen, S.: Serious games: games that educate, train and inform. Thomson Course Technology, Boston (2006)
2. Susi, T., Johannesson, M., Backlund, P.: Serious Games: An overview. Institutionen för kommunikation och information, Skövde (2007)
3. Othlinghaus-Wulhorst, J., Hoppe, H.U.: A technical and conceptual framework for serious role-playing games in the area of social skill training. Front. Comput. Sci. **2**(28) (2020). https://doi.org/10.3389/fcomp.2020.00028
4. Naidu, S., Ip, A., Linser, R.: Dynamic goal-based role-play simulation on the Web: a case study. Educ. Technol. Soc. **3** (2000)
5. Sauvé, L., Renaud, L., Kaufman, D.: Games, simulations, and simulation games for learning: definitions and distinctions. Educ. Gameplay Simul. Environ. Case Stud. Lessons Learn., 1–26 (2010). https://doi.org/10.4018/978-1-61520-731-2.ch001
6. Struppert, A.: "It's a whole new fun fifferent way to learn". students' perceptions of learning with an electronic simulation: selected results from three case studies in an Australian, an American and a Swiss middle school. Int. J. Learn. Annu. Rev. **17**(9), 363–376 (2010). https://doi.org/10.18848/1447-9494/CGP/v17i09/47255
7. Rodrigues, R., Ferreira, P.D.C., Prada, R., Paulino, P., Simao, A.M.V.: Developing children's regulation of learning in problem-solving with a serious game. IEEE Comput. Graph. Appl. **40**(5), 26–40 (2020). https://doi.org/10.1109/MCG.2020.3011616
8. Driscoll, A., Lehmann, M.: Scaling innovation in climate change planning: serious gaming in Portland and Copenhagen. In: Action Research for Climate Change Adaptation: Developing and Applying Knowledge for Governance, pp. 130–147. Routledge (2015)
9. Neset, T.-S., Andersson, L., Uhrqvist, O., Navarra, C.: Serious gaming for climate adaptation-assessing the potential and challenges of a digital serious game for urban climate adaptation. Sustainability **12**(5), 1789 (2020). https://doi.org/10.3390/su12051789
10. Cruz-Cunha, M.M. ed: Handbook of research on serious games as educational, business and research tools: IGI Global (2012). https://doi.org/10.4018/978-1-4666-0149-9

11. Caltabiano, C.: Economics, common core state standards, and the fourth R. Soc. Stud. Rev. **52**, 32–37 (2013)
12. Boulding, K.E.: Economic education: the stepchild too is father of the man. J. Econ. Educ. **1**(1), 7 (1969). https://doi.org/10.2307/1182430
13. Meszaros, B., Suiter, M.: The case for economics in the elementary classroom. Reg. 10453369. **12**(4), 38 (1998)
14. Ramsett, D.E.: Toward improving economic education in the elementary grades. J. Econ. Educ. **4**(1), 30 (1972). https://doi.org/10.2307/1182569
15. Council for Economic Education: Survey of the States. Council for Economic Education (2022)
16. Kapralos, B.: A course on the design and development of serious games and virtual simulations. In: 2012 IEEE International Games Innovation Conference, pp. 1–4. IEEE, Rochester, NY (2012). https://doi.org/10.1109/IGIC.2012.6329837
17. Michigan Department of Education: Michigan K-12 Standards: Social Studies. Michigan Department of Education
18. Australian Curriculum: F-10 Curriculum | Economics and Business 7–10 - Year 7, 8, 9, 10. https://v9.australiancurriculum.edu.au/f-10-curriculum/learning-areas/economics-and-business-7-10/year-7_year-8_year-9_year-10?view=quick&detailed-content-descriptions=0&hide-ccp=0&hide-gc=0&side-by-side=1&strands-start-index=0&subjects-start-index=0,lastaccessed2023/03/11
19. Yamane, E.: Social and economic education in the Japanese elementary school national curriculum. Citizsh. Soc. Econ. Educ. **1**(1), 31–44 (1996). https://doi.org/10.2304/csee.1996.1.1.31
20. Curriculum for the compulsory school: preschool class and school-age educare 2011 revised 2018. Skolverket, Stockholm (2018)
21. Ministry of Education Singapore: Social studies teaching and learning syllabus: Lower and upper secondary normal (technical) course. Ministry of Education Singapore (2020)
22. Ministry of Education Ecuador: BGE and UGB: Social Sciences. Ministry of Education Ecuador
23. National Curriculum Development Centre Uganda: Primary Seven Curriculum. National Curriculum Development Centre Uganda (2012)
24. State of Kuwait: Kuwait National Curriculum - Primary Education: Curriculum and Standards - Social Studies. State of Kuwait (2016)
25. State of Kuwait: Kuwait National Curriculum - Intermediate Education: Curriculum and Standards - Social Studies. State of Kuwait (2016)
26. Hense, J., Mandl, H.: Learning in or with games?: Quality criteria for digital learning games from the perspectives of learning, emotion, and motivation theory. In: Sampson, D.G., Ifenthaler, D., Spector, J.M., and Isaias, P. (eds.) Digital Systems for Open Access to Formal and Informal Learning, pp. 181–193. Springer, Cham (2014). https://doi.org/10.1007/978-3-319-02264-2_12
27. Cohen, M.S., Freeman, J.T., Thompson, B.: Critical thinking skills in tactical decision making: a model and a training strategy. In: Cannon-Bowers, J.A., Salas, E. (eds.) Making Decisions Under Stress: Implications for Individual and Team Training, pp. 155–189. American Psychological Association, Washington (1998). https://doi.org/10.1037/10278-006
28. Wu, W.-H., Hsiao, H.-C., Wu, P.-L., Lin, C.-H., Huang, S.-H.: Investigating the learning-theory foundations of game-based learning: a meta-analysis: Exploring the learning-theory bases of GBL. J. Comput. Assist. Learn. **28**(3), 265–279 (2012). https://doi.org/10.1111/j.1365-2729.2011.00437.x

29. National Academies of Sciences, E., and Medicine: How People Learn II: Learners, Contexts, and Cultures. The National Academies Press, Washington, DC (2018). https://doi.org/10.17226/24783

30. National Research Council: Improving Adult Literacy Instruction: Options for Practice and Research. The National Academies Press, Washington, DC (2012). https://doi.org/10.17226/13242

31. Quintana, C., Reiser, B.J., Davis, E.A., Krajcik, J., Fretz, E., Duncan, R.G., Kyza, E., Edelson, D., Soloway, E.: A scaffolding design framework for software to support science inquiry. J. Learn. Sci. **13**(3), 337–386 (2004). https://doi.org/10.1207/s15327809jls1303_4

32. Jacobs, R.S.: Winning over the players: investigating the motivations to play and acceptance of Serious Games. Media Commun. **9**(1), 28–38 (2021). https://doi.org/10.17645/mac.v9i1.3308

A Reusable Serious Game Model for Natural Hazard Risk Communication: Evaluation of a Tsunami-Focused Case Study

Steven Hawthorn[1]([✉]) [iD], Rui Jesus[2] [iD], and Maria Ana Baptista[3] [iD]

[1] Universidade NOVA de Lisboa, 1099-085 Lisbon, Portugal
s.hawthorn@googlemail.com
[2] ISEL, Instituto Politécnico de Lisboa, 1959-007 Lisbon, Portugal
[3] Instituto Dom Luiz, Faculdade de Ciências da Universidade de Lisboa, 1746-016 Lisbon, Portugal

Abstract. This paper outlines the challenges around communicating natural hazard risk to children, due to the nature and concept of risk. It utilizes trusted disaster risk reduction advice to form the learning objectives of a serious game prototype for tsunami hazard. The study proposes an activity model that could form the basis of a game applicable to twelve different natural hazard scenarios thereby reducing resource input and reaching a significant number of learners in the formal education system. Evaluation of the prototype using an attitudinal survey suggests an adventure role playing game centered on challenges which use risk information is a viable concept for a serious game for communicating natural hazard risk.

Keywords: Serious games · natural hazard risk · children · disaster risk reduction · tsunami · active learning

1 Introduction

While disasters are nothing new, the evidence of overlapping disasters presents a considerable preparedness challenge in a multi-hazard world [1]. Risk has gained focus as a societal phenomenon as a by-product of new technologies. It is a standalone concern and also as a combination of natural hazard events with severe technological consequences. Preparing communities to face multi-hazard situations comprises three main challenges; communicating the polysemous nature of risk to the widest audience while providing information to inform appropriate actions for both the individual and the community.

This paper proposes Serious Games (SG) as a potential learning tool to help address these challenges. One option for addressing this challenge is through dissemination of Action-Oriented information as Key Messages (AOKM) from Disaster Risk Reduction (DRR) organisations [2]. This combined with innovative technologies allows the communication of risk information through SG as part of formal education of children in response to an increase in natural risk as an area of interest in education [3].

The complexity of risk communication as part of science education and education for sustainability (EfS) was highlighted during the COVID 19 pandemic. In this paper,

P. Dondio et al. (Eds.): GALA 2023, LNCS 14475, pp. 97–106, 2024.
https://doi.org/10.1007/978-3-031-49065-1_10

SGs are considered pieces of software with an educational purpose as part of a video game structure which are entertaining to use [4].

This paper briefly outlines the challenges of communicating action-oriented risk information from DRR specialists to a wide audience and addresses the suitability of SGs as a medium for teaching children in a classroom environment. It then describes a natural hazard game concept model (based on a tsunami risk communication prototype) that can be reused for other natural hazard scenarios. The paper finally presents player test evaluation of the tsunami prototype.

2 Communicating Risk: Pedagogic Approaches and SGs

2.1 Risks and Uncertainty

The ongoing debate related to teaching science to the general public includes risk communication and decision making under uncertainty [5]. Including risk and uncertainty in Education for Sustainability (EfS) means that methods to convey risk concepts in an engaging way are greatly sought after. These need to embrace uncertainty rather than viewing science as robust, highly reliable and delivering robust solutions.

Being polysemous in nature, 'risk' is defined in various ways. This can complicate risk assessment and pose a teaching challenge. Schenk *et al.* presented nine specialized definitions of risk [6], but identified key elements to provide consistency: uncertainty, probability, and consequence. Consequently, risk can be seen as referring to a future event with potentially negative outcomes. Decision making under uncertain conditions requires evaluation of response options, potential outcomes, and selection of a course of action. This requires the ability to engage in hypothetical reasoning, contemplating "what if" scenarios.

Despite ongoing debates about the conceptualization of risk in science education, it is suggested that SGs offer an interactive environment where learners can explore risk, decisions and consequences, without becoming overwhelmed in complex debate.

2.2 Focusing on Children

The focus on children as our main target-learners can be explained as follows.

Firstly, children are disproportionally affected by disasters and can effectively behave as risk communicators; their disaster education can trickle down and inform others in the community. As such children can be considered central to community-based DRR initiatives and to developing resilient communities.

Secondly, childhood is the stage in life where education is generally provided and young children are open to new ideas and concepts. They also have a right to information that could inform their own decision-making, particularly during emergency situations.

Thirdly, the formal education system has a role to clarify confusing and conflicting information and can address the health and well-being of children in emergency situations. Schools can provide a measured approach to controversial subject areas, (e.g. the intersection of climate science and natural hazard events) and have a significant role in children's disaster education.

The classroom is a structured environment with trained educators, which supports materials and links to discussions, and can provide support for learners who find risk material upsetting. As a consequence, the deployment of such a SG in a classroom environment is considered an appropriate way to address a wide audience of learners.

2.3 Pedagogic Considerations

Child development theories frequently embrace the notion of developmental stages with constructivist theory identifying the final operational stage during which abstract thinking and hypothetical evaluation is developed [7]. Cognitive processes can be categorized into a hierarchy of six levels of increasing complexity, where lower-level thinking skills include remembering (recall or recognition of information without necessarily applying it in a new context) and higher order thinking skills (HOTS), such as analysis, evaluation and justification of decisions. HOTS activities are considered a desirable departure from traditional knowledge retention (frequently assessed through recall and completion of routine exercises), and SGs provide an ideal environment where these kinds of activities can be undertaken [8]. Conventional teaching techniques, on the other hand, have been criticized for failing to address future hypothetical scenarios related to climate change education and sustainability which requires hypothetical, future-focused thinking [9].

Facilitating Active Learning: Learning can be undertaken using experimental, interactive activities where 'what if' scenarios can be examined and evaluated. This complements experiential learning where experience is translated through reflection into concepts thereby helping refine understanding through learner experimentation [10]. This active learning approach, where learners actively process information, is considered more desirable and effective than traditional learning.

Actionable Oriented Key Messages (AOKMs): DRR organizations complement simple awareness raising information with AOKMs, which go beyond simply conveying information about the risks and provide clear guidance on what actions to take [2]. Following a review of existing tsunami games [11] and a mapping of AOKM to existing tsunami SG [12] it was evident that the coverage of AOKM in games could be more comprehensive. AOKMs can be included as learning objectives in an SG scenario where learners apply the information to inform critical decisions in the game.

With an increase in the incidence and severity of natural hazard events related to planetary warming, a game with actionable DRR advice could help prepare learners to make appropriate decisions. Games can provide a simulated environment where decision making can be undertaken and key messages are communicated during the process. Applying key messages in active learning scenarios (game challenges) can induce information familiarity and facilitate appropriate decision making.

Engaging the Learner Using Storytelling: Controversial subjects such as planetary warming can produce denial, fatalistic attitudes and dichotomous views of such events, reducing the participants into deniers and accepters, which can serve to paralyse the debate. Activities which increase learner engagement are desirable and evidence in the literature suggests that SG can result in improved learner motivation and engagement. Using a SG facilitates participation in an interactive, hypothetical situation based on factual past events which would be impossible to replicate in reality. This approach helps circumvent focus on controversies around the climate change debate hence reducing doubt and denial and increasing engagement in the learning activity.

In the case of EfS (which includes risk communication) researchers have adopted a variety of different communication approaches. Storytelling has emerged as a strategy that can provide inaccessible information in a narrative framework by tapping into archetypal patterns for orientation and knowledge transmission [13] and facilitate reframing and shared understanding. Significant research highlights how indigenous communities have employed storytelling to transfer traditional knowledge, understanding and responsibilities for environmental artefacts and legal principles. More recently storytelling is seen as an important pedagogic tool for making sustainability more accessible.

Storytelling is a fundamental method for learners to interpret the experience of others and engage our inclination for connecting characters, events and experiences. Educators can exploit this predisposition to enhance the learning experience by engaging learner emotions and cognitive abilities through the connection of stories to the targeted learning objectives. In an educational context storytelling facilitates information delivery in a context and provides an emotional dimension to a social experience. This helps learners relate information (in our case AOKM) to their own experience (making decisions in the game). Placing the story into the interactive environment with challenges and learner feedback can be achieved by using a role-playing adventure game.

The previous section has summarized the pedagogic context which influenced the conceptual approach to a SG for risk communication. The following section outlines the development of the game concept into a working prototype.

3 Game Concept

This section outlines the prototype concept development and explains the reusability of the tsunami prototype to other forms of natural hazard.

The focus of the study was developing a SG prototype and as such the game concept development began by identifying a reliable source and a set of specific learning goals.

The game concept was designed to support communities where the perception of tsunami risk was considered extremely low or knowledge of natural warning signs (NWS) of tsunami could be improved [12]. The subsequent step involved selecting a deployment method that would offer a supportive environment for reaching a wide range of appropriate learners.

The formal education system was identified as the suitable platform, targeting 11–14-year-old learners. The most suitable game genre (partly inspired by Campo Santos's Firewatch[1]) was considered a story based, adventure game incorporating challenges that would directly relate to the learning objectives. Our prototype embraces a game loop which uses AOKMs in the form of challenges which oblige the learner to use information to complete the challenge and progress in the game.

---

[1] https://www.firewatchgame.com/.

3.1 Game Concept Development

The concept development prioritized the educational component using an International Red Cross publication as the origin of learning objectives [2]. The document is aimed at providing trusted, actionable information for households and schools. The advice relates to twelve specific natural hazard scenarios[2], and contain a series of actionable steps which can be completed at low cost and can significantly reduce risk should the hazard event occur. Actions can also be undertaken during a hazard event, which can inform a later critical decision making, (for example, counting the duration of earthquake ground shaking can inform the tsunami evacuation decision).

This approach empowers individuals to make decisions rather than wait for a warning which may not arrive in sufficient time, as in the case of near field tsunamis. The game loop activity diagram illustrates the relationship between game, scenes and the learning objectives. It follows the approach taken by De Lope *et al.* [14].

The interface design employed on-screen instructions at the start of each scene, speech dialogue bubbles to convey AOKM to the player and on-screen quizzes to assess the player understanding of the situation. An on-screen display shows the 'time remaining' and 'probability of survival' as a feedback to player decisions made.

3.2 Working Concept Prototype

The game prototype (referred to as "Tendenko Tsunami") comprises a dialogue driven, 3D role playing adventure game developed in the Unity[3] game engine.

Context Setting: Initial activities are focussed on context setting and providing background information, as the basis of the storyline. The initial dialogues inform the learner of the proximity to the ocean and that the principle character is unfamiliar with the local geography. The core game loop uses sequences of scenes, featuring characters who respond in an 'event – process information – response' paradigm.

The stages outlined in Fig. 1 can be described as follows.

Introduction: The core game loop comprises three processes; event, challenge and response. Each scene involves a series of small but important responses which are separated into Sub-Process[4] events each of which has a corresponding Sub-Process challenge and Sub-Process response. E.g. while the main (natural hazard) event is earthquake, an example of Sub-Process event is initiate the 'drop, cover, hold' response until the ground shaking has stopped.

Information Provision: Designed for uninformed players, the information required during game challenges is provided as part of a narrative. This is supplied using a storytelling approach, in which the Grandma character summarises an historic account

---

[2] Drought, Extreme heat/heat wave, Extreme cold and winter storms/cold wave, Major epidemic/pandemic diseases, Earthquakes, Landslides, Tsunami and storm surge, Volcanic eruptions, Tropical cyclones, Floods, Hailstorms, Wildfires.

[3] https://unity.com/products/unity-engine.

[4] https://www.ibm.com/docs/en/opw/9.0.0?topic=objects-sub-processes.

of a previous tsunami. However, information could be provided through a number of other methods. Grandma's story contains AOKMs which inform the sub process challenges.

Sub-process Events: These are mini-events triggered in the story which require specific information (AOKM) to facilitate a specific response. Each scene's main event comprises a number of Sub-Process events which combine to make an appropriate response and increase the probability of survival (PoS) of the player. Examples include recognising the earthquake and counting the duration of shaking.

Sub-process Challenges: Each Sub-Process event has a corresponding challenge. The primary function of the challenges is to oblige the learner to use the information from the AOKMs and thereby compel the learner to familiarise themselves with the information and its utility.

Sub-process Challenge Responses: The challenges are designed to output information that will help the player make an informed response from the learner in order to make progress in the game. An example, is the assessment Sub-Process challenge following the immediate evacuation uses information from the big wave story (i.e. Wave arrival was 20 min after the ground shaking) to allow the player to calculate the expected time of arrival of the wave and start a countdown clock to provide a sense of urgency in the game). With the Sub-Process challenge output, the player can make an informed response to the Sub-Process challenge and move to the next activity in the loop.

Once all the Sub-Processes are complete, the player should reach the concluding state of the game where the wave arrival time has counted down to zero and the player is either at the safe space (success state) or not (fail state). The player can restart the game if desirable. The same model can be used for a tsunami event and adapted for other natural hazard events.

4   Concept Prototype Evaluation

Following the development of a concept prototype and initial usability and play testing within the project team, the concept prototype was tested with school aged learners (Fig. 3).

4.1   Method and Results

The aim of the evaluation was to test both usability and playability of the prototype and validate the game concept prior to learning effectiveness evaluation in a later, more comprehensive trial. The survey questions were based on 'The Game Experience Questionnaire' [15] but were adapted to address a classroom deployable SG, and were validated by co-authors. The participants (comprising 6 male and 4 female respondents aged 15–18) were invited to play through the prototype and respond to a post-test survey. Although the game is aimed at 11–14-year-olds, the nature of the (Beta) test required more mature testers and reduced the need for direct interaction with the school. The survey comprised 24 Likert items (12 of which were reversed coded) and 6 questions focused on demographic information. Responses registered the degree of agreement or disagreement to

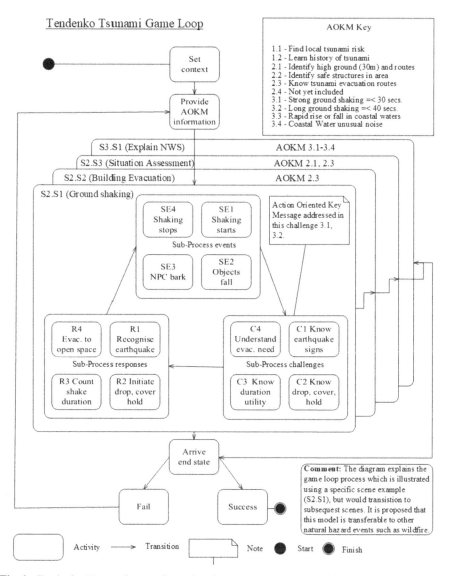

Fig. 1. Tendenko Tsunami game loop showing 'event – process of information – response' approach applicable to other natural hazard scenarios

the items, with five possible responses; strongly disagree; disagree; neither agree nor disagree; agree; and strongly agree. Results of positively and negatively worded items were combined and a summary of 11 items is presented in the diverging bar chart shown in Fig. 2.

Fig. 2. Shows how information provided in the 'Big Wave Story' needs to be utilized by the player in a later scene to estimate time available to evacuate.

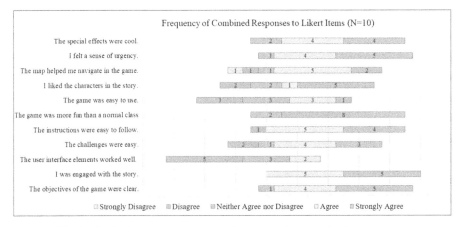

Fig. 3. Tendenko tsunami prototype player experience evaluation summary.

4.2 Results

The diverging stacked bar chart (Fig. 2) presents frequency of responses to the key Likert items presented in the survey. Items related to usability showed that 5/10 respondents did not experience a satisfactory interface interaction, with 3/10 giving a neutral response. Similarly, 3/10 respondents disagreed that the prototype was easy to use, with 3/10 neutral. In terms of player experience, all respondents were positive about engagement with the game story with 5/10 strongly agreeing. This suggests the interactive nature of the SG presents a suitable environment for active learning of AOKMs. The special effects were considered 'cool' by 8/10 respondents and 9/10 responded positively to feeling a sense of urgency while playing. Regarding the ludic educational balance, respondents overwhelming (8/10) reported having more fun than when attending a normal class. These results suggest validation of the adventure game concept in which learners use risk information to inform response in the scene challenges. However, development work focused on the user interaction is required to improve the game usability and player experience.

5   Conclusion

The authors believe that the factors outlined in this paper provide a strong argument in favor of further testing of a serious game approach for communicating natural hazard risk. This is primarily due to the complexity of addressing risk in an interactive, engaging and interesting way through a medium with which learners enjoy using. SG can provide an environment for experimentation and are aligned to established pedagogic approaches where support and follow-up discussion activities are provided.

The development of a generic model could help address multiple natural hazard events where the 'event – information process - response' paradigm could be reused. Ongoing work will extend the prototype evaluation to include the assessment of learning effectiveness in a future trial with a larger population of participants.

Acknowledgement. This work is supported by NOVA LINCS (UIDB/04516/2020) with the financial support of FCT.IP.

Conflict of Interest Declaration.   No potential competing interests were reported by the authors.

References

1. International Federation of Red Cross and Red Crescent Societies. World Disasters Report (2022). https://www.ifrc.org/sites/default/files/2023-01/20230130_2022_WDR_DataAnnex.pdf
2. IFRC. Save the Children International. Public awareness and public education for disaster risk reduction: action-oriented key messages for households and schools, 2nd edn. (2018). https://www.ifrc.org/sites/default/files/PAPE-2.0-English.pdf
3. Komac, B., Zorn, M., Ciglič, R.: European education on natural disasters – a textbook study. Nat. Hazards Earth Syst. Sci. Discuss. **1**(3), 2255–2279 (2013). https://doi.org/10.5194/nhessd-1-2255-2013
4. Ra, G., Sung, J., Yu, H., Min, H.: Analysis of serious games based on pedagogical features and proposal of civil defence training game. Int. J. Comput. Vis. Robot. **6**(3), 235–243 (2016). https://doi.org/10.1504/IJCVR.2016.077354
5. Doyle, E.E.H., Johnston, D.M., Smith, R., Paton, D.: Communicating model uncertainty for natural hazards: a qualitative systematic thematic review. Int. J. Disaster Risk Reduct. **33**, 449–476 (2019). https://doi.org/10.1016/j.ijdrr.2018.10.023
6. Schenk, L., et al.: Teaching and discussing about risk: seven elements of potential significance for science education. Int. J. Sci. Educ. **41**(9), 1271–1286 (2019). https://doi.org/10.1080/09500693.2019.1606961
7. Bélanger, P.: Three main learning theories. In: Egetenmeyer, R. (ed.) Theories in Adult Learning and Education, pp. 17–34. Verlag Barbara Budrich, Opladen & Farmington Hills (2011). https://doi.org/10.2307/j.ctvbkjx77.6
8. Obikwelu, C., Read, J.C.: The serious game constructivist framework for children's learning. Procedia Comput. Sci. **15** (2012). https://doi.org/10.1016/j.procs.2012.10.055
9. Lautensach, A.: Educating for sustainability: curriculum reform in the age of environmental crisis. Sustainability 1–15 (2011). https://sciforum.net/manuscripts/596/original.pdf
10. Ranglund, O.J., et al.: Using games for teaching crisis communication in higher education and training. In: Conference on Information Technology Based Higher Education and Training (ITHET) (2016). https://doi.org/10.1109/ITHET.2016.7760752

11. Hawthorn, S., Jesus, R., Baptista, M.A.: A review of digital serious games for tsunami risk communication. Int. J. Serious Games **8**(2), 21–47 (2021). https://doi.org/10.17083/ijsg.v8i 2.411

12. Hawthorn, S., Jesus, R., Baptista, M.A.: Tsunami risk communication: assessing knowledge gaps and suitable serious games. Sci. Tsunami Hazards **40**(1), 54–76 (2022). http://www.tsu namisociety.org/STHVol41N1Y2022.pdf

13. Dahlstrom, M.F.: Using narratives and storytelling to communicate science with nonexpert audiences. Proc. Natl. Acad. Sci. U. S. A. (2014). https://doi.org/10.1073/pnas.1320645111

14. De Lope, R.P., Medina-Medina, N., Urbieta, M., Lliteras, A.B., Mora García, A.: A novel UML-based methodology for modeling adventure-based educational games. Entertain. Comput. **38** (2021). https://doi.org/10.1016/j.entcom.2021.100429

15. IJsselsteijn, W.A., de Kort, Y.A.W., Poels, K.: The Game Experience Questionnaire. Technische Universiteit Eindhoven, Eindhoven (2013). https://research.tue.nl/en/publications/the-game-experience-questionnaire

Serious Games for Health, Wellbeing and Social Impact

Does Players' Prosocial Behavior in Computer Game Predict Their Well-Being in Real Life?

Kazuhisa Miwa[✉]

Nagoya University, Nagoya 4648601, Japan
kazuhisa.miwa@gmail.com

Abstract. This study investigates the correlation between players' prosocial behavior in computer games and their well-being in real life. Participants were invited to engage in a simple computer game where their task was to assist others in enhancing their mobility to reach the goal. The primary objective of this study was to determine whether the characteristics of this supportive behavior in the game could predict the participants' well-being in real life. Participants' prosociality was evaluated from two perspectives: a subjective evaluation of their prosocial behavior in daily life, as measured by the Altruistic Personality Scale (APS), and the number of assists provided in the game. While controlling for key demographic variables, the study examined the effect of participants' prosociality on their level of well-being. The results revealed that players who exhibited more prosocial behavior in the game also reported higher levels of well-being outside the game context.

Keywords: Prosocial behavior · Well-being · Hierarchical regression model

1 Introduction

1.1 Consistency of Behaviors in Serious Games and Real-Life Settings

The relationship between serious games and the real world is a critical area of research. Many studies have demonstrated an interactive relationship between the two, showing that experiences in serious games can influence real-world behaviors.

This correlation suggests that serious games can have both positive and negative societal impacts. A substantial amount of research indicates that playing violent video games can lead to several harmful effects on social behavior. Anderson and Dill (2000) conducted a study to investigate the effects of violent video games on aggression and socially problematic behavior [3]. They discovered that exposure to violent games in laboratory environments correlates positively with aggressive behavior in real-life situations. Other research has also highlighted the negative impacts of violent games on real-life activities [2,25].

© The Author(s), under exclusive license to Springer Nature Switzerland AG 2024
P. Dondio et al. (Eds.): GALA 2023, LNCS 14475, pp. 109–118, 2024.
https://doi.org/10.1007/978-3-031-49065-1_11

Greitemeyer et al. (2010) noted that there is limited evidence on the effects of prosocial video games compared to the numerous studies indicating various negative effects of playing violent video games [19]. Despite this, through four experiments, they confirmed the hypothesis that playing a prosocial game increases helping behavior. Gentile et al. (2009) conducted three separate studies with participants from different countries, and found an association between playing prosocial video games and increased prosocial behavior in real-life settings [15]. In a related meta-analytic review, the authors examined the effects of violent and prosocial video games on social outcomes, such as aggression and prosocial behavior [18]. They concluded that there is a significant link between video game content and real-life social behavior.

For considering the link, the findings that participants actively associate their own traits with the characters of agents in serious games are important. In one study [32], it was demonstrated that avatars were used to accurately reflect their owners' offline selves; this was deduced from twenty participants customizing an avatar while thinking aloud. Conversely, another study suggested that World of Warcraft players created their main character more akin to their ideal self than to their actual selves [4]. Furthermore, in the same study, participants who were content with their lives created avatars resembling themselves in terms of personality traits, while dissatisfied users created avatars that were dissimilar.

These studies collectively suggest that serious game participants project themselves into the game and connect their in-game experiences to the real world, indicating an interactive relationship between the serious gaming community and the real world.

1.2 Prosocial Behaviors and Well-Being

Our primary research question is: how can the behavioral characteristics of participants in a simple computer game predict their real-life social activities and life issues? In this study, we investigate the relationship between prosocial behavior and well-being.

Prosocial behavior is a type of social conduct that benefits others or society as a whole. Among the numerous studies on prosociality, there has been growing interest in the relationship between exhibiting prosocial behavior and one's personal well-being. Central to these studies is the question of whether engaging in prosocial behavior benefits not only the receiver but also the giver. A substantial body of research supports a positive correlation between givers' prosocial behavior and their well-being [21,24].

Volunteering, a notable example of prosocial action, has been found to be associated with increased well-being and a reduced risk of depression [22,31]. This correlation is likely due to the social support and sense of purpose that are often found in community-oriented efforts.

Another form of prosocial behavior, monetary generosity towards others, has also been linked to increased well-being. Dunn et al. (2008) found that those who spend more of their income on others reported greater happiness, both in cross-sectional and longitudinal studies [13]. Aknin et al. analyzed survey data from 136 countries and demonstrated that prosocial spending is associated with greater happiness worldwide, regardless of the country's economic status [1].

Lastly, expressing gratitude, another form of prosocial behavior, has been found to enhance well-being, increase positive emotions, and improve relationships. Emmons and McCullough (2003) found that participants who were encouraged to express gratitude in an experimental group reported higher well-being compared to a control group, particularly regarding the impact on positive emotions [14]. Additionally, Seligman et al. discovered that three of the interventions they studied, including expressing gratitude, resulted in a sustained increase in happiness and a decrease in depressive symptoms [28].

1.3   The Current Study

As previously mentioned, there are serious games that simulate prosocial activities. Some studies have indicated that engaging in these games positively impacts real-life social behaviors. However, to date, no studies have examined the relationship between participants' behavioral characteristics in these games and their overall well-being in real life.

In this study, participants are asked to engage in a simple computer game where they assist others' mobility. We aim to determine if the characteristics of this helping behavior in the game can predict the participants' real-life well-being.

Helping others move, such as pushing them from behind, taking their hand for support, or pulling them up, constitutes small acts of kindness that are part of everyday life. Some studies have indicated that these small acts of kindness in daily life improve the well-being of those performing the acts [26,33]. For example, Raposa et al. (2016) demonstrated that kind gestures, such as holding open a door, assisting with schoolwork, and asking someone if they need help, can mitigate the effects of stress on overall mental health.

We predict that the well-being of individuals who exhibit more helping behavior in the game will be higher than that of those who exhibit less helping behavior. This suggests that the measurement of prosocial behaviors in the game functions as a predictor of their real-life well-being.

In addition to the in-game behavior predictor, another easily measurable predictor is the subjective rating of one's own prosociality through a questionnaire. Various scales exist for measuring prosociality, such as PTM: Prosocial Tendencies Measure [5], PBQ: Prosocial Behavior Questionnaire [34], VFI: Volunteer Functions Inventory [6], and APS: Altruistic Personality Scale [27]. It has been found that some of these scales predict well-being levels. For instance, all six factors comprising the VFI contribute to well-being [30].

In the current study, we first examine the possibility that questionnaire scores predict participants' well-being levels, then we investigate whether the participants' helping behavior in the game serves as a predictor for their well-being.

2   Experiment

2.1   Measurements

Well-Being. Subjective well-being is considered to encompass two aspects: cognitive and affective [10,11]. In this study, we employed the Satisfaction with Life Scale (SWLS), which is a widely-used self-report tool for measuring the cognitive aspect of subjective well-being [9].

For the affective aspect, we utilized the Scale of Positive and Negative Experience (SPANE) [12]. The SPANE is a self-report measure designed to assess the emotional aspects of well-being. This scale aims to capture both the frequency and intensity of positive and negative emotions experienced by an individual.

Prosociality. We used a questionnaire to measure participants' prosociality. In Japan, a Japanese translation of the original Altruistic Personality Scale (APS) [27], developed by Rushton et al., is widely used [20].

Demographic Variables. We measured the following five demographic variables: gender, age, household income, highest level of education, marital status, along with two additional variables, namely, the number of friends and health status, as control variables.

2.2   Game Environment

The game was developed by a member of the author's lab. A screenshot of the game screen used in the experiment is shown in Fig. 1. In this game, participants utilize the arrow keys to navigate their marker (the red-colored point) up, down, left, and right, with the objective of crossing the goal line at the top of the screen within a specified time limit. In addition to the participant's marker, there are three other markers (gray-colored points) on the screen, which represent other players.

Due to the slower movement of the other markers compared to the participant's marker, some of them would not be able to cross the goal line unassisted. Participants can aid other markers in reaching the goal by maneuvering their own marker to push the others upward.

2.3   Procedures

The experiment was conducted online. After explaining the experimental procedures, participants first practiced moving their marker using the arrow keys in a practice phase before the actual experiment. This also allowed them to understand how they could assist the other markers.

Following the practice phase was the main experimental phase. Participants completed 30 trials in total. For the analysis, we used the average number of times each participant assisted other markers across the 30 trials. There were

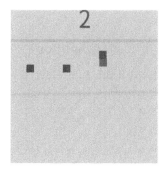

Fig. 1. An example screenshot of the experimental environment. The red square is assisting the rightmost gray square by lifting it. The remaining time is 2 s (Color figure online).

rare instances when a single marker was assisted multiple times; however, this was still counted as one instance of assistance.

Two factors were manipulated in the experiment:

Factor 1: Participant Responsibility. In one condition (High condition), participants were informed that they assumed the role of an instructor and had certain responsibilities concerning the other three participants reaching the goal. In the other condition (Low condition), participants were told that they were simply one of four participants.

Factor 2: Time Limit Format. In one condition (Fixed condition), the time limit was set at 10 s, and a countdown clock was displayed on the screen. In the other condition (Random condition), the time limit averaged 10 s (ranging from a minimum of 8 s to a maximum of 12 s), with a countdown clock appearing two seconds before the trial's end.

Participants were randomly assigned to one of the four 2×2 conditions described above. In each condition, participants were not explicitly instructed to help others, nor were they given any incentives to help.

After the game, participants answered 20 questions on the APS, followed by the well-being questionnaire, including SWLS and SPANE. Lastly, demographic variables were assessed.

2.4 Participants

Participants were recruited using a crowdsourcing service, and each participant was paid an honorarium of 400 yen. The total number of participants was 580 (age: mean = 41.15, SD = 9.02, gender: 251 males and 329 females) with 144, 149, 141, and 146 being assigned to the High (Responsibility) and Random (Time format), High and Fixed, Low and Random, and Low and Fixed conditions respectively.

3   Results

3.1   Number of Assists in Each Condition

First, as a preliminary analysis, Table 1 displays the average number of times participants assisted others in each of the 2 (Responsibility) × 2 (Time Limit Format) conditions.

Table 1. Average number of assists in each of the experimental conditions.

Time Format	Responsibility	mean	SD
Random	Low	37.1	12.1
	High	41.6	11.1
Fixed	Low	36.8	9.4
	High	41.8	9.4

A 2 × 2 ANOVA reveals a significant main effect of the responsibility factor $(F(1, 576) = 28.60, p < .001, \eta^2 = .047)$, with the number of assists being higher in the high responsibility condition compared to the low responsibility condition. Neither the main effect of the time limit format factor nor the interaction effect between the two factors reached a significant level $(F(1, 576) < 1, \text{n.s.}, F(1, 576) < 1, \text{n.s.})$.

3.2   Effect of Prosociality and Assist Behavior in Game

Hierarchical regression analysis was used to identify the unique contribution of specific variables to the prediction of the target variable, with the variables entered into the model in a specific order. First, we input demographic variables into the model (Model 1). Next, we entered the APS score into the model to assess its effect on well-being scores (Model 2A). Finally, we entered the average number of assists that the participants gave in the game, instead of the APS score, into the model to evaluate the effect of this variable on well-being scores (Model 2B).

Table 2(a) shows how each of the models predicts life satisfaction (SWLS score). In the initial model (Model 1), the demographic variables were used to predict life satisfaction, accounting for 35.0% of the variance in life satisfaction $(R^2 = 0.350, F(8, 572) = 38.36, p < 0.001)$.

In Model 2A, the addition of APS explained an additional 1.0% of the variance in life satisfaction $(\Delta R^2 = 0.010, F(8, 572) = 35.62, p < 0.001)$, bringing the total variance explained to 36.0%. The benefit of entering the APS variable is significant $(p < 0.01)$.

In Model 2B, the addition of the number of assists explained an additional 0.8% of the variance in life satisfaction $(\Delta R^2 = 0.008, F(8, 572) = 35.27, p <$

Table 2. Results of hierarchical regression analysis for predicting life satisfaction (SWLS) and emotional states of well-being (SPANE).

(a) Life satisfaction

	Model 1	Model 2A	Model 2B
Gender	0.910 +	0.711	1.097 *
reference = male			
Age	-0.000	-0.013	0.014
Education	0.616 *	0.530 *	0.594 *
Income	0.389 ***	0.359 ***	0.387 ***
Marriage	3.793 ***	3.636 ***	3.798 ***
Marriage (others)	0.722	0.648	0.963
reference = unmarried			
Relationship	0.178 ***	0.136 **	0.179 ***
Health	1.697 ***	1.672 ***	1.684 ***
APS in questionnaire		0.057 **	
# of assists in game			0.060 **
R^2	0.350	0.360	0.358
ΔR^2		0.010 **	0.008 **
Adj R^2	0.340	0.350	0.348
F-statics	38.36 ***	35.62 ***	35.27***

(b) Positive emotions

	Model 1	Model 2A	Model 2B
Gender	1.584 ***	1.372 **	1.699 ***
reference = male			
Age	-0.006	-0.019	0.003
Education	0.145	0.053	0.131
Income	0.132	0.100	0.131
Marriage	2.154 ***	1.987 ***	2.157 ***
Marriage (others)	-0.178	-0.257	-0.029
reference = unmarried			
Relationship	0.094 *	0.050	0.095 *
Health	1.378 ***	1.351 ***	1.370 ***
APS in questionnaire		0.061 ***	
# of assists in game			0.037 *
R^2	0.269	0.289	0.274
ΔR^2		0.020 ***	0.005 *
Adj R^2	0.259	0.278	0.263
F-statics	26.29 ***	25.70 ***	23.94 ***

(c) Negative emotions

	Model 1	Model 2A	Model 2B
Gender	0.568	0.534	0.525
reference = male			
Age	-0.081 ***	-0.083 ***	-0.084 ***
Education	-0.192	-0.207	-0.187
Income	-0.231 **	-0.236 **	-0.230 **
Marriage	0.480	0.453	0.479
Marriage (others)	2.446 *	2.434 *	2.392 *
reference = unmarried			
Relationship	-0.030	-0.038	-0.031
Health	-1.590 ***	-1.595 ***	-1.587 ***
APS in questionnaire		0.010	
# of assists in game			-0.014
R^2	0.210	0.210	0.211
ΔR^2		0.001	0.001
Adj R^2	0.199	0.198	0.198
F-statics	18.94 ***	16.86 ***	16.88 ***

0.001), bringing the total variance explained to 35.8%. The benefit of entering the number of assists variable is also significant ($p < 0.01$).

With regards to SPANE, the results suggest that both the APS and the number of assists in the game contribute to predicting the positive aspect of emotional well-being. However, neither variable significantly influences the prediction of the negative aspect. See the detailed results with statistical analysis in Tables 2(b) and (c).

4 Discussion and Conclusions

In this study, we first investigated whether the APS score (participants' self-rated prosociality) predicted their level of well-being while controlling for relevant demographic variables (Model 2A). Additionally, examined whether the volume of supportive behavior participants exhibited towards others in the game predicted their well-being levels, again controlling for demographic variables (Model 2B).

First, there was no correlation observed between the value of APS and the number of assists in the game ($r = -0.02$, n.s.). This suggests that these variables represent distinct aspects of participants' prosociality each independently contributing to the explanation of well-being levels.

Regarding the cognitive aspect of well-being, the results for both variables (APS score and number of assists) entered in Models 2A and 2B were consistent. Both variables effectively explained participants' life satisfaction, representing the cognitive aspect of well-being. In other words, participants with higher APS scores and those who provided more assists in the game reported higher levels of well-being. Overall, although affective well-being is more susceptible to fluctuations influenced by daily experiences and emotional states, cognitive well-being tends to exhibit greater stability over time, reflecting a person's satisfaction and evaluation of life [10]. Especially, employing indicators that consider multiple perspectives, such as the Satisfaction with Life Scale (SWLS), can help maintain a certain degree of stability in measuring well-being [23].

When it comes to predicting stable indicators of well-being such as life satisfaction, we found that two variables related to prosociality were valid. On the other hand, it has been confirmed that the emotional aspect of well-being is susceptible to short-term fluctuations. For example, emotional states undergo rhythmic changes throughout the day [29], week [7], or even across different seasons [16].

Regarding the affective aspect of well-being, the effects were not consistent in the explanation for positive and negative affective well-being level. Both APS and the number of assists in the game demonstrated a association with positive affect, while neither of them significantly improved the explanation for negative emotions. Many studies have pointed out that positive and negative emotions are not attributes of a single dimension in opposite directions, but rather, they represent two distinct dimensions [8]. Thus, it's possible for both positive and negative emotional states to be high or low at the same time. The results of this study suggest that indicators, such as prosociality, contribute differently to these various dimensions of emotional well-being.

Although the demographic variables accounted for 35.0% of the variance in well-being ratings related to life satisfaction and 26.9% related to the positive affect of well-being, the increase in explanatory power due to the inclusion of both variables was minimal—approximately 1% for both aspects. In the current experiment, participants played the game from a third-person perspective. Gorisse et al. (2017) concluded that a first-person viewpoint enables maximal user inclusion within the virtual environment, largely due to the natural transposition of our perceptual mechanisms [17]. This suggests that the contribution of in-game behaviors to the explanation might be more significant if we allowed participants to adopt a first-person perspective by modifying the game environment.

This study discussed the relationship between two variables related to prosocial behavior and three variables related to subjective well-being. It should be noted, however, that this is a correlational study and causal relationships between these variables cannot be discussed.

Acknowledgement. The experimental environment was developed by Mr. Yuki Fujita as part of his graduation study. The author expresses gratitude to Mr. Fujita and Dr. Mayu Yamakawa, both of whom made beneficial contributions to the earlier phase of this research project.

References

1. Aknin, L.B., et al.: Prosocial spending and well-being: cross-cultural evidence for a psychological universal. J. Pers. Soc. Psychol. **104**(4), 635 (2013)
2. Anderson, C.A., et al.: The influence of media violence on youth. Psychol. Sci. Public Interest **4**(3), 81–110 (2003)
3. Anderson, C.A., Dill, K.E.: Video games and aggressive thoughts, feelings, and behavior in the laboratory and in life. J. Pers. Soc. Psychol. **78**(4), 772 (2000)
4. Bessière, K., Seay, A.F., Kiesler, S.: The ideal elf: identity exploration in world of warcraft. Cyberpsychol. Behav. **10**(4), 530–535 (2007)
5. Carlo, G., Randall, B.A.: The development of a measure of prosocial behaviors for late adolescents. J. Youth Adolesc. **31**, 31–44 (2002)
6. Clary, E.G., et al.: Understanding and assessing the motivations of volunteers: a functional approach. J. Pers. Soc. Psychol. **74**(6), 1516 (1998)
7. Csikszentmihalyi, M., Hunter, J.: Happiness in everyday life: the uses of experience sampling. J. Happiness Stud. **4**, 185–199 (2003)
8. Diener, E., Emmons, R.A.: The independence of positive and negative affect. J. Pers. Soc. Psychol. **47**(5), 1105 (1984)
9. Diener, E., Emmons, R.A., Larsen, R.J., Griffin, S.: The satisfaction with life scale. J. Pers. Assess. **49**(1), 71–75 (1985)
10. Diener, E., Oishi, S., Tay, L.: Advances in subjective well-being research. Nat. Hum. Behav. **2**(4), 253–260 (2018)
11. Diener, E., Suh, E.M., Lucas, R.E., Smith, H.L.: Subjective well-being: three decades of progress. Psychol. Bull. **125**(2), 276 (1999)
12. Diener, E., et al.: New well-being measures: short scales to assess flourishing and positive and negative feelings. Soc. Indicators Res. **97**, 143–156 (2010)
13. Dunn, E.W., Aknin, L.B., Norton, M.I.: Spending money on others promotes happiness. Science **319**(5870), 1687–1688 (2008)
14. Eamons, B., Mc Cullough, M.E.: Counting blessings versus burdens: an experimental investigation of gratitude and subjective well-being in daily life. J. Pers. Soc. Psychol. **84**(2), 377–389 (2003)
15. Gentile, D.A., et al.: The effects of prosocial video games on prosocial behaviors: international evidence from correlational, longitudinal, and experimental studies. Pers. Soc. Psychol. Bull. **35**(6), 752–763 (2009)
16. Golder, S.A., Macy, M.W.: Diurnal and seasonal mood vary with work, sleep, and daylength across diverse cultures. Science **333**(6051), 1878–1881 (2011)
17. Gorisse, G., Christmann, O., Amato, E.A., Richir, S.: First-and third-person perspectives in immersive virtual environments: presence and performance analysis of embodied users. Front. Robot. AI **4**, 33 (2017)

18. Greitemeyer, T., Mügge, D.O.: Video games do affect social outcomes: a meta-analytic review of the effects of violent and prosocial video game play. Pers. Soc. Psychol. Bull. **40**(5), 578–589 (2014)

19. Greitemeyer, T., Osswald, S.: Effects of prosocial video games on prosocial behavior. J. Pers. Soc. Psychol. **98**(2), 211 (2010)

20. Kikuchi, A.: The Science of Caring: The Psychology and Skills of Prosocial Behavior. Kawashima-shoten (1988)

21. Lyubomirsky, S., King, L., Diener, E.: The benefits of frequent positive affect: does happiness lead to success? Psychol. Bull. **131**(6), 803 (2005)

22. Musick, M.A., Wilson, J.: Volunteering and depression: the role of psychological and social resources in different age groups. Soc. Sci. Med. **56**(2), 259–269 (2003)

23. Pavot, W., Diener, E.: The affective and cognitive context of self-reported measures of subjective well-being. Soc. Indic. Res. **28**, 1–20 (1993)

24. Post, S.G.: Altruism, happiness, and health: it's good to be good. Int. J. Behav. Med. **12**(2), 66–77 (2005)

25. Prescott, A.T., Sargent, J.D., Hull, J.G.: Metaanalysis of the relationship between violent video game play and physical aggression over time. Proc. Nat. Acad. Sci. **115**(40), 9882–9888 (2018)

26. Raposa, E.B., Laws, H.B., Ansell, E.B.: Prosocial behavior mitigates the negative effects of stress in everyday life. Clin. Psychol. Sci. **4**(4), 691–698 (2016)

27. Rushton, J.P., Chrisjohn, R.D., Fekken, G.C.: The altruistic personality and the self-report altruism scale. Personality Individ. Differ. **2**(4), 293–302 (1981)

28. Seligman, M.E., Steen, T.A., Park, N., Peterson, C.: Positive psychology progress: empirical validation of interventions. Am. Psychol. **60**(5), 410 (2005)

29. Stone, A.A., Schwartz, J.E., Schkade, D., Schwarz, N., Krueger, A., Kahneman, D.: A population approach to the study of emotion: diurnal rhythms of a working day examined with the day reconstruction method. Emotion **6**(1), 139 (2006)

30. Stukas, A.A., Hoye, R., Nicholson, M., Brown, K.M., Aisbett, L.: Motivations to volunteer and their associations with volunteers' well-being. Nonprofit Volunt. Sect. Q. **45**(1), 112–132 (2016)

31. Thoits, P.A., Hewitt, L.N.: Volunteer work and well-being. Journal of health and social behavior, pp. 115–131 (2001)

32. Vasalou, A., Joinson, A., Bänziger, T., Goldie, P., Pitt, J.: Avatars in social media: balancing accuracy, playfulness and embodied messages. Int. J. Hum. Comput. Stud. **66**(11), 801–811 (2008)

33. Weinstein, N., Ryan, R.M.: When helping helps: autonomous motivation for prosocial behavior and its influence on well-being for the helper and recipient. J. Pers. Soc. Psychol. **98**(2), 222 (2010)

34. Weir, K., Duveen, G.: Further development and validation of the prosocial behaviour questionnaire for use by teachers. J. Child Psychol. Psychiatry **22**(4), 357–374 (1981)

Pro(f)Social: A Serious Game to Counter Cyberbullying

Nádia Pereira, Paula Ferreira(✉), Sofia Francisco,
and Ana Margarida Veiga Simão

Faculdade de Psicologia, CICPSI, Universidade de Lisboa, Lisbon, Portugal
{nadia,sofia.francisco}@campus.ul.pt,
paula.ferreira@edu.ulisboa.pt, amsimao@psicologia.ulisboa.pt

Abstract. This study proposes to present the design and face validity of a serious game prototype, Pro(f)Social, as part of a blended learning teacher training program based on social-emotional ethical learning to promote pro-social behavior and well-being among children, through changes in teachers' emotion regulation and moral involvement with cyberbullying and their social-emotional competence to deal with the phenomenon. Teachers are often unaware of aggressive acts among their students, and even when they are, many consider that they are not responsible for resolving cyberbullying issues. Therefore, it is fundamental to develop resources based on human-machine collaboration to attain several milestones in designing serious games to prevent and intervene in cyberbullying by providing teachers with know-how through interactive training with artificial intelligence. The game presented, along with its face validity (n = 290 units for content analysis), offer technology professionals the necessary knowledge to develop future interventions to counter cyberbullying.

Keywords: Serious games · Social agents · Cyberbullying · Teachers

1 Introduction

1.1 Cyberbullying and the Role of Teachers

Cyberbullying is intentional and repeated cruel behavior towards peers, through electronic media when online, which is not often disclosed by participants [1]. Cyberbullying may influence academic performance, cause absenteeism and learning difficulties and lead to feelings of anger, loneliness, anxiety and health-harming behavior [2]. Moreover, different social-cognitive and affective reactions to cyberbullying may emerge due to the lack of contextual information and emotional cues [3]. It involves social interaction in context and how individuals react to it, may include individual variables, such as emotion and moral factors [4, 5].

However, evidence has shown that teachers feel unprepared to manage cyberbullying and are unsure of how to respond to students who are victimized, thus needing training [6]. Students' interpersonal interactions and relationships with teachers and peers can

P. Dondio et al. (Eds.): GALA 2023, LNCS 14475, pp. 119–128, 2024.
https://doi.org/10.1007/978-3-031-49065-1_12

impact their social behavior through modeling/advice, behavioral goals and expectations [6]. Thus, there is a need for awareness, understanding, and training for teachers regarding cyberbullying, as they have little to no training with this phenomenon [2]. Creating interventions that strengthen the relationship between teachers and students seems to be more effective, as these professionals serve as role models and youth become more engaged at school [5]. The role of teachers is pertinent to investigate in order to foster their social-emotional skills and strategies to intervene in an adaptive manner. Serious games are digital games aimed toward purposes other than entertainment, such as problem-solving [7]. Serious games have been reported to be a beneficial resource to foster these competencies and prosocial behavior [4, 5].

This study proposes to present the design and face validity of a serious game prototype as part of a blended learning teacher training program concerning cyberbullying. This study's innovative nature is two-fold. To understand teachers' emotional and moral involvement with cyberbullying, it uses an integrated approach of a cyclical modular appraisal framework of emotion [8, 9] and a social cognitive perspective of moral agency [10]. In moral agency, personal, behavioral and environmental factors contribute to guide individual functioning, whereas appraisal theories consider different evaluations, namely, whether events are perceived as the individuals' responsibility, are probable, unexpected, desirable, and morally good or bad.

1.2 Serious Games to Counter Cyberbullying

Serious games can be used as an innovative way to teach strategies to counter cyberbullying with an immersive experience, which in turn, raises awareness and empathy with victims [11]. Previous research with serious games for students has shown that these resources are significant and valid tools to teach adolescents about situations that are associated to violence [4, 5].

Research on serious games, such as CyberBullet [12], The #StopBully app [13], the Inn Inoue game [14], the Bully Book [15], Cyberhero Mobile Safety game [16], and Cooperative Cybereduca 2.0 [17] and Conectado [18] presented their design and development as games for students, whereas we propose a game for teachers. Games for students, such as Conectado [18], along with others such as FearNot! [19] had a single game session, whereas we propose four sessions, which will enable a longitudinal analysis of teachers' performance. Moreover, the NNLazarinis game presented various short stories about online behavior with different characters [20], similar to what we propose to do with different social agents portraying students and teacher colleagues. In a systematic review of serious games to prevent cyberbullying among children and adolescents [11], the main mechanics used in these types of games have been based on making choices, providing adventure with scenarios and exploration, enabling dialogues, and customizing features [11]. In accordance, this study presents a game for teachers based on cyberbullying scenarios within a common storyline that includes students and colleague teachers. Previous research has found that serious games can minimize bullying behavior [21] and that using simulation of interactions on social networks (i.e., Bully Book) is an essential element of gameplay. In view of this, we present a game which incorporates a fictitious social network into the game to contextualize the storyline with the different cyberbullying scenarios. Previous research has suggested that these types of scenarios [5] have various response options incorporated into the game, which we also include. It is also imperative to provide context and social feedback with interactive entities, such as social agents, to understand how players may react to specific situations. Social agents are the technologies that interact with other agents and humans by how they are designed and applied so that they mimic human-to-human interaction [22]. Research has provided evidence of the importance of players establishing a relationship with the social agents because this type of virtual interaction may influence their emotional and behavioral reactions to the situations [23]. In accordance, we also took this aspect into consideration, as these agents may improve social interaction in educational applications [4]. In fact, social agents can help build a context and create a sense of social belonging, which is what we intend to do.

To contribute to previous studies, we expect that the game we present will foster emotion regulation and moral involvement with cyberbullying and develop social-emotional competence to deal with the phenomenon. By developing a new game for teachers, which as far as we know, is unique, we can contribute with innovative design criteria and features which inform the development of future games.

2 Pro(f)Social, the Game

2.1 Conceptualizing and Developing the Game

This serious game prototype has an introductory session (0) for teachers to learn how to play, and 4 subsequent sessions which include: (1) a diagnostic phase to examine if they identify a cyberbullying situation by observing warning signs and to identify the knowledge and moral engagement they have with cyberbullying; (2) to reflect on emotion regulation and empathy related with the presented cyberbullying situation; and (3) to reflect about prevention and intervention strategies. Teachers receive feedback regarding their choices throughout the game on how they can improve pro-sociality. The game is played individually and the player's main objective is to adopt pro-social behavior to help solve 4 cyberbullying situations from Com@Viver [4, 5] with virtual social agents, while executing different teachers' daily tasks.

2.2 Providing Context in the Game

Session 1 begins with break 1 which includes "everyday" dialogue situations between students in different school spaces, which the teacher can observe. Situation 1 occurs during this break and is related to the cyberbullying case. It refers to a dialogue in the schoolyard between three female students about another female student (victim): a bystander from the teacher's class who supports the bully and two bystanders from another teacher's class who support the bully. In situation 2, the teacher goes into the classroom to start the first lesson. Inside the classroom is a group of students: bystanders from the teacher's class intending to help the victim; a bystander from the teacher's class intending to ignore the situation; and a bystander from the teacher's class intending to support the bully. The teacher witnesses a dialogue (Fig. 1).

The second lesson of session 1 consists of the teacher viewing the post related to the cyberbullying case, following break 2. A teacher appears at the entrance of the

Fig. 1. Interaction between social agents who portray students

classroom and mentions that a student sent him a post, showing his cell phone. Lastly, situation 3 takes place during break 3, where a dialogue occurs between the cyberbully, surrounded by other students: observers from another teacher's class who support the bully; an observer from the teacher's class who supports the victim; and an observer from the teacher's class who ignores the situation.

2.3 Identifying Warning Signs During Gameplay

In break 1, task 3 and 4 are teacher "everyday" tasks (e.g., sending an urgent email). Task 5 consists of identifying warning signs and is related to the cyberbullying case, i.e., finding out who the student in the post is. Situations that constitute warning signs of cyberbullying victims appear besides the "everyday" situations between students, which also appear in different school spaces. The teacher will have the option to indicate whether they have finished the task at any point during the break by going to the teachers' room, where a yes or no question appears ("Were you able to identify which student is in the post?") and indicate a reason through an open response option.

Break 2 has the same structure as break 1. It includes "everyday" dialogue situations between students in different school spaces, which the teacher can observe. Task 6 and 7 are "everyday" teacher tasks (e.g., making photocopies of tests in the library). Task 8 is related to the cyberbullying case and consists of finding out which student posted the picture. Similarly to break 1, to accomplish task 8 the teacher must identify warning signs of cyberbullying aggressors and will have the option to indicate whether they have finished the task at any point in the teachers' room, answering to a yes or no question and justifying it ("Were you able to determine which student posted the picture?").

2.4 Measuring Moral (Dis)engagement and Bystander Intervention During Gameplay

Moral (dis)engagement [10], interpreting the situation as an emergency and taking responsibility for the situation from the Bystander Intervention Model [24] will be measured during the interaction of the player facing situation 1. A question appears, in a thought format ("To what degree do I attribute severity to this situation?"). The teacher has to choose one option from a 4-point scale reflecting to which degree they consider the situation as serious. Next, a set of sentences appears (e.g., "It's just a joke between girls. Nothing special."). The teacher will have the possibility to show their degree of agreement for each of the sentences regarding situation 1, on a 3-point scale ("agree", "neither agree nor disagree", "disagree").

In break 3, which includes "everyday" dialogue situations between students in different school spaces, which the teacher can observe, task 9 and 10 are teacher "everyday" tasks (e.g., preparing an activity for the next day). Task 11 is a cyberbullying-related task in the teacher's room and consists of reflecting on how to intervene as a bystander [24] in the face of the cyberbullying post. Moreover, teacher interaction with situation 3 includes knowing how to intervene and intervention strategies [24]. Two options (i.e., "I will not get involved" and "I'm going to do something") appear, in a thought format, to the question "What do I do regarding what I know about Nando's post about Tatiana?" Similar to the previous situation, after answering the question, a set of sentences and the same gamified format appear, but this time, these options depend on whether the teacher chooses to intervene (e.g., "Report the situation to the Principal") or not (e.g., "I don't think I would be able to change the situation").

2.5 Measuring Empathic Concern, Emotion and Emotion Regulation During Gameplay

The teacher gets to interact with the game regarding situation 2 and show their level of empathic concern with regards to the situation, responding to a question which appears, in a thought format ("To what degree does this situation concern me?"). The teacher must choose one option from a 4-point scale reflecting in which degree they worry with the situation. Like situation 1, after assessing their degree of empathic concern about situation 2, sentences in the same gamified format appear related to empathy in relation to different social agents (e.g., "I understand that Tatiana is going through a difficult situation"). The teacher will have the possibility to show his or her degree of agreement for each of the sentences, on a 3-point scale ("agree", "neither agree nor disagree", "disagree"). During lesson 2, the player is instructed to think about how they felt about the post their colleague showed him/her on his cell phone. Then, the same gamified format as in situation 1 and 2 appears with a set of sentences pertaining to emotion regulation guided by Gratz and Roemer's [25] model of emotional (dys)regulation.

2.6 Feedback Provided During Gameplay and at the End of the Game

Feedback throughout the sessions is given regarding the specific options the player agrees with in each of the three situations and on the tasks related to the cyberbullying case, to reinforce/guide him/her towards adopting pro-social behavior and promote proactivity throughout the session (e.g., Response: "I understand why classmates are being supportive of Tatiana." Feedback: "You understand the perspective of students who are supporting a classmate who is being bullied."). Feedback can be received during the gameplay in the coordinator's room. The player will be able to choose whether to consult the feedback they receive, which can be consulted at any time. At the end of the session, a summary table appears with all the feedback given throughout the session, followed by feedback on the score the teacher got for that session in the format of percentage of pro-social behavior.

3   User Study

3.1   Sample Characteristics

The validation session was attended by 6 teachers from a High School in the Lisbon Metropolitan area. The participants' ages ranged from 33 to 67 years old. Regarding years of service, the sample was quite heterogeneous, ranging from 1 year of service to 40 years. Table 1 shows the participants' socio-demographic description.

Table 1. Socio-demographic variables of the participants.

Sample	Sex	Age	Years of service	Subject taught	Professional situation	Students' grade
1	Male	33	1	Technology/Visual Arts	Temporary contract	9/10
2	Male	60	34	Portuguese	Effective	9/10/12
3	Male	63	35	Portuguese/Special Education	Effective	7/8/9
4	Male	49	25	Portuguese/French	Temporary contract	7/8/9
5	Male	47	1	Math	Temporary contract	7/10/Night classes
6	Female	67	40	Portuguese/French	Effective	7/8/12

3.2   Instruments and Procedures

We used a questionnaire composed of 6 closed-ended questions and 6 open-ended questions. Concerning the closed-ended questions, two items assessed the level of experience and familiarity with game play (e.g., "How frequently do you play games?"), one item evaluated previous training in cyberbullying (i.e., "Did you have any training about cyberbullying?"), and three items assessed the level of pertinence of the game in training about cyberbullying (e.g., "To what extent did you find the game useful for a teacher training about cyberbullying?"). The open-ended questions evaluated participants' perspectives about the game, namely learning experiences. Seven items included in this questionnaire were used to assess participants' sociodemographic characteristics. A semi-structured group interview was conducted with 30 open-ended questions: (1) global game experience (e.g., "How did you feel during the game?"), (2) learning experience (e.g., How do you compare the learning experience using the game with others?"), (3) adaptability (e.g., What did you enjoy the most in the game?"), (4) usability (e.g., "Did you find any errors?"), (5) fidelity (e.g., "Do you identify with the situations and game characters?").

We held a 90-min audio recorded session with the target audience of the game (6 in-service teachers) to validate the game prototype and concept of the game.

3.3 Data Analysis

Content analysis was performed using a mixed method with NVivo 14 software (i.e., deductive, based on the literature and inductive (what emerges from participants' utterances during the interview) The analysis was based on 290 of the participants' verbalizations – units of analysis). A categorization system based on five main categories was used: (1) Global game experience (i.e., level of interest, flow, immersion, challenge, tension, effort, competence, fun, pleasant/unpleasant emotions); Learning experience (i.e., whether the game content facilitates teachers' learning regarding cyberbullying); Adaptability (i.e., whether the game fits teachers' needs concerning cyberbullying); Fidelity (i.e., adequacy of the level of realism offered by the game and the learning context); Usability (i.e., whether the game's interface and mechanisms allow for functional gameplay).

3.4 Results

The questionnaire results indicated that all participants considered they learned during the game. Two participants partially agreed that the serious game led to reflections about cyberbullying, and 4 totally agreed. All participants considered the game very useful as part of a teacher training on cyberbullying. Four participants found the game very interesting in the context of a teacher training on cyberbullying, and 2 found it extremely interesting. The content analysis of the interviews revealed that from the total 290 units of analysis, that the most frequently mentioned category was fidelity, followed by usability, game experience, learning experience and adaptability (Fig. 2).

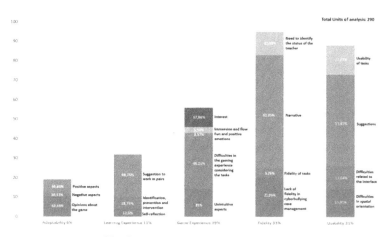

Fig. 2. Results of the content analysis

Within the fidelity category, the most frequent aspects referred by the participants were related with the game narrative, specifically the lack of fidelity (63,79%; e.g., "because as teachers we don't walk around here listening to the conversations") versus fidelity (36,21%; e.g., "the story, the episode, the situations are believable, so they are…even the dialogues…"), followed by issues related to the cyberbullying case management (e.g., "Only if in the real sharing of a message that a student and a teacher received… Could we know about it."). Regarding usability, participants focused more on tasks' usability and giving suggestions (e.g., "ah yes, that is, we had already identified but there was no step…."). The suggestions referred mostly (51,06%) to issues about the interface (e.g., "… when the game starts, to have a kind of initial presentation of that menu where our class is, so that we clearly understand that that's our class") and the need for greater interaction between the characters (34,04%; e.g., "So those conversations that take place between them(…)by the way between the teacher and another colleague"). In the game experience category, participants made reference with more frequency to their difficulties with the game experience concerning the tasks (e.g., "we had that time to do certain things and we had already wasted a lot of time listening to the conversations");and unintuitive aspects (e.g., "We have failed badly on the identification issue, and we don't understand why"). In the Learning experience category, participants gave suggestions about working with others (e.g., "exactly, working in pairs would be interesting"), then, mentioned aspects related to identifying, preventing and intervening in cyberbullying (e.g., "I think it's to get us thinking about the principles of conflict prevention and mediation in educational settings"). Lastly, in the adaptability category, participants gave their opinions (e.g., "The fact that the game is an excellent way to put us into the orbit of…this very serious problem"), then focused on positive aspects (e.g., "I think the game is important for us, it alerts us, leads us to reflect, to pay attention to the signs that are out there") and negative issues (e.g., "and not being able to go back, sometimes it came in handy").

4 Conclusions

The practical implications of this study constitute a step forward to a human-machine collaboration to provide teachers with know-how through interactive training with artificial intelligence. This game for teachers is an innovative approach to dealing with cyberbullying since most games are directed for students [11]. Firstly, players are offered the option to make responsible decision-making [24] through human-agent interactions [26], which complements previous studies on game design. Secondly, players are given the freedom to either morally engage or disengage from the situation [10] by interpreting the situation [24] through feedback given by social agents to offer a more realistic social interaction, which is integrated into the game and adds to previous research on game design [27]. Thirdly, players are given the opportunity to think about whether they can resolve the situation by examining their self-efficacy beliefs to intervene [3], which is constitutes a step forward in game design features [11]. Fourthly, players have the freedom to choose whether they intend to intervene and with appropriate strategies [24] by being offered options to interact with social agents [27]. Fifthly, players are able to choose to intervene or not by reflecting on the situation through a feedback loop provided by the game, a feature which enables them to remember their trajectory throughout the game, which is innovative when compared to previous games for students [11]. Moreover, the game enables not only assessment of specific moral and emotion variables, but it is also a training resource with various sessions, unlike most games for students [18, 19]. Although this first prototype of the game provided positive results in the user study, it is still in development based on continuous testing. For future works, it would be interesting to diversify the participants.

Acknowledgements. This study was funded by the Portuguese Foundation for Science and Technology (PTDC/PSI-GER/1918/2020) CICPSI–UIDB/04527/2020, UIDP/04527/2020.

References

1. Francisco, S., Veiga Simão, A.M., Ferreira, P.C., Martins, M.J.: Cyberbullying: the hidden side of college students. Comput. Hum. Behav. **43**, 167–182 (2015)
2. Veiga Simão, A.M., Ferreira, P.C., Freire, I., Caetano, A.P., Martins, M.J., Vieira, C.: Adolescent cybervictimization: who they turn to and their perceived school climate. J. Adolesc. **58**, 12–23 (2017)
3. Ferreira, P.C., Veiga Simão, A.M., Paiva, A., Ferreira, A.: Responsive bystander behaviour in cyberbullying: a path through self-efficacy. Behav. Inf. Technol. **39**, 511–524 (2020)
4. Ferreira, P.C., et al.: Exploring empathy in cyberbullying with serious games. Comput. Educ. **166**, 104155 (2021)
5. Ferreira, P.C., Veiga Simão, A.M., Paiva, A., Martinho, C., Prada, R., Rocha, J.: Serious game-based psychosocial intervention to foster prosociality in cyberbullying bystanders. Psychosoc. Interv. **31**, 83–96 (2022)
6. Green, V.A., Johnston, M., Mattioni, L., Prior, T., Harcourt, S., Lynch, T.: Who is responsible for addressing cyberbullying? Perspectives from teachers and senior managers. Int. J. Sch. Educ. Psychol. **5**, 100–114 (2016)
7. Pilote, B., Chiniara, G.: The many faces of simulation. In: Elsevier eBooks, pp. 17–32 (2019)
8. Gratch, J., Marsella, S.: Appraisal models. In: Calvo, R.A., D'Mello, S.K., Gratch, J., Kappas, A. (eds.) The Oxford Handbook of Affective Computing, pp. 54–67 (2015)
9. Scherer, K.R.: Appraisal considered as a process of multilevel sequential checking. In: Scherer, K.R., Schorr, A., Johnstone, T. (eds.) Appraisal Process in Emotion: Theory, Methods, Research, pp. 92–120 (2001)
10. Bandura, A.: Moral Disengagement: How People Do Harm and Live with Themselves. Macmillan, New York (2016)
11. Calvo-Morata, A., Alonso-Fernández, C., Freire, M., Martínez-Ortiz, I., Fernández-Manjón, B.: Serious games to prevent and detect bullying and cyberbullying: a systematic serious games and literature review. Comput. Educ. **157**, 103958 (2020)
12. Mikka-Muntuumo, J., Peters, A., Jazri, H.: Cyberbullet - Share your story (2018)
13. Neo, H.F., Teo, C.-C., Boon, J.L.H.: Mobile edutainment learning approach (2018)
14. Higashino, M., Imado, T., Inoue, M.: Design of a computerized educational system about risks of social networking services for children (2019)
15. De Troyer, O., Helalouch, A., Debruyne, C.: Towards computer-supported self-debriefing of a serious game against cyber bullying. In: Bottino, R., Jeuring, J., Veltkamp, R.C. (eds.) GALA 2016. LNCS, vol. 10056, pp. 374–384. Springer, Cham (2016). https://doi.org/10.1007/978-3-319-50182-6_34

16. Hswen, Y., Rubenzahl, L., Bickham, D.S.: Feasibility of an online and mobile videogame curriculum for teaching children safe and healthy cellphone and internet behaviors. Games Health J. **3**, 252–259 (2014)

17. Garaigordobil, M., Martínez-Valderrey, V.: Technological resources to prevent cyberbullying during adolescence: the CyberProgram 2.0 program and the cooperative CyberEduca 2.0 videogame. Front. Psychol. **9**, 745 (2018)

18. Calvo-Morata, A., Rotaru, D.C., Alonso-Fernandez, C., Freire-Moran, M., Martínez-Ortiz, I., Fernández-Manjón, B.: Validation of a cyberbullying serious game using game analytics. IEEE Trans. Learn. Technol. **13**, 186–197 (2020)

19. Paiva, A., et al.: Learning by feeling: Evoking empathy with synthetic characters. Appl. Artif. Intell. **19**, 235–266 (2005)

20. Lazarinis, F., Alexandri, K., Panagiotakopoulos, C., Verykios, V.: Sensitizing young children on internet addiction and online safety risks through storytelling in a mobile application. Educ. Inf. Technol. **25**, 163–174 (2019)

21. Antequera, J.G., Estudio Evaluativo de Prevención del Acoso Escolar con un Videojuego, Doctoral dissertation, Universidad de Extremadura (2017)

22. Luria, M.: Beyond ChatGPT: 'Social Agents' & the Policy Gap (2023). https://cdt.org/insights/beyond-chatgpt-social-agents-the-policy-gap/#:~:text=Computer%20scientists%20and%20other%20academics,human%2Dto%2Dhuman%20interaction

23. Hideki, H., Sugawara, K., Kinoshita, T., Uchiya, T.: Flexible distributed agent system and its application. In: 5th Joint Conference of Knowledge-based Software Engineering, pp. 72–77. Amsterdam, IOS Press (2002)

24. Latané, B., Darley, J.M.: The Unresponsive Bystander: Why Doesn't He Help? Prentice Hall, Hoboken (1970)

25. Gratz, K.L., Roemer, L.: Multidimensional assessment of emotion regulation and dysregulation: development, factor structure, and initial validation of the difficulties in emotion regulation scale. J. Psychopathol. Behav. Assess. **26**, 41–54 (2004)

26. Ohmoto, Y., Morimoto, T., Nishida, T.: Effects of the perspectives that influenced on the human mental stance in the multiple-to-multiple human-agent interaction. Procedia Comput. Sci. **112**, 1506–1515 (2017)

27. Yalcin, Ö.N., DiPaola, S.: A computational model of empathy for interactive agents. Biologically Inspired Cogn. Architectures **26**, 20–25 (2018)

Balancing Inequalities: A Board Game for Young People from Coastal Communities to Discuss Plausible Futures

Vanissa Wanick[1](✉) ⓘ, Cara Black[1](✉) ⓘ, Craig Hutton[1] ⓘ, Mary Barker[1] ⓘ, and Adam Watts[2]

[1] University of Southampton, University Road, Southampton SO17 1BJ, England
vwv1n12@ecs.soton.ac.uk, C.M.Black@soton.ac.uk
[2] Nucleolus Software, Preston Park House, Brighton, Brighton and Hove, Brighton BN1 6SB, England

Abstract. This paper describes and summarises the design process of making a board game for young people from coastal communities in England to engage and discuss perspectives about their futures. The board game was created around imagining plausible futures and aimed at providing scenarios for players to make decisions about their futures considering social, economic and health inequalities. The paper showcases an exploratory approach of identifying game design elements based on co-design sessions with stakeholders (young people between the ages of 14–17) and experts, while using real-world scenarios and game design balancing techniques. The contributions of the paper are twofold: 1) it describes the process of making the board game via stakeholder participation, game design systems and game balancing; and 2) it provides a research-through-design method in which the design of the game reflects the intrinsic system in which young people live and suggests ways to overcome barriers established by these systems. The paper concludes with suggestions for future research such as the use of the game in participatory design sessions, mentoring classes and as an initial framework for serious games that can emerge from the discussions (e.g., teaching life skills, entrepreneurship competencies, etc.).

Keywords: Board Game Design · Places and Inequalities · Coastal communities · Plausible Futures · Young People · Game Balancing · Gamification

1 Introduction

In England, coastal communities have one of the worst health outcomes, with low life expectancy and high rates of major health diseases, including a vast range of physical and mental health conditions. The CMO's 2021 annual report describes how the UK's coastal communities exemplify the inequalities in health associated with geography and socio-economic status [1]. Deprivation is much higher in coastal communities when compared to non-coastal communities, particularly with regards to health, employment, education, and skills and training [2]. Thus, young people from coastal communities tend to leave their town and some never return, which makes it even more difficult for local business to thrive and retain talent. Coastal communities include concentrations of both older people attracted by the idea of retiring by the seaside, and some of the poorest groups in the UK. Many of these communities were also created around single industries which have diminished, such as fishing, where employment opportunities are scarce or seasonal. Thinking about the future therefore becomes a complex and problematical task for young people. How might young people engage in creating new futures for their communities? How do they see their futures in these places? How might games facilitate this conversation? Although the motivation for this project was based in local UK communities, the issues presented in this paper are relevant to many deprived communities across the world.

This paper showcases the process of developing a board game, originated from a gamified version of previous research on plausible futures scenario development [3,4]. The research questions that we address in this paper are: *How might games facilitate and elicit conversations about plausible futures for young people in coastal communities? What is the design process of making this game?*

To address the research question posed in this paper and design project, we will i) look at evidence collected from playtests. And ii) highlight key theories and thought processes behind game design, inequalities, and games about the future. This is a research-through-design process [5], in which via the development of an artefact (game), we aim at identifying an emerging design process.

2   Related Work and Research Background

2.1   Young People and the Future

Deprivation has a profound effect on communities as a whole and young people are no exception. It has been documented through several studies that the effects of deprivation on young people create specific health challenges and adverse outcomes which are exacerbated in the adult population [6–8]. Specific problems noted in later years include reduced employment status, income and wealth, poor life satisfaction and mental & physical health [6]. In recent years there has been an increased interest in adolescent health and wellbeing in research and policy. Studies have shown that adolescents are developmentally primed to engage with interventions that focus on improved health and wellbeing [7], thereby reducing the prevalence of adverse outcomes later on in adult life [8]. In this way young people can be powerful agents of social change and given the opportunity, have the ability to promote their own health and wellbeing [9]. To elevate the health and wellbeing of whole communities, we need to focus on reducing inequalities experienced by young people within these communities and equip them with the skills they need to create healthy habits. There are many factors that play a role in the health and wellbeing of young people. Among these factors, recent research has pointed to where people live or, place, as a significant aspect in shaping the relationships, opportunities and identities of young people [10]. Places such as coastal communities have inherent challenges that create unique problems which young people need to overcome. Struggles such as material inequalities, access to education and cultural assets and poor transport links create an environment that is unstimulating and uninviting for young people [10]. Informed by previous research and our own experiences, young people living in coastal communities feel that they are isolated from opportunities such as a lack of access to further education and skills-building programmes, which are more readily available in cities [10]. This was the main reason the young people we spoke to wanted to leave their local area. The explanations we received from young people in our own experience, fit in with existing research which shows that a lack of opportunities leads to a mass exodus of young people from coastal communities who are in search of better education or labour experiences [10]. This exacerbates inequalities within coastal communities even further by creating an aged population with fewer opportunities and a decreased focus on young people [10].

2.2 Discussing Futures and Inequalities via Games for Serious Contexts

When looking at the intersection between games and future thinking, design disciplines (e.g., Design Fiction [11]) can be merged with games design aspects, such as procedural rhetoric [12]. This enables designers to understand the meaning of 'time' in game systems. In 2016, Coulton, Burnett and Gradinar drew an insightful line between these disciplines, proposing the use of games for speculative design practice [13]. This intersection has shown that the sense of time is not linear, but a coexisting process, in which the perception and the future is linked to the players experience of the past and the present. One of the findings from Coulton, Burnett and Gradinar [13]'s design of the game *Cold Sun* is that speculative games should provide plausible scenarios and should be co-designed with experts, in order to avoid downfalls and possible misconceptions. Yet, the field of speculative game design is still underdeveloped and requires further research. Current research in games and future thinking has been tackling anticipatory governance via game design elements, such as role-playing and collective imagination [14]. Thinking about the future has become a need, particularly due to uncertainties already experienced in the real-world. However, it is challenging to think about a future in which current systems carry a historical legacy that might be difficult to change. Games are rhetorical systems and since dealing with issues such as climate change requires system 'thinking', games can offer an innovative way for people to learn how to solve complex problems [14].

The core context and motivation of this paper is grounded on the underlying health, social and economic inequalities that are inherent within the lives of young people. As such, it is crucial to understand how conflict and inequalities are represented in games, in order to inform our design process. Since conflict is a game design element that relies on the rules of the game, shaping victory and loss conditions is also intrinsically important in this context [15]. Inequalities can also come in different forms, such as asymmetric play, very common in multiplayer games. When choosing asymmetry in games design, it is expected that players will be given different abilities and resources. The board game *Pandemic*, for instance is an asymmetric game that requires thoughtful teamwork, but players start with different roles. The interesting aspect of 'conflict' in the case of asymmetric games is that there is conflict between players as they are starting the game with different abilities/advantages that need to be 'fair' throughout the game [16]. Thus, this influences how game designers balance the game and is one of the approaches we brought in our design method later in this paper.

When dealing with geographical inequalities, games can be used to entice negotiation. Serious games can be used as a platform for decision making when it comes to consensus building and negotiation strategies. One example is the game *You Place It!*, developed by Monachesi [17], created to enable negotiation amongst players and spatial and financial obstacles players may encounter in the process. The use of different player roles is also a design strategy in serious games that tackle crisis management [18]. Role-playing games in particular have a large system of goals (e.g., the ones set by the game master or the ones set by your own character) and relies more on achieving these goals instead of having an established victory 'condition' [15].

All these aspects reflect a systematic approach based on procedural rhetoric, since it represents ways of thinking from both the designer and the player spectra.

3   Gamifying Plausible Futures

3.1   Developing Scenarios: Plausible Futures

The co-development of effective simulations (outputs) from scenarios (inputs) can be explored in several ways. These include *explorative* scenarios where the participants consider the consequences of specific interventions or phenomena or *normative* where a future state is envisaged and the pathways to achieving that state are considered [19]. In this work we have asked young people to explore normative scenarios of what their future might look like based upon pre-determined axis that address plausible choices, as opposed to issues, that are likely to face them [3, 4]. This approach allows stakeholders to consider future state axis that intersect to produce a matrix of fours future 'worlds'. Participants are then requested to identify, with a given time frame, where they might place themselves in the following context. Firstly, where they believe they are today, then where might they believe they would plot if current trends continued or Business as Usual (BaU) and finally where they would, plausibly, like to be at the future date. The information comes from the difference between these plots which can be linked to characteristics of the participants where permission has been gained.

In this work the axes are a continuum between 'Comfortable and Safe' and 'Independent and Adventures' on the horizontal axis and prioritising between 'Money and Work' and 'Health and Wellness' on the Vertical Axis (see Fig. 1). These were derived from early engagement with young people and were retained in order to keep a consistency of results across the various young people stakeholder groups. Critically participants are rarely anticipated to select any extreme end member across a given axis, rather to consider the relative balance between the extremes and select an appropriate point on each axis that then provides a single point within the matrix. The matrix consists of four 'worlds' that can be named by the stakeholders. This process of naming allows the different plausible future or scenario to be discussed and given a name that is reflective of the group's perspective. So, for example one group identifies the matrix quadrant that resulted from the combination of 'Money & Work' and 'Independent and Adventurous' as 'Entrepreneur World' reflecting the sort of risk taking and financially driven nature of this combination as perceived by the young people.

The result is that each young person is asked to provide 3 points on the matrix. These are, as mentioned above, Today, BaU and Plausibly ideal. Then a line is drawn between these in that order. This information provides a context for how they view the word today in the broadest sense, how they feel their lives are likely to turn out if thing carry on in the current trend (note, not exactly as today but in the current trend of change) and where they would like to be. The scale and direction of movement can be very revealing of the perspectives, hopes and fears of the young people and their futures.

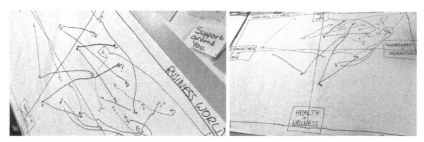

Fig. 1. Paths emerged from the Plausible Futures (PF) workshop with young people with already set axes.

3.2 Extracting and Identifying Game Design Elements

To identify the most relevant game design elements based on Plausible Futures (PF), we have looked at two general design questions: 1) what are the stakeholder's requirements and current conflicts/obstacles for young people? 2) which game design elements are more appropriate for the design (asymmetrical design, role-playing, negotiation)?

The project team was composed of experts in Sustainable Sciences (SS), Psychology and Behavioural Sciences (PBS) and game designers. Usually, games designed for specific contexts might have experts as content providers. In the case of our paper, the experts had a role to play in the design process, either as providers of realistic design constraints, or just players who had extensive knowledge and research not just about young people but also board games. In this case, 'ludo literacy' [20] was a factor that influenced the dynamics of the design of the game. Our first tactic to design was to utilise the axes from the PF exercise as a board, using them as underlying rules from our emerging game. This step was completed via an expert workshop, in which we identified key components and game requirements. Later these were redefined during a workshop with young people at a school in the Isle of Wight (see Fig. 2).

Additional components emerged after the PF exercise with students from the Isle of Wight. Initially, the PF exercise allowed participants to have a set of criteria, identify the axes, name the worlds, identify where they are now and think about scenarios in 10 years' time. Due to time constraints, researchers began giving predefined axes to participants, but it was their choice to identify where they were in each stage of their present and 'future' lives. This allowed them to visualise how they could move from today's world to a 'plausible' future. Based on this interaction and observations from the workshops, we have identified this as the main goal of the game (see Table 1). From this, we had to identify barriers and facilitators for this, 'main goal' to happen. The next step was looking for a winning/losing condition for the game, which then helped us design the first version of the game.

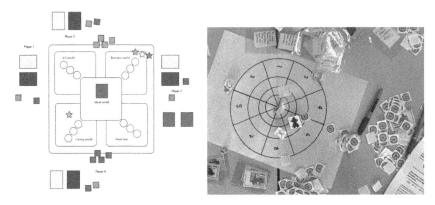

Fig. 2. First iteration of the board game (left) and current version (right)

Table 1. Initial design requirements

Component	Technical and design requirements based on stakeholder conversations
Number of players	12 (initially), later changed to 4–8
Expected age group	Year 10 UK (usually aged between 13.5 and 15)
Gameplay length	50 min to fit into a standard school lesson
Game platform	Board or table-top game
Goal	Move from 'today's' world to a plausible future. Thus, BaU was removed, and the main 'journey' was represented from today's position to a 'generic' plausible world at the center of the board

4   The Game

4.1   Collaboration, Competition, or Both?

Initial discussions around gameplay included thinking about if players would have a common goal if they were going to work together or compete to achieve this goal. As part of the discussion, we identified potential barriers and facilitators for players to achieve their goal (the plausible future). With that in mind, there was a need to discover barriers and facilitators (changed to 'obstacles' and 'opportunities' respectively), which was identified during a workshop with young people prior to the game design. During the workshop, such obstacles included GCSE marks, managing their mental health, not having money, the possibility that they could change their minds and death. As for opportunities, they mentioned having self-belief, having support around them, confidence, and good grades. While discussing these results with experts in the project, we have identified three aspects: the need to learn 'life' skills as different stages in the game, balancing wellness and wealth and having individual aptitudes such as 'superpowers'. From our market analysis and research background, we have identified that having different roles and starting in an asymmetric way could make the game more engaging for the target audience. This was considered in the design, together with resources available in each of the axes ('wealth' and 'wellness'). In this case, each player would not start with the same amount of resources and the number of tokens was determined by the position they chose on the board (which was relative to the axes of the PF workshop). Negotiation was one element mentioned by experts after the first iteration and was included in the subsequent version of the game (see Fig. 2).

4.2   Identifying the Nature of Conflict and Game Balancing

Our next approach was to identify and frame the game as a system, in the same way that it was presented to young people. Since the context of our game does not belong to a fantasy world, we have replicated a few elements from the 'real-world' as a system, following the systemic approach from [15] of objects, attributes, internal relationships and environment (see Table 2). Players had to first select who would be their partner and then they would receive a character card each. Each character card had a specific set of

Table 2. Game System and board design

Elements	Applied elements in the current version of the game
Objects	One board with different stages, cards (obstacles, opportunities, superpowers, character cards), $2\times$ dice, tokens (wellness and wealth), meeples
Attributes	Each stage in the board represents an obstacle leading towards the center (the main goal); character cards show different tokens available to each player in each round; superpower cards provide an advantage for the player in 2 rounds; obstacle cards provide information about how many tokens are required to overcome it; opportunity cards provide a chance for players to acquire more tokens; each dice provide 50/50 chance for players to receive tokens of wellness or wealth, meeples represent where players are (these were customizable)
Internal relationships	Players start with different amounts of tokens and need to think about how they might obtain more tokens to overcome obstacles; players do not know which obstacle they will encounter in each round. Every round the players need to get an obstacle or an opportunity card. If they cannot pass the obstacle, they do not move on the board
Environment	Players play in pairs and trade tokens with their partner; they should not have a 'shared' pile of resources. Players win when their team reaches the center

resources available to the player. Players can only win if they reach the centre together by overcoming obstacles via token 'exchange'.

The game had conflicts within its own system such as 'economic' conflict. In the case of our game, the economic conflict posits a real-world scenario as 'wealth' representing 'money' and 'wellness' as also a unit of value. It is possible that the game had a 'territorial' conflict since players could win the game once their team reaches the centre of the board. However, the game main loop was attached to its economic value due to overcoming obstacles and working together. Without defeating the obstacles, players were not allowed to progress; thus, trading was a game strategy.

We have conducted 3 playtests (see Table 3). During the third playtest with a school in the Isle of Wight, we held a discussion after gameplay that allowed young people to step back from the game for a reflection. Players mentioned that they were aware of the inequalities in the real-world and therefore could understand why they were starting at different stages.

Table 3. Playtesting session summary

Playtesting sessions	Findings and elements evaluated
Version # 1 - Participants: Postgraduate students and game designers (online)	**Collaboration vs competition**: we have decided to keep both elements after playtesting two different set of rules. With the game designers, we found that there is a need to balance risk and reward
Version #2 – Participants: Researchers and research assistants from the team; game designers	**Difficulty**: Players were using the trading mechanism as a 'one pot' that belongs to the whole team. We had to add to the rules that each player should have their own set of resources and could choose to trade or not. The game had too many rounds
Version #3 – Participants: Young people (age 14 years old) in the Isle of Wight	**Engagement and understanding;** Round rules were difficult to remember in each round; players stayed engaged in the game but had difficulties remembering all elements combined

5   Conclusion and Next Steps

Based on the research questions proposed in Sect. 1, this paper has introduced the design and process of making a board game that facilitates conversations around inequalities. This paper opens a discussion for interdisciplinary research in serious games and addresses current and new challenges in the field. The process has been documented by experts via a research through design approach. Compared to other projects with similar themes [13, 17, 18], this paper showcases a mechanics-driven iterative process. Yet, although the game itself promotes conversations, one of the limitations of the current game is that it requires a knowledgeable facilitator (which may be the tutor or researcher), a short debriefing stage and a reflective stage. Since this is a prototype, there is still a need to include a narrative element to the cards to give them meaning to the players. We are working together with the experts in the next stage of the design to incorporate youth specific narratives.

We have also identified potential learning outcomes that could emerge from gameplay such as life skills or acquiring entrepreneurial skills to achieve their life goals. Expansions of the game might be a way to address these ideas in the future, to support sessions like mentoring and career competences that can help young people to thrive in their environment. Therefore, the game itself can be a tool to generate other games, according to player's needs. We hope to explore this aspect in the future as this opens the scope for research-through-design and through game making. Since most of serious games for learning are designed with learning objectives at their core, our design approach identifies these later in the process. In addition, the process of gamifying plausible futures adds to the literature mechanisms in which interdisciplinary researchers can work together on the same level but bring their own expertise to the design of the game.

We also expect our game can be utilised as a participatory design method/game, to elicit conversations about difficult questions. With this in mind, we hope our game is a starting point for the design of games that could aid young people in coastal communities and further afield, not just to express their ideas about the future but to be able to be active agents of change in their own lives and their communities.

References

1. Whitty, C.: Chief Medical Officer's annual report 2021: Health in Coastal Communities (2021)
2. CLG Ministry of Housing: The English Indices of Deprivation 2019. Natl. Stat. (2019)
3. Hutton, C.W., et al.: Stakeholder expectations of future policy implementation compared to formal policy trajectories: scenarios for agricultural food systems in the Mekong delta. Sustainability **13**, 5534 (2021). https://doi.org/10.3390/su13105534
4. Marcinko, C.L.J., et al.: The development of a framework for the integrated assessment of SDG trade-offs in the Sundarban biosphere reserve. Water (Switzerland). **13**, 528 (2021). https://doi.org/10.3390/w13040528
5. Zimmerman, J., Forlizzi, J., Evenson, S.: Research through design as a method for interaction design research in HCI. In: Conference on Human Factors in Computing Systems - Proceedings (2007)
6. Villadsen, A., et al.: Clustering of adverse health and educational outcomes in adolescence following early childhood disadvantage: population-based retrospective UK cohort study. Lancet Public Heal. **8**, e286–e293 (2023). https://doi.org/10.1016/S2468-2667(23)00029-4
7. Yeager, D.S., Dahl, R.E., Dweck, C.S.: Why interventions to influence adolescent behavior often fail but could succeed. Perspect. Psychol. Sci. **13**, 101–122 (2018). https://doi.org/10.1177/1745691617722620
8. Ciocanel, O., Power, K., Eriksen, A., Gillings, K.: Effectiveness of positive youth development interventions: a meta-analysis of randomized controlled trials. J. Youth Adolesc. **46**, 483–504 (2017). https://doi.org/10.1007/s10964-016-0555-6
9. Bröer, C., et al.: Recruiting and engaging adolescents in creating overweight and obesity prevention policies: the CO-CREATE project. Obes. Rev. **24**, e13546 (2023). https://doi.org/10.1111/obr.13546

10. Wenham, A.: "Wish you were here"? Geographies of exclusion: young people, coastal towns and marginality. J. Youth Stud. **23**, 44–60 (2020). https://doi.org/10.1080/13676261.2019.1704408

11. Dunne, A., Raby, F.: Speculative Everything: Design. Fiction and Social Dreaming. MIT Press, Cambridge (2013)

12. Bogost, I.: The rhetoric of video games. The Ecology of Games: Connecting Youth, Games, and Learning, pp. 117–139 (2008). https://doi.org/10.1162/dmal.9780262693646.117

13. Coulton, P., Burnett, D., Gradinar, A.: Games as speculative design: allowing players to consider alternate presents and plausible features. DRS Bienn. Conf. Ser. **4** (2016). https://doi.org/10.21606/DRS.2016.15

14. Vervoort, J.M.: New frontiers in futures games: leveraging game sector developments. Futures. **105**, 174–186 (2019). https://doi.org/10.1016/j.futures.2018.10.005

15. Salen, K., Zimmerman, E.: Rules of Play: Game Design Fundamentals. Massachusetts Institute of Technology (2004)

16. Siitonen, M.: Conflict. In: Wolf, M.J.P., Perron, B. (eds.) The Routledge Companion to Video Game Studies. Routledge, Milton Park (2014)

17. Monachesi, P.: Overcoming space inequalities in city building games through negotiation. Commun. Comput. Inf. Sci. **852**, 487–493 (2018). https://doi.org/10.1007/978-3-319-92285-0_67/FIGURES/5

18. Di Loreto, I., Mora, S., Divitini, M.: Collaborative serious games for crisis management: an overview. In: Proceedings of the Workshop on Enabling Technologies: Infrastructure for Collaborative Enterprises, WETICE, pp. 352–357 (2012). https://doi.org/10.1109/WETICE.2012.25

19. Börjeson, L., Höjer, M., Dreborg, K.H., Ekvall, T., Finnveden, G.: Scenario types and techniques: towards a user's guide. Futures **38**, 723–739 (2006). https://doi.org/10.1016/j.futures.2005.12.002

20. Grace, L.D.: Social impact games, a probable future illuminated by looking back. ACM Games Res. Pract. **1**, 1–3 (2023). https://doi.org/10.1145/3583986

The C3C Game: Serious Games and Community-Centered Design for Improved Pandemic Decision Making

Francesca de Rosa[1(✉)], Mark Escott[2], Douglas Havron[3], Desmar Walkes[4], and Lauren Ancel Meyers[1,5,6]

[1] Center for Advanced Preparedness and Threat Response Simulation, Austin, TX 78701-1524, USA
francesca.derosa@captrs.org
[2] City of Austin, Office of the Chief Medical Officer, Austin, TX 78721, USA
[3] Capital Area of Texas Regional Advisory Council, Austin, TX 78613, USA
[4] Austin Public Health, Austin, TX 78702, USA
[5] The University of Texas at Austin, Austin, TX 78712, USA
[6] Santa Fe Institute, Santa Fe, NM 87501, USA

Abstract. Serious games have long been used in domains like defense, management, finance, and environmental protection to improve plans and procedures. In the aftermath of the COVID-19 pandemic, public health and emergency management organizations are beginning to use such games to enhance their preparedness and readiness activities. In this paper, we present a Knowledge Acquisition Analytical Game (K2AG) focused on understanding and providing training for command, control, coordination, and communication (C3C) functions during an infectious disease outbreak. Unlike traditional game-based exercises, which target strategic, operational and tactical decision making, the K2AG games focus on the cognitive level at which decision-making under uncertainty takes place. Specifically, the C3C Game collects data reflecting the cognitive processes by which players gain situational awareness, make decisions, and take actions. The C3C Game was created through a community-centered design process and leverages methods from human factor engineering, including hierarchical task analysis. This paper describes the game, presents results from a pilot exercise conducting with public health and emergency response decision makers from a large US metropolitan area, and discusses the potential for such games to improve pandemic preparedness and resilience.

Keywords: Serious Game · Community-Centered Design · Human-Centered Design · Exercise · Pandemic Preparedness · Decision Making · Command and Control

This material is based upon work supported by the National Science Foundation under Grant No. 2200169.

1   Introduction

Organizations are starting to include serious games as part of their preparedness and readiness exercises. For example, the United States Federal Emergency
Management Agency (FEMA) includes games as a subcategory of discussion-
based exercises. Different forms of games have been traditionally used to improve
decision-making at strategic, operational and tactical level in several fields, such
as the military domain (i.e., wargames), finance, management and environmental protection [9]. Recent work is exploring how serious games could expand
the focus to the cognitive [2,3,19] and meta-cognitive (e.g., [1]) aspects of
decision-making. Knowledge Acquisition Analytical Games (K2AGs) [17] focus
on decision-making underpinning processes, such as the ones attaining information handling strategies and reasoning under uncertainty. To this end, the
players' decision-making related processes are unfolded following human-factors
models. For example, the decision-making cycle is modelled following Endsley [5],
which identifies three main building blocks (i.e., situational awareness, decision
and action) and the related interfering factors (e.g., stress, workload and complexity). These are directly linked to game elements and game mechanics. Previous K2AGs have focused mainly on situational awareness and partially on the
decision component. In fact, they focused on how the players process uncertain
information to build a mental situational picture. Specifically, participants are
requested to perform threat assessments and reflect on how these assessments
influence the propensity towards some of the possible response options. In this
paper we introduce a new K2AG called Command, Control, Coordination and
Communication (C3C) Game that has been developed as part of a US federally
funded project on Predictive Intelligence for Pandemic Preparedness (PIPP). We
discuss the conceptual design approach, which is based on community-centered
design principles and human factor engineering techniques. Moreover, we present
the preliminary results of a small-scale in-person exercise employing the C3C
game. The remainder of the paper is organized as follows: Sect. 2 summarizes
relevant work on crisis management serious games; Sect. 3 introduces the C3C
Game; Sect. 4 provide an overview of the conceptual game design; Sect. 5 present
the first exercise employing the C3C Game and Sect. 6 reports conclusions and
future work.

2   Crisis and Decision Making Serious Games

Several crisis management and disaster relief serious games have been developed in the last few decades, as described in literature reviews [4,11]. They have
focused on different types of crises (e.g., fires, terrorist attacks, mass casualties
and natural disasters), they focus on different phases of the crisis management
cycle and they might target professionals or the general public. Often, they aim
at improving rescue operations proficiency [11], for example by enhancing spatial
thinking [22]. Some games focus on improving team coordination (e.g., [13]), procedures knowledge (e.g., [8]) and ethics in rescue operations (e.g., [26]). However,

the literature reviews highlight a gap with respect to games focusing on decision-making in relation to command and control approaches. Moreover, reviews show that they often demonstrate only a partial interdisciplinary knowledge integration (e.g., social science and natural science knowledge) [10]. Little attention appears to be devoted also to the integration of decision-making theories. In fact, many of these games look at improving decision-making under uncertainty and high-stress conditions, but the techniques employed tend to treat decision-making as a monolithic element, in which inputs are provided to the players and only their response actions are observed. K2AGs, instead, focus on the different underpinning processes that lead to a certain decision and action. This gaming technique has been used and validated in previous exercises focusing on maritime security and safety emergency management (e.g., Reliability Game [19], MARISA Game [16] and MUST Game [20]) and to collect insights regarding the use of innovative data sources for pathogen threat surveillance. With the C3C Game we aim at understanding and improving C3C related decisions when facing a pathogen threat with pandemic potential.

3   The C3C Game

Command, control, coordination and communication (C3C) are essential functions in every crisis and emergency management activity. Overall guidance on them can be found in a considerable amount of planning instruments at federal, state, regional and local level. However, the complexity of the problem space makes it difficult to: (i) navigate between the different plans, (ii) identify the best approaches and (iii) understand which command, control and coordination structure might be more effective and efficient in a specific situation. In fact, the nature of the threat, the contextual situation, the geographical and time extension of the event, the resources available and the regulations in place are only some of the factors that impact on such decisions. The recent COVID-19 pandemic highlighted several weakness with respect to these functions. The C3C Game objective is to support better decision making in relation to C3C. It extends the scope of previous K2AGs by increasing the factors tracked and analysed during gameplay both in relation to the players' situational awareness (i.e., vulnerability assessment and impact assessment) and decision (i.e., declaration of emergency, activation of emergency operation centers and setup of specific command, control and coordination structures). All these factors are monitored and tracked through a specific game board (Fig. 1), which includes data gathering areas that takes advantage of geometrical features of simple shapes (e.g., a triangle) to easily collect players' beliefs and attitudes [18]. These beliefs can be translated to subjective probabilities or other mathematical quantities. The primary objectives of the game are to: (i) provide a safe-to-fail environment to pressure test and critique current plans and concept of operations, (ii) provide an educational and training experience for the decision-makers involved (by allowing them understanding of the perspective of other organizations and by improving their coordination capability and semantic interoperability) and

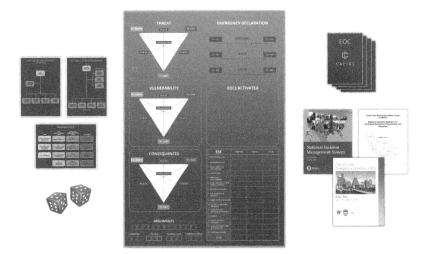

Fig. 1. Command, Control, Coordination and Communication (C3C) Game elements: game board (central), flashcards (left), game cards and supporting plans (right).

(iii) conduct research to improve efficiency, effectiveness and resilience of the command and control structures during emergencies.

In the C3C Game players are divided in two teams, an emergency response team (ERT) and a challenge team (CT). The game is organized in five rounds in which an evolving threat situation is presented. In each round players receive a new situational report. At first, each participant has time to perform a set of individual assessments. Specifically, they will perform: (i) a situational assessment (which includes a risk assessment), (ii) an assessment on the need for a disaster declaration (at local, state or national level), (iii) an assessment on which Emergency Operations Centers should be activated and the adequate activation level, (iv) the assessment of the proper command and control structure to be setup together with staffing considerations and (v) the assessment of which emergency function services should be ensured. After the individual assessments the ERT has to discuss and generate a consensus answer for all the above listed points and generate a set of arguments to support their decisions. The CT generates a set of counter-arguments. An adjudicator evaluates the validity of the arguments and counter-arguments and the relative strengths, that will determine the likelihood of successful implementation of the proposed solution. In fact, the stronger the counter-arguments, the lower this likelihood becomes.

The scenario adopted includes a pathogen threat with pandemic potential. Specifically, some cruise ship passengers are dying after showing the symptoms of a new virus. While the game unfolds, additional details are revealed to the participants, both about the pathogen itself and the current situation (e.g., number and location of new cases, time to produce a vaccine and social unrest). The scenario is a modification of a scenario used in a two year exercise series [6]. The modification mainly consists of moving the triggering event (e.g., the disembarkation of the sick travellers and consequent death) to a different geographical area (i.e., Texas), changing the season of the year and adding additional details regarding the unfolding threat in the different rounds. The decision to use a scenario developed for previous exercises was due to the desire to showcase that pre-existing validated scenarios could be easily integrated into the new game (potentially with no modification) and to assess additional or complementary results that could be obtained with the new game-based exercise approach. We tailored the game elements to a pathogen threat to improve pandemic decision-making. However, the game is based on an all-hazard response paradigm, as specified in the US National Incident Management System and National Response Framework [7]. Therefore, it allows to explore the problem space of C3C at different levels (e.g., local, regional, state, national or international) and to address threats of different nature (e.g., pathogens, climate induced threats, incidents and security issues).

4   Design Approach

Research has highlighted the need for multi-layered design approaches to the creation of serious games [9]. Specifically, it has been recognized that the game artifact design should be preceded by design activities accounting for the socio-technical systems issues it tries to inform or support [9]. In order to design targeted and effective K2AG, conceptual modelling becomes key [15]. The conceptual model of K2AGs is a solution and platform independent description of the problem space [17]. It should describes the objectives, inputs, outputs, content, assumptions and simplifications of the simulated game world [14], including aspects related to operational or cognitive processes. The conceptual model can act as the bridge between the game artifact, the problem space, the operational context in which the problem needs to be addressed and the scientific theories that might be integrated [15]. Conceptual modelling requires a deep understanding of the application domain. The importance of collaboration with domain experts has been often highlighted in relation to serious game design. However, knowledge elicitation activities can be time consuming, not targeted and if not well structured it might be difficult to acquire tacit knowledge [25]. Some uses of structured approaches are reported in the literature (e.g., task models derived from human-computer interaction for game scenario generation [23]), but a systematic use of validated approaches appears to be missing. In order to address such aspects, while expanding the scope of the K2AG framework and creating a new K2AG to support pandemic preparedness, we adopted a community-centered design (CCD) approach enhanced with the rigorous structure provided by human factors engineering methods such as hierarchical task analysis (HTA). HTA supports enhanced user-centered design, as it allows describing the activities and workflows under analysis as a hierarchy of goals, sub-goals, operations and plans [21]. CCD is a specific human-centered design approach, in which the stakeholder community (i.e., the emergency response decision-makers) and

Table 1. Players demographic details.

Category	Value
Age (range)	
18–24	0 (0%)
25–34	1 (5.9%)
35–44	3 (17.6%)
45–54	7 (41.2%)
55–64	6 (35.3%)
65+	0 (0%)
Gender	
Male	10 (58.8%)
Female	7 (41.2%)
Other	0 (0%)
Prefer not to specify	0 (0%)
Nationality	
US	17 (100%)
Years of relevant experience	
Mean	21.0
Standard deviation	10.5

designers co-create the solution to the problem. CCD appears to be a promising approach when dealing with complex socio-technical systems. In fact, it engages the community not only to co-design the solution, but also to become part of the design objectives [24]. Moreover, it enhances solution acceptance and the inclusion of the perspectives of minorities in the target community. In the C3C Game design CCD has been enhanced with HTA to capture the processes characterizing the specific operational community under investigation and the activities that should be performed as part of crisis management. The resulting structure allowed: (i) the identification of key areas that should be the focus of the serious game (e.g., critical areas, error prone activities or under-researched aspects), (ii) the identification of factors' correlation and (iii) an informed decision on which elements not to include in the design. Moreover, the resulting HTA structure supports the game validation activities and might serve as starting point for conceptual design of new games in the same application domain.

5   First Pandemic Preparedness Exercise

A pilot exercise has been run to assess the C3C Game design and to collect insights on the utility of the proposed extension to the K2AGs to improve decision making when facing a pathogen threat with pandemic potential. Participants to the one-day in-person event included operational and political decision-

Fig. 2. Game participants during the PIPP game-based exercise.

makers involved in emergency and crisis management at local (city and counties) and regional (e.g., Trauma Service Areas) level in the State of Texas (Fig. 2). Demographic details of the players ($n = 17$) are included in Table 1. One of the exercise participants was not included as active player, but as part of the exercise control team. In fact, he helped refining and validating the scenario and acted as adjudicator during gameplay.

In addition to the in-game data, we collected pre-game player profiling data and post-game data (i.e., Game Experience Questionnaire - GEQ [12], verbal feedback and written feedback). The post-game data shows that the game was overall positively perceived by the participants. GEQ results (Fig. 3) show how participants felt content during gameplay (58.8%), were interested in the game's story (94.1%), were fully occupied with the game (82.4%) and perceived it as a rich (82.4%) and enjoyable experience (94.1%). Moreover, most of the participants appreciated the aesthetic dimension of the game (76.5%). Most participants, did not express negative feelings such as boredom, irritation, annoyance or frustration. Many participants felt deeply concentrated (58.8%), however, further attention should be devoted to understand the reasons why some participants did not (e.g., length of the exercise) and the potential impacts on the exercise objectives. While several participants (52.9%) reported to feel challenged, others felt only moderately (35.3%) or not challenged (11.7%). This aspect should be further investigated to understand if it might be mainly correlated to the scenario or to the game mechanics. Finally, most players reported that they felt able to explore things in the game (76.5%). From the written general feedback (Fig. 4) it appears that players understood well the purpose of the game (70.6%) and considered the topics explored as operationally very relevant (94.1%). Most players considered the game very realistic (70.6%). Moreover, they stated how the game

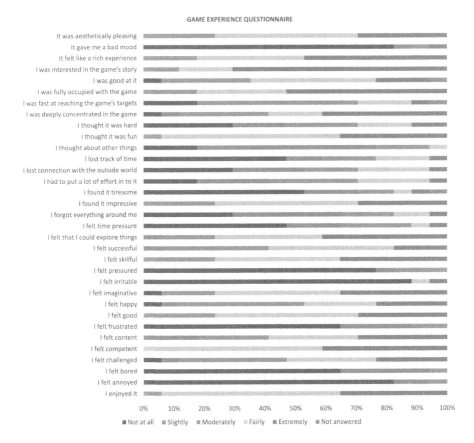

Fig. 3. Game Experience Questionnaire (GEQ) ratings results for the first pilot.

provided an educational and training component (76.5%), as well as an awareness increase (82.3%). Verbal feedback highlighted how the game allowed them to understand perspectives of other organizations, improving their coordination capability and semantic interoperability. For example, a political decision-maker explained how they are part of the emergency management process, but do not receive formal training. Therefore, the game allowed to familiarize with procedures, approaches, responsibilities and meaning of different terms. Finally, most of the participants reported that they considered the future inclusion of game-based exercises in their organizations very useful (88.2%). This is considered an important outcomes as 82.3% of the players participate regularly into different kinds of exercises, but only 23.5% had been previously exposed to game-based exercises.

Fig. 4. Participants' written feedback answers for the first pilot.

6 Conclusion

In this paper we introduced the C3C Game, which aims at improving decision making related to command, control, coordination and communication during a pandemic crisis. The results of the first pilot game-based exercise in which we deployed the game provided positive outcomes. Future work will include further validation activities to ensure the flexibility to scale across geographical areas (when the threat scenario calls for a large scale response) and the ability to quickly change threat type without the need for specific changes to the game structure. Moreover, future research should investigate the ability to quickly adapt the game to be employed in countries that might have different response paradigms and structures.

References

1. Azevedo, R., Gašević, D.: Analyzing multimodal multichannel data about self-regulated learning with advanced learning technologies: issues and challenges. Comput. Hum. Behav. **96**, 207–210 (2019)
2. Dass, S., Barnieu, J., Cummings, P., Cid, V.: A cognitive task analysis for an emergency management serious game. In: The Interservice/Industry Training, Simulation, and Education Conference: I/ITSEC. Interservice/Industry Training, Simulation, and Education Conference, No. 16244 (2016)
3. Daylamani-Zad, D., Spyridonis, F., Al-Khafaaji, K.: A framework and serious game for decision making in stressful situations; a fire evacuation scenario. In. J. Hum.-Comput. Stud. **162**(102790) (2022)
4. Di Loreto, I., Mora, S., Divitini, M.: Collaborative serious games for crisis management: an overview. In: 2012 IEEE 21st International Workshop on Enabling Technologies: Infrastructure for Collaborative Enterprises, pp. 352–357 (2012)
5. Endsley, M.R.: Toward a theory of situation awareness in dynamic systems. Hum. Factors **37**(1), 32–64 (1995)

6. Federal Emergency Management Agency: Pandemic Accord 2013 Continuity of Operations Pandemic Tabletop Exercise Summary of Findings Report (2013)

7. Federal Emergency Management Agency: National Incident Management System (2017)

8. Hullett, K., Mateas, M.: Scenario generation for emergency rescue training games. In: 4th International Conference on Foundations of Digital Games, pp. 99–106 (2009)

9. Klabbers, J.H.G.: The Magic Circle: Principles of Gaming & Simulation, 3rd and revised edn. Sense Publishers (2009)

10. Mochizuki, J.: Review of serious gaming applications in humanitarian operations and disaster risk management: state-of-the-art and future directions for research. In: IDRiM 2016 7th International Conference on Integrated Disaster Risk Management Disasters and Development: Towards a Risk Aware Society (2016)

11. Ning, H., Pi, Z., Wang, W., Farha, F., Yang, S.: A review on serious games for disaster relief. In: 2022 4th International Conference on Data Intelligence and Security (ICDIS), pp. 408–414 (2022)

12. Norman, K.L.: GEQ (game engagement/experience questionnaire): a review of two papers. Interact. Comput. **25**(4), 278–283 (2013)

13. Granlund, R., Johansson, B., Persson, M.: C3Fire: a microworld for collaboration training in the ROLF environment. In: 42nd Conference on Simulation and Modelling, Simulation in Theory and Practice (2001)

14. Robinson, S.: Conceptual modelling for simulation part I: definition and requirements. J. Oper. Res. Soc. **59**(3), 278–290 (2008)

15. de Rosa, F., Strode, C.: Improving decision support systems and disruptive technology adoption with analytical serious games. In: Correia, A., Simões-Marques, M. (eds.) Handbook of Research on Decision-Making Capabilities Improvement With Serious Games. IGI Global (2023)

16. de Rosa, F., De Gloria, A.: An analytical game for knowledge acquisition for maritime behavioral analysis systems. Appl. Sci. **10**(2), 591 (2020)

17. de Rosa, F., De Gloria, A.: Design methodology of analytical games for knowledge acquisition. Int. J. Serious Games **8**(4), 3–23 (2021)

18. de Rosa, F., De Gloria, A., Jousselme, A.L.: Analytical games for knowledge engineering of expert systems in support to situational awareness: the Reliability Game case study. Expert Syst. Appl. **138**, 112800–112811 (2019)

19. de Rosa, F., Jousselme, A.L., De Gloria, A.: A reliability game for source factors and situational awareness experimentation. Int. J. Serious Games **5**(2), 45–64 (2018)

20. de Rosa, F., Strode, C.: Games to support disruptive technology adoption: the MUST Game use case. Int. J. Serious Games **9**(2), 93–114 (2022)

21. Stanton, N.A., Salmon, P.M., Walker, G.H., Baber, C., Jenkins, D.P.: Human Factors Methods: A Practical Guide for Engineering And Design. Ashgate Publishing Company, Brookfield (2006)

22. Tomaszewski, B., et al.: Supporting disaster resilience spatial thinking with serious geogames: project Lily Pad. ISPRS Int. J. Geo-Inf. **9**(405) (2020)

23. Vidani, A.C., Chittaro, L.: Using a task modeling formalism in the design of serious games for emergency medical procedures. In: 2009 Conference in Games and Virtual Worlds for Serious Applications, pp. 95–102 (2009)

24. Villari, B.: Community-centered design: a design perspective on innovation in and for places. Int. J. Design Soc. **16**(1), 47–58 (2021)

25. Chergui, W., Zidat, S., Marir, F.: An approach to the acquisition of tacit knowledge based on an ontological model. J. King Saud Univ. - Comput. Inf. Sci. **32**(7), 818–828 (2020)
26. Wahyudin, D., Hasegawa, S.: Mobile serious game design for training ethical decision making skills of inexperienced disaster volunteers. J. Inf. Syst. Educ. **14**(1), 28–41 (2015)

JOYRIDE: Mobile Robot-Integrated Gamified Exercise Tour for Increasing Physical Activity Among Elderly People

Mirka Leino[1] , Taina Jyräkoski[1(✉)] , Tommi Lehtinen[1], Jussi-Pekka Aaltonen[1], Sandra Herrnegger[1], Johanna Virkki[2], and Sari Merilampi[1]

[1] RoboAI Research and Development Centre/Faculty of Technology, Satakunta University of Applied Sciences, 28130 Pori, Finland
taina.jyrakoski@samk.fi
[2] Tampere Institute for Advanced Study/Faculty of Information Technology and Communication Sciences, Tampere University, 33720 Tampere, Finland

Abstract. This study presents development of JOYRIDE, a light-hearted gamified exercise tour, which is built around a mobile robot for Finnish elderly people, who also played with the system in practice. The user testing results, despite the starting challenges during these first testing rounds, can be considered positive: elderly people are willing to welcome technology to improve their functioning and enhance social interaction. It was discovered that the design and size of the robot, the user interface, as well as the layout of the route, are crucial factors when mobile robots are implemented into these kinds of applications and environments.

Keywords: Activation · Elderly · Exercises · Gamification · Mobile Robots

1 Introduction

1.1 Role of Physical Activity for the Elderly

Globally, there is a growing number of elderly people with longer life expectancy, for whom aging causes a decline in muscle strength, mobility, and balance without active exercising [1, 2]. The deteriorating physical condition, loneliness, depression, and memory disorders make it difficult for many to function and survive independently. Due to all the evidence regarding the benefits of exercising for the elderly, it would be unethical not to implement exercise programs for the elderly as part of healthcare. It is estimated that being more active could not only extend the life expectancy by 7,5% but provide a better quality of life, better health, and more independence [3]. Thus, it is no longer the question of whether exercising should be implemented as part of the daily lives of the elderly, but the question of how it can be implemented [4].

P. Dondio et al. (Eds.): GALA 2023, LNCS 14475, pp. 150–159, 2024.
https://doi.org/10.1007/978-3-031-49065-1_15

1.2 Gameful Technology for Motivating Physical Activity

During past years, gamification and gameful technology has become a major trend. Promising studies have been done about the benefits of gameful interventions for the elderly, suggesting they may benefit from gameful technology and gamification, especially in the health domain [5]. So far, gameful technology has mostly focused on games played on screens [5–9], usually on tablet devices.

This study targeted at providing one gameful technology-enabled solution on the urgent question on how to get older people motivated to exercise on their own – as there will not be enough instructors in the future. We present development of JOYRIDE, a light-hearted exercise tour, which is built around a mobile robot. The system was designed for Finnish elderly people, who also tested the system in practise. The user experience results are reported in this study.

2 Practical Implementation

2.1 Mobile Robot System

The practical implementation was carried out with a mobile robot, on top of which a cabinet was built and additional technology was integrated to implement all the required functions (MiR250 mobile robot, Fig. 1). The cabinet was painted red to make it easy to recognize and remember. The cabinet had a large drawer opening on both sides and space for the needed electronics. RFID (Radiofrequency identification) reader antennas and speakers were installed on the sides of the cabinet. A touch screen was attached to the back wall of the cabinet, and 4 cameras were added on top of the cabinet, as shown in Fig. 1. The touch screen was adjustable, so that it could be turned to the optimal angle for the user: more vertical position for wheelchair users and more inclined for standing users.

Thus, the system worked as a combination of mobile robot and additional electronics including a computer (Intel NUC with external graphics processing unit), a switch, an RFID reader (Impinj Speedway R420), a transformer that worked in the power supply of additional electronics, as well as a touch screen (ASUS ZenScreen Touch) integrated into the cabinet, RFID antennas (BRRFID BRA-02SR), cameras (Opticam i5 IP cameras), speakers, and a safety circuit with emergency stop switches and acknowledgment buttons.

2.2 User Interface

The user interface of the system consisted of two parts – main view and navigation. The main view contained the visual content of the application, while the navigation consisted of controls for volume and robot speed, as well as navigational components, such as the buttons for starting, skipping or aborting the task at hand. When the application started (Fig. 2), the user was offered a choice of three options – THE STARLING, an exercise-based memory game, JOYRIDE, a light-hearted exercise tour, and FAMILIARIZATION, an introductory tour either for residents, staff members or visitors, each of whom had their own version of the tour.

Fig. 1. A player carrying out JOYRIDE guided by MiR250 mobile robot (Mirkku).

Fig. 2. User interface: When the application starts, the user is offered a choice of three options –
THE STARLING, JOYRIDE, and FAMILIARIZATION.

The application was a one-page-website, running on a local server, with client-side
rendering (CSR) of the page using HTML and JavaScript, and the server running on
node.js and express framework that handles the data fusion elements (communication
with the robots and the RFID reader) of the application. On the client side, the application
used jQuery library to handle sending AJAX requests to the server as needed. The server
used the node version of the Fetch API (application programming interface) to make
GET, POST, and PUT HTTP requests to the REST API of the robot. During testing, the

persons were identified based on their robot tester cards with individual passive RFID tags, which were read with the RFID reader.

2.3 Gameful Approach for Exercising

The gamified exercises and the dose were designed based on the current guidelines of physical activity for the elderly, focusing on functional balance and strength, including all muscle groups, especially targeting the prevention of falls [3, 10–12]. The JOYRIDE consisted of 12 gameful exercises that covered all main body movements targeting to above mentioned aspects. The implemented goals were motivation and encouragement for movement by providing a way of exercising that is new and fun, in order to reach the required amount of activity. Here, cultural and geographical aspects and landscape characteristics (see e.g., [13] for their importance) were included into the design and creation process of the exercise program by including well-known Finnish birds (see Fig. 2), as the themes of the exercises and guiding elderly people to mimic birds' movements.

Firstly, before the JOYRIDE began, there were overall instructions for the activities and how to proceed with the robot. The instructions for the exercises were given through videos, where two physiotherapists showed the movements with quiet background music. Oral instructions with natural human voice clarified the movements and gave reasoning for the exercises. Elderly people were also guided to adjust the exercising based on their individual state of health and functional ability. Exercises could be performed in a sitting or in a standing position, and it is possible to use the support of a rail or a chair. After instructions, a time bar visualized a 30 s period for performing each exercise along the physiotherapists. Each exercise could be done through, interrupted, or skipped if wanted/needed. Before each video, there was a button for "skip". During the whole instructions and videos of each exercise, buttons for "quit" and "next" were shown.

The mobile robot guided the person through the ride from the starting point back to starting point (See Fig. 3). In the first spot, the exercises were for upper body mobility and included arm movements like flying and bending the spine like a swan moves its neck while greeting. In the second location, the focus was on the strength of thigh muscles and balance. One task was to lift legs in a sitting position, imitating a white wagtail wagging its tail. Another task was to stand on toes and heels or alternatively done in sitting position. The exercises in the third spot focused on balance and lower extremity strength and mobility. The tasks were lifting the legs like a stork, standing up from sitting and steering back like checking eggs while brooding, and stretching back of lower extremities while diving down like a duck. The last exercises were done in the starting location, where they walked following the robot, trying to remember the steps of an old Finnish dance (Letkajenkka). Here, the person could sit down and relax for a while imagining themself in an eagle nest listening to birds singing. After relaxation, a feather dance was done to improve creativity and mobility while moving their upper extremities freely. Finally, it was time to shake their body like a wet bird shakes its feathers for loosening tensions, and the last task is to do a self-hug by opening and closing the arms, breathing deeply, and rotating upper spine. When the person had done the required number of exercises, they earned a trophy, which was a bronze, silver, or gold egg, each achieved after seven (or more) exercises.

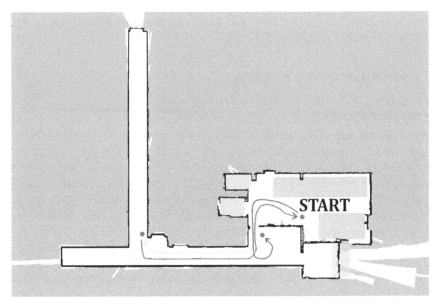

Fig. 3. Mobile robot route during JOYRIDE

3   User Study for JOYRIDE

A user study was carried out for JOYRIDE in a building containing apartments for the elderly. All the residents had the possibility to participate in the testing and eight voluntary seniors (referred to as players) tested it on the first-floor premises of the building. The participants were all independently living older adults from the apartments of the test place. JOYRIDE was selected from the mobile robot's touch screen (Fig. 1 and Fig. 2). The players identified themselves to the mobile robot using their robot tester cards, so the player could come back at any time and do a new tour. This made it possible to reward the players, as they collected prizes for the exercise performances.

The user study was organized so that the exercise tour with Mirkku mobile robot was tested by the residents for two weeks on weekdays from 9 a.m. to 3 p.m., one player at a time. There was always one observer (altogether two observers during the study) and one technical support person from the research team following the test tours. The observer gave the player instructions in case needed and observed the JOYRIDE tour from start to finish while writing down the notes to a pre-planned observation frame made according to Jesse Garrent's user experience framework [14]. The observations were covering different elements of user experience: (user needs, functional specifications and requirements, interaction design, information design and visual design) and the following themes were especially investigated: Reactions, emotions and feelings, Need for support and understanding the instructions & game play, Interaction with the robot & the game content; Interaction with the observer, Interaction with others; Spontaneous comments; General usability issues. The notes were taken with pen and paper. Right after each test, the notes were digitized. The digitized observation notes were clustered as presented in the next section, where they are discussed.

4 Observation Results and Discussion

4.1 Starting the Ride and Understanding the Instructions

Despite all the players testing the gamified exercise ride, the JOYRIDE, independently one by one, there were great similarities in the observations. Before starting the first tour, all players except one seemed exited, but after starting got more relaxed. Six of the players came for the trial eagerly. *"I will try everything there is!"* said one. Two of the players only wanted to try after a long talk with the observer. These two wanted to have confidence in their ability to play (physical abilities and skills with computers). Based on this discussion, the tour was adjusted to one person so that the person only performed exercises in one place, not following the robot in the corridor. The other person was willing to try after the discussion *"(I could now try, as nobody else is here to see")*. Two players were not able to start the tour on their own and three needed oral guidance from the observer (*"So what do I push now?"*). Mainly the observer just needed to cheer and support (*"Now you can press"*).

After starting the JOYRIDE, the robot moved a bit, to a spot it was programmed to start the exercise tour from, which made the players think the robot was leaving somewhere. In most cases, the player was standing too close to the robot in this location, which made the robot stop. That is why the observer needed to guide the player to the correct starting point. Additionally, the wheels were making a loud sound, as the robot speed was low, and some of the instructions were missed due to this. This needs to be developed further in the next version.

In all test days, the robot had lost its position first, as there was a lot of furniture in the room, and they were in different places than on the day the map was done for the robot. Thus, Mirkku-robot was lost at first for two test persons, but both persons remained calm and were waiting patiently as the staff members were doing adjustments. *"Machines are machines"*, said one player.

In general, all participants understood the instructions well. Some were repeating the instructions given. All except one player could see the screen well. For that one player, the observer operated the robot according to the person's wishes. In this case, the observer skipped the exercises, which were meant to be done in the corridor.

All participants were both reading the instructions from the screen as well as hearing the instructions. Some players had their fingers on the screen following the text. One person also read aloud the instructions on the screen.

4.2 Interaction with the Robot

All players experienced challenges with the touch screen at some part of the tour: Three accidentally "double clicked" and skipped an exercise or guidance, because the skip button was located exactly the same place as the next button (only text changed). This will be fixed by placing these buttons apart from each other. With one player, it was agreed the observer was operating the software, but two other players also asked the observer to click "next", when sitting a bit far from the robot. All seven players operating the software themselves used the software more independently as the tour proceeded. All of them learned how to operate it quickly, despite the challenges with the touchscreen identifying the click. The players were typically pushing the button quite long instead of a quick tap. *"Annoying"* said one person after multiple trials. As a solution, the players were given a touch screen pen, which improved the situation significantly. These results are in line with the results in [7], in which dry skin of the seniors as well as challenging clicking style were also noticed and the solution was a touch screen pen.

All players (except the one not operating the software and following the robot to the corridor) were following the robot intuitively and kept a reasonable distance without any guidance (distance between the person and the mobile robot was usually naturally kept at 1–1,5 m). Even for players with a walking aid or electric wheelchair, the speed of the robot was found to be good. The only part where the speed was too fast, was the exercise, in which a player should do dance movements while following the robot (*"Where does it run now?"*). As a result, the speed was lowered, which made the situation better, but on the other hand, the robot started to sound louder, which caused trouble for hearing the voice of the robot. Thus, in addition to focusing on the noise created by the robot at slow speed, another important step is to focus on optimizing the speed of the tour.

Multiple times there was a sudden obstacle on the way (chair, another person, rollator, wheelchair), which needed to be moved. In these cases, the robot just stopped, which ensured safety but of course disturbed the tour. In general, the robot seemed quite big and clumsy in such an environment, especially when there were other people and equipment present. Thus, a smaller mobile robot will be equipped with similar electronics for future steps of research.

During the relaxation exercise, two players gave comments about the previous exercises instead of concentrating on relaxation. All the others closed their eyes, but were checking every now and then, to see if the exercise was still on-going. There was a slight delay when the bird singing ended before the eyes were opened again, which caused a bit of confusion. At the end, when the robot returned to the starting place, one comment was *"Are the same exercises now repeated again?"*, which indicates the player does not know how many exercises there are left before the tour ends. *"So, this was it?"*, a player was asking when the tour ended. *"How long will I do this?"*, asked another player. It is clear that the progress of the player during the tour and the end of the tour must be made clearer, e.g., by using visualization and/or by adding sounds. Additionally, four players asked about their scores or wanted feedback about their performance from the observer (*"I don't know if I am doing these just as they are supposed to."*, *"Somehow you should make sure the player understood the movement correctly."*) This also indicates the need for further visualizing the rewards and adding feedback for the player.

4.3   Feelings, Expressions, and Comments

All the players were smiling, at least in some parts of the tour. Many were also laughing aloud and commenting on the tour. Players were paying attention to the content and generally they were in a good mood and interested. The robot was also given nicknames, such as "Klohmo" (the clumsy big one). It seems the discussion with the observer and the interview was making the experience more enjoyable, which affects the findings. There is also identified bias in answers, as all the volunteers were willing to test a robot, so the potential negative thinkers did not even participate.

The comments related to the exercises were positive or neutral: *"Well, this is quite nice, I have stiff legs.", "This is fun", "This is good for my shoulders, they are jammed.", "Great, these are not too hard", "Well, that raised the heartbeat"*. Some comments and ideas were given related to the exercise difficulty levels: *"You could do 2–3 different levels, so that everybody can find their own training program, and nobody feels like I cannot do this."*

Also, the mobile robot functionalities caused comments: *"It now goes back to its home nest to take some electricity.", "Does the sound come from there?"*. One was commenting on its appearance *"I am glad the robot is not black, that would be scary."*. Also new ideas about the content, which the robot should have, were proposed: *"In the screen there could also be the day program!"*. Some free comments were also given that the screen should be bigger, as the robot itself is also big. This is an important finding. A bigger screen would also allow the creation of group activities.

One player commented about possible real-world rewards: *"Do I get rewards, when I get points, it is very important for seniors, we will get something small like key rings"*. This is an element that is important to consider, especially if the robot would be in everyday use among the residents.

In many cases there were other people in the corridor during testing. In these situations, a lot of discussion was initiated (*"What's the top speed?", "Does it spread some diseases?", "It cannot open doors, right?"*). In most cases, the other people in the corridor did not disturb the player and most people in the corridor were curious and smiling. In some cases, the other people in the corridor also had an effect on the players. One player following the robot with dance movements quit dancing after seeing others and started dancing again when others were gone. One player showed "shhh" expression to some people talking, so they would be quiet, as the player was doing the exercises and listening the instructions. One player waived to say "hi" to a friend during the tour. Twice other people were asked to move a bit from a spot in which the robot was programmed to stop.

During the testing days, at least three players were telling the researchers how much discussion the robots have caused among the residents. Some were very proud to be part of the trial, explaining it is meaningful for them. One person was afraid of rents getting higher, if robots are purchased. Some were worried about losing human contact. Mainly people did not have anything against robots, but the consequences of having robots around. Thus, it is extremely important to further research and learn together to find out in which activities robots are acceptable and reasonable and highlight the potential of robots in allowing more resources for nurses to perform the care work and meaningful discussions, while robots would perform routine tasks. Thus, robots would be there to help and provide something extra, instead of replacing human contact.

Due to small number of participants, further research in needed to make far reaching conclusions. Our future work includes structured interviews on topics, like what it was like to cooperate with the robot and did players find the exercising enjoyable, effective and easy. This study was made in a project which focused on the seniors' needs and ideas how to use mobile robots in home-like environment. Further game design is needed as only early prototype concept was used. Well-known MDA framework [15] will be applied in the advanced game design process, as the "entertainment" element will play crucial role in the next development steps. Earlier successful senior serious games will be bench marked as well.

5   Conclusions

This study introduced one mobile robot-enabled solution on the urgent question on how to get older people motivated to exercise on their own. JOYRIDE, a light-hearted exercise tour, was designed for Finnish elderly people, who also tested the system in practise. The results show that while the number of professionals will decrease in the future, elderly people are willing to welcome technology to improve their functioning and enhance social interaction. Despite the starting challenges during these first testing rounds, the user testing results can be considered positive. The design and size of the robot and the user interface, as well as the layout planning of the route, are crucial factors when mobile robots are implemented into these kinds of applications and environments. Based on the achieved results, in addition to the physical exercise, the trial added social interaction among the residents as well as with the staff members. The robot-integrated game was arising much more discussion compared with the other games researched in earlier studies of the same research group. It is extremely important to learn and research the role of technology together with the users and search for maximal value for technical investments. It should be especially noted that the exercise program is not designed for replacing an individualized training program or therapy but offers a motivating alternative activation option that can be performed independently without the guidance of healthcare professionals.

References

1. Sigelman, C.K., Rider, E.A.: Life-Span Human Development. Cengage Learning, Canada (2014)
2. Rantakokko, M., Mänty, M., Rantanen, T.: Mobility decline in old age. Exerc. Sport Sci. Rev. **41**, 19–25 (2013)
3. OECD/WHO: Step Up! Tackling the Burden of Insufficient Physical Activity in Europe. OECD Publishing, Paris (2023)
4. Izquierdo, M., et al.: International exercise recommendations in older adults (ICFSR): expert consensus guidelines. J. Nutr. Health Aging **25**, 824–853 (2021)
5. Koivisto, J., Malik, A.: Gamification for older adults: a systematic literature review. Gerontologist **61**(7), e360–e372 (2021)
6. Merilampi, et al.: Implementing mobile games into care services—service models for Finnish and Chinese elderly care. Information **10**(2), 13 (2019)
7. Merilampi, S., et al.: The cognitive mobile games for older adults - A Chinese user experience study. In: Proceedings of 5th IEEE International Conference on Serious Games and Applications for Health (2017)
8. Pyae, A.: The potential of digital games in promoting older people's active ageing in developing countries: the case of Myanmar. Int. J. Educ. Ageing **4**, 19–34 (2017)
9. Wang, X., Niksirat, K.S., Silpasuwanchai, C., Wang, Z., Ren, X., Niu, Z.: How skill balancing impact the elderly player experience? In: Proceedings of the 13th IEEE International Conference on Signal Processing (2016)

10. Demet, G., et al.: Comparison of physical activity, exercise barriers, physical performance, and fall risks in frail and nonfrail older adults. Top. Geriatr. Rehabil. **39**(1), 58–65 (2023)

11. Sherrington, C., et al.: Exercise for preventing falls in older people living in the community: an abridged Cochrane systematic review. Br. J. Sports Med. **54**, 885–891 (2020)

12. Rodrigues, F., Domingos, C., Monteiro, D., Morouço, P.: A review on aging, sarcopenia, falls, and resistance training in community-dwelling older adults. Int. J. Environ. Res. Public Health **19**, 874 (2022)

13. Li, D., Xu, H., Kang, Y., Steemers, K.: Systematic review: landscape characteristics correlated with physical activity of the elderly people. Land **12**, 605 (2023)

14. Garret, J.J.: The Elements of User Experience, 2nd edn. New Riders, Berkeley (2011)

15. https://users.cs.northwestern.edu/~hunicke/MDA.pdf. Accessed 11 Sept 2023

The Gamification Elements Speech-Language Pathologists Use to Motivate Children for Speech Therapy Training

Charlotta Elo[1](✉) ⓘ, Tiina Ihalainen[2] ⓘ, Tanja Vihriälä[1] ⓘ, and Johanna Virkki[1,3] ⓘ

[1] Faculty of Information Technology and Communication Sciences, Tampere University, Tampere, Finland
`charlotta.elo@tuni.fi`
[2] Faculty of Social Sciences, Tampere University, Tampere, Finland
[3] Tampere Institute for Advanced Study, Tampere University, Tampere, Finland

Abstract. Motivation is an important factor in paediatric speech therapy. Rehabilitation is often long-term work that requires many repetitions and home training with parents. Therefore, one of the most important tasks of paediatric speech-language pathologists (SLPs) is to find different ways, over and over again, to motivate children for training. As different types of games themselves have already been identified as important motivational tools used by SLPs, the purpose of this study was to investigate what kind of gamification elements SLPs use in therapy, in addition to the games themselves, to motivate children for training. 26 Finnish SLPs responded to an online questionnaire consisting of four open-ended questions. Our results indicate that SLPs typically use several different motivational methods, which they aim to personalize as much as possible to individually support motivation. SLPs make a special effort to increase children's intrinsic motivation by employing motivational features commonly used in gamification, such as playfulness, the child's own interests, and goal setting.

Keywords: Motivation · Gamification · Speech Therapy · Survey

1 Introduction

Motivation is a complex psychological and behavioural component that aims to explain why individuals act as they do and what makes them make different decisions about, for example, the use of time and energy [1, 2]. Motivation can be divided into intrinsic and extrinsic motivation [1, 3]. Intrinsic motivation means that a person is motivated to do something because the thing itself gives the person pleasure or enjoyment [1, 3]. An intrinsically motivated person does something because they are interested in it, and because doing it brings them value. If a person is intrinsically motivated to do something, their actions are not influenced by external factors. As opposed to an externally motivated person who will do something because doing it will lead to the desired result [1, 4]. This result could be, for example, getting a reward or social acceptance [1]. Studies indicate that a person can also be both intrinsically and extrinsically motivated to do something [5, 6].

P. Dondio et al. (Eds.): GALA 2023, LNCS 14475, pp. 160–169, 2024.
https://doi.org/10.1007/978-3-031-49065-1_16

Motivation also plays an important role in rehabilitation processes [7, 8], including speech therapy. Speech therapy rehabilitates children and adults with challenges in areas such as communication, social interaction, language, and swallowing [9, 10]. It is often long-term work and requires many repetitions. Especially in the rehabilitation of children with speech motor challenges, such as childhood apraxia of speech, high repetition rates play an important role in successful rehabilitation [11]. Thus, one of the most important tasks of paediatric speech-language pathologists (SLPs) is to find ways, over and over again, to motivate the children and their parents to engage in speech therapy, which has proven challenging in previous studies [12, 13].

Gamification refers to the use of game elements for non-gaming purposes to make them more engaging and motivating [14]. Gamification has been found to positively influence targeted behavioural outcomes, cognition, and user experience in health and well-being related interventions. Previous research indicates that different types of games themselves are one of the most recognised motivational tools used by SLPs [12, 15–17]. It is therefore important to explore how the constantly evolving field of gamification can bring new opportunities for rehabilitation. In this study, we explore their ways of gamifying speech therapy, i.e., what kind of gamification elements SLPs use in therapy, in addition to the games themselves, to motivate children for training.

2   Methods

2.1   Study Design and Participants

The data was collected through an online questionnaire. The questionnaire targeted SLPs of any grade or place of employment in Finland. A voluntary participation request and a link to the online questionnaire, seen as an appendix, was sent to several social media communities for SLPs in December 2021 and a total of 26 responses were received. To maximize anonymity, occupation was the only demographic information collected.

The research team developed the first version of the questionnaire, which was edited based on feedback from an external SLP. After editing, the questionnaire was tested with another external SLP. This version was accepted as final. The online survey contained 4 items: (1) How have you made speech motor exercises motivating for a child? Give at least three concrete ideas, (2) Give at least three concrete examples of tasks that motivate to practice speech motor skills at home, (3) In your experience, what practical factors prevent the implementation of home practice? and (4) Free comments on the topic. With the exception of one participant, all respondents answered all three first questions. Twelve participants also expressed their free comments.

2.2   Analysis

The data were analyzed, and themes created inductively [18]. Firstly, the researchers familiarized themselves with the data, and focused in particular on the responses including ideas related to motivation. Next, the first researcher collected every motivational tool or idea mentioned by SLPs and thematized the responses. Ideas directly related to actual games were left out because they have already been covered in another published article [12]. However, some ideas were accepted for this article that were also selected for inclusion in the previous article on games published from the same data. In these ideas, elements of gamification emerged in addition to the specific game ideas. Following that, the rest of the research team checked that all of the motivation-related responses had been identified and commented on the thematization. Based on the feedback and discussion, the thematization was refined. Finally, all of the researchers reviewed the thematization together and discussed the differences until they reached a conclusion about the themes, resulting in a codebook containing six major themes, one of which has two subthemes.

3   Results and Discussion

As seen in Table 1, the motivational tools identified by participants are divided into the following six main themes: (1) the expertise of a speech-language pathologist (2) extrinsic motivators, (3) playfulness, (4) concretizing progress, (5) child's interests, and (6) environment. Theme 1 is further divided into two subthemes: (1A) ideas related to practices, and (1B) interaction and therapeutic relationship. It is worth noting that there is also a slight overlap between themes 2 and 4, as four responses contained ideas related to both of these two different themes, and therefore were placed in both of the themes. Similarly, one response was placed under both theme 1 and 3.

The Expertise of a Speech-Language Pathologist.   The largest theme was motivational ideas related to SPLs. The first subtheme included ideas concerning practices, both the ones done with the SLP and the ones SLP instructed to be done at home with the parents. The ideas mentioned in this subtheme were related to the number, duration, content, and difficulty of the exercises, which SLPs said they aim to personalize as much as possible, so that the child and their parents are motivated by the home exercises provided. For example, electronic, tablet-based exercises were mentioned as motivational in many of the responses, which has been noted also in previous studies. For example, Zajc et al. [19] mentioned that mobile technologies can increase children´s motivation to speech therapy and also the duration of exercises.

Interaction and therapeutic relationship between the SLP, the child and their parents were mentioned as another way to maintain and increase motivation for speech therapy training. Our results suggest that trust and positive interaction between the therapist and the child play an essential role in motivation, as do giving positive feedback, verbalizing progress, and having fun while doing the exercises.

Extrinsic Motivators.   The second largest theme was motivational tools and ideas related to extrinsic motivators. SLPs generally mentioned the use of rewards as a motivating factor, but also gave more details about the rewards they use, such as stickers, treats, checklists, and tablet games. Although gamification is mostly based on increasing intrinsic motivation [20], it can often include elements that increase extrinsic motivation [21], such as (virtual) prizes, scoring, and ranking of players. The use of external motivation seems to be one of the motivational tools used by SLPs, but the results suggest that they do not use it as the only motivational tool, but rather as an aid when the child's intrinsic motivation is weaker. SLPs also work with very young children, who may not yet understand the purpose of the exercises and therefore do not yet have a strong intrinsic motivation to exercise, so it is understandable why they also rely on external motivational tools in their work.

Playfulness. The third largest theme consisted of motivational tools and ideas related to playfulness and functionality in speech therapy training both with SLP and with parents at home. For example, lego building, tag, feeding the training pictures to a figure, throwing paper airplanes, ninja kicks, and jumping on a trampoline were mentioned. This theme was unsurprising given that several prior studies have shown that there is a relationship between playfulness and motivation [22–24], as playfulness is a component of intrinsic motivation that encourages participation in games [22, 25]. By adding game elements and

Table 1. Themes and subthemes related to motivational tools identified from the data, with examples mentioned by SLPs and the number of ideas related to each theme.

Theme	Subtheme	Examples of the motivational tools mentioned (with respondent ID in parentheses)	The number of ideas related to this theme
The expertise of a speech-language pathologist			34
	Ideas related to practices	"It is the therapist's responsibility to commission exercises at the appropriate level and to highlight and reinforce progress." (SLP 15) "Varied and diverse types of exercises" (SLP 17) "Electronic exercises: speech motor exercises can easily be added to a theme that motivates the child, e.g., a Minecraft game" (SLP 11)	21
	Interaction and therapeutic relationship	"The therapeutic relationship is the main motivating factor!" (SLP 15) "Use of funny words and pictures" (SLP 12) "Asking parents about the child's progress" (SLP 18) "I also take into account the child's initiatives" (SLP 10)	13

(*continued*)

Table 1. (*continued*)

Theme	Subtheme	Examples of the motivational tools mentioned (with respondent ID in parentheses)	The number of ideas related to this theme
Extrinsic motivators		"Fast and clear enough rewards" (SLP 2) "I have advised families about external motivators, e.g., sticker board, beads in a jar, practice first then playtime…" (SLP 5) "A cereal exercise to train oral motor skills: children love cereal, so a training session is a treat at the same time" (SLP 10)	27
Playfulness		"Practising while playing" (SLP 9) "By making the training functional and relevant to the child's world" (SLP 23)	26
Concretizing progress		"A training calendar at home, in which you always note when you have practised" (SLP 24) "Using different timers on your tablet" (SLP 2)	23
Child's interests		"The exercises include pictures of your child's favourite characters (Minegraft, Starwars, Minions, Angry birds…)" (SLP 6) "Exercises based on the child's interests" (SLP 24)	15

(*continued*)

Table 1. (*continued*)

Theme	Subtheme	Examples of the motivational tools mentioned (with respondent ID in parentheses)	The number of ideas related to this theme
Environment		"Usually, the best motivator is an enthusiastic parent who encourages the child to practise. Home practice rarely works if the parents are not interested." (SLP 3) "By mapping the family's daily routines and brainstorming together to link the exercise to a familiar habit/moment." (SLP 23)	10

playfulness in therapy exercises, SLPs may be able to strengthen the child's feelings of competence, autonomy, and relatedness, and thus increase the child's intrinsic motivation [25, 26, 28].

Our results suggest that playfulness and functionality can increase a child's motivation and improve performance even if sitting still at a desk is challenging for the child, for example because of attention and concentration challenges. As one SLP (SLP 25) pointed out, they use functional exercises if the child is very mobile and desk work is therefore challenging.

Concretizing Progress. The fourth theme consisted of ideas related to concretizing progress. The ideas cited included, e.g., calculators, training grids and tables, and training calendars. Responses echoed the idea that these different monitoring methods allow the child to see how much training they are doing and how they progress. As one SLP (SLP 14) explained, "child's understanding of the importance of practice and progress, e.g., on a pictorial scale, is motivating". Gamification and serious games can be valuable tools to illustrate the process and its goals and importance [31]. The visualization of progress, e.g., through a training calendar, is often based on the fact that at the end of the calendar there is a goal created together with the child and the family, e.g., a certain number of repetitions achieved. As previous studies have shown, there is a strong link between goal setting and motivation [29–31]. It has been studied that when children and parents are involved in goal setting, they have a high level of engagement in achieving it [27]. In addition to the autonomy of the child and their parents in relation to goal setting, other means of goal setting that increase motivation to achieve goals are appropriate attention and commitment, and task persistence [27, 32].

Child's Interests. The fifth largest theme involved responses on how the child's interests are taken into account in speech therapy practices. SLPs listed different characters and themes that they have used to motivate children to do exercises. Examples of these include Paw Patrol, Frozen, Minions, and dinosaurs. These characters and themes have been used by SLPs, e.g., by adding pictures of favorite characters to exercises or by choosing words to practice according to a motivating theme. This finding mirrors prior findings of studies by Lanou et al. [33], in which using child's own interests made the strategy used for self-monitoring and asking for help meaningful and motivating, and by Vassileva [34] wherein it was described that since motivation is personal, also personalization can be considered essential.

Environment. The sixth largest, final major theme was motivational ideas related to the environment. The responses addressed the role of parents in motivating children to participate in home practice; SLPs highlighted the importance of a motivated parent and the importance of the SLPs in motivating parents to participate. As one SLP (SLP 3) pointed out in their response "home practice rarely works if parents are not interested". The lack of parental motivation and engagement has also been highlighted in several previous studies [12, 35]. The lack of motivation and commitment may be influenced by factors, such as a lack of understanding of the importance of home practice or a lack of belief in its benefits [12, 35–37]. For these reasons, it is particularly important for the SLP to work closely with the child's family members and share information and guidance for them. Our results also suggest that one way to engage and motivate children and their parents in speech therapy home practice is to send practice videos to parents and ask parents to send videos of home practice to the SLP. This can also serve as a way to increase parents' understanding of speech therapy training and provide a low-threshold avenue for asking for help.

Our study contained some limitations that could be addressed in future studies. Firstly, in this study, we were interested in the motivational ideas used by speech-language pathologists in general, regardless of the age of the children they work with. Thus, based on this study, we cannot say which game elements motivate children of a certain age. Further, as it is understandably possible that therapists are not aware of all the possibilities of game elements and gamification, potential future work should include the identification of gamified possibilities from a game design perspective. For example, a focus group or a design group activity to put game designers and therapists together would be an interesting study.

4   Conclusions

It is known that motivation has a significant impact on speech rehabilitation processes, which are often long and challenging. Adding gamific elements to therapy practices, i.e., gamification of therapy, has the potential to address the discussed major challenge of pediatric speech therapy, as they can make training activities more internally motivating and engaging, for example by generating automated, accurate positive feedback that contributes to the feeling of competence and, consequently, improves intrinsic motivation [38]. This study provided data on what kind of gamification elements SLPs use in therapy, in addition to the games themselves, to motivate children for training.

The findings of the present study indicate that SLPs use versatile game elements to motivate children and their parents to do speech therapy exercises. The mentioned methods and tools employed motivational features like playfulness, continuous guided progress paths, feedback, and individual goal setting, as well as tangible rewards, for example, stickers, which are fundamental parts of gamification [14,31].

Our future goal is to build on the game elements successfully used by SLPs to create a framework to gamify speech therapy training, so that not only the children but also their parents would be motivated to do the training at home, as it is known that a motivated parent plays an essential role in the child's rehabilitation process. The results of this study provide an excellent starting point for this further work.

Acknowledgments. We thank Eveliina Autio and Mauri Inkinen for their help in the data collection process of this study.

Appendix

Participation Request

Questionnaire on motivation for speech motor training for speech-language pathologists.

A key problem, especially in the rehabilitation of children's speech motor skills, is the successful implementation of home practice: it is challenging to get children to do exercises on a long-term basis. In this short questionnaire, we collect experiences on motivation to practice and barriers to home practice.

Participation in this research is completely voluntary. The information you provide will be used in theses and scientific articles published on the research data. The data collected will only be accessible to the people working at the university who carry out this research. The study data will be destroyed at the latest one year after the publication of the study. The privacy notice of the study is available here: XXXX.

For further information on the study, please contact Johanna Virkki, Docent (tel. 0408490618, johanna.virkki@tuni.fi).

1. How have you made speech motor exercises motivating for a child? Give at least three concrete ideas.
2. Give at least three concrete examples of tasks that motivate to practice speech motor skills at home.
3. In your experience, what practical factors prevent the implementation of home practice?
4. Free comments on the topic.

Thank you for your answers! The privacy notice of the survey is available here: XXXX.

I have read the privacy notice.

[] yes.

By selecting "I agree!" and by submitting the form, you consent to the use of the information you provide for research purposes as described in this form.

[] I agree!

References

1. Filgona, J., Sakiyo, J., Gwany, D.M., Okoronka, A.U.: Motivation in learning. Asian J. Educ. Soc. Stud. **10**, 16–37 (2020)
2. Graham, S., Weiner, B.: Motivation: past, present, and future. In: Harris, K.R., Graham, S., Urdan, T., McCormick, .CB., Sinatra, GM., Sweller, J. (eds.). APA Educational Psychology Handbook, vol. 1, Theories, Constructs, and Critical Issues. American Psychological Association (2012)
3. Usher, A., Kober, N.: What is motivation and why does it matter? Center on Education Policy (2012)
4. Pintrich, P.R.: A motivational science perspective on the role of student motivation in learning and teaching contexts. J. Educ. Psychol. **95**(4), 667–686 (2003)
5. Rigby, C.S., Deci, E.L., Patrick, B.C., Ryan, R.M.: Beyond the intrinsic-extrinsic dichotomy: self-determination in motivation and learning. Motiv. Emot. **16**(3), 165–185 (1992)
6. Murray, A.: Montessori elementary philosophy reflects current motivation theories. Montessori Life **23**(1), 22–33 (2011)
7. Barry, J.: Patient motivation for rehabilitation. Cleft Palate J. **2**(1), 62–68 (1965)
8. Griffiths, L., Hughes, D.: Typification in a neuro-rehabilitation centre: Scheff revisited? Sociol. Rev. (Keele) **41**(3), 415–445 (1993)
9. Houtrow, A., et al.: Prescribing physical, occupational, and speech therapy services for children with disabilities. Pediatrics (Evanston) **143**(4), e20190285 (2019)
10. Brownlee, A., Bruening, L.M.: Methods of communication at end of life for the person with amyotrophic lateral sclerosis. Top. Lang. Disord. **32**(2), 168–185 (2012)
11. Kaipa, R., Peterson, A.M.: A systematic review of treatment intensity in speech disorders. Int. J. Speech Lang. Pathol. **18**(6), 507–520 (2016)
12. Elo, C., Inkinen, M., Autio, E., Vihriälä, T., Virkki, J.: The role of games in overcoming the barriers to paediatric speech therapy training. In: Kiili, K., Antti, K., de Rosa, F., Dindar, M., Kickmeier-Rust, M., Bellotti, F. (eds) Games and Learning Alliance, GALA 2022, Lecture Notes in Computer Science, vol 13647, pp. 181–192. Springer, Cham (2022). https://doi.org/10.1007/978-3-031-22124-8_18
13. Sugden, E., Munro, N., Trivette, C.M., Baker, E., Williams, A.L.: Parents' experiences of completing home practice for speech sound disorders. J. Early Interv. **41**(2), 159–181 (2019)
14. Johnson, D., Deterding, S., Kuhn, K.-A., Staneva, A., Stoyanov, S., Hides, L.: Gamification for health and wellbeing: a systematic review of the literature. Internet Interv. Appl. Inf. Technol. Mental Behav. Health **6**, 89–106 (2016)
15. Ahmed, B., Monroe, P., Hair, A., Tan, C.T., Gutierrez-Osuna, R., Ballard, K.J.: Speech-driven mobile games for speech therapy: user experiences and feasibility. Int. J. Speech Lang. Pathol. **20**(6), 644–658 (2018)
16. Saeedi, S., Bouraghi, H., Seifpanahi, M.-S., Ghazisaeedi, M.: Application of digital games for speech therapy in children: a systematic review of features and challenges. J. Healthcare Eng. **2022**, 4814945–4815020 (2022)
17. Javkin, H., et al.: A motivation-sustaining articularity/acoustic speech training system for profoundly deaf children. In: 1993 IEEE International Conference on Acoustics, Speech, and Signal Processing, vol. 1, pp. 145–148 (1993)
18. Guest, G., MacQueen, K.M., Namey, E.E.: Applied Thematic Analysis. SAGE, Thousand Oaks (2012)
19. Zajc, M., Istenič Starčič, A., Lebeničnik, M., Gačnik, M.: Tablet game-supported speech therapy embedded in children's popular practices. Behav. Inf. Technol. **37**(7), 693–702 (2018)
20. Xiao, R., Wu, Z., Hamari, J.: Internet-of-gamification: a review of literature on IoT-enabled gamification for user engagement. Int. J. Hum. Comput. Interact. **38**(12), 1113–1137 (2022)

21. Csikszentmihalyi, M.: Flow: The Psychology of Optimal Experience. Harper and Row, New York (1990)
22. Ríos-Rincón, A.M., Adams, K., Magill-Evans, J., Cook, A.: Playfulness in children with limited motor abilities when using a robot. Phys. Occup. Ther. Pediatr. **36**(3), 232–246 (2016)
23. Keleş, S., Yurt, Ö.: An investigation of playfulness of pre-school children in Turkey. Early Child Dev. Care **187**(8), 1372–1387 (2017)
24. Loukatari, P., Matsouka, O., Papadimitriou, K., Nani, S., Grammatikopoulos, V.: The effect of a structured playfulness program on social skills in kindergarten children. Int. J. Instr. **12**(3), 237–252 (2019)
25. Rigby, S., Ryan, R.M.: Glued to Games: How Video Games Draw us in and Hold us Spellbound. Praeger, Santa Barbara, CA (2011)
26. Deci, E.L., Ryan, R.M.: The 'what' and 'why' of goal pursuits: Human needs and the self-determination of behavior. Psychol. Inq. **11**(4), 227–268 (2000)
27. Ryan, R.M., Deci, E.L.: Intrinsic and extrinsic motivations: classic definitions and new directions. Contemp. Educ. Psychol. **25**(1), 54–67 (2000)
28. Ryan, R.M., Rigby, C.S., Przybylski, A.: The motivational pull of video games: a self-determination theory approach. Motiv. Emot. **30**(4), 344–360 (2006)
29. Bryan, J.F., Locke, E.A.: Goal setting as a means of increasing motivation. J. Appl. Psychol. **51**(3), 274–277 (1967)
30. Poulsen, A.A., Ziviani, J., Cuskelly, M., Ryan, R.: Goal Setting and Motivation in Therapy: Engaging Children and Parents. Jessica Kingsley Publishers, London (2015)
31. Krath, J., Schürmann, L., von Korflesch, H.F.O.: Revealing the theoretical basis of gamification: a systematic review and analysis of theory in research on gamification, serious games and game-based learning. Comput. Hum. Behav. **125**, 106963 (2021)
32. Locke, E., Latham, G.: New Developments in Goal Setting and Task Performance. Routledge, Taylor and Francis, New York, NY (2013)
33. Lanou, A., Hough, L., Powell, E.: Case studies on using strengths and interests to address the needs of students with autism spectrum disorders. Interv. Sch. Clin. **47**(3), 175–182 (2012)
34. Vassileva, J.: Motivating participation in social computing applications: a user modeling perspective. User Model. User-Adap. Inter. **22**(1–2), 177–201 (2012)
35. Lim, J., McCabe, P., Purcell, A.: Challenges and solutions in speech-language pathology service delivery across Australia and Canada. Eur. J. Person Centered Healthc. **5**(1), 120–128 (2017)
36. Sugden, E., Baker, E., Munro, N., Williams, A.L., Trivette, C.M.: An Australian survey of parent involvement in intervention for childhood speech sound disorders. Int. J. Speech Lang. Pathol. **20**(7), 766–778 (2018)
37. Watts Pappas, N., McLeod, S., McAllister, L., McKinnon, D.H.: Parental involvement in speech intervention: a national survey. Clin. Linguist. Phon. **22**(4–5), 335–344 (2008)
38. Deci, E.L., Ryan, R.M.: Motivation, personality, and development within embedded social contexts: an overview of self-determination theory. In: The Oxford Handbook of Human Motivation. Oxford University Press (2012)

Application of a Serious Game for Emotion Elicitation Under Socio-Economic and Trust Based Decision-Making Scenarios for Autistic Adolescents

Fahad Ahmed[1,2](✉) ⓘ, Riccardo Berta[2]ⓘ, Francesco Bellotti[2]ⓘ,
Federica Floris[3]ⓘ, Luca Lazzaroni[2]ⓘ, Giacinto Barresi[4]ⓘ,
and Jesus Requena Carrion[1]ⓘ

[1] Queen Mary University of London, Mile End Road, Bethnal Green,
London E1 4NS, UK
{fahad.ahmed,j.requena}@qmul.ac.uk
[2] University of Genoa, Via All'Opera Pia, 15, 16145 Genoa, Italy
{fahad.ahmed,luca.lazzaroni}@edu.unige.it,
{riccardo.berta,francesco.bellotti}@unige.it
[3] Piccolo Cottolengo Genovese di Don Orione, Via Benvenuto Cellini 22,
16143 Genova, Italy
federicafloris@pcdo.it
[4] Rehab Technologies Lab, Istituto Italiano di Tecnologia, Via Morego, 30,
16163 Genoa, Italy
giacinto.barresi@iit.it

Abstract. The relationship between decision-making and emotions has been extensively studied in both theoretical and empirical research. Game Theory-based paradigms utilizing socio-economic and trust-based contexts have been established to elicit specific emotional responses in autistic individuals. Serious games, incorporating cohesive storylines and multiple interactions within these contexts, can serve as engaging tools for emotion elicitation in autistic individuals. As autistic adolescents tend to show higher engagement with games, we aimed to investigate applicability in this population. To achieve this, we developed a mobile serious game that combines four socio-economic and trust-based game paradigms, aiming to evoke specific emotions of varying intensities during different interactions. This paper presents the outcomes of a preliminary experiment involving thirteen participants. The results show that the game's designed interactions successfully elicited emotional responses aligning with the expectations derived from literature in non-game applications.

Keywords: Affective Computing · Serious Games · Emotion Elicitation · Game Theory · Autism · Depression · Decision-making

Supported by Queen Mary University of London & University of Genoa.

P. Dondio et al. (Eds.): GALA 2023, LNCS 14475, pp. 170–180, 2024.
https://doi.org/10.1007/978-3-031-49065-1_17

1 Introduction

Emotions play a significant role in decision-making, influencing various aspects of our daily lives, such as behavior, clothing choices, dietary preferences, and investments [15]. Classification and detection of emotions have wide-ranging applications in fields like e-commerce, financial trading, and mental health (e.g., [22]). Discovery of patterns in emotional responses, particularly in individuals with social anxiety, depression, and borderline personality disorder, has been studied in different applications [20]. Various games incorporate well-known Game Theory paradigms, such as socio-economic tasks and dilemmas, which elicit specific emotional responses in both mentally healthy individuals and those with mental illnesses [8]. Table 1 showcases the emotional response patterns observed in different typical scenarios and Table 2 provides the description for the same scenarios.

Table 1. Decision-Making & Emotional Response Patterns in Socio-Economic and Trust Based Scenarios.

Interaction Type	Type of Pattern	Pattern Observed
Ultimatum Game (UG)*	Decision-Making	Favours accepting only fair offers and rejecting unfair ones as responder and makes fair but lower offer to maximize profit
	Emotion Elicitation	Induces sadness and disgust when unfair offer is presented and happiness when fair offer is presented
Trust Game (TG)*	Decision-Making	Favours investing smaller amounts in the beginning and donate more often as trustee
	Emotion Elicitation	Induces sadness and anger when trustee does not return profit shares and happiness for the contrary
Dictator Game (DG)*	Decision-Making	Favours making lower allocations to recipients
	Emotion Elicitation	Induces happiness in being able to provide any amount of resource to the responder
Prisoner's Dilemma Game (PDG)**	Decision-Making	Favours non-cooperative behaviour
	Emotion Elicitation	Induces anger, sadness and sometimes disgust when betrayed and happiness for the contrary

* [9,23]
** [18]

Studies have indicated that autistic adolescents exhibit greater comfort in interacting with Non-Player Characters (NPCs) in games than with real people [3], especially if they have depression. The popularity of Role Playing Games on mobile platforms has made decision-making games widely accessible, enabling their use in various real-world contexts as well [1]. Hence, we hypothesize that socio-economic interactions with NPCs in a compelling mobile digital game can elicit similar emotional responses as observed in previous studies in in-person serious game applications. Being able to demonstrate this will indicate that decision-making games can effectively support and investigate activities for autistic individuals by inferring their mental state, satisfaction level, and socio-economic inclinations, etc. This paper presents the design of a mobile serious game which employs Game Theory paradigms to evoke various emotions in autistic adolescents with varying levels of depression. Preliminary experiment results support our hypotheses and suggest the potential for further testing and deployment.

2   The Game Design

2.1   Game Storyline, Dynamics and Mechanics

The designed game features "Joe", a character living on the island of Laniakea. Joe's daily tasks involve interacting with locals to complete objectives using limited resources (money, food, and health) to satisfy the Overlord. In a new town called Caldwell, Joe encounters NPCs and engages in socio-economic and trust-based decisions. Following game mechanics, Joe must complete the level [4], experiencing a mix of interactions, from borrowing money from a rude individual to being rewarded for trusting a stranger. This design aims to create positive uncertainty, engaging the player and encouraging him/her to minimize future uncertainties [6]. NPC engagement is a crucial element, with the player assuming Joe's perspective in first-person during interactions, enhancing immersion.

After each interaction, NPCs indicate the next destination. Interactions affect resources positively or negatively, reflecting the economic aspect. To complete the level, the player needs sufficient levels of two out of three resources. Staying within road bump barriers while moving maintains the player's focus and introduces the risk of health reduction [14]. This is visualised by a heart symbol that appears on the 'Joe' every time he hits a road barrier. A navigation arrow and map aid the player in locating NPCs and their current position (Fig. 1a). In order to avoid unpredictable emotional responses, the socio-economic interactions do not hinder game progression [8]. Requiring two resource levels ensures no direct link between socio-economic interactions and failure.

2.2   UI Elements

Figure 1 displays game UI snapshots. Figure 1a showcases the default UI with the player status panel, white arrow indicating NPC location, navigation map button, joystick for character control, and 'Jump!' button. The positioning of these UI elements was updated from the version presented in [2] to improve the affordance of the joystick, as placing it near the playing character would make it easier for the players to map its movements to that of the players [10]. The player status panel features health, money, and food bars, representing their respective levels. Clicking the navigation map icon reveals a top angled view of the scene, displaying task markers and Joe's real-time position (Fig. 1c).

To capture emotional responses, self-reporting is integrated into the gameplay itself, following literature standards [19]. After each socio-economic interaction, players use the UI in Fig. 1b to self-report their emotional state. The self-report options encompass the six basic emotions: Happy, Surprise, Sad, Angry, Fear, and Disgust, and their intensities, which serve as foundational components for deriving complex emotions from collected data [7]. The UI for self-reports was translated to Italian for this study.

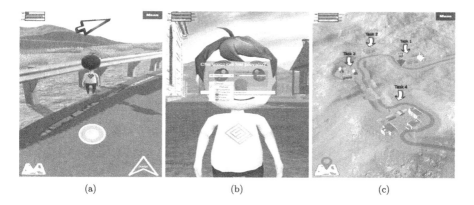

(a)   (b)   (c)

Fig. 1. Game UI, Emotion Self-Reporting & Navigation elements

2.3   Decision-Making Interactions

The overall game implements four decision-making interactions (discussed in Table 2). Three of them are of socio-economic type: Ultimatum Game (UG), Trust Game (TG), and Dictator Game (DG) in Figs. 2a, 2c, and 2d. One is trust-based: Prisoner's Dilemma Game (PDG) in Fig. 2e and 2f. In comparison with a previous version of the game [2], the on-screen dialogues were translated to Italian, with emotive Italian voice-overs for the NPC dialogue lines added to the game for increasing immersion for the target audience. Additionally, soothing background sounds of rustling leaves in a gentle wind with birds chirping around, were added to further increase the immersive nature of the game. Also, a feature of prompting to progress in a conversation was added to ensure the players had the opportunity to read the dialogues completely before the conversation would move on, seen in Fig. 2b.

3   Data Collection Using the Game

3.1   The Experiment

Our experiment utilized a "within-subjects" design without control groups, following established efficacy for affect measurement in laboratory settings [13]. A small-scale data collection involved 14 adolescents, with 13 fully participating,

(a) UG NPC   (b) Repeat or Progress   (c) TG NPC

(d) DG NPC   (e) PDG Prisoner NPC   (f) PDG Jailer NPC

Fig. 2. NPC interactions

of whom 7 had varying levels of depression (1 to 3) while 6 did not. Participants were selected based on their age (10 to 19), autism diagnoses (level 1 to 3), their ability to read and comprehend in Italian and have the willingness to join in-person experiments. External collaborators conducted assessments using the WISC-IV for IQ measurement [25], K-SADS-PL-DSM-5 for depression level [12] on a scale of 0 (no depression) to 3 (symptoms of depression are visible), as shown in Fig. 3b, and ADOS-2 and ADI-R [11,16] to classify their autism level on a scale of 0 (autism traits not apparent) to 2 (autism traits hinder the daily activities) of the participants. Except for one (autism Level 2), all participants were in autism level 1. The participant numbers for depression levels 0, 1, 2 and 3 were 6, 3, 3 and 1 respectively. Ethics approval was obtained from the University of Genoa's ethics review committee.

The participants, aged 11 to 16 ($\mu = 12.96$, $\sigma = 2.06$, their distribution given in Fig. 3a). The experimental setup ensured a distraction-free environment by removing colorful images and multimedia devices from the air-conditioned room. The therapist who provided care to the participating adolescents from the collaborating team was present to ensure participant safety and provide support if needed, as it is a standard practice when working with vulnerable individuals [21]. The number of participants was determined based on the requirements for preliminary usability testing, following Turner et al.'s suggestion that approximately 5 participants would cover 90% of usability issues [24]. After playing the

Table 2. Game Theory Paradigms utilised in designing our player-NPC interactions.

Type	Game	Description	Our Implementation
Socio-economic Games [23]	UG	In this scenario, there are two players: a Proposer and a Responder. The Proposer is provided with a sum of money and is tasked with proposing a division of the amount to the Responder. The Responder has the option to either accept or reject the offer. If the Responder accepts, both players receive the agreed-upon amount. However, if the Responder rejects the offer, neither player receives any money	In our game, the NPC assumes the role of the 'proposer' while Joe becomes the 'responder'. The NPC presents an unfair offer, creating a negative interaction characterized by condescending and slightly rude dialogues. However, the interactions are not offensive, as previous research on Ultimatum game settings has demonstrated that such interactions elicit distinct negative emotional responses with high intensity. Figure 2a illustrates a portion of the dialogue between Joe and the NPC
	TG	In this scenario, there are two players: a Trustor and a Trustee. The Trustor is provided with a resource, such as money, and is instructed to propose a division of the resource with the Trustee. The Trustee has the choice to accept or reject the offer. In the game, whatever amount is given to the Trustee is multiplied by two or three. However, the Trustee has the freedom to decide whether or not to repay any portion of the resource to the Trustor	In our game, Joe acts as the 'trustor' while the NPC assumes the role of the 'trustee'. If Joe decides to trust the NPC with his food, the NPC reciprocates by rewarding Joe and returning his share of the profit. The interaction has a positive polarity, characterized by uplifting dialogues and the NPC expressing gratitude. This positive tone serves two purposes. Firstly, it balances the negativity of the NPC in the Ultimatum Game, as prolonged negativity could potentially impact the player's decision-making. Secondly, positive interactions in Trust Game settings promote cooperation. Figure 2c depicts a section of the dialogue between Joe and the NPC
	DG	In this scenario, there are two players: a Dictator and a Responder. The Dictator is provided with a sum of money and is tasked with deciding whether to donate a portion or the entirety of the amount to the Responder. The Responder is obligated to accept the donation. The Dictator also has the option to choose not to donate any amount, and the recipient (Responder) does not have any say in this game	In our game, Joe assumes the role of the 'Dictator' while the NPC becomes the 'responder'. This interaction is designed such that if Joe chooses to donate some of his money, the NPC expresses gratitude for his generosity. However, even if Joe decides not to donate, the NPC remains polite, maintaining a positive polarity throughout the interaction. This positive polarity is crucial to establish that the previous trust game interaction, which also had a positive polarity, was not an isolated occurrence. It reinforces the idea that not all NPCs are rude. Moreover, this positive tone sets the stage for the subsequent interaction, which has a negative polarity, as narrative changes tend to evoke stronger emotional responses in players. Figure 2d illustrates a section of the dialogue between Joe and the NPC
Trust-based game [18]	PDG	In this scenario, there are three players: a Jailer, Prisoner A, and Prisoner B. The prisoners are being interrogated by the Jailer for a crime they are accused of. If both prisoners accuse each other, they will both receive a sentence of 1 year in prison. If neither prisoner accuses the other, they will both be sentenced to 5 years in prison. However, if one prisoner, let's say Prisoner A, accuses Prisoner B while B remains silent, Prisoner A will be set free while Prisoner B will receive a sentence of 10 years in prison.	In our game, the NPCs assume the roles of the 'jailer' and 'prisoner B', while Joe takes on the role of 'prisoner A'. The interaction is designed to involve Joe assisting the prisoner-NPC in completing the final task, which aligns him with the prisoner-NPC and makes him an accomplice to the jailer-NPC. This interaction is intentionally crafted to orchestrate a betrayal from the prisoner-NPC, aiming to elicit a strong negative emotional response from the player. Figure presents a section of the dialogue between Joe and the prisoner NPC, while Figs. 2e & 2f displays a portion of the dialogue between Joe and the jailer NPC

game, participants were asked to provide feedback on their engagement using the Game Engagement Questionnaire (GEQ) by Brockmyer et al. [5]. The GEQ score can be used to understand how well the participants engaged with the game [5,17].

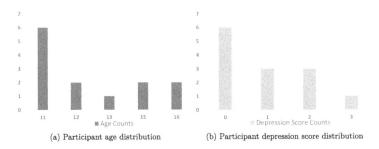

(a) Participant age distribution   (b) Participant depression score distribution

Fig. 3. Participant Information.

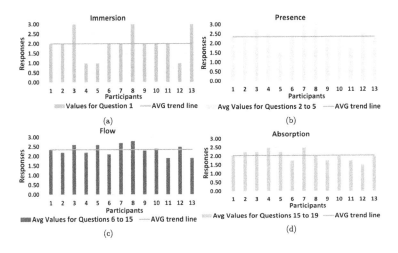

Fig. 4. GEQ responses according to the four areas of engagement assessed by the questionnaire.

3.2   Analysis of the Collected Data

The GEQ contained 19 questions that can be clustered to represent four different aspects of player engagement: Immersion (question 1), Presence (questions 2 to 5), Flow (questions 6 to 15) and Absorption (questions 16 to 19) [5]. Each question had three possible answers, 'No', 'Maybe' and 'Yes', which were coded to 1, 2 and 3, respectively, in a Lickert scale. Figure 4 shows the responses for each of the aspects of engagement. The responses for the latter three aspects were averaged for each participant over the range of questions for each aspect. The orange horizontal line in the response charts shows the average response score for each aspect, which was 2.0 for Immersion, 2.4 for Presence, 2.45 for Flow and 2.04 for Absorption. Hence, the average trend shows that players tended to respond positively ("Yes") to all aspects of player engagement. This indicates that the players had a good level of engagement with the game, which can be interpreted as the reported emotions to be related with the game interactions [17]. Due to the varied distribution between participant age ranges as mentioned earlier, it was not possible to find significant differences in engagement between participant of different age ranges.

Figure 5 shows the self-reported emotional response patterns from the participants. The emotion with the highest self-reported intensity by a player for each decision-making interaction was chosen as the dominant emotion experienced by that player during that interaction and thus, as the emotion label for that interaction for that player. The aim was to simplify visualizing players' emotional responses. Only 4 out of 13 participants provided intensities for multiple emotions, with their dominant emotion being reported as double or more intense than other their emotions. In UG, most players reported being 'Angry', followed by 'Sad' and 'Disgusted', seen in Fig. 5a and the dominant emotions for PDG and TG are shown in Figs. 5b and 5c respectively. Finally, Figs. 5d and 5e show the emotion response polarity for the interactions, where proportion of positive emotions (happy and surprised) and negative emotions (sad, angry, scared and disgusted) are represented for UG, PDG and TG. Notably, for both in UG and PDG, the players experienced exactly the same and greater levels of negative emotions while in TG, the players experienced greater levels of positive emotions. Figure 5 does not include a visualisation for DG as all players reported 'Happy' as their dominant emotion. These findings are in line with literature, as discussed in Subsect. 2.3 and observed in Table 2 for each type of NPC interaction we implemented in the game. Some decision making patterns, however, deviated from the literature. For instance, in an unfair UG, 7 out of the 13 participants accepted the Proposer's offer, while everyone chose to collaborate with the jailer NPC in PDG. Due to the small sample size for this study, no conclusive understanding for such deviations in decision-making patterns. Also, as 6 out 13 (46%) of the participants did not have depression symptoms and there were very few samples for the depression levels 1 to 3 (3 participants in level 1, 3 participants in level 2 and 1 participant in level 3) the effect of depression in autism on emotion elicitation patterns could not be conclusively determined.

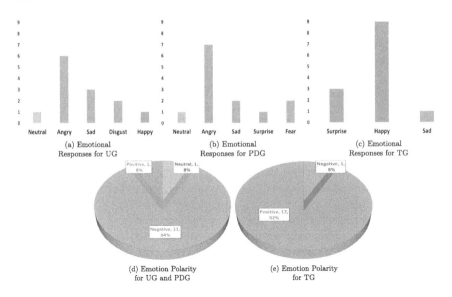

Fig. 5. Emotional responses of players for the different decision-making interactions.

4   Conclusion

The paper has presented a mobile game design incorporating socio-economic and trust-based interactions, and demonstrated its ability to consistently elicit intense specific emotions from autistic adolescent players. These findings substantially agree with the literature in non-game settings and suggest the potential of serious games as a novel tool for emotional elicitation in this population. Furthermore, the game's application extends to the detection of abnormal emotional responses and inference of potential affective disorders.

While the current game's scope is constrained by the limited number and type of player-NPC interaction narratives, the promising preliminary results warrant further research to explore additional scenarios that can elicit predictable emotional responses. This would enhance the game's variety, appeal, and the variety of interactions available to players.

References

1. 23+ mobile gaming statistics for 2022. https://techjury.net/blog/mobile-gaming-statistics/#gref
2. Ahmed, F., et al.: Socio-economic decision making and emotion elicitation with a serious game in the wild. Appl. Sci. **13**(11), 6432 (2023). https://doi.org/10.3390/app13116432
3. Ahmed, F., Carrión, J.R., Bellotti, F., Barresi, G., Floris, F., Berta, R.: Applications of serious games as affective disorder therapies in autistic and neurotypical individuals: a literature review. Appl. Sci. **13**, 4706 (2023). https://doi.org/10.3390/APP13084706

4. Almeida, M.S.O., da Silva, F.S.C.: A systematic review of game design methods and tools. In: Anacleto, J.C., Clua, E.W.G., da Silva, F.S.C., Fels, S., Yang, H.S. (eds.) ICEC 2013. LNCS, vol. 8215, pp. 17–29. Springer, Heidelberg (2013). https://doi.org/10.1007/978-3-642-41106-9_3

5. Brockmyer, J.H., Fox, C.M., Curtiss, K.A., McBroom, E., Burkhart, K.M., Pidruzny, J.N.: The development of the game engagement questionnaire: a measure of engagement in video game-playing. J. Exp. Soc. Psychol. **45**, 624–634 (2009). https://doi.org/10.1016/J.JESP.2009.02.016

6. Deterding, S., Andersen, M.M., Kiverstein, J., Miller, M.: Mastering uncertainty: a predictive processing account of enjoying uncertain success in video game play. Front. Psychol. **13**, 924953 (2022). https://doi.org/10.3389/fpsyg.2022.924953

7. Ekman, P.: An argument for basic emotions. Cogn. Emot. **6**, 169–200 (1992). https://doi.org/10.1080/02699939208411068

8. Harlé, K.M., Allen, J.J., Sanfey, A.G.: The impact of depression on social economic decision making. J. Abnorm. Psychol. (2010). https://doi.org/10.1037/a0018612

9. Hu, Y., et al.: The effects of social comparison and depressive mood on adolescent social decision-making. BMC Psychiatry **21**, 1–15 (2021). https://doi.org/10.1186/s12888-020-02928-y

10. Jiow, H.J., Lim, S.S.: The evolution of video game affordances and implications for parental mediation. Bull. Sci. Technol. Soc. **32**(6), 455–462 (2012). https://doi.org/10.1177/0270467612469077

11. Luyster, R.: Autism diagnostic observation schedule, (ADOS-2) manual (part II): toddler module (2012)

12. Nishiyama, T., et al.: The kiddie schedule for affective disorders and schizophrenia present and lifetime version (K-SADS-PL) for DSM-5: a validation for neurodevelopmental disorders in Japanese outpatients. Compr. Psychiatry **96**, 152148 (2020). https://doi.org/10.1016/j.comppsych.2019.152148

13. Pallavicini, F., Pepe, A.: Virtual reality games and the role of body involvement in enhancing positive emotions and decreasing anxiety: within-subjects pilot study. JMIR Serious Games **8**(2), e15635 (2020). https://doi.org/10.2196/15635

14. Perttula, A., Kiili, K., Lindstedt, A., Tuomi, P.: Flow experience in game based learning - a systematic literature review. Int. J. Serious Games **4** (2017). https://doi.org/10.17083/IJSG.V4I1.151

15. Rilling, J.K., Sanfey, A.G.: The neuroscience of social decision-making. Annu. Rev. Psychol. **62**(1), 23–48 (2011). https://doi.org/10.1146/annurev.psych.121208.131647

16. Rutter, M., Le Couteur, A., Lord, C., et al.: Autism diagnostic interview-revised. Los Angeles CA: Western Psychol. Serv. **29**(2003), 30 (2003)

17. Sackl, M., Steinmaurer, A., Cheong, C., Cheong, F., Filippou, J., Gütl, C.: sCool: impact on human-computer interface improvements on learner experience in a game-based learning platform. In: Auer, M.E., Rüütmann, T. (eds.) ICL 2020. AISC, vol. 1328, pp. 439–451. Springer, Cham (2021). https://doi.org/10.1007/978-3-030-68198-2_41

18. Sally, D., Hill, E.: The development of interpersonal strategy: autism, theory-of-mind, cooperation and fairness. J. Econ. Psychol. (2006). https://doi.org/10.1016/j.joep.2005.06.015

19. Spink, A., et al.: Psychophysiology of digital game playing: the relationship of self-reported emotions with phasic physiological responses. In: 6th International Conference on Methods and Techniques in Behavioral Research (2008)

20. Staebler, K., Gebhard, R., Barnett, W., Renneberg, B.: Emotional responses in borderline personality disorder and depression: assessment during an acute crisis and 8 months later. J. Behav. Ther. Exp. Psychiatry **40**, 85–97 (2009). https://doi.org/10.1016/J.JBTEP.2008.04.003

21. Stige, S.H., Barca, T., Lavik, K.O., Moltu, C.: Barriers and facilitators in adolescent psychotherapy initiated by adults-experiences that differentiate adolescents' trajectories through mental health care. Front. Psychol. **12**, 633663 (2021). https://doi.org/10.3389/fpsyg.2021.633663

22. Suslow, T., Junghanns, K., Arolt, V.: Detection of facial expressions of emotions in depression. Percept. Mot. Skills **92**(3 Pt 1), 857–868 (2001)

23. Tamarit, I., Sánchez, A.: Emotions and strategic behaviour: the case of the ultimatum game. PLoS ONE **11**, e0158733 (2016). https://doi.org/10.1371/JOURNAL.PONE.0158733

24. Turner, W.C., Lewis, J.R., Nielson, J.: Determining usability test sample size. Int. Encycl. Ergon. Hum. Factors **3**, 3132–3136 (2006). https://doi.org/10.1201/9780849375477-616

25. Wechsler, D., Kodama, H.: Wechsler Intelligence Scale for Children, vol. 1. Psychological Corporation, New York (1949)

User Experience, User Analysis and User Assessment in Serious Games

Not (Only) a Matter of Position: Player Traits Which Influence the Experience with the Leaderboard in a Digital Maths Game

Pierpaolo Dondio[1(✉)], André Almo[1], Maíra Amaral[1], Ephrem Tibebe[1], Mariana Rocha[1], and Attracta Brennan[2]

[1] School of Computer Science, Technological University Dublin, Dublin, Ireland
{pierpaolo.dondio,andre.almo,maira.amaral,mariana.rocha}@tudublin.ie,
D22125038@mytudublin.ie
[2] Computer Science Department, University of Galway, Galway, Ireland
attracta.brennan@universityofgalway.ie

Abstract. Leaderboards have often been shown to increase engagement and motivation in digital serious games, supporting better learning outcomes and positively affecting players' game experience. However, few studies show how the player's position on the leaderboard can be a demotivating factor and how the presence of a leaderboard can increase competition and social pressure on players to the point of hindering their game experience. In examining the relationship between a leaderboard and the player's game experience, we sought to identify the significant factors influencing whether or not a player liked the presence of a leaderboard in a digital maths game. We conducted an experimental study involving 434 Irish primary school children who participated in a 6-week digital game-based learning (DGBL) programme playing the game Seven Spells, which included a game leaderboard. Results indicated that the players' enjoyment of the leaderboard depended not only on their in-game performance (i.e. their position on the leaderboard), but also on their level of maths anxiety and how much they enjoyed different play modes such as playing versus a classmate or playing alone. These results suggest that game designers should consider the non-cognitive traits of players when deciding on the inclusion of a leaderboard in a digital maths game, in order to mitigate its potential negative effects on the players' game experience.

Keywords: game-based learning · game design · maths anxiety

1 Introduction

Digital game-based learning (DGBL) is defined as "the use of games within an existing lesson, classroom, or other instructional contexts where the intent is at least as much to learn rather than to (exclusively) have fun" (p. 144) [27]. The efficacy of game-based learning has been widely demonstrated [7]. As an example, learning through games can support problem-solving and critical thinking

P. Dondio et al. (Eds.): GALA 2023, LNCS 14475, pp. 183–193, 2024.
https://doi.org/10.1007/978-3-031-49065-1_18

and can help students comprehend abstract mathematical concepts [17]. A recent meta-analysis by [28] investigated the impact of digital games on students' learning achievements in different STEM subjects. The authors included 33 studies published in the last ten years and reported an overall moderate effect size of 0.629 for mathematics. [14] suggests that learning through games positively promotes engagement and increases pupils' self-confidence, in addition to fostering positive attitudes towards maths. DGBL is also regarded as a potential intervention to support the integration of creativity within mathematics teaching [18,20], foster positive views on mathematics and mitigate maths anxiety (MA), despite the evidence to date being inconclusive [10].

The efficacy of DGBL is related to the quality of the games used, and the ability of the game designer to incorporate game features and game mechanics supporting enjoyment, active learning and engagement, all of which are interconnected [7,18]. The choice of game design features and game mechanics in DGBL can influence a player's game experience [20] and, consequently, a player's learning experience. The use of game features to promote challenge and competition has been proven to foster engagement and result in a deeper knowledge of the learning content [25,26]. Moreover, the social aspect of competition is frequently perceived to motivate and engage players [5]. One of the most used features in gamified educational settings is the use of a leaderboard showing the game scores achieved by players [23]. A leaderboard can be employed to implement competition, goals, performance-based feedback and/or relative comparison between players [22,23].

Leaderboards have been shown to be effective in enhancing a player's engagement and self-reported levels of motivation [3,22,23]. Leaderboards however, do not affect all players equally. In a classroom setting, a leaderboard's display of student achievement can increase social comparison and peer-pressure to the point of becoming detrimental for the game experience of other students, especially those unable to cope with higher levels of competition, social anxiety and/or stress [24,29]. Studies on the use of a leaderboard in a mathematics game team competition found that although the leaderboard tended to motivate the students, less successful teams were less motivated by the presence of the leaderboard [22]. Similarly, previous research has shown that students positioned in the lower ranks of the leaderboard can often feel inadequate and may not respond to the leaderboard due to a negative comparison of themselves against those players who are higher placed [23]. In a 2013 study, students considered the leaderboard to be a demotivating factor, acknowledging that the growing gap between the highest scoring students and the rest of the class discouraged them from scoring more points in the game [21].

In this paper, we seek to identify traits that can influence a player's experience with the leaderboard. The predictors which were used include gender, age, position on the leaderboard, level of mathematics anxiety, level of mathematics and literacy cognitive skills, and video game habits. We conducted an experimental study where 434 Irish primary school children participated in a 6-week DGBL programme, playing the digital maths game *Seven Spells*. We focused on the following two research questions:

- **RQ1.** What are the significant factors predicting whether or not a player will report a positive or negative experience with the leaderboard in a digital maths game?
- **RQ2.** What level of accuracy can be achieved by a model predicting a player's opinion of the leaderboard?

While RQ2 is an open question, our hypothesis regarding RQ1 is that the players' experience with the leaderboard is not driven solely by their game performance (i.e. their position on the leaderboard), but may also be influenced by other traits such as the players' aversion to peer-comparison in the context of mathematics (measured by maths anxiety) and by the propensity of the player to play socially rather than individually. The answers to the above research questions can help game designers consider to what extent leaderboards should be used in a learning context and also how to adaptively emphasize or diminish the use of leaderboards based on the profile of the players.

2   Methods

Data collection was performed from January 2022 to May 2022 in the context of *Happy Maths* [1], a research project investigating the effect of game-based learning on primary school students' numerical cognition and maths anxiety.

The participants of this study were 434 students from 25 classrooms of five Irish primary schools. The age of the participants ranged from 8 to 11 years, corresponding to 3rd, 4th, 5th and 6th classes of the Irish education system. The study was a quasi-experimental intervention with a pre-post design and one hour weekly game-based sessions delivered in class for six consecutive weeks. During the study's six weeks, students engaged with the digital maths card game *Seven Spells* [1], developed by the authors. In this game, players enter a fictional martial arts academy, learning the ancient art of number fighting. Their goal

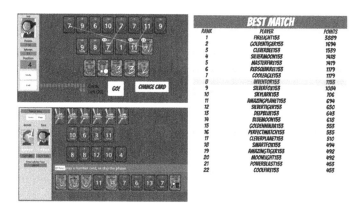

Fig. 1. The *Seven Spells solo* mode (top left), the *versus a human* mode (bottom left). and the *solo* mode leaderboard (right).

is to capture number cards using their mathematics skills, including arithmetic operations (addition, subtraction, multiplication, and division), knowledge of mathematical concepts (even and odd numbers, prime numbers, numeric tables, intervals, greater and smaller, etc.) and their ability to combine and manipulate numbers. The game can be played in a *solo* mode (i.e. without an opponent) or in *vs human* mode (i.e. against another human player) (see Fig. 1).

In this study, we focused on the infinite design leaderboard [22] of the *solo* game mode, which showed all players in the class in an ordered ranking. Players could access a class leaderboard showing the performance of only those students in their class. The class leaderboard was also displayed on the classroom white-board during the game sessions and the in-class activities. The class leaderboard was updated in real-time so that whenever a player performed a move which generated points, they and other players could see their position in the rankings change as they played.

At the beginning of the study, information on children's game habits was collected in addition to cognitive and non-cognitive measurements. The children were asked about how much they enjoyed playing video games (on a scale of 1 to 5) and how much time they spent playing video games daily. They were also asked to complete the Modified Abbreviated Maths Anxiety scale (mAMAS) [8], a validated scale for primary school children to measure their level of maths anxiety (MA). Maths anxiety is defined as negative feelings (i.e. stress, apprehension, tension and anxiety) in relation to mathematics problems, exercises and tests [6,8,16]. As maths anxious students might be sensitive to peer-pressure and social comparison [16], MA was introduced as a predictor potentially inversely correlated with the enjoyment of the leaderboard. Using the Irish national standardized tests for maths and English, two cognitive measures were collected for each student: their level of maths ability and their literacy ability [2]. These scores are provided in a STEN scale from 1 to 10. The gender and class grade of each student were also collected. After the end of the sixth session, students answered a short feedback survey about their game experience. The survey included a question asking the students whether they enjoyed the presence of a leaderboard in the game. Students were also asked to rate the *solo* and *vs. human* game modes on a scale from 1 to 10. The ratings assigned to the game modes were introduced as key control variables. While the leaderboard introduces a form of social comparison and competition, playing against a classmate is another form of social comparison (a peer comparison rather than a class comparison) that can measure a player's openness to playing the game socially rather than individually. Moreover, a low score for the *vs. human* game mode could act as a proxy for the social anxiety that a player might experience when facing an opponent. Our hypothesis is therefore that the rating of the *vs. human* game mode would be positively correlated with their enjoyment of the leaderboard. The description of the variables collected in this study are presented in Tables 1 and 2. Of the data collected, 380 out of 434 records were complete.

Data analysis was carried out using R, with the binary predictor outcome being whether or not the players enjoyed the game's leaderboard. The predictors used in the models are shown in Tables 1 and 2. In order to answer our research questions, we fitted a Logistic Regression model, a Random Forest and an XGBoost model to describe the relationships. The importance of each variable (RQ1) was captured by looking at the significant factors of the Logistic Regression model and by considering the mean decrease in accuracy for the machine learning models (Random Forest and XGBoost) [15]. As can be seen from Table 2, the majority of the players liked the leaderboard (81.3%), resulting in an imbalanced dataset. To deal with this imbalance, the SMOTE oversampling technique was applied [9]. In order to have a better estimate of each model's accuracy, we report the average of 100 models, each of which was trained on a different test/train dataset split.

Table 1. Numerical study variables (N = 380).

Variable	Description	Mean	SD	Range
MA	Maths Anxiety score (mAMAS)	20.7	7.47	9–45
MS	Maths Score	6.02	2.09	1–10
LS	Literacy Score	5.98	1.92	1–10
Pos	Normalized Rank of a player in the class leaderboard (1 = highest rank)	0.5	0.3	0–1
RateHum	Rate to the *vs. human* game version	9.11	1.52	1–10
RateSolo	Rate to the *solo* game version	6.84	2.21	1–10

3   Results

The dataset contained complete data for 380 players. The binary target variable Y (liked/did not like the leaderboard) contained 71 negative outcomes (18.7%) and 309 positive (81.3%) outcomes, showing that players generally enjoyed the leaderboard. Tables 1 and 2 show the descriptive statistics for each variable, including mean, standard deviations (SD) and range. The variable *pos* measured the position of a player on the class leaderboard normalized in relation to each class, so that the top position in each class has a value of 1 and the bottom position has a value of 0. It was therefore converted into a uniformly distributed variable between 0 and 1. We note how the children enjoyed playing the *vs. human* game mode, with an average score of 9.1 out of 10. The variable is strongly right skewed, with 55% of students giving a score of 10 and only 11% of children assigning a score less than 5. The same can be said for the variable measuring how much a player liked playing video games, with only 4.7% of the players reporting that they did not like to play (Table 1). The rating given to the *solo* game mode was much lower than the rating for the *vs. human* game mode,

Table 2. Categorical study variables considered (N = 380). The variable *Class Yr* refers to levels in the Irish school system: 3rd class refers to 8 year-old children, 4th class refers to 9 year old children, 5th class refers to 10 year old chidlren and 6th class refers to 11 year-old children.

Variable	Description	Distribution of levels
Class Yr	Class grade	24 (3rd), 106 (4th), 166 (5th), 84 (6th)
Gender	Binary variable M,F	F = 203 (53.4%), M = 177 (46.6%)
Likevideo	Do you like video games? Likert scale (1 = love 5 = hate)	1: 53.4%, 2: 28.4%, 3: 13.4%, 4: 2.6%, 5: 2.1%
PlayTime	How much do you play video games daily?	Never (9.2%), ≤ 1 h (20%), 1–2 h (34.6%), ≥ 2 h (36.2%)
Y	Did you like the leaderboard?	Yes = 309 (81.3%) No = 71 (18.7%)

with an average of 6.84. We also found that the enjoyment of the leaderboard was strongly associated with the enjoyment of the entire game. Players that liked the leaderboard gave an average rating to the *solo* and *vs. human* game modes of 8.13 (SD = 1.74) while the group that did not like the leaderboard gave an average rating of 7.33 (SD = 2.2). A t-test was significant (p < 0.0001, t = 4.9).

In order to answer RQ1 and RQ2, we fitted several machine learning models, including Logistic Regression, Random Forest and XGBoost. Table 3 shows the Logistic Regression model fitted to the entire datasets of 380 observations. There were three significant variables in the model: the position in the leaderboard, the score given to the *vs. human* game mode (both with a positive association) and MA (negative association). The score of the *vs. human* game mode was the most significant factor (1 extra point increased the log-odds ratio like over dislike by .36, i.e. the probability of liking the leaderboard incremented by a factor of 1.43), followed by the MA score (1 point increase in the MA score corresponded to a decrease of 7% in the probability of linking the leaderboard) and leaderboard position (an increase of 1 position in the leaderboard in a typical class of 30 students incremented the probability of liking the leaderboard by a factor of 1.07). None of the other features were significant. Finally, the value of Tjur's R^2 of 0.21 represented the mean difference between the prediction of the two levels of the target variable. This value suggests a medium effect-size fit.

The importance of each variable was also measured using the mean decrease in accuracy (MDA) of the machine learning tree-based models. We report only the results for Random Forest (the best performing model), excluding XGBoost that held similar results. Figure 2 shows the importance of the predictor variables ranked by MDA. The values represent the average of 100 random forest models fitted on a different test/train split. The rating given to the *vs. human*

Table 3. Logistic Regression model. Target variable: Y (like the leaderboard).

Predictor	β	Pr($> \lvert z \rvert$)	Predictor	β	Pr($> \lvert z \rvert$)
Intercept	−2.31	0.15	class year	0.024	0.90
Video like	−0.06	0.74	**MA**	**−0.07**	**0.003**
Gender = M	−0.13	0.67	**pos**	**1.88**	**0.005**
Game time ≤1 h	1.07	0.28	**rate human**	**0.36**	**≤ 0.001**
Game time: 1–2 h	0.44	0.66	MS	−0.01	−0.076
Game time ≥2 h	0.64	0.52	LS	0.18	0.12
rate solo	0.07	0.42			
Observations = 380, R^2 (Tjur) = 0.21					

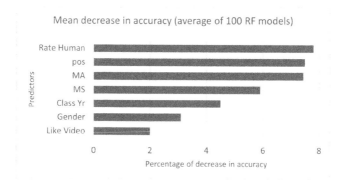

Fig. 2. Mean decrease in accuracy for each predictor. The average of 100 random forest is presented.

Table 4. Accuracy of machine learning models predicting the liking of the leaderboard.

Models	Test Accuracy	Training Accuracy
Random Forest	83.7%	98.7%
XGBoost	79.3%	96.7%
Logistic Regression	69.7%	91.1%

game mode, the position on the leaderboard and MA were the top three most important predictors with respect to model accuracy. *Gender* and *Like video* were ranked as the two bottom features. The results substantially confirmed the significant factors of the Logistic Regression model. In order to answer RQ2, we trained various machine learning algorithms such as Logistic Regression, XGBoost and Random Forest and evaluated the performance of these models on the test dataset. Note how the values are the mean of 100 random test/train dataset split, each with a 20:80 ratio. The dataset was perfectly balanced using SMOTE. The randomized search cv method was used to adjust the parameters of the model for optimization. As can be seen from Table 4, Random Forest out-performed all of the other models on the testing set. The best performing model was Random Forest, followed by Gradient Boosting, both of which aggregate multiple decision trees learned from data. Statistical models such as Logistic Regression had a performance in the high 60 s. In general, our results show how the leaderboard game experience can be predicted with an accuracy above 80%. Since the dataset used in the analysis has been perfectly balanced, the accuracy shown is also the balanced accuracy of each model.

4   Discussion

In this paper we sought to identify: those player traits which predict a player's experience of a leaderboard in a digital maths educational game (RQ1), and the accuracy to which such experiences can be predicted (RQ2). Regarding our first research question, the most significant factors predicting whether or not players liked the leaderboard were the MA score (negatively associated), the score given to the vs. human game mode, and the position on the leaderboard (both positively associated). As expected, a player's position on the leaderboard was a strong significant predictor. Indeed, it is reasonable to expect that players enjoyed seeing their names at the top of the leaderboard whilst contrarily, not enjoying a display of their poor performance to their fellow classmates. These findings are also indirectly compatible with previous research suggesting how a player's position on the leaderboard was directly linked to how much they felt motivated in the game [22,23].

Excluding position on the leaderboard, our results also confirmed how factors unrelated to game performance were also important. Our most interesting result was that MA was a significant factor even in the presence of other predictors (such as leaderboard position, gender, age, player's maths ability). This means that anxious students might indeed have a negative reaction to game elements emphasizing competitiveness and social comparison such as a leaderboard, even when their scores are as good as non-anxious players. The accentuation of social comparison by the leaderboard can trigger the negative effects of MA, that could include not only a negative game experience with the leaderboard, but more than likely, a detrimental experience with the entire game, as suggested by the strong association between liking the leaderboard and the average ratings assigned to the game. A well-known negative effect of MA is the avoidance of maths tasks [16] which can lead to less engaged players, thereby undermining the potential of the game as a learning tool. Indeed, the leaderboard could possibly trigger those negative effects of MA that game-based interventions are actually trying to mitigate. Our results support previous studies where social comparison was shown to be a significant predictor of MA [13] and where MA was discovered to be related not only to the manipulation of numbers, but also to the social experience of doing mathematics tasks in the classroom in front of peers [30]. This is in line with [19], who suggested that a number of in-class behaviours (e.g. embarrassment in front of their classmates) are related to a student's maths anxiety. The rating given to the *vs. human* game mode significantly predicted the leaderboard experience, while the rating given to the *solo* game mode did not, confirming again that non-cognitive factors (i.e. the extent to which social play is enjoyed) can affect the leaderboard experience.

Neither the maths national score nor the literacy national score were significant predictors, possibly reflecting the fact that the leaderboard position was sufficient to capture the players' maths abilities. Gender was not a significant factor in predicting whether the students liked the leaderboard as supported by studies highlighting that girls are as competitive as boys at school in physical and playful activities [4,12]. Our results suggest how differences in the perception of competition are driven by anxiety rather than being a gender specific trait. Indeed, gender was not significant in the presence of maths anxiety and the rating assigned to the *vs. human* mode as predictors. Students' game habits were also not a significant factor in predicting whether they liked the leaderboard. While class year was moderately important in the tree based models, it was not a significant factor in the Logistic Regression model. Furthermore, age was not a significant factor on liking the leaderboard. Although MA and awareness of social comparison increase with age [11], it may be that these effects are already included in other factors (such as the MA score itself), thus diminishing the importance of age in predicting the leaderboard experience. Overall, our results reinforce the need for educators and game designers to consider how the introduction of competitive elements might affect anxious students.

Regarding RQ2, the machine learning models showed how a set of easily obtainable non-game variables can accurately predict the player experience with the leaderboard with an accuracy above 80%. Such models can be used to adaptively emphasize or diminish the leaderboard element in an educational game to safeguard the quality of the players' user experience.

5 Conclusions

In this paper, we examined factors which predict player experience with a leaderboard in a digital maths educational game. Whilst leaderboards are one of the most common elements in game design, their effect is debated, with some studies showing that leaderboards can motivate players and other studies highlighting their negative impact on both the player's enjoyment of the game and their educational experience by increasing peer-pressure.

Our results show how the player's experience of the leaderboard is not only driven by their game performance, but also by their emotional traits. Maths anxious students were sensitive to the presence of a leaderboard and the social competition dynamic introduced by it. Maths anxiety was one of the main factors which predicted a player's negative experience with the leaderboard, even after controlling for the position of the player on the leaderboard, their gender, age and numerical abilities. Even if the results were weighted by the minority of players who reported a negative experience with the leaderboard, this minority represented a non-negligible 20% of the participant cohort.

Our best predictive model had an accuracy above 83% in predicting player experience with the leaderboard. Such models can be used to adaptively emphasize or diminish the leaderboard element of a digital educational game to maximize player experience. Our results can also support game designers in better understanding the impact of a player's emotional traits on the game experience whilst also helping educators understand the effect of introducing competitive games or gamified activities in the classroom on the most anxious students.

References

1. The happy maths programme. www.happymaths.games. Accessed 31 May 2013
2. Primary test, eductional research centre. www.tests.erc.ie/primary-paper-tests. Accessed 11 June 2013
3. Balci, S., Secaur, J.M., Morris, B.J.: Comparing the effectiveness of badges and leaderboards on academic performance and motivation of students in fully versus partially gamified online physics classes. Educ. Inf. Technol. **27**(6), 8669–8704 (2022)
4. Booth, A., Nolen, P.: Choosing to compete: how different are girls and boys? J. Econ. Behav. Organ. **81**(2), 542–555 (2012)
5. Boyle, E.A., Connolly, T.M., Hainey, T., Boyle, J.M.: Engagement in digital entertainment games: a systematic review. Comput. Hum. Behav. **28**(3), 771–780 (2012)
6. Buratta, L., Piccirilli, M., Lanfaloni, G.A., Ilicini, S., Bedetti, C., Elisei, S.: Mathematics anxiety and cognitive performance in adolescent students. Psychiatr. Danub. **31**(suppl 3), 479–485 (2019)
7. Byun, J., Joung, E.: Digital game-based learning for k-12 mathematics education: a meta-analysis. Sch. Sci. Math. **118**(3–4), 113–126 (2018)
8. Carey, E., Hill, F., Devine, A., Szűcs, D.: The modified abbreviated math anxiety scale: a valid and reliable instrument for use with children. Front. Psychol. **8**, 11 (2017)
9. Chawla, N.V., Bowyer, K.W., Hall, L.O., Kegelmeyer, W.P.: Smote: synthetic minority over-sampling technique. J. Artif. Intell. Res. **16**, 321–357 (2002)
10. Dondio, P., Gusev, V., Rocha, M.: Do games reduce maths anxiety? A meta-analysis. Comput. Educ. **194**, 104650 (2023)
11. Dowker, A., Sarkar, A., Looi, C.Y.: Mathematics anxiety: what have we learned in 60 years? Front. Psychol. **7**, 508 (2016)
12. Dreber, A., Von Essen, E., Ranehill, E.: Outrunning the gender gap-boys and girls compete equally. Exp. Econ. **14**, 567–582 (2011)
13. Erdoğan, A., Kesici, Ş., Şahin, İ.: Prediction of high school students' mathematics anxiety by their achievement motivation and social comparison. Ilkogretim Online **10**(2) (2011)
14. Gil-Doménech, D., Berbegal-Mirabent, J.: Stimulating students' engagement in mathematics courses in non-stem academic programmes: a game-based learning. Innov. Educ. Teach. Int. **56**(1), 57–65 (2019)
15. Han, H., Guo, X., Yu, H.: Variable selection using mean decrease accuracy and mean decrease gini based on random forest. In: 2016 7th IEEE International Conference on Software Engineering and Service Science (ICSESS), pp. 219–224. IEEE (2016)

16. Hill, F., Mammarella, I.C., Devine, A., Caviola, S., Passolunghi, M.C., Szucs, D.: Maths anxiety in primary and secondary school students: gender differences, developmental changes and anxiety specificity. Learn. Individ. Differ. **48**, 45–53 (2016)
17. Homer, B.D., Raffaele, C., Henderson, H.: Games as playful learning: implications of developmental theory for game-based learning. In: Handbook of Game-Based Learning, pp. 25–52 (2020)
18. Hwa, S.P.: Pedagogical change in mathematics learning: harnessing the power of digital game-based learning. J. Educ. Technol. Soc. **21**(4), 259–276 (2018)
19. Jackson, C.D., Leffingwell, R.J.: The role of instructors in creating math anxiety in students from kindergarten through college. Math. Teach. **92**(7), 583–586 (1999)
20. Moyer-Packenham, P.S., et al.: How design features in digital math games support learning and mathematics connections. Comput. Hum. Behav. **91**, 316–332 (2019)
21. Nicholson, S.: Exploring gamification techniques for classroom management. Games+ Learn.+ Soc. **9**, 21–27 (2013)
22. Ninaus, M., De Freitas, S., Kiili, K.: Motivational potential of leaderboards in a team-based math game competition. In: Marfisi-Schottman, I., Bellotti, F., Hamon, L., Klemke, R. (eds.) GALA 2020. LNCS, vol. 12517, pp. 242–252. Springer, Cham (2020). https://doi.org/10.1007/978-3-030-63464-3_23
23. Park, S., Kim, S.: Leaderboard design principles to enhance learning and motivation in a gamified educational environment: development study. JMIR Serious Games **9**(2), e14746 (2021)
24. André de la Porte, S., et al.: Exploring the inner workings of the leaderboard for use in educational contexts. Master's thesis (2022)
25. Rubin-Vaughan, A., Pepler, D., Brown, S., Craig, W.: Quest for the golden rule: an effective social skills promotion and bullying prevention program. Comput. Educ. **56**(1), 166–175 (2011)
26. Tan, J.L., Goh, D.H.L., Ang, R.P., Huan, V.S.: Participatory evaluation of an educational game for social skills acquisition. Comput. Educ. **64**, 70–80 (2013)
27. Eck, R.N.: SAPS and digital games: improving mathematics transfer and attitudes in schools. In: Lowrie, T., Jorgensen (Zevenbergen), R. (eds.) Digital Games and Mathematics Learning. MEDE, vol. 4, pp. 141–173. Springer, Dordrecht (2015). https://doi.org/10.1007/978-94-017-9517-3_9
28. Wang, L.H., Chen, B., Hwang, G.J., Guan, J.Q., Wang, Y.Q.: Effects of digital game-based stem education on students' learning achievement: a meta-analysis. Int. J. STEM Educ. **9**(1), 1–13 (2022)
29. Werbach, K., Hunter, D., Dixon, W.: For the Win: How Game Thinking Can Revolutionize Your Business, vol. 1. Wharton Digital Press, Philadelphia (2012)
30. Wu, S.S., Barth, M., Amin, H., Malcarne, V., Menon, V.: Math anxiety in second and third graders and its relation to mathematics achievement. Front. Psychol. **3**, 162 (2012)

An AI Approach for Analyzing Driving Behaviour in Simulated Racing Using Telemetry Data

Fazilat Hojaji[✉] [ID], Adam J. Toth, John M. Joyce, and Mark J. Campbell

Esports Science Research Laboratory, Lero Irish Software Research Centre, University of Limerick, Limerick, Ireland
{Fazilat.Hojaji,Adam.Toth,John.M.Joyce,Mark.Campbell}@ul.ie

Abstract. The emerging and rapid progress of esports (competitive computer gaming) currently lacks approaches for ensuring high-quality analytics to augment performance in professional and amateur esports teams. In this paper, we demonstrate the application of Artificial Intelligence (AI) and Machine Learning (ML) techniques in the esports domain, particularly in simulation (sim) racing, for analyzing drivers' behaviour based on telemetry data from race drivers. To achieve this, we used a professional racing simulator to collect a wide range of feature-rich telemetry data from 93 participants through MoTec telemetry software and the ACC sim racing gaming platform. An objective assessment of the characteristics of the driver's behaviour was then obtained through a set of predefined lap-based metrics derived from telemetry data. Additionally, a comparison of driving styles was carried out using machine learning approaches for grouping the acquired laps based on performance (lap time). The findings from our analysis contribute to a better understanding of how elite drivers differ from low skilled drivers based on their telemetry. Furthermore, our findings provide researchers with key metrics to develop more efficient training tools and techniques to improve sim racing performance.

Keywords: MoTec · Sim racing · Machine Learning · Artificial Intelligence

1 Introduction

Esports analytics, which may be considered a part of game analytics or sports analytics [1, 2], refers to the method of analyzing esports-related data to uncover significant patterns and trends in the data and then transmitting these patterns using visualization approaches to support decision-making processes [3]. Esports analytics has benefited from a variety of community-based projects aimed at helping players access, analyze, and derive meaning from data. In recent years, many new data analysis techniques have been used for processing and analyzing data to extract new knowledge, and these techniques have been well leveraged for improving players' performance [4]. However, there is a lack of tools that provide player performance feedback and suggestions for how to improve [5]. This opens plenty of new opportunities for esports research to determine what makes a gamer successful.

P. Dondio et al. (Eds.): GALA 2023, LNCS 14475, pp. 194–203, 2024.
https://doi.org/10.1007/978-3-031-49065-1_19

In this paper, we focus on simulated motorsport, which is one of the oldest genres in the world of esports. The phrase "sim racing" refers to any computer programs that attempt to properly simulate car racing, along with real-world elements like gasoline consumption, damage, tyre wear and grip, and suspension settings [6]. To be successful in sim racing, a driver must be knowledgeable about all the aspects of vehicle handling that make real-world racing so challenging [7], including threshold braking, maintaining control of a vehicle as the tires lose traction, and correctly entering and exiting turns without losing speed. Technological enhancement in the computer-based simulator domain of simulated driving contributes to the direct improvement of the team and sim racer performance [8]. In this case, solutions, and strategies for becoming the fastest driver are of utmost importance, with various methods of data analysis and data collection tools being used for sim racers. (See [9–12] as examples).

One challenge that researchers face in understanding how elite racers control vehicles at the limits of handling is the lack of ability to obtain data from highly dynamic driving. Racing organisations may have access to this information for internal analysis, but it is not publicly available. Until relatively recently, researchers only used in-game data to analyze driver behaviour and estimate a driver's performance. In this case, the ability to compare experimental and simulated driving behaviour is limited by available sensor information. The public may now obtain telemetry data from sim racing video games thanks to APIs and telemetry tools (e.g., vTelemetry PRO [13] and Motec [14]). Using such tools, the physical and control parameters of the simulation may be tracked and saved as telemetry files [8]. It allows sim racers to gather all the information provided by the vehicle and analyze the data captured during a race or session [15]. Insights from telemetry data lead to a better understanding of the corresponding strengths and weaknesses of the drivers' behaviour and can foster performance improvements through more accurate tuning of their car setup as well as informing them on driving strategies and techniques [16]. By leveraging sim telemetry data collected from sim racers and utilising the state of-the-art AI approach, the purpose of this study is to model and analyze race driver behaviour that may reflect a wide range of driver control features and, as a result, provide adaptations for many of the characteristics of human drivers.

While there are number of studies that investigate simulated driving style for general road cars [17, 18], few efforts have been made to analyze driving behaviour in a simulated racing environment. Some models, such as those employed in Formula One driving [19, 20] or related types of automated or more idealised driver performance, are primarily concerned with achieving perfect performance [15, 21]. These studies rarely include sim telemetry data from entire racing circuits. Even if they rely on telemetry data in their analysis [15, 22], they utilize only a limited number of parameters (i.e., steering wheel, throttle, pedal, and brake pedal) in their analysis and most of the telemetry in-game data is omitted.

This study combines sim telemetry data for entire laps from 93 sim racers through MoTec telemetry software and the ACC sim racing game and presents a structural method to define a set of lap-based metrics that objectively characterise various driving styles. Using ML techniques, these metric sets were then used to cluster elite and low skilled driver behaviour. Insights from this study will lead to a better understanding of the driver's behaviour and the key components that augment learning and performance.

2 Data and Methods

2.1 Apparatus

To address the research goal, we applied the following approach to data collection in the experimental design. Through the ACC simulated racing game, we employed a professional racing simulator to gather a variety of feature-rich telemetry data from 93 participants. The steering wheel, manual gearbox, and control pedals (brake, clutch, and accelerator; Logitech the Logitech Pro wheel and pedals) formed up the simulator's vehicle control interface. The participants were instructed to drive as quickly as they could while keeping the car on the track during the driving task. Before the driving session, general questions were posed about driving passenger cars. 85% had a driving licence and drove on average 10.14 (SD = 10.04) hours a week. In addition, the participants provided a self-assessment of their driving skills in video racing games, which resulted in an average of 12.32 (SD = 9.29) hours a week.

We augmented ACC with MoTec i2 Pro (v1.1.5, Melbourne, Victoria, Australia), a professional telemetric data analysis application, and routed all telemetric data to the data analysis package. The vehicle telemetry was recorded for all participants. Vehicle telemetry includes numerous channels, from which we chose those related to vehicle control. To extract telemetry data, we used Motec i2 Pro available from the MoTec website. We used Python (3.9) as our programming language on the Anaconda3 (Spyder 5.2) platform for the development of the pre-processing and analysis processes.

2.2 Data Analysis

Data preprocessing, we extracted all data channel statistics corresponding to in-game driver and vehicle features. Note that Motec records data for up to 84 metrics, including the driver's input data, chassis and suspension data, brake and tyre data, engine data, wheel data, balancing data, g-force, and car position data. To capture the driver's behaviour, time series data with a sample rate of 50 Hz were extracted. As a result, three types of data files, including a summary file of lap times, channel statistic data, and time series driving data, were obtained for each participant. Following a preliminary screening and cleaning of the data in accordance with Tabachnick and Fidell's [23] recommendations, 12 invalid laps, including laps with zero lap time caused by MoTec disconnection, were omitted from the analysis. We also excluded out laps—the first lap taken after the driver exits the pit lane—and in laps—the laps taken just before the driver returns to the pits, as both are slow laps not representative of the instructed task. A total of 571 laps remained that were subjected to additional criteria for outlier removal using the z-score normalization method [24]. After removing the outliers, 557 laps remained for further analysis. In addition, we did some general descriptive analysis to determine the distribution of data and identify any trends.

Vehicle Control Features, being that all participants used the same car and track, a driver's lap time is a representation of the activities they performed during that lap as well as their driving patterns (braking, throttling, steering, and car speed). Thus, the performance during a lap may be anticipated by evaluating the driving patterns and the driver's behaviour during the lap. Thus, for assessing the driving patterns, which was the main objective of this study, we relied on telemetry data retrieved from MoTec that contained data channels such as speed, RPMS, the steering angle, acceleration, the brake pedal position, and the throttle as a function of the travelled distance in the lap. RPMS describes the engine's rotations per minute and is a function of the gear used by the driver as an indication of when to change gear. Steering angle displays the angle of the steering wheel that is being input into the car at any given time. Lateral acceleration and longitudinal acceleration indicate the level of acceleration of the car in a specific direction, whether longitudinal (forward and backward) or lateral (side to side). More accurately, the higher the longitudinal acceleration, the more extreme acceleration the car has undergone, which means the car has more grip when accelerating [25]. The same can be applied through a corner using the lateral acceleration; the acceleration rate is higher for a car under the absolute limit of cornering grip.

Furthermore, to assess a participant's performance during the session, we obtained new behavioural and car control measures from telemetry data. Based on the steering angle data channel, we defined lane deviation, oversteer, and understeer. Lane deviation is the value of the difference between the car's lateral position and the centre of the lane. Understeer and oversteer are two car control factors, especially in corners. The most common sign of understeer is when the front wheels lose grip due to excessive speed or hard braking through a corner, which can lock the front wheels. The same active variables that contribute to understeer also contribute to oversteer. Oversteer is typically brought on by strong acceleration in a rear-wheel-drive car or braking through a corner [22]. Steering reversal rate is the number of times the driver crossed the centred position of the wheel. Based on brake pedal position, we defined Trail braking application as the percentage of the distance between maximum brake and brake release divided by the length of braking zone. Similarly, we defined throttle release application as the distance covered from throttle application to throttle release.

Time-series telemetry data for each participant were used to produce the measurements for the new metrics and the data channels as well. We employed a sliding window of 200 frames (at a frequency of 50 Hz) for each of the data channels in order to record patterns of such variations in controls, and we then calculated the mean and the standard deviation for those windows. It is worth nothing that we had to apply a custom normalization method to all driver time-series data prior to taking these measurements. Because the number of rows for each lap varies depending on the length of the laps (i.e., a shorter lap has fewer rows in telemetry data), we constructed one row per lap distance indicator by averaging all the data related to that lap distance. Finally, a dataset of 93 time series data files was produced and exported as csv files, each referring to a participant data file that contains all of the participant's valid laps.

3 Results

3.1 Performance Level Analysis

In line with the aim of this study to understand key differences between elite and low skilled racers, we first attempted to categorize the laps into performance levels. To do this, we used a dataset containing 557 laps resulting from the pre-processing step for analyzing performance throughout the course of a lap. We analyzed two K-value selection algorithms, namely the elbow method [26] and Silhouette Coefficient [27], to determine the optimal number of clusters for the data set, then used the k-means method, the most commonly used clustering algorithm in both sport science (e.g., [15, 28]) and research conducted outside of the context of gaming literature [29, 30]. Table 1 presents the results of clustering as well as the statistics of the corresponding groups. The cluster names refer to the lap time, i.e., SLOW points to a low skilled's laptime and FAST points an elite racer's lap time. These clusters give an acceptable model with an accuracy of **81.42%**. Figure 1 shows the distribution of groups using a density plot as well as violin plots displaying the means and distributions within each group. Violin plots display the means and distributions of the two clusters. Wider areas of the violin plot represent a higher density of laps in the cluster for the given value, while a smaller population is represented by smaller sections. Both groups have a normal distribution, as we observe similar mean and median values.

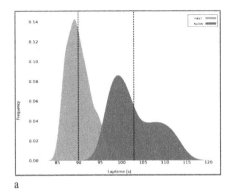 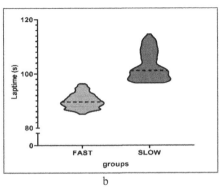

a   b

Fig. 1. Clustering visualization showcasing (a) density plot of lap-time across clusters, each density plot shows the data point's cluster distribution (filled area) and the mean of each cluster data point (vertical dash line). (b) violin plots displaying the means and distributions, within each cluster. The thick line in the centre of each plot represents the median, while the two blue lines represent the interquartile range.

Table 1. Lap time statistics for performance levels for the Brands Hatch track.

Group	Number of laps	mean	std	min	max	median
SLOW	115	102.86	5.09	96.47	114.61	101.16
FAST	441	89.93	2.65	85.04	96.32	89.58

3.2 Driving Patterns Analysis

Using the clustering results, the average of the time series lap data, explained in Sect. 2.2.2, for each metric was calculated for both the slow and fast groups. Figures 2–3 show driving patterns for different metrics for the Brands Haches circuit. They provide a comparison between human driver laps from groups FAST (red) and SLOW (blue). In order to make a better sense of the track, we incorporated section lengths of the track that we obtained from professional drivers. The vertical grey lines in Figs. 2–3 depict the track sections' boundaries. (e.g., S1 and T1 refer to the first straight and turn, respectively). It is clear that all groups of drivers race in the same manner on straight sectors while performing differently in corners. We can identify the distinction between various groups of drivers in terms of vehicle control features. To be more precise, the fast drivers accelerate earlier and more quickly after each corner, with a sharp throttle, higher brakes, and stable steering control. We can also observe how quickly the steering decreases when the throttle is increased in the fast laps. Additionally, how much turning is done while the brakes are fully applied? Moreover, it is obvious that fast drivers have more *throttle release application*, which is the act of applying the throttle more strongly and earlier while releasing the brake later. Similarly, when looking at the brake trace, there is greater *trail braking application* for fast drivers. They reach the peak very quickly, then modulate the brake and release the brake slowly as they get closer to the corner. The brake maximum and median are greater for laps with shorter times. It is interesting to see that the braking and longitudinal acceleration change proportionally for each driver group. However, there is no discernible trend in the acceleration feature (i.e., lateral and longitudinal acceleration).

Looking at Fig. 3, it appears that fast drivers apply a higher amount of steering angle when approaching corners, resulting in more amplitude in lane deviation. Regarding understeering and oversteering, as we observe, fast laps experience *understeer* situations almost twice as often as slow laps, while fast laps have far less *oversteer* than slow laps. While the results indicate greater turning in fast laps, they also imply less normal variation in steering angle.

As we examine the traces in greater detail, we can observe that the beginning part of the track has the most differences between the groups. The difference is more obvious in the first three corners, especially T2, which is kind of a hairpin corner that requires threshold braking in a straight line. Looking at the trace line for both groups, we see that when Fast drivers apply the brakes earlier before the entry of the corner, they trail off just as they begin to turn. They are doing this to aid in the initial rotation of the car and to help them reach the first apex of the corner so they can turn. Thus, the Fast driver keeps a tidier, tighter line through this section and then manages to roll on the throttle a little bit smoother and more consistently than the other one. Looking at T3, we see the Slow drivers get on the brakes earlier and off the throttle earlier than the Fast drivers, ending up with less speed and slowing the corner. Regardless of the big difference in the first section of the track, there is a little variation in the last section of the track (i.e., the last three corners), showing that both groups of drivers got off the throttle at about the same time and used roughly the same amount of brake pressure entering.

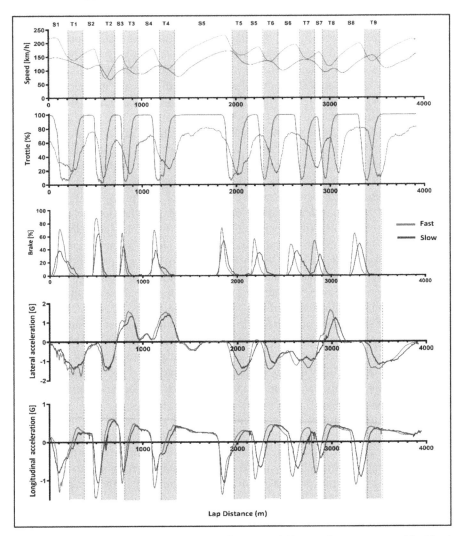

Fig. 2. Different features of driving behaviour for Fast and Slow performance group. The Y-axis (from top to bottom): speed, throttle position, brake position, lateral acceleration, longitudinal acceleration (Color figure online).

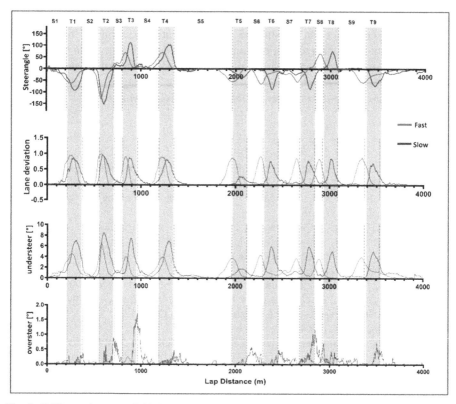

Fig. 3. Different features of driving behaviour for Fast and Slow performance group. The Y-axis (from top to bottom): steering angle, lane deviation, understeer, oversteer.

4 Conclusion

In this work, we provided an AI-enabled solution for analysing driver behaviour in sim racing. Given telemetry data from 93 race drivers, a cluster analysis was used to divide the resulting laps into two groups based on performance (lap-time), and then an in-depth analysis was conducted by defining a set of lap-based metrics derived from telemetry data and examining the car trajectory, steering behaviour, and car control features of different racer groups. From the results, we can conclude that over the course of the whole lap, a higher value of the speed mean, a longer throttle release application, and a higher lane deviation led to a shorter laptime. By deeply analyzing telemetry data for different sections of the track, we were able to determine indicators on how much turning is increased during cornering, how quickly the steering decreases, and how strong acceleration or braking is through a corner. The findings of this research might be used to improve the effectiveness and efficiency of sim racing performance, including software tools to train the drivers and manufacturers to evaluate the configurations and various parameters of the car. Furthermore, the findings from our analysis contribute to a better understanding of the human driver and pave the way to enhance sim racing performance with consideration of elite-racer driving styles.

Our work opens future research directions, including analyzing driving behaviours on various types of tracks and utilising the model to identify the channels that are more challenging to professional racers. Furthermore, time-series telemetry data can be used to forecast several features such as the lap time. The knowledge from this analysis can be transferred to self-driving vehicles to apply reinforcement learning or to offer a technique to enhance their driving style can be applied for self-driving vehicles.

References

1. Lindsey, G.R.: Tatistical data useful for the operation of a baseball team. Oper. Res. **7**(2), 197–207 (1959)
2. Drachen, A., El-Nasr, M.S., Canossa, A.: Game Analytics: Maximizing the Value of Player Data. Springer, London (2013)
3. Schubert, M., Drachen, A., Mahlmann, T.: Esports analytics through encounter detection. In: MIT Sloan Sports Analytics Conference. MIT Sloan (2016)
4. Chu, W.C.-C., et al.: Artificial intelligence of things in sports science: weight training as an example. Computer **52**(11), 52–61 (2019)
5. Roose, K.M., Veinott, E.S.: Leveling up: using the tracer method to address training needs for esports players. In: Proceedings of the Human Factors and Ergonomics Society Annual Meeting. SAGE Publications Sage CA: Los Angeles, CA (2020)
6. Bob, B.: Game Design (2004)
7. Ricmotech. *What is Sim Racing?* (2016). https://www.ricmotech.com/What is Sim Racing s/1553.htm.
8. de Frutos, S.H., Castro, M.: Assessing sim racing software for low-cost driving simulator to road geometric research. Transp. Res. Procedia **58**, 575–582 (2021)
9. Tango, F., et al.: Field tests and machine learning approaches for refining algorithms and correlations of driver's model parameters. Appl. Ergon. **41**(2), 211–224 (2010)
10. Baldisserri, L., et al.: Motorsport driver workload estimation in dual task scenario. In: Sixth International Conference on Advanced Cognitive Technologies and Applications. Citeseer (2014)
11. Tjolleng, A., et al.: Classification of a Driver's cognitive workload levels using artificial neural network on ECG signals. Appl. Ergon. **59**(Pt A), 326–332 (2017)
12. Chihara, T., Kobayashi, F., Sakamoto, J.: Evaluation of mental workload during automobile driving using one-class support vector machine with eye movement data. Appl. Ergon. **89**, 103201 (2020)
13. *vTelemetry PRO*. https://www.renovatio-dev.com/vtelemetry-pro
14. Forum, K.: MoTeC telemetry and dedicated ACC workspace. https://www.assettocorsa.net/forum/index.php?threads/motec-telemetry-and-dedicated-acc-workspace.55103/
15. Remonda, A., Veas, E., Luzhnica, G.: Comparing driving behaviour of humans and autonomous driving in a professional racing simulator. PLoS ONE **16**(2), e0245320 (2021)
16. Sim Racing Telemetry. https://www.simracingtelemetry.com/
17. Constantinescu, Z., Marinoiu, C., Vladoiu, M.: Driving style analysis using data mining techniques. Int. J. Comput. Commun. Control **5**(5), 654–663 (2010)
18. Erséus, A., Driver-vehicle interaction: identification, characterization and modelling of path tracking skill. KTH (2010)
19. Casanova, D., Sharp, R.S., Symonds, P.: On minimum time optimisation of formula one cars: the influence of vehicle mass. Proc. AVEC **2000**, 22–24 (2000)
20. Metz, D., Williams, D.: Near time-optimal control of racing vehicles. Automatica **25**(6), 841–857 (1989)

21. Kegelman, J.C.: Learning from Professional Race Car Drivers to Make Automated Vehicles Safer. Stanford University, Stanford (2018)
22. Bugeja, K., Spina, S., Buhagiar, F.O.: Telemetry-based Optimisation for User Training in Racing Simulators. In: 2017 9th International Conference on Virtual Worlds and Games for Serious Applications (VS-Games). IEEE (2017)
23. Tabachnick, B.G., Fidell, L.S., Ullman, J.B.: Using Multivariate Statistics, vol. 5. Pearson, Boston (2007)
24. Smiti, A.: A critical overview of outlier detection methods. Comput. Sci. Rev. **38**, 100306 (2020)
25. Lopez, C.: Going Faster! Bentley Publishers, Cambridge (1997)
26. Géron, A.: Hands-on Machine Learning with Scikit-Learn, Keras, and TensorFlow: Unsupervised Learning Techniques. O'Reilly Media, Sebastopol (2019)
27. McCallum, A., Nigam, K., Ungar, L.H.: Efficient clustering of high-dimensional data sets with application to reference matching. In: Proceedings of the Sixth ACM SIGKDD International Conference on Knowledge Discovery and Data Mining (2000)
28. Odierna, B.A., Silveira, I.F.: MMORPG player classification using game data mining and k-means. In: Arai, K., Bhatia, R. (eds.) FICC 2019. LNNS, vol. 69, pp. 560–579. Springer, Cham (2020). https://doi.org/10.1007/978-3-030-12388-8_40
29. Abdullah, D., et al.: The application of K-means clustering for province clustering in Indonesia of the risk of the COVID-19 pandemic based on COVID-19 data. Qual. Quant. **56**(3), 1283–1291 (2022)
30. Ashari, I.F., et al.: Application of data mining with the k-means clustering method and davies bouldin index for grouping IMDB movies. J. Appl. Inform. Comput. **6**(1), 07–15 (2022)

The Influence of Personality Traits and Game Design Elements on Player Enjoyment: An Empirical Study on GWAPs for Linguistics

Rosa Lilia Segundo Díaz[1,2](✉)⑩, Gustavo Rovelo[3]⑩, Miriam Bouzouita[4]⑩, Véronique Hoste[2]⑩, and Karin Coninx[1]⑩

[1] HCI and eHealth, Hasselt University, Hasselt, Belgium
`rosalilia.segundodiaz@uhasselt.be`
[2] LT3 Language and Translation Technology Team, Department of Translation, Interpreting and Communication, Ghent University, Ghent, Belgium
[3] Expertise Centre for Digital Media, Hasselt University - tUL - Flanders Make, Hasselt, Belgium
[4] Institut für Romanistik, Humboldt-Universität zu Berlin, Berlin, Germany

Abstract. The present research investigates the effects of Personality Traits (PTs) and Game Design Elements (GDEs) on Player Enjoyment (PE) in the context of serious games. Three Games With A Purpose (GWAPs) were created to revise and correct automatically tagged Parts-of-Speech (PoS) of the *Corpus Oral y Sonoro del Español Rural* (COSER, [5], 'Audible Corpus of Spoken Rural Spanish'), the most extensive collection of spoken dialectal Spanish data. The ultimate goal of the project is to build a morpho-syntactically annotated and parsed corpus of the European Spanish dialects through a crowd-sourced gaming environment, whereby players assign a PoS, i.e., a grammatical category (e.g., verb, noun, adjective, pronoun), to a word in an input text thereby confirming or correcting the automatically tagged PoS. This task has been implemented in three GWAPs: *Agentes*, *Tesoros*, and *Anotatlón*. Each game concept includes a set of GDEs (e.g., rewards, challenges, leaderboards, among others) to investigate their influence on PE. This study, which includes 54 participants, shows associations between PTs and GDEs, and some GDEs yielded a positive correlation with PE. These findings hold the potential to inspire future research and guide the design of future serious games.

Keywords: Serious Games · Games With A Purpose · Game Design Elements · Personality Traits · Player Enjoyment · Part-of-Speech Tagging

1 Introduction

Games With A Purpose (GWAPs) are a subset of serious games that generate, collect, and validate data while people play a game [21]. They constitute a

P. Dondio et al. (Eds.): GALA 2023, LNCS 14475, pp. 204–213, 2024.
https://doi.org/10.1007/978-3-031-49065-1_20

promising approach within Natural Language Processing (NLP) to create large annotated corpora. This approach is more cost and time efficient compared to manual data annotation or other data collection methods (e.g., Mechanical Turk) [3]. Further, they can improve the accuracy of the output thanks to the consensus of multiple players. However, designing a GWAP for linguistics is a challenge because linguistic tasks can be complex, specialised, and tedious, and thus difficult to include in an entertaining game for the player [17]. Therefore, to succeed in creating and annotating corpora, the games' attractiveness must be ensured to engage the crowd and thus get them to contribute to the project. As part of our research, we designed three games to annotate the part-of-speech (PoS) of the COSER corpus (*Corpus Oral y Sonoro del Español Rural*, 'Audible Corpus of Spoken Rural Spanish' [5]), currently the most extensive collection of Spanish oral dialect data. Each game concept integrates different Game Design Elements (GDEs) to increase Player Enjoyment (PE). These variations in the game concepts will, of course, influence how participants perceive them. Hence, the purpose of the current study is to discover which game concept is preferred in terms of PE, and whether links between GDEs and the participants' Personality Traits (PTs) influence that preference.

2   Related Work

Users' motivations for participating in an activity have been linked to human personality. The Big-Five model of personality [11] is one of the most popular models used in game studies and counts with different questionnaires (e.g., [7,9]) to measure the following five PTs: Openness to Experiences, Conscientiousness, Extraversion, Agreeableness, and Neuroticism/Emotional Stability. Openness to Experiences is defined as the tendency to generate new ideas and follow different values. Conscientiousness involves planning and organising tasks. Extraversion implies the search for new opportunities. Agreeableness is defined as helping others and expecting help in return. Finally, Neuroticism/Emotional Stability concerns the degree to manage fear, sadness, and stress. This model has been used to clarify how the game affects different groups of players or how players perceive them and have an effect on PE, which has been described as the positive experience that players undergo during a gaming session [2]. PE has been recognised as a crucial game aspect that not only motivates players [13], but is decisive in sustaining their interest in the game [1]. For games used in crowdsourcing, where all types of players might initially be attracted to participate, it is challenging to please every possible player. Therefore, to provide a more general approach to create PE for most players, we need also to understand the links between the GDEs and PTs and their effects on PE.

Previous studies have demonstrated interesting relationships between GDEs and PTs. Jia et al. [10] presented demo videos of the GDEs for the participants to evaluate. They found that people with high Conscientiousness perceive progress and levels to be very motivating factors. People that are more extravert find their motivation in leaderboards and levels, whereas players with lower Emotional Stability scores consider rewards and badges more enjoyable. Nagle et al. [14]

used a custom-made first-person shooter game to evaluate four conditions for difficulty adaptation: (1) Dynamic Difficulty Adjustment (DDA), (2) Plateau, (3) Reverse, and (4) Rest. While DDA intends to adjust the difficulty based on player skill, Plateau, Reverse, and Rest adhere to a specific difficulty curve. Their findings revealed links between the difficulty conditions and PTs, which in turn contributed to moderate PE levels. Tondello and Nacke [20] investigated the effects of a personalised online gameful application to classify images, whereby participants interact with a customised (selected GDEs) or generic (no selection of GDEs) version of the app. They found significant unexpected correlations between PTs and GDEs. In the context of linguistic GWAPs, which aim is to reach a specific scientific goal and not only to offer a personalised experience, the relationship between PTs and GDEs may help to design games for a broad audience. However, those relationships are still unexplored. There is no evidence of whether the participants' PTs and perception of certain GDEs influence the level of PE when the same linguistic task is presented in different game concepts. Thus, this study aims to evaluate three GWAP concepts to explore potential correlations between PTs and the implemented GDEs that influence the PE levels.

3   Methodology

This study aims to test how participants with different PTs perceive PE when different GDEs are implemented in a GWAP context. Participants were split into three groups to evaluate two game concepts. The decision to separate participants this way was taken to avoid biases due to the fatigue of performing more than two playing and evaluating sessions. Additionally, for each group, the order of the games was reversed for half of the players to ensure equal weight for each game and prevent the order from affecting the results. The play session was a free-playing session that lasted about 15 min. After this, participants evaluated their perceptions of the game by answering two questionnaires. The following paragraphs describe the games used for the study, the participants, and the evaluation instruments.

3.1   GWAPs and Game Design Elements

Three game concepts (see Fig. 1) were designed to incorporate the PoS tagging task, whereby the player assigns a morpho-syntactic category (e.g., verb, noun, adjective, pronoun, among others) to a word in order to confirm or correct the automatically assigned tags. The web-based, single-player games are presented in a training and playing mode. Both modes have the same mechanics, showing a highlighted word together with random categories of the Universal Dependencies (UD) [15] including the automatically annotated category. Similar to Phrase Detectives [4] and Zombilingo [6], the training mode was designed to familiarise players with the games and the complex task of assigning a grammatical category. The training mode is essential given that not all UD tags might be familiar

Fig. 1. Screenshots of the three GWAPs.

to non-linguist players, e.g., a determiner is not a tag commonly taught during education, but an article is. In addition, the training also helps the players remember the grammatical terminology of the categories (e.g., adverb) that they learned at one point but might have forgotten. Once the player completes the training, the playing mode is activated, and participants start helping with the confirmation or correction of tags. In **Agentes**, players must drag highlighted words to the corresponding grammatical categories (e.g., verb, noun, etc.) that are randomly positioned around the sentence in order to annotate the word in question. **Tesoros** is a platform game that aims to give more sense of progress and achievement to the player by building a path where an avatar can walk, collect coins and win a treasure chest at the end of the path. After the player annotates the word, the avatar moves automatically. **Anotatlón** is a race car game that aims to give more control to the players: they can move a car to avoid obstacles and at the end of the track they choose a PoS. Also, the level of game difficulty can be adapted. Four GDEs have been implemented in all games, namely leaderboards, levels, rewards, and theme, as they can contribute positively to the PE [19]. In order to increase the PE levels of each game further, other GDEs have also been implemented, as shown in Fig. 2: these include storyline, adaptation, and customisation.

Fig. 2. Implemented GDEs per GWAP.

3.2   Participants

54 participants (30 males, 24 females) took part in the study, who were recruited via convenience sampling through the researchers' professional networks. 42 participants were native Spanish speakers, while 12 were proficient. They were randomly assigned to one of the three groups (n = 18 in each), where they played

and evaluated two games (group A: Agentes-Tesoros; B: Agentes-Anotatlón; C: Tesoros-Anotatlón). Thus, each game was played by 36 participants.

3.3   Measurement

Standardised and custom-designed questionnaires were used as instruments in the formal experiment with the three designed GWAPs. The **Ten-Item Personality Inventory** (TIPI) consists of 10 questions to measure the Big-Five PTs. This instrument provides a brief measure with still adequate levels of reliability [9]. The **Intrinsic Motivation Inventory** (IMI, [12]) is a well-established and thoroughly tested questionnaire used to assess the subjective experience of intrinsic motivation to play a game. IMI helps to measure needs satisfaction and to evaluate dimensions of intrinsic motivation, such as Interest/Enjoyment (PE)[1] [18]. The **Custom Designed Questionnaire** is used to obtain the players' perceptions on the GWAPs they played. The questions target two levels: the implementation of GDEs and the preferred/favourite GDEs. First, players evaluated the extent to which they feel that the GDE is implemented. Note that the players can select the option "Does not apply" if they consider that the element is not implemented. Second, participants were asked to sort the GDEs from most to least favourite by dragging them to the desired position in a ranking, whereby position one corresponded to the most favourite and ten to the least. GDEs previously marked as not implemented were not shown in this ranking.

4   Personality Traits, Game Design Elements and Player Enjoyment

This study was designed to evaluate how players' PTs influence PE when various GDEs are implemented. Analysis of the experimental data yielded the following.

As shown in the upper part of Table 1, no significant differences were found between the three GWAPs for the PTs: the mean value for Agreeableness in Anotatlón's participants is closest to being significantly different, especially as Agentes and Tesoros exhibit the same mean value for this PT ($Mean = 5.35$). Given this result, we will focus now on the distribution of the players' PTs per GWAP. More specifically, in the % column, the proportion of participants with medium-high and high scores for the PT are provided, which are calculated using the norms of the bottom part of Table 1 where the ranges for the low, medium-low, medium-high, and high values are given [8]. Whereas Extraversion, Conscientiousness, Emotional Stability, and Openness to Experiences present similar proportions of players with medium-high and high scores in the three GWAPs, the same cannot be said for Agreeableness: in Anotatlón 78% is recorded while in Tesoros and Agentes only 53%. Other PTs with a high percentage are Openness to Experiences (61%) in both Agentes and Anotatlón, as well as Emotional

---

[1] In this study, the terms 'Interest/Enjoyment' and 'PE' are used interchangeably since the former serves as a measure for the latter.

Table 1. Top table: descriptive statistics of participants' PTs per GWAP. Bottom table: norms used to identify whether a PT is low, medium-low, medium-high or high.

Personality Trait	All GWAPs		Agentes			Tesoros			Anotatlón		
	Mean	SD	Mean	SD	%	Mean	SD	%	Mean	SD	%
Extraversion	3.90	1.31	4.03	1.32	33%	3.90	1.37	36%	3.76	1.24	31%
Agreeableness	5.51	0.99	5.35	1.01	53%	5.35	0.98	53%	5.83	0.91	78%
Conscientiousness	5.27	1.10	5.32	1.07	53%	5.24	1.09	50%	5.25	1.15	53%
Emotional Stability	4.97	1.26	4.82	1.33	56%	4.99	1.25	56%	5.11	1.20	61%
Openness	5.47	0.89	5.51	0.81	61%	5.38	0.94	56%	5.53	0.91	61%
Personality Trait	Norms										
	Low		Medium-Low			Medium-High			High		
Extraversion	[0.0, 2.99)		[2.99, 4.44)			[4.44, 5.89)			[5.89, 7]		
Agreeableness	[0.0, 4.12)		[4.12, 5.23)			[5.23, 6.34)			[6.34, 7]		
Conscientiousness	[0.0, 4.08)		[4.08, 5.40)			[5.40, 6.72)			[6.72, 7]		
Emotional Stability	[0.0, 3.41)		[3.41, 4.83)			[4.83, 6.25)			[6.25, 7]		
Openness	[0.0, 4.31)		[4.31, 5.38)			[5.38, 6.45)			[6.45, 7]		

Stability (61%) for the latter. Interestingly, Extraversion is a minor PT among participants of these three GWAPs (around a third of participants per game).

As for the interplay between PTs and PE, for Tesoros, a positive correlation exists between Emotional Stability ($r = .47, p < .05$) and PE. Its players showed at least medium-high values for this PT. A possible explanation for this result might be that Tesoros reflects some of the characteristics that are associated to this PT, e.g., being relaxed, not anxious, not moody, not easily upset, and not easily stressed [9]. Agentes shows a negative correlation with Conscientiousness ($r = -.38, p < .05$) as participants with higher Conscientiousness scores displayed lower PE levels. One possible explanation could be that, as progress indicators were not implemented in this GWAP, players were less stimulated, following Jia et al. [10] who observed that the sense of progress can motivate people with high Conscientiousness. Therefore, adding the GDE progress to the game could encourage more PE. For Anotatlón, no significant correlations were found.

4.1 Player Enjoyment and Perceptions on GDE Implementation

Participants who played Anotatlón presented the highest PE ($Mean = 5.46, SD = 1.15$), followed by Tesoros ($Mean = 5.18, SD = 1.30$), and Agentes ($Mean = 4.49, SD = 1.5$). Correlations between PE and the player perceptions on GDE implementation have also been tested. The four shared GDEs (bolded in Table 2) were identified as implemented in the three GWAPs. In Agentes, positive correlations between PE and three GDEs were documented: challenges, levels, and theme. Tesoros was associated with higher PE for six GDEs: adaption, challenges, customisation, levels, rewards, and theme. Anotatlón showed correlations between PE and four GDEs: challenges, customisation, leaderboards, and levels. In other words, challenges and levels are positively linked to PE in the three GWAPs, whereas theme only for two GWAPs (Agentes-Tesoros). Recall that challenges, in contrast to levels was, in fact, not implemented in Agentes (see Fig. 2), though players perceived it as such. Similarly, customisation, despite not being implemented in Tesoros, yielded a positive correlation with PE for this GWAP. Of the other shared GDEs, rewards was positively linked to PE in Tesoros, while leaderboards in Anotatlón.

Table 2. Descriptive statistics and correlation matrix between perceptions on GDEs and PE, and perceptions on GDEs and PTs. *: $p < .05$; **: $p < .01$; ***: $p < .001$.

GDE	Agentes			Tesoros					Anotatlón				
	Mean	SD	PE	Mean	SD	PE	A	ES	Mean	SD	PE	E	O
Adaptation	6.97	2.34		**7.61**	2.37	0.49 **			7.53	2.20			
Avatar	2.74	2.49		6.72	2.95				6.05	3.55			
Challenges	**7.43**	2.13	0.36 *	7.31	2.24	0.57 ***			**7.91**	2.08	0.60 ***		
Customisation	3.29	2.88		5.00	3.56	0.46 *			8.03	2.99	0.41 *		
Leaderboards	**7.91**	1.84		7.47	2.57				7.75	2.41	0.37 *		
Levels	**7.15**	2.58	0.45 **	7.31	2.84	0.60 ***			7.40	2.78	0.36 *	-0.35 *	
Progress	5.88	3.09		7.57	2.68		0.48 **		6.50	3.06		-0.35 *	
Rewards	6.89	2.76		**8.69**	1.72	0.36 *			**8.39**	1.68		-0.39 *	0.44 **
Storyline	5.58	2.88		5.11	2.59				4.53	2.84			
Theme	6.47	2.55	0.42 *	**7.69**	2.10	0.56 ***		0.45 **	7.29	2.97			

The correlations between player perceptions on GDE implementation and players' PTs have also been analysed: few significant relationships have been found, as shown in Table 2, which only shows the significant results. For Agentes, no significant correlations between PTs and GDEs were found. In contrast, for Tesoros, Agreeableness (A) presents a positive correlation with progress: more precisely, in this GWAP all participants have at least medium-high scores for this PT and they appear to have a predilection for this GDE. This is in line with Park et al. [16], who found a link between this PT and achievement. Nonetheless, it contradicts the claims of Jia et al. [10], who suggest that low or high Agreeableness scores do not influence the preference for specific GDEs. Note that the preference for this GDE is not positively linked to PE. A positive correlation between Emotional Stability (ES) and theme is also found for Tesoros. Contrarily to Agreeableness and progress, there is a highly significant correlation between this PT-GDE pair and PE. In Anotatlón, negative correlations were found between Extraversion (E) and levels, progress, and rewards. This could suggest a weak link between this PT and the sense of achievement that these GDEs provide. As for the positive correlation between Openness to Experiences (O) and rewards, it is known that people with this PT prefer a balance between seeking challenges and building skills [14]. This could suggest that the received rewards have been perceived as the consequence of newly acquired skills that help the players face the challenge.

Table 3. Descriptive statistics and correlation matrix between GDE preferences and PE and between GDE preferences and PTs. *: $p < .05$; **: $p < .01$; ***: $p < .001$.

GDE	All GWAPs			Agentes		Tesoros				Anotatlón			
	Mean	SD	PE	Mean	SD	Mean	SD	PE	C	Mean	SD	PE	E
Adaptation	**3.80**	2.29		**3.44**	2.16	**4.06**	2.46			**3.89**	2.26		
Avatar	6.44	2.90		8.05	1.99	5.69	2.88			6.10	3.16		
Challenges	**3.24**	1.94		**3.40**	1.82	**3.28**	1.88			**3.03**	2.16		
Customisation	6.68	2.63		7.10	2.30	7.45	2.54			5.83	2.76		
Leaderboards	5.79	2.31	0.33***	5.23	2.35	6.22	2.40	0.40 *		5.89	2.14	0.38 *	
Levels	4.66	2.13		4.59	2.30	4.81	2.18		0.47 **	4.60	1.97		0.43 **
Progress	5.78	1.98		5.76	1.69	5.43	2.17			6.15	2.02		
Rewards	4.59	2.33		5.37	2.28	4.42	2.32			**4.00**	2.26		
Storyline	6.62	3.11		5.24	3.39	7.41	2.44			7.79	2.70		
Theme	**4.20**	2.88		**4.03**	2.97	**4.00**	2.86			4.57	2.84		

4.2   Player Enjoyment and GDE Preferences

GDE preferences, as well as the correlations between these and PE, and between GDE preferences and PTs have also been tested. The more preferred GDEs, which have lower means, are shown in bold in Table 3. Note also that the ranking question only included those GDEs considered by the players to be present. Challenges, adaptation, and theme are the most preferred GDEs generally. Leaderboards was the only one that correlates very significantly with PE overall, while a positive link is also observed for Tesoros and Anotatlón. As concerns each of the GWAPs, adaptation and challenges are the two GDEs that were the most preferred in each of the three GWAPs. Interestingly, both were not implemented in Agentes (see Fig. 2). No GDE correlated significantly with PE for Agentes. Of the four shared GDEs, theme is one of the more preferred GDEs for Agentes and Tesoros, rewards for Anotatlón, whereas levels and leaderboards were not selected among the more preferred GDEs. The least liked GDEs are (1) avatar in Agentes, (2) storyline in Anotatlón and Tesoros, and (3) customisation in Tesoros and Agentes. As concerns GDE preferences and the players' PTs, Agentes does not present any correlations. For Tesoros, a strong positive correlation between Conscientiousness (C) and levels is observed and for Anotatlón between Extraversion (E) and levels.

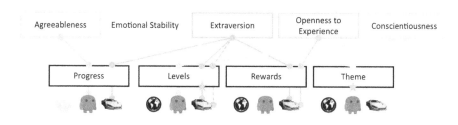

Fig. 3. Links between PTs, GDEs, and PE.

5   Conclusions

Despite the small sample, some associations between PTs and GDEs have been found, as illustrated in Fig. 3, where solid lines represent GDE implementation, dotted ones preferred GDEs, and stars links with PE. As for PTs and GDE implementation, (1) Agreeableness is associated with progress in Tesoros, (2) Emotional Stability with theme in Tesoros, (3) Extraversion is negatively correlated to levels, progress, and rewards in Anotatlón, (4) and Openness to Experiences positively with rewards in Anotatlón. Additionally, as concerns perceptions on GDE implementation and PE, Tesoros presents the most positive correlations between PE and the implemented GDEs (adaption, challenges, levels, rewards, and theme), ranking this GWAP in second place. Anotatlón had overall the highest PE values and was thus the favourite game. We conclude that PE plays a role in GWAPs' preference, whether considering the entire game or individual GDEs. As for GDE preferences, overall challenges, adaptation, and theme were the most preferred ones. Leaderboards correlated positively with PE overall and in Tesoros and Anotatlón (but not in Agentes). Levels was associated with the PT of Conscientiousness in Tesoros and Extraversion in Anotatlón.

More extensive studies with larger samples, longer playing sessions, and which explore other factors are recommended to shed more light on the precise relationship between PTs, GDEs and PE.

Acknowledgements. This research is part of the project 'A (Respeaking and) Collaborative Game-Based Approach to Building a Parsed Corpus of European Spanish Dialects' funded by the Flemish Research Fund (FWO; I000418N; PI: M. Bouzouita; 2018–2023).

References

1. Boyle, E.A., Connolly, T.M., Hainey, T., Boyle, J.M.: Engagement in digital entertainment games: a systematic review. Comput. Hum. Behav. **28**(3), 771–780 (2012). https://doi.org/10.1016/j.chb.2011.11.020
2. Caroux, L., Isbister, K., Le Bigot, L., Vibert, N.: Player-video game interaction: a systematic review of current concepts. Comput. Hum. Behav. **48**(C), 366–381 (2015). https://doi.org/10.1016/j.chb.2015.01.066
3. Chamberlain, J., Fort, K., Kruschwitz, U., Lafourcade, M., Poesio, M.: Using games to create language resources: successes and limitations of the approach. In: Gurevych, I., Kim, J. (eds.) The People's Web Meets NLP. TANLP, pp. 3–44. Springer, Heidelberg (2013). https://doi.org/10.1007/978-3-642-35085-6_1
4. Chamberlain, J., et al.: Phrase detectives: a web-based collaborative annotation game. In: Proceedings of the International Conference on Semantic Systems (I-Semantics 2008), pp. 42–49. Verlag der Technischen Universität Graz, Graz (2008)
5. Fernández-Ordóñez, I.: Corpus Oral y Sonoro del Español Rural (2005-present). http://www.corpusrural.es. Aaccessed 20 Sept 2023
6. Fort, K., Guillaume, B., Chastant, H.: Creating zombilingo, a game with a purpose for dependency syntax annotation. In: ACM International Conference Proceeding Series, pp. 2–6. Association for Computing Machinery, New York (2014). https://doi.org/10.1145/2594776.2594777

7. Goldberg, L.R.: The development of markers for the big-five factor structure. Psychol. Assess. **4**, 26–42 (1992)
8. Gosling, S.D., Rentfrow, P.J., Potter, J.: Norms for the ten item personality inventory. Unpublished data (2014)
9. Gosling, S.D., Rentfrow, P.J., Swann, W.B.: A very brief measure of the Big-Five personality domains. J. Res. Pers. **37**(6), 504–528 (2003). https://doi.org/10.1016/S0092-6566(03)00046-1
10. Jia, Y., Xu, B., Karanam, Y., Voida, S.: Personality, targeted gamification: a survey study on personality traits and motivational affordances. In: Conference on Human Factors in Computing Systems - Proceedings (CHI 2016), pp. 2001–2013. Association for Computing Machinery, New York (2016). https://doi.org/10.1145/2858036.2858515
11. John, O.P., Srivastava, S.: The Big Five trait taxonomy: history, measurement, and theoretical perspectives. Handb. Personal. Theory Res. **2**(510), 102–138 (1999)
12. McAuley, E.D., Duncan, T., Tammen, V.V.: Psychometric properties of the intrinsic motivation inventory in a competitive sport setting: a confirmatory factor analysis. Res. Q. Exerc. Sport **60**(1), 48–58 (1989). https://doi.org/10.1080/02701367.1989.10607413
13. Mekler, E.D., Bopp, J.A., Tuch, A.N., Opwis, K.: A systematic review of quantitative studies on the enjoyment of digital entertainment games. In: Conference on Human Factors in Computing Systems - Proceedings, pp. 927–936. Association for Computing Machinery, New York (2014). https://doi.org/10.1145/2556288.2557078
14. Nagle, A., Wolf, P., Riener, R.: Towards a system of customized video game mechanics based on player personality: relating the Big Five personality traits with difficulty adaptation in a first-person shooter game. Entertain. Comput. **13**, 10–24 (2016). https://doi.org/10.1016/j.entcom.2016.01.002
15. Nivre, J., et al.: Universal dependencies v2: an evergrowing multilingual treebank collection. In: Proceedings of The 12th Language Resources and Evaluation Conference, pp. 4034–4043. European Language Resources Association, Marseille (May 2020). https://www.aclweb.org/anthology/2020.lrec-1.497
16. Park, J., Song, Y., Teng, C.I.: Exploring the links between personality traits and motivations to play online games. Cyberpsychol. Behav. Soc. Netw. **14**(12), 747–751 (2011). https://doi.org/10.1089/cyber.2010.0502
17. Poesio, M., Chamberlain, J., Kruschwitz, U.: Crowdsourcing. In: Ide, N., Pustejovsky, J. (eds.) Handbook of Linguistic Annotation, pp. 277–295. Springer, Dordrecht (2017). https://doi.org/10.1007/978-94-024-0881-2_10
18. Ryan, R.M., Mims, V., Koestner, R.: Relation of reward contingency and interpersonal context to intrinsic motivation: a review and test using cognitive evaluation theory. J. Pers. Soc. Psychol. **45**(4), 736–750 (1983). https://doi.org/10.1037/0022-3514.45.4.736
19. Segundo Díaz, R.L., Rovelo Ruiz, G., Bouzouita, M., Coninx, K.: Building blocks for creating enjoyable games-a systematic literature review. Int. J. Hum Comput Stud. **159**, 102758 (2022). https://doi.org/10.1016/j.ijhcs.2021.102758
20. Tondello, G.F., Nacke, L.E.: Validation of user preferences and effects of personalized gamification on task performance. Front. Comput. Sci. **2**, 29 (2020). https://doi.org/10.3389/fcomp.2020.00029
21. Von Ahn, L., Dabbish, L.: Designing games with a purpose. Commun. ACM **51**(8), 58–67 (2008). https://doi.org/10.1145/1378704.1378719

UX and Serious Games—A Research Agenda

Gerda Huber[1]([✉]) [iD] and David Rückel[1,2]([✉]) [iD]

[1] Department of Computer Sciences, University of Applied Sciences Technikum Wien,
Höchstädtplatz 6, 1200 Wien, Austria
{huberg,rueckel}@technikum-wien.at
[2] Institute of Business Informatics - Information Engineering, Johannes Kepler University Linz,
Altenberger Straße 69, 4040 Linz, Austria

Abstract. User experience (UX) research entails the research and design processes of all user experiences with a product, while serious games have been increasingly gaining importance to facilitate otherwise unappealing or tedious activities in education, health, or business contexts. The players, their willingness to play the game, and the games' effects on them are crucial in the design and development of games and serious games. The established concepts and methods for research and design of user experience constitute a reasonable starting point for locating methods to employ when designing and developing serious games. To identify gaps and form a research agenda, we adopted grounded theory-based literature review as a method to research the current state of UX concept integration in serious games' development. While integrating evaluation methods is well under-way, there is still significant unfulfilled potential around user research and design. In particular, lacking awareness of existing research concepts and methods poses a significant hurdle.

Keywords: User Experience · Usability · Serious Games · Gamification · Research Agenda

1 Introduction

The use of serious games or gamification in an organizational context has been increasing for years, ranging from individual or organizational development to teaching, learning, or steering measures to change the behavior of individuals or groups [1]. Conferences or conference tracks with corresponding goals indicate this phenomenon. In practice, the focus on serious games or gamification is often more on software products or components of software products intended for this purpose than on broader or non-digital concepts. Methods applied consistently producing software products are subsumed under the term user experience (research)—UX for short— and may find applications in other disciplines or areas. According to the definition given in ISO 9241 [2], UX deals with all aspects of anticipated, actual, and previous interaction with a system product or service, and UX methodology aims to create systems, products, or services that support the users and help them fulfill their goals.

P. Dondio et al. (Eds.): GALA 2023, LNCS 14475, pp. 214–222, 2024.
https://doi.org/10.1007/978-3-031-49065-1_21

UX has high importance in designing and implementing serious games and gamification. Research in this area starts from the fundamental position that as the application domain approaches the human individual or group, the importance of using methods from UX increases. The skills commonly associated with creating serious games are (1) game design/development, (2) domain knowledge, (3) teaching skills, (4) software design and development, and (5) UX engineering [3]. Based on an initial exploratory literature search, the literature attempting to combine the concepts of serious gaming or gamification and UX research seems relatively sparse. We found no literature covering the overall integration of UX and serious games development.

Consequently, a merging of academic concepts may not yet exist. We derive our research goal from this research gap, laying the groundwork for a research agenda based on the state of research integrating UX methods and approaches into the de-sign and development of serious games and an analysis of the methods and approaches. We derive the following research questions from this background:

(1) What is the state of the field toward the integration of UX methods and concepts in the design and development of serious games?
(2) Which UX methods and approaches are applied?
(3) What elements could be part of a future research question?

The next chapter of the paper introduces the methodology applied to answering these questions. In Sect. 3 we introduce the main concepts discussed in the selected articles. Section 4 details the facts we determined when analyzing the articles, followed by interpretation of these facts in Sect. 5. Section 6 presents the derived research agenda and Sect. 7 the limitations to our findings.

2 Methodology

To answer the research questions proposed above, we applied a structured literature review [4] based on a grounded theory approach [5]. Common databases, ACM Digital Library (ACM), SpringerLink (SL), ScienceDirect (SD), IEEE Explore (IEEE), the Directory of Open Access Journals (DOAJ), and Hindawi, were systematically searched prior to the conference submission deadline to find the overlap between methods and concepts used in UX and methods and terminology geared toward users and their experience in serious game development. The phrases "user experience" AND "serious games" served as search terms without restriction on dates or locations within the content, leading to an initial search result of 2319 scientific articles: ACM: 385; SL: 1253; SD: 462; IEEE: 138; DOAJ: 48; Hindawi: 33.

Next, titles and abstracts were scanned; only papers that discuss the methods used in the development of the games or gamified applications that come from a catalog of methods used in UX (e.g., field studies, persona building, journey mapping, usability testing) or that do literature reviews regarding the use of methods from the field of UX research were considered. Direct applications of methods were excluded. Several papers deal with gamification instead of serious games; these were included, as gamification is often used synonymously with the term "serious games," even if that is not strictly correct. This step led to the following 101 remaining results: ACM: 34; SL: 46; SD: 5;

IEEE: 5; DOAJ: 3; Hindawi: 8. The next step was to analyze the content to find papers that discuss methods used in the development of the games that come from the methods used in UX or do literature reviews regarding the use of methods from UX research. The language was limited to English or German. This step led to the final total of 57 articles, divided among the following: ACM: 17; SL: 30; SD: 5; IEEE: 2; DOAJ: 1; Hindawi: 3.

Due to space restrictions within this publication, we did not include the complete list of articles within the reference section. However, we published a cloud-hosted document with information for all 57 included articles (including publication year, author, and title; listed in ascending order by publication year)[1]. We reference these articles in the results section with the row number and the prefix A set in parentheses; (A_3) would thus reference the article in row 3 of the results list.

After analysis of the articles we categorized the findings cooperatively, which led to the proposed research questions.

3 Concepts

As a topic, serious games have been gaining relevance in recent years. Although the selected literature did not offer a universal definition for them, the consensus is that serious games have a purpose beyond entertainment, which may include education, physical or mental training, and attitudinal or behavioral change. Whether board games, role-playing games, or diverse digital games, these serious games are still developed using game elements and design methods.

The community has agreed on the definition of gamification presented by Deterding [6]: "Using game design elements in non-game contexts to motivate and increase user activity and retention." Crucially, however, the resulting product is not a game. It may instead be an exercise, application, or process that utilizes game elements. Of course, the precise distinction between a game and a gamified application may be blurred in certain instances.

According to Juul, "A game is a rule-based formal system with a variable and quantifiable outcome, where different outcomes are assigned different values, the player exerts effort in order to influence the outcome, the player feels attached to the outcome, and the consequences of the activity are optional and negotiable" [7]. Thus, games are distinguishable from play, which is rule-free, spontaneous, and improvisational [8]. Formalism implies that identifiable elements exist that form a game or can be used for gamification that can be considered building blocks of games. No single one is necessary for a game, but they are usually associated with gaming. Such game elements may include narrative context, avatars, time constraints, achievements, and unlockable content. However, actual classifications vary [6, 9–12].

Games, serious games, and gamified applications each target an audience of users, whether to entertain, educate, train, or meet many of those goals at once. The field of human-computer interaction has long examined how applications can interact with users to optimally support them in reaching their goals or performing their tasks. Through this research, scholars and designers have developed the terms "usability" and "user

---

[1] https://docs.google.com/spreadsheets/d/1Js4mNMKRhg2xlXwsjHc6ZALzVZNcA5g4Du-l4YAH4-E/edit?usp=sharing.

experience" and outlined the human-centered design process to ensure that users are considered and included in the design and development of applications. One product of this discussion is ISO 9241, "Ergonomics of Human-System-Interaction," where the relevant definitions for the following terms can be found.

Usability is the "extent to which a system, product, or service can be used by specified users to achieve specified goals with effectiveness, efficiency, and satisfaction in a specified context of use" [13]. Usability is tied to the actual use of a product, system, or service; to optimize it, we must know who the users are (e.g., demographics, previous knowledge, experience), what they want to accomplish with the product, and where they are going to use it (e.g., environment, stress, noise, and light conditions, criticality, devices). The product has to be designed so that the goals are reached (effectiveness) efficiently (i.e., with the least possible use of resources) and satisfactorily. The importance of those three constraints varies by application. Efficiency is crucial in an often-used system (e.g., a cash register), whereas satisfaction is more relevant in entertainment (e.g., music streaming).

User experience is defined as a "person's perceptions and responses resulting from the use and/or anticipated use of a product, system or service," [2] implying that everything concerning that product, system, or service contributes to a user's experience—hearing about it, searching for it, seeing advertisements, or otherwise encountering it, and then acquiring it, installing or unpacking it, using it, and thinking and communicating about it after use. Therefore, usability is a distinct part of the user experience.

ISO 9241–210 presents the human-centered design process: an iterative process that involves researching the context of use (users, scenarios, goals, environment), deriving requirements from that research, designing solutions based on the requirements, and evaluating the solutions. Human-centered designers run evaluations to discern errors made in previous steps and revisit them as needed (iteration). Here, a fundamental concept is the inclusion of end-users as much as possible. This process must be integrated into actual development processes to facilitate user-centricity in product development.

The community is aware of these developments, and some researchers have sought to implement these concepts and processes. However, such implementations have generally dealt with various discrete applications, from flight control to radiology equipment operation, speech-controlled devices, and much more. When applying the above-outlined concepts to games, serious games, or gamification, one's focus must narrow to reflect the characteristics of such applications.

One such distinction lies in the purpose of games, including serious games. For example, one study noted that "in contrast to the productivity-focused roots of HCI [human computer interaction], digital games have traditionally been designed to entertain" [14]. Still, although the satisfaction dimension's importance is high among all applications, UX cannot be reduced to emphasizing "fun" as a concept, as observed with player frustration or stress from challenges. Fun and challenges are each essential game elements in keeping the player interested, even if some elements must be eliminated due to bad interface or design decisions [15].

Another term to carefully consider is efficiency. Users expect to fail in a game and adopt different approaches to reach a goal—they would likely consider a game boring without challenges.

Finally, errors must be placed in context. When they occur within the game, they may be expected (e.g., failing in a mission due to unsuitable tactics) and ascribed to game difficulty. However, when a save of the game fails due to bad interface design, the design must be reconsidered: "According to a more careful definition of error, game interfaces should be as error-free as productivity software interfaces" [16].

4   Results

Of the 57 selected articles, 21 contained literature reviews; all used multiple libraries or journals as **resources**. Most searched ACM Digital Library and IEEE Explore (about 70% consulted one of each, but not always both), followed by ScienceDirect (about 40%) and Scopus (about 40%). Springer Link, Google Scholar, and Web of Science each were accessed by about 30% of the literature reviews. Ten additional resources were used once or twice. The research topics ranged from very specific—researching guidelines for measuring the usability of educational video games for smartphones (A_ 36) or researching which methods have been employed to evaluate games for computing education (A_ 27)—to broad-based overviews regarding methods (A_ 29), (A_ 43), (A_ 49), and (A_ 56).

Publication years of all articles ranged from 2009 to 2023. A peak was reached in 2017 with nine articles. Twentynine articles were published in the following years.

The **authors' analysis** shows the following result: The average number of authors is 3.44 (median: 3; SD: 1.96), the minimum is 1, and the maximum is 11. The authors are associated on average with 1.84 affiliations (median: 2; SD: 1.06), the minimum is again 1, and the maximum is 6. The affiliations are divided, on average, into 1.33 nations, with a median of 1, a standard deviation of 0.71, a minimum of 1, and a maximum of 4. A closer look at the 23 participating nations shows that 42% of the participating institutions are from Europe, just under 23% from South America, 14% from North America, 12% from Asia, 5% from Australia-Oceania, and just under 4% from African nations. The nations with the most participating authorships are Brazil (9), Spain (8), Germany (6), the USA (6), and finally, Great Britain and Australia (3).

There was little **cross-referencing** within the 57 results. An article by Deterding et al. [6] that proposes a definition for gamification and discusses the distinctions between games, serious games, and gamification was cited eight times. Next is an article by Moreno-Ger et al. [15] that presents an adapted method for user testing, cited twice. Four other articles were cited once each: one presenting a framework for serious game design and development (A_ 9), one detailing the elements of user experience in educational games (A_ 14), one presenting the methods used in the usability evaluation of serious games (A_ 29), and one about a framework for serious educational games (A_ 34).

Among the sample, reliance on **definitions or standards** was infrequent. ISO 9241 was referenced in 11 articles, three articles referenced ISO 25000 Software-Engineering – Quality Requirements and Evaluation (SQuaRE), and three references cited its predecessor, ISO 9126, which was replaced by ISO 25000 in 2011 and later withdrawn. The most frequently defined terms were "serious game" (13 times), "usability" (10 times), "UX" (9 times), and gamification (8 times) out of 14 total defined terms. The other definitions occurred no more than twice; no work offered more than four definitions. Twenty-one articles offered no definitions.

User experience or UX is mentioned in 20 of the articles (in some of these papers, the term "player experience" is used; as it is not well-defined, we merged the findings under the term UX). One article (A_ 34) describes it as based on two elements, the graphic interface and the interaction experienced through it. Two articles—(A_ 15) and (A_ 26)—directly link UX to the interaction. (A_ 25) describes its research as an ill-defined field; eight articles, (A_ 6), (A_ 12), (A_ 26), (A_ 27), (A_ 32), (A_ 43), (A_ 57), and (A_ 58), list components or evaluation factors.

The **evaluation** of games and serious games predominates as a topic, with 34 of the selected articles pertaining to it. Ten of them are literature reviews. The most used method for evaluating games, serious games, or gamified applications is play-testing, where persons from the target group play a version of the game. The chosen method for gathering relevant data is through post-test questionnaires. Sometimes, interviews or observation (data tracking, thinking-aloud) are employed during the test. The questionnaires may be ad-hoc or one of a considerable number of standardized questionnaires. SUS, or System Usability Scale, was mentioned in four works, followed by UEQ, or User Experience Questionnaire, which was mentioned three times. We encountered about 15 other standard questionnaires that were mentioned twice (PENS, UPEQ, IMI, GAMS, GEQ) or only once.

Another method of evaluating a product is by gathering **expert opinions**. In cases where a product is not yet playable or access to the players is difficult, experts can offer insight and help avoid problems quickly and with less effort. Experts usually employ a set of heuristics to review a product. These heuristics can also identify possible pitfalls and problems during product design. Six articles discussed heuristics with varying degrees of specialization. (A_ 11) compares various sets, (A_ 17) and (A_ 34) compile new sets for varying target user groups and application domains. Building on previous work, (A_ 38) set out to unify the various specific heuristics and formulates a new modular set tailorable to specific areas. Two articles, (A_ 51) and (A_ 56), advocate for heuristics in development and evaluation without specifying them.

Another dominant topic is **development methods**, game/gamification/design models, and frameworks. Twenty works discussed this topic, five of which were literature reviews. (A_ 34) offers an overview of the evolution of game design models from the perspectives of Mechanics, Dynamics, and Aesthetics (MDA), Design, Play, and Experience (DPE), Design Dynamics and Experience (DDE), and Learning Games Design Model (LGDM) and proposes a new model for the design of educational digital games. (A_ 42) summarizes the topic similarly and develops another model considering virtual reality. Regarding game development, serious games, and gamified applications, researchers tend to agree that development is iterative and that an interdisciplinary approach should be used. Several articles, (A_ 3), (A_ 9), (A_ 25), (A_ 34), and (A_ 42), present different lists that include psychologists, pedagogical experts, game designers, computer scientists, domain experts, and project managers. Regarding the development of games, the concept of participatory design, where users are actively included in all design process steps, is mentioned in eight articles, while human- or user-centered design is mentioned in nine articles. (A_ 6), (A_ 19), (A_ 46), and (A_ 50) report their experience after implementing those methods.

Several articles emphasize the importance of considering or **including end-users** in the development process: (A_ 5), (A_ 6), (A_ 15), and (A_ 47). Others such as (A_ 22), (A_ 32), (A_ 36), (A_ 50), and (A_ 58) discuss user models that classify the users of different applications, e.g., in museums, for knowledge repositories, or at schools. Two articles, (A_ 39) and (A_ 46), describe user participation in the development process, providing input into the research. One article (A_ 47) emphasizes the need to define and research user groups clearly.

5   Discussion

Research regarding serious games, concepts, and methodologies is active and ongoing, but the necessity for considering users in developing serious games is undisputed.

When examining the works analyzed, it seems notable that most publications were penned by two to four authors, with a median of three. Only about one-tenth of the publications have a single author, yet despite the low proportion of sole authorships, over half of the publications are attributed to only one affiliation. Only about one-third of the publications were authored by authors from two academic institutions, perhaps indicating a reluctance to engage in cross-organizational or frequent trans- or interdisciplinary collaborations—a thesis supported when observing the nations involved, as almost 80% of the sampled research was authored from one nation. Another 15% are publications with two nationalities involved. Thus, cross-institutional, and cross-national cooperation both appear scarce in the literature. Notably, upon examining those most frequently involved, four nations of authors publish more frequently than average: Brazil, Spain, Germany, and the United States. These four nations are spread over three continents and do not share a first language. Unfortunately, the hypothesis that geographic proximity leads to higher levels of collaboration, such as within the European Union through regional funding, cannot be confirmed. None of the publications from Germany and Spain show an overlap in authorship.

Unfortunately, there also seems to be little discussion of the research, as can be concluded from the dearth of cross-references within the selected articles. The visibility of existing research is seemingly not high enough across databases, conferences, and journals. In some cases, the research for an appropriate method was done by looking for methods others had applied in similar situations. A best-practice approach seems preferable when entering a new domain, yet if highly suitable methods are new or have not been used for other reasons, they are virtually nonexistent with such an approach and cannot be utilized.

To answer RQ (1): Integration of UX methods and concepts into the design and development of serious games has started and is still under way with a large area seemingly still left unexplored.

To answer RQ (2): The evaluation of serious games is well-established, and the preferred method seems to be a summative evaluation occurring relatively late or at the end of development. In contrast, formative evaluation, which happens during development, allows for recognizing and repairing errors with comparatively lower cost and effort.

Although a definition for user experience is available, it is still often used intuitively, differing from the definition, or even becoming interchangeable with usability in some instances. As such, no agreed-upon definition apart from the one in ISO 9241 exists, so that many misconceptions may arise through the undefined use of user experience or usability. Discussing (measurable) user experience or usability factors depends on agreed-upon definitions. Again, this is a problem of visibility and accessibility of research, definitions, and standards.

There is no question about the value of interdisciplinary teams, yet none of the lists contained UX experts who can help select and apply appropriate user research and evaluation methods beyond questionnaires and tracking.

6   Research Agenda

Consequential to the findings mentioned in the description of the results and the discussion, we derived the following possible research questions (PRQs) in answer to RQ (3):

PRQ1: What are the specifics of games and/or serious games that necessitate adaptation of concepts and methods? Which concepts and methods need to be adapted and how?

PRQ2: Which insights into users and user types regarding games/serious games exist? How can those insights be integrated into a unified concept that supports user research? How does such a concept influence existing user research methods?

PRQ3: Which evaluation methods are used in the context of games/serious games? What adaptations were implemented to allow for game-specific circumstances? How can/need existing evaluation methods be adapted to support the needs of evaluations in games/serious games?

PRQ4: How can content be made more readily available and accessible across research field borders?

PRQ5: What is the degree of scientific maturity of the research published regarding serious games or gamification and UX concepts and methods? To which degree do articles clearly state the employed scientific method and the underlying definitions and concepts?

Aside from specific research questions, we need more cooperation and collegiality across disciplines and national borders to facilitate a well-founded and established understanding of the factors contributing to successful serious games. This can constitute the basis for creating new and innovative applications to enhance the experiences in education, health, business, and others.

7   Limitations

Although the databases we identified as most important were searched, relevant literature available in other databases may have been excluded from this study.

Some literature was inaccessible to the authors and may contain relevant information.

Relevant research may have been published in languages other than English and German. Unfortunately, automatic translation is not yet to the level of trustworthiness sufficient for scientific content.

Relevant information may be in publications that use different terminology and thus was not found using the above search terms.

References

1. Moizer, J.: An approach to evaluating the user experience of serious games. Comput. Educ. **136**, 141–151 (2019). https://doi.org/10.1016/j.compedu.2019.04.006
2. International Organization for Standardisation: ISO 9241–210 (2019). https://www.iso.org/standard/77520.html. Accessed 14 July 2023
3. Vanden Abeele, V., et al.: P-III: a player-centered, iterative, interdisciplinary and integrated framework for serious game design and development. In: De Wannemacker, S., Vandercruysse, S., Clarebout, G. (eds.) ITEC/CIP/T 2011. CCIS, vol. 280, pp. 82–86. Springer, Heidelberg (2012). https://doi.org/10.1007/978-3-642-33814-4_14
4. Watson, R.T., Webster, J.: Analysing the past to prepare for the future: writing a literature review a roadmap for release 2.0. J. Decis. Syst. **29**, 129–147 (2020). https://doi.org/10.1080/12460125.2020.1798591
5. Wolfswinkel, J.F., Furtmueller, E., Wilderom, C.P.M.: Using grounded theory as a method for rigorously reviewing literature. Eur. J. Inf. Syst. **22**, 45–55 (2013). https://doi.org/10.1057/ejis.2011.51
6. Deterding, S., Dixon, D., Khaled, R., Nacke, L.: From game design elements to gamefulness: defining "gamification." In: Proceedings of the 15th International Academic MindTrek Conference: Envisioning Future Media Environments, pp. 9–15. Association for Computing Machinery, New York, NY, USA (2011). https://doi.org/10.1145/2181037.2181040
7. Juul, J.: Half-Real: Video Games between Real Rules and Fictional Worlds. The MIT Press, Cambridge, MA (2011)
8. Caillois, R.: Man, Play, and Games. University of Illinois Press, Urbana, Chicago (2001)
9. Furtado, L.S., de Souza, R.F., Lima, J.L. dos R., Oliveira, S.R.B.: Teaching method for software measurement process based on gamification or serious games: a systematic review of the literature. Int. J. Comput. Games Technol. **2021**, e8873997 (2021). https://doi.org/10.1155/2021/8873997
10. Pereira de Aguiar, M., Winn, B., Cezarotto, M., Battaiola, A.L., Varella Gomes, P.: Educational digital games: a theoretical framework about design models, learning theories and user experience. In: Marcus, A., Wang, W. (eds.) DUXU 2018. LNCS, vol. 10918, pp. 165–184. Springer, Cham (2018). https://doi.org/10.1007/978-3-319-91797-9_13
11. Costa, C.J., Aparicio, M., Aparicio, S., Aparicio, J.T.: Gamification usage ecology. In: Proceedings of the 35th ACM International Conference on the Design of Communication, pp. 1–9. Association for Computing Machinery, New York, NY, USA (2017). https://doi.org/10.1145/3121113.3121205
12. Heintz, S., Law, E.L.-C.: Digital educational games: methodologies for evaluating the impact of game type. ACM Trans. Comput.-Hum. Interact. **25**, 8:1–8:47 (2018). https://doi.org/10.1145/3177881
13. International Organization for Standardisation: ISO 9241–110 (2020). https://www.iso.org/standard/75258.html. Accessed 14 Jul 2023
14. Khaled, R.: Muse-based game design. In: Proceedings of the Designing Interactive Systems Conference, pp. 721–730. Association for Computing Machinery, New York, NY, USA (2012). https://doi.org/10.1145/2317956.2318065
15. Moreno-Ger, P., Torrente, J., Hsieh, Y.G., Lester, W.T.: Usability testing for serious games: making informed design decisions with user data. Adv. Hum.-Comput. Interact. **2012**, e369637 (2012). https://doi.org/10.1155/2012/369637
16. Yáñez-Gómez, R., Cascado-Caballero, D., Sevillano, J.-L.: Academic methods for usability evaluation of serious games: a systematic review. Multimed. Tools Appl. **76**, 5755–5784 (2017). https://doi.org/10.1007/s11042-016-3845-9

Does Playing Video Games Give a Child an Advantage in Digital Game-Based Learning?

Pierpaolo Dondio[✉]

Technological University Dublin, School of Computer Science, Dublin, Ireland
`pierpaolo.dondio@tudublin.ie`

Abstract. In this paper we first investigated the relationship between game habits of primary school children and their school achievements and anxiety levels. Then, we investigated if children habitually playing video games at home have an advantage when it comes to learning using educational games. In order to answer these questions, we exploited the data coming from the digital game-based learning (DGBL) intervention *Happy Maths*, a 6-week programme run in Irish primary schools aimed to increase maths abilities and decrease maths anxiety (MA). The dataset contained the academic achievements, the video game habits and the intervention data of 952 pupils. Our results show how playing games at home that are not age-appropriate was associated with higher MA and lower maths score, while time spent playing was associated with higher MA and lower literacy score. Regarding the efficacy of the DGBL intervention, there was no difference in the efficacy of the intervention between gamers and non-gamers. However, habitual video gamers were faster in executing their game moves, and they achieved higher scores, learning the game better. Overall, the study underlines the importance of playing age-appropriate games, and it provides evidence that, although kids playing video game might have a good advantage when it comes to educational games, the efficacy of such games is the same for gamers and non-gamers.

Keywords: digital game-based learning · academic achievements

1 Introduction

It is estimated that almost 3 billion people played video games in some capacity in 2022, with a prevalence among adolescent of about 75%, approaching 90% in industrialized countries [16]. Since video gaming is such a widespread activity, the link between playing video games and the cognitive and emotional traits of players has been subject to extensive attention. Multiple reasons have been proposed to explain the potential link between video gaming and academic achievements. In [11], authors summarise previous relevant theories. According to the *time displacement* hypothesis, computer gaming replaces time that should be invested in academic activities [22], causing lower academic scores. According

P. Dondio et al. (Eds.): GALA 2023, LNCS 14475, pp. 223–233, 2024.
https://doi.org/10.1007/978-3-031-49065-1_22

to the *sleep displacement* hypothesis [14], computer gaming reduces both the quantity and the quality of sleep, causing lack of attention and poorer cognitive abilities [9]. In the *attention deficit* hypothesis [10], it is assumed that prolonged computer gaming takes away time from tasks that would otherwise contribute to the development of sustained attention and therefore decrease players' cognitive performance and their ability to focus. In contrast to these negative views, the *cognitive enhancement* hypothesis [20] suggests that games might also act as training programs for various cognitive skills, such as attentional capacity, visual orientation, and memory, which might improve players' cognitive abilities.

Experimental studies to date seem to support both perspectives. Some studies reported poorer test performance for students spending a lot of their time playing games [3,17], but several researchers found significantly better performance on standardized tests of cognitive abilities among gamers as compared with non-gamers [13,18], or no effects at all [8]. In [4], a meta-analysis found that regularly playing computer games was associated with cognitive gains corresponding to Cohen's d between .30 to .70. A large study of the PISA results of more than 192000 students from 22 countries [16] found only a negligible difference in academic performance across the relative frequencies of videogame use, concluding that video games had little impact on academic achievements. While these studies were cross-sectional, and therefore can only report an association between games and academic achievements, a recent large-scale longitudinal study on 3500 German adolescents found that playing computer and video games can result in a noticeable, albeit small, loss of educational achievements, but it does not affect basic competences [11].

The effect of video games was found to be dependent on the type of game played. In [5] the author found that multi-player gaming, rather than single-player gaming, was linked with lower performance in reading. In [15], the authors focused on a group of 70 kids aged 6–10 and found a negative correlation between academic scores and time spent playing games, but only for violent video games. Educational games were related to good academic achievements.

Video games have been investigated also in relations to depression and anxiety. While a moderate use of video games does not seem to have relationship with anxiety, problematic game behaviour and excessive use were clearly linked with anxiety and depression. Excessive use of video games can lead to IGD (internet gaming disorder), a recognized mental disorder that has an estimated prevalence of 10.6% among teenagers [21] and it is strongly correlated with anxiety. Indeed, a recent study has found that 92% of players suffering from IGD also have anxiety [12], providing further evidence of the strong correlation between the two conditions. However, the directionality between game habits and anxiety has not been disentangled. There is evidence that anxiety might precede problematic game behaviour, but it has also been observed that excessive gaming can increase an existing anxiety. Evidence to date on the link between gaming and anxiety is inconsistent.

A recent study of 97 21-year-old participants [2] found no statistically significant difference in anxiety levels or daytime sleepiness between expert and non-expert players, where expert and non-expert players were identified by the time spent playing action video games. There is indeed a line of research investigating how games can be used to alleviate anxiety. A recent meta-analysis [7] investigated the effect of game-based interventions to reduce maths anxiety, reporting a small positive effect size of 0.24.

The present study seeks to investigate further the link between video games and some cognitive and emotional traits of players with novel contributions. In the first part of the paper, a traditional cross-sectional study is presented, in which we studied the relationship between game habits and three outcome variables, namely students' maths scores, literacy scores and maths anxiety. Therefore, our first set of research questions was:

RQ1. *Are game habits associated with academic performance in (a) maths, (b) literacy and with (c) maths anxiety in primary school kids (age 8–11)?*

Our cross-sectional study provides new evidence in a still inconsistent landscape. It focuses on primary school children, for which fewer studies have been published. Moreover, a novel predictor was considered, namely the *age rating* of the games habitually played by each participant, introduced in order to understand if the games played were appropriate to the age of the child. Our hypothesis is that, when it comes to young children, the age rating of the game, rather than the content, could significantly impact the above outcome variables.

In the second part of the paper, we investigated a novel research question. We wondered if the familiarity with video games can impact the efficacy of a maths digital game-based learning (DGBL) intervention in school. In other words, we wondered if habitual gamers have an advantage when learning using (educational) games. Multiple hypothesis supports this statement: (1) habitual gamers could be more engaged and motivated when learning with games than non-habitual gamers, (2) they could be less sensitive to computer or technology anxiety and (3) they might have acquired specific skills by playing digital games that could make more effective the way they learn with educational games. We were interested in testing two related aspects. The first is whether players' video game habits can affect players' performance in an educational game. Game performance in an educational game is not merely an indicator of how good a player is, but it is indeed a proxy for maths performance and, according to studies in game-based assessment, it can be a more fair and precise form of assessment for certain groups of students. The second aspect is whether habitual gamers learn in the same way as non-gamers after a DGBL intervention, where learning is measured by comparing the results of a relevant maths test administered before and after the DGBL intervention. Our second set of research questions was therefore the following:

RQ2. *Do game habits of students predict students' performance in an educational game? Do game habits of students predict the effects of a DGBL intervention?*

In order to answer RQ1 and RQ2, we exploited the data of the DGBL intervention *Happy Maths*, including a set of in-game data and the results of the paper maths test administrated pre- and post- intervention. It is important to report that data from the *Happy Maths* programme [1] showed that, after the *Happy Maths* DGBL intervention, children had a lower number of errors in the post maths test (effect size of 0.35) and a reduced maths anxiety (effect size 0.19). Here, we wondered if such positive effects were associated with the game habits of the participants.

2   Methods

Data collection was performed from January 2022 to May 2023 in the context of *Happy Maths* [1], a research project investigating the effects of DGBL on primary school students' numerical cognition and maths anxiety. The study was a quasi-experimental intervention with a pre-post design and weekly game sessions delivered in class for six consecutive weeks. At the beginning of the study, information on children's game habits was collected via a questionnaire containing items about how much time the respondents spent playing video games daily, how much they enjoyed playing videogames and the list of favourite videogames usually played. For each game, we collected its age rating as suggested by the Entertainment Software Rating Board (ESRB), that assigns to each game one of the following categories: E (everyone), E10+ (everyone above 10-year-old), T (teenager), M (mature player) and A (adult).

Additional measures were collected. Pupils were asked to fill the Modified Abbreviated Maths Anxiety scale [6], a validated scale for primary school kids to measure their level of maths anxiety (MA). Data were collected pre- and post-intervention. In a similar way, pupils were asked to fill a maths test pre- and post- intervention. The test covered the maths content of the games. Moreover, for each student, their maths score and literacy score were gathered by collecting the results obtained in the Irish national standardize test for maths and English. Results were provided in the range 1 to 10. Demographic data such as gender and age were also collected.

Fig. 1. The *Seven Spells solo* mode (left) and *versus a human* mode (right).

Children took part in a 6-week DGBL intervention in class called *Happy Maths*. Each week a 1-hr session was delivered by at least two members of the *Happy Maths* research team. The intervention is designed around the digital game Seven Spell [1], a card game to stimulate problem-solving, numerical skills and strategic thinking (Fig. 1). Aim of the game is to capture the other player's number cards using various maths abilities, including arithmetic computations, knowledge of mathematical concepts (even and odd numbers, prime numbers, numeric tables, intervals, greater and smaller, etc.) and players' ability to combine and manipulate numbers. The more cards a player captures, the higher their score. A good move requires the player to combine multiple cards, allowing players to build from simple to very complicated moves and to exercise their own creativity and tactics. In order to answer RQ2, we used game logs and game performance data and we extracted the following in-game measurements: the average score of each player at week 1 and at week 6 (that is at the end of the intervention) and the average duration of each move across the 6 in-class sessions.

3   Results

The dataset contained complete data for 952 players. Tables 1 and 2 show the descriptive statistics for the numerical and categorical variables included in the study. A total of 216 games was mentioned; the most frequently mentioned games were Fortnite, FIFA, Minecraft and Roblox. Boys' and girls' game preferences were quite segregated; only 45 games (20.8%) were played by both boys and girls, 54 by girls only and 117 by boys only. However, the 45 games in common were the most popular, and they were played by 79.4% of girls and 75.7% of boys. The game mostly played by girls was Roblox (played by 48.7% of girls and only 12% of boys) and the game mostly played by boys was FIFA (6.9% of girls vs. 32.7% boys), while Minecraft was the most *equally* played game (28.4% of girls vs. 25.3% of boys).

Table 1. Numerical study variables (N = 952).

Variable	Description	Mean	SD	Range
MA	Maths Anxiety score (mAMAS)	20.7	7.47	9–45
MS	Maths Score	5.88	2.14	1–10
LS	Literacy Score	5.87	1.99	1–10

Table 2. Categorical variables considered (N = 952). The variable *Class Yr.* refers to the levels in the Irish school system: 3rd class refers to 8-year-old children, 4th class refers to 9-year-old, 5th class refers to 10-year-old and 6th class refers to 11-year-old children.

Variable	Description	Distribution of levels
Class Yr.	Class grade	14.5% (3rd), 20.8% (4th), 32.5% (5th), 32.2% (6th)
Gender	Binary variable M,F	F = 394 (41.4%), M = 558 (58.6%)
Likevideo	Do you like video games? Likert scale (1 = hate 5 = love)	1: 4.2%, 2: 2.8%, 3: 8.0%, 4: 25.8%, 5: 59.2%
PlayTime	How much do you play video games daily?	Never: 6.8%; ≤ 1 h: 21.4%; 1–2 h: 36.1%; ≥ 2 h: 35.7%
ESRB	ESRB Rating	E: 30.7%; E10+: 23.1% T: 36.8%; M: 9.4%

3.1 Impact on Academic Achievements and Maths Anxiety

Table 3 shows the results of three linear regression models, each of them predicting one of the outcome variables of interest: maths anxiety (MA), maths score (MS) and literacy score (LS). The predictors used were gender, class year, the *age rating* of the games played by each player, the time spent playing videogames (variable *Timep*) and how much video games are enjoyed (variable *like VG*). For each player, the value of the *age rating* variable was computed as the highest ESRB age rating among the games played by the player. The ratings M (mature) and A (adult) were grouped into the M rating. Therefore, the *age rating* was a categorical variable with four levels (E, E10+, T, M). The idea behind the *age rating* variable was to measure if a player was habitually exposed to content that was not appropriate to their age. In the regression models of Table 3, the rating E was used as reference. The significant predictors are shown in bold, and the p-value for each predictor is reported in parentheses. The variables describing game habits were significant: *age rating* was significant in the model predicting MA and MP, *TimeP* was significant for MA and LS, while *Like VG* for MP.

We also noticed how the average level of MA varied by the age rating of the games, but the variation was mainly for girls and not for boys, as shown in

Table 3. Linear regression models to predict maths anxiety (MA), maths score (MS) and literacy score (LS) using predictors related to game habits (p-values are shown in parentheses, significant predictors at 0.05 level are shown in bold).

Y	Gender = M	Class Yr.	E10+	T	M	TimeP	LikeVG	R^2
MA	**−3.82*** (<0.001)**	−0.14 (0.61)	0.62 (0.51)	**1.76** (0.015)**	1.86 (0.053)	**1.43 (<0.001)**	−0.19 (0.58)	9.55
MS	**0.55*** (<0.001)**	0.02 (0.75)	0.29 (0.26)	**−0.60*** (<0.001)**	−0.32 (0.41)	−0.19 (0.068)	**−0.22* (0.017)**	5.33
LS	0.09 (0.56)	−0.003 (0.96)	**0.78** (0.004)**	0.32 (0.15)	0.10 (0.72)	**−0.28** (0.007)**	−0.17 (0.087)	4.41

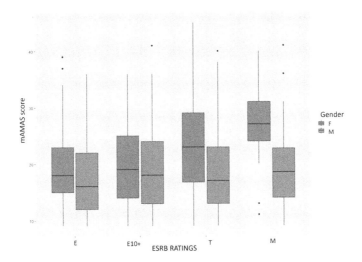

Fig. 2. Average maths anxiety by gender and by the age rating of the games habitually played by each student.

Fig. 2. We therefore fitted a model including an interaction term between gender and age rating. Table 4 shows the result of the obtained model: the interaction term was significant and the R^2 of the model was improved.

3.2 Impact of Video Game Habits on the DGBL Intervention

We tested the effect of video game habits on the outcomes of the *Happy Maths* intervention and on the game performance achieved in the educational game. In the introduction of this paper we reported how the *Happy Maths* programme [1] was effective in reducing the number of errors in a post-intervention maths test (effect size of 0.35) and maths anxiety levels (effect size 0.19). However, even if the intervention had an effect, we wondered if the effect of the intervention could be explained by the game habits of the participants. Moreover, by looking at game logs, we wanted to understand if video game habits at home affected the way children played the educational game. We studied the following outcome variables: the pre-post difference in maths anxiety (Δ_{MA}), the pre-post difference in the number of errors in the paper maths test (Δ_{ME}) and the following three in-game measures: average duration of a move, game performance (measured by the average of the two highest scores achieved in the game by each player), and the difference in game performance between the first and the last week of the intervention (Δ_{Score}). We added to the list of predictors maths score, literacy score and maths anxiety, in order to fully test if the effect of the game habits variables was present even after controlling for the cognitive abilities and anxiety levels of the players. Results are shown in Table 5, where each line represents a linear regression model for one of the outcome variables considered.

Table 4. Linear regression model to predict Maths Anxiety containing an interaction term between gender and the age rating of the games played.

Predictor	β	$Pr(> |z|)$	Predictor	β	$Pr(> |z|)$
Gender (M)	1.02	0.27	TimeP	1.31	(<0.001)
Class Yr.	−0.16	0.54	LikeVG	−0.23	0.51
E10+	0.40	0.82	Gender(M)*E10+	−0.25	0.91
T	**3.55**	**0.024***	Gender(M)*T	−2.99	0.068
M	**7.41**	**0.002****	**Gender(M)*M**	**−6.76**	**0.009****
Observations $= 952$, $R^2 = 10.95$					

Table 5. Linear regression models to predict the effect of a DGBL intervention using players' game habits (p-values are shown in parentheses, significant predictors at 0.05 level are shown in bold).

Outcome	Gender (M)	Class Yr.	MP	LS	MA	TimeP	LikeVG	R^2
Δ_{MA}	0.49 (0.26)	0.33 (0.25)	0.24 (0.14)	−0.18 (0.28)	–	0.53 (0.13)	−0.02 (0.96)	1.1
Δ_{ME}	0.51 (0.21)	**−0.49* (0.02)**	**−0.48*** (<0.001)**	−0.03 (0.78)	0.03 (0.37)	0.02 (0.92)	0.09 (0.73)	10.2
Mean Duration	**−2.99 (<0.001)**	−0.26 (0.18)	**0.53*** (<0.001)**	−0.19 (0.22)	**0.10*** (<0.001)**	**−1.06*** (< 0.001)**	**0.63* (0.04)**	14.7
Mean Score	15.4 (0.40)	**25.4*** (<0.001)**	**41.07*** (<0.001)**	3.65 (0.49)	**−3.05** (0.01)**	**20.2* (0.05)**	6.08 (0.57)	21.1
Δ_{Score}	**−33.4* (0.05)**	8.49 (0.19)	**28.3 (<0.001)**	−4.27 (0.40)	**−2.58* (0.03)**	**22.1* (0.02)**	4.84 (0.61)	14.1

4 Discussion

Regarding the effect of game habits on school achievements and maths anxiety (RQ1), our data showed how the age rating of the games played was a significant predictor even after accounting for player's gender and age. Regarding MA, playing games rated for teenagers (T) or for a mature audience (M) increased the maths anxiety of the player by about 1.8 point (about 0.26 SD). However, the most interesting result was the interaction between gender and the age rating of the games played, whereby the effect of *age inappropriate* videogames was stronger for girls than for boys. In the model without an interaction term, girls had an average MA level 3.82 points higher than boys, while in the interaction model girls playing games rated M had an average MA level 5.74 points higher than boys. The model with the interaction term was a better fit for the data (R^2 of 10.95 compared to 9.55).

Age rating was also significant for maths score and literacy score. Playing games rated T decreased maths score by 0.60 (on a scale 1–10), while playing games rated for everyone (E) increased literacy score by 0.78, This is consistent with [15], that found an association between playing violent video games and lower academic achievements. However, by considering the age rating of each game, our study goes beyond [15]. Indeed, age rating is not only assigned considering the level of violence in a game, but many other factors such as language, sex, tension, storyline, how safe the communication among online players is and so forth. Our study suggests the importance for children to play games appropriate to their age and the importance of supervision when playing.

Regarding the time spent playing video games, it had a significant effect on increasing MA. An explanation could be that habitual players might be the ones at risk of developing problematic game behaviour, that is strongly associated with anxiety [12,19]. Time spent playing also affected literacy score negatively, while it did not affect maths score, in accordance with [5].

In the second part of our analysis we wondered if the effect of a DGBL intervention depended on the game habits of players (RQ2). We found no significant associations between the learning outcome of the *Happy Maths* intervention (variable Δ_{ME}) and the players' game habits (variables *TimeP* and *LikeVG*). The same was true for MA reduction (variable Δ_{MA}). Therefore, even if the intervention had an effect, it was not explained by the game habits of players.

Habitually playing video games gave an advantage in the educational game, since *TimeP* was a significant positive predictor of higher game scores even after controlling for cognitive abilities, age and maths anxiety of the student. Playing games habitually gave also a significant advantage in terms of how much a student improved their game scores from week 1 to week 6 of the intervention. Likewise, habitual gamers and video games lovers (variable *LikeVG*) were much faster in executing their moves in the game, as evidence of their higher familiarity with the mechanics of digital games.

In summary, being a habitual player did not give an advantage in learning measured by traditional assessment methods, however it gave an advantage with respect to the performance in the educational game. Since scoring a high score in the game requires to perform maths tasks similar to the ones presented in the pre- and post- paper maths test, we wondered why habitual players had higher game scores but not higher test scores. Several explanations are possible. One explanation could be that the game environment might have engaged and stimulated kids differently, with some players more enthusiastic to play and motivated by the competition aspects of the game and some other less motivated. Moreover, players might have felt less motivated or focused doing a test on paper, since the test was not linked to any reward. Other explanations could be that the game and the test, although similar, were not perfectly aligned in terms of content, or that the game did not affect maths abilities outside the game. However, data from the *Happy Maths* programme evaluation show how after playing the game kids improved their paper test scores, as evidence that the educational game had an effect. In addition to all of these explanations, we also mention that test anxiety might have been present in the paper test and absent in the game, while technology-related anxiety could have been present in the game and absent in the test, both factors influencing students' performance. In order to fully answer our question, further analysis and controlled studies should be implemented to isolate the reasons why the performance of some students differed between the game and the test. As they stand, our results are interesting to show that habitual players played educational games in a more effective way than non-habitual players, suggesting that game-based learning could be a more truthful form of assessing the maths level of this group of children.

5   Conclusion

In this paper we contributed to the study of the relationship between game habits and cognitive and non-cognitive traits of players. In the first part of the paper, we described a cross-sectional study investigating the relationship between game habits with three outcome variables: maths score, literacy score and maths anxiety. Our results showed how playing games that are not age-appropriate was associated with higher MA and a lower maths score, while time spent playing was associated with higher MA and a lower literacy score. In the second part of the paper, we tested if game habits affected the outcome of a DGBL intervention in school. Our results showed that there was no difference in the efficacy of the intervention between habitual gamers and non-gamers with respect to MA reduction and maths learning. However, habitual video gamers were faster in executing their game moves, they achieved higher scores and learnt the game better. Overall, the study underlines the importance of playing age-appropriate games, and it provides evidence that, although kids playing video game might have good advantage when it comes to educational games, the efficacy of such games is the same for gamers and non-gamers. We also showed that habitual players played educational games in a more effecting way, suggesting that game-based learning could be a more truthful form of assessment for these students.

References

1. The Happy Maths Programme. https://www.happymaths.games. Accessed 31 May 2013
2. Alsaad, F., et al.: Impact of action video gaming behavior on attention, anxiety, and sleep among university students. Psychol. Res. Behav. Manag. 151–160 (2022)
3. Anand, V.: A study of time management: the correlation between video game usage and academic performance markers. Cyber Psychol. Behav. 10(4), 552–559 (2007)
4. Anderson, C.A., et al.: Violent video game effects on aggression, empathy, and prosocial behavior in eastern and western countries: a meta-analytic review. Psychol. Bull. 136(2), 151 (2010)
5. Borgonovi, F.: Video gaming and gender differences in digital and printed reading performance among 15-year-olds students in 26 countries. J. Adolesc. 48, 45–61 (2016)
6. Carey, E., Hill, F., Devine, A., Szűcs, D.: The modified abbreviated math anxiety scale: a valid and reliable instrument for use with children. Front. Psychol. 8, 11 (2017)
7. Dondio, P., Gusev, V., Rocha, M.: Do games reduce maths anxiety? a meta-analysis. Comput. Educ. 194, 104650 (2023)
8. Drummond, A., Sauer, J.D.: Video-games do not negatively impact adolescent academic performance in science, mathematics or reading. PLoS ONE 9(4), e87943 (2014)
9. Dworak, M., Schierl, T., Bruns, T., Strüder, H.K.: Impact of singular excessive computer game and television exposure on sleep patterns and memory performance of school-aged children. Pediatrics 120(5), 978–985 (2007)
10. Gentile, D.A., Swing, E.L., Lim, C.G., Khoo, A.: Video game playing, attention problems, and impulsiveness: evidence of bidirectional causality. Psychol. Pop. Media Cult. 1(1), 62 (2012)
11. Gnambs, T., Stasielowicz, L., Wolter, I., Appel, M.: Do computer games jeopardize educational outcomes? a prospective study on gaming times and academic achievement. Psychol. Popular Media 9(1), 69 (2020)
12. González-Bueso, V., et al.: Internet gaming disorder in adolescents: personality, psychopathology and evaluation of a psychological intervention combined with parent psychoeducation. Front. Psychol. 9, 787 (2018)
13. Green, C.S., Seitz, A.R.: The impacts of video games on cognition (and how the government can guide the industry). Policy Insights Behav. Brain Sci. 2(1), 101–110 (2015)
14. Hale, L., Guan, S.: Screen time and sleep among school-aged children and adolescents: a systematic literature review. Sleep Med. Rev. 21, 50–58 (2015)

15. Hastings, E.C., Karas, T.L., Winsler, A., Way, E., Madigan, A., Tyler, S.: Young children's video/computer game use: relations with school performance and behavior. Issues Ment. Health Nurs. **30**(10), 638–649 (2009)
16. Islam, M.I., Biswas, R.K., Khanam, R.: Effect of internet use and electronic gameplay on academic performance of Australian children. Sci. Rep. **10**(1), 1–10 (2020)
17. Jackson, L.A., Von Eye, A., Fitzgerald, H.E., Witt, E.A., Zhao, Y.: Internet use, videogame playing and cell phone use as predictors of children's body mass index (BMI), body weight, academic performance, and social and overall self-esteem. Comput. Hum. Behav. **27**(1), 599–604 (2011)
18. Kovess-Masfety, V., et al.: Is time spent playing video games associated with mental health, cognitive and social skills in young children? Soc. Psychiatry Psychiatr. Epidemiol. **51**(3), 349–357 (2016)
19. Männikkö, N., Ruotsalainen, H., Miettunen, J., Pontes, H.M., Kääriäinen, M.: Problematic gaming behaviour and health-related outcomes: a systematic review and meta-analysis. J. Health Psychol. **25**(1), 67–81 (2020)
20. Powers, K.L., Brooks, P.J., Aldrich, N.J., Palladino, M.A., Alfieri, L.: Effects of video-game play on information processing: a meta-analytic investigation. Psychonom. Bullet. Rev. **20**, 1055–1079 (2013)
21. Singh, Y.M., Prakash, J., Chatterjee, K., Khadka, B., Shah, A., Chauhan, V.S.: Prevalence and risk factors associated with internet gaming disorder: a cross-sectional study. Ind. Psychiatry J. **30**(Suppl 1), S172 (2021)
22. Subrahmanyam, K., Renukarya, B.: Digital games and learning: identifying pathways of influence. Educ. Psychologist **50**(4), 335–348 (2015)

Are Game Elements Fueling Learners' Motivation via Positive Affect?

Stefan E. Huber[1]([✉]) [ID], Antero Lindstedt[2] [ID], Kristian Kiili[2] [ID],
and Manuel Ninaus[1,3] [ID]

[1] Department of Psychology, University of Graz, Graz, Austria
stefan.huber@uni-graz.at
[2] Faculty of Education and Culture, Tampere University, Tampere, Finland
[3] LEAD Graduate School and Research Network, University of Tübingen, Tübingen, Germany

Abstract. The use of game elements in learning tasks is often motivated by the aim of utilizing their motivational capabilities. Even if game elements do not directly affect cognitive learning outcomes, they can keep learners engaged and support long-term loyalties. In this contribution, we present an investigation of the effect of game elements with a specific focus on affective and motivational aspects. In particular, we report a value-added online experiment, comparing a game-based version with a non-game-based version of an association learning task. In total, 61 participants completed the experiment. While we find comparable cognitive learning outcomes, we find medium and large differences in affective and motivational outcomes. Game elements are associated with an increase in positive affect and increased perceived competence compared to the non-game-based task. The game-based task was further perceived significantly more attractive and stimulating. Mediation models revealed that the increased cognitive cost introduced by game elements was effectively balanced by their benefits regarding motivation. The latter was partially mediated by changes in positive affect. In sum, the net cognitive outcome was the same for both tasks, but learners in the game-based condition were more positively affected, more motivated and felt more competent. Implications and future research directions are discussed.

Keywords: game elements · association learning · cognition · motivation · affect

1 Introduction and Theoretical Background

The use of games in educational contexts is often based on the aim to leverage their capabilities in capturing and holding people's attention and in fostering sustained engagement and motivation [1]. While previous reviews yielded mixed results regarding outcomes of game-based learning, recent meta-analyses support their effectiveness concerning cognitive and motivational outcomes for learning in school [2] and higher education [3]. Meta-analyses have further shown that already the inclusion of specific, separable game features in digital tasks (gamification) can enhance engagement [4] and motivation [5]. While game-based learning and gamification are certainly distinct approaches, the motivational capabilities of their common feature of game elements have been corroborated for both game-related pedagogies [6].

P. Dondio et al. (Eds.): GALA 2023, LNCS 14475, pp. 234–243, 2024.
https://doi.org/10.1007/978-3-031-49065-1_23

However, the exact mechanisms by which game elements exert their effects during learning are far from being fully elaborated [7]. The Integrated Cognitive Affective Model of Learning with Multimedia (ICALM) [8] provides a theoretical framework which can shed light on how cognitive and motivational aspects may be related. This contribution attempts to clarify further the relations between game design features, cognition, affect, and motivation during learning within the framework provided by ICALM.

Theoretical Background. A crucial point in the ICALM model [8] is that cognitive processes are inseparably intertwined with affective processes induced by the learning environment. If attributable to a specific source these affective processes are subjectively experienced as emotions, whereas otherwise they may persist unattributed as mood. Affect that involves appraisal is subjectively experienced in the form of interest or motivation. In any of these forms, affect influences selection and organization processes in working memory and is finally integrated also into emotionally laden schemas stored via long-term memory.

The important point for the present work is that affective dynamics provide a link between design features of the learning environment and motivational learning outcomes [7]. In other words, design features may induce affect, which may enhance motivation. Research in the framework of self-determination theory [1] has shown that high levels of motivation, particularly intrinsic need satisfaction for autonomy, competence, and relatedness, are characteristics of high-quality learning. Hence, the affective dynamics initialized by game elements may fuel learners' motivation which in turn may enhance cognitive outcomes.

However, according to ICALM [8], affective processes also pose additional demands on cognitive resources. According to multimedia learning research [9], this may finally lead to a zero net effect on cognitive outcomes, as found in earlier studies [10–12], via the mutual cancelation of motivational benefits with cognitive demands.

Present Study. The present study aimed to test these theoretical considerations empirically by utilizing the well-established value-added research paradigm [13]. To do so, we aimed for clarification of the following hypotheses.

Informed by our previous study focusing on behavioral engagement during a similar task [10], we did not expect a net difference between task versions regarding cognitive learning outcomes. However, we hypothesized that the task versions differ regarding affective or motivational outcomes. We further hypothesized that the motivational benefits of game elements counter-balance their higher cognitive processing demands and are partially mediated by affective outcomes.

By testing these hypotheses, we aimed to answer the following research questions. Can specific, separable game features influence cognitive, affective, or motivational learning outcomes in an association learning task? Are motivational effects accompanied or mediated by affective effects as suggested by the ICALM model? Are game elements associated with (partially) antagonistic motivational and cognitive effects?

2 Methods

Participants. In total, 61 participants (44 female, 15 male, 2 diverse) completed the study. The participants' age ranged from 18 to 64 years ($M = 27.56$, $Mdn = 24$, $SD = 11.54$, $MAD = 4.45$; all in units of years). Most of the participants were students (51 of 61). Psychology students were compensated for study participation by course credit. All study participants provided informed consent. The study was approved by the Ethics Committee of the University of Graz.

Study Design. We conducted a value-added research experiment (see Fig. 1). Participants were randomly assigned to one of two experimental conditions. The two experimental conditions comprised two learning task versions differing solely in the use of specific, separable game elements, described below.

Before (pre-task survey) and after (post-task survey) the task, participants were administered questionnaires regarding affective and motivational constructs (besides socio-demographic data). Details on the used questionnaires are given below. Both surveys were implemented with LimeSurvey. After completing data acquisition, appropriate measures of effect size (see below) were computed for all outcome variables regarding differences between the two experimental conditions.

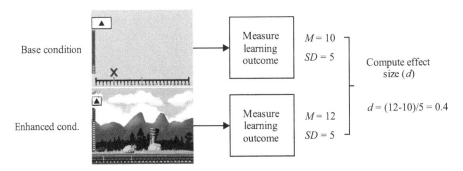

Fig. 1. Study design illustrating condition comparison using fictional descriptive statistics.

Learning Task. The goal of the participants was to memorize associations between 20 symbols and numbers over five consecutive levels. For each symbol, participants had to indicate a number, distributed spatially on a visual number line ranging from 0 to 26 (see Fig. 1) by using the left and right arrow keys of the keyboard and pressing the spacebar to confirm their choice. Each symbol corresponded exactly to one location along the number line specified by its respective number. These associations between symbols and numbers were fixed over the entire task, but initially unknown to the participants. Participants had 20 s for each symbol to select a number and confirm their choice. After each response (or after expiration of the maximum response time of 20 s) participants would receive corrective feedback (see Fig. 1). A green vertical bar would indicate the correct position/number associated with the currently presented symbol and some visual aesthetic, which differed between game and non-game task versions (see below), would indicate if the choice was correct.

The differences between the non-game and game task versions comprised a narrative, visual aesthetics, and a virtual incentive system. The narrative in the game version of the task consisted of a dog walking in a forest searching for bones hidden by an enemy. The only hint the dog would have for the location of the bones was a set of symbols, each associated with a certain position in the ground. By memorizing the associations between symbols and numbers, the participants could assist the dog in finding the hidden bones. In the game version of the task, the cursor's movement was accompanied by a walking animation of the dog. The placement of the cursor (by pressing the spacebar) would initiate a digging animation. Correct positioning resulted in the dog wagging its tail and the bone count increasing by one (incentive system). In the case that the position was incorrect, the dog would cry instead, and the correct position was shown (i.e., corrective feedback). In the non-game version, a green check mark and a red X-symbol would indicate correct and incorrect responses, respectively. The non-game version would also lack all described visual aesthetics. Instead, a constant, empty, grey background was presented (see Fig. 1).

Learning Outcome Measures. Regarding learning outcome measures, we discern between cognitive, affective, and motivational outcome measures. Regarding cognitive outcomes, we discern further between learning efficacy (i.e., did participants learn over the course of the task?) and learning efficiency (i.e., how fast did participants learn?). Efficacy was measured by the number of correct responses for each task level. Efficiency was measured by fitting an exponential learning curve [14] to the series of those numbers for each participant:

$$N_{corr,i}(L) = N_{max}\{1 - exp[-C_i(L - 1)]\} \tag{1}$$

In Eq. (1), $N_{corr,i}(L)$ denotes the number of correct responses of the i-th participant at task level L, $N_{max} = 20$, and the coefficient C_i denotes the rate constant indicating the learning efficiency of the i-th participant.

Affective and motivational outcomes were assessed using self-report questionnaires. Positive and negative affect was assessed before and after the learning task using the positive and negative affect schedule [15]. PANAS provides 20 adjectives describing feelings and emotions like "excited" or "distressed". Participants are asked to indicate the intensity with which they were experiencing these emotions on a 5-point scale ranging from "not at all" to "very much". Ten adjectives are associated with each positive and negative affect. Regarding affect, we compared the two conditions regarding the change in affect from before to after the learning task and testing condition equivalence before the learning task.

To assess motivational outcomes, we used the two subcomponents *interest* (items like "The activity in the learning task was fun") and *perceived competence* (items like "I am satisfied with my performance in the learning task") of the short scale to measure intrinsic motivation developed by Wilde et al. [16]. The two subcomponents comprise 3 items each. All items were answered on a 5-point rating scale ranging from "does not apply at all" to "applies completely". The subscales *perceived choice* and *pressure/tension* were not included since the mechanics of the learning task did not allow for customization of the learning activity.

Motivational outcomes were complemented by the *attractivity* and *stimulation* subscales of the user experience questionnaire [17]. Both subscales consist of several items, each presenting two opposing adjectives, forming the endpoints of a 7-point rating scale, on which participants indicate their experience of the task. In particular, *attractivity* aims to assess how enjoyable, good, pleasing, pleasant, attractive, and friendly a product (or task) is perceived. *Stimulation* aims to assess how valuable, exciting, interesting, and motivating a product (or task) is perceived. Regarding their face validity, the two subscales are thus closely related to qualities associated with (intrinsic) motivation. All motivational outcomes were assessed after the learning task.

Internal consistency of all scales was satisfactory, $\alpha > 0.87$. All scales were administered in German.

Data Analysis. Count data were analyzed regarding statistical significance using Fisher's exact test. Differences between means were statistically analyzed using robust methods based on trimmed means (Yuen's test, robust ANOVA) provided by the WRS2 package [18] with trimming kept at 0.2, if assumptions for parametric tests (t-test, parametric ANOVA) were not met (normality, homogeneity of variances and covariances). Trimmed means are denoted by the symbol M_t. For reporting effect sizes in the case of robust comparisons, we refer to the effect size δ_t suggested by Algina et al. [19] as a robust alternative for Cohen's *d*. Associations between variables were assessed using percentage bend correlations ρ_{pb} (i.e., a robust correlational measure [18]). Mediation models were based on robust regression using *M*-estimators [20]. Indirect effects were tested using Zu and Yuan's robust approach [21]. 95% confidence intervals (CIs) are reported directly following the respective quantity in squared brackets. All statistical analyses were conducted using R [22].

3   Results

Condition Equivalence. Of 61 participants, 33 and 28 participants completed the non-game and game condition of the learning task, respectively. The conditions were equivalent regarding gender distribution, $p > 0.999$, and regarding counts of student and non-student participants, $p = 0.488$. In the non-game condition, the participants' age ranged from 18 to 64 years ($Mdn = 23$, $MAD = 4.45$), while in the game condition, it ranged from 19 to 61 years ($Mdn = 24.5$, $MAD = 5.19$), yielding also no significant difference, $Y_t = 0.30, p = 0.775$.

The conditions were also equivalent regarding participant attrition during the learning task, $p = 0.526$. In the non-game condition, 49 persons started the task and 33 completed it. In the game condition, 47 started the task and 28 completed it. The conditions were further equivalent regarding positive affect before the task (non-game: $M = 3.02, SD = 0.80$; game: $M = 2.90, SD = 0.72$), $t(58.76) = 0.61, p = 0.547$. The conditions were also equivalent regarding negative affect before the task (non-game: $Mdn = 3.10, MAD = 0.89$; game: $Mdn = 3.00, MAD = 0.74$), $Y_t = 0.73, p = 0.476$.

Cognitive Outcomes. Learning efficacy was not significantly different between conditions at any task level. In particular, a robust two-way between-within subjects ANOVA

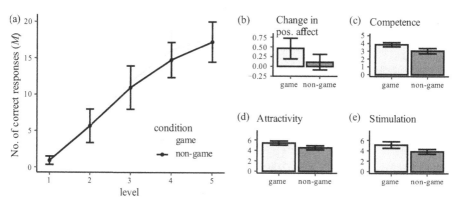

Fig. 2. (Trimmed) means and their 95% CIs for some cognitive, affective and motivational outcome measures.

yielded a significant main effect of level, $Q_{level}(3, 28.19) = 167.76$, $p < 0.001$, yet no significant main effect of condition, $Q_{condition}(1, 33.87) = 0.30$, $p = 0.590$, and also no significant interaction, $Q_{level,condition}(3, 28.19) = 0.52$, $p = 0.673$. The trimmed means and their 95% CIs are provided for each task level in Fig. 2(a).

Learning efficiency was also not significantly different between the game ($M_t = 0.53$ [0.40, 0.65]) and the non-game ($M_t = 0.46$ [0.28, 0.63]) conditions, $\Delta M_t = 0.07$ [-0.13, 0.26], $Y_t = 0.48$, $p = 0.479$, $\delta_t = 0.18$ [-0.32, 0.62].

Affective and Motivational Outcomes. The results for the comparisons between task conditions regarding affective and motivational outcomes are summarized in Table 1. We obtained a significantly larger increase in positive affect from pre- to post-task in the game than in the non-game condition, yielding a medium effect. The means of the change in positive affect for the two conditions and their 95% CIs are depicted in Fig. 2(b). Negative affect decreased from pre- to post-task in the non-game condition, while it increased slightly in the game condition; however, the difference between conditions was not significant, but was again close to a medium effect. We obtained no notable difference in reported interest. Perceived competence was significantly higher in the game than in the non-game condition, see also Fig. 2(c), accounting for a large effect. Also, the task's attractivity and stimulation by the task were rated significantly higher in the game than in the non-game condition, see Fig. 2 (d&e), accounting in both cases for large effects.

Correlational Analyses. Changes from pre- to post-task in negative and positive affect were not significantly correlated with each other ($p > 0.05$). Neither was the change in negative affect significantly correlated with any of the motivational variables ($p > 0.05$). In contrast, the change in positive effect was significantly correlated with all motivational variables ($p < 0.01$), yielding medium associations with $0.34 < \rho_{pb} < 0.44$. Interest was significantly correlated with the other motivational variables ($p < 0.05$), yielding also medium associations with $0.29 < \rho_{pb} < 0.33$. Perceived competence, attractivity, and stimulation were highly correlated among each other ($p < 0.001$), yielding large

Table 1. Results of comparisons between groups concerning the considered affective and motivational outcomes.

Outcome measure	Test statistics	Effect size
Change in pos. affect	$t(53.78) = 2.01, p = 0.049$	$d = 0.52\ [-0.01, 1.06]$
Change in neg. affect	$Y_t = 1.67, p = 0.090$	$\delta_t = 0.48\ [-0.11, 1.06]$
Interest	$Y_t = 0.56, p = 0.538$	$\delta_t = 0.16\ [-0.46, 0.57]$
Competence	$t(58.42) = 3.52, p < 0.001$	$d = 0.89\ [0.37, 1.44]$
Attractivity	$Y_t = 3.00, p = 0.003$	$\delta_t = 0.82\ [0.39, 1.33]$
Stimulation	$Y_t = 3.17, p < 0.001$	$\delta_t = 0.87\ [0.24, 1.69]$

associations with $0.78 < \rho_{pb} < 0.86$, indicating that any of them may be utilized as a proxy for (intrinsic) motivation.

The effect of task condition (non-game or game) on learning efficiency was mediated by attractivity, see Table 2. While we obtained a significant, small indirect effect, both direct and total effects of condition on efficiency were insignificant, indicating that game elements yielded not much of an effect on cognitive outcomes anyway. Replacing attractivity with any of the other two motivational measures yielded very similar, but slightly smaller effects.

The effect of task condition on attractivity was further partially mediated by the change in positive affect, see Table 3. The small significant indirect pathway somewhat reduced the condition's total effect on attractivity, while the dominant contribution was still retained in the direct pathway.

Table 2. Results obtained for the robust mediation model with attractivity mediating the effect of condition (non-game or game) on learning efficiency.

Type	Effect	β	p
Component	Condition → Attractivity	0.73 [0.31, 1.15]	<0.001
	Attractivity → Efficiency	0.26 [0.04, 0.48]	0.020
Indirect	Cond. → Attr. → Eff	0.24 [0.03, 0.55]	0.021
Direct	Condition → Efficiency	−0.12 [−0.56, 0.31]	0.572
Total	Condition → Efficiency	0.09 [−0.33, 0.53]	0.659

4 Discussion

Altogether, we find that specific, separable game features influenced cognitive, affective, and motivational aspects in our association learning task. In particular, they affected the development of positive affect rather than negative affect, which agrees with an earlier

Table 3. Results obtained for the robust mediation model with change in positive affect (ΔPA) mediating the effect of game elements on attractivity.

Type	Effect	β	p
Component	Condition $\rightarrow$ ΔPA	0.46 [−0.06, 0.98]	0.080
	ΔPA $\rightarrow$ Attractivity	0.32 [0.11, 0.53]	0.004
Indirect	Cond. $\rightarrow$ ΔPA $\rightarrow$ Attr	0.17 [0.01, 0.42]	0.038
Direct	Condition $\rightarrow$ Attractivity	0.58 [0.16, 0.99]	0.008
Total	Condition $\rightarrow$ Attractivity	0.73 [0.31, 1.15]	<0.001

finding of the capability of game-based learning to elicit especially positive (epistemic) emotions [23]. Our correlational analyses indicated that the two assessed dimensions of user experience [17] in the form of attractivity and stimulation may be utilized as proxies for (intrinsic) motivation. Doing so in subsequent mediation analyses revealed that motivation appears at least partially mediated by these changes in positive affect. Finally, and in line with earlier studies [9, 10], our mediation analysis (Table 2) provides some evidence that game elements are associated with antagonistic effects on cognitive outcomes, i.e., their motivational benefits may effectively balance their their slightly higher demand on cognitive resources.

It should be noted that the task did not represent a very favorable context for game elements taking effect at all. In earlier studies on fraction estimation [12, 24], basically the same game elements were intrinsically integrated into the learning task. Choosing the correct location along the number line required to estimate a given fraction accurately and a suitable game narrative elaborated why the information about the location was given in form of a fraction in the first place. In the present implementation of the task, however, the associations between symbols and locations along a numbered line were neither tied to the visual aesthetics nor to the background narrative. Neither was there any further meaning to the incentive system apart from providing feedback on learning progress. Overall, the intrinsic integration of game elements can be regarded as relatively low in the present case. Yet the more noteworthy seem the effects of those game features regarding affective and motivational outcomes (also considering the small sample size). The coherence principle developed within multimedia learning research would advocate avoiding any additional, unnecessary information [25], which would certainly apply to our game elements in the present context from a mere cognitive perspective. In line with a more integrative perspective [9], we arrive, however, at a very different conclusion. Cognitively, the additional costs introduced by game elements are effectively balanced by their indirect effects along the affect-motivation-cognition pathway in line with the ICALM model [8]. However, regarding their affective and motivational effects, they may come with substantial benefits.

Limitations and Outlook. The limited characterization of the assessed participant sample does not allow us to determine if and how our results, particularly positive and negative affect baselines, may depend on comfort or familiarity with (serious) games. Besides investigating these relations, future studies are also required to scrutinize how the effects of game elements are related to prior knowledge or existing expertise with memorization tasks by extending the study beyond the assessment of (mainly) university students. The influence of the value assigned to such a specific learning task by the participants must also be addressed in future research. The latter may further illuminate if differences between game and non-game conditions can be traced back to individual components of game elements, for instance, if differences in feedback attractiveness could underlie differences in perceived competence. Another pathway for future research is seen in investigating long-term memory effects of game elements beyond short-term efficacy in the present work. Finally, our correlational analysis cannot confirm causal relations. Causation also implies temporal directionality and exclusion of alternative causation pathways. Regarding temporal directionality, our results cannot confirm that attractive design elements lead to a positive, affective response, which, in turn, leads to enhanced motivation. The latter might indeed be a foundation of the persistent activity players can show when immersed in a well-designed game, which, according to SDT [1], is a characteristic of high-quality learning. However, illuminating this requires digging deeper into the microstructure of the learning process. One way (among others) to approach this would be to temporally resolve the development of affective dynamics by, for instance, leveraging the potential of multimodal assessment of physiological correlates in future studies besides longitudinal, repeated sampling of situational interest, motivation, and emotion.

References

1. Ryan, R.M., Rigby, C.S.: Motivational foundations of game-based learning. In: Plass, J.L., Mayer, R.E., Homer, B.D. (eds.) Handbook of Game-Based Learning, pp. 153–176. MIT Press, London (2020)
2. Barz, N., Benick, M., Dörrenbächer-Ulrich, L., Perels, F.: The effect of digital game-based learning interventions on cognitive, metacognitive, and affective-motivational learning outcomes in school: a meta-analysis. Rev. Educ. Res., 003465432311677 (2023)
3. Hu, Y., Gallagher, T., Wouters, P., Van Der Schaaf, M., Kester, L.: Game-based learning has good chemistry with chemistry education: a three-level meta-analysis. J. Res. Sci. Teach. **59**, 1499–1543 (2022)
4. Looyestyn, J., Kernot, J., Boshoff, K., Ryan, J., Edney, S., Maher, C.: Does gamification increase engagement with online programs? A Syst. Rev. PLOS ONE **12**(3), e0173403 (2017)
5. Sailer, M., Homner, L.: The gamification of learning: a meta-analysis. Educ. Psychol. Rev. **32**(1), 77–112 (2020)
6. Zhang, Q., Yu, Z.: Meta-analysis on investigating and comparing the effects on learning achievement and motivation for gamification and game-based learning. Educ. Res. Int., 1519880 (2022)
7. Loderer, K., Pekrun, R., Plass, J.L.: Emotional foundations of game-based learning. In: Plass, J.L., Mayer, R.E., Homer, B.D. (eds.) Handbook of Game-Based Learning, pp. 111–151. MIT Press, London (2020)
8. Plass, J.L., Kaplan, U.: Emotional design in digital media for learning. In: Tettegah, S.Y., Gartmeier, M. (eds.) Emotions, Technology, Design, and Learning, pp. 131–161. Academic Press, Cambridge (2016)
9. Park, B., Flowerday, T., Brünken, R.: Cognitive and affective effects of seductive details in multimedia learning. Comput. Hum. Behav. **44**, 267–278 (2015)

10. Huber, S.E., Cortez, R., Lindstedt, A., Kiili, K., Ninaus, M.: Game elements enhance engagement and mitigate attrition in online learning tasks. Comput. Hum. Behav. **149**, 107948 (2023)
11. Bernecker, K., Ninaus, M.: No pain, no gain? Investigating motivational mechanisms of game elements in cognitive tasks. Comput. Hum. Behav. **114**, 106542 (2021)
12. Ninaus, M., et al.: The added value of game elements: better training performance but comparable learning gains. Educ. Technol. Res. Dev. (2023)
13. Mayer, R.E.: Cognitive foundations of game-based learning. In: Plass, J.L., Mayer, R.E., Homer, B.D. (eds.) Handbook of Game-Based Learning, pp. 83–110. MIT Press, London (2020)
14. Leibowitz, N., Baum, B., Enden, G., Karniel, A.: The exponential learning equation as a function of successful trials results in sigmoid performance. J. Math. Psychol. **54**, 338–340 (2013)
15. Breyer, B., Bluemke, M.: Deutsche Version der Positive and Negative Affect Schedule PANAS (GESIS Panel). Leibniz-Institut für Sozialwissenschaften, Mannheim (2016)
16. Wilde, M., Bätz, K., Kovaleva, A., Urhahne, D.: Überprüfung einer Kurzskala intrinsicher Motivation (KIM). Zeitschrift Didaktik Naturwissenschaften **15**, 31–45 (2009)
17. Schrepp, M., Hinderks, A., Thomaschewski, J.: Die UX KPI - Wunsch und Wirklichkeit. In: Hess, S., Fischer, H. (eds.) Mensch und Computer 2017 - Usability Professionals, pp. 117–125. Gesellschaft für Informatik e.V., Regensburg (2017)
18. Mair, P., Wilcox, R.R.: Robust statistical methods in R using the WRS2 package. Behav. Res. Methods **52**, 464–488 (2020)
19. Algina, J., Keselman, H.J., Penfield, R.D.: An alternative to Cohen's standardized mean difference effect size: a robust parameter and confidence interval in the two independent groups case. Psychol. Methods **10**(3), 317–328 (2005)
20. Venables, W.N., Ripley, B.D.: Modern Applied Statistics with S, 4th edn. Springer, New York (2002). https://doi.org/10.1007/978-0-387-21706-2
21. Zu, J., Yuan, K.: Local influence and robust procedures for mediation analysis. Multivar. Behav. Res. **45**(1), 1–44 (2010)
22. R Core Team: R: A language and environment for statistical computing. R Foundation for Statistical Computing, Vienna (2022). https://www.R-project.org
23. Kiili, K., Siuko, J., Cloude, E., Dindar, M.: Motivation and emotions in a health literacy game: insights from co-occurrence network analysis. In: Kiili, K., Antti, K., de Rosa, F., Dindar, M., Kickmeier-Rust, M., Bellotti, F. (eds.) Games and Learning Alliance. GALA 2022, LNCS, vol. 13647, pp. 149–159. Springer, Cham (2022). https://doi.org/10.1007/978-3-031-22124-8_15
24. Kiili, K., Moeller, K., Ninaus, M.: Evaluating the effectiveness of a game-based rational number training—In-game metrics as learning indicators. Comput. Educ. **120**, 13–28 (2018)
25. Mayer, R.E. (ed.): The Cambridge Handbook of Multimedia Learning. Cambridge University Press, New York (2005)

An Introduction to Game-Based Competence Assessment Based on Cognitive Diagnostic Models

Michael D. Kickmeier-Rust[✉] [ID], Corsin Niggli, and Katharina Richter

St.Gallen University of Teacher Education, St.Gallen, Switzerland
{michael.kickmeier,katharina.richter}@phsg.ch,
corsin.niggli@student.phsg.ch

Abstract. In Serious Games, in particular in learning and training games, the assessment of competencies and skills is crucial for monitoring learning progress, tailoring learning experiences, and providing individual formative feedback. A sound psychometric diagnostic of competencies is not trivial, however. Conventional scoring techniques have severe shortcomings in terms of accuracy and the degree to which actionable information can be drawn from them. In this paper we introduce Cognitive Diagnostic Models and in particular Competence-based Knowledge Space Theory as theoretical underpinnings of in-game competence assessments. We exemplify the approach by a gamified mathematics learning scenario named Mathiade and illustrate the steps of developing, implementing, and evaluating competence models.

Keywords: Competence Assessment · Cognitive Diagnostic Models · Competence-based Knowledge Space Theory · Mathematics

1 Introduction

Digitization is changing education; there is a strong movement toward stronger competence-orientation, formative and contextualized assessments, as well as evidence-based personalization of learning. Along with these developments, digital games are about to play an increasingly important role. Educational games, in a very natural way, focus on the learners' competencies and skills, they can provide clear goals and rules, a relevant learning context, an engaging storyline, immediate feedback, a high level of interactivity, challenge and competition, random elements of surprise, and rich and appealing learning environments. These factors not only determine motivation to play but are also considered important for successful and effective learning. Meta-reviews [1–3] revealed that digital games can significantly increase learning success as opposed to conventional learning media, even though the effect sizes are generally moderate. A substantial body of research reported that a key element of a serious game's success is a suitable personalization and balancing of learning and gaming experiences [4]. This endeavor, however, requires a solid understanding of individual learning processes, strengths, weaknesses, knowledge gaps, and learning dispositions by a game

P. Dondio et al. (Eds.): GALA 2023, LNCS 14475, pp. 244–253, 2024.
https://doi.org/10.1007/978-3-031-49065-1_24

as an autonomous tutorial system. In other words, individualized learning and gaming require valid, reliable, and accurate assessments [5]. The approaches to in-game assessment and non-invasive adaptation of games have been refined significantly over the past decade [6]. State-of-the-art psychometric methods include the concept of stealth assessment [7], which is a method for embedding assessment seamlessly into games. A different approach to stealth assessment was introduced by [8]; it applies recurrent neural networks (long short-term memory networks) models for assessment. In addition, there exist structural, combinatorial models [9], cognitive classification models [10], Bayesian approaches [11], latent variable models [12] and methods from the fields of learning analytics research [13] and machine learning [14]. The likely most popular combinatorial methods are Cognitive Diagnostic Models (CDM) [15].

1.1 Cognitive Diagnostic Models and Knowledge Space Theory

Cognitive Diagnostic Models (CDMs) or Diagnostic Classification Models represent a psychometric framework for collecting, analyzing, and reporting diagnostic data. CDMs provide discrete multivariate fine-grained diagnostic feedback information about learners' strengths and weaknesses for developing targeted instruction and personalized support [16]. Knowledge Space Theory (KST) [17] can be considered a member of the CDM family. [18] for example, have elaborated on the relationships between CDM and KST. It represents a structural, combinatorial approach, which may serve as a counterpart to the statistical models. The starting point is the notion of a so-called knowledge domain, which is a set of problems taken from a certain area. For instance, additions, subtraction, multiplication, and division of positive integers are problems of the domain basic algebra. To provide an example, assume that the knowledge domain $Q = \{a, b, c, d, e, f\}$ consists of six problems a, b, c, d, e, and f. The performance state of a person is represented by the subset of problems from Q that the person can solve. However, if we look at the answer patterns a sufficiently large number of subjects exhibit on these six problems, then most certainly not all possible subsets (there are $2^{|Q|} = 64$ subsets in our example) will actually occur. A person who can solve a problem that requires multiplying two positive integers will also be capable of solving a problem that involves an addition of two positive integers. This means that from a correct solution to the first problem we can surmise a correct solution to the second problem. This kind of mutual dependency is captured in a so-called prerequisite relation. By this relation, the number of performance states is restricted: items cannot establish a performance state without their prerequisite items. The collection of the performance states corresponding to a prerequisite relation is called a (quasi-ordinal) performance space (or knowledge space). The original concept of KST only operated on the observable performance dimension. To account for the underlying latent cognitive processes, the approach has been extended, emphasizing the underlying latent competences, which are necessary to solve a problem. Such extensions came, for example, from [19–21]. We subsume the approaches, specifically that of [21], under the term Competence-based Knowledge Space Theory (CbKST). Competences (skills, knowledge, aptitude) can be defined as a fine-grained (often termed atomic) latent theoretical construct which determines a person's observable behavior respectively performance, i.e., if a person solves a test item/task or not. Competence and performance structures can be mapped to each other utilizing interpretation respectively representation functions. On this basis, a latent, structural competence model can be established, describing individual competence states and learning paths. A particular advantage is that learning processes – from the stage of holding none of the skills and competencies of a domain to possessing all – are not seen as a linear, unidimensional approach but a rather multidimensional processes with multiple, individual learning paths [5]. KST models have been advanced in various applied directions [17], and they have been applied in the field of adaptive serious games.

KST provides several standard validation methods. These methods investigate the consistency of empirical answer patterns and the patterns hypothesized by a knowledge (or competence) structure. Different numerical measures have been proposed, for example, the Discrepancy Index [22] or the Distance Agreement Coefficient [23] or the Minimal Symmetric Set Difference [24], which likely is the most common metric. An important quality indicator for the structural competence modelling approach KST is a size-fit trade-off; with increasing model size (number of competence/performance states) the fit (the number of explained empirical answer patterns) increases automatically. A validation method to account for this trade-off was presented by [25]. The principal idea is to compare all possible prerequisite relations for a given set of competences (or items) and select the one that offers the best fit to a set of empirically observed answer patterns. The method offers statistical data about the relations between the cumulative relative frequencies of partial order types, number of relations in a partial order, and a certain goodness-of-fit-criterion.

In this paper we demonstrate the potential of CDM in general and CbKST in particular, to conduct a fine-grained competence-oriented assessment. We exemplify the approach in high school mathematics in the domain of fractions. In a first step we explain the development of a competence model and in a second step we evaluate the model with the data from a gamified math app.

1.2 Modelling the Domain of Fraction Arithmetic

Fraction arithmetic presents students with complex challenges and requires students to have a solid understanding of the basic concepts in arithmetic. We started the generation of a CbKST-type competence model by analyzing curricula, for example, LehrplanPLUS (www.lehrplanplus.bayern.de) and the relevant literature in math didactics (e.g., [27]). A systematic content analysis revealed a set of key skills (cf. Table 1). The level of granularity of the model depends on the nature of tasks. In other words, with certain task types it is possible to identify certain skills and sets of skills. To avoid an unnecessary large model, the key skills have been grouped into nine distinct competencies (Table 1).

In a next step, we developed the CbKST-type surmise relation among the competencies. The surmise relation states whether we can assume from mastering one task the mastery of another. This relation is shown in Fig. 1, left panel. This graphical representation is identical with the Q matrix of CDMs. The graph reads from bottom to top; lower competencies are considered prerequisites of higher ones (e.g., $c1$ is a prerequisite of $c3$). Competence $c9$ is considered independent from the others, which are built upon each other. From the surmise (or prerequisite) relation we can derive the competence structure by set inclusion (Fig. 1, right panel). The competence structure (depending on its mathematical properties, it is called competence space or learning space [17]) is the set of all admissible states – i.e., the combination of competencies – in which a learner can be if the assumed surmise relation is true. The competence structure includes the empty and the full set of competencies. The edges of the graph indicate admissible learning paths.

Table 1. Competencies in the domain of fraction arithmetic.

Level	Description	Skill	Competency
1	Basic mathematical concept	a_1	c_1
2	Whole number arithmetic	b_1	c_2
	Mathematical symbols	b_2	
	Non-symbolic representations	b_3	
	Non-symbolic proportional reasoning	b_4	
	Number line estimation	b_5	
	Equivalence of ratios	b_6	
3	Multiplication with whole number	c_1	c_3
	Division with whole number	c_2	
	Addition with whole number	c_3	
	Subtraction with whole number	c_4	
4	Recognizing equivalent fractions	d_1	c_4
	Ordering fractions	d_2	
	Describing fractions in different form	d_3	
	Knowledge of fraction magnitudes	d_4	
5	Multiplication with fractions	e_1	c_5
	Division with fractions	e_2	c_6
	Subtraction with fractions	e_3	c_7
	Addition with fractions	e_4	c_8
6	Reduce fractions	f_1	c_9

1.3 *Mathiade*: A Gamified Math Competition

In educational settings, gamification is utilized primarily to facilitate learners' motivation, engagement, concentration, probably decrease frustration and thus – as the ultimate consequence – improve (learning) performance [28]. There is a broad range of studies investigating the effects of various gamification applications in education. *Mathiade* is a gamification scenario for an entire lesson in a classroom setting that combines competition and cooperation in mathematics learning, both are supposed to be strong facilitators of performance. In educational settings, leaderboards represent rankings of learners according to certain measurable variables, including performance, achievements, diligence, and perseverance [29]. Leaderboards compare these variables of individuals with several opponents and, thereby, induce a competitive environment. Competition, in turn, is considered a key element of game and play, that is supposed to encourage learners to persistently carry out certain tasks. As [30] pointed out, the board leaders may provide others with a (more or less desirable) goal to reach, that is, keeping up with the leaders. This goal could improve performance by guiding attention, improving motivation and persistence, and promoting the use of goal-relevant strategies. The second gamification element in our scenario is cooperation. Cooperation can be seen as a behavior that is facilitated by gamification, but it also can be considered a game mechanic on its own [31]. Cooperation supports a mutual exchange of ideas, knowledge, and skills on the one hand, and it influences psychological variables and sentiment (e.g., group norms and social identity), which in turn raise motivation, engagement, and perseverance [32].

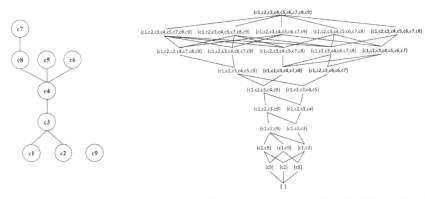

Fig. 1. The left panel shows the surmise relation for the domain described in Table 1; the right panel shows the resulting competence structure.

First, the students were arranged in groups of three or four students by the teacher. The groups evenly included stronger and weaker students as well as high and low communicative students. The groups competed for points by solving mathematics tasks in an online interface (Fig. 2). Each student worked separately, however, in the interface the students always saw the live results (i.e., the tasks completed and the points) of other group members. Assuming that each member (especially the high performers and students with highly competitive characteristics) of a group wanted to win the competition, collaboration and mutual help were possible. High performers were intended to support other group members when they encountered those who underperformed. The way the students communicated and collaborated was open. On a center screen in the classroom, all students saw the live rankings of the groups (Fig. 2) – without information about the performance of individuals. By having a public ranking via the group leaderboard, low performers were less exposed and perhaps stigmatized due to possibly poor performance. This approach was intended to reduce the perception of stress and other socially and emotionally detrimental effects for individuals. Technically, the interface has been realized in HTML 5 as a browser-based app. Dynamic functions (i.e., display of tasks, scoring, display of live results, data storage) have been realized with PHP and JavaScript. The backend was a mySQL database. The application consisted of an item pool, the student interface, the group leaderboard, and additional administrative functions.

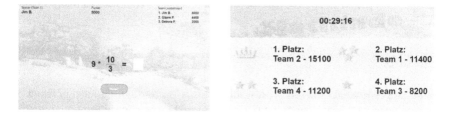

Fig. 2. Screenshots of the *Mathiade* app.

2 Study Implementation

To exemplify the CbKST assessment procedure, we implemented Mathiade for the 10th grade in a secondary school in Switzerland. We investigated general performance measures, and we used the students' response data to evaluate and revise the competence model. The research question is whether the gamification scenario is superior to a conventional, non-gamified setting.

2.1 Participants

In total, 43 students participated in the study. We recruited four classes of a 10th grade of a secondary school in Liechtenstein with 10 to 12 students in each class. The average age of the students was 17 years. For the study the class teacher formed heterogenous groups (in terms of performance and openness) of 2 to 4 students. For practical reasons we assigned the students of the entire classes to either control or experimental group.

2.2 Procedure and Materials

All classroom activities were administered by the regular class teacher. Beforehand, the teachers were instructed about the procedures and specifically about keeping systematic logs about collaborative events during the lesson. First, we made a baseline survey on student motivation. A week later, we carried out the mathematics competition scenario in two groups, one with and one without gamification. Another week later we carried out the scenario again and changed control and experimental group. For the mathematics competition students had exactly 30 min. In both groups, communicating and working together in groups was allowed but not explicitly required. Directly after the session, we issued the motivation questionnaire again. During the sessions, teachers kept logs about any events, specifically collaborative events. For the mathematics competition we developed a set of 120 test items in the domain of fraction arithmetic. The items cover the basic arithmetic operators addition, subtraction, multiplication and division. Devisor as well as dividend were either integers or fractions. Examples are 5 + 3/8, 7/9 - 8y, and 6/12 * 7/24. The results had to be entered in text fields, either as integer or as a fraction (Fig. 2). In the control group, the students worked on the tasks in the form of a paper-and-pencil test. The students were instructed to complete as many items as possible within 30 min.

3 Results

In terms of performance (i.e., correctly solved tasks) we did not find a significant difference in the gamification condition (GC) as opposed to the control (non-gamification) group (CG). In the GC the number of correctly solved tasks was somewhat lower (M = 41.89, SD = 15.74) than in the CG (61.00, SD = 22.77). The session date (gamification in the first session, no gamification in the second and vice versa) had an effect as well; in the first session the results were higher (M = 48.87, SD = 29.56) in comparison to the second session (M = 32.58, SD = 19.89). Given the study setup, where the cooperation of students was the focus, absolute performance plays a subordinate role, however. More important is the loss in performance from session 1 to session 2, which is an indicator of the students' motivation. In the gamification condition (GC) the loss in performance (22%) is clearly lower than in the CG (69%). Which is a remarkable difference. A repeated measures ANOVA yielded a non-significant main effect for condition (p = .157), however, a significant main effect of time (F(1,23) = 17.59, p = .001) and a significant interaction (F(1,23) = 13.64, p = .003). This result provides some evidence that gamification can indeed sustain motivation in repeated tasks. The domain modelling (Sect. 3) resulted in a surmise relation (Fig. 1, left panel), from which we derived the latent competence structure (Fig. 1, right panel). This structure denotes all admissible combinations of competences a learner may hold. This is a latent model, meaning that the competencies cannot be observed directly. Therefore, we link the competencies to the tasks. In terms of CbKST this linkage is named representation function. It specifies all the competencies that are necessary to master a certain task (cf. Table 2). This linkage results in the set of possible test results, that is, the set of mastered and not mastered tasks. If a learner possesses all the competencies that are necessary to master a task, this student should in fact master that task. Given that the real answer patterns of students may include errors such as slips and lucky guesses the identification of competence states is not unique. Therefore, we applied the minimal symmetric set distance (MSSD) [24] to analyze the data. This metric represents the difference between a given empirical response pattern and the closest competence state. The corresponding algorithm is described by [33]. For the hypothesized model (Fig. 1), the mean MSSD was 9.03 (SD = 3.69); the maximum set difference for 120 tasks is N/2 = 60. The number of identified competence states was 6, including the full and the empty set. The identified states are bolded in Fig. 1. The average number of tasks presented to students was 75.83 (SD = 37.02) a mean MSSD of 9.03 is satisfying in terms of identifying the competencies of learners; it means – on average – that 9 of 75 tasks results (12%) deviated from the hypothesized model.

Table 2. Representation function – linkage of competencies and tasks

Competencies										
		c1	c2	c3	c4	c5	c6	c7	c8	c9
Tasks	1	1	1	1	1				1	
	2	1	1	1	1				1	
	...	...								
	119	1	1	1	1		1			1
	120	1	1	1	1		1		1	1

The evaluation of a model's goodness of fit, typically arises from the comparison of several models, given that there is no ground truth. Such comparisons are beyond of the scope of this paper.

4   Discussion

In the present paper, we have demonstrated the use of CbKST, a family member of CDM, to conduct assessment in situations with a large degree of freedom, as it usually occurs in serious games. As opposed to a conventional approach to performance or competence assessment, the approach does not result in a single value, e.g., the percentage of correctly solved tasks, but in a set of probabilities with which a student may hold each of the competencies of a domain. In the presented *Mathiade* setting, the advantage is obvious. In the data, we found rather heterogenous and often contradictory results, where equivalent tasks were solved and not solved by the same student. When, however, computing the solution frequencies we obtain a mean of 0.49 with a SD of 0.19. By the CbKST-based assessment we could identify the competencies the learners hold, ranging from all to none of the competencies. The biggest advantage of the approach is that it uncovers actionable information about learners. From the identified competence states tailored interventions (e.g., providing individual learners with concrete learning content) or highly specific feedback can be derived. One can argue that the certainty of assessments may be weak. However, the same goes for computing solution frequencies, as discussed above. Other psychometric approaches, for example, Item Response Theory, are much more demanding, they require, for example, standardization studies of tasks. In serious games, this is most likely not possible for cost reasons. And, more importantly, in serious games all sorts of actions can be linked to certain available and lacking competencies. This concept has been described under the term micro adaptivity [34]. The technical implementation, in turn, is more challenging since the CbKST approach requires (a) a detailed modelling of the domain and (b) the implementation of assessment algorithms. There do exist, however, comprehensive introductions including *R* Shiny demonstrations (cf. Tquant.eu). The modelling procedures described in this paper follow the framework of Evidence Centered Design (ECD) [35], which serves as a scaffolding for the realization of CbKST based in-game assessments.

References

1. Clark, D.B., Tanner-Smith, E.E., Killingsworth, S.S.: Digital games, design, and learning: a systematic review and meta-analysis. Rev. Educ. Res. **86**(1), 79–122 (2016)
2. Wouters, P.J.M., van Oostendorp, H.: A meta-analytic review of the role of instructional support in game-based learning. Comput. Educ. **60**, 412–425 (2013)
3. Wouters, P.J.M., Van Nimwegen, C., Van Oostendorp, H., Van Der Spek, E.D.: A meta-analysis of the cognitive and motivational effects of serious games. J. Educ. Psychol. **105**, 249–265 (2013)
4. Wouters, P., van Oostendorp, H.: Overview of instructional techniques to facilitate learning and motivation of serious games. In: Wouters, P., van Oostendorp, H. (eds.) Instructional Techniques to Facilitate Learning and Motivation of Serious Games. AGL, pp. 1–16. Springer, Cham (2017). https://doi.org/10.1007/978-3-319-39298-1_1
5. Kickmeier-Rust, M.D., Albert, D.: Educationally adaptive: balancing serious games. Int. J. Comput. Sci. Sport **11**(1), 15–28 (2012)
6. Bellotti, F., Kapralos, B., Lee, K., Moreno-Ger, P., Berta, R.: Assessment in and of serious games: an overview. Adv. Hum.-Comput. Interact. **2013**, 1–11 (2013)
7. Shute, V., Ke, F., Wang, L.: Assessment and adaptation in games. In: Wouters, P., van Oostendorp, H. (eds.) Instructional Techniques to Facilitate Learning and Motivation of Serious Games. AGL, pp. 59–78. Springer, Cham (2017). https://doi.org/10.1007/978-3-319-39298-1_4
8. Akram, B., Wookhee, M., Wiebe, E., Mott, B., Boyer, K.E., Lester, J.: Improving stealth assessment in game-based learning with LSTM-based analytics. In: Proceedings of the Eleventh International Conference on Educational Data Mining, Buffalo, New York (2018)
9. Nyamsuren, E., van der Maas, H.L.J., Maurer, M.: Set-theoretical and combinatorial instruments for problem space analysis in adaptive serious games. Int. J. Serious Games **5**(1), 5–18 (2018)
10. Heller, J., Stefanutti, L., Anselmi, P., Robusto, E.: On the link between cognitive diagnostic models and knowledge space theory. Psychometrika **80**, 995–1019 (2015)
11. Käser, T., Klingler, S., Schwing, A.G., Gross, M.: Dynamic Bayesian Networks for student modeling. IEEE Trans. Learn. Technol. **10**(4), 450–462 (2017)
12. Mislevy, R.J., Oranje, A., Bauer, M., von Davier, A.A., Hao, J., et al.: Psychometric Considerations in Game-Based Assessment. GlassLab, Redwood City, CA (2014)
13. Kickmeier-Rust, M.D.: Learning analytics for an in serious games. In: Proceedings of the Joint Workshop of the GALA Network of Excellence and the LEA's BOX Project at EC-TEL 2014, 17 September 2014, Graz, Austria (2014)
14. Rowe, J., Lester. J.: Improving student problem solving in narrative-centered learning environments: a Modular Reinforcement Learning Framework. In: Proceedings of the Seventeenth International Conference on Artificial Intelligence in Education, Madrid, Spain (2015)
15. de la Torre, J., Carmona, G., Kieftenbeld, V., Tjoe, H., Lima, C.: Diagnostic classification models and mathematics education research: opportunities and Challenges. In: Izsák, A., Remillard, J.T., Templin, J. (Eds.), Psychometric Methods in Mathematics Education: Opportunities, Challenges, and Interdisciplinary Collaborations, pp. 53–72. National Council of Teachers of Mathematics, Reston, VA (2016)
16. Xin, T., Wang, C., Chen, P., Liu, Y.: Editorial: cognitive diagnostic models: methods for practical applications. Front. Psychol. **13**, 895399 (2021)
17. Falmagne, J.-C.: Thirty years of knowledge space theory: the beginning, the core ideas, and the assessment spaces. Paper presented at the EMPG Meeting 2015 at Padua, Italy, 01–03 September (2015)

18. Heller, J., Stefanutti, L., Anselmi, P., Robusto, E.: Erratum to: on the link between cognitive diagnostic models and knowledge space theory. Psychometrika **81**, 250–251 (2016)
19. Doignon, J.: Probabilistic Assessment of Knowledge. In: Albert, D. (ed.) Knowledge Structures, pp. 1–56. Springer, New York (1994). https://doi.org/10.1007/978-3-642-520 64-8_1
20. Düntsch, I., Gediga, G.: Skills and knowledge structures. Br. J. Math. Stat. Psychol. **48**, 9–27 (1995)
21. Korossy, K.: Modelling knowledge as competence and performance. In: Albert, D., Lukas, J. (eds.) Knowledge Spaces: Theories, Empirical Research Applications, pp. 103–132. Lawrence Erlbaum Associates, Mahwah, NJ (1999)
22. Kambouri, M., Koppen, M., Villano, M., Falmagne, J.-C.: Knowledge assessment: tapping human expertise by the QUERY routine. Int. J. Hum. Comput. Stud. **40**, 119–151 (1994)
23. Schrepp, M., Held, T., Albert, D.: Component–based construction of surmise relations for chess problems. In: Albert, D., Lukas, J. (eds.) Knowledge Spaces: Theories, Empirical Research, and Applications, pp. 41–66. Lawrence Erlbaum Associates, Mahwah, NJ (1999)
24. Schrepp, M.: A method for comparing knowledge structures concerning their adequacy. J. Math. Psychol. **45**, 480–496 (2001)
25. Albert, D., Kickmeier-Rust, M.D., Matsuda, F.: A formal framework for modelling the developmental course of competence and performance in the distance, speed, and time domain. Dev. Rev. **28**, 401–420 (2008)
26. Obersteiner, A., Dresler, T., Bieck, S.M., Moeller, K.: Understanding fractions: Integrating results from mathematics education, cognitive psychology, and neuroscience. Construct. Num.: Merg. Perspect. Psychol. Math. Educ., 135–162 (2019)
27. Padberg, F.: Didaktik der Bruchrechnung für Lehrerausbildung und Lehrerfortbildung, 4th edn. Spektrum, Heidelberg (2009)
28. Oliveira, W., Hamari, J., Shi, L., et al.: Tailored gamification in education: a literature review and future agenda. Educ. Inf. Technol. **28**, 373–406 (2023)
29. Nebel, S., Beege, M., Schneider, S., Rey, G.D.: The higher the score, the higher the learning outcome? Heterogeneous impacts of leaderboards and choice within educational videogames. Comput. Hum. Behav. **65**, 391–401 (2016)
30. Landers, R.N., Bauer, K.N., Callan, R.C.: Gamification of task performance with leaderboards: a goal setting experiment. Comput. Hum. Behav. **71**, 508–515 (2017)
31. Erickson, L.V., Sammons-Lohse, D.: Learning through video games: the impacts of competition and cooperation. E-Learn. Digit. Med. **18**(1), 1–17 (2021)
32. Reza Keramati, M., Gillies, R.M.: Teaching cooperative learning through cooperative learning environment: a qualitative follow-up of an experimental study. Interact. Learn. Environ., 1–13 (2022)
33. Hockemeyer, C.: Documentation of the libsrbi Library (2000). https://kst.cord-hockemeyer. info/techreports/libsrbi_TechRep_FWF00.pdf
34. Kickmeier-Rust, M.D., Albert, D. (eds.): An Alien's Guide to Multi-adaptive Educational Games. Informing Science Press, Santa Rosa, CA (2012)
35. Kim, Y.J., Almond, R.J., Shute, V.: Applying evidence-centered design for the development of game-based assessments in physics playground. Int. J. Test., 1–22 (2016)

A Teacher-Configurable Scoring System for Serious Games

Alessandro Pighetti[1]([✉]) [iD], Luca Forneris[1] [iD], Francesco Bellotti[1],
Alessio Capello[1] [iD], Marianna Cossu[1] [iD], Giuseppe Gioco[2], and Riccardo Berta[1] [iD]

[1] Department of Electrical, Electronic and Telecommunication Engineering (DITEN),
University of Genoa, Via Opera Pia 11a, 16145 Genoa, Italy
`{alessandro.pighetti,luca.forneris,alessio.capello,`
`marianna.cossu}@edu.unige.it, {francesco.bellotti,`
`riccardo.berta}@unige.it`
[2] Wondertech Srl, Via Marcello Staglieno, 10/9, 16129 Genoa, Italy
`giuseppe.gioco@wondertechweb.com`

Abstract. Serious Games (SGs) are versatile tools that entertain while addressing serious issues through digital or analog gameplay. However, ensuring continuous supervision during gameplay can be challenging. To overcome this, we propose a flexible scoring system that automates procedure evaluation, empowering learners and promoting independent skill development. By conceptualizing procedures as ordered actions with specific information, our approach enriches the learning experience, making SGs more effective educational instruments. This research advances SGs, allowing students to take control of their learning journey and improving information retention through practical experiences. With this innovative scoring mechanism, SGs hold the promise of becoming even more impactful in addressing critical educational challenges.

Keywords: Serious Games · Scoring System · Procedure Evaluation · Learning Experience · Educational Instruments

1 Introduction

Procedural learning is a crucial skill that involves developing perceptual and motor abilities through extensive practice, since it enables efficient processing and automatic responses to complex environmental events. Serious Games (SG) have emerged as a valid tool for education and training on procedures [1].

This paper introduces a flexible scoring system with the goal of enhancing the learning process of SGs without requiring the continuous supervision from a teacher. Our proposed approach involves encapsulating the teacher's knowledge within an automated system to evaluate procedure execution. A key aspect of our system is the conceptualization of procedures as sequences of ordered actions. We incorporate a Golden Path (GP) which pertains to a precise sequence of actions indicating the correct procedure in detail. The comprehensive evaluation of SGs should include player performance assessment, as these games are intended to support knowledge acquisition. Therefore, SGs should be capable of evaluating the learning progress, ensuring that rewards and game advancement are closely linked to it [2].

The remainder of the paper is organized as follows: Sect. 2 explores the current state of SGs, Sect. 3 explains the approach used in the study, specifically focusing on the proposed method for implementing a scoring system, Sect. 4 presents an example of our approach based on the medical sector and the Sect. 5 highlights the key factor of the presented work and addresses its limitations and discusses potential avenues for future enhancements.

2 Related Works

Relevant research lines in the SGs context include Moreno-Ger et al. [3] discussing key elements needed for such a system to be more mainstream, Lameras et al. [4] examining how learning attributes and game mechanics can be integrated into lesson plans, Laamarti et al. [5] proposing a taxonomy for digital SGs, Codreanu et al. [6] proposing a home system for older adults in healthcare, [7, 8] presenting two SGs for medic field training. Simulators are crucial in developing and designing SGs, providing an immersive, realistic environment for training and education. Limited availability of dedicated engines requires entertainment-based game development tools. Cowan et al. [9] list common frameworks and game engines, while Brown et al. [7] implement a combat medic simulator using physiology engines and human-computer interfaces.

2.1 Scoring System Management

Designing scoring systems in social games is crucial for player satisfaction and engagement [4]. The GP represents the optimal sequence of actions for task completion, aiding supervisors in analyzing player performance [7]. Lee et al. [10] emphasize perceivability, controllability, and achievement are primary considerations in scoring system design. Lazzaroni et al. [11] propose a data toolchain for SG analytics within a trivial game scene, emphasizing the importance of gathering data in SG context.

2.2 Adaptability

Adapting SGs to individual players is a significant challenge. Differences in players' knowledge and skills can result in games that are either too easy and dull or excessively difficult, leading to frustration. To enhance effectiveness of these games, it may be useful to incorporate an adaptive engine that can dynamically adjust non-player characters and game difficulty according to the players' abilities. For instance, Bellotti et al. [12] propose a design methodology using an experience engine that can adapt the game flow even without predefined target knowledge levels.

Tan et al. [13] introduce an adaptive artificial intelligence architecture designed to adjust the difficulty level according to the player's skill level in the Gomoku game. Rasim et al. [14] present a survey of various adaptive frameworks and adaptive engine algorithms for SGs.

3   Methodology

In order to facilitate the learning of a procedure within a SG that lacks a scoring system, it becomes necessary for a supervisor (i.e., the teacher) to evaluate the player (i.e., the learner) performance during the procedure. To avoid the need for continuous support and feedback from the supervisor, which may be a strict requirement, it is beneficial to encapsulate the knowledge of the teacher into a system that automatically assesses the weaknesses of the students to focus further training on those areas. For these reasons, we decided to implement a flexible scoring system by conceptualizing a procedure as a sequence of ordered actions, containing comprehensive information on how to perform it (i.e., duration, order's importance, etc.). Our method was designed specifically for virtual game simulations, but the main concepts are applicable to real-world games, while the implementation may require some tweaking. We propose the GP as the only correct way to perform the given procedure, which has been implemented as a list of actions named GA. Such list has no ramifications and is unique, implying that to perform a specific procedure the player can obtain the highest score only by performing the specific sequence of actions which corresponds precisely to GP. Similarly, in parallel with the concept of GP, the actions performed by the player, known as Player Actions (PAs), are recorded in a list called Player Path (PP). This structure mirrors the behavior of the Golden Path (GP) and provides a straightforward means of computing the score. A visual representation of GP and PP is shown in Fig. 1.

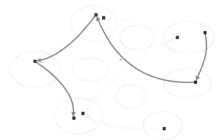

Fig. 1. This representation of the action space indicates actions as ellipses and a possible Golden Path, colored in yellow, and Player Path colored in blue. (Color figure online)

The usage of our scoring system involves two phases, namely Definition and Usage:

- Definition: The supervisor defines all the GAs comprising the GP, specifying the importance of each action, the required quantity involved (if applicable), the correct timing, and other relevant details.
- Usage: The student executes a procedure, and the recorded PAs in the generated PP are compared to the GAs stored in the GP. This comparison results in a score that reflects the overall execution quality of the procedure. Additionally, individual scores are assigned to each action, thereby highlighting areas where the student can improve.

The concept of the GP is designed to allow supervisors to define a linear path without branches. This design choice is rooted in the teaching of rigorous procedures, where deviations from the original path are generally not encouraged. Additionally, defining a branched GP would impose greater complexity on the supervisor. Moreover, our approach empowers supervisors to customize GPs based on different types of students.

3.1 Simulation Engine

To deploy and test the proposed scoring system, we utilized a medical-procedure simulation framework [8], that offers a range of customizable medical scenarios, catering to various types of medical procedures. Exploiting the simulator's versatility, we modified our system during testing to fit a generic plot for the medical use-case. Within the simulation environment, players can interact among each other and execute procedures by performing actions using appropriately reproduced tools. Tools are the only way for player to interact with the simulated environment (i.e., perform an action), hence is possible to record the whole execution as a series of PAs.

3.2 Golden Action

A Golden Action (GA) incorporates detailed information regarding the precise execution of a single step within the procedure, encompassing factors such as timing, quantities involved, and tools to be used. To enable the system to provide scores after each student's attempt, the supervisor is responsible for specifying the relevant values for all the actions within the GP. This ensures that the scoring system can accurately assess the player's performance. Values defined into each GA are shown inside Table 1. Description of each parameter composing the GA. Additionally, for each of the order index, quantity, duration, and start time parameters both a weight, ranging from 0 to 1, and a maximum difference threshold should be specified.

Table 1. Description of each parameter composing the GA.

Parameter name	Description
Action score	The maximum score assigned to this action, reflecting its importance in the overall procedure
Tool name	The name of the instrument or tool required to perform this action (e.g., scalpel, hammer, drug)
Order index	The ordinal number of this action in the sequence of steps within the procedure
Quantity	The quantity of the tool or item required for this action (if applicable)
Duration	The duration of time required to complete this action
Start time	The designated time for initiating this action relative to the beginning of the procedure
Safe time	The designated time window within which penalties for deviations are considered zero. Actions performed within this time window are considered to be within an acceptable range and do not incur penalties
Timeout time	The maximum allowable time to perform the action. If the action exceeds this threshold, maximum penalties are assigned

3.3 Player Action

The scoring framework is ready to determine the score for each execution of the procedure once the supervisor has finished defining all GAs in the GP. To make this possible, the SG needs to connect to the scoring system and broadcast all the PAs, which are recorded in the PP list. The PA is defined by:

- Tool name: The name of the instrument or tool that has been used by the player.
- Start time: The specific time instant at which the action was initiated.
- Quantity: The quantity of the tool used by the player during the action.
- Duration: The duration of the action performed by the player.
- Order index: The ordinal number of this action in the sequence of actions executed by the player.

3.4 Score Computation

Once the player has completed the procedure simulation, the score is determined. The PP contains all the activities of the player for the process, and the scoring framework can output the outcome value. The framework assumes that a tool is only used once during each procedure, hence the first stage of the algorithm is to match a PA in the PP with the corresponding GA in the GP. The GA-PA pair is used to compute costs for each action used to calculate the penalty for each action, then the final score is calculated. The costs of each action parameter are calculated based on two main concepts: the variation between the parameters of the action performed by the user and those described in the GP, and the impact of each action on the total penalty.

The uniqueness of a procedural sequence is defined by the specific ordering of its constituent actions. In our case, both the GP and the PP sequences differ when the order of their respective actions varies. The difference cannot exceed a defined threshold to avoid an excessive penalty on the final score for all the described costs. In the following formulas, the subscript symbols "Idx", "W", "TH", and "diff" stand in order for index, weight, threshold, and difference of the term they subscript.

$$order_{Cost} = \left[\min\left(|GA_{orderIdx} - PA_{orderIdx}|, GA_{order\ diff\ TH} \right) \cdot GA_{orderW} \right]$$

The quantity of tools used in specific scenarios holds significance. In certain situations, specific tools require central focus, and any wastage of these tools (e.g., medicines to be administered) may lead to unfavorable outcomes. Conversely, underdosing a tool may not be an appropriate choice.

$$quantity_{Cost} = \left[\min\left(|GA_{quantity} - PA_{quantity}|, GA_{quantity,\ diff\ TH} \right) \cdot GA_{quantityW} \right]$$

The application of a tool is a delicate procedure, as highlighted in the earlier discussion regarding start time. It is crucial to allocate an appropriate amount of time when applying a tool, as both excessive and insufficient time can lead to unfavourable outcomes.

$$duration_{Cost} = \left[\min\left(|GA_{duration} - PA_{duration}|, GA_{duration\ diff,\ TH} \right) \cdot GA_{durationW} \right]$$

Initiating a procedure strictly following a timeline is crucial, particularly in sensitive use cases. Starting an action too late could result in wasted time on other actions, whereas initiating it too early may indicate a player's lack of thoroughness in completing the preceding action.

$$time_{Cost} = \left[\min\left(|GA_{start\ time} - PA_{start\ time}|, GA_{start\ time\ diff\ TH}\right) \cdot GA_{start\ timeW}\right]$$

The maximum cost is calculated multiplying all the max value for all the quantities (i.e., the thresholds) by their weight. It is required to normalize the costs when calculating the penalty.

$$Max_{Cost} = \left[(GA_{order\ diff\ TH}) \cdot GA_{orderW}\right] + \left[(GA_{quantity\ diff\ TH}) \cdot GA_{quantityW}\right]$$
$$+ \left[(GA_{duration\ diff\ TH}) \cdot GA_{durationW}\right]$$
$$+ \left[(GA_{start\ time\ diff\ TH}) \cdot GA_{start\ timeW}\right]$$

Penalties are computed considering the following cases:

- When action is performed within the safe time
  penalty $= 0$
- When action is performed between the safe time and the timeout time defined in the corresponding GA

$$penalty = \frac{(order_{Cost} + quantity_{Cost} + duration_{Cost} + time_{Cost})}{Max_{Cost}} \cdot GA_{actionscore}$$

- When the action is performed beyond the timeout time.

$$penalty = GA_{action\ score}$$

Actions that are found only in the GP are taken into account when computing the score; unexpected behaviors are disregarded because they have no bearing on how the procedure is carried out. Effects of spurious actions are naturally included into non-spurious action parameters; for example, the start time and index values change when other actions are carried out. The formula to calculate the final score is as follows:

$$score = \sum_i^{GA-PA\ pairs} GA_{i\ action\ score} - PA_{i\ penalty}$$

The score also includes all the costs and contributions for each action to assess the performance in detail. Supervisor and player can then exploit this data to focus the further training on the detected weaknesses.

3.5 Use Case

To highlight the inner mechanisms and procedures of our system, we provide a simple medical scenario use-case. Here, the player must treat a patient with an arm injury caused by a shard of glass. The necessary steps for this procedure are the following: (1) disinfect

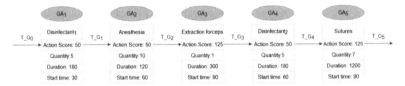

Fig. 2. Golden Path related to the use-case just described. For each GP is the achievable score, the amount of tool to be administered, and the duration of tool application.

the injury; (2) administer a local anaesthesia; (3) remove the shard; (4) clean the wound; (5) suture the wound. In Fig. 2 we present the GP for this sequence.

Figure 3 and Fig. 4 show two possible examples of actual PP. Specifically, the first one has a PP similar to the reference GP, while the latter depicts a divergent one. We show how the score is computed for both paths. The final score will be higher for the more similar PP with respect to the GP.

Fig. 3. Example of possible well-performed PP, similar to the GP.

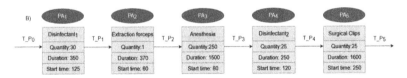

Fig. 4. Example of possible badly performed PP, divergent to the GP.

The parameters set by the teacher are shown in both Table 2 and Table 3. Particularly, the former presents the weights for each performed action, while the latter shows the upper thresholds for value differences between GA and PA pairs along with execution time indications.

By applying the formulas presented in Sect. 3 using values of GP and PPs shown in Fig. 2, Fig. 3, and Fig. 4 the PAs and total player's scores are obtained, as shown in Table 4.

Table 2. Weight values for actions in the GP.

Tool name	Order index	Quantity	Duration	Start time max
Disinfectant1	1.0	0.9	0.8	0.5
Anesthesia	1.0	1.0	0.9	0.65
Extraction forceps	1.0	1.0	0.7	0.35
Disinfectant2	1.0	0.9	0.8	0.65
Sutures	1.0	1.0	0.9	0.2

Table 3. Maximum difference and timing values for actions in the GP.

Tool name	Max order difference threshold	Max quantity difference threshold	Max duration difference threshold	Max start time difference threshold	Safe time	Timeout time
Disinfectant1	10	2	100	20	140	260
Anesthesia	10	1	80	140	70	390
Extraction forceps	10	0	140	300	200	1650
Disinfectant2	10	2	100	20	75	355
Sutures	10	2	300	20	900	2000

Table 4. Total and single score reached by the users.

Tool name	GA score	PA1 score	PA2 score
Disinfectant1	50	29.7	4.9
Anesthesia	50	30.7	9.2
Extraction forceps	125	106.5	65.4
Disinfectant2	50	26.6	16.2
Sutures	125	83.5	4.4
Total	400	277.0	100.1

4 Discussion

Considering the specific simulator used in our study, our method takes into consideration several factors inherent to the simulation environment. Our scoring system operates on the basis of actions, which are defined by the simulator and serve as the sole means of interaction with the simulated environment.

Once the simulated environment is prepared for use the teacher can deploy the Golden Path (GP) to execute a procedure just by populating a configuration file with values for each action. Configuring the GP requires a thorough understanding of the target procedure, as it involves assessing the significance of each action parameter, such as the order of execution, timing, and other relevant factors. However, the role of the teacher extends beyond defining the GP, as they can leverage the detailed scores generated by our system to provide guidance to students on specific actions within the procedure. The proposed work does not tackle the remedial teaching aspect of a SG. The remedial strategy is left to the teacher which can guide the learner after the evaluation. The presented system does not incorporate the possibility to define branched or multiple GP or to assess the performance of the students among all of them together, as it is intended for rigid, well-defined procedure.

5   Conclusion

Given the importance of assessment in SGs, this work presented the concept of a scoring system for procedural instructional games, independent from the game itself. It relies on the concept of GP, which enables the teacher to specify and define the optimal solution for the game. Furthermore, it allows for significant adaptations tailored to the individual students. The role of the teacher does not end with the definition of the GP, in fact the proposed tool can be helpful during the teaching process to highlight student's weaknesses. Each PA is evaluated individually so that the teacher can obtain a detailed overview of the student interactions during simulation. This leads to a more constructive assessment of the players capabilities in the target context and enables targeted future learning experiences.

In the proposed medical use-case, the scoring system has shown its ability to properly assess the player from the procedural point of view. The system is currently integrated within a single simulator, but further research will be devoted to the development of a library that can seamlessly interface with any SG or simulation environment. Future works include the modelling and integration of unforeseen events and non-linear GPs to create more realistic simulations and effectively handle highly dynamic scenarios. The design could also be improved exploiting psychometric frameworks (e.g., Cognitive Diagnostic Models, Micro Adaptivity, etc.). Moreover, a testing phase including several teachers and students utilizing the system in custom created environments, may be conducted to assess the user experience provided by the proposed work. Another possible topic for research involves upgrading the system by incorporating user profiling and consequently enabling adaptivity.

References

1. Torrente, J., et al.: Development of game-like simulations for procedural knowledge in health-care education. IEEE Trans. Learn. Technol. **7**, 69–82 (2014). https://doi.org/10.1109/TLT.2013.35
2. Bellotti, F., Kapralos, B., Lee, K., Moreno-Ger, P., Berta, R.: Assessment in and of serious games: an overview. Adv. Hum.-Comput. Interact. **2013**, e136864 (2013). https://doi.org/10.1155/2013/136864

3. Moreno-Ger, P., Martinez-Ortiz, I., Freire, M., Manero, B., Fernandez-Manjon, B.: Serious games: a journey from research to application. In: 2014 IEEE Frontiers in Education Conference (FIE) Proceedings, pp. 1–4. IEEE, Madrid, Spain (2014)

4. Lameras, P., Arnab, S., Dunwell, I., Stewart, C., Clarke, S., Petridis, P.: Essential features of serious games design in higher education: Linking learning attributes to game mechanics: essential features of serious games design. Br. J. Edu. Technol. **48**, 972–994 (2017). https://doi.org/10.1111/bjet.12467

5. Laamarti, F., Eid, M., El Saddik, A.: An overview of serious games. Int. J. Comput. Games Technol. **2014**, 1–15 (2014). https://doi.org/10.1155/2014/358152

6. Codreanu, I.A., Florea, A.M.: A proposed serious game architecture to self-management healthcare for older adults. In: 2015 17th International Symposium on Symbolic and Numeric Algorithms for Scientific Computing (SYNASC), pp. 437–440. IEEE, Timisoara, Romania (2015)

7. Brown, R., McIlwain, S., Willson, B., Hackett, M.: Enhancing combat medic training with 3D virtual environments. In: 2016 IEEE International Conference on Serious Games and Applications for Health (SeGAH), pp. 1–7 (2016)

8. De Gloria, A., et al.: 3D software simulator for primary care training. In: Proceedings of the 8th International Workshop on Innovative Simulation for Healthcare (IWISH 2019), pp. 114–119. CAL-TEK srl (2019)

9. Cowan, B., Kapralos, B.: A survey of frameworks and game engines for serious game development. In: 2014 IEEE 14th International Conference on Advanced Learning Technologies, pp. 662–664. IEEE, Athens, Greece (2014)

10. Lee, C.-I., Chen, I.-P., Hsieh, C.-M., Liao, C.-N.: Design aspects of scoring systems in game. Art Des. Rev. **05**, 26–43 (2017). https://doi.org/10.4236/adr.2017.51003

11. Lazzaroni, L., Mazzara, A., Bellotti, F., De Gloria, A., Berta, R.: Employing an IoT framework as a generic serious games analytics engine. In: Marfisi-Schottman, I., Bellotti, F., Hamon, L., Klemke, R. (eds.) Games and Learning Alliance, pp. 79–88. Springer International Publishing, Cham (2020). https://doi.org/10.1007/978-3-030-63464-3_8

12. Bellotti, F., Berta, R., De Gloria, A., Primavera, L.: Adaptive experience engine for serious games. IEEE Trans. Comput. Intell. AI Games **1**, 264–280 (2009). https://doi.org/10.1109/TCIAIG.2009.2035923

13. Tan, K.L., Tan, C.H., Tan, K.C., Tay, A.: Adaptive game AI for Gomoku. In: 2009 4th International Conference on Autonomous Robots and Agents, pp. 507–512. IEEE, Wellington (2009)

14. Rasim, R., Langi, A.Z., Munir, M., Rosmansyah, Y.: A survey on adaptive engine technology for serious games. Presented at the Bandung, Indonesia (2016)

Evaluating and Assessing Serious Games Elements

Exploring Immersive Learning Environments in Human-Robot Interaction Use Cases

Daniel Majonica[1,2]([⊠]), Nardie Fanchamps[2], Deniz Iren[2], and Roland Klemke[1,2]

[1] Cologne Game Lab, Technische Hochschule Köln, Cologne, Germany
daniel.majonica@th-koeln.de
[2] Open University, Heerlen, The Netherlands

Abstract. This paper describes a focus group study that explores immersive learning in the field of Human-Robot Interaction (HRI). We examine four categories of HRI cases: robot-led, human-led, autonomous, and collaborative. For each case, we evaluate the potential risks and human learning outcomes. Our findings include interaction styles that can be applied in HRI as well as the directionality and (multi)modality of these interaction styles. We identified several areas of risk, including miscommunication, privacy concerns, and injuries. Lastly, we explored common human learning outcomes based on the interaction categories. Our findings fill a gap in the literature by providing an analysis of immersive learning outcomes and risks in the field of HRI. Our results contribute towards the establishment of a framework that can improve the development of immersive learning environments.

Keywords: human-robot interaction · multimodal interaction · learning-related risks · learning outcomes

1 Introduction

Robotics, artificial intelligence, and immersive technologies present new possibilities for education in the field of human-robot interaction (HRI). Developing immersive learning environments (ILEs) for HRI entails a comprehensive examination of both technical and pedagogical aspects. Therefore, a framework is needed to guide the creation of ILEs that facilitate safe, effective, and efficient learning of human interaction and collaboration with robots. This paper specifically focuses on utilizing ILEs to enhance the skills of aspiring professionals in HRI. The study concentrates on exploring foundational principles and potential interactions and modalities, aiming to identify opportunities for educational optimization and establish a framework for ILE development.

We expect to derive relevant findings regarding the interaction and communication modality, the risks involved in HRI, and a representation of a) affective; b) cognitive; and c) psychomotor domains of Bloom's taxonomy [5]. Our study uses qualitative research comprising interviews with experts in technology-enhanced learning (TEL) and Computational Thinking (CT). Our study aims at tackling the following research questions (RQs).

- RQ1: What interaction styles apply in HRI?

    - RQ1.1: What difference in directionality (i.e., human to robot/robot to human) of interaction styles in HRI can be identified?
    - RQ1.2: What are common multimodal combinations in HRI?

- RQ2: What are learning-related risks of HRI?
- RQ3: What are potential learning outcomes in HRI?

To address these RQs we categorise interaction styles, risks of HRI, and learning outcomes in HRI. To define learning-related risks of HRI we acknowledge that there is knowledge transfer between the human and the robot. Learning-related risks are focusing on the risks for people when they learn new interactions with robots. We define learning outcomes in HRI as the acquisition of knowledge or skills by a human by interacting with a robot and getting multimodal support from the ILE.

2 Related Work

HRI can contain multiple categories of interaction. Based on the literature, we distinguish four different HRI aspects: modality, interaction styles, immersive technologies, and risks. Fig. 1 gives an overview of the different aspects and their categories.

Modality describes a particular mode in which something exists or is experienced or expressed. Different modalities can be combined to create a multimodal experience. Blattner and Glinert [4] have categorised modalities into visual, auditory, and haptic/kinesthetic modalities, further classifying the haptic modality into touch, hand movement, and head movement. Turk [27] lists modalities as visual, auditory, touch, and other sensors, highlighting the benefits of multimodality. In this paper, we adopt Turk's [27] taxonomy and add gestures as a separate modality, resulting in four modalities: visual, auditory, haptic, and gestures. We add gestures because it was listed under multiple modalities. This indicates the uniqueness of this modality.

Interaction styles provide high-level abstractions that fundamentally determine the type of information received by the user's task performance. Interaction styles have been classified into tasks such as selection, manipulation, navigation, and system control by LaViola [14]. More focused on HRI, Schulz et al. [24] describe robot-led, human-led, and autonomous interactions. Keller et al. [13] add collaborative interactions. We follow the HRI focus and combine these two categorizations into one taxonomy as seen in figure 1. Each interaction style can be instigated by either one or both sides in HRI and is therefore multi-directional.

Previous research on the use of *ILEs* in HRI focuses on remote control using ILEs [1, 22]. Instead, we concentrate on robots and humans interacting with immersive technologies. These usually include Augmented Reality (AR), Virtual Reality (VR), and Mixed Reality (MR) or low immersive environments [23] such as screens. Matsas et al. [19] emphasise the importance of mental models and awareness of moving robots and describe a VR training system focusing on the interaction with the robot.

Literature indicates that required safety levels during HRI are important aspects of *risks* [17, 29]. It has been shown that safety is a major concern when humans have

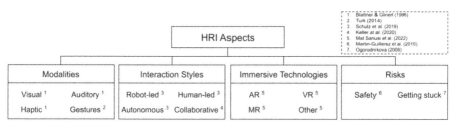

Fig. 1. HRI aspects derived from literature to form a basis for focus group discussions [4, 13, 17, 20, 23, 24, 27].

physical contact with robots. Safety issues include injury which can be either human-related or due to a robot system failure [20]. Robot system failures can result in the robot getting stuck without human injuries involved. Other types of risks such as privacy or miscommunication are often neglected in papers on risks in HRI. However, Martin-Guillerez et al. [17] mention how their analysis leads to the need for communication between the user and the robot.

3 Theoretical Framework

HRI is an interdisciplinary field focusing on the design, development, application, and evaluation of robots that interact with humans [6, 18, 30]. The theory underlying HRI encompasses a range of concepts drawn from various disciplines, including computer science [30], psychology [6], and sociology [6, 30]. At its core, HRI is about understanding how humans and robots can effectively communicate, interact and cooperate with each other [26]. One of the goals is to develop robots capable of perceiving, interpreting, and responding to human social signs, such as gestures, facial expressions, and speech [25]. HRI requires robots designed to adapt to changing environments and to respond appropriately to unexpected events [26]. HRI research covers social robots that can effectively communicate and interact with humans in a wide range of contexts, from manufacturing and healthcare to entertainment and education, where robots are not only functional and efficient, but also contribute to social and emotional development [8, 12].

While some effort in HRI is made in the development of social robots [3, 7], using ILEs as an intermediate step in-between robots and humans can help bridge the gaps in communication and interaction [16]. Since researchers are becoming increasingly aware that new methods, methodologies and a theoretical and conceptual basis need to be formed, the combination of HRI with ILE could provide promising new insights [9].

Modality refers to the mode or channel of information transmission and perception, such as visual, auditory, haptic, or gestures. It determines the types of cues and feedback that can be used [2] and is related to the quality and effectiveness of the interaction. The parallel use of multiple modalities (i.e. multimodality) can be beneficial to this quality and effectiveness [10]. Thus, understanding modalities, and how they can be combined and coordinated, is important for designing effective and engaging HRI systems.

Human-centred areas in robotics focus on designing robots that meet the specific needs and preferences of human users. This approach considers human capabilities, limitations, and preferences during robot design and development [15]. Social robotics, on the other hand, concentrate on creating robots capable of engaging with people in social and emotional ways. These robots are intended to be companions, assistants, and interactive partners for humans [15, 18, 30]. Establishing trust between humans and robots is crucial for successful HRI: how trust is formed and maintained, considering factors like robot behavior, appearance, and performance [11].

4 Methodology

The study includes an expert focus group study which was conducted on two different occasions. In total, the study includes 77 experts from various academic backgrounds (18+ years old) which were novices to the technology and which were asked by the conducting researchers to form groups of 2–4 people. This resulted in 22 groups. On the first occasion, 17 groups of experts in the TEL domain were tasked with describing four use cases each in these four different categories and evaluate the risks and human learning outcomes associated with each case:

1. *robot-lead interaction*, where the robot takes the lead in the interaction.
2. *human-led interaction*, where the human takes the lead in the interaction.
3. *autonomous interaction*, where the robot acts independently of the human.
4. *collaborative interaction*, where the human and robot work together to achieve a common goal.

On the second occasion, 5 groups of experts in the field of CT were tasked with describing three use cases each in different categories and evaluate the risks and human learning outcomes associated with each case. Three categories where humans could encounter robots were identified and for the second occasion presented as follows:

1. *residential setting*, in which the robot interacts with the user at their home.
2. *commercial setting*, in which the robot takes a service tasks.
3. *industrial setting*, where the robot is placed in a factory/work scenario.

The reason why CT experts were given different categories than TEL experts was due to the iterative process of this study. We've found out in the first iteration with TEL experts that the associated categories result in mostly residential/commercial settings and neglect the industrial setting. Overall, industrial setting was present in only 17.7% of the resulting use cases in the first study. Because of this, we decided to give CT experts different categories to create a bigger variety in use cases and spread the answers over more topics than before.

We selected the participants by their respective fields of expertise. The time of the tasks were about 45 minutes in total. While experts in the TEL domain were coming mostly from a learning domain, these participants were researchers who showed interest in HRI. Similarly, the experts in the field of CT showed interest in HRI and were researchers with expertise in computer-assisted learning. The groups of experts were randomly included on a voluntary basis and therefore no HRI experts were present. However, these TEL and CT experts showed interest in the topic of HRI and voluntarily participated in the study.

Data was collected through an open survey where participants brainstormed use cases from their own experience, received background information on ILEs, and evaluated learning-related risks and outcomes in the form of free text. The collected free text as data were coded using Atlas.ti under three criteria: 1) *modality*, describing the interaction style which is crucial for HRI; 2) *learning-related risks*, analysing what risks are listed regarding HRI; and 3) *learning outcomes*, categorising the data in different learning domains. Bloom's taxonomy [5] was used to categorize the data, although it is not specifically tailored for HRI. Categories emerged from the qualitative data analysis of the free text collected. Perceivable findings to address research questions RQ1, RQ2, and RQ3 using focus group research were reported and discussed in the final step.

5   Results

The results of the data collected are reported in three different topics: modality, risk, and potential learning outcomes.

5.1   Modality

The majority of interactions between humans and robots are initiated by the robot and directed toward the human. The least commonly mentioned modality in HRI, compared to visual, auditory, and haptic, was gestures. While multimodality was commonly used, an important observation relates to directionality, i.e., the interaction direction from human to robot or vice versa. Imbalances were observed for each modality, as shown in Table 1. The table also displays how the interaction directionality from the robot to the human is almost exclusively auditory and visual (91.4%). This partially answers RQ1.1 in terms of differences in directionality that exist in HRI and shows how different modalities are more commonly used in one direction than being bi-directional. For example, visual being used mostly from the robot to the human. On the other side, some modalities are used in the opposite direction. For example, haptic being used mostly from the human to the robot.

Table 1. Results split up by modality and directionality.

modality	visual	auditory	haptic	gestures
from human	18	27	**34**	**10**
from robot	**58**	**59**	9	2

Haptic modality, including the sense of touch, was the most common when humans interacted with robots. The modality data were further analyzed in terms of possible multimodal combinations, as shown in Table 2. The first column represents the base modality and its occurrence count. Gestures had only 12 occurrences in the data. Each row in the table indicates the combination of modalities *with* the *base* modality. The most frequent multimodal combination, with an absolute value of 71% or 54 out of 76 occurrences, was visual and auditory together. Among the 43 haptic occurrences, visual was the most common modality, accounting for 81.4% or 35 instances. It's important to note that the percentage values in the gestures row should be considered in the context of only 12 gesture occurrences. Among those 12 occurrences, 11 also included the haptic modality, resulting in the highest percentage (91.7%) due to the low number of gesture occurrences.

Table 2. Base Modality combined with other modalities.

Base/With	visual	auditory	haptic	gestures
visual (n=76)		71%	42.1%	9.2%
auditory (n=76)	62.8%		39.5%	10.4%
haptic (n=43)	81.4%	69.7%		32.5%
gestures (n=12)	50%	75%	91.7%	

5.2 Risks

The findings of the qualitative data analysis indicate that most errors identified in the interaction between humans and robots were related to the robot itself (76.6%) rather than the human (29.8%). The analysis revealed that the risk of hurting the human was a more common concern (13%) than the risk of damaging the robot (6.5%).

It was showing that the most common error on the robot side in HRI was miscommunication. Miscommunication was also found to be the most common error on the human side. The second most significant error for the robot was found to be the robot getting stuck. The most common risk associated with HRI was found to be injury to humans, while the second significant risk is related to human privacy.

5.3 Learning Outcomes

We observed that experts in the field of TEL and CT almost never discussed the learning or training of robots and focused instead on human learning (2.5%). In general, the cognitive domain is most commonly used when interacting with a robot. The psychomotor domain may also be used, especially if the robot requires physical interaction with its environment. For example, a person operating a robotic arm may need to use physical skills to manipulate the robot's controls and move the arm into position. The affective domain may also come into play in some cases, particularly if the robot has social or emotional components. For example, a person interacting with a robot designed to provide emotional support may need to use affective skills to establish rapport and communicate effectively with the robot. In summary, while all three domains of learning are involved when interacting with a robot, the cognitive domain is typically the most commonly used.

6 Discussion

This section aims to provide an in-depth interpretation and analysis of the findings presented in the results section. We, therefore, discuss the modalities, risks, and learning outcomes. In the following list we summarized findings from the data. These show the major findings of this study summarized from the Results section.

- Modality: "Gestures" are less common
- Modality: Human to Robot communication is most commonly "haptic"
- Multimodality: All modalities examined in this study have an imbalance in interaction directionality
- Multimodality: Most common combination is "visual" & "auditory"
- Learning-related risks: Most errors described were robot related
- Learning-related risks: Most common error on both robot and human side was "Miscommunication"
- Learning-related risks: Most common risks are "injury of human" and "human privacy"
- Learning outcome: "Cognitive domain" is more prominent than "affective domain" and "psychomotor domain"

6.1 Modality

The data indicates a higher interaction-rate from the robot-side in HRI, suggesting the robot's role as a facilitator and provider of feedback and guidance. Robots also might be seen as mostly autonomous and only actively communicate when needed. Gestures are used less frequently, which may suggest it might not be effective or intuitive as other modalities, and limited generalizability in HRI scenarios. The under-representation of gestures in existing systems and the collected data may contribute to this. The findings suggest that touch-based haptic feedback may play a significant role in human communication, especially in contexts like healthcare. Incorporating touch feedback in robot design can improve HRI quality. However, including touch also increases haptic interaction occurrences, as it encompasses physical and digital touch interactions. This prevalence of haptic feedback can be attributed to the fundamental nature of the interaction, according to the researchers.

6.2 Risks

The majority of risks in HRI are related to human injuries, indicating the need for greater attention to the robot's robustness, reliability, and safety. Additionally, privacy emerges as the second most mentioned risk for humans, emphasizing the importance of considering safety and privacy in robot design and deployment. The most common errors for robots are miscommunication and getting stuck, highlighting the necessity of improving communication and movement capabili-ties. Similarly, humans also commonly experience miscommunication errors, underscoring the importance of communication skills in robot design and human training. Future ILE designs should facilitate successful bidirectional communication.

6.3 Learning Outcomes

This study reveals a focus on human learning outcomes in HRI, with limited emphasis on robot learning outcomes, possibly influenced by the expertise of TEL and CT professionals. Machine learning [21, 28] and developmental learning using social robots in HRI [3, 7] are potential areas for investigation in ILEs.

Cognitive domain emerges as the most frequent in learning outcomes, while affective and psychomotor domains are mentioned less frequently. This suggests a potential bias towards cognitive skills or a focus of TEL and CT experts. However, broader availability of ILEs could enhance learning in affective and psychomotor skills. The cognitive domain is dominant in HRI due to the need for users to comprehend robot capabilities, programming, problem-solving, and mental models [13].

7 Limitations

The findings of our study should be interpreted with caution. First of all, our conducted exploration concerns a limited number of respondents concerning the focus group experts who either have a background in TEL or CT and therefore also have different perceptions of the applicability of HRI. It is recommended to repeat the survey with a larger number of respondents originating from a multitude of disciplines, including participants with previous experience of HRI.

The selection included in our study for an analysis and elaboration of the four different categories concerning aspects of HRI is only a limited representation of the possibilities that HRI could harbour. Despite the fact that the literature review we carried out beforehand indicated the prominence of the four categories selected, it is recommended to further expand the research area to include additional aspects.

8 Conclusion

The proceeds and findings of our study provide a foundation for further research on the importance of HRI. The results from expert focus groups offer opportunities for other researchers to contribute to discussions on ILEs in HRI. Our research identified interaction styles in terms of directionality and multimodal combinations (RQ1.1&RQ1.2), as well as learning-related risks (RQ2) and learning outcomes (RQ3). However, limitations prevent us from providing a conclusive list of all learning-related risks and outcomes. The results are constrained by the predetermined categories chosen.

9 Future Research

The study's findings provide a basis for future research in ILEs in HRI. The outlined research agenda includes theoretical exploration, comparing ILEs in HRI to traditional teaching methods, using virtual robots for HRI training without instructors, and evaluating new approaches to ILEs in HRI. The inclusion of touch in haptic feedback increased its occurrences, suggesting the need for a more detailed approach to this modality.

Existing taxonomies in learning domains [5] primarily focus on human learning without considering robots, highlighting the necessity for a new taxonomy specific to learning in HRI. Additionally, exploring privacy and miscommunication in learning-related risks of HRI is crucial, as current literature predominantly focuses on injury and safety, creating a research gap. Another potential avenue for future research involves examining machine learning and the learning process on the robot-side, as this aspect was underrepresented in the collected data. To obtain a more comprehensive understanding of modalities addressed, learning-related risks, learning outcomes in HRI, and the correlations to possibly be expected between these categories, more research in this field is needed. We see these lines of research as promising directions for future research.

References

1. Adami, P., et al.: An immersive virtual learning environment for worker-robot collaboration on construction sites. In: 2020 Winter Simulation Conference (WSC), pp. 2400–2411. IEEE (2020)
2. Baltru˘saitis, T., Ahuja, C., Morency, L.P.: Multimodal machine learning: a survey and taxonomy. IEEE Trans. Pattern Anal. Mach. Intell. **41**(2), 423–443 (2018)
3. Baranes, A., Oudeyer, P.Y.: Active learning of inverse models with intrinsically motivated goal exploration in robots. Robot. Auton. Syst. **61**(1), 49–73 (2013)
4. Blattner, M.M., Glinert, E.P.: Multimodal integration. IEEE Multimed. **3**(4), 14–24 (1996)
5. Bloom, B.S., Englehart, M.D., Furst, E.J., Hill, W.H., Krathwohl, D.R.: Taxonomy of Educational Objectives: Handbook I. Cognitive Domain. David McKay, New York (1956)
6. Burke, J.L., Murphy, R.R., Rogers, E., Lumelsky, V.J., Scholtz, J.: Final report for the DARPA/NSF interdisciplinary study on human–robot interaction. IEEE Trans. Syst. Man Cybern. Part C (App. Rev.) **34**(2), 103–112 (2004). https://doi.org/10.1109/TSMCC.2004.826287
7. Ceha, J., Law, E., Kuli´c, D., Oudeyer, P.Y., Roy, D.: Identifying functions and behaviours of social robots for in-class learning activities: Teachers' perspective. Int. J. Soc. Robot. 1–15 (2022)
8. Chuah, S.H.W., Yu, J.: The future of service: the power of emotion in human-robot interaction. J. Retail. Consum. Serv. **61**, 102551 (2021)
9. Dautenhahn, K.: Methodology & themes of human-robot interaction: a growing research field. Int. J. Adv. Rob. Syst. **4**(1), 15 (2007)
10. Di Mitri, D., Scheffel, M., Drachsler, H., Borner, D., Ternier, S., Specht, M.: Learning pulse: a machine learning approach for predicting performance in self-regulated learning using multimodal data. In: Proceedings of the seventh International Learning Analytics & Knowledge Conference, pp. 188–197 (2017)
11. Hancock, P.A., Billings, D.R., Schaefer, K.E., Chen, J.Y., De Visser, E.J., Parasuraman, R.: A meta-analysis of factors affecting trust in human-robot interaction. Hum. Factors **53**(5), 517–527 (2011)
12. Hong, A., et al.: A multimodal emotional human–robot interaction architecture for social robots engaged in bidirectional communication. IEEE Trans. Cybern. **51**(12), 5954–5968 (2020)
13. Keller, T., Majonica, D., Richert, A., Klemke, R.: Prerequisite knowledge of learning environments in human-robot collaboration for dyadic teams. In: Proceedings. ISSN 1613, 0073 (2020). https://ceur-ws.org
14. LaViola, J.J., Jr., Kruijff, E., McMahan, R.P., Bowman, D., Poupyrev, I.P.: 3D User Interfaces: Theory and Practice. Addison-Wesley Professional, Boston (2017)

15. Leite, I., Martinho, C., Paiva, A.: Social robots for long-term interaction: a survey. Int. J. Soc. Robot. **5**, 291–308 (2013)
16. Limbu, B., Fominykh, M., Klemke, R., Specht, M., Wild, F.: Supporting training of expertise with wearable technologies: the wekit reference framework. In: Yu, S., Ally, M., Tsinakos, A. (eds.) Mobile and Ubiquitous Learning. PRRE, pp. 157–175. Springer, Singapore (2018). https://doi.org/10.1007/978-981-10-6144-8_10
17. Martin-Guillerez, D., Guiochet, J., Powell, D., Zanon, C.: A uml-based method for risk analysis of human-robot interactions. In: Proceedings of the 2nd International Workshop on Software Engineering for Resilient Systems, pp. 32–41. Association for Computing Machinery, New York, NY, USA (2010)
18. Mataric, M.J.: The role of embodiment in assistive interactive robotics for the elderly. In: AAAI Fall Symposium: Caring Machines, pp. 75–77 (2005)
19. Matsas, E., Vosniakos, G.C.: Design of a virtual reality training system for human– robot collaboration in manufacturing tasks. Int. J. Interact. Des. Manuf. (IJIDeM) **11**, 139–153 (2017)
20. Ogorodnikova, O.: Methodology of safety for a human robot interaction designing stage. In: 2008 Conference on Human System Interactions, pp. 452–457 (2008)
21. Rani, P., Liu, C., Sarkar, N., Vanman, E.: An empirical study of machine learning techniques for affect recognition in human–robot interaction. Pattern Anal. Appl. **9**, 58–69 (2006)
22. Rukangu, A., Tuttle, A., Johnsen, K.: Virtual reality for remote controlled robotics in engineering education. In: 2021 IEEE Conference on Virtual Reality and 3d User Interfaces Abstracts and Workshops (VRW), pp. 751–752. IEEE (2021)
23. Sanusi, K.A.M., Iren, D., Klemke, R.: Experts' evaluation of a proposed taxonomy for immersive learning systems. In: Kiili, K., Antti, K., de Rosa, F., Dindar, M., Kickmeier-Rust, M., Bellotti, F. (eds.) Games and Learning Alliance: 11th International Conference, GALA 2022. LNCS, vol 13647, pp. 247–257. Springer, Cham (2022). https://doi.org/10.1007/978-3-031-22124-8_24
24. Schulz, R., Kratzer, P., Toussaint, M.: Preferred interaction styles for human-robot collaboration vary over tasks with different action types. Front. Neurorobot. **12**, 36 (2018)
25. Seibt, J., Nørskov, M., Andersen, S.S.: What Social Robots Can and Should Do: Proceedings of Robophilosophy 2016/TRANSOR 2016, vol. 290. IOS Press (2016)
26. Sheridan, T.B.: Human–robot interaction: status and challenges. Hum. Factors **58**(4), 525–532 (2016)
27. Turk, M.: Multimodal interaction: a review. Pattern Recogn. Lett. **36**, 189–195 (2014)
28. Wang, J., Pradhan, M.R., Gunasekaran, N.: Machine Learning-Based Human-Robot Interaction in its. Inf. Process. Manage. **59**(1), 102750 (2022)
29. Zacharaki, A., Kostavelis, I., Gasteratos, A., Dokas, I.: Safety bounds in human robot interaction: a survey. Saf. Sci. **127**, 104667 (2020)
30. Żarkowski, M.: Multi-party turn-taking in repeated human–robot interactions: an interdisciplinary evaluation. Int. J. Soc. Robot. **11**(5), 693–707 (2019). https://doi.org/10.1007/s12369-019-00603-1

Skill Check: Some Considerations on the Evaluation of Gamemastering Models for Role-Playing Games

Santiago Góngora[1](✉) [iD], Luis Chiruzzo[1] [iD], Gonzalo Méndez[2] [iD],
and Pablo Gervás[2] [iD]

[1] Universidad de la República, Montevideo, Uruguay
{sgongora,luischir}@fing.edu.uy
[2] Universidad Complutense de Madrid, Madrid, Spain
{gmendez,pgervas}@ucm.es

Abstract. In role-playing games a Game Master (GM) is the player in charge of the game, who must design the challenges the players face and narrate the outcomes of their actions. In this work we discuss some challenges to model GMs from an Interactive Storytelling and Natural Language Processing perspective. Following those challenges we propose three test categories to evaluate such dialogue systems, and we use them to test ChatGPT, Bard and OpenAssistant as out-of-the-box GMs.

Keywords: Role-playing Games · Natural Language Processing · Interactive Storytelling · Computational Creativity · Dialogue Systems

1 Introduction

Probably no one wants to hear somebody say *"Watch out! Behind that door there's a giant monster!"*; except if they are playing a role-playing game (RPG), using their imagination to visit endless worlds and having lots of fun.

Tabletop role-playing games (TTRPGs) consist of two or more players that collaborate in order to create a story, while acting as characters. One of these players is the Game Master (GM), who is the one in charge of creating the world where the narrated events take place, describing the non-playable characters the human players meet and the situations they face. Having a player acting as the GM is one of the characteristics that most TTRPGs share [12].

Capturing the essence of RPGs has long been one of the goals of Interactive Storytelling (IS) research [21,25]. However, through the years only limited solutions have been found, typically by having a lot of premade scenes that can be mixed to generate other narrative structures[1], but pushing the player's freedom aside[2] [25]. To automate a GM is a big challenge for Natural Language Processing (NLP) and Artificial Intelligence, due to its complexity on dialogue and creativity [8].

---

[1] For example "Call of Cthulhu: The Official Video Game", an adaptation of the RPG.
[2] An interesting example of this is "The Stanley Parable", a novel videogame that makes the players think about free will and the impact of their actions.

P. Dondio et al. (Eds.): GALA 2023, LNCS 14475, pp. 277–288, 2024.
https://doi.org/10.1007/978-3-031-49065-1_27

Our long-term goal is to model the diverse set of skills that a GM needs to play RPGs. This long path must lead to an explainable, grounded and controllable model, so human-in-the-loop features should be taken into consideration to meet the needs reported by [1] and [30].

In this paper we will take a first step by proposing, inspired in core aspects of RPGs, a set of unit test categories to evaluate such GM models. We also use these brand new tests to evaluate ChatGPT[3], Bard[4] and OpenAssistant[5] [16] as out-of-the-box automated GMs, both for Spanish and English.

2   Previous Work

The study of the role of GMs in narrative is nothing new and also some efforts have been made to explicitly model their capabilities. [27] reflects on the core concepts of RPGs and gamemastering. [21,22] consider GMs and RPGs as a framework to build IS systems, in order to tackle the *Interactive Dilemma*, the conflict and balance between the player's will and the designer's choices. Closely related to this concept is the GM's skill to improvise some aspects of a scene due to unexpected players' actions, and [18,19] discuss concepts, approaches and architectures taking that into account. As they present insightful discussions about modelling narrative improvisation, they are some of the most clarifying works for us to date.

Most of the latest works pursue the modelling of GMs for *Dungeons & Dragons* (D&D), called *Dungeon Masters* (DMs), since it is the most popular RPG and finding data is easier than for other games. For example [8] describes the complexity of modelling the (D&D) game, performing experiments with neural models and using *control features* to guide their outputs. They also describe a *gameplay dataset* in English used for training. [28] tries to create a DM model with the ability to predict player's actions, modelling the *Dungeon Master-Player* interactions using Theory-of-Mind and Reinforcement Learning. The recent published datasets are also centered on modelling the D&D game. [24] presents one of the most complete datasets to study D&D interactions, consisting of transcriptions of the popular *Critical Role* web show. [17,29] also present datasets of D&D players' interactions from online text-based playing sessions.

It is important to note that all of these recent works are about D&D, while our main objective is to work on the general aspects of a GM, regardless of the specific game or theme. Additionally, all of them rely on English resources.

3   A List of Gamemastering Challenges

Most of the works mentioned in the previous section discuss difficulties faced while modelling some aspects of RPGs. However, as a way of introducing some

---

[3] https://openai.com/blog/chatgpt.
[4] https://bard.google.com.
[5] https://huggingface.co/chat/.

details that guide our long-term goal and justify the test categories we propose, we would like to convey our thoughts on some challenges that a GM must face while running an RPG session. This list is not exhaustive and there may be other challenges that are not described here.

I. World and Story Design. As storytellers, GMs must create and manage a rich and coherent world, populated with diverse forms of life (e.g. plants and animals) and characters. In this fictional world is where the players' characters will live and act. They also need to create some interesting places (e.g. an old library) and challenges for the players, which can be logic puzzles, tactic battles, complex dialogues with characters, or other challenges (e.g. the library has hidden rooms). Usually these situations are intended to be solved by teaming up with other characters, collaborating and using the different skills that they may master. It is useful if a GM can also measure how interesting these challenges are for the players, and how meaningful they are for the development of their characters or other characters that live in the fictional world. That is the reason why it is important that such a model can take *creative responsibility* [7,10] while being able to explain what the plan and objectives of each utterance are.

II. Extract Player's Actions from Input. Since TTRPGs are played through a discussion between the players, these games have an inherent *conversational nature*. Therefore classic research problems related to dialogue systems [9] are fundamental to model GMs. More specifically, in order to *understand* (i.e. semantically represent) the actions taken by the players, decide if they are possible in the fictional world and then determine the outcomes, the GM model should have the ability to semantically analyze their inputs.

III. Commonsense Reasoning. Commonsense reasoning is an important research area within NLP [26], and despite the great advances made in the area it remains as one of the hardest tasks [11], even for the recent Large Language Models (LLMs) like ChatGPT [23]. The relation between this classic task and the challenges for a GM is direct: since commonsense is an inherent part of our human identity, it naturally arises when playing RPGs. It is important to note that this challenge is related but different to the previous challenge: a model can semantically represent what a human is saying, but maybe the action does not make sense in some context. For instance, sometimes players may want to do actions that are possible in the real world but not in the fictional world (e.g. a character wants to play basketball but there is no gravity in her world).

IV. Track the Game State. One of the core aspects of RPGs is to let the players act as they wish, what in IS is usually called *user agency* [25]. Making the players feel this way while thoroughly tracking the state of items (i.e. objects) and characters is one of the greatest problems for IS [6,18]. To track some component of the game is to know where it is, how hurt (in case of a living being) or damaged it is (in case of an object), and other properties that it may have (e.g. intensity of the magic property of a sacred object). This game state must be constantly updated as the world changes and the story moves forward.

Finally, we would like to mention other relevant aspects for this long path. In first place, we think it is crucial that the narrative structure and the game state may be represented using a human-readable format. Since RPG games are used in educational [13] and therapy environments [2], such GM models could be used to create serious games with a wide range of objectives. Having the possibility of visualizing and customizing the boundaries of an RPG session is extremely crucial for that kind of applications.

In second place, it is fundamental that these models generate respectful and *ethical* outputs, to make the players feel safe and included. In modern RPGs like "Alice is Missing"[6] there are mechanics to silently communicate the rest of players that something recently said was hurtful or uncomfortable. This is crucial when working with neural systems or LLMs, which are known to *hallucinate* [14] and generate offensive outputs [4].

Last but not least, we have to keep in mind that GMs are constantly adapting the game to fit the players' choices, so they have the additional requirement of facing every challenge described here on the fly. That big challenge is related to what [18] previously described as *open-world improvisational storytelling*.

4   How to Evaluate Such Models?

The procedure to evaluate creative systems (i.e. appropriate experiments and metrics) has long been a subject of debate, and remains one of the main problems of the field [10,15]. Since TTRPGs can be modelled as a series of utterances in a complex dialogue [12], we will assume that a GM model will always have a *conversational nature*, as we mentioned in *challenge II*. This gives us a general guideline: there is always a player who is asking or trying to do something, and another player answering or reacting to it.

The first idea that comes to mind could be to ask humans to play and evaluate the models based on their reaction. Although we consider important to measure how fun it is to play with the models, the humans' judgments can be very subjective, not very specific, and also biased by the fluency of the generated text [3]. This bias can be stronger when working with LLMs, since they are trained to sound very natural to the human reader (exploiting the patterns behind the form of massive amounts of texts [5]), what can lead to distract the evaluators from their goal of judging specific characteristics of the models' output.

Hence, we would like to take an approach on evaluating basic, almost essential, skills that a GM should master. We propose three different test categories related to the previously described challenges: *commonsense reasoning*, the capacity to track *items* in the world and the ability to coherently design *maps*. These categories were designed reflecting on core characteristics of RPGs, so we think they can be used to evaluate any system trying to model a GM, independently of the theme and features of the modelled game, and the technology used to play it. We also hope these categories work as a guide for human

---

[6] https://www.huntersentertainment.com/alice-is-missing.

evaluators, helping them to judge models while reducing the subjectivity, the mentioned biases and the evaluation noise as possible. We will describe each of them next.

4.1 GM-P-GM Pattern

In *challenges II* and *III* we discussed the importance of pragmatics and commonsense reasoning for a GM model. In order to evaluate the performance on this challenges we propose the GM-P-GM pattern, a formalization of the most elemental interaction between a GM and a player [12]. Specifically, we propose to evaluate the model's ability to judge the feasibility of a player's action:

– GM_1: Narrates a **situation** to solve in some **context**.
– *Player*: Describes the **actions** to overcome that **situation**.
– GM_2: Validates if those **actions** are feasible for that **context**, and next narrates the **outcomes**.

To run this test we give the model the GM_1 and *Player* contradictory utterances and ask it to generate the GM_2 utterance. If the GM model prevents the action and explains why it is an inconsistency, the test is passed. A failure case is shown in Table 1.

Table 1. An example of a *GM-P-GM* unit test.

GM	You enter the building to look for the lost suitcase. However, the door is covered in flames. To your right you see a fire extinguisher, which seems to be ready to use. You can't use anything from your backpack because you can hardly move your arms. What will you do?
Player	I take a bucket of water from my backpack and put out the fire
GM	As the player grabs the bucket of water from their backpack, they realize it's not nearly enough to put out the flames completely. However, they quickly pour the water onto the fire, creating a small opening in the flames (...)
Result	Failed

4.2 Item Tracking

As we described in *challenge IV*, item tracking is one of the fundamental problems for gamemastering. It is important both to track items that are located in specific places (e.g. on the ground, inside a safe) and to track items that belong to the characters. The latter is usually referred as the *inventory* of each character but, in order to avoid the use of specific RPG words, in this test we will use *bag* or *backpack* as more neutral words for a similar concept. To test if the model can track objects inside or outside the *backpack*, we follow this scheme:

1. *Player*: "What is in my backpack?"
2. *GM*: $Object_1, Object_2, Object_3, Object_4, ...$
3. *Player*: "I take $Object_K$ and leave it on *another location*'"
4. *GM*: *Narrates outcome*
5. *Player*: "What is in my backpack?"
6. *GM*: $Object_1, Object_2, Object_3, ...$
7. *Player*: "What is on *another location* ?"
8. *GM*: $Object_A, Object_B, ...$

If the lists given in steps #2 and #6 are the same or contain other unrelated objects, then the test is failed. In case the object is not listed in step #6, the step #8 tries to check if the model updated its new location. A failure case is shown in Table 2.

Table 2. An example of an *Item tracking* unit test.

GM	(...) Aside from the mysterious key, your backpack also contains the usual adventurer's equipment: a sturdy rope, a grappling hook, a water flask, some dried rations, a small first-aid kit, a compass, a map of the surrounding area, and a trusty dagger at your side
Player	I take the rope, the map and the key and I leave them on the floor
GM	You carefully set the rope, map, and key down on the floor, making sure they are within reach in case you need them later. (...)
Player	What's in my backpack?
GM	As you take a closer look at your backpack, you notice that it contains a few essential items that any adventurer would find useful: A sturdy rope: (...) this rope is perfect for climbing or rappelling down steep surfaces. (...) A map of the surrounding area: this map shows the nearby landmarks, towns, and topography of the region, allowing you to plan your route. (...)
Result	Failed

4.3   Map Design

When GMs create a fictional world they also have the challenge to design an interesting and coherent concrete map for the players to explore, as we described in *challenge I*. Although we also justified the importance of having interesting situations for the players, for now we do not focus on how attractive, large or complex the maps generated are.

Inspired in the scheme of the *Item tracking* category, we propose to ask the model to describe the accessible locations from the current location. Then the player must choose to move to one of those locations and go back again to the original location, in order to test the map's coherence. If during this process the available locations are coherent, the test is passed. A successful case is shown in Table 3.

Table 3. An example of a *Map design* unit test.

GM	(...) Current place: You find yourself standing at the entrance of a dark and damp cave. The entrance is surrounded by tall trees, and the sound of running water can be heard in the distance
	Accessible places: Inside the cave, Back to the forest, Along the river
Player	I want to explore the cave
GM	(...) Current place: Inside the cave
	Accessible places: The cave entrance, Deeper into the cave
Player	I want to go outside
GM	(...) Current place: Outside the cave
	Accessible places: Inside the cave, Along the river, Deeper into the forest
Result	Passed

5   Large Language Models as Out-of-the-Box GMs

In order to perform some experiments with our three proposed categories, we wrote five unit tests in Spanish and English for each of them. We then used those unit tests to evaluate the out-of-the-box GM skills of three LLMs: ChatGPT[7], Bard[8] and the LLaMA-based OpenAssistant chatbot[9]. We consider these three LLMs appropriate since they are dialogue systems (i.e. they have a *conversational nature*), a fundamental requirement for a GM model.

Since these are only preliminary experiments we consider really important to make the experimental logs open, because it can help the reader to critically examine the results reported here and reflect on the real flaws and strengths of both our proposed test categories and the evaluated models. Therefore, the detailed logs of the experiments and their results are accessible on GitHub[10].

We detail the analysis in two subsections, the quantitative results and the qualitative observations.

---

[7] "ChatGPT Mar 14 Version. Free Research Preview".
[8] Bard Experimental. Accessed on the 17th of July, 2023.
[9] "Model: OpenAssistant/oasst-sft-6-llama-30b". Accessed on the 14th of July, 2023.
[10] https://github.com/sgongora27/skill-check-GM-tests.

Table 4. Number of passed tests for each of the categories described in Sect. 4, testing OpenAssistant (OA), Google's Bard and ChatGPT (CGPT), both for English and Spanish. The last row shows the sum of the passed tests for each model-language pair.

Category	OA [ES]	BARD [ES]	CGPT [ES]	OA [EN]	BARD [EN]	CGPT [EN]
GM-P-GM	0 out of 5	1 out of 5	1 out of 5	1 out of 5	1 out of 5	0 out of 5
Item	0 out of 5	0 out of 5	2 out of 5	0 out of 5	3 out of 5	1 out of 5
Map	0 out of 5	3 out of 5	3 out of 5	0 out of 5	2 out of 5	3 out of 5
Total	0 out of 15	4 out of 15	6 out of 15	1 out of 15	6 out of 15	4 out of 15

5.1 Quantitative Results

After we ran the tests using the aforementioned models, we carefully examined the outputs and determined the results for each test, shown in Table 4. As can be seen, the performance on the *GM-P-GM* category is really low, regardless of the language or model. This result is aligned with those in [23], where common-sense reasoning was one of the remarkable flaws of ChatGPT. However, *Item tracking* and *Map design* tests were quite good both for ChatGPT and Bard. Although these preliminary experiments do not report a big gap in the results for ChatGPT or Bard between languages, they do unveil their strength over OpenAssistant. In most cases OpenAssistant just could not finish the test, due to generating nonsensical outputs that had nothing to do with the narrated events. That problem was even deeper for the tests in Spanish.

5.2 Qualitative Observations

The first and most important observation is that ChatGPT and Bard are really good at making the user feel that is playing with a real GM. There is a world to interact with, characters to meet and items to use. Everything seems perfect if the player chooses an action from those suggested by the model, although it is far from perfect when having to improvise new scenes and keep it coherent. OpenAssistant, however, struggles to deliver a minimum interactive experience and the tests had to be repeated several times to obtain a reasonable output. Our evaluation methodology does not distinguish that kind of errors, hence this aspect cannot be inferred by just comparing the quantitative results for each category between models (e.g. Bard failed the Spanish *Item tracking* tests due to wrongly list the available items, while OpenAssistant failed them because could not even give a proper output). However, we think that the quantitative results do represent the strengths and weaknesses of each model (e.g. ChatGPT is better at world coherence than commonsense reasoning) but also the "Total" scores provide an accurate comparison of the experience provided by the different models.

The second observation is about the contents generated by the models when taking the *creative responsibility*. Almost every scene *generated* by the models took place in a medieval-fantasy setting. This relation between RPGs and a medieval setting is aligned with the previous comments in Sect. 2: most of the available data about RPGs is in fact about D&D. As LLMs reproduce the biases in their training data [4], this shows that more work on other RPGs with different themes is needed. There is also a notorious absence of diversity of plots; after playing a few hours the narrated events and the available places start to repeat. Although this is related to the previous comment about the medieval settings and the biased data, it is important to have in mind that a great diversity of plots can be created using a medieval-fantasy setting[11], so they are independent flaws and might be studied separately.

Our third observation is about these models' tendency to constantly adjust the output to the prompt. If the player says or tries to do something then the output will try to adjust the narrative to it, without letting the player to feel any mystery about the plot. This is not a good sign for the skills we described in *challenge I*.

5.3   Limitations

Although we propose the test categories to assist the evaluation of GM models, the human subjectivity is still there. In addition to the difficulties faced to decide whether or not the test was passed, this subjectivity can also be present in the prompts design as well, as in the case of the *GM-P-GM* tests which need a specific human-designed case in order to run (i.e. a situation to solve and a player's solution to it). To perform a deeper evaluation and extract stronger conclusions we would need a diverse team of human evaluators and a bigger number of tests.

It is important to highlight that the difficulties faced when evaluating a creative system, added to the nearly-infinite input space that RPGs offer, make the evaluation even harder. Furthermore, the LLMs show a tendency to irregularly move the story forward: sometimes the model's output narrates a single event happening immediately and sometimes narrates long scenes. Not having a reliable mechanism (e.g. a symbolic representation) to restrict the model makes the execution of these tests more unpredictable, forcing the human evaluator to take unexpected decisions on the fly. For example, it would be positive for the *Map design* tests to have some kind of constraints and visualization components, to perform an in-depth analysis of the different reachable places in a given scene but without moving the story forward. Also, these dialogue models compute the utterances each time a new input is sent, what makes the replication experiments harder. Additionally we share the same limitations found by [23] regarding the needed time to run a small set of tests.

---

[11] This is evidenced by the massive amount of adventures published for RPGs with this theme, such as *Dungeons & Dragons* or *Pathfinder*.

6   Conclusions and Future Work

In this paper we discussed some challenges to face in order to model the skills that GMs need to play RPGs, like creating and managing a fictional world, tracking the game state and understanding the players' actions.

Following those challenges we proposed three test categories to evaluate any kind of GM model. Although these tests are domain specific, we think they can inspire other evaluation methodologies for dialogue systems.

We also used those test categories to perform preliminary experiments with ChatGPT, Bard and OpenAssistant. We found that ChatGPT and Bard can provide a satisfying gaming experience, but also they struggle when dealing with commonsense reasoning. OpenAssistant was unable to maintain the GM role during most of the tests. All 90 unit tests are available on GitHub.

The difficulties faced to control the models' outputs while running the tests make us think that in the future more *neuro-symbolic* approaches should be explored. We think that would help to keep the test phase more controllable, and also allow the players to examine the narrative details, avoid some scenes that they do not want to play and add another elements that they do.

In the future we would like to improve these test categories and design more to test other gamemastering skills (e.g. model the emotional variation of a character during an interaction with other character [20]).

Acknowledgements. This paper has been partially funded by ANII (Uruguayan Innovation and Research National Agency), Grant No. $POS\_NAC\_2022\_1\_173659$ and by the project CANTOR: Automated Composition of Personal Narratives as an aid for Occupational Therapy based on Reminescence, Grant No. $PID2019 - 108927RB - I00$ (Spanish Ministry of Science and Innovation).

References

1. Acharya, D., Mateas, M., Wardrip-Fruin, N.: Story improvisation in tabletop role-playing games: towards a computational assistant for game masters. In: 2021 IEEE Conference on Games (CoG), pp. 01–08 (2021). https://doi.org/10.1109/CoG52621.2021.9619006

2. Arenas, D.L., Viduani, A., Araujo, R.B.: Therapeutic use of role-playing game (RPG) in mental health: a scoping review. Simul. Gaming **53**(3), 285–311 (2022)

3. Behnke, H., Fomicheva, M., Specia, L.: Bias mitigation in machine translation quality estimation. In: Proceedings of the 60th Annual Meeting of the Association for Computational Linguistics (Volume 1: Long Papers), pp. 1475–1487. Association for Computational Linguistics, Dublin (2022). https://doi.org/10.18653/v1/2022.acl-long.104

4. Bender, E.M., Gebru, T., McMillan-Major, A., Shmitchell, S.: On the dangers of stochastic parrots: can language models be too big? In: Proceedings of the 2021 ACM Conference on Fairness, Accountability, and Transparency, FAccT 2021, pp. 610–623. Association for Computing Machinery, New York (2021). https://doi.org/10.1145/3442188.3445922

Some Considerations on the Evaluation of GM Models for RPGs

287

5. Bender, E.M., Koller, A.: Climbing towards NLU: on meaning, form, and understanding in the age of data. In: Proceedings of the 58th Annual Meeting of the Association for Computational Linguistics, pp. 5185–5198. Association for Computational Linguistics, Online (2020). https://doi.org/10.18653/v1/2020.acl-main.463

6. Benotti, L.: Implicature as an interactive process. L'implicature comme un Processus Interactif. Ph.D. thesis, Henri Poincaré University, Nancy, France (2010)

7. Botelho, L.M.: A guided journey through non-interactive automatic story generation (2021)

8. Callison-Burch, C., Tomar, G.S., Martin, L., Ippolito, D., Bailis, S., Reitter, D.: Dungeons and dragons as a dialog challenge for artificial intelligence. In: Proceedings of the 2022 Conference on Empirical Methods in Natural Language Processing, pp. 9379–9393. Association for Computational Linguistics, Abu Dhabi (2022)

9. Chen, H., Liu, X., Yin, D., Tang, J.: A survey on dialogue systems: recent advances and new frontiers. SIGKDD Explor. Newsl. **19**(2), 25–35 (2017). https://doi.org/10.1145/3166054.3166058

10. Colton, S., Wiggins, G.A.: Computational creativity: the final frontier? In: European Conference on Artificial Intelligence (2012)

11. Davis, E., Marcus, G.: Commonsense reasoning and commonsense knowledge in artificial intelligence. Commun. ACM **58**(9), 92–103 (2015)

12. Durall, J., Perrin, S.: Basic Roleplaying: Universal Game Engine. Chaosium Inc. (2023)

13. Gatsakou, C., Bardis, N., Drigas, A.: Role playing vs RPGs as teaching strategies in educational procedure. Technium Soc. Sci. J. **26**, 186 (2021)

14. Ji, Z., et al.: Survey of hallucination in natural language generation. ACM Comput. Surv. **55**(12), 1–38 (2023). https://doi.org/10.1145/3571730

15. Jordanous, A.: A standardised procedure for evaluating creative systems: computational creativity evaluation based on what it is to be creative. Cogn. Comput. **4**(3), 246–279 (2012). https://doi.org/10.1007/s12559-012-9156-1

16. Köpf, A., et al.: OpenAssistant conversations - democratizing large language model alignment (2023)

17. Louis, A., Sutton, C.: Deep dungeons and dragons: learning character-action interactions from role-playing game transcripts. In: Proceedings of the 2018 Conference of the North American Chapter of the Association for Computational Linguistics: Human Language Technologies, Volume 2 (Short Papers), pp. 708–713. Association for Computational Linguistics, New Orleans (2018). https://doi.org/10.18653/v1/N18-2111

18. Martin, L.J., Harrison, B., Riedl, M.O.: Improvisational computational storytelling in open worlds. In: Nack, F., Gordon, A.S. (eds.) ICIDS 2016. LNCS, vol. 10045, pp. 73–84. Springer, Cham (2016). https://doi.org/10.1007/978-3-319-48279-8_7

19. Martin, L.J., Sood, S., Riedl, M.O.: Dungeons and DQNs: toward reinforcement learning agents that play tabletop roleplaying games. In: INT/WICED@AIIDE (2018)

20. Oñate, A., Méndez, G., Gervás, P.: Emolift: elevator conversations based on emotions. In: International Conference on Innovative Computing and Cloud Computing (2019)

21. Peinado, F., Gervás, P.: Transferring game mastering laws to interactive digital storytelling. In: Göbel, S., et al. (eds.) TIDSE 2004. LNCS, vol. 3105, pp. 48–54. Springer, Heidelberg (2004). https://doi.org/10.1007/978-3-540-27797-2_7

22. Peinado, F., Gervás, P.: Automatic direction of interactive storytelling: formalizing the game master paradigm. In: Cavazza, M., Donikian, S. (eds.) ICVS 2007. LNCS, vol. 4871, pp. 196–201. Springer, Heidelberg (2007). https://doi.org/10.1007/978-3-540-77039-8_18

23. Qin, C., Zhang, A., Zhang, Z., Chen, J., Yasunaga, M., Yang, D.: Is ChatGPT a general-purpose natural language processing task solver? (2023). https://doi.org/10.48550/ARXIV.2302.06476

24. Rameshkumar, R., Bailey, P.: Storytelling with dialogue: a critical Role Dungeons and Dragons Dataset. In: Proceedings of the 58th Annual Meeting of the Association for Computational Linguistics, pp. 5121–5134. Association for Computational Linguistics, Online (2020). https://doi.org/10.18653/v1/2020.acl-main.459

25. Riedl, M.O., Bulitko, V.: Interactive narrative: an intelligent systems approach. AI Mag. **34**(1), 67 (2012). https://doi.org/10.1609/aimag.v34i1.2449

26. Sap, M., Shwartz, V., Bosselut, A., Choi, Y., Roth, D.: Commonsense reasoning for natural language processing. In: Proceedings of the 58th Annual Meeting of the Association for Computational Linguistics: Tutorial Abstracts, pp. 27–33. Association for Computational Linguistics, Online (2020). https://doi.org/10.18653/v1/2020.acl-tutorials.7

27. Tychsen, A., Hitchens, M.: The many faces of role-playing games. Int. J. Role-Play. **1**(1), 3–21 (2009)

28. Zhou, P., et al.: An AI dungeon master's guide: learning to converse and guide with intents and theory-of-mind in dungeons and dragons (2022). https://doi.org/10.48550/ARXIV.2212.10060

29. Zhu, A., Aggarwal, K., Feng, A., Martin, L., Callison-Burch, C.: FIREBALL: a dataset of dungeons and dragons actual-play with structured game state information. In: Proceedings of the 61st Annual Meeting of the Association for Computational Linguistics (Volume 1: Long Papers), pp. 4171–4193. Association for Computational Linguistics, Toronto (2023)

30. Zhu, A., Martin, L.J., Head, A., Callison-Burch, C.: CALYPSO: LLMs as dungeon masters' assistants. UMBC Faculty Collection (2023)

Assessment of Input Modalities for Control and Accessibility in Fully Immersive Virtual Reality Educational Game

Hubert Cecotti[1]([✉]) [iD], Louis van der Putten[2], Robin Coste[3], and Michael Callaghan[4] [iD]

[1] California State University, Fresno, CA, USA
hcecotti@csufresno.edu
[2] Polytech Montpellier, Montpellier, France
louis.van-der-putte@etu.umontpellier.fr
[3] CESI Ecole d'Ingenieurs, Toulouse, France
robin.coste@viacesi.fr
[4] Ulster University, Derry/Londonderry, Northern Ireland, UK
mj.callaghan@ulster.ac.uk

Abstract. Educational video games need to be fully accessible and inclusive. Fully immersive virtual reality (VR) must consider and address the needs of diverse user groups. In this paper, we propose to assess user performance, task completion and input modality preferences for a range of different gameplay modes, in either a standing or sitting position, in the educational game "Numbers and Letters". We assess the performance and usability of three input modalities: 1) a hand laser pointer for pointing and a trigger for selection, 2) a head laser pointer for pointing and a trigger for selection, and 3) a head laser pointer and a dwell time for selection, then assess differences in user performance between the sitting and standing positions for these three input modalities. The analysis was carried out with 14 users. The most preferred input modality was the hand laser pointer in the sitting position. The results stress the need to develop multimodal VR games where users can determine the way they interact with the environment.

Keywords: Virtual Reality · Educational Game · Input Modality · Multimodal interface

1 Introduction

Increasing accessibility and inclusion in video games is critical for educational games [1]. It is particularly true for games using fully immersive virtual reality (VR). The main challenge for accessibility in VR is ensuring that individuals with disabilities or special needs can fully participate and benefit from VR games or experiences [4,8]. Multiple barriers can prevent users from appreciating VR based video games. These include physical accessibility, visual impairments, cognitive and neurological disabilities. Firstly, VR systems typically require users

P. Dondio et al. (Eds.): GALA 2023, LNCS 14475, pp. 289–298, 2024.
https://doi.org/10.1007/978-3-031-49065-1_28

to interact with physical controllers, headsets, or other equipment. Gamers with mobility impairments may face difficulties in operating these devices or accessing the physical environment where the VR game takes place. Designing inclusive hardware and providing alternative input methods, e.g., voice commands or adaptive controllers, can help address this challenge. Secondly, VR heavily relies on visual content that poses challenges for individuals with visual impairments or blindness. Game designers and developers need to consider audio-based cues, haptic feedback, and alternative ways of conveying information to make VR games accessible to these users. This may involve providing detailed audio descriptions, incorporating text-to-speech features, or utilizing accessible user interfaces. Thirdly, some individuals with cognitive or neurological disabilities, such as autism or attention deficit disorder, may find it challenging to engage with VR experiences due to sensory overload, difficulties in understanding complex instructions, or problems with spatial awareness. Creating customizable settings, reducing sensory stimuli, providing clear instructions, and offering structured experiences can enhance accessibility for these users. Motion sickness and vestibular disorders are also critical important elements that must be addressed to make the technology fully inclusive and accessible [16]. There are large numbers of players and participants who suffer from motion sickness [10]. VR can induce motion sickness or exacerbate symptoms in individuals with vestibular disorders, causing discomfort, dizziness, or nausea. Multiple questionnaires existing for assessing and quantifying VR sickness symptoms and causes [14]. In order to mitigate these effects game developers should focus on optimizing frame rates, reducing latency, and providing customizable comfort settings. Additionally, offering choices and using alternative forms of locomotion, e.g., teleportation or smooth locomotion with adjustable speed, can help users with motion-related challenges [5]. Social inclusion is often mentioned as a challenge in VR. VR games and experiences often involve social interactions that may present barriers for individuals with social anxiety, communication disorders, or those who rely on sign language [6]. Implementing features that accommodate diverse communication styles, facilitating non-verbal communication through avatars or gestures, and providing supportive environments can enhance social inclusion within these environments. Finally, affordability and availability still represents a barrier for many users. Fully immersive VR technology (VR headset + controller) can be expensive, limiting access for individuals with lower incomes or in regions with limited resources. Addressing affordability and ensuring widespread availability of accessible VR hardware and software can help overcome this barrier [2]. Promoting the development of inclusive VR content can ensure that users with diverse needs can find meaningful experiences.

Games in fully immersive virtual reality typically require multimodal interfaces where actions can be performed in different ways. Locomotion and player movement is one of the main challenges in VR games, where users are given multiple choices to navigate the VR environment in different ways: through teleportation (with/without blinks), by moving to predefined points, or by moving directly using the trackpad or stick.

In this paper, we investigate the impact of different input modalities for interacting with the graphical user interface and the game elements by assessing usability, workload of the game, and virtual reality sickness symptoms. We compared three input modalities for item selection: the laser pointer with the selection performed by the trigger of the controller (baseline condition), the head laser pointer with the selection performed by the trigger of the controller, and the head laser pointer with the selection performed by a dwell time, i.e., the user has to keep the pointer on an item for a predefined duration. Furthermore, we assess these three modalities in two positions: sitting and standing where the gameplay is set in relation to their position e.g., in the sitting position, the user interface and game items are presented only in front of the user.

The remainder of the paper is organized as follows. First, we describe the game under consideration for the experiments in Sect. 2. The results of the experiments are provided in Sect. 3. Finally, the impact of the results are discussed in Sect. 4.

2 Methods

2.1 Game Overview

Numbers and Letter VR is a fully immersive virtual reality learning environment which allows users to develop their mathematical thinking skills. The game provides a practical example and case study of using the (LM-GM) framework [3] in the design of a game-based learning (GBL) approach for the applied use of the four basic mathematical operations to improve numeracy through flexible mathematical thinking and the adaptive use of arithmetic strategies [9]. The core gameplay is based on the game Countdown, where the player has to reach a target number by combining 6 different numbers that are selected randomly among a set of numbers. The game mechanics, integrated learning content and game implementation allows the users to perform fast paced mental calculations using mathematical operators and operands to explore and understand the role of numerical relations and operators in mathematical problem solving to achieve the objectives and learning outcomes, underpinned by appropriate theory. It develops their adaptive number knowledge skills and mathematical proficiency by facilitating searching for solutions and using different strategies for problem solving with mechanisms to quantify, rate and assess their accuracy and efficiency [15]. Successful completion of game levels indicates the students have met the objectives, achieved the learning outcomes, and understood the underlying theory. The game offers a fully immersive and interactive virtual reality learning environment which combines a range of engaging puzzles, levels, and environments using achievements and leader boards to ensure a high level of user engagement, retention, and game replay ability through the inclusion of competitive elements. The main menu of the game is presented in Fig. 1.

Fig. 1. Left: main menu of the game, Right: representative scene of the game with the selection of two numbers.

2.2 Input Modalities

The sitting and standing positions differ in two key ways: 1) the placement of the graphical user interface is different, the height is changed for both conditions, so the main controls are directly accessible in front of the user (see Fig. 2). An icon in the game indicates the current position. The graphical user interface turns in relation to the direction the user is facing; the user can lock/unlock the direction of the graphical user interface. With the head control modalities, the graphical user interface is locked.

Fig. 2. Position of the graphical user interface in the game. Left: sitting position, Right: standing position.

The visual feedback for the head laser pointer with the dwell time is depicted in Fig. 3. It includes a circle around the dot corresponding to the end of the laser pointer. The circle fills in direct relation to the dwell time duration. This type of visual feedback allows the user to predict when an item will be selected. If the user does not want to select an item, he/she can move the pointer to a different location. During the experiments, we have chosen a dwell time of 2 s.

2.3 Experiments

14 healthy adults took part in the experiment (age=21.5 ± 0.94; 3 females, 11 males; 13 right handed, 8 with vision correction). The experiments took place at the Intelligent Systems Research Centre, Derry, UK. Prior to the experiment,

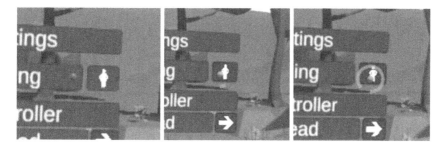

Fig. 3. Dwell time. Left: no selection of a button (red), Middle: selection of a button (green), Right: selection of a button with the circle getting filled. (Color figure online)

participants were informed about the purpose of the study, the procedure(s) undertaken and the use of the VR headset. No financial aid was provided to the participants in the study. The study followed the Helsinki Declaration of 2000 to conduct experiments with healthy human participants.

Participants in the experiment were asked to play the game in both standing and sitting positions. For each position, they had to play the game in the arcade mode (12 "puzzles") using each of the three input modalities: the laser pointer coming from the hands with the trigger used to select the buttons and items in the game, the head pointer with the triggers, and the head pointer with the dwell time and its associated feedback. Participants played the easiest difficulty level in the game where only a single operation is required to determine and solve the target number. The order of the conditions was randomized across participants. An HTC Vive and its controllers were used for the experiments. The left and right controllers have the same functions in the game.

The input modalities were assessed through questionnaires after the experiment. We used the NASA-TLX test to assess the workload [11,12], the System Usability Score (SUS) for the game usability [7], and the Virtual Reality Sickness Questionnaire (VRSQ) [13] to assess the overall experience. As there is a total of 6 different conditions, we only have questions related to the preference of the position and the input modality related to the 6 performance categories of the NASA-TLX test (mental, physical, temporal, performance, effort, and frustration), and 3 additional questions to determine the favorite position and input modality. Finally, we measure the average time for completing the 12 puzzles in each experimental condition.

3   Results

All of the 14 participants had previous experience playing video games; 86% of participants play first person shooter games; all the participants have used a VR headset before; and only 43% play VR games regularly. The results for the assessment of the workload with the NASA-TLX test are presented in Table 1. The average workload is 39.35 ± 19.01, which can be categorized as somewhat

Table 1. NASA-TLX test performance [11].

	Type	Questions	Score (mean ± sd)	Skew
1	Mental Demand	"How mentally demanding was the task?"	8.14 ± 3.39	1.63
2	Physical Demand	"How physically demanding was the task?"	7.79 ± 4.98	−0.10
3	Temporal Demand	"How hurried or rushed was the pace of the task?"	8.29 ± 6.38	0.40
4	Performance	"How successful were you in accomplishing what you were asked to do?"	8.93 ± 4.08	0.80
5	Effort	"How hard did you have to work to accomplish your level of performance?"	9.07 ± 5.05	0.46
6	Frustration	"How insecure, discouraged, irritated, stressed, and annoyed were you?"	8.64 ± 7.47	0.41
	Total	(0–100)	39.35 ± 19.01	0.08

Table 2. SUS test performance [7].

	Questions	Score (mean ± sd)	Skew
1	"I think that I would like to use this feature frequently"	2.43 ± 1.02	0.99
2	"I found the feature unnecessarily complex"	2.07 ± 1.14	0.57
3	"I thought the feature was easy to use"	4.14 ± 0.86	−1.14
4	"I think that I would need the support of a technical person to be able to use this feature"	1.29 ± 0.47	1.07
5	"I found the various functions in this feature were well integrated"	3.43 ± 1.09	−0.62
6	"I thought there was too much inconsistency in this feature"	2.36 ± 1.15	0.94
7	"I would imagine that most people would learn to use this feature very quickly"	4.21 ± 1.05	−0.96
8	"I found the feature very cumbersome to use"	2.71 ± 1.20	0.03
9	"I felt very confident using the feature"	3.57 ± 1.22	−0.78
10	"I needed to learn a lot of things before I could get going with this feature"	1.36 ± 0.63	1.69
	Total (0–100)	70.00 ± 11.73	−0.75

high. The performance related to usability is given in Table 2. The average system usability score is 70, suggesting a good, acceptable level of usability.

Table 3. Virtual Reality Sickness Questionnaire performance with values between 0 and 6.

	Category	Type	Score (mean ± sd)	Skew
1	General body symptoms	General discomfort	1.29 ± 1.59	0.79
2	General body symptoms	Fatigue	1.07 ± 1.44	0.94
3	General body symptoms	Boredom	1.5 ± 2.03	1.26
4	General body symptoms	Drowsiness	0.64 ± 1.01	1.38
5	General body symptoms	Headache	0.50 ± 1.29	2.41
6	General body symptoms	Dizziness	0.29 ± 0.83	3.20
7	General body symptoms	Difficulty concentrating	0.71 ± 1.33	1.77
8	General body symptoms	Nausea	0.21 ± 0.80	3.74
1	Eye related symptoms	Tired eyes	0.93 ± 1.33	1.30
2	Eye related symptoms	Sore/aching eyes	0.43 ± 1.09	3.13
3	Eye related symptoms	Eyestrain	0.79 ± 1.05	0.96
4	Eye related symptoms	Blurred vision	0.86 ± 1.17	0.99
5	Eye related symptoms	Difficult focusing	0.64 ± 1.22	2.01
	Total (0–6)		0.76 ± 0.09	1.38

Table 4. Ranking for the positions (values in %).

Question	Sitting	Standing	No pref
Most mentally demanding condition	21.43	21.43	57.14
Most physically demanding condition	14.29	78.57	7.14
Most hurried or rushed feeling condition	7.14	42.86	50
Most successful condition	57.14	33.71	7.14
Most convenient condition	35.71	50	14.29
Most frustrating condition	21.43	28.57	50
Preferred condition	35.71	64.29	0
Easiest condition to use	50	42.86	7.14
Most confident in using	42.86	50	7.14
Easiest condition to learn	42.86	50	7.14

The results for the VRSQ are given in Table 3. Only 3 participants have a score of 0 across the 13 criteria, while there is one person with a score of 3, 9 participants out of 14 have an average score below 1. The ranking of the different positions is given in Table 4 while the ranking of the different input

Table 5. Ranking for the input modalities (values in %).

Question	Hands	Head+Hand	Head+Dwell time	No pref
Most mentally demanding condition	0	7.14	71.43	21.43
Most physically demanding condition	21.43	0	64.29	14.29
Most hurried or rushed feeling condition	21.43	21.43	28.57	28.57
Most successful condition	57.14	35.71	0	7.14
Most convenient condition	50	42.86	7.14	0
Most frustrating condition	0	0	85.71	14.29
Preferred condition	64.29	28.57	0	7.14
Easiest condition to use	78.57	21.43	0	0
Most confident in using	71.43	28.57	0	0
Easiest condition to learn	85.71	7.14	7.14	0

modalities is provided in Table 5. The results indicate a greater preference for the hand laser pointer. As expected, the modality that does not require the use of the hands is more difficult. While the standing position is the most demanding condition, it is also the most preferred condition, giving more freedom to the participants to interact with the items and objects in the VR environment. The time for completing the game in the different conditions is presented in Fig. 4. A Wilocoxon signed rank test revealed no difference between the standing and sitting positions for the game performance. Similarly, there were no difference between the hand laser pointer with trigger and head with laser pointer. However, there is a difference between the hand laser pointer, the head laser pointer, and the hand with dwell time ($p < 10e-4$). The best average performance is obtained with the hand laser pointer in the sitting position with an average of 12.07 s per puzzle.

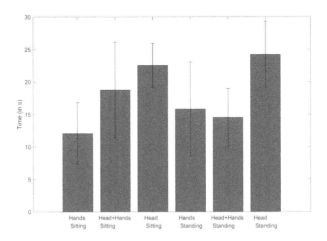

Fig. 4. Average time (in second) for completing the puzzle in the arcade mode in the different conditions.

4   Discussion

Games in fully immersive virtual reality require consideration of the needs of a diverse cohort of end users with different requirements in the design of intuitive, user-friendly, and accessible interfaces. To overcome these challenges, it is crucial for VR developers, hardware manufacturers, and content creators to prioritize accessibility from the early stages of the design and development process. Collaborating with individuals from disability communities, incorporating accessibility guidelines, and continuously seeking feedback can lead to more inclusive and accessible VR experiences for everyone, in particular for students with physical disabilities.

In this paper, we have considered and embraced the principles of universal design, e.g., simplicity, consistency, and effective feedback mechanisms. The UI elements developed, including the buttons and game objects in the VR environment, are large enough to be easily seen and interacted with, and avoid relying solely on colour cues. We have proposed, implemented, and assessed three interaction methods based on a laser pointer control to accommodate different user capabilities.

The evaluation of the input modalities was performed with students as participants. Their experience playing video games and using video game controllers would certainly an impact on the evaluation. The input modalities using the head as a pointer, and in particular with the dwell time, should be assessed with participants who have severe disabilities and who would not be able to use or hold a regular controller. Nonetheless, the evaluation provides some key insights about the need to develop multimodal VR games, which can be played in different conditions, i.e., sitting and standing with different control mechanisms.

Future work on this educational video game will include voice commands, brain-computer interfaces, and adaptive controllers, e.g., a mouth switch to replace the trigger of the controller with the head laser pointer. The condition with the head laser pointer and the dwell time could be enhanced with a subject-specific dwell time.

5   Conclusion

In this study, we have presented the evaluation of an educational game related to Mathematics in fully immersive reality by comparing three input modalities and two playing positions. We have highlighted the need to create multimodal interfaces that can be fully accessible. The results show that the hand laser pointer and the standing position were the preferred conditions.

References

1. Aguado-Delgado, J., Gutierrez-Martinez, J.M., Hilera, J.R., de Marcos, L., Otón, S.: Accessibility in video games: a systematic review. Univ. Access Inf. Soc. **19**, 169–193 (2020)

2. Amer, A., Peralez, P.: Affordable altered perspectives: making augmented and virtual reality technology accessible. In: IEEE Global Humanitarian Technology Conference (GHTC 2014), pp. 603–608. IEEE (2014)

3. Arnab, S., et al.: Mapping learning and game mechanics for games analysis. Br. J. Educ. Technol. **46**, 391–411 (2015)

4. Bierre, K., Chetwynd, J., Ellis, B., Hinn, D.M., Ludi, S., Westin, T.: Game not over: accessibility issues in video games. In: Proceedings of the 3rd International Conference on Universal Access in Human-Computer Interaction, pp. 22–27 (2005)

5. Boletsis, C.: The new era of virtual reality locomotion: a systematic literature review of techniques and a proposed typology. Multimodal Technol. Interact. **1**(4), 24 (2017)

6. Bravou, V., Oikonomidou, D., Drigas, A.S.: Applications of virtual reality for autism inclusion. a review. Retos: nuevas tendencias en educación física, deporte y recreación (45), 779–785 (2022)

7. Brooke, J.: SUS: a "quick and dirty" usability scale. In: Jordan, P.W., Thomas, B., Weerdmeester, B.A., McClelland, A.L. (eds.) Usability Evaluation in Industry. Taylor and Francis, London (1986)

8. Brown, M., Anderson, S.L.: Designing for disability: evaluating the state of accessibility design in video games. Games and Cult. **16**(6), 702–718 (2021)

9. Cecotti, H., Callaghan, M.: Practical application of the learning mechanics-game mechanics framework for serious games design and analysis for the development of mental computation in virtual reality. In: 2021 IEEE International Conference on Engineering, Technology & Education (TALE), pp. 1067–1072 (2021). https://doi.org/10.1109/TALE52509.2021.9678639

10. Chattha, U.A., Janjua, U.I., Anwar, F., Madni, T.M., Cheema, M.F., Janjua, S.I.: Motion sickness in virtual reality: an empirical evaluation. IEEE Access **8**, 130486–130499 (2020)

11. Hart, S.G., Staveland, L.E.: Development of NASA-TLX (task load index): Results of empirical and theoretical research. In: Advances in psychology. vol. 52, pp. 139–183 (1988)

12. Hart, S.G.: Nasa-task load index (NASA-TLX); 20 years later. In: Proceedings of the human factors and ergonomics society annual meeting. vol. 50, pp. 904–908. Sage publications Sage CA: Los Angeles, CA (2006)

13. Kim, H.K., Park, J., Choi, Y., Choe, M.: Virtual reality sickness questionnaire (VRSQ): motion sickness measurement index in a virtual reality environment. Appl. Ergon. **69**, 66–73 (2018)

14. Lee, S., Kim, S., Kim, H.G., Ro, Y.M.: Assessing individual VR sickness through deep feature fusion of VR video and physiological response. IEEE Trans. Circuits Syst. Video Technol. **32**(5), 2895–2907 (2022). https://doi.org/10.1109/TCSVT.2021.3103544

15. McMullen, J., Brezovszky, B., Rodríguez-Aflecht, G., Pongsakdi, N., Hannula-Sormunen, M., Lehtinen, E.: Adaptive number knowledge: exploring the foundations of adaptivity with whole-number arithmetic. Learn. Individ. Differ. **47**, 172–181 (2016)

16. Strupp, M., Dlugaiczyk, J., Ertl-Wagner, B.B., Rujescu, D., Westhofen, M., Dieterich, M.: Vestibular disorders: diagnosis, new classification and treatment. Dtsch. Arztebl. Int. **117**(17), 300 (2020)

Assessing the Complexity of Gaming Mechanics During Science Learning

Daryn A. Dever[1]([envelope]) [iD], Megan Wiedbusch[1] [iD], Saerok Park[1], Andrea Llinas[1],
James Lester[2] [iD], and Roger Azevedo[1] [iD]

[1] University of Central Florida, Orlando, FL 32828, USA
daryn.dever@ucf.edu
[2] North Carolina State University, Raleigh, NC 27695, USA

Abstract. Game-based learning environments (GBLEs) incorporate game mechanics, i.e., learning and assessment mechanics, to increase domain knowledge while maintaining learner engagement. Although GBLEs have been developed to improve science learning, learners have attained lower science achievement scores over the past decade as they progress through school. As such, there is a need to better understand how learners use game mechanics as they learn about science content. This study aimed to understand how learners generally use and transition between learning and assessment mechanics while learning about science with a GBLE and how those transitions were related to learning outcomes (i.e., learning gains, game success). High-school students (N = 137) were recruited to play Crystal Island, a GBLE about microbiology. Results found that participants used static learning mechanics (e.g., virtual books about microbiology) most often, followed by game and content assessment mechanics, and lastly followed by aid and dynamic learning mechanics. Further results found that several sequential transition probabilities were related to lower learning outcomes with a few transitions positively relating to game completion success. Findings from this study also show that the type of game mechanic, as well as the direction of transitions across game mechanics significantly relate to learning outcomes. These findings provide insights into how to develop scaffolding techniques for improving science learning outcomes.

Keywords: Game-based Learning · Gaming Mechanics · Transition Matrices · Science Learning

1 Introduction

A 2019 report from the U.S. National Center for Education Statistics (NCES) showed that since 2009, as grade level increases (i.e., 4th, 8th, 12th grades), the percentage of students labeled at or above NAEP basic and proficient achievement levels decreases, and conversely the percentage of students labeled as below the basic NAEP level in-creases from 27% to 41% across 4th and 12th grade students [1]. Addressing this decline, several game-based learning environments (GBLEs) have been used to increase learning outcomes across science domains (e.g., [2–5]). These GBLEs include game mechanisms

P. Dondio et al. (Eds.): GALA 2023, LNCS 14475, pp. 299–308, 2024.
https://doi.org/10.1007/978-3-031-49065-1_29

that help learners increase their domain knowledge and achieve game goals (i.e., learning mechanics) and assess learning outcomes (i.e., assessment mechanics). Because seventy percent of schools have reported using technology to supplement classroom instruction [6], researchers and educational game developers must understand how learners use game mechanics during learning to develop GBLEs that better support learning. This study examines high school students' behaviors while learning microbiology with Crystal Island, a GBLE, and identifies how learners' overall use and sequential transitions between game mechanics relate to science learning outcomes.

2   Game Mechanics

GBLEs are platforms where game mechanics are embedded to enhance learning outcomes without sacrificing learners' engagement and interest [7]. Game mechanics have been described and defined as tools embedded within a GBLE with which learners interact during the game [8]. GBLEs typically encompass design elements that are used to increase learning outcomes and maintain learner engagement. This relationship is detailed in Plass et al.'s [7] Integrated Design Framework for Playful Learning, describing how game design elements (i.e., game mechanics, visual design, sound design, narrative design, incentive systems) and types of engagement (i.e., affective, behavioral, cognitive, social/cultural) interact to elicit playful learning and promote learners' cognitive, affective, metacognitive, motivational, and social processes for increased learning outcomes. According to the Integrated Design Framework for Playful Learning, game mechanics can be categorized as either learning or assessment mechanics. This study examines how game mechanics, i.e., learning and assessment mechanics, are used within a virtual GBLE to promote learning outcomes, including domain knowledge acquisition and game completion.

2.1   Learning Mechanics

Learning mechanics are operationally defined as tools and materials that promote a learning goal and have been designed using a learning theory [7]. While learning mechanics have been shown to enhance learning outcomes (see [9]), many of these mechanics need to explicitly incorporate learning theories to dictate how information is presented to learners and the tools that support learners' understanding of instructional materials (e.g., Winne's [10] Information Processing Theory). For example, Dever et al. [11] showed that learning gains increased when learners were prompted to reflect on their progress using an embedded reflection tool. These findings are similar to those in a recent review [12] highlighting that learning outcomes increase when learning mechanics are designed to support cognitive and metacognitive processes during learning.

Overall, current literature shows that not only is it essential for researchers to understand how learning mechanics within GBLEs are designed, but how these mechanics improve learning outcomes. It is equally important for researchers to focus on how learning is assessed during game-based learning and how learners' use of learning mechanics may be influenced by their usage of assessment mechanics within GBLEs.

2.2 Assessment Mechanics

Game mechanics incorporate assessment mechanics, operationally defined as embedded tools that aim to address a diagnostic goal using testing theories. Related to the current study, assessment mechanics can identify learning outcomes such as learners' understanding of instructional materials related to increased domain knowledge and learners' ability to use skills needed to successfully complete the game [7, 13].

GBLEs are uniquely positioned to evaluate learning outcomes through more direct means in which a questionnaire is used within the study design, or more indirect methods in which the game itself collects information about learners' developing understanding. In a systematic review of learning assessments during game-based learning [14], most studies generally assessed learning using questionnaires or standardized tests, where a small portion of the studies used learners' interactions with game elements as a form of assessment. This suggests that studies should use both direct and indirect measures of learning. Because of this, it is important to understand how assessment mechanics within GBLEs can be developed for enhancing learning outcomes.

The most common assessment mechanic within GBLEs is stealth assessment, in which a stream of data is collected in real-time (e.g., time on the game, actions completed; [15]) to evaluate learners' developing content understanding [4, 16]. The current study argues that assessment mechanics can also be classified as tools that evaluate learners' content understanding while simultaneously progressing the game narrative. Across all studies examining the role of game mechanics on learning outcomes, very few studies examine the temporal sequencing of how learners transition between both learning and assessment mechanics while learning about science with a GBLE. It is important to fully understand these transitions to design GBLEs that better support transitions for increased learning outcomes. Because of this, the current study aims to address this gap by using log files collected during game-based learning to examine how learners generally use game mechanics and how the transition between and across learning and assessment mechanics relate to learners' science learning outcomes.

3 Current Study

The current study aimed to examine how learners use and transition between gaming mechanics (i.e., learning and assessment mechanics) while learning microbiology using Crystal Island, a GBLE. We relate these transitions to learning outcomes, i.e., learning gains and game completion, to identify how different game mechanics support multiple learning outcomes. To address gaps in current literature, we asked: (1) How often are different game mechanics used during game-based learning?; (2) To what extent do learners' transitions within learning and assessment mechanics relate to learning outcomes?; (3) To what extent do learners' transitions across learning and assessment mechanics relate to learning outcomes?

We first hypothesize that learners will demonstrate greater use of learning mechanics rather than assessment mechanics as prior research has shown that learners focus on gathering information related to learning goals during game-based learning (RQ1; [17]). Additionally, we hypothesize that transitions between components of learning mechanics will positively relate to learning gains (RQ2; [17]), where greater transitions across assessment mechanics will have a positive relationship with game success [18, 19] as the goals of the learning mechanics align with learning goals and assessment mechanics align with testing learners about their knowledge to complete the game [10]. Finally, we hypothesize that learners' transitions across learning and assessment mechanics will be positively related to all learning outcomes where learning outcomes are promoted due to learners' constant learning and testing (RQ3; [13, 14]).

4   Method

4.1   Participants

This study recruited 148 (19.5% female) participants from a public North American high school, ages 14 to 18 years ($M_{age} = 15.5$; $SD_{age} = 1.05$). Due to missing post-test scores, 11 participants were removed from analyses, resulting in our final dataset of 137 participants analyzed for this study. As participants were recruited during school hours during regular class time, participants were not paid for their involvement.

4.2   Crystal Island: A Game-Based Learning Environment

Crystal Island is a GBLE that promotes microbiology knowledge and scientific reasoning skills [2, 20] where participants were tasked with identifying a mysterious disease that has infected researchers on the island. There were several resources to develop knowledge about microbiology and apply that knowledge to achieving game goals. Participants learned about microbiology concepts through posters, books, and research articles. Concept matrices allowed participants to demonstrate their understanding of the material. Participants can interact with non-player characters (NPCs; e.g., nurses, patients, researchers) that guide them in their tasks, convey symptoms and possible transmission sources, and provide instructional information about microbiology. Participants could synthesize information about diseases and their symptoms using a diagnostic worksheet. Using a diagnostic worksheet, participants could synthesize information about diseases and their symptoms. To complete the game, participants were required to provide the name, source, and treatment of the disease. We outline how each of these mechanics are classified as learning or assessment mechanics below.

4.3   Experimental Procedure and Apparatus

Participants began by completing 15-min pre-task questionnaires on demographics, task motivation, and a 17-item pre-test on microbiology. Participants then played the computer-based game for 60 min before being directed to transition to post-task questionnaires similar to those completed at the beginning of the session. If participants completed Crystal Island before 60 min, the platform immediately transferred them to post-task questionnaires. Participants then completed post-task questionnaires lasting approximately 15 min. This included a 17-item post-test on microbiology knowledge that was similar, but not identical, to the pre-test. Feedback was not provided on either the pre- or post-tests. Participants were then thanked and debriefed.

Log files were collected to capture participants' behaviors during game-based learning with Crystal Island. Logged behaviors include if participants solved the mystery successfully, timestamps of events, and in what order events occurred. Events studied within this study include the following: when participants opened books, research articles, and posters, talked with NPCs, edited or viewed the worksheet, completed concept matrices, scanned food items for diseases, and submitted their final diagnosis.

4.4 Coding and Scoring

Learning Outcomes. Learning outcomes were measured with two indicators - learning gains as a measure of domain learning and game success as a measure of game understanding. Learning gains were calculated using normalized change score [21]. *Game success* was identified using log files where participants either provided a correct diagnosis to complete the game or did not submit a correct diagnosis.

Learning Mechanics. Within this study, we defined learning mechanics as materials or tools that aid participants in increasing microbiology knowledge by providing domain-specific information or allows for participants to consolidate knowledge without assessment or feedback. This includes interactions with books, research articles, posters, NPCs, and editing/viewing the diagnostic worksheet. We identified three components: (1) *static* where participants could not directly change or navigate their interactions (i.e., books, research articles, posters); (2) *dynamic* where participants could change their interactions with the mechanics (i.e., dialog with NPCs); and (3) *aid* where participants were provided a tool to consolidate knowledge (i.e., diagnostic worksheet) that was not assessed until the final submission (see Assessment Mechanics).

Assessment Mechanics. Within this study, we defined assessment mechanics as tools that identified participants' current knowledge in relation to both (1) content knowledge and (2) game progress. Concept matrices determined content knowledge during interactions with instructional materials. Game progress was determined using participants' interactions with the scanner to hypothesize about the disease and source and the final diagnosis submission. Both assessment mechanics categorized in this study were formative assessments that always provided outcome-oriented feedback in which the concept matrices highlighted the cell in red when the submitted answer was incorrect. The scanner and the final diagnosis submission both were formative assessments that also provided outcome feedback in the terms of informing the participant if their answer was either correct or incorrect via text.

4.5 Data Preparation

To examine how participants used game mechanics, a transition matrix was constructed and analyzed for Research Questions 2 and 3. Transition matrices identified the probability each participant transitioned between states (i.e., gaming mechanics; see Coding and Scoring section). A total of 25 possible transitions within and across gaming mechanics were identified and quantified for each participant (see Fig. 1).

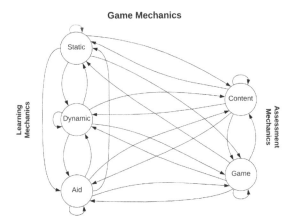

Fig. 1. Possible transitions across game mechanics.

5 Results

5.1 Research Question 1: How Often are Different Game Mechanics Used During Game-Based Learning?

A Friedman test examined differences in participants' frequency of game mechanics. Results found that frequency significantly differs across gaming mechanics ($X^2(4) = 128.0, p < .01$; Kendall's $W = 0.234$). A pairwise Wilcoxon signed rank test with Bonferroni correction ($p < .005$) found significant differences across most game mechanics (see Table 1). Participants used static learning mechanics most often, followed by game and content assessment mechanics, and lastly aid and dynamic learning mechanics.

Table 1. Pairwise comparisons of game mechanics.

Mechanic Component	M	SD	1	2	3	4
1. Static	22.38	9.35				
2. Dynamic	11.47	4.29	455.0*			
3. Aid	11.99	6.49	466.0*	4317.5		
4. Content	18.08	9.45	2155.5*	6736.5*	2402.5*	
5. Game	18.88	11.17	2948.0*	1599.5*	1497.0*	4313.5

Note. Values indicate the Wilcoxon signed rank test statistic. *indicates $p < .05$.

5.2 Research Question 2: To What Extent do Learners' Transitions Within Learning and Assessment Mechanics Relate to Learning Outcomes?

Learning Mechanics. Two regression models examined the extent to which the transitions within learning mechanics components (i.e., static, dynamic, aid) related to learning outcomes (i.e., learning gains, game completion). Due to multicollinearity, a correlation matrix was used for dimension reduction where, if the variables were significantly correlated ($p < .05$), the variable with the higher correlation coefficient to the outcome variable was kept while the other was dropped from analyses. We used four final transition probabilities as predictor variables: (1) static to static; (2) static to dynamic; (3) static to aid; and (4) dynamic to static. A multiple linear regression found a nonsignificant relationship between the learning mechanic transitions and learning gains ($p > .05$). A multiple logistic regression ($X^2(5) = 9.7, p > .05$) found that as the probability learners transition from static learning mechanics to dynamic learning mechanics increased, the likelihood learners completed the game decreased by 3.88% ($z = -2.91, p < .01$).

Assessment Mechanics. Two regression models were constructed to identify the extent to which the transition probabilities within assessment mechanics are related to learning outcomes. For both models, there were three transition probabilities as predictors: (1) content to content; (2) game to game; and (3) game to content. One transition probability, content to game, was removed as no participants engaged in that transition sequence. A multiple linear regression model identified a significant relationship between assessment mechanic transition probabilities and learning gains ($F(3,133) = 6.69, p < .001; R^2 = 0.13$) with significant main effects where, as participants increased in their recursive content transitions ($t = -3.95, p < .001$) and game to game ($t = -2.40, p < .05$) transitions, learning gains decreased. A multiple logistic regression model found a significant relationship ($X^2(4) = 10.4, p < .05$) between assessment mechanics and game completion. As the probability participants transitioned from content to content assessment mechanics increased, the likelihood of learners completing the game decreased by 5.52% ($z = -2.88, p < .01$).

5.3 Research Question 3: To What Extent do Learners' Transitions Across Learning and Assessment Mechanics Relate to Learning Outcomes?

Two regression models identified the extent to which the transitions across learning and assessment mechanics were related to learning outcomes. Across all 17 possible transitions, participants did not engage in two transitions (i.e., content to dynamic, content to aid). Due to multicollinearity, a correlation matrix was used as a dimension reduction method where, if the variables were significantly correlated ($p < .05$), the variable with the higher correlation coefficient to the outcome variable was kept while the other was dropped from analyses. This resulted in the use of six final transition probabilities as predictor variables: (1) dynamic to content; (2) aid to aid; (3) aid to the game; (4) content to static; (5) game to game; and (6) game to aid.

A multiple linear regression model found a nonsignificant relationship between transitions across learning and assessment mechanics and learning gains ($p > .05$). A multiple logistic regression was then conducted to examine relationships between learning and assessment mechanics and game completion. Results found an overall significant model ($X^2(7) = 22.6, p < .01$) with several significant main effects: (1) aid to game ($z = 3.22, p < .05$); (2) content to static ($z = -2.18, p < .05$); (3) game to game ($z = 2.59, p < .01$); and (4) game to aid ($z = -3.81, p < .01$). Overall, results showed that as learners' transitions between aid to game and game to game increased, their probability of game completion increased by 243.8 and 58.2 respectively. Conversely, an increase in the transitions from content to static and game to aid results in a decreased likelihood of game completion by 0.14 and 0.02 respectively (Fig. 2).

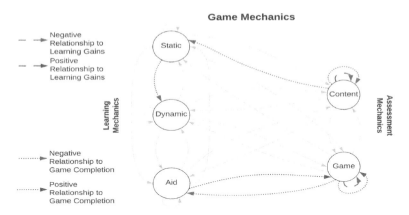

Fig. 2. Significant transitions across Research Questions 2 and 3.

6 Discussion

The goal of this study was to address current gaps in game-based learning literature by examining how learners' use of game mechanics were related to science learning outcomes. The first research question aimed to understand how learners used different game mechanics during game-based learning. Hypotheses were not supported by results. Findings showed that learners demonstrated a mixed frequency of game mechanics use across both learning and assessment mechanics. While this may indicate that learners place a large value in the information provided by static learning mechanics, the balance between learners' game mechanics use is noteworthy. This finding provides implications for how games can present game mechanics to learners, with assessment mechanics intertwined with learning mechanics rather than current literature on stealth assessments (e.g., [4, 16]).

The second and third research questions examined the probability that transitions between game mechanics were related to learning outcomes. Results from these research questions were not fully consistent with hypotheses or prior literature [4, 14, 17–19]. Results showed that learning outcomes decreased as most transition within and across game mechanics increased in probability. Two exceptions to this rule were found where the transitions from aid to game and game to game were positively related to game completion. One transition of particular note was the relationship between aid and game. Findings indicated a positive relationship with game completion when learners transitioned from aid to game, but a negative relationship with the same learning outcome when learners transitioned back from game to aid. This implies that not only are transitions across game mechanics important to consider for GBLE mechanic design, but that the directionality of transitions is essential to consider. The findings of this paper may be due to limitations of the game environment and incorporation of game mechanics. For example, learning mechanics and assessment mechanics are highly related to each other as well as the learning outcomes assessed.

7 Implications and Future Directions

This research has several theoretical, methodological, analytical, and applied implications for the future design and development of GBLE research. While Plass et al.'s [7] framework details relationships between game design elements and learning processes, more work should be directed towards understanding how game mechanics interact with other design elements to promote learning. This intersects with design implications of this research in which the narrative elements of GBLEs should be designed to both promote and diminish transitions within and across specific game mechanics. Specifically, to promote learning outcomes and game completion, games should scaffold learners' interactions with game mechanics according to the findings of this study. While this study addresses the gaps in current GBLE and science learning literature on how learners interact with game mechanics over time and how this is related to learning outcomes, future research is needed to: (1) examine the generalizability of these study results to other GBLEs and domains; (2) fully understand how cognitive, affective, metacognitive, motivational, and social processes interact with learners' behaviors to produce learning outcomes; (3) use additional methodological and analytical methods for capturing learners' interactions with game mechanics; and (4) incorporate a theory-based approach to studying how learners transition between game mechanics.

References

1. National Center for Education Statistics (NCES): Science Performance. Condition of Education, U.S. Department of Education, Institute of Education Sciences (2022). https://nces.ed.gov/programs/coe/indicator/cne/science-performance
2. Dever, D.A., Amon, M.J., Vrzakova, H., Wiedbusch, M.D., Cloude, E.B., Azevedo, R.: Capturing sequences of learners' self-regulatory interactions with instructional material during game-based learning using auto-recurrence quantification analysis. Frontiers 13, 1813577 (2022)
3. Lester, J.C., Spires, H.A., Nietfeld, J.L., Minogue, J., Mott, B.W., Lobene, E.V.: Designing game-based learning environments for elementary science education: a narrative-centered learning perspective. Inf. Sci. 264, 4–18 (2014)
4. Shute, V.J., et al.: Maximizing learning without sacrificing the fun: Stealth assessment, adaptivity and learning supports in educational games. J. Comput. Assist. Learn. 37(1), 127–141 (2021)
5. Kiili, K., Ojansuu, K., Lindstedt, A., Ninaus, M.: Exploring the educational potential of a game-based math competition. Int. J. Game-Based Learn. 8(2), 14–28 (2018)
6. Gray, L., Lewis, L.: Use of educational technology for instruction in public schools: 2019–20 (NCES 2021–017). US Department of Education. National Center for Education Statistics, Washington, DC (2021). https://nces.ed.gov/pubsearch/pubsinfo.asp?pubid=2021017
7. Plass, J.L., Homer, B.D., Mayer, R.E., Kinzer, C.K.: Theoretical foundations of game-based and playful learning. In: Plass, J.L., Mayer, R.E., Homer, B.D. (eds.) Handbook of Game-based Learning, pp. 3–24. The MIT Press, Cambridge (2020)

8. Pawar, S., Tam, F., Plass, J.L.: Emerging design factors in game-based learning: Emotional design, musical score, and game mechanics design. In: Plass, J.L., Mayer, R.E., Homer, B.D. (eds.) Handbook of Game-based Learning, pp. 347–365. The MIT Press, Cambridge (2020)

9. Ravyse, W.S., Blignaut, S., Leendertz, V., Woolner, A.: Success factors for serious games to enhance learning: a systematic review. Virtual Reality **21**, 31–58 (2017)

10. Winne, P.H.: Cognition and metacognition within self-regulated learning. In: Schunk, D.H., Greene, J.A. (eds.) Educational Psychology Handbook Series, Handbook of Self-Regulation of Learning and Performance, pp. 36–48. Routledge/Taylor & Francis Group, London (2018)

11. Dever, D.A., Cloude, E.B., Azevedo, R.: Examining learners' reflections over time during game-based learning. In: Roll, I., McNamara, D., Sosnovsky, S., Luckin, R., Dimitrova, V. (eds.) Artificial Intelligence in Education. LNCS (LNAI), vol. 12749, pp. 129–133. Springer, Cham (2021). https://doi.org/10.1007/978-3-030-78270-2_23

12. Zhao, J., Peng, H.: How to support and evaluate self-regulation in a game-based learning environment: A review. In: Chang, M., Chen, N.-S., Dascalu, M., Sampson, D. G., Tlili, A., Trausan-Matu, S. (eds.) International Conference on Advanced Learning Technologies, pp. 112–116. IEEE, Bucharest, Romania (2022)

13. Rahimi, S., Shute, V.J.: Stealth assessment: a theoretically grounded and psychometrically sound method to assess, support, and investigate learning in technology-rich environments. Educational Technology Research and Development (2023)

14. Gris, G., Bengtson, C.: Assessment measures in game-based learning research: a systematic review. Int. J. Serious Games **8**(1), 3–26 (2021)

15. Min, W., et al.: DeepStealth: game-based learning stealth assessment with deep neural networks. IEEE Trans. Learn. Technol. **13**(2), 213–325 (2020)

16. Smith, G., Shute, V.J., Rahimi, S., Kuba, R., Dai, C.P.: Stealth assessment and digital learning game design. In: McCreery, M.P., Kach, K. (eds.) Games as Stealth Assessments. IGI Global (in press)

17. Dever, D.A., Azevedo, R., Cloude, E.B., Wiedbusch, M.: The impact of autonomy and types of informational text presentations in game-based environments on learning: converging multi-channel processes data and learning outcomes. Int. J. Artif. Intell. Educ. **30**, 581–615 (2020)

18. Park, S., Wiedbusch, M., Azevedo, R.: What do log-files and learning outcomes reveal about developmental differences in self-regulated learning with serious games? In: Slotta, J., Charles, L., Breuleux, A., Laferriere, T., Cassidy, R., Beck, S. (eds.) Proceedings of the 3rd Annual Meeting of the International Society of the Learning Sciences. ISLS (in press)

19. Taub, M., Mudrick, N.V., Azevedo, R., Millar, G.C., Rowe, J., Lester, J.: Using multi-channel data with multi-level modeling to assess in-game performance during gameplay with crystal Island. Comput. Hum. Behav. **76**, 641–655 (2017)

20. Rowe, J., Shores, L., Mott, B., Lester, J.: Integrating learning, problem solving, and engagement in narrative-centered learning environments. Int. J. Artif. Intell. Educ. **21**, 115–133 (2011)

21. Marx, J.D., Cummings, K.: Normalized change. Am. J. Phys. **75**, 87–91 (2007)

Serious Games and Game Design

Inside the System - Designing VR Serious Games for Computer Science Education

David Baberowski[1]([✉])[iD], Thiemo Leonhardt[2][iD], and Nadine Bergner[2][iD]

[1] TUD Dresden University of Technology, Dresden, Germany
`david.baberowski@tu-dresden.de`
[2] RWTH Aachen, Aachen, Germany
{`bergner,leonhardt`}`@informatik.rwth-aachen.de`

Abstract. This paper argues, that VR learning games are a promising approach to build motivating interactive learning experiences for abstract learning content in computer science education (CSE). This can be achieved, by using suitable metaphors, letting learners get in touch with abstract learning content in an immersive hands-on experience. In order to implement a successful game design that supports the learning content while utilizing the possibilities of VR, a design process is proposed. This process uses conceptual models in order to find suitable metaphors and connecting learning content with game design. The process is demonstrated for two VR learning games that are part of the Inside the System series of CSE serious games.

Keywords: virtual reality · computer science education · game design

1 Motivation

Serious games are a well-established and widely used approach to computer science education (CSE) [6]. However, for VR applications, most of the applications are related to programming contexts, while other areas of computer science (CS) are less well covered [8]. One reason for this imbalance could be the abstract nature of computer science content (automata, formal languages, networks and logic). These require finding suitable metaphors and transferring them into a game design. For this purpose, this paper extends established approaches of game design by aspects of abstract learning content. Using two applications of the Inside the System series (ITS) as examples, this approach is then demonstrated.

2 Related Work

Mental models (MM) are representations of situations and domains that learners use to build knowledge, reason and think [2]. A MM is constructed, by setting into relation the important objects of a learning content. According to Norman a MM can be incomplete and incorrect, but must be functional, learnable and

P. Dondio et al. (Eds.): GALA 2023, LNCS 14475, pp. 311–320, 2024.
https://doi.org/10.1007/978-3-031-49065-1_30

usable [7]. Learners interact with the learning content based on them. By doing that, the model is constantly evolving, changing the objects and relations that make up the MM. This can be harder if the learning content is abstract, so this process is often supported by analogies. Norman further describes conceptual models (CM) as representation of learning content that supports the constructing of MM [7]. They are created by educators, scientists and designers as tools for the understanding of a system. They are therefore factual correct, consistent with the learning content and complete.

The relation of learning content, metaphor, CM and MM is rather complex. The following example about the abstract CS topic of cryptography will illustrate the connection of these concepts. Cryptography is an important and abstract content in CSE. Data is encrypted using complex algorithms, protocols and calculation. A CM for symmetric cryptography could describe two kinds of objects, a data-object that can be encrypted or decrypted and a key-object that must be present to de- or encrypt the data-object (see Fig. 1). Another property of these objects is the strict one-to-one-relation where only one certain key-object can be used in combination with one specific data-object. Even though this CM is valid for the learning content of cryptography it does not support learning on its own, but enables the use of fitting metaphors. Here a key-lock metaphor is also compatible with the CM and therefore the learning content, since key and lock behave exactly as the key- and data-object. With this analogy in mind, the learner can then construct a MM that is compatible with the CM and the learning content. At the same time, the metaphor can only work if the learner has already constructed a MM about the function of a key and a lock, in order to transfer the important attributes of these objects and their relations to cryptography. Doing this allows to construct a basic mental model for the processes in symmetric cryptography without the need for complex calculations and protocols. The CM combined with a matching metaphor for a specific learning content are the main parts of the didactic design for a learning game in CSE.

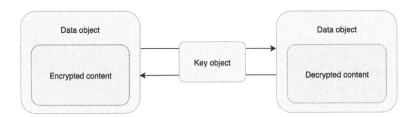

Fig. 1. Visualization of the conceptual model (CM), that is the basis of the key-lock metaphor.

2.1 VR as a Learning Medium

According to Schnotz, it is primarily through the organization of visual impressions and the subsequent selection of themes, that mental models are formed. Visual processing stimulates the process of analogical structure mapping in the learner, as opposed to the analysis of symbolic structures during the textual reception of information [10]. This is one of the strengths of VR, as it is able to block out visual stimuli other than the intended content. Therefore, it has potential for learning and constructing MMs for abstract content. Another benefit of VR applications is their highly immersive nature, when immersion is defined as the objective level of sensory fidelity provided by a VR system [11]. In contrast to the concept of immersion, the feeling of actually being in another place is referred to as presence. Research in CSE has shown, that immersion is a contributing factor to presence and beneficial for learning [1]. In his *Immersion Principle* Mayer evaluates different studies and comes to the conclusion, that high presence can facilitate deeper learning, in part due to higher motivation [5]. At the same time some studies show poorer performance after immersive media lessons, than in the control group. Mayer suggests, that this is because immersion can also increase cognitive load [12], which hinders learning. This makes game design with the specifics of VR in mind all the more important. Mayer also suggests, not all design principles for multimedia learning transfer directly to immersive environments and learning contents. Especially declarative knowledge does not seem to be easily transferable into VR, where process knowledge and affective skills, on the other hand, seem to benefit.

Even though Mayer suggests how different design principles of multimedia learning can translate to immersive media, further research is needed to examine individual influencing factors in more detail. ITS is an approach to do this for the special domain of abstract CS learning content. In order to systematically change different factors, the game design as a whole must be based on a sound didactic design by following a standardized process to produce comparable results.

2.2 Game Design

There are several approaches to facilitate a systematic game design process. According to Schell [9] a game design is divided into four parts: technology, mechanics, aesthetics and story. The *technology* of a game design refers to all means and interaction measures that enable the game. For VR games this is of course the headset, but there are important distinctions like the available degrees of freedom (DOF[1]) and the usage of controllers or hand tracking. The presented ITS series is aimed at stand-alone 6 DOF Headsets with controller support. *Game mechanics* govern the ways the player can interact with the game. On one hand the mechanics are dependent on the technology in terms of possible inputs and outputs, on the other hand the rules and procedures of a game are also part

---

[1] e.g. 3DOF means looking around is possible, 6DOF means one can move around inside the VR.

of the game mechanic. For the ITS series the game mechanics change in each title to make use of the different metaphors, used to make the abstract concepts interactive. The *aesthetics* of a game are expressed in the design of the game objects and the scene. Thus, a conscious decision can be made between simple or more realistic representations in order to reduce cognitive load or increase the fidelity of the virtual environment. The *story* relates to the contextualization of the task. The aim of a story is to motivate the learner and to tie together the other elements of the game design into a cohesive experience.

3   Game Design for Abstract Learning Content

In this chapter we want to suggest a game design process that utilizes CMs, metaphors and the strengths of VR (see Fig. 2). In a first step the learning content must be clarified. This includes constructing a CM by finding the most important objects and their interaction with another. A special focus lies on the interactions, since the goal is to foster process knowledge and not declarative knowledge. After this, a suitable metaphor must be found to support the assimilation process from the CM to the MM of the learner, that is coherent, reduced and familiar.

In order to utilize a metaphor to help the learner construct a MM for the intended learning content, it must be *coherent* with the CM. This means that the objects of the CM are represented by objects of the metaphor and behave similar to each other. Moreover, to provide an advantage to the learner, the metaphor should be easier to grasp than the learning content itself. Therefore, the metaphor should be *reduced*, that is, contain important and neglect unimportant information. In this way, the focus can be directed and cognitive overload avoided, so that the relevant relations between the attributes and objects can be included in the new MM of the learner. To support the learner, the metaphor should be from a *familiar* domain. In this way, existing MMs can be referenced and their structure, such as the relationship between objects, can be used to adapt existing knowledge and construct a new MM. At the same time, it follows that a clarification of the object of the metaphor and their correspondence in the learning content is important.

If a suitable didactic design is created, the remaining steps of the design process aim to make the analogy interactive, using an immersive environment. Aesthetics, mechanics and story then aim to foster strengths of VR like motivation and presence. The whole process should be implemented iterative, in order to check if the game design still supports the learning content.

3.1   Inside the Router

The learning content of *Inside the Router* (ITR) is located in the subject context of computer networks. The goal of the learning game is to understand the dataflow inside a home router and the rules, the router uses to receive and send

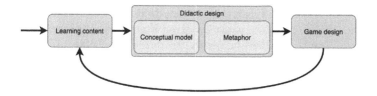

Fig. 2. The Process of Game Design with Conceptual Models (CM).

data packages in a network via IP addresses and ports. In the didactical reduced learning content, the home router has only three possible types of packages.

Local packages travel from one local client to another. A data package like this contains the direct address of its destination. Outgoing packages are destined for clients outside the local network. The destination address of such a package is not part of the local network. Incoming packages, that are mostly answers to previous outgoing packages, are all addressed to the public address of the router. The routing decision is based on the port number. Depending on the type of package, a router uses different strategies and attributes of a data package to forward it to the correct target.

After the clarification of the learning content, a CM was designed (see Fig. 3). The model consists of the data-object, that has to be sorted to a target object, according to different strategies, based on the type of the data object and its properties.

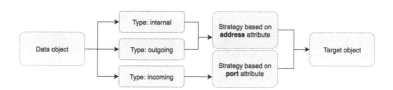

Fig. 3. Visualization of the conceptual model (CM) for ITR.

The used metaphor is based on a pneumatic tube system. This system consists of tubes, that stand for the connections to the different clients and capsules that stand for the data packages, traveling along those tubes. Since the goal of this application is to learn about routing in computer networks based on IP addresses and ports these are directly included in this metaphor. Each tube has a label with the address of the connected client, and each capsule shows the source and destination IP.

The metaphor is *coherent* with the learning content since the interactable objects (capsules and tubes) represent the central elements of routing (data objects and target objects). At the same time the objects are *reduced* in comparison to the learning content, since the content of the capsules and the properties about the clients are unknown. The IP addresses and ports on the other hand are so central to the learning content that they are directly included in the metaphor as labels on the capsules. Even if few students know what a pneumatic tube system is, the metaphor can utilize the knowledge about the sending and receiving of packages in a post system, what should be *familiar* since early childhood. The relation of sender, recipient, deliverer and addresses from a MM in most students that can be referenced in this new context.

After the CM is described, the game design utilizes VR as follows. The task of the learner is to sort the capsules into the correct tubes (mechanics). Different interactions were tested to maintain high motivation during the practice of this task. Catch and throw interactions were chosen in the end, letting the learner catch packages that come flying out of the tubes and then decide in which tube the package should get thrown back into. The capsules gain extra speed when they are thrown and self-correct small errors in aiming. If a capsule did not hit a tube or was not caught in the first place, it respawns in front of the player. If a player throws a capsule into a wrong tube, the capsule will bounce back and the player has another chance of choosing correctly. The mechanics aim to motivate the player by using engaging interactions and prevent frustration.

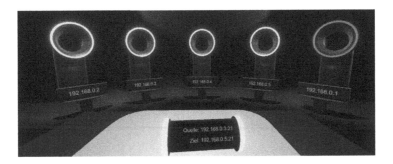

Fig. 4. First person view of ITR: a visually reduced pneumatic tube system, with a capsule in front of the tubes.

The aesthetics of ITR aim to reduce distraction and at the same time increase presence. The 3D objects are clearly identifiable as tubes and capsules, but do not contain any unnecessary detail or textures. The surrounding room is sparsely lit with only five spotlights illuminating the tubes. This way it should be clear to the player which objects are important during the game and distractions should be minimized (see Fig. 4). The controllers are not visualized inside the game, instead a virtual hand that is animated according to the controller input is shown to increase immersion. At the same time this visualization fits well with the grab interaction the user performs. Besides the tubes, the room contains only a table on that the packages are landing and respawning if they are not caught. This fixed point in the room gives the player an orientation where to stand.

The story of ITR is the premise that the learner has to perform the tasks of a router in order to ensure the operation of a local home network. The learner is also told, that fast routing will lead to a higher download speed. Since the overwhelming majority of students will have a local network at home, a reference to the home Wi-Fi is sufficient to establish a connection to everyday life. This whole scenario is setup in a short tutorial before the main game, where a little animated personified router named Routi guides the player through the basic interactions. The story of ITR is limited, because the main focus is on learning process knowledge in a limited time frame.

ITR leverages VR by drawing on its strengths in learning process knowledge [5]. This is done by frequent repetition of a task, while trying to minimize errors with the help of feedback from the system. Since this is a repetitive task, an engaging interaction is used to keep the player motivated. In a usability and learning performance study, learners performed significantly better in learning performance (repetition tasks as well as transfer tasks) after playing the game while high motivation was measured [3]. Even though the virtual environment did not contain complex or realistic textures in order to reduce cognitive load, high presence in users could be measured.

3.2   Inside the CPU

In Inside the CPU (ITC) the goal is to learn how a processor in a computer works. Modern computers are based on the von Neumann architecture. Here a processor consists of different components, that can interchange data via the data and address bus. One such component is the memory, that holds the program instructions as well as data. Each datum can be retrieved or saved via its address. If an address is written to the address bus, the memory writes the corresponding datum or instruction to the data bus from where other components like the instruction register can read it. Here the instructions, given in macro code, are translated into microcode. The difference between macro and micro code is, that macro code only describes the required operation like LOAD, STORE or ADD, while micro code describes in detail which components of the von Neumann computer have to perform together to actually achieve this.

In ITC the function of the von Neuman architecture will be the focus, by translating macro into micro code and executing it. Therefore, the CM is based on a macro-object that gets translated into multiple micro-objects in sequence (see Fig. 5). In order to execute this sequence, different components have to be activated and data-objects exchanged. Therefore, the CM is about the dataflow between the different components of the architecture to execute basic algorithms.

The metaphor consists of an industrial factory plant with distinct components. Each component stands for a component of the von Neumann architecture. Data is represented as cardboard box, that is transported between the components. If a component operates on this data it can get unpacked and the content gets accessible. It then can for example get combined and repackaged into another box, which would be the analogy for adding up two values stored in memory.

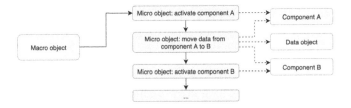

Fig. 5. Visualization of the conceptual model (CM) for ITC.

The metaphor is *coherent* with the von Neumann architecture, since all components are symbolized and behave accordingly. Also, the metaphor is *reduced* since the inner workings of the components are excluded from the metaphor. Instead, its focus lies on the control of the dataflow between the components. The metaphor of an abstract machine that is used to process something should be familiar, since it is already learned in elementary school and does not address specific knowledge. In the metaphor the product is the cardboard box symbolizing the data, that is processed by a machine in several steps. Learners therefore can infer the importance of the order of sequence and by watching the components work also the kind of task each one is responsible for.

Fig. 6. First person view of ITC: A factory plant as visualization for the components of a von Neumann machine.

The goal of the game is to process all the macro code instructions from the memory, by helping the machine to execute the corresponding micro code. This is done by transporting the data to the components of the machine from the user and processing it there automatically in each case. Therefore, the VR game uses a room scale environment, in that the player can walk around to access the different components. The player can also throw packages to complete the task faster.

The game uses a high detailed steam punk design of the machine to support the effect of the metaphor on feeling present in a factory (see Fig. 6). Every component has pipes, pressure tanks, gears and gauges, while the textures use metallic reflective materials. Every component is animated when activated and motionless when not. The animations symbolize the task performed by the component, like using robotic arms to unpack a cardboard box or using flamethrowers to destroy the content of the accumulator when a reset button is pushed. Each animation is accompanied by appropriate sound effects, while the entire application uses factory-like background sounds. This way the aesthetics aim to contribute to presence as well as visualizing the different micro code actions.

The game is designed story less. The development of a matching story, that fits the requirements between the metaphor, aesthetics and the learning goal, was complex and a working solution was not found yet.

ITC showed how important the iterative approach to didactic game design is. In an earlier version of the design, the focus was more on the structure of the von Neuman architecture, by letting the player control the machine from the distance with a good overview over all the components and animate the dataflow between the components. ITC showed high presence, low motion sickness, high user experience and high interactivity aud standardized scales in a first study [4]. Even though this was consistent with the learning content, the interactions (using a static control panel) did not utilize the CM. So, the game mechanics were refined with a focus on the processes of the von Neumann architecture during operation and the metaphor and game design adjusted as well. Now ITC uses VR to let the learners directly execute the dataflow by themselves, based on the CM for the dataflow inside a computer. Since in the final design the learner has to walk to transport the cardboard boxes, it is assumed that by repeatedly walking to the different components, knowledge is constructed about their linkage and the process of instruction processing. This still has to be confirmed in future studies.

4   Conclusion

The presented game design approach thus enables the integration of the conceptual model into the learner's mental model by interacting with the information technology system. This is done by having the learner perform the internal process of a system (e.g. routing or execution of instructions). The visualized metaphors are intended to activate prior knowledge and establish an everyday reference (e.g. the functioning of a postal system or the structure and operation of an industrial production line).

Conceptual models can be the basis for metaphors, that help learners construct mental models for abstract content in CSE. VR is a suitable approach to interact with these metaphors and therefore help learners to construct mental models, while it is also beneficial for learning through higher motivation and presence than other media. To build successful VR serious games a game design approach was suggested, that utilizes the generation of conceptual models to find suitable metaphors as starting point for the game design. The process was used on two applications, ITR and ITC. While the design of ITR already showed, that the didactic design process can lead to motivating and effective learning experiences, the design of ITC showed the importance of the iterative approach and the focus on processes and interactions for VR games.

The goal of the ITS series, besides creating good serious games for CSE, is to experiment with the influence of different design decisions on immersion, motivation and learning success. Further research in this area needs more examples of VR serious games following this game design approach.

Acknowledgements. The results presented were developed in the PraxisdigitaliS project. This project is part of the "Qualitätsoffensive Lehrerbildung", a joint initiative of the Federal Government and the Länder which aims to improve the quality of teacher training. The programme is funded by the Federal Ministry of Education and Research. The authors are responsible for the content of this publication.

References

1. Dengel, A.: Effects of Immersion and Presence on Learning Outcomes in Immersive Educational Virtual Environments for Computer Science Education. Ph.D. thesis, Universität Passau (2020)
2. Gentner, D.: Mental Models, Psychology of. In: International Encyclopedia of the Social & Behavioral Sciences. Elsevier (2001). https://doi.org/10.1016/B0-08-043076-7/01487-X
3. Leonhardt, T., Baberowski, D., Bergner, N.: Inside the router: an interactive VR learning application to practice routing and network address translation. Gesellschaft für Informatik e.V. (2022). https://doi.org/10.18420/delfi2022-018
4. Leonhardt, T., Lilienthal, L., Baberowski, D., Bergner, N.: The tension between abstract and realistic visualization in VR learning applications for the classroom (2023). https://doi.org/10.18420/DELFI2023-31
5. Mayer, R.E.: Multimedia learning. Cambridge University Press, Cambridge (2021)
6. Miljanovic, M.A., Bradbury, J.S.: A review of serious games for programming. In: Göbel, S., et al. (eds.) JCSG 2018. LNCS, vol. 11243, pp. 204–216. Springer, Cham (2018). https://doi.org/10.1007/978-3-030-02762-9_21
7. Norman, D.A.: Some observations on mental models. Psychol. Press (2014). https://doi.org/10.4324/9781315802725-5
8. Pirker, J., Dengel, A., Holly, M., Safikhani, S.: Virtual reality in computer science education: a systematic review. In: 26th ACM Symposium on Virtual Reality Software and Technology. VRST 2020, Association for Computing Machinery, New York, NY, USA (2020). https://doi.org/10.1145/3385956.3418947
9. Schell, J.: The art of game design, 3rd edition (2019)
10. Schnotz, W., Hauck, G., Schwartz, N.H.: Multiple mental representations in picture processing. Psychol. Res. **86**, 903–918 (2022). https://doi.org/10.1007/s00426-021-01541-2
11. Slater, M.: A Note on Presence Terminology. Presence Connect 3 (2003)
12. Sweller, J., Ayres, P.L., Kalyuga, S.: Cognitive load theory. Explorations in the learning sciences, instructional systems and performance technologies, Springer, New York (2011). https://doi.org/10.1007/978-1-4419-8126-4

Generator of Personalised Training Games Activities: A Conceptual Design Approach

Bérénice Lemoine[(✉)] [ID] and Pierre Laforcade [ID]

LIUM Computer Science Laboratory, Le Mans Université, Laval, France
{berenice.lemoine, pierre.laforcade}@univ-lemans.fr

Abstract. Memorizing declarative knowledge requires repetition, which can become wearing for learners. In addition, redundant game activities, offering unbalanced challenges in relation to the player's skills, can also lead to a sense of boredom. To reduce this feeling, learning games must provide adapted and varied activities. Automated generation is one way of building such activities. This article proposes a conceptual framework for the design of activity generators for training declarative knowledge in Roguelite games. The framework has been applied in the context of the AdapTABLES project aiming at multiplication tables training.

Keywords: Modelling · Training · Generation Design · Serious Games

1 Introduction

Long and short term memorization of declarative knowledge (DK), such as facts and laws, requires repetition [9]. However, repetitive tasks can become boring for learners [17], which can lead to their abandonment. Furthermore, serious games that offer redundant activities with challenges that do not match their skills can also become wearing for learners [18]. Thus, to limit the feeling of boredom, serious games aimed at working on DK must offer a wide variety of varied and adapted activities. Adaptation can be implemented in various ways and can be aimed at one or more targets (e.g., game preferences, learning content, difficulty). Personalisation can be defined as the use of models for the purpose of tailoring systems to each person [1,7].

Literature in cognitive psychology has shown that the process of retrieving concepts or facts through testing increases their long-term acquisition [3]. In our work, *training* on DK consists of repeatedly providing the learners-players with various forms of questions on facts. In addition, *activity generation* is a solution for designing adapted and varied training activities that few works address in Technology-Enhanced Learning [2] (TEL). Generators are software components that use structured data to create elements (e.g., text, documentation, activities). Building activity generators involves identifying and specifying the necessary elements for generation and their interactions. **Our interest lies in the design of generators of learner-player personalized and varied game activities for DK training**. To that extent, this article presents a conceptual approach for the design of such generators.

P. Dondio et al. (Eds.): GALA 2023, LNCS 14475, pp. 321–331, 2024.
https://doi.org/10.1007/978-3-031-49065-1_31

2 Research Context

Related Works. Although not widely addressed in TEL, content generation has been approached from three main angles: non-adapted content, learner-adapted content and player-adapted content. Most of these works have one thing in common: they use models to represent and structure the data required for generation (e.g., game elements, targeted knowledge, targeted content structure). Only, these models tend to be domain-dependant. Moreover, the elements not captured by the models, such as the adaptations rules, are captured in algorithms. Holohan et al. [6] defined an ontology to allow the description of relational databases. They then use this ontology to automatically generate online exercises for learning procedural knowledge (i.e., relational databases). Carpentier and Lourdeaux [5] have proposed an approach for dynamically generating scenarios adapted to learners' abilities and pedagogical needs in virtual environments. Their approach is part of a framework based on three models: the domain (i.e., static description of the world, its elements and their relationships), the activity (i.e., hierarchical structure of the observed activity), the causality (i.e., expresses the relevant causal chains occurring in the environment). Sehaba and Hussaan [16] have proposed a general architecture for learner-adapted (i.e., competencies, skills, needs) game scenarios generation. This architecture is based on several models: the *domain model* models the domain concepts and their relations; the *learner model* models learners' personal information, motivation, skills and interactions; the *presentation model* describes the structures of the scenarios; the *serious game model* associates game resources to pedagogical ones. Moreover, adaptation knowledge is represented as a rule-based system. Laforcade and Laghouaouta [10] have proposed a Model Driven Engineering (MDE) approach to understand the specification of generators of activities sequences (i.e., game scenario) adapted to individual learner's needs. This approach is based on [16], and mainly use the same models. Callies et al. [4] have proposed an adaptive architecture consisting in generating adapted pedagogical plans as well as in adapting the behaviours of the non-player characters according to the players' actions in simulation-type games. This work is based on a player model composed of their game and domain knowledge, as well as an adaptation module.

Outside a generation standpoint, some works propose architectures to guide the design of personalised learning systems. Roepke et al. [15] proposed a modular, component-based architecture for implementing personalised pipelines for learning games for anti-phishing education. A pipeline is a three steps process: data collection, content generation, content delivery. Ismail and Belkhouche [7] proposed a reusable architecture for the design of personalised learning software systems decomposed in 4 units: learner (i.e., maintains data about the learner), knowledge (i.e., maintains learning resources), personalisation (i.e., maps learner's model to learning resources), and presentation (i.e., represents the software environment). However, although the design of game activity generators requires choices to be made about game design, their design varies from pure game design. Furthermore, Tang and Hanneghan [19] discovered that there was no game model that offered a complete representation of game concepts from a design viewpoint for the use of MDE. Therefore, they propose a game ontology representing design aspects of video games for simulation and role-play genres, which also describes concepts linked to game activities.

Research Positioning. Our work targets declarative knowledge training (i.e., repeatedly providing the learners-players with various forms of questions on facts), independently of a specific didactic domain, through games. Consequently, the proposal must be reusable in a similar way to [7] in order to be extended to domain-specific DK. Training requires repetitive activities [9] as well as varied and personalised activities to avoid boredom caused by redundancy and inadequate challenges [17,18]. Depending on the genre, the structure of a game activity changes completely. Therefore, it was necessary to select a suitable game genre for DK training. Roguelite is a dungeon-like genre that meets DK training needs [12]. It is mainly characterized by the procedural generation of dungeons with pseudo-random content, permanent death (each death of the avatar forces the player to start a new game), and the limited possession of unlockable elements (e.g., avatars, items, power-ups). Therefore, a *training game activity* is a *dungeon*, i.e., a set of interconnected rooms in which the avatar moves around and in which the training takes place. In our context, adaptation focuses on both educational dimension and game dimension by considering teachers' viewpoint on training for each learner, learners' progress in their training, and players' preferences. Consequently, our research questions are as follows: 1) What are the elements involved in an activity generator? 2) What are the relationships between these elements? 3) How can the elements and their relations be structured to construct such generators? and 4) How to consider DK independently of a specific didactic domain? Our proposition is a framework extensible to domain specific DK. This extensible framework is a conceptual and software infrastructure composed of models and tools to formalize and guide the implementation of varied and adapted activity generators. This is a contribution in engineering research of TEL systems [20] contributing to the exploration and orientation of solutions for the generation of adapted activities. This article **focuses on the conceptual aspects** of the framework, describing the different models involved in the generation process, how they are built, and their relationships.

3   Activity Generation Needs

Activity generators are software components that take structured data as input and provide detailed descriptions of activities as output (e.g., XML files). They are composed of knowledge about the structure of the data they need and a generation algorithm (e.g., rule-based system, procedural generation) they follow to create activities. Dungeon generators for DK training require different models to work, cf. Figure 1. First, a *domain model* describing the training path and the facts to be worked on. Second, a *learner-player model* that keeps track of the learners progress in their training and in the game, and their game preferences so that the generator can personalise the activity on the basis of these data. Next, a *game model* which describes the game elements available (e.g., gameplays, game objects). Then, a *relation model* that describes the relations between the game elements and the training elements so that the generator builds coherent activities. In the literature, relationships are often implemented directly in the generation algorithm and rarely made explicit or modelled. Finally, to build an activity, the generators need to know its structure, which is why the *dungeon activity model* describes the structure of a dungeon for DK training.

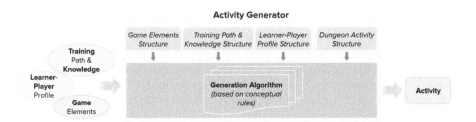

Fig. 1. Training Game Activity Generator Overview.

3.1 Domain Model: Training Paths and Knowledge

In the context of the AdapTABLES project, that aims at building a game for multiplication tables training, we conducted an exploratory research [11] with the help of experts in mathematics (i.e., teachers and didacticians). The exploratory research had two main objectives: 1) how to organize training, and 2) what adaptations to consider for training on multiplication tables (i.e., source and targets of adaptation). This led us to organize training into a structure called training path. A *training path* is a set of objectives to achieve, ordered by prerequisite relationships. An objective concerns a set of facts to work on, and is unlocked when its prerequisites are met (i.e., making training a step-by-step process with increasing difficulty). Each objective is decomposed into progressive difficulty levels. A level is composed of a series of tasks, having domain-specific parameters, which the learner must complete in order to progress in the training. Such training paths, from objectives to task parameters, are defined by a teacher for a learner or a group of learners. Therefore, each path is adapted, based on the teacher's viewpoint, to each learner individually.

DK are specific to the targeted didactic domain. For example, a multiplication table fact can be represented as an object with three integers x (operand), y (table) and res (result). On the other hand, a historical date would rather be represented by an object with a string (event) and a date or a period (integers). In addition, level and task parameters are also domain-dependant. For example, multiplication tables facts can be built in different ways, operand × table or table × operand, which is solely dependent on the domain of mathematics. Moreover,

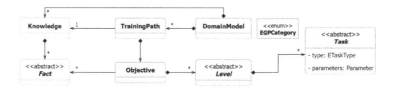

Fig. 2. Simplified UML class diagram of the domain model.

for a task consisting of completing facts with a missing element (e.g., find the historical date, the result of a multiplication), the element sought depends on the domain too (e.g., result, operand, or table for multiplication, and event or date for history). As a result, this model needs to be extended, by an engineer, on the basis of data provided by the teacher, at three strategic points: Fact, Level, Task. Figure 2 presents a simplified overview of the model, extension points are represented as abstract classes. On the basis of this study and discussions with history-geography teachers, specific tasks were defined for each field. Observation of these tasks led to the definition of four types of task (i.e., super-classes of the different tasks): Completion (i.e., completing a fact with missing elements), Order (i.e., ordering facts using a heuristic), Identification (i.e., attesting of the validity or invalidity of facts) and Membership Identification (i.e., identifying elements sharing a given property).

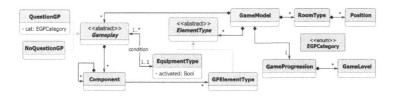

Fig. 3. Simplified UML class diagram of the game model.

3.2   Game Model: Game Elements Structure

Prensky [14] said that the main reason for learning game failure lies in their lack of gameplay. To that extent, we decided to provide a variety of gameplay (i.e., action that the avatar can perform within a dungeon that impacts the learner-player's progress). On the basis of informal interviews with game designers, we designed gameplays and gameplay categories (i.e., they do not claim to be exhaustive) for DK training through Roguelite: SELECT (i.e., selecting objects with the right answer), MOVE (i.e., moving the correct objects to the expected areas), ORIENT (i.e., orienting the objects to the right answers), POSITION (i.e., placing the avatar in the right positions) and DIRECT RESPONSE (i.e., typing in the right answers) [12]. Consequently, the game model is composed of gameplays. There are two types of gameplays: gameplays for answering questions and gameplays purely for gaming. Question gameplays all fall into one of the five categories mentioned above. The other gameplays describe game elements such as traps to avoid, objects to break to get more coins, and so on. Every gameplay are described by components that refer to a concrete type of game element (i.e., element that can be used within gameplays, such as pots, statues, traps).

Roguelites often feature an economic game mechanic, meaning that coins are collected throughout the levels, enabling the player to buy and activate items such as equipments. It is important to note that the creation of a game activity generator **does not require** the creation of a game (as it is an independent software component). However, creating game activities does require choices to be made in terms of game design. For this reason, our design choices included this mechanism. As a result, our game model features equipment and items that learner-players can purchase and activate according to their preferences. To ensure that these preferences have an impact on generation, and are not just aesthetic preferences, our choice was to offer items which, once activated, unlock new gameplays. So if a learner does not like a gameplay, they can deactivate the item and make it unavailable to the generator. In order to have a variety of rooms, we have chosen to model room types that describe the different room shapes that the generator can use. Finally, the game model describes the progression of the game in terms of difficulty levels. A game level can modify the size of the dungeon (i.e., the number of rooms), its shape (i.e., linear or labyrinthine) and the possible traps (i.e., difficulty and number). This model must be specified by game designers or engineers. Figure 3 presents an overview of the model.

Fig. 4. Simplified UML class diagram of the relation model.

3.3   Relation Model

For the purpose of generating coherent activities, the generator must be able to associate the game and training elements correctly. In order to define the relationships between our elements, we proposed a systematic method for defining machine-readable relationships between gameplay categories and task types for DK training. The method is described here [13]. The resulting relationships associate a gameplay category and a task type with a condition (i.e., a set of valued parameters required to associate them within an activity). Figure 4 describe an overview of the relation model. This model must be defined by engineers.

3.4   Learner-Player Model

Facts present in the domain model are raw information such as $3 \times 5 = 15$. Depending on the task and its parameters, the questions about the facts to practice changes. For example, completing a fact with a missing element will yield questions such as $3 \times ? = 15$, while identifying if elements share a given property will yield questions such as "Which ones are results of table three? $\{3, 5, 9, 13\}$". Therefore, like the facts, levels and tasks, these questions need to be modelled dependently of the didactic domain (i.e., another extension point). The questions present in the dungeon will have both correct and incorrect propositions (when the answer modality is Choice). From a didactic perspective, it is more interesting if the incorrect answers vary constantly. However, in order to compare learners' results on a given fact, it is necessary to have a common base that does not change (i.e., keep the question format but not the elements that vary). To this end, we propose a two-stage fact transformation process. First, questionable facts are built based on the raw facts present in the domain model. A questionable fact represents a question about a fact without incorrect propositions. Such facts are used to retain learners' results in the learner-player model (e.g., response times, given answers). Secondly, questioned facts are built based on questionable facts (i.e., they are questionable facts with incorrect answers). These facts will be those present in the activity (cf. Figure 6).

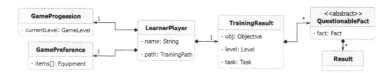

Fig. 5. Simplified UML class diagram of the learner-player model.

As mentioned earlier, players' preferences reside in the items they purchase and activate. As a result, the learner-player model keeps track of which items are purchased/activated. In addition, the model keeps track of the player's game level (i.e., game progression). Figure 5 presents an overview of this model.

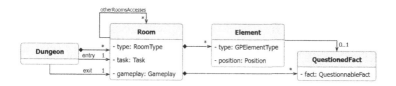

Fig. 6. Simplified UML class diagram of the activity model.

3.5   Dungeon Activity Model

Figure 6 describes the simplified structure of a Roguelite-like activity for DK training. An activity is a dungeon composed of rooms including an entry and an exit. A room disposes of accesses to other rooms (i.e., its neighbours) as well as a type (i.e., its shape) and a gameplay (cf. Section 3.2). Moreover, rooms with question gameplays are also associated to a specific task and a set of questioned facts (i.e., facts that are questioned in the room). Finally, each room is described by their concrete positioned game elements that can be linked to questioned facts (e.g., elements wearing choices or statements).

4   A Design Framework of Activity Generators

4.1   Design Framework: Presentation

For proof-of-concept purposes, the presented conceptual design approach has been implemented inside a framework (i.e., software infrastructure composed of models and tools) using Model-Driven Engineering [8] tools and principles. The aim of this framework is to guide the implementation of varied and adapted game activity generators for DK training.

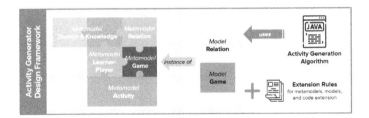

Fig. 7. Activity Generator Design and Implementation Framework Overview.

The framework (cf. Figure 7) is composed of machine-interpretable models that are translations of each conceptual model presented. Accordingly, it is made up of *metamodels* (i.e., models whose instances are also models), *models* (i.e., instances of the metamodels), an *activity generation algorithm* implemented in Java, and a set of *extension rules* (i.e., description of the different parts of meta-models, models and code to extend in order to build a domain-specific activity generator). The framework also includes an instance of the relation and game metamodels (i.e., models) as default. However, domain/knowledge model and learner-player model (i.e., only their personal information, such as name) must be instantiated and their metamodel extended by following the extension rules. As the framework guides the design of software components (i.e., generators), it is evaluated through the generators it builds, which are then assessed by means of system/integration tests and model checking (not presented in this article).

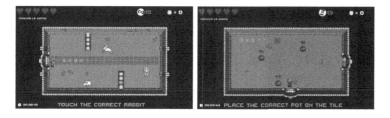

Fig. 8. Example of SELECT and MOVE gameplays for a Completion Task.

4.2 Design Framework: Application to AdapTABLES

AdapTABLES is a research project that aims at building a game for multiplication tables training. Currently, a game prototype has been implemented. It uses an activity generator built by using the framework presented in Sect. 4 (i.e., creation of an extension of the framework for multiplication tables). The generator provides XML files describing the dungeons (i.e., each element and its position), which the game player (i.e., prototype) interprets to create a playable dungeon. Figure 8 shows screenshots of the prototype displaying two different gameplays. Both gameplays are questioning the same fact: $3 \times 5 = 15$. Both questioned facts were built from the same questionable fact (cf. Section 3.4) but are different in terms of their possible incorrect answers. In addition, one gameplay is of the SELECT category (i.e., the player must touch the correct rabbit) while the second is of the MOVE category (i.e., the player must place the correct pot on the tile). It illustrates that a generator can produce a variety of questioned facts and gameplay for the same questionable fact.

5 Conclusion and Perspectives

In conclusion, this article describes a conceptual approach for the design of game activity generators for DK training. This conceptual approach has been implemented in a model-driven engineering framework that is extensible to specific didactic domains. This framework has been extended to build an activity generator for multiplication table training that is currently being used in a game prototype. The main limitation of our work is that the models and metamodels present within the framework are dependent on the game genre, in the way that they target DK learning through Roguelite activities (i.e., dungeons). In addition, there are many ways of modelling the information presented, and each of our choices can be argued according to different viewpoints. In the future, we intend to extend that framework to a second didactic domain: history-geography facts of the *Diplôme National du Brevet*, an exam taken in Year 10 in France.

References

1. Bakkes, S., Tan, C.T., Pisan, Y.: Personalised gaming: a motivation and overview of literature. In: Proceedings of The 8th Australasian Conference on Interactive Entertainment: Playing the System, pp. 1–10. ACM, Auckland New Zealand (2012)
2. Bezza, A., Balla, A., Marir, F.: An approach for personalizing learning content in e-learning systems: a review. In: Second International Conference on E-Learning and E-Technologies in Education, pp. 218–223. IEEE, Lodz, Poland (2013)
3. Brame, C.J., Biel, R.: Test-enhanced learning: the potential for testing to promote greater learning in undergraduate science courses. LSE **14**(2), es4 (2015)
4. Callies, S., Sola, N., Beaudry, E., Basque, J.: An empirical evaluation of a serious simulation game architecture for automatic adaptation. In: R. Munkvold & L. Kolas, Proceedings of the 9th ECGBL, pp. 107–116 (2015)
5. Carpentier, K., Lourdeaux, D.: Generation of learning situations according to the learner's profile within a virtual environment. In: Filipe, J., Fred, A. (eds.) ICAART 2013. CCIS, vol. 449, pp. 245–260. Springer, Heidelberg (2014). https://doi.org/10.1007/978-3-662-44440-5_15
6. Holohan, E., Melia, M., McMullen, D., Pahl, C.: The generation of E-learning exercise problems from subject ontologies. In: 6th International Conference on Advanced Learning Technologies, pp. 967–969. IEEE, Kerkrade, Netherlands (2006)
7. Ismail, H., Belkhouche, B.: A reusable software architecture for personalized learning systems. In: 2018 International Conference on Innovations in Information Technology (IIT), pp. 105–110. IEEE, Al Ain (2018)
8. Kent, S.: Model driven engineering. In: Butler, M., Petre, L., Sere, K. (eds.) IFM 2002. LNCS, vol. 2335, pp. 286–298. Springer, Heidelberg (2002). https://doi.org/10.1007/3-540-47884-1_16
9. Kim, J.W., Ritter, F.E., Koubek, R.J.: An integrated theory for improved skill acquisition and retention in the three stages of learning. Theor. Issues Ergon. Sci. **14**(1), 22–37 (2013)
10. Laforcade, P., Laghouaouta, Y.: Generation of adapted learning game scenarios: a model-driven engineering approach. In: McLaren, B.M., Reilly, R., Zvacek, S., Uhomoibhi, J. (eds.) CSEDU 2018. CCIS, vol. 1022, pp. 95–116. Springer, Cham (2019). https://doi.org/10.1007/978-3-030-21151-6_6
11. Laforcade, P., Mottier, E., Jolivet, S., Lemoine, B.: Expressing adaptations to take into account in generator-based exercisers: an exploratory study about multiplication facts. In: 14th CSEDU. Online Streaming, France (2022)
12. Lemoine, B., Laforcade, P., George, S.: An analysis framework for designing declarative knowledge training games using roguelite genre. In: Proceedings of the 15th CSEDU, Volume 2, Prague, Czech Republic, April 21–23, pp. 276–287 (2023)
13. Lemoine, B., Laforcade, P., George, S.: Mapping task types and gameplay categories in the context of declarative knowledge training. In: Proceedings of the 15th CSEDU, Volume 2, Prague, Czech Republic, April 21–23, pp. 264–275 (2023)
14. Prensky, M.: Computer Games and Learning: Digital Game-Based Learning. Handbook of Computer Game Studies (2005)
15. Roepke, R., Drury, V., Schroeder, U., Meyer, U.: A modular architecture for personalized learning content in anti-phishing learning games. In: Software Engineering (Satellite Events) (2021)
16. Sehaba, K., Hussaan, A.M.: GOALS: Generator of adaptive learning scenarios. IJLT **8**(3), 224 (2013)

17. Smith, R.P.: Boredom: a review. Hum. Factors **23**(3), 329–340 (1981)
18. Streicher, A., Smeddinck, J.D.: Personalized and adaptive serious games. In: Dörner, R., Göbel, S., Kickmeier-Rust, M., Masuch, M., Zweig, K. (eds.) Entertainment Computing and Serious Games. LNCS, vol. 9970, pp. 332–377. Springer, Cham (2016). https://doi.org/10.1007/978-3-319-46152-6_14
19. Tang, S., Hanneghan, M.: Game content model: an ontology for documenting serious game design. In: 2011 Developments in E-systems Engineering, pp. 431–436. IEEE, Dubai, United Arab Emirates (2011)
20. Tchounikine, P., Mørch, A.I., Bannon, L.J.: A computer science perspective on technology-enhanced learning research. In: Balacheff, N., Ludvigsen, S., de Jong, T., Lazonder, A., Barnes, S. (eds.) Technology-Enhanced Learning. Springer, Dordrecht (2009). https://doi.org/10.1007/978-1-4020-9827-7_16

Haptic Recording Experience

The Iceberg Model as a Serious Game for Decision Making in Systemic Design Oriented Leadership (SDOL)

Pelin Celik[✉]

Hochschule Für Technik Und Wirtschaft, Wilhelminenhofstr. 75 A, 12459 Berlin, Germany
pelin.celik@htw-berlin.de

Abstract. The Iceberg Model, derived from Systems Thinking, is one of the powerful methods for understanding the hidden dynamics and complexities that influence decision making. By examining the various layers of the iceberg metaphorically, one can gain a deeper understanding of the interconnectedness and interdependencies within systems, enabling to make more informed and connected decisions and foster sustainable change in a complex world.

By applying the Iceberg Model in the context of serious games, Systemic Design Oriented Leadership (SDOL) in particular could gain a holistic understanding of the hidden dynamics that determine behaviour and outcomes within their organizations. A serious game of this nature has the capacity to augment a leadership learning culture that fosters the investigation of cognitive frameworks, the interrogation of presumptions, and the cultivation of critical thinking. Through dialogue and reflection, SDOL could surface underlying beliefs and values. SDOLthat embraces the gamification of the Iceberg Model might effectively drive sustainable change in a playful manner. By focusing the gameplay on levels such as "mental models" and "systemic structures", SDOL can design interventions that address the root causes of challenges rather than applying quick fixes. The Iceberg Model as a serious game fosters a culture of continuous improvement and adaptability, positioning the organization for long-term success.

This paper explores the application of the Iceberg Model as a physical serious game in SDOL, highlighting its significance in identifying and addressing underlying factors that impact organizational behavior and performance.

Keywords: serious games · leadership · iceberg model · systems thinking

1 Introduction

The role of leaders in this present complex and interconnected world might demand a Systems Thinking oriented approach in leadership that goes beyond traditional command-and-control structures. Companies are faced with major economic challenges and also societal expectations that are shaped by values and sustainability [1]. These conditions require a systemic perspective in order to address the complexity and the "wicked problems" [2]. Leadership could be aware of these conditions and be able to take active action but this requires not only the right methods and an interconnected thinking, but also the implementation of serious games.

© The Author(s), under exclusive license to Springer Nature Switzerland AG 2024
P. Dondio et al. (Eds.): GALA 2023, LNCS 14475, pp. 332–341, 2024.
https://doi.org/10.1007/978-3-031-49065-1_32

Systemic Design Oriented Leadership (SDOL) can be such an approach to leadership that emphasizes understanding and addressing complex problems from a systemic perspective [3] as well serious games can be used to recognize different leadership styles and their impact on organizational dynamics [4].

The Iceberg Model, as one of the tools in Systems Thinking and based on General Systems Theory that offers valuable insights into the hidden aspects of organizational and societal systems, helping leaders recognize and navigate the deeper layers of complexity [5]. The model serves as a metaphor to illustrate the deeper dynamics of a system. While there is not a specific book or publication solely dedicated to "The Iceberg Model" terminology, authors such as Senge [6] introduce the concept of Systems Thinking and have a clear explanation into the direction of an iceberg metaphor. He discusses the importance of looking beyond surface-level events (visible) and addressing underlying systemic structures in order to understand the mental models (invisible). Authors such as Stroh [7] explore the Systems Thinking principles and their application to social change and explicitly refer to the Iceberg Model terminology.

Stroh's [7] sketch of the iceberg metaphor is the starting point for questioning the two-dimensional model and asking for serious games to train SDOL in Systems Thinking within a playful setting. Serious games can play a valuable role in promoting social and sustainable leadership. Authors such as Bonteaux & Sweeney [8] conclude that serious games can promote systemic understanding and future oriented strategy development in leadership. Morini [9] discusses the use of game design elements and Systems Thinking in participatory mapping, which helps participants develop systems modeling skills. Nordby [10] focuses on a pervasive game developed to teach sustainability and Systems Thinking, showing positive results in terms of learning outcomes. Sajjadi et al. [11] conclude that serious games promote Systems Thinking and allow more exploration in testing decisions.

This paper presents the implementation of a physical three-dimensional iceberg model as a serious game that supports the management of increasing complexity by using the Systems Thinking approach to enable Systemic Design Oriented Leadership in a playful way.

2   The Iceberg Model

The Iceberg Model as a metaphor is used in Systems Thinking to understand the underlying dynamics and behavior of complex systems [9]. It encourages systems thinkers to go beyond simple cause-and-effect relationships and to consider the complexity and interconnectedness of the various elements within a system [12]. The observations on the surface represent only a partial aspect of the system, while the majority of the essential components and influences remain hidden below the surface, similar to the metaphor of an iceberg where only a modest part is perceptible above the waterline.

The model is a powerful tool for Systems Thinking and analysis, helping Systemic Design Oriented Leadership and organizations to move beyond superficial observations and address the root causes of complex problems. It highlights the need for holistic thinking and the recognition that changes in one part of the system can have unintended consequences elsewhere [13]. In the context of Systems Thinking, the iceberg model in Fig. 1 illustrates two main components of a system: the visible and the invisible [7].

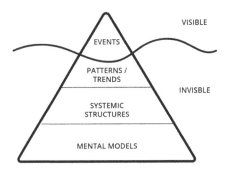

Fig. 1. The Iceberg Model. Source: Adopted from Senge, Peter, The fifth Discipline, 2006.

Visible Components:
These are the observable elements of a system that are easily recognized and measured. They include the tangible aspects such as events, processes and outcomes. These visible components are usually the focus of attention and can be addressed through direct actions and interventions. Most decisions of leaders are taken at this level only treating the symptoms and overcoming situations as quick as possible instead of looking underneath the problems to achieve long lasting solutions [13].

Invisible Components:
These are the underlying factors that are not immediately apparent but greatly influence the behavior and outcomes of the system. They are typically less visible, harder to measure and often involve intangible aspects such as mental models, patterns, trends, systemic structures and models (values, beliefs, assumptions).These invisible components are the driving forces behind the visible aspects and play a significant role in shaping the system's behavior over time [7].

By addressing the invisible components, Systemic Design Oriented Leadership might gain a deeper understanding of the system's behavior, identify leverage points for intervention and create more sustainable decisions [3].

Overall, the Iceberg Model as a serious game in Systems Thinking might be a useful tool for visualizing and analyzing complex systems, enabling practitioners to uncover hidden dynamics, challenge assumptions and develop more comprehensive solutions.

3   Haptic Recording Experience - The Physical Iceberg Model as a Serious Game

3.1   Overview

Applied methods from Systems Thinking such as Causal Loop mapping or Iceberg Model have so far remained represented on a two-dimensional level and cannot fully illustrate complexity in a three-dimensional framework [7]. A physical realization of the iceberg as a serious game could make the concept both playful and tangible. The model might be observed, touched and manipulated to develop a better understanding of the different layers and their relationships to each other. The physical presence of the model might make the static concept of the iceberg more tangible. In turn, the visible components in this serious game refer to the elements and progression indicators of the game that are observable and interacting with the player [9]. These components are part of the gameplay environment and have a crucial role in conveying information, facilitating interaction and achieving the game's educational objectives. The invisible components in the iceberg model as a serious game are play-based personal objectives such as benefits, learnings, decisions, hesitations and emotions between the players. Therefore the aim of the author was to design a serious game of the iceberg called the "Haptic Recording Experience" which is part of an ongoing research work in ludic leadership development [14]. The game is based on Stroh's Iceberg Model, which has four stages, starting on the visible iceberg component "Event", followed by "Trends& Patterns" and then focusing on the invisible component "Systems structures" and "Mental Models". The model is read top-down. The layers of different iceberg models start from three to five layers [13]. The Haptic Recording Experience game uses only three layers of systemic analysis: "event" as the visible layer or game setup and "pattern/ structures" and "mental models" as the invisible layer or level 1 and level 2 (see Fig. 2).

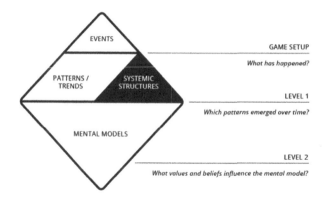

Fig. 2. Three levels of the Iceberg Model for Haptic Recording Experience.

This game is supposed being applied to specific ecological, economic or social problems within an organization in order to deal with the complexity of systems in playful way through dialogue and interaction. Players are confronted with an event as the starting point of the game, the deeper causes of which they have to explore from level 1 to level 2 and which usually finds no place for discussion in everyday work because it is too complex or too difficult to achieve a compromise notwithstanding the conflict.

3.2 Game Elements and Tokens

Event Cards: An event card describes an event that players will deal within the game setup. The events are graded in the level of complexity. **Mobilé:** The hanging artefact "mobilé" is the main structure of the serious game. it is made of acrylic glass and symbolizes the iceberg model in three layers, where the dialogue between the players takes place. The first layer is determined by the event cards for the game setup, then players can deal with the second layer the underlying patterns/structures in game level 1 and mental models in the third layer with game level 2. **Speech bubbles:** The speech bubbles are made of metal and are labelled in dialogue with key terms from general perspectives of the players on the event card and attached to the second layer (patterns/structures) and third layer (mental models) of the mobilé. **Comments and emojis:** Comments and emojis have a magnet to attach them to the speech bubbles. comments are labelled with personal perspectives and experiences of the players. Alternatively speech bubbles can also be annotated with emojis, which simplifies the game dynamic and makes interactions of the players visible. **Interconnection ropes:** Interconnections consist of a yellow rope to connect the speech bubbles systemically and across levels (Fig. 3).

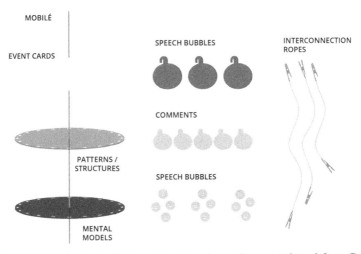

Fig. 3. Play components of Haptic Recording Experience. Source: Adapted from Celik et al., Ludic Innovation Experiences, 2023 [16].

3.3   Play Mode

In this first round of the game multiple players are confronted with everyday situations that they are allowed to deal within a systemic perspective in order to approach the game sequences. In the second round the complexity of the events increases and the event cards describe global events that require Systems Thinking. In the third round multiple players are tasked with addressing events they have personally defined, which may originate from leadership or organizational scenarios by utilizing blank cards.

3.4   Game Sequences

The players choose an event card from the three stages of complexity and label the first layer of the mobilé with the event by attaching it to the string. Then the speech bubbles are labelled and attached to the second layer of the mobilé ("Patterns/Structures"). This is repeated on the third layer of the "mental models".

After the second and third layer have been labeled with speech bubbles, players have the opportunity to step back and reflect on the dynamic construction. After the reflection, players are motivated to leave reactions in the form of comments and emojis on the speech bubbles. They are then allowed to connect the commented speech bubbles with each other across layers. Again, there should be a moment of reflection in which players can observe and reflect on the new construct. The haptic phase is finished.

Afterwards the players are divided into groups. From the observations made earlier, players should now select an area from the construct and create a speculative question. Once the question has been formulated, the group has to develop a scenario (determine the time, describe the environment, set the scene, distribute roles,…). The scenarios are presented by the players in a Speculative Role Enactment. Finally, the space for a final reflection is opened.

4   Results

The serious game was assessed through a three-hour workshop involving ten players from the University administration, specifically from the School of Design and Culture at HTW Berlin, to evaluate the game. The pedagogical objective and educational goal was to develop Systems Thinking skills, to encourage behavioral change and to facilitate the transfer of knowledge from the game environment to real-world situations. The event was dedicated to the topic of "Cultural Appropriation in Design", as it has triggered a number of debates, especially in design, and is considered as a so-called wicked problem. After a short introduction, the game rules and tokens were explained. To commence, the players were tasked with game testing using an everyday situation event card titled "Secretly you are annoyed because the elderly woman in front of you in the supermarket takes so long to count her coins," a selection made by the group. Each player was allocated a total of 15 min to navigate through all the gameplay sequences and delve into mental models. Following the warm-up exercise, the topic of "cultural appropriation," a subject that has garnered significant attention in social media, was introduced (Designer Isabel Marant facing legal action and backlash due to allegations of cultural appropriation of Mexican indigenous cultural heritage). Subsequently, the Systems Thinking training, featuring the physical and serious Iceberg Model game, commenced.

This workshop was the first testing of the physical Iceberg Model as a serious game with the title Haptic Recording Experience. During the game, numerous impressions were gathered from the players by observations and a recorded feedback, which will be included in the further development of the game (Fig. 4).

The visual, haptic, and interactive elements of the game received the highest positive ratings for their aesthetics. Similarly, all players expressed a high level of appreciation for the opportunity to engage in the exchange of tangible items. Three of the players had the impression that if the workshop had only taken place with notes on paper, the content would have been "just written down and left there". But this way they reported that they had to be much more careful with what they wrote on the acrylic sheets: *"(...) I think if it had been just a few pieces of paper again, we might have all fallen on our necks. That is why I found the care with which everything was prepared, and also the interesting fragility of the construct, that you have such an edifice of thoughts in front of*

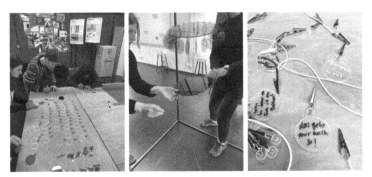

Fig. 4. Players attaching speech bubbles. Photo credits: Leona Goldstein.

you, reflecting the whole thing relatively well (...)." This statement can be attributed to the pedagogical aspects of knowledge transfer and behavior change.

Eight of the players opened up to the topic on the day of the play and experienced moments of vulnerability, both in dealing with the topic itself and in recounting personal experiences. In this regard, one player stated that she was *"in the here and now"* during the workshop and had managed not to think about anything else during the workshop. In fact, seven players verified this pedagogical aspects of motivation and engagement in the serious game by emphasizing how quickly the three hours had passed: *"(...) But I found it a pity that it was so short. I think it would be great if it was actually a course and you could go deeper into it."* A further statement in the aspect of developing skills was: *"In addition, I would like to emphasize again that the encounter itself was great, especially working in a group that you do not know and where this topic is perhaps not yet so easy. I thought it was good that we approached each other while working and then sought distance again, just like the distribution of the whole thing in stations. (...)"*. Furthermore, the speculative component did not work as intended. Players were able to form speculative scenarios, but did not get to the actual role play. Instead, players requested a longer discussion and feedback session, which validates the aspects of knowledge transfer in the game.

There is also the alternative of asking players to make a statement for the future instead of a speculative role-play: *"The only thing I could imagine additionally would be to hear some positions and ideas from the perspective of the community and the relevant stakeholders. Via audio, text, video or if possible even in real life as experts on site. That would certainly expand the thinking by a few completely new levels."*

The systemic complexity of the chosen issue, although there was still a sense of insecurity in the room at the beginning, was easier to deal with and the exchange took place both in the room and on the object: *"You can see the complexity of the topic very well. (...) But it reflects the mindset in people's heads quite well. In order to extract things from it, you would have to be able to transfer the contents again somehow. (...) On the other hand, it promoted the exchange very well: the togetherness, this sneaking around, searching around, handling the materials carefully"* (Fig. 5).

The application of the Iceberg Model was thus perceived as positive by the players as a whole, especially due to the fact that they were able to visually observe and reflect

Fig. 5. Players discussing the result. Photo credit: Leona Goldstein.

on these different game levels: *"(...) What was nice in any case was how we dealt with it in a totally sensitive way. For me, that also means mindful reflection.(...) Today I also discovered for myself that I have thought about it much more: What am I writing now? Because then I might have to go down to another level...Going to a deeper level myself was, I think, quite good, also for one's own reflections on the points that one had already stated."*

5   Discussion

The architect and designer Otl Aicher was called a thinker on the object because he believed that "touching and grasping - the relations between thinking and the body are so close that what happens in thinking is often described in the language of the hands". This Gestalt philosophy of Aicher's is also expressed in the serious game "Haptic Recording Experience". This serious game demonstrates how important it is not only to reflect on the own attitude and systemic understanding in leadership - discussing in words with others - but also to play and create an object that make these words and thoughts tangible.

The Haptic Recording Experience game as a physical Iceberg Model is a multiplayer game to experience thoughts, reactions and linkages in relation to a specific event, in order to identify the underlying structures and to understand the mental models in a system. The pedagogical objectives in this serious game refers to learning outcomes such as behavioral change, developing skills, knowledge transfer and motivation and engagement. The game might enable SDOL for more collaboration and discussion with different stakeholders as the physical Iceberg Model acts as a common frame of reference. By moving and linking the game components SDOL could explore the impact on the overall dynamics of a system. This promotes a deeper understanding of the underlying patterns and relationships.

In the very first game testing players were asked not only to react to an event, but also to gradually examine and reflect systemically on the underlying causes and mental models that led to the event. By adding or removing game tokens of the model, the effects on the system could be explored. This allowed a playful approach to complex problems and encouraged creative approaches to solving them. In addition, the players learned the basics of Systems Thinking completely unconsciously by addressing a case of systemic scale in exchange with others and through explorative actions.

The physical Iceberg Model game might serve as a long-term tool to maintain awareness of the underlying dynamics and principles. It could also be placed in a central location to serve as a reminder and reference point for systemic thinking and action. SDOL could refer to the model regularly to broaden their perspective and improve their decision-making.

The game is still in testing mode and it has to be evaluated if a physical, gamified Iceberg Model can train SDOL in practicing Systems Thinking methods. For further development, it should also be explored what causes players to lose the sense of time and the pressure to work performance while playing.

6 Conclusion

The structure of the Iceberg Model was used as the guiding method for the game. The Iceberg Model shows that events and patterns are caused by systemic structures and mental models, that are often hidden under the "water level". Behaviors in an organization or system derive from these underlying structures, that are established over time due to mental models [15]. Leaders have to understand the systemic structures and underlying mental models to make sustainable decisions. Systemic Design Oriented Leadership might recognize the ethical dimensions of managers decisions and actions. This type of leadership is particularly relevant in the contemporary world, where many challenges, such as climate change, inequality, and social issues, require holistic and innovative approaches to drive meaningful change [5].

The Haptic Recording Experience play shall encourage SDOL to a holistic perspective and promote the exploration of the deeper layers that shape the visible outcomes. It might consider the social, environmental and ethical implications of the choices and strive to act responsibly and with integrity.

The three-dimensional gamified representation and interaction in space, as well as touching and discussing, connections and communication might be an opportunity for SDOL to capture complexity physically and playful and identifying leverage points for interventions.

References

1. Nilsson, J., Jansson, J., Vall, G.H., Modig, F.: The importance of market and entrepreneurial strategic orientations among companies committed to sustainability values and practices. Bus. Strat. Sustain. (2018)
2. Beehner, C.G.: System Leadership for Sustainability, 1st edn. Routledge, London (2019)
3. Mugadza, G., Marcus, R.: A systems thinking and design thinking approach to leadership. Expert J. Bus. Manage. 7(1), 1–10 (2019)
4. Almeida, F., Buzady, Z.: Recognizing leadership styles through the use of a serious game. J. Appl. Res. High. Educ. 14(4), 1592–1602 (2022)
5. Garrity, E.: Using systems thinking to understand and enlarge mental models: helping the transition to a sustainable world. Systems 6, 15 (2018)
6. Senge, P.: The Fifth Discipline. Doubleday, New York (1990). Revised 2006
7. Stroh, D.P.: Systems thinking for social change: a practical guide to solving complex problems, avoiding unintended consequences and achieving lasting results. Chelsea Green Publishing, White River Junction, Vermont (2015)

8. Bontoux, L., Bengtsson, D., Rosa, A., Sweeney, J.A.: The JRC scenario exploration system-from study to serious game. J. Futures Stud. **20**(3), 93–108 (2016)

9. Morini, L.: Playful participatory mapping: co-creating games to foster systems thinking. In: European Conference on Games Based Learning (2022)

10. Nordby, A., Øygardslia, K., Sverdrup, U.U., Sverdrup, H.U.: The art of gamification; teaching sustainability and system thinking by pervasive game development. Electron. J. e-Learn. **14**, 152–168 (2016)

11. Sajjadi, P., et al.: Promoting systems thinking and pro-environmental policy support through serious games. Front. Environ. Sci. **10**, 957204 (2022)

12. Foster-Fishman, P., Nowell, B., Yang, H.: Putting the system back into systems change: a framework for understanding and changing organizational and community systems. Am. J. Community Psychol. **39**, 197–215 (2007)

13. Al-Homery, H.A., Ashari, H., Ahmad, A.: The application of system thinking for firm supply chain sustainability: the conceptual study of the development of the iceberg problem solving tool (IPST). Int. J. Supply Chain Manage. **8**, 951–956 (2019)

14. Celik, P., Schönbohm, A., Hidalog Miranda, O., Walther, J.-H.: Ludic innovation experiences – führungskräfteentwicklung mit spiel und system, Berlin (2023)

15. Hemmelgarn, A.L., Glisson, C.: The role of mental models in organizational change. In: Building Cultures and Climates for Effective Human Services: Understanding and Improving Organizational Social Contexts with the ARC Mode, pp. 93–111. Oxford Academic, New York (2018).https://doi.org/10.1093/oso/9780190455286.003.0008

Mapping Facts to Concrete Game Elements for Generation Purposes: A Conceptual Approach

Bérénice Lemoine[(⊠)] and Pierre Laforcade

LIUM Computer Science Laboratory, Le Mans Université, Laval, France
{berenice.lemoine,pierre.laforcade}@univ-lemans.fr

Abstract. Designing serious games or serious game activities requires mapping the educational elements and the game elements. This mapping is mainly addressed from a high-level game design perspective. Moreover, low-level mapping methods are generally domain-specific. Our aim is to address this problem, at an algorithmic level, in the context of activity generation (i.e., automatic creation of activities) for declarative knowledge training. This paper presents a generic modelling approach of questioned facts and gameplays, and an algorithm for the automatic and domain-independent generation of various gameplays for training purposes. The approach has been applied to multiplication tables training.

Keywords: Modelling · Generation · Gameplay · Serious Games

1 Introduction

Recently, the design and use of learning games has become a recurrent theme [3]. Designing learning game activities requires to map the game elements with the educational elements [12]. This mapping requirement is more important in the context of game activity generation, since the generation algorithm needs to know the relations between elements to automatically build a coherent activity. The relations between elements might vary in regard to the game genre, the targeted knowledge, and the didactic domain. Some works propose methods for mapping game elements and educational elements during game general design [1, 8]. However, to the best of our knowledge, no work guides the implementation of these relations at an algorithmic level.

Declarative knowledge (DK), i.e., factual information, is part of the necessary knowledge to perform a task. Their memorisation, generalisation, and retention requires repetition [9]. Retrieval practice is a form of test-based learning, which has been shown to improve long-term retention of facts [14]. In our context, *training* on DK is considered a form of retrieval practice that involves repeatedly providing learner-players with various forms of questions about facts. Such training can generally be performed through formative quizzes or dedicated serious games. In order to reduce the feeling of boredom caused by repetition,

P. Dondio et al. (Eds.): GALA 2023, LNCS 14475, pp. 342–352, 2024.
https://doi.org/10.1007/978-3-031-49065-1_33

serious games designed for declarative knowledge training must offer a wide variety of activities. However, existing training games are often lacking variety (e.g., no variation of gameplays, no aesthetic variation of the activities). In addition, these games are always specific to a single didactic domain. Activity generation is a solution for designing varied training activities that few works addresses in Technology-Enhanced Learning [2].

This article tackles the domain-independent mapping of questioned facts (i.e., questions on facts/declarative knowledge) to gameplays (i.e., fun things that can be controlled, decided and achieved by players [12], which are described by game elements) at the implementation level. Our proposal is a generic modelling of questioned facts and gameplays, as well as a domain-independent algorithm for gameplay (i.e., structured game elements) generation.

2   Research Context

2.1   Related Works

Several works have approached the mapping problem between game and educational elements by proposing relations between high-level concepts. Rapeepisarn et al. [13] proposed an extension of Prensky's work [12] by adding the relationships between learning styles to the existing relationships between game genres, knowledge to be learned and learning activities. Gosper and McNeill [7] defined relationships between learning outcomes, learning processes, assessment and game genres. Moreover, Dondi and Moretti [6] attempted to link knowledge types and learning objectives to high-level game features (e.g., content engine, evaluation engine) that the game should possess. Although very interesting for the general design of learning games, these relationships cannot be used at the implementation level to match learning content to concrete game elements.

Some works offer methods to guide the specification of relations (i.e., either to analyse or conceive games). Arnab et al. [1] proposed the LM-GM framework that supports the transition between learning objectives and game mechanics (e.g., collaboration, orientation, exploration) through concepts called Serious Game Mechanics. The game mechanics considered are high-level concepts that can have many concrete implementations in a game. Hall et al. [8] proposed a method that guides designers in defining the transition between learning content to core-gameplays, by having them answer questions from both real-world and game-world perspectives. Although interesting, this work is also more aimed at general game design.

In conclusion, mappings between learning elements and game elements are not addressed from a low-level design standpoint, but only at high conceptual levels or at low-level in studies for very specific contexts [4]. Indeed, it is not easy to propose reusable techniques at a sufficiently generic level of abstraction.

2.2   AdapTABLES Project

AdapTABLES is a research project that aims to build a Roguelite-oriented game for multiplication tables training. This project includes a user group composed of mathematics experts who have also been involved in the game design (e.g., training specification, gameplays evaluation).

Roguelite has been shown to be an adequate genre for DK training [10]. A Roguelite training activity is a dungeon (cf. Fig. 1), i.e., a set of interconnected rooms traversed by an avatar in which the training takes place. A dungeon has an entry room and an exit room. A room has accesses to others rooms (i.e., its neighbours), is associated to a training task (e.g., complete the fact, identify the correctness of a fact) and a gameplay, i.e., a set of positioned game elements that can be interactive (e.g., blocks to be pushed by the avatar, pots to be moved) or not (e.g., decoration blocks, texts). Based on the gameplay, and facts questioned, a room has a set of positioned elements. A positioned element has a type (i.e., game element that it implements, e.g., a chest, a pot, an enemy) and a position in the room. These elements can also have zero to multiple display values that displays facts propositions or statements of a specific questioned fact, or simple textual information. To enable the game to evaluate learners' actions, when a positioned element proposes choices or expects responses, it must declare whether it represents a correct response (i.e., *isAnswerElement*) or what values it expects (i.e., *expectedAnswers*).

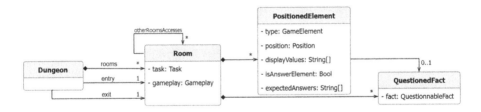

Fig. 1. Conceptual Modelling of Roguelite Activities for DK Training.

2.3   Research Questions

Our overall objective concerns the generation of Roguelite-oriented activities for training DK. In previous work, we identified training tasks with teachers and education specialists in mathematics and history-geography, such as *complete a fact where the multiplicand is missing, place historical dates in chronological order, identify the results of a table, name and locate countries of the European Union*, and so on. For a genericity purpose, an abstraction of these tasks led us to define four task types: Completion (i.e., completing a fact with missing elements), Order (i.e., ordering facts using a heuristic), Identification (i.e., attesting the validity or invalidity of facts) and Membership Identification (i.e., identifying elements sharing a given property). In addition, the definition of gameplays for Roguelite activities led us to define 5 gameplay categories inspired by the game classification of Djaouti et al. [5]: SELECT (i.e., selecting objects with the right answer), MOVE (i.e., moving the correct objects to the expected areas), ORIENT (i.e., orienting the objects to the right answers), POSITION (i.e., placing the avatar in the right positions) and DIRECT RESPONSE (i.e., typing in the right answers). In order to design such activities independently of any specific didactic domain (i.e., consider declarative knowledge in general), we identified 4 design questions:

1. How can training tasks be mapped onto gameplays? *(mapping)*
2. How can the facts questioned (i.e., build from tasks) be defined domain-independently in order to be used generically? *(modelling)*
3. How can gameplays be defined in terms of variable game elements? *(modelling)*
4. Once a task is paired with a compatible gameplay. How can these questioned facts be transformed into specific game elements? *(instantiation)*

To answer #1, we proposed a systematic approach for mapping task types (e.g., Completion, Order) to gameplay categories (e.g., SELECT, MOVE) [11]. This approach guides the specification of machine-readable relations that describe the conditions under which a gameplay category is compatible with a task type. Thus, to select a gameplay for a given task, the algorithm must sort the gameplays according to their categories (i.e., the categories that are compatible on the basis of the defined relations). It is important to note that some gameplays may be specially designed for a specific task type and thus have a parameter restricting their availability to that type only.

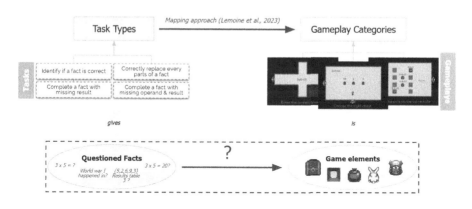

Fig. 2. Research Problem Illustration.

Facts are raw information such as $3 \times 5 = 15$. Depending on the task and its parameters, the questions about the facts to practice changes. For example, completing a fact with the missing operand will yield questions such as $3 \times ? = 15$, while identifying if elements share a given property will yield questions such as "Which ones are results of tables three? $\{3, 5, 9, 13\}$". These *questioned facts* have different structures. In addition, gameplay also have different structures and elements (e.g., some elements can wear one proposition, others can wear multiple propositions, some game elements are simple elements, others are composites). Preliminarily, it would seem that the association of questioned facts with gameplays must be performed specifically for each task/gameplay pair. To that extent, our question (cf. Fig. 2) concerns #2, #3, and #4: *How to model facts being questioned and gameplays to drive the generation of corresponding game elements?* Our proposal consists in modelling both concepts (i.e., the facts being questioned and the gameplays) at a sufficient level of abstraction. Such modelling would allow coverage of different forms of questioned facts, as well as variety in terms of game elements available for a given gameplay.

3   A Conceptual Design Approach

This section presents our proposal for modelling the questioned facts, the gameplays as well as a possible generation algorithm. In this article, the illustrative examples focus on multiplication tables.

3.1   Questioned Facts Model

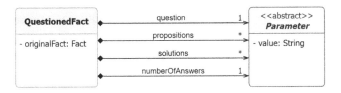

Fig. 3. Proposed modelling of questioned facts.

Questioned facts are questions about facts. To represent questioned facts generically, our main idea is to consider them as elements with possible parameters. Accordingly, each parameter is instantiated if necessary. Although the form of the questioned facts varies according to the training task concerned, the concepts that compose questioned facts are generic. Let's take two tasks T1 and T2 as an example. T1 consists in choosing from a set of propositions the answer corresponding to the multiplication result for each fact. From the parameters of T1, the facts questioned would be constructed to give a question such as $2 \times 6 = ?$ and a set of propositions such as $\{8, 12, 14\}$ for example. T2 consists in choosing from a set of propositions those that are the possible results of a given table. From the parameters of T2, the constructed questioned facts would give questions such as "Which elements are results of table 3?" as well as a set of propositions such as $\{3, 5, 7, 9, 12\}$. It can be seen that, although the questions associated with the facts do not have the same form, the facts from both tasks are composed of a question (i.e., a text) and a set of propositions. Consequently, a questioned fact has a parameter *question*, describing the question to be asked, and a parameter *propositions*, representing the list of possible choices for answering. Since questioned facts represent questions about facts, they need to know their solutions. Knowing the question and the propositions alone is not enough to assess a learner's answer. To this extent, the facts questioned have another parameter which indicates the correct solutions to the corresponding question. Furthermore, from an automation standpoint, it is necessary to know the number of expected answers (e.g., for a question such as $3 \times ? = ?$, two answers are expected) to declare whether a learner has entirely answered a question or not. It is important to note that this parameter could be deduced from the number of solutions, but for the sake of clarity we decided to make it explicit.

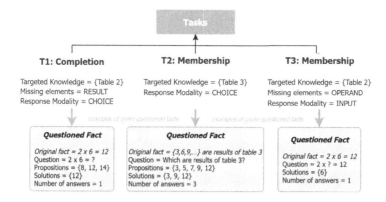

Fig. 4. Examples of questioned facts in generic form.

Furthermore, our previous example of tasks only considered tasks where the response modality was *choice* (i.e., selecting from a list of propositions). Let's consider a task T3, which consists, for each fact, of typing the answer corresponding to the operand of the multiplication. A questioned fact built from T3 would have a *question* such that $2 \times ? = 12$, its *propositions* parameter would not be instantiated, its *solutions* parameter would contain 6, and the *expected answers* parameter would be equal to 1. Figure 4 presents the questioned facts examples built in a generic form from the different tasks. It is obviously important to note that facts can be constructed in a generic form, but that their construction necessarily depends on the domain.

3.2 Gameplays Model

In a game, gameplay is represented by the set of elements with which the players interact or which provide them with information. Statically defining gameplays in terms of specific game elements allows a certain level of variety. However, it creates two principal constraints: 1) it is time-consuming, i.e., gameplays have to be described one by one according to the game elements available; and 2) it is static, i.e., adding a game element means having to specify new gameplays for that element. Our proposal, cf. Fig. 5, is to use *abilities* to describe gameplays

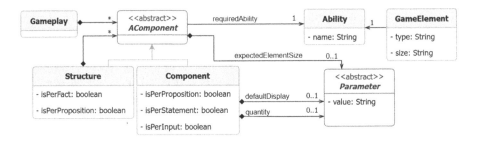

Fig. 5. Proposed modelling of gameplays & game elements.

through variable game elements. This involves describing game elements in terms of abilities, such as: a block can be pushed (i.e., *pushable*), a pot can be moved (i.e., *movable*), a bridge can be crossed (i.e., *crossable*), etc. Abilities capture the elements' behaviour (i.e., how avatars can interact with them). This enables the definition of different elements with the same ability, for example: a cube and a pot can be moved (i.e., *movable*). Such modelling of game elements allows gameplays to be described in terms of components[1] that rely on a specific ability rather than a specific game element. Thus, it creates gameplay variability in the sense that the ability is known, but the actual game element will be chosen by the algorithm. There are two types of gameplays components: simple component, i.e., elements that are not composed of other components (e.g., chest, pots, enemies), and 2) structure components, i.e., elements that are composed of other components (e.g., components that describe blocks to be pushed on specific tiles: *structure* = [*block*, *tile*])). As the context is DK training, gameplay components have an intention. They can represent a fact, a statement, a proposition, and so on. Structures (i.e., composite components) can be instantiated for each fact questioned in a room or for each proposition of a fact (cf. Fig. 6).

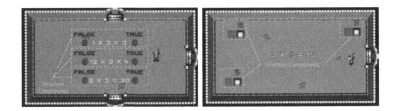

Fig. 6. Gameplays with structures per fact (left)/per propositions (right).

Simple components can be instantiated to represent statements, propositions, or input area. These component parameters are necessary for the algorithm to

---

[1] Gameplays are described by means of components, since this is a conceptual description of the gameplays and not a description of their implementation in the activities. The concrete gameplay elements of activities are called *PositionedElement* in Fig. 1.

correctly instantiate the game elements corresponding to the gameplay, as they allow the algorithm to know which parts of questioned facts must be associated to which components. Some simple components can describe decoration elements or answer areas (e.g., tiles where the player must place elements). These elements can therefore have a default display or specify a default necessary quantity that can depend on the expected number of answers to the question. In addition, game elements are described according to their size. Therefore, a specific ability can be represented by different sized elements. As a result, a game component can specify an expected size so that the algorithm maintains consistency when instantiating a gameplay.

3.3   Generation Algorithm

As mentioned in the previous sections, our overall objective is to generate training activities (i.e., dungeons) for DK training. A dungeon is a set of interconnected rooms that are associated to a training task and a corresponding gameplay. The game elements composing the gameplay (i.e., called positioned elements) must be built based on the questioned facts to work on. Algorithm 1 describes the main structure of the generation algorithm. The general idea is to go through the gameplay components and, depending on the type (i.e., Structure or Simple Component), to call the corresponding method, to build positioned elements, with the required parameters.

Algorithm 1: Generate Room Positioned Elements (simplified)

1 **Function** createRoomElements(*gameplay, facts, room*):
2   **for** *AComponent comp: gameplay.getComponents()* **do**
3   room.element.addAll(buildComponentElements(*comp, facts, []*));

4 **Function** buildComponentElements(*comp, facts, listElems*):
5   gameE ← findGameElement(*comp*.getAbility(), *comp*.getSize());
6   **if** *comp is Structure* **then**
7   *listElems*.add(buildElement(*comp, facts, gameE*));
8   **for** *AComponent sComp: comp.getComponents()* **do**
9   **return** buildComponentElements(*sComp, facts, listElems*);
10   **else**
11   **return** *listElems*.add(buildElement(*comp, facts, gameE*);

For example, let's take the following questioned fact $QE1 = \{question=$"2 × ? = 12", $propositions=[8, 4, 6]$, $solutions=[6]$, $numberOfExpectedAnswers=1\}$ and a gameplay $G1 = \{Structure1, Component1\}$. $Structure1 = \{isPerFact=$false, $isPerProp=$true, $ability=$HORIZONTAL, $components=[StrComp1, StrComp2]\}$ describes a horizontal structure that must be instantiated for each proposition of a questioned fact (i.e., the number of structure in the room equals the number of propositions of the questioned fact). $StrComp1 = \{isPerProp$=true, $isPerState$-$ment$=false, $isPerInput$=false, $ability$=PUSHABLE$\}$ is a simple component that describes that each horizontal structure must comprise a pushable element that bears one of the facts propositions. $StrComp2 = \{isPerProp$ =false, $isPerState$-$ment$=false, $isPerInput$=false, $ability$=DETECTOR, $expectedSize$=small$\}$ is a simple component that describes that each horizontal structure must comprise a small element that can detect another element (i.e., the pushable element). $Component1 = \{isPerProp$=false, $isPerStatement$=true, $isPerInput$=false, $ability$=DISPLAY$\}$ is a simple component that describes that the room must contain an element to display the statement (i.e., question). This description can instantiate gameplays such as the one shown on the right in Fig. 6.

Hence, building the positioned elements of a room consists in: 1) finding a game element with the correct size and ability, 2) selecting a position in the room, 3) linking questioned facts parameters values to positioned elements parameters values based on component parameters, 4) adding the built positioned element to the room. Figure 7 shows an example of positioned elements that can be generated from game elements, a gameplay description, and a questioned fact.

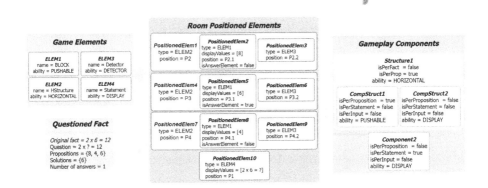

Fig. 7. Example of generated positioned elements.

3.4   Real-Case Study Application

The proposed approach has been applied for the implementation of an activity generator dedicated to multiplication table training. Our activity generator is implemented in Java and uses the Eclipse Modelling Framework (EMF) to model every piece of data required for generation. This generator produces detailed XML descriptions of dungeons that are currently being used in a game prototype developed in the context of AdapTABLES project. The prototype acts as a *game player* which interprets XML files and translates them into playable dungeons. Figure 6 presents screenshots of the prototype.

4   Conclusion and Perspectives

To conclude, this article proposes an approach to model questioned facts and gameplays generically. Our research work targets game-based activities for declarative knowledge training. The proposed approach enables abstraction from any didactic domain and facilitates the variety of gameplays proposed for the purpose of game activity generation. The approach has been implemented in an activity generator for multiplication table training. This generator is currently being used in a prototype designed as part of the AdapTABLES project. Furthermore, we intend to implement the approach in a second didactic domain about history-geography facts.

References

1. Arnab, S., et al.: Mapping learning and game mechanics for serious games analysis: mapping learning and game mechanics. Br. J. Educ. Technol. **46**(2), 391–411 (2015)
2. Bezza, A., Balla, A., Marir, F.: An approach for personalizing learning content in e-learning systems: a review. In: Second International Conference on E-Learning and E-Technologies in Education, pp. 218–223. IEEE, Lodz (2013)
3. Codish, D., Ravid, G.: Detecting playfulness in educational gamification through behavior patterns. IBM J. Res. Dev. **59**(6), 1–14 (2015)
4. Debabi, W., Champagnat, R.: Towards Architecture for Pedagogical and Game Scenarios Adaptation in Serious Games (2017)
5. Djaouti, D., Alvarez, J., Jessel, J.P., Methel, G., Molinier, P.: A gameplay definition through videogame classification. In: IJCGT, pp. 1–7 (2008)
6. Dondi, C., Moretti, M.: A methodological proposal for learning games selection and quality assessment. BJET **38**(3), 502–512 (2007)
7. Gosper, M., McNeill, M.: Implementing game-based learning: the MAPLET framework as a guide to learner-centred design and assessment. In: Ifenthaler, D., Eseryel, D., Ge, X. (eds.) Assessment in Game-Based Learning: Foundations, Innovations, and Perspectives, pp. 217–233. Springer, New York (2012). https://doi.org/10.1007/978-1-4614-3546-4_12
8. Hall, J.V., Wyeth, P.A., Johnson, D.: Instructional objectives to core-gameplay: a serious game design technique. In: Proceedings of the 1st ACM SIGCHI Annual Symposium on (CHI PLAY 2014), pp. 121–130. ACM, Toronto (2014)
9. Kim, J.W., Ritter, F.E., Koubek, R.J.: An integrated theory for improved skill acquisition and retention in the three stages of learning. Theor. Issues Ergon. Sci. **14**(1), 22–37 (2013)
10. Lemoine, B., Laforcade, P., George, S.: An analysis framework for designing declarative knowledge training games using roguelite genre. In: Proceedings of the 15th CSEDU, Prague, 21–23 April 2023, vol. 2, pp. 276–287 (2023)
11. Lemoine, B., Laforcade, P., George, S.: Mapping task types and gameplay categories in the context of declarative knowledge training. In: Proceedings of the 15th CSEDU, Prague, 21–23 April 2023, vol. 2, pp. 264–275 (2023)
12. Prensky, M.: Computer games and learning: digital game-based learning. In: Handbook of Computer Game Studies (2005)

13. Rapeepisarn, K., Wong, K.W., Fung, C.C., Khine, M.S.: The relationship between game genres, learning techniques and learning styles in educational computer games. In: Pan, Z., Zhang, X., El Rhalibi, A., Woo, W., Li, Y. (eds.) Edutainment 2008. LNCS, vol. 5093, pp. 497–508. Springer, Heidelberg (2008). https://doi.org/10.1007/978-3-540-69736-7_53

14. Roediger, H.L., Pyc, M.A.: Inexpensive techniques to improve education: applying cognitive psychology to enhance educational practice. J. Appl. Res. Mem. Cogn. **1**(4), 242–248 (2012)

Collectible Content – Towards a Modular Ecosystem of Intrinsically Integrated Gameplay: The Case of Fractions

Georgios Thoma[1]([✉]) [ID], Korbinian Moeller[1,2,3] [ID], Manuel Ninaus[2,4] [ID], and Julia Bahnmueller[1,2] [ID]

[1] Department of Mathematics Education, Loughborough University, Loughborough, UK
g.thoma@lboro.ac.uk
[2] LEAD Graduate School and Research Network, University of Tübingen, Tübingen, Germany
[3] Leibniz-Institut Fuer Wissensmedien, Tübingen, Germany
[4] Institute of Psychology, University of Graz, Graz, Austria

Abstract. Designing a good game is hard. Designing a learning game might be even harder as it requires engaging game elements to be aligned with the respective learning content. However, when this alignment is successful—referred to as intrinsic integration—games become effective tools for learning. In this article, the idea of *collectible content* is introduced as one way to achieve or make more pervasive use of intrinsic integration to support learning. Similar to an in-game currency system, learning content may be incorporated as in-game collectibles whose collection and manipulation are central aspects of gameplay. To substantiate the beneficial effects of *collectible content*, it is repeatedly presented, explored, and analyzed through various gameplay tasks. Through its characteristics of duality, consistency, and uniqueness/uniformity, *collectible content* evolves and adapts offering continuous opportunities for the development of conceptual understanding of the respective content—along with practice of procedures and acquisition of fact knowledge for the tasks at hand. To illustrate the idea and highlight affordances and potential impact of intrinsic integration, we present a prototype design of a fraction learning game to showcase a modular ecosystem focused on *collectible content* gameplay.

Keywords: Intrinsic Integration · Game-based learning · Fractions · Equivalent · Number line · Mathematics

1 Introduction

Digital games for learning (mathematics) are becoming more and more prevalent and popular [1]. However, digital learning games face several fundamental issues that have been frequently highlighted in the literature. Many games merely seem to replicate paper-pencil based approaches to learning (mathematics) instead of embracing and exploiting the affordances which digital learning games provide [2]. To reach their full potential for facilitating more in-depth learning compared to other media, digital learning games need

P. Dondio et al. (Eds.): GALA 2023, LNCS 14475, pp. 353–362, 2024.
https://doi.org/10.1007/978-3-031-49065-1_34

to overcome what has been termed "Frankensteinian mashups" [3, p. 2]. For example, such existing games often follow a "carrot and stick" approach where the learning content acts as a barrier players must overcome to be allowed to access the engaging game content (e.g., "Answer these questions to play this cool snake game. Oops! Question time again."). The learning content might also be "painted on top" a popular game genre with little to no consideration of how the respective game elements might facilitate it. Even to this day, the difficulty persists to design and develop a game that is not only engaging and fun to play, but also conveys the respective learning content successfully. In this spirit, the present article introduces the *collectible content* ecosystem—reflecting learning content as in-game collectibles whose collection and manipulation are central aspects of gameplay.

For illustration and comprehensibility *collectible content* is presented within the context of a prototypical game for learning about the magnitude of fractions using number lines. While simultaneously describing and showcasing the ecosystem, it also provides a first proof of concept of how existing learning games may evolve through *collectible content*. In the following, key concepts of digital learning games as well as defining features of existing digital fraction number line games are introduced. Subsequently, the idea of *collectible content* is outlined alongside its implementation in the mentioned prototype—highlighting its characteristics of duality, consistency, and uniqueness/uniformity. We then present additional systems to expand a modular gameplay ecosystem before the conclusion.

2   Background

Regarding games for learning, Plass and colleagues [4] highlight five game elements as crucial building blocks: game mechanics, visual aesthetics, musical score, incentives, and narrative. Collectively, these are used to make any game. A sixth element, learning content and skills, dictates what the learning game aims to cover or introduce. Game-based learning can be more effective when the first five game elements properly integrate and align with the learning content—leading to what has been described as *intrinsic integration* [5].

In a game, collectibles refer to collectable objects that the player needs to find, can store, display, or use in the game for different gameplay or personal reasons [6]. Collectibles range from those with purely cosmetic purposes (e.g., a new skin that visually changes the player's avatar) to those that directly influence gameplay (e.g., giving power ups or working as progression devices for incentives and narrative). Depending on the game, a storage system or menu helps to record and keep track of this acquisition of— and progression through—collectibles. As such, collectibles seem to offer a promising opportunity to intrinsically integrate learning content into the gameplay.

As highlighted in a recent review by Kiili and colleagues [7], a considerable number of games have been designed to assist, engage, and motivate learners in fraction learning. However, the review also indicated that intrinsic integration of the learning content was neither considered regularly and systematically nor implemented in the design of the majority of fraction games. Interestingly, many of the games that were identified as having their learning content intrinsically integrated were using a number line—a seemingly powerful educational tool for conveying mathematical content [8].

In a typical fraction number line game [7, 10]: a fraction is presented (see "a" in Fig. 1), and points are awarded ("b") if the player—through their avatar ("c")—estimates on the number line ("d") by maneuvering the avatar's position ("e") sufficiently close to the hidden magnitude of the fraction ("f"), and confirms their estimation. Thereafter— or depending on the game, when the player is (un)successful—the fraction's position is revealed ("f"). Serving as *corrective feedback*, this revealing provides an explanation as to why (or why not) points were awarded (based on the difference between the estimate "e" and the correct position "f").

Many learning games such as these tend to focus on specific aspects of the learning content (e.g., fraction magnitude). Even if integrated intrinsically to make a successful game, such a focus may not always reflect the richness of the learning content (e.g., magnitude is only one aspect of fractions). Therefore, it is desirable to think of a modular ecosystem of game elements that allow for an easy adaptation of game projects to better consider the richness of the respective learning content.

From the popularity and effectiveness of these number line games, three questions arise: i) Can a game, which mainly addresses fraction magnitude understanding, be expanded to support learning of other concepts related to fractions—such as fraction equivalence? ii) For such an expansion, how can new modules fit organically in the existing ecosystem? And iii) can these be generalized and adapted to future learning game design applications?

In efforts to take advantage of various game affordances and towards creating an intrinsically integrated game addressing more fraction aspects, prototypical systems and design choices are presented below to help illustrate the idea of *collectible content* as a modular ecosystem guiding game design.

Subsequent sections showcase game modules that evolved from the fraction number line game considering more aspects of the rich learning content (from Fig. 1 to the evolved Fig. 5).

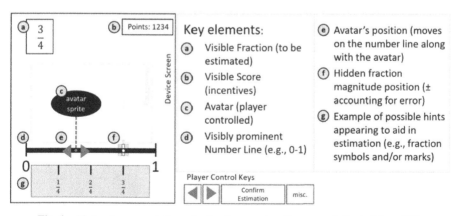

Fig. 1. Abstract representation of a fraction number line game (adjusted from [9]).

3   Collectible Content

Collectible Content is a game design idea, supporting learning by creating a modular ecosystem of intrinsically integrated gameplay. Fusing educational content and gameplay, it focuses on designing and materializing the learning content as in-game "collectables" (e.g., in the form of items/objects/creatures) that players collect and manipulate. Examples of the *collectible content* idea could be applied to any educational content that is set towards exploring the relations between units (e.g., letters, words, sentences; chemical elements, compounds, and reactions; cytoplasmic organelles, cells, organs, etc.). Modular tasks can evolve around these collectibles, each task exploring a content's property or relation between them. Wholistically, these modular tasks create an ecosystem, which highlights the complexity of the chosen content.

To better illustrate this, three characteristics are identified that allow for exploration and evolution of *collectible content* within a game: i) Duality—educational content and its properties, existing and manipulated in the game world. ii) Consistency—remaining in its essence unchanged regardless of task, manipulation, or different representations. iii) Uniqueness/Uniformity—each *collectible content* is distinguishable from others due to its unique values/yet all can be reduced to each of their properties depending on the task. While the *collectible content* concept may apply to any learning content as above, we illustrate these characteristics for fractions as our use case.

3.1   Narrative and the Characteristic of Duality

The game prototype is set in an isolated underground village where limited supplies of energy make it difficult for the inhabitants to survive. The player falls underground and must aid the villagers to be able to escape. The narrative themes of escape and survival aid in supporting and maintaining the urge to explore and make careful use of the few resources available. Early in the game, it is revealed that laser-cats (Fig. 2) living in the sewers produce energy once captured. From thereon, capturing, storing, and processing these laser-cats, becomes the core aim of the game. Hence, laser-cats are introduced as the *collectible content* of the game.

Fig. 2. Properties of *collectible content*: laser-cat states of matter reflecting different fraction representations. (a) Solid: symbolic; Gas: part-whole area model; Liquid: length on the number line. (b) Plasma: shooting upwards as a green line of energy (adjusted from [9]).

Laser-cats swim in the underground sewer sludge. To capture them, the position of the respective laser-cat needs to be estimated on the number line as described above (see also Fig. 1). The player moves an avatar on a number line ranging from 0 to 1, represented as a horizontal metal platform. Each laser-cat represents a specific magnitude (cf. Fig. 2a)—which is indicated by the position on the number line at which a laser-cat shoots upward, as a literal laser beam of energy-filled plasma (Fig. 2b). Mathematically, the green laser shot reflects a specific fraction magnitude as a position on the number line. Game-wise, it is an attribute of the laser-cats. In combination, it is a property of *collectible content*.

This duality is the first core characteristic of *collectible content* and is explored and portrayed through all aspects of the game. By aligning (mathematical) content with in-game collectibles in such a way, different tasks can be designed that make sense regarding both the learning content (e.g., estimating a fraction's magnitude), and gameplay (e.g., capturing a laser-cat). This characteristic works toward intrinsic integration of the learning content into gameplay, informing the game elements' design.

Thereby, *collectible content* expands the incentive system [4]. Point-based incentive systems (see "b" in Fig. 1) are mostly an extrinsic way to measure, score, and motivate players. Collectible game objects can work in the same way (i.e., "How many more laser-cats can you catch?") [6]. Moreover, captured laser-cats also reflect a player's acquired resource which links with other functionalities that allow for transfer to and between other gameplay modules (as described in the next chapters).

When players' estimates are close to the position of plasma emission (i.e., the fraction magnitude on the number line, "f", Fig. 1), they capture the laser-cat which shot up (Fig. 2b). When in the line of fire, but not sufficiently close, they do not capture the whole laser-cat but only gather some residual energy. This way several important points are considered: i) The scoring/incentive system is tied to the narrative as laser-cats are a source of energy and the player gets more/captures more laser-cats—in case their estimates are sufficiently close to the correct position on the number line. ii) Corrective feedback ("f", Fig. 1; Fig. 2b) is provided visually and narratively integrated (e.g., "if you are in the plasma fire, you get energy/ laser-cats"). iii) It is clearly discernable to the player why or why not points were awarded, justifying the permitted error area and consequently, their degree of success. iv) Mathematically, it highlights the correct position of a fraction on the number line is, but also how far the estimate is off, allowing for reflection and possibly better future estimations.

3.2 The Village Lab and the Characteristic of Consistency

To balance fraction estimation and capturing laser-cats, players can return to the village, where the gameplay is less intense. The village works as a hub world, intertwined with the narrative and incentives [4], where players see their progress, interact with the locals, and gradually experience more of the storyline. The village's lab is where successfully captured laser-cats are stored, processed and repurposed (Fig. 3). It is also here where an additional characteristic of *collectible content* is revealed.

Design-wise, living up to their almost mythical internet popularity as well as historical, cultural, and mythological representations, laser-cats extend to all states of matter (i.e., solid, liquid, gas, and plasma, Fig. 2). This property facilitates and aligns well with the complex nature of fractions and their representations (e.g., symbolic, non-symbolic as length on the number line or part-whole relation). Expanding the metaphor, the molecular structure of a laser-cat (i.e., its fraction magnitude) is invariable despite any physical change it might exhibit from one state of matter to another reflecting different fraction representations. Thus, the magnitude of the symbolic fraction 1/4 remains the same in its solid laser-cat form, when depicted as length on the number line in liquid form, or as parts of a whole on a pie-chart in gas form. This narrative is also tied with the aforementioned fourth state of matter of laser-cats shooting upwards as plasma, indicating them as a position on the number line.

Importantly, this reflects the second characteristic of *collectible content*: it stays constant throughout the game. Its appearance might change (i.e., in different states) highlighting different conceptual ideas and properties, but the core content (i.e., the respective fraction) is always the same. The same laser-cat regardless of state of matter, always reflects the same fraction magnitude (Figs. 2 & 3). This consistency should foster comprehensive conceptual understanding of learners, but may also allow the game to be further expanded towards other areas of the content (e.g., fraction equivalence as shown below), while strengthening the links between them.

In the village lab, with intrinsically integrated educational opportunities in mind, tasks (Fig. 3a) are designed around the respective fraction representations—thus jointly considering the first two characteristics of *collectible content*: duality and consistency. For simplicity and ease of access, the tasks follow the same approach: automatically moving parts are controlled to stop with just one key press. If the player aligns the part at the correct position, the task is successful, and the freshly captured laser-cats, being processed one by one, move from one state of matter to the other.

One-by-one, captured solid laser-cats enter the machine (Fig. 3a), and their symbolic fraction magnitude is revealed (1st requiring alignment of the numerator). Then, laser-cats turn to a liquid state, reflected as length on the number line (2nd alignment of the magnitude position on the number line). Finally, to a gas state, as part of a whole on a pie-chart (3rd clockwise alignment of the radius). Once these tasks are done, laser-cats are bottled up in glass-batteries, ready to be repurposed—allowing the *collectible content* ecosystem to be further extended (described in the next sections).

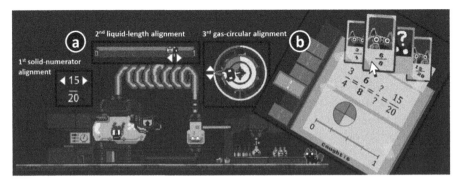

Fig. 3. (a) The lab: three mini-game tasks reflective of the fraction representations, shown with white arrows the automatic movement that needs to be aligned. (b) The Bestiary: photos taken, symbolic fractions, visual representations of part-whole, magnitude on the number line.

3.3   The Bestiary and the Characteristic of Uniqueness/Uniformity

After a laser-cat is processed as described above, its details (i.e., magnitude and representations) are registered automatically in the Bestiary—along with their picture (Fig. 3b). The Bestiary is a frequent system in games, providing information of common statistics and tracking the player's progress. It can be accessed by the player using a menu during specific parts of gameplay, showcasing how many and which laser-cats have been captured, what their magnitude and representations look like, etc. This also incentivizes players towards capturing and learning more about the *collectible content* by progressively completing their Bestiary records [6]. Taking this system further towards intrinsic integration, players can sort their Bestiary by magnitude, denominator, numerator etc., but also compare and order fractions to help identify equivalent fractions and group them on the same page (Fig. 3b).

The third characteristic of *collectible content* is that it is uniform but also unique—like a real life set of coins in a currency system. In this metaphor, each laser-cat, each *collectible content*, is like an ancient coin. Each *collectible content*—coin—shares a set of properties (size, weight, denomination, historical era etc.) but might also have its own unique story (was melted to create a ring or vice versa, it stopped a bullet, etc.). Each one brings joy to the collector. However, in the end, they can be stripped down to their general properties: used for their currency value to purchase things, ordered in size or date of minting, as raw metal materials to be melted, etc.

Similarly, properties of *collectible content* are showcased through different tasks while simultaneously being part of the world's narrative and systems. In the prototype, all laser-cats are uniform: they each represent fraction magnitudes, shoot upwards as a green line of plasma on the number line, can turn to solid, liquid, gas. But they are also unique: e.g., the 1/5 laser-cat is the first cat a player has collected, it might share the same denominator, yet is very different from 4/5 in terms of magnitude, but it is equivalent to 21/105—even if they look different—and so on. In consequence, one game task might be focused on ordering fractions based on their magnitude, another by grouping their denominators when they are multiplied by 7. Focusing on properties allows modular gameplay tasks to stay rich and relevant, intrinsically integrated as they are deeply embedded in game elements and learning content. For example, a laser-cat is collected through magnitude estimation, but also processed and registered into other representations. (e.g., symbolic, part-whole). This allows gameplay to expand the same content to more than one task, modularly, but also linked in the ecosystem. Additionally, tasks in the Bestiary of curating the collectibles [6] for example, might be considered as existing outside the core gameplay experience yet contribute substantially to the learning aims—ordering, fraction equivalence, etc.

4   Growing the Modular Ecosystem

Based on the three core characteristics of *collectible content*—duality, consistency, uniqueness/uniformity—below examples give an idea of the evolution of the number line estimation game towards richer and player driven tasks. Through the energy gathered from laser-cats, these modular expansions make use of the *collectible content* ecosystem, allowing players to develop new in-game tools to capture and process more laser-cats, simultaneously exploring more of fractions mathematical richness.

4.1 "Flower Blooming" and "Meowing Booming" Systems.

In fraction number line games, marks appear ("g", in Fig. 1) by segmenting the number line or otherwise hinting the correct location of a fraction [7, 10]. However, the following systems go a step further towards making the player aware of fraction equivalence—"flower blooming" visually and "meowing booming" audibly.

Visually, in the fraction estimation task, different types of flowers may bloom along with the appearance of a fraction ("a", Fig. 1; Fig. 4a). After the estimation, as corrective feedback, the same type of flowers may bloom from the start point at 0 to the position of the respective fraction ("f", Fig. 1; Fig. 4b). This works as a subtle nudge of identifying equivalence. For example, if the fractions 1/5 or 2/10 appear, the same orange flower would accompany them—after the estimation, orange flowers would bloom from 0 to 0.2 on the number line (Fig. 4a then 4b).

Accompanying the visual "flower blooming" system, "meowing booming" associates each fraction's magnitude, to a unique sound. Each time a laser-cat appears, it is accompanied by a unique meowing cry (when spawning, captured, being processed, accessed in the Bestiary etc.). In consequence, laser-cats reflecting equivalent fractions sound the same regardless of their symbolic presentation or segmentation.

Fig. 4. Marking tools: (a) along with the fraction, the "blooming flower" system appears; (b) same on the number line after a fraction estimation, marking 1/5. (c) The wheel system, rolling across the number line—segmenting it in sixths.

4.2 The Wheel System and Parallel Number Lines

The wheel system draws on the part-whole aspect of fractions (e.g., a pie-chart) and translates it to a magnitude on the number line. Also, it is a tool for players to dynamically segment the number line with their own marks (e.g., in sixths, Fig. 4c). This tool is connected directly to laser-cats—used to arm and fuel the wheel—and indirectly—the segmentation could help players be more accurate in their future cat-captures.

Regarding equivalence, the above-described upward shooting laser-cats (Fig. 2b; "f", Fig. 5), allow more than one 0–1 parallel number lines/horizontal platforms to be hit simultaneously. When a laser shot goes up at a specific magnitude (e.g., at ¾) the shot will register in different platforms with a different symbolic representation (3/4, 6/8, 9/12 etc. multiples of 4 denominators). Thus, being at the same position on the parallel number lines, it illustrates their equivalence in terms of overall magnitude (see [9] for a more detailed description of these two systems).

4.3   The Enriched Number Line Estimation Prototype

Compared to the number line game presented at the start (Fig. 1), the prototype now reflects *collectible content* incorporation (Fig. 5): ("a") The appearance of a fraction is connected to the Bestiary and the visual-audio b(l)ooming systems. The relevance of collected energy points and laser-cats ("b"), more than just incentives, they are now intrinsically expanded to this and other areas of the game. The avatar sprite ("c") changes visually communicating the availability of different tools. Taken together, the number line as a platform ("d") and player position ("e") both expand to take advantage of the vertical laser-cat plasma shot ("f"). Finally, the new b(l)ooming marking systems—along with the wheel—segment and offer hints ("g").

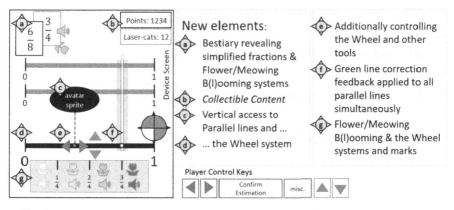

Fig. 5. Evolved Abstract representation of a fraction number line game. Based on Fig. 1.

5   Conclusion

This conceptual article introduces the idea of *collectible content* within a modular ecosystem as a learning game design approach for intrinsically integrating learning content with gameplay elements. Future studies and research are needed to evaluate the effectiveness of *collectible content*—or any of its effects on learning or student engagement—in comparison to more traditional educational approaches. As a first step, it seems sensible to conduct user experience studies to identify if and how players engage (more) with *collectible content*. If user experience indicates good playability of games with a fused *collectible content* ecosystem, its additional elements, and representations, it would be interesting to evaluate any benefits to learning in controlled intervention studies.

To summarize, taking the form of laser-cats, *collectible content* was presented alongside a game prototype that expands on the fraction number line estimation. Examples from the prototype—illustrating the intrinsic integration of different aspects of fractions (e.g., magnitude, part-whole, equivalence)—were used to showcase *collectible content's* three characteristics: duality, between game and learning content; consistency, across representations and properties; uniqueness/uniformity, allowing the modular expansion of tasks. Against this background, we are confident that the idea and implementation of *collectible content* can facilitate intrinsic integration and may be expanded successfully to other content areas (even beyond mathematics). Particularly, it may help design teams to integrate learning content better into their game mechanics, visual and audio aesthetics, narrative and incentives, by placing *collectible content* as the core of the gameplay.

References

1. Byun, J., Joung, E.: Digital game-based learning for K–12 mathematics education: a meta-analysis. Sch. Sci. Math. **118**, 113–126 (2018). https://doi.org/10.1111/ssm.12271
2. Devlin, K.: Mathematics Education for a New Era: Video Games as a Medium for Learning. A K Peters/CRC Press, New York (2011).https://doi.org/10.1201/b10816
3. Van Eck, R.N., Shute, V.J., Rieber, L.P.: Leveling up: game design research and practice for instructional designers. Pap. Knowl. Media Hist. Doc. **7**, 107–115 (2014)
4. Plass, J.L., Homer, B.D., Kinzer, C.K.: Foundations of game-based learning. Educ. Psychol. **50**, 258–283 (2015). https://doi.org/10.1080/00461520.2015.1122533
5. Habgood, M.P.J., Ainsworth, S.E.: Motivating children to learn effectively: exploring the value of intrinsic integration in educational games. J. Learn. Sci. **20**, 169–206 (2011). https://doi.org/10.1080/10508406.2010.508029
6. Toups, Z.O., Crenshaw, N.K., Wehbe, R.R., Tondello, G.F., Nacke, L.E.: The collecting itself feels good": towards collection interfaces for digital game objects. In: Proceedings of the 2016 Annual Symposium on Computer-Human Interaction in Play. pp. 276–290. ACM, Austin Texas USA (2016). https://doi.org/10.1145/2967934.2968088
7. Kiili, K., Koskinen, A., Ninaus, M.: Intrinsic integration in rational number games – A systematic literature review (2019).https://ceur-ws.org/Vol-2359/
8. Sidney, P.G., Thompson, C.A., Rivera, F.D.: Number lines, but not area models, support children's accuracy and conceptual models of fraction division. Contemp. Educ. Psychol. **58**, 288–298 (2019). https://doi.org/10.1016/j.cedpsych.2019.03.011
9. Thoma, G., Bahnmueller, J., Ninaus, M., Moeller, K.: From research to prototypes: developing a digital game to foster fraction equivalence. In: 17th European Conference on Games Based Learning (2023). (To be published)
10. Gresalfi, M.S., Rittle-Johnson, B., Loehr, A., Nichols, I.: Design matters: explorations of content and design in fraction games. Educ. Technol. Res. Dev. **66**, 579–596 (2018). https://doi.org/10.1007/s11423-017-9557-7

A Comprehensive Classification of the Elements in Video Games - Explorative, Ludic, Narrative, Sociable

Michael Riesner[✉][iD]

Technische Universität Dresden, Software Technology Group,
Nöthnitzer Str. 46, 01187 Dresden, Germany
michael.riesner@tu-dresden.de

Abstract. Video games are complex and interdisciplinary objects. For a comprehensive analysis it is essential to have a classification that describes and includes all the game aspects and their interactions with the player. This paper provides a holistic approach with focus on general functional entities, the elements of video games and their relations and associations. The basic idea is a subdivision of video games into meaningful individual game aspects, into elements which belong to one or more classes on the basis of terms and definitions. Based on these element associations, the game itself can be classified as a whole, analyzed and compared on an abstract level.

Keywords: classification · video game · elements · entities · game studies · player · interaction · explorative · ludic · narrative · sociable

1 Introduction

1.1 Motivation and Goals

For an analysis and comprehensive discussion of the object "video game" it is essential to have a classification that can describe and include all the aspects of games and interactions with the player. But is it possible to do so and meet the demands of analysts in the game studies and the needs of game designers and makers? What is needed when you want to compare the essence of games, what to design and plan a new one? This paper provides a holistic approach with focus on **general functional entities** and the relations between the game and the player. Video games do not only consist of code, video and sound... they also interact with the player, the environment and the hardware.

Being the subject of scientific debates since the end of the last millennium there are still no generally applicable terms or suitable methods for analyzing the medium as a whole. Researchers usually concentrate only on aspects, using their traditional repertoire of literature review or game theory or focus on technical aspects. Like in the parable of the blind men and the elephant [1], where blind men are tasked to touch an elephant in order to describe it. They all touch different parts of the body and that's why they end up describing a completely different animal. But only the sum of all gathered data forms an adequate interpretation of the whole elephant's body. So far video games are interactive narratives for film and literature scientists, rule systems for ludologists, human-machine interactions for psychologists and program code made up of functions and variables for computer scientists [7].

1.2   Terms

The terms narrative and ludic are referring to the history of games studies.

Narratology: Narratologists transferred their tools and methods for analyzing texts and stories unchanged to digital games. They declared games as another form of narrative, just like books, movies and theater [3,8]. The narrative is a general communicative concept for the "construction of meaning". Narratologists approach the medium within their perspective of literature science and concentrate in particular on the narrative elements of games like background stories, cutscenes or dialogues. For them even abstract games like chess or tetris are considered a narrative.

Ludology: Ludologists, on the other hand, are convinced that video games and narratives have only a few things in common and rely on familiar theories from game theorists like Johan Huizinga or Roger Caillois [5]. They analyze the object like a classic analog game [2,6]. The focus of their considerations is the interaction between the player and the simulation of a virtual environment, set by certain rules. The most important criteria for ludologists is the game process, based on the rules, and the player's interactions.

Exploration: Children explore the world with intrinsic curiosity, learn to deal with challenges and use the experiences they made in a beneficial way in the future. Such activities increase their knowledge, enabling them to better adapt to their environment and further challenges. Such behavior, if successful, results in a massive release of endorphins [11]. But that is not restricted to children only. For adults this is referred to as the "exploratory behavior". Explorative video games provide a framework or sandbox with possibilities to pursue the game on someone's own interests and pace.

1.3   Approach

In my analysis of the evolution of video games in 2009 [10] it was shown that modern video games consist of a characteristic and often unique distribution of elements. These are part of at least one class, no matter what type of input or output they require, what genre the games belong to, or how many people are involved in the game. This work will update and extend the classification with new thoughts from the perspective of a developer, a player and a researcher but also integrate aspects from already existing theories of ludology, game theory and narratology.

2   Classification of Video Game Elements

The basic idea of this classification is the subdivision of the game into meaningful individual game aspects, into parts that belong together semantically and that can be compared. I will use the terms **elements** or **entities** (equivalently). Elements can overlap and vary in size and dimension and are not limited to physical or software aspects only, the interaction with the player and the environment is also taken into account. My classification, using the **concept of elements and classes**, is based on definitions for each class. Every element of the video game can be part of one or several of the classes. I choose them to be specific enough to be unambiguous, but also leave enough room for interpretation to include all existing and currently conceivable computer game aspects.

2.1   Explorative Elements

The central and unique aspects, the essence of video games are the **explorative elements** [10]. They are the parts of the game, that encourage discovery and exploration. Game elements like: an open world that encourages exploring and examining, riddles to solve, processes to optimize, finding the right way or just trying out different possible inputs or commands. Explorative elements are also important for long-term motivation [10], especially in games utilizing player-created content that continuously generate new game aspects.

Definition 1. *An element of a game is explorative, when it is explorable or encourages exploration.*

But what motivates the player to do so? For Herodotus[1] intrinsic curiosity was the main reason that let him become a historian, for the Ionian natural philosophers it was the drive to look "beyond things" and for Plato it was the beginning of all philosophy. Curiosity ensures that we explore and play games, want to finish and master it. Curiosity is mostly stimulated by sensory perceptions. In video games this can be unusual colors or movements, objects in unusual spatial positions, above-average details or conspicuous noises [11]. Explorative elements can further be divided into two subclasses.

Definition 2. *Explicit explorative elements arouse an intrinsic motivation to deal with the element or with elements connected.*

They could also be called the motivational ones. Entities in this class can be "built" and/or placed inside the game and its game world. Explicit explorative elements for example are: the game world (with rooms, corridors, houses, landscapes), interaction elements (switches, doors, items), Non-Player-Characters (NPCs) or possible inputs (movements, commands). The second subclass centers on the player and the interaction between him and the game.

---

[1] Herodotus was a Greek historian and geographer.

Definition 3. *Implicit explorative elements provide opportunities for the players to prove himself, to show that they have mastered the game and its mechanics.*

The cognitive component predominates in the case of the implicit explorative elements. That is primarily manifested in the ability to gain relevant information, understand correlations and distinguish important from unimportant data when dealing with a challenge. The player has to try out, anticipate, combine, analyze, learn and apply certain ways of thinking or a specific behavior or certain motoric input patterns. The goal: being in control and gaining power through the new learned competencies and thereby proving being worthy [4]. Implicit explorative elements for example are: puzzles, riddles, obstacles or strategic challenges.

2.2 Ludic Elements

The term ludic originally comes from the non-mathematical game theory (ludology) [5]. The homo ludens (lat. "the playing human") improves his abilities through playing and develops new skills and abilities according to his made experiences. Transferred to video games the purpose of playing is game mastery. Players have to learn the rules and prohibitions and have to develop sensorimotor skills and behaviors to gain more and more control. This challenge is the main motivating factor in ludic games [4]. **Ludic entities** regulate, like the game instructions, the game board, game figures or cards in classical board or card games. They all specify the possibilities as well as prohibitions.

Definition 4. *An element of a game is ludic, if it is regulating something or is part of the ruleset.*

An element regulates the game by creating rules or applying them. In a video game every possibility of interaction or movement has to be created. That's why prohibitions are often less important or absent, in contrast to non-digital games, where rules often has to restrict the natural repertoire of the abilities of the human being. For example not to use hands when playing football. Ludic elements can be separated into active and passive ones.

Definition 5. *Active ludic elements regulate the game.*

These entities are often subsumed as gameplay mechanics and directly linked to the gameplay implementation in the program code. The player has to learn the correct and most beneficial way of using these elements while playing the game. Active ludic elements for example are: motion and command elements (moving, interacting, commanding), background processes (physics, economic cycles, simulations), game events without restrictions on interaction and manipulation possibilities (triggers, timers, scripts), artificial intelligence or status and configuration elements (character values, points).

Definition 6. *Passive ludic elements are the interactive game pieces of the ruleset.*

Passive ludic elements make the game interactive. Without that possibility, the player would be degraded to a passive observer in a kind of walk-through movie or picture. A virtual reality in which you can look but not touch. Ludic entities therefore influence the course of the game, by creating new states in a predefined way, triggering game events or processes or giving the player new needed information or directions. Passive ludic elements for example are: interaction elements (switches, doors, objects), NPC actions, camera perspectives (possibilities and restrictions) or situational display of information.

2.3   Narrative Elements

Analogous to previous definitions the term for the third class of elements originates from literature and film studies: the "narratology". **Narrative elements** (from the Latin verb "narrare" for "to tell") are correspondingly storytelling elements.

Definition 7. *An element of the game is narrative when it tells something or possesses meaning.*

Narrative elements can be compared to words in languages. In narrative entities the story of the game is told through direct entities such as videos, dialogs and texts or indirectly through the transfer of meaning or metaphorization.

Definition 8. *Direct narrative elements tell the narrative of the game.*

The direct narrative elements tell or explain the story or meaning of the game and were often conceived by authors for specific moments. Such entities continue or expand the game plot in a classic literary way. Direct narrative elements for example are: video sequences with absence of possible interactions (intro, cutscenes), text overlays, dialogues with NPCs, monologues of a character or story collectibles (books, videos or tapes). Sequences where the player loses the ability to interact can be compared to conventional movies. The game is paused and the sequence is played to create a transition to new game states or just to motivate or reward the player for completed tasks. But they all have one in common: in direct narrative elements the player is exclusively passive and degraded to a recipient only.

Definition 9. *Indirect narrative elements possess and transport meaning for the gameplay.*

Indirect narrative elements are not immediately perceived as part of the narrative, often versatile and subconsciously acting. Indirect narrative elements for example are: game events without loss of possible interactions (triggers, timers, scripts), player quests, tasks or metaphorized elements like well-known names, shapes, textures, sounds or music. Non-restrictive game events can be explorative, ludic, narrative or any combination of them, depending on if they create new gameplay challenges through newly emerging game situations, if they change the game mechanics, or if they tell something and advance the plot. Quests or tasks also contribute significantly to the narrative. They intentionally push the players in certain directions without them mostly being aware of. Many elements in the game world use already known objects, people or places as a template for their names, shapes, textures or sounds. The reason: the game then does not have to explain everything in detail and the player can anticipate how to assess and use the element or what to expect from it. This metaphorization is also called "transfer of meaning" and describes the association of an entity of the game with the meaning of this entity in the cultural and moral framework of the player [4]. As a primitive example the entity door "tells" us by its position: "I am a component of the room", by its texture: "I am made of a solid material" and by its rectangular shape: "I am stable".

2.4   Sociable Elements

For some people the most important aspect of games is establishing and maintaining contact with the other players: chatting with or meeting them, building relationships and communities and playing cooperatively or competitively in front of one device or in separate physical spaces connected by the internet [9]. To provide these functionalities games need their own elements, the **sociable** ones.

Definition 10. *A game element is sociable, when it encourages player to player communication or coordination.*

Sociable elements must be part of games where players have to cooperate or compete. For example, in competitive arcade games, without the ability to interact, you could replace one of the players with an AI without the other players noticing. That is why that type of game is usually played locally with the players communicating directly or by using voice chat over the internet. In many of the player versus player games one team competes against another one. To win, players have to show their individual skills in the ludic parts, but also have to communicate, organize and play as a team.

Definition 11. *Communicative sociable elements encourage the player to communicate with others.*

If a game wants the players to cooperate and establish and maintain contacts it needs appropriate entities. The communicative sociable elements are responsible for enabling players to do so with different tools, depending on the players and the game type. Communicative sociable elements for example are: text and voice chat, forum and boards or special character animations and commands (emotes).

Definition 12. *Coordinative sociable elements encourage the player to cooperate with others.*

The world's most popular sports are team sports [12]. Their players need a lot of technical and physical skills. But also they have to act "as a team": structure and organize roles and responsibilities. In video games, the coordinative sociable elements are the aspects that encourage or even force the players to cooperate, either against the game itself or another team. Coordinative sociable elements for example are: cooperative tasks and riddles (positions, roles, strengths and weaknesses of player characters) or responsibilities and arrangements. These aspects often also have ludic parts or relations to ludic elements that enforce or reward the player, because games mostly have to demand cooperation. Players usually only do so, when they gain benefit.

2.5   Groups and Relations of the Element Classes

Using the four element classes and their subclasses all kinds of current video games can be analyzed. The differentiation in subclasses helps to specify the entities, highlight similarities and differences. The single aspects also can be analyzed more in detail, if desired, using traditional methods of ludology, narratology, the game studies or sociology. Some element subclasses have larger intersections with others. Implicit explorative, passive ludic, indirect narrative and coordinative sociable elements are more often overlapping with other classes. These classes can be labeled as **secondary classes**. Entities of the **primary classes**: explicit explorative, active ludic, direct narrative and communicative sociable on the other hand are often exclusively part of their classes (Fig. 1).

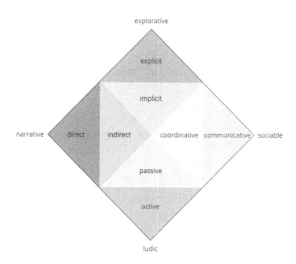

Fig. 1. Groups of element classes of video games.

The classification is made to support adaptation to the task by choosing the matching level of abstraction, in determination of how detailed the ranking of the entities is. Using Fig. 1 a game element could be defined as a point or an area. Also only the four main classes can be used without the primary and secondary ones. Another possibility is to use a Kiviat-Graph, to display elements as a n-dimensional graph.

2.6   Layers of Video Games

Video games do not only exist in the program code and in the game assets it's shipped with. Even more important is the interactions between the game and the player and the mental and emotional processes it triggers. That is why watching someone else playing can be a lot of fun, it also triggers them for the watchers [13]. But what kind of relations exist between the player and the game? Figure 2 illustrates the relations using layers. It shows player activities on top, program aspects on the bottom while the defined terms build their associations, connecting the player and the program layer in a **meta layer**.

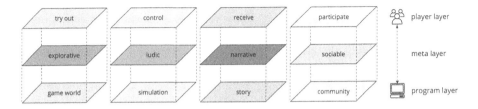

Fig. 2. 3 layers of video games and their class associations.

The **player layer** consists of all the processes running at the player: his physical and motor activities, intrinsic and extrinsic motivations and his thoughts and ideas. In the **program layer** all game processes, the program code, the data structures and all kinds of audiovisual contents are included. The explorative, ludic, narrative and sociable aspects link and combine both layers by establishing a bidirectional association. The player tries out explorative elements in the game world, controls ludic elements of the simulation, receives narrative story elements and participates socially in the game community. What is a player without a game or a game without a player?

3   Discussion and Limits

It is now possible to compare video games on the basis of their game aspects and thus to specifically examine **differences and similarities**. To do so, the analyst has to set and specify concrete (significance-) criteria and scales. Criteria for a comparison could for example be: the time the player interact with certain elements (relative or in total), the quantity of player interactions, the quantity of game elements in specific classes, the share of code of the entities or any combination. The scales and criteria for the specific analysis should be adjusted to serve the purpose of the research. Do elements occur only once or multiple times and how to weigh them, if they are part of multiple classes? Also the rating has to be consistent if the goal is to get comparable results. Figure 3 shows an exemplary simple comparison of four popular video games, which are roughly rated according to the relative occurrence and significance of their game elements, displayed as a Kiviat graph.

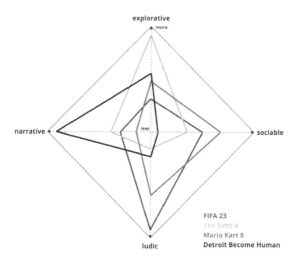

Fig. 3. Exemplary comparison of some popular video games.

A subdivision of complex objects into aspects or elements is a proven method to analyze and rate them. This classification defines terms and relations to do so and compare all different kinds of video games on an meta level. It supports adaptation to the task by choosing the matching level of abstraction in determination of how detailed the ranking of the entities should be. But assigning a game entity to one of the classes does not state anything about the quality of the element. Depending on the type, the quality of an element can be measured. For example by a detailed analysis using suitable criteria, scales and proven methods of the narratology or ludology. Nevertheless identifying key aspects, while designing and planning a game, can help to improve the overall quality. Because core elements of the game have more impact on the player experience than the less important ones. Besides the quality, there is also no direct statement about the quantity and the kind of content. One possibility could be to count the quantity of elements. The more elements a video game has, the more content the player has to explore. Also further research should investigate the relation between the game content and the player's motivation. The expectation for further evaluation: the motivation should be high, when there are many unexplored elements and descend while playing and processing the game.

4 Conclusion

Today there are corresponding representatives for every possible combination of elements in diverse genres, offering a large variety of games to the passionate player. If you want to compare them you need a holistic classification to name, analyze and describe the games and their entities on an abstract level. Thereby exploration is the most important aspect in video games. "A player picks up a game, explores it, and puts it down" [6]. But also the ludic, narrative and sociable elements are essential parts and used in most video games to motivate, teach, test and reward the player. When the player has tried out all explorative elements, has mastered all ludic elements, has received all story elements and has participated in all of the sociable events, the game is finished.

References

1. Blind Men and an Elephant (2023). https://en.wikipedia.org/wiki/Blind_men_and_an_elephant. Accessed 08 Dec 2022
2. Aarseth, E.: Allegories of space: the question of spatiality in computer games (1998). http://www.hf.uib.no/hi/espen/papers/space/Default.html. Accessed 18 May 1998
3. Consalvo, M., Dutton, N.: Game analysis: developing a methodological toolkit for the qualitative study of games. Game Stud. **6**(1) (2006). http://gamestudies.org/0601/articles/consalvo_dutton
4. Fritz, J.: Warum eigentlich spielt jemand computerspiele? (2005). http://www.staff.uni-marburg.de/feldbusc/page12/files/17FRITZ.PDF. Accessed 06 Dec 2005
5. Huzinga, J.: Homo Ludens. Vom Ursprung der Kultur im Spiel. No. 435 in Rowohlt Enzyklopädie, Rowohlt, Reinbeck b. Hamburg, 1sd edn, pp. 113–115 (1987)
6. Juul, J.: A certain level of abstraction (2007). http://www.jesperjuul.net/text/acertainlevel. Accessed 28 Sept 2007
7. Moller, S., Schmidt, S., Beyer, J.: Gaming taxonomy: an overview of concepts and evaluation methods for computer gaming QoE (2013). https://doi.org/10.1109/qomex.2013.6603243
8. Neitzel, B.: Gespielte geschichten. struktur- und prozessanalytische untersuchungen der narrativität von videospielen (2008). http://deposit.ddb.de/cgi-bin/dokserv?idn=970619278. Accessed 09 Oct 2008
9. Peng, W., Crouse, J.: Playing in parallel: The effects of multiplayer modes in active video game on motivation and physical exertion. Cyberpsychol. Behav. Soc. Netw. **16**, 423–427 (2013). https://doi.org/10.1089/cyber.2012.0384
10. Riesner, M.: Ludisch, narrativ, explorativ - Eine Taxonomie zur Klassifikation des Mediums Computerspiel. mathesis, Technische Universität Dresden (2009)
11. Stangel, W.: Neugier - ein spezielles motiv (2008). http://www.stangl-taller.at/ARBEITSBLAETTER/MOTIVATION/Neugier.shtml. Accessed 02 Jan 2009
12. Veroutsos, E.: The most popular sports in the world (2022). https://tinyurl.com/3n3a89fz. Accessed 18 June 2023
13. Weightman, C.: Crucible: the science behind why watching others playing video games has become so popular (2020). https://tinyurl.com/yvpyutr4. Accessed 12 Sept 2023

A Hat-Integrated HCI System for Serious Games–Proof-of-Concept Applications in Focus Detection and Game Controlling

S. M. Musfequr Rahman[1]([✉]) [iD], Asif Shaikh[1], Henna Mattila[1], Tarmo Lipping[1], Merilampi Sari[2], Pasi Raumonen[1], and Johanna Virkki[1]

[1] Tampere University, 33100 Tampere, Finland
`smmusfequr.rahman@tuni.fi`
[2] Satakunta University of Applied Sciences, 28130 Pori, Finland

Abstract. This paper presents the first prototype and proof-of-concept applications of an everyday hat-integrated human-computer interaction (HCI) system for serious games. Copper textile-based electrodes are integrated into a basic hat, and an HCI system is built around OpenBCI Ganglion device. As proof-of-concept applications, focus detection based on electroencephalography (EEG) and mobile game controlling based on electrooculogram (EOG) are presented. The functionality of these applications is tested by four participants. Based on the achieved results, this hat-integrated HCI system with copper-based textile electrodes can be an effective HCI medium for versatile serious games applications. Calibration of the system must be done for each participant, which will be the focus of our next study in this field. The results of this study are steps towards more user-friendly human-technology interfaces and game controllers, which can be integrated into our daily clothing for versatile serious games applications.

Keywords: EEG · EOG · electrode · focusing · games · OpenBCI · textiles · wearables

1 Introduction

Human-computer interaction (HCI) is a multidisciplinary field and of great importance in the field of serious games. Examples of the versatile studied topics include person identification through eye movement [1], gaze- and sound-based focus estimation [2], electromyography (EEG)-based gesture recognition [3], multimodal attention detection for reading [4], electrooculogram (EOG)-controlled games, such as a baseball game on a computer [5], a virtual reality game that uses eyeblink and eye gaze [6], and a parkour game designed for adolescents and for those with hyperactivity disorders, which employs human attention and EOG [7].

P. Dondio et al. (Eds.): GALA 2023, LNCS 14475, pp. 373–382, 2024.
https://doi.org/10.1007/978-3-031-49065-1_36

EEG and EOG are important methods of electrophysiological monitoring. EEG is the easiest, safest, and least invasive way to get a neurophysiological response. It records the brain's electrical activity from the scalp's surface [8]. EOGs, on the other hand, detect the potential difference between the retina and the cornea to determine eye movement [9]. Instead of current wearable devices for EEG or EOG using rigid electrodes (e.g., from Emotiv, interaXon, NeuroSky, and OpenBCI, whose use in research projects in the field is booming [10–14]), it has been found that clothing-integrated electrodes would create more favorable user experiences compared to such devices [15]. A clothing-integrated system can be more easily accepted by users, as it offers comfort and appears like regular clothing. This paper presents the first prototype and initial technical testing of an everyday hat-integrated HCI system with textile electrodes. As proof-of-concept applications in the field of serious games, focus detection based on EEG and game controlling based on EOG are presented.

2   Hat Prototype Fabrication

Based on information gained from our prior study about textile electrodes, the electrode diameter was selected to be 10.00 mm [16]. Copper textile-based electrodes, which were made of 'Pure copper polyester taffeta' fabric supplied by Less EMF Inc., were cut with scissors. This fabric is a polyester-based textile with copper plating and a surface resistance of less than 0.05 Ω/square [16,17]. It has been found to be a suitable electrode material in our previous study [16].

A readymade electrode is shown in Fig. 1. The electrodes were attached to an everyday hat (Fig. 1) with a touch fastener. The 10–20 system for EEG measurements is a widely accepted electrode placement system [18]. Here, odd numbering is on the left side and even numbering is on the right, while the skull and head area are divided into 23 standard positional points. From these points, fronto-polar 1 (FP1) and fronto-polar 2 (FP2), which were used in this study, are on the frontal lobe area, i.e., forehead. In addition, A1 and A2 electrodes are located at earlobes and used as a driven ground and a reference pin, respectively, for the OpenBCI. A four-channel OpenBCI Ganglion device, connected to a laptop using Bluetooth low energy, was placed in a textile pocket inside the hat (See Fig. 1 for a ready hat prototype).

In this study, both dry and semi-dry (saline water-wetted) copper textile-based electrodes were tested. The saline water solution was made according to the Florida Research Instruments, Inc. Manual [19]. Before the measurements, the saline water solution was applied to the electrode substrate, which was basic dishcloth material (yellow material in Fig. 1), and the substrate acted as an electrolyte dispenser during the measurements.

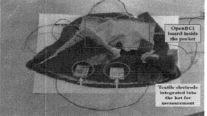

Fig. 1. Fabricated electrode structure from copper-based textile (left) and textile electrodes integrated into the hat (right).

3 Proof-of-Concept Applications

3.1 Focus Detection Using EEG

In a focus detection system, Arduino Mega 2560 microcontroller was used. The board's main control unit is ATmega2560. It has 54 digital input/output pins, of which 15 can be used as plus width modulation (PWM) outputs. It also has 16 analog inputs, 4 universal asynchronous receiver-transmitter (UARTs) (hardware serial ports), a USB port, a power jack, an in-circuit serial programming (ICSP) header, and a reset button. The USB port was used to power the Arduino. A single red light emitting diode (LED) and a 16 × 2 liquid-crystal display (LCD) were connected to the Arduino. USB cable was used to connect the computer and Arduino. The laptop was Bluetooth-connected to the OpenBCI. Laptop and OpenBCI board measured raw EEG data and filtered it with a 50 Hz notch filter and a 1–100 Hz bandpass filter. OpenBCI's focus widget determines the focus state based on the predefined algorithm of beta and gamma brain wave [20].

In Task 1, the participants were asked to focus. When participant was focused, the focus widget sent the signal to the Arduino and Arduino send the signal to turn on a LED. Thus, if the participant wasn't focused, the LED was turned off. The full workflow is shown in Fig. 2. In Task 2, the participants' focus state was measured during reading tasks. Here, Arduino was programmed to show the total time the user was focused. An LCD display was used to show the exact in milliseconds is shown in Fig. 2. The focused time starts as soon as the signal arrives from OpenBCI board, and the timer stops as soon as there is no signal. The full workflow is shown in Fig. 3.

3.2 Game Controlling Using EOG

Next, a mobile game controlling system was created. Bluetooth Module HC-05 was used to connect an Android mobile phone with the Arduino (same Arduino Mega 2560 microcontroller as in focus detection system) for playing a self-developed (via MIT app inventor) mobile game using EOG signal from OpenBCI. In this simple game, balloons appear randomly on the screen and the user blinks their eyes to shoot an arrow and pop the balloons, as shown in Fig. 4. Each popped balloon is counted as a score.

As in focus detection system, raw EEG data was filtered with a 50 Hz notch filter and a 1–100 Hz bandpass filter. As shown in the working procedure of the mobile game play system in Fig. 5, a network feature of OpenBCI was used [20]. It streamed the data

Fig. 2. Focus detection system: When the user is focused, Arduino is programmed to turn on the LED (left) or to record the focused time and display it in the LCD display (right).

Fig. 3. Working procedure of the EEG-based focus detection system.

to the computer. A Python script, which received the data, decided if it hit the threshold value and threshold time or not. This eye blink threshold value and threshold time were stored in the Python script, and they can be modified for each user. The threshold value was normalized to range from 0 to 1 from the raw EEG data. The threshold time is the time that must pass before an output is triggered, i.e., an arrow is shot in the game.

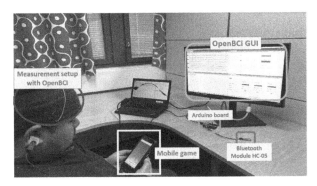

Fig. 4. Participant testing EOG-based mobile game controlling.

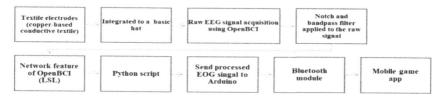

Fig. 5. Working procedure of the EOG-based game controlling system.

4 Test Procedures

Four participants tested the functionality of the proof-of-concept applications. The goal was to evaluate if this hat-integrated system with copper-based textile electrodes can be a HCI medium for future serious games. As explained, the electrodes were tested as dry and semi-dry. All the participants were aged between 24–35; among them, two were female and two were male. Each participant was measured four times with the same procedures.

Firstly, for focus detection, the participants were asked to focus on turning an LED. Next, they were given scientific articles to be read from papers and from a screen. The participants were not familiar with the scientific articles they were provided. The full measurement protocol is shown in Fig. 6.

Next, for the mobile game controlling, the participants played the game with different eyeblink threshold levels for EOG from (0.2 to 0.8). The threshold time was set to be 300 ms. The participants were instructed to play the game until they have popped 20 balloons with the arrow, i.e., achieved 20 points in the game. The full measurement protocol is shown in Fig. 7.

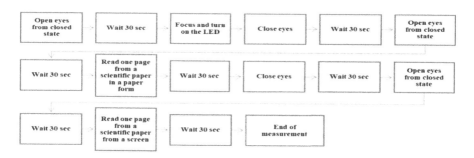

Fig. 6. Measurement protocol for focus detection with EEG.

Fig. 7. Measurement protocol for controlling a game with EOG.

5   Results and Discussion

5.1   Focus Detection System Results

All participants were always (four times) successful in turning on the LED with dry and semi-dry electrodes. Thus, all of them were found to be able to achieve the focused state in OpenBCI Ganglion device, which was successfully monitored by the developed hat-integrated HCI system. Next, the focus detection results were calculated using Eq. (1):

$$\text{Focus time}(\%)\frac{Time\ in\ focused\ state}{Total\ time\ taken\ to\ finish\ the\ task} \times 100 \qquad (1)$$

Figure 8 and 9 show the results from the focus detection measurements using dry and semi-dry electrodes, respectively. These figures display the median values and the standard deviation. The time in the focused state varies among participants and tasks, as can be expected. However, it can be seen, e.g., that most participants were more attentive during the reading task when reading from a paper than when reading from a screen. Table 1 shows the focus time mean and standard deviation (SD) with two different types of electrodes and two different types of measurement setups for all the participants. Based on these initial results, both types of electrodes, dry and semi-dry, integrated into an everyday hat can be an effective medium to be combined with the created HCI system for detecting human focusing during different tasks. This is a very promising result, as the dry electrodes are very convenient for daily life measurement when compared to the semi-dry electrodes that would require use of saline water.

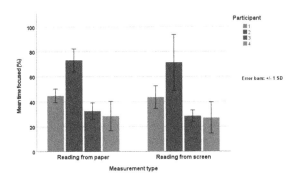

Fig. 8. Focus detection while using dry textile electrodes.

The ability to control one's attention and to ignore distractions while focusing on the task at hand is essential. Cognitive research demonstrates that it is necessary for success in any field requiring skilled performance, and it is a vital component of human well-being [21, 22]. An increasing amount of information is present and available in our daily life, which causes distractions. Losing focus is easy. The ability to focus can vary during the day, while different people are able to concentrate in different ways. According to previous research, factors such as task difficulty, time of the task, fatigue/tiredness

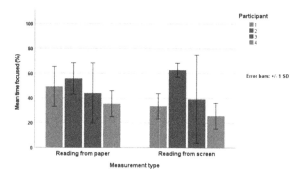

Fig. 9. Focus detection while using semi-dry textile electrodes.

Table 1. Focus time mean and SD with two different types of electrodes and two different types of measurement setups for all the participants.

				Time focused	
				Mean	SD
Measurement type	Reading from paper	Electrode type	Dry	44.64%	19.27%
			Semi-Dry	46.07%	16.83%
Measurement type	Reading from screen	Electrode Type	Dry	42.61%	22.01%
			Semi-Dry	40.21%	22.42%

(how well you have slept), attentional resources (how much attentional resources you have), negative emotionality (negative mood, or negative thoughts), mind wandering, how interesting the task is /boredom (how interesting the text is for the reader), and how familiar the task is for the participant (how familiar the text topic is for the reader) all influence the focusing ability of individuals [23–27]. Thus, the need for this type of everyday clothing-integrated focus detection measurement system is clear. Next, the hat prototype must be compared to more traditional setups to further evaluate its accuracy.

5.2 Game Controlling System Results

The game controlling system results are shown in Table 2. The data reveals the mean and SD of successful (i.e., arrow shot in the game when tried to shoot) and non-successful (i.e., arrow not shot in the game when tried to shoot) EOG inputs and false inputs (i.e., arrow shot in the game without trying to shoot). The results show that the optimal threshold for dry and semi-dry electrodes for successful eyeblink detection and gameplay is 0.20 and 0.40, respectively.

Based on these results, an everyday hat with both dry and semi-dry electrodes is a potential medium for controlling a mobile game, although the results are not comparable to existing commercial solutions yet. It is likely that a calibration of threshold for EOG is needed for each player, which will also support the removal of false hits. This kind of automatic calibration is our next goal.

Using EOG in HCI can especially benefit individuals who have limitations in motor skills. EOG signal is simple to acquire and has versatile applications [28–30]. However, frequent recalibration is required due to factors like user fatigue and variation in skin impedance as well as environmental lightning [28–30].

Table 2. Game controlling system results: Successful (i.e., arrow shot in the game when tried to shoot) and non-successful (i.e., arrow not shot in the game when tried to shoot) EOG inputs and false inputs (i.e., arrow shot in the game without trying to shoot).

Electrode type	Threshold for EOG	Successful	Successful	Non-successful	Non-successful	False hit	False hit
		Mean	SD	Mean	SD	Mean	SD
Dry	0.20	20.00	0.00	0.25	0.50	12.00	4.08
	0.40	17.00	6.00	9.00	17.34	3.75	3.59
	0.60	17.00	6.00	8.75	14.95	1.25	1.50
	0.80	15.00	10.00	15.50	26.41	2.00	4.00
Semi-dry	0.20	19.50	1.00	0.00	0.00	10.50	5.80
	0.40	20.00	0.00	2.00	2.31	3.25	1.50
	0.60	17.75	4.50	11.50	15.11	2.25	3.86
	0.80	15.00	10.00	17.75	18.71	2.50	3.00

6   Conclusion

We presented the first prototype and proof-of-concept applications of an everyday hat-integrated HCI system for serious games. As a proof-of-concept, we showed successful focus detection based on EEG and game controlling based on EOG. Calibration of the system must be done for each participant, which will be the focus of our next study in this field. Also, our goal is to compare these measurements to those done with standard rigid (Ag/AgCl) electrodes and with existing measurement setups and carry out measurements with more participants.

The results of this study are steps towards more user-friendly human-technology interfaces and game controllers, which can be integrated into our daily clothing for more inclusive serious games. We especially see the value of such clothing-integrated system for people who are sensitive for wearing traditional devices or simply find them clumsy for long-term use.

References

1. Abdulin, E.R., Komogortsev, O.V.: Person verification via eye movement-driven text reading model. In: 2015 IEEE 7th International Conference on Biometrics Theory, Applications and Systems (BTAS), pp. 1–8. IEEE, Arlington, VA, USA (2015). https://doi.org/10.1109/BTAS.2015.7358786

2. Stiefelhagen, R., Yang, J., Waibel, A.: Estimating focus of attention based on gaze and sound. In: Proceedings of the 2001 workshop on Perceptive User Interfaces, pp. 1–9. ACM, Orlando Florida USA (2001). https://doi.org/10.1145/971478.971505

3. Bulling, A., Roggen, D., Tröster, G.: It's in your eyes: towards context-awareness and mobile HCI using wearable EOG goggles. In: Proceedings of the 10th international conference on Ubiquitous Computing, pp. 84–93. ACM, Seoul Korea (2008). https://doi.org/10.1145/1409635.1409647

4. Li, J., Ngai, G., Va Leong, H., Chan, S.: Multimodal human attention detection for reading. In: Proceedings of the 31st Annual ACM Symposium on Applied Computing, pp. 187–192. ACM, Pisa Italy (2016). https://doi.org/10.1145/2851613.2851681

5. Lin, C.-T., Wu, S.-L., Jiang, W.-L., Jyun-Wei Liang, Chen, S.-A.: A wireless Electrooculography-based human-computer interface for baseball game. In: 2013 9th International Conference on Information, Communications & Signal Processing, pp. 1–4. IEEE, Tainan, Taiwan (2013). https://doi.org/10.1109/ICICS.2013.6782884

6. Kumar, D., Sharma, A.: Electrooculogram-based virtual reality game control using blink detection and gaze calibration. In: 2016 International Conference on Advances in Computing, Communications and Informatics (ICACCI), pp. 2358–2362. IEEE, Jaipur, India (2016). https://doi.org/10.1109/ICACCI.2016.7732407

7. Wang, P., Yang, Y., Li, J.: Development of parkour game system using EEG control. In: 2018 International Symposium on Computer, Consumer and Control (IS3C), pp. 258–261. IEEE, Taichung, Taiwan (2018). https://doi.org/10.1109/IS3C.2018.00072

8. Webster, J.G., Clark, J.W. (eds.): Medical instrumentation: application and design. John Wiley & Sons, Hoboken, NJ (2010)

9. Heo, J., Yoon, H., Park, K.S.: A novel wearable forehead EOG measurement system for human computer interfaces. Sensors 17(7), 1485 (2007). https://doi.org/10.3390/s17071485

10. Sawangjai, P., Hompoonsup, S., Leelaarporn, P., Kongwudhikunakorn, S., Wilaiprasitporn, T.: Consumer grade EEG measuring sensors as research tools: a review. IEEE Sensors J. 20, 3996–4024 (2020). https://doi.org/10.1109/JSEN.2019.2962874

11. Wei, C.-C., Ma, M.-Y.: Influences of visual attention and reading time on children and adults. Read. Writ. Q. 33, 97–108 (2017). https://doi.org/10.1080/10573569.2015.1092100

12. Vourvopoulos, A., Liarokapis, F.: Evaluation of commercial brain–computer interfaces in real and virtual world environment: a pilot study. Comput. Electr. Eng.. Electr. Eng. 40, 714–729 (2014). https://doi.org/10.1016/j.compeleceng.2013.10.009

13. Patsis, G., Sahli, H., Verhelst, W., De Troyer, O.: Evaluation of attention levels in a tetris game using a brain computer interface. In: Carberry, S., Weibelzahl, S., Micarelli, A., Semeraro, G. (eds.) User Modeling, Adaptation, and Personalization, pp. 127–138. Springer, Berlin (2013). https://doi.org/10.1007/978-3-642-38844-6_11

14. Crowley, K., Sliney, A., Pitt, I., Murphy, D.: Evaluating a brain-computer interface to categorise human emotional response. In: 2010 10th IEEE International Conference on Advanced Learning Technologies, pp. 276–278. IEEE, Sousse, Tunisia (2010). https://doi.org/10.1109/ICALT.2010.81

15. Baskan, A., Goncu-Berk, G.: User experience of wearable technologies: a comparative analysis of textile-based and accessory-based wearable products. Appl. Sci. 12, 11154 (2022). https://doi.org/10.3390/app122111154

16. Rahman, S.M.M., Mattila, H., Janka, M., Virkki, J.: Impedance evaluation of textile electrodes for EEG measurements. Text. Res. J. 93, 1878–1888 (2023). https://doi.org/10.1177/00405175221135131

17. Less EMF: Pure Copper Polyester Taffeta. https://lessemf.com/product/pure-copper-polyester-taffeta/

18. Marcuse, L.V., Fields, M.C., Yoo, J., Rowan, A.J.: Rowan's primer of EEG. Elsevier, Edinburgh (2016)

19. Florida Research Instruments Inc: FRI-2147-OpenBCI. http://www.floridaresearchinstru ments.com/manuals/saline-openBCI-1-1-printing-version.pdf

20. OpenBCI Documentation: GUI Widget Guide. https://docs.openbci.com/Software/OpenBC ISoftware/GUIWidgets/

21. Moran, A.: Concentration: attention and performance. In: Murphy, S.M. (ed.) The Oxford Handbook of Sport and Performance Psychology, pp. 117–130. Oxford University Press (2012). https://doi.org/10.1093/oxfordhb/9780199731763.013.0006

22. Näsi, M., Koivusilta, L.: Internet and everyday life: the perceived implications of internet use on memory and ability to concentrate. Cyberpsychol. Behav. Soc. Netw.. Behav. Soc. Netw. 16, 88–93 (2013). https://doi.org/10.1089/cyber.2012.0058

23. Chayer, C., Freedman, M.: Frontal lobe functions. Curr. Neurol. Neurosci. Rep.. Neurol. Neurosci. Rep. 1, 547–552 (2001). https://doi.org/10.1007/s11910-001-0060-4

24. Robertson, I.H., Manly, T., Andrade, J., Baddeley, B.T., Yiend, J.: 'Oops!': performance correlates of everyday attentional failures in traumatic brain injured and normal subjects. Neuropsychologia 35, 747–758 (1997). https://doi.org/10.1016/S0028-3932(97)00015-8

25. Heilman, K.M., Valenstein, E., Heilman, K.M. (eds.): Clinical neuropsychology. Oxford Univ. Press, New York (2012)

26. McGough, O.H., Mayhorn, C.B..: In Response to warnings: exploring individual differences in sustained attention performance. In: Proceedings of the Human Factors and Ergonomics Society Annual Meeting, vol. 66, 231–235 (2022). https://doi.org/10.1177/107118132266 1095

27. Rooth, M.: A theory of focus interpretation. Nat. Lang. Seman. 1, 75–116 (1992). https://doi. org/10.1007/BF02342617

28. Barea, R., Boquete, L., Mazo, M., Lopez, E.: System for assisted mobility using eye move- ments based on electrooculography. IEEE Trans. Neural Syst. Rehabil. Eng. 10, 209–218 (2002). https://doi.org/10.1109/TNSRE.2002.806829

29. Golrou, A., Rafiei, N., Sabouri, M.: Wheelchair controlling by eye movements using eog based human machine interface and artificial neural network. IJCA 184, 12–18 (2022). https://doi. org/10.5120/ijca2022922465

30. Hosni, S.M., Shedeed, H.A., Mabrouk, M.S., Tolba, M.F.: EEG-EOG based virtual keyboard: toward hybrid brain computer interface. Neuroinform 17, 323–341 (2019). https://doi.org/10. 1007/s12021-018-9402-0

Posters

A Game Design-Centric Taxonomy for Feedback Features in Digital Serious Games

André Almo[1]([✉]) [iD], Mariana Rocha[1] [iD], Attracta Brennan[2] [iD],
and Pierpaolo Dondio[1] [iD]

[1] Technological University Dublin, Dublin, Ireland
andre.almo@tudublin.ie
[2] National University of Ireland Galway, Galway, Ireland

Abstract. As with other pedagogical approaches, feedback is crucial in digital game-based learning, providing information to players and impacting their learning and motivation. However, the design of feedback features varies throughout different serious games, as feedback includes many distinct characteristics. This paper proposes a comprehensive taxonomy for feedback features in serious games, building on previous classifications and emphasising game design aspects. The *Taxonomy for Feedback Design in Serious Games* provides nuanced descriptions of different feedback aspects and defines clearer distinctions among different feedback characteristics, creating eight new descriptive categories. This paper discusses the characteristics of feedback features, as well as the potential contributions of this new taxonomy for research and practice in the area of education and game science.

Keywords: digital game-based learning · game features · feedback · taxonomy

1 Introduction

Digital Game-Based Learning (DGBL) is a pedagogical strategy that has proven to positively affect cognitive and non-cognitive factors [1–5]. Different games, however, have distinct features which can influence user experience and learning [3, 4, 6–9]. Among these, feedback features are particularly important as they respond to players' actions and provide information on their performance, as well as present further knowledge and possible alternatives to amend incorrect choices [10–12]. They may also vary in design, including content, timing and other characteristics [11, 12, 14]. Variations in feedback can lead to different outcomes depending on the game and who plays it [11, 12, 14].

Studies show a paucity of comprehensive clarity and detail in feedback descriptions in addition to conflicting terminology [12–14]. While previous works have described and classified feedback features [10, 12, 14, 15], a game design-centric taxonomy which provides more detailed explanations and well-defined categories is required. This paper introduces eight new feedback categories and a game design-focused taxonomy for feedback features in serious games. The goal of this taxonomy, entitled the *Taxonomy for Feedback Design in Serious Games*, is to present feedback features in a more replicable

P. Dondio et al. (Eds.): GALA 2023, LNCS 14475, pp. 385–389, 2024.
https://doi.org/10.1007/978-3-031-49065-1_37

manner, with more nuanced descriptions, systemise their characteristics and aid and inform serious game designers/developers and researchers.

2 Methods

The *Taxonomy for Feedback Design in Serious Games* builds on previous research on feedback features in serious games [10–12, 14–16]. This taxonomy provides additional categories encompassing different characteristics. It aims to offer more explicit, descriptive and replicable feedback features to the field of serious games.

3 The Taxonomy for Feedback Design in Serious Games

The *Taxonomy for Feedback Design in Serious Games* has 14 main categories with each category being further divided into several subcategories.

Type: Defines what the feedback feature is: accuracy feedback (informs players if their choice was correct or not), scores/points (gives players points for correct choices), a leaderboard (informs players of their position in comparison to other players) or a dashboard (performance data, number of matches, wins/losses, etc.).

Content: The content and amount of information given to the player can vary across different feedback features. Outcome feedback, also known as 'Corrective'/ 'Evaluative' feedback, informs players whether or not their actions were correct [11, 12, 15]. Subtypes of outcome feedback include knowledge of outcome (informs the player whether their actions were correct/positive or incorrect/negative [12]), knowledge of correct response (informs the player of the correct choice [12]), accuracy percentage [12], error flagging (informs the player which choices were incorrect [12]), self-comparison (compares the player's performance to their previous performance(s) [12]) and normative/social comparison (compares the player's performance to other players' performance(s) [12]). Elaborative feedback, also known as 'Process'/'Explanatory' feedback, further elaborates on reasons behind success or failure [11, 12]. Elaborative feedback can be informational (the player is given a reminder of the topic relevant to the current task [12]), topic-specific (the player receives specific information related to the content [12]), response-specific (the player is provided with information as to why a given answer is correct/incorrect [12]) or can include hints [12].

Timing: Feedback features can be put into effect at different times depending on player activity in the game [10]. Immediate feedback is given immediately after a specific action. Delayed feedback is delayed for a certain time after the player's action is completed, while requested feedback is only delivered if requested by the player.

Duration: Feedback may disappear automatically (automatic) or the player may be required to end it (player action required).

Modality: Feedback can be delivered through different senses. Auditory feedback includes verbal or non-verbal effects [10]. Visual feedback uses either text/dialogue or non-textual visual effects [10, 11]. Haptic feedback uses the sense of touch; it may be related to the position of the body (proprioception), body movement (kinesthesia), or the tactile/cutaneous system, including texture and temperature [16].

Expression: Feedback can be expressed implicitly (usually through dialogue with a non-playable character (NPC)) or explicitly (given outside of the narrative, through the interface, such as written or audio messages, scores and progress bars) [14].

Agent: Delivers the feedback. It may be an NPC, the game's interface, another player, and/or external agents, including teachers, colleagues or facilitators [14, 15].

Input: The feedback feature uses data inputted or implicitly provided by players during gameplay e.g. score, errors and/or time spent playing the game, a match, or completing a certain task. This data may be collected from one or more players and can include data from one or more matches.

Trigger: Feedback features are triggered by the player completing an action, by the action being correct and/or incorrect [10] or given in response to other events, including physiological measures [17], time spent on a task, or by the player reaching a performance target, such as a score.

Adaptation: Feedback content, timing, modality, expression, agent, trigger, purpose, action and/or consequence may adapt based on player characteristics, including native language, gender, age, individual preferences, prior knowledge, emotional state, motivation and/or performance [12, 18, 19].

Purpose: Feedback features may be used for different purposes, such as cognitive (e.g. learning) and non-cognitive (e.g. enjoyment, motivation and/or interest) [19].

Follow-Up Action: After an incorrect answer, players may be requested to perform a follow-up action, such as restarting the task, correcting the mistake(s), changing their choices or simply continuing the game.

Consequence: Gameplay may be influenced positively, negatively or neutrally by feedback. With positive consequences, the player progresses in the game, earns time, scores/points and/or earns other rewards. In contrast, with negative consequences, there is a block or loss of progress, time, points, rewards and/or attempts [20]. With neutral consequences, there are no rewards or penalties.

Voluntariness: Players may have the choice to receive the feedback or not (voluntary), or feedback may be mandatory within the game (involuntary).

4 Discussion

This paper provides a new taxonomy for more nuanced descriptions of distinct characteristics of feedback features. This taxonomy builds on previous research [10–12, 14–16], whilst introducing eight new categories: 'Type', 'Duration', 'Agent', 'Input', 'Purpose', 'Action', 'Consequence' and 'Voluntariness'. The 'Haptic' modality is a new subcategory, which has been studied and commented on before, but not included in recent feedback classifications. Other categories (i.e. content, timing and modality) are adapted from previous work on feedback features [10, 12, 14], including slight changes to nomenclature, hierarchy and classification in order to achieve clearer descriptions.

The *Taxonomy for Feedback Design in Serious Games* will be useful for researchers and game developers/designers who want to analyse, describe, compare, design and/or evaluate feedback features in serious games. It can aid further research on feedback in serious games, exploring the effects of different feedback characteristics on learning outcomes and motivation of different student populations through different games, as well as the interactions between feedback features and other game design features. This taxonomy will be evaluated through its use by serious game designers and researchers, who will classify feedback features using the taxonomy and provide the authors with comments. The results of the classification by different professionals will be compared, their comments analysed, and their inter-rater reliability measured by Cohen's kappa coefficient.

Acknowledgements. This work was conducted with the financial support of the Science Foundation Ireland Centre for Research Training in Digitally-Enhanced Reality (d-real) under Grant No. 18/CRT/6224. For the purpose of Open Access, the author has applied a CC BY public copyright licence to any Author Accepted Manuscript version arising from this submission.

References

1. Connolly, T., et al.: A systemic literature review of empirical evidence on computer games and serious games. Comput. Educ. **59**, 661–686 (2012). https://doi.org/10.1016/j.compedu.2012.03.004
2. De Freitas, S.: Are games effective learning tools? a review of educational games. Educ. Technol. Soc. **21**(2), 74–84 (2018)
3. Moyer-Packenham, P.S., et al.: How design features in digital math games support learning and mathematics connections. Comput. Hum. Behav. **91**, 316–332 (2019). https://doi.org/10.1016/j.chb.2018.09.036
4. Vanbecelaere, S., et al.: The effects of two digital educational games on cognitive and non-cognitive math and reading outcomes. Comput. Educ. **143**, 103680 (2020). https://doi.org/10.1016/J.COMPEDU.2019.103680
5. Theofylaktos, A., et al.: Digital game-based learning and serious games in education. Inter. J. Adv. Sci. Res. Eng. **4**, 139–144 (2018). https://doi.org/10.31695/IJASRE.2018.33016
6. Clark, D.B., et al.: Digital games, design, and learning: a systematic review and meta-analysis. Rev. Educ. Res. **86**(1), 79–122 (2016). https://doi.org/10.3102/0034654315582065
7. Dondlinger, M.: Educational video game design: a review of the literature. J. Appli. Educ. Technol.. **4**(1), 21–31 (2007)
8. Fairuzabadi, A., Supianto, A.: An overview of learning support factors on mathematic games. kinetik: game technology, information system. Comput. Netw. Comput. Electron. Control **4**(2), 169–178 (2019). https://doi.org/10.22219/kinetik.v4i2.761
9. Laamarti, F., et al.: An overview of serious games. Intern. J. Comput. Games Technol. **358152**, 1–15 (2014). https://doi.org/10.1155/2014/358152
10. Boyer-Thurgood, J. M.: The Anatomy of Virtual Manipulative Apps: Using Grounded Theory to Conceptualize and Evaluate Educational Apps that Contain Virtual Manipulatives. All Graduate Theses and Dissertations, vol. 6178 (2017). https://digitalcommons.usu.edu/etd/6178
11. Gauthier, A., et al.: I Don't usually listen, i read: how different learner groups process game feedback. In: Proceedings of the 2022 CHI Conference on Human Factors in Computing Systems (CHI 2022), Article 88, pp. 1–15 Association for Computing Machinery, New York (2022). https://doi.org/10.1145/3491102.3517480

12. Johnson, C.I., Bailey, S.K.T., Van Buskirk, W.L.: Designing effective feedback messages in serious games and simulations: a research review. In: Wouters, P., van Oostendorp, H. (eds.) Instructional Techniques to Facilitate Learning and Motivation of Serious Games, pp. 119–140. Springer International Publishing, Cham (2017). https://doi.org/10.1007/978-3-319-392 98-1_7

13. Pan, Y., Ke, F., Xu, X.: A systematic review of the role of learning games in fostering mathematics education in K-12 settings. Educ. Res. Rev. **36**, 100448 (2022). https://doi.org/10.1016/j.edurev.2022.100448

14. Mozdzer, M.: A State of the Art on Feedback in Serious Games (2021)

15. De Freitas, S., et al.: Efficacy of the 4F feedback model: a game-based assessment in university education. Information **14**(2), 99 (2023). https://doi.org/10.3390/info14020099

16. Menelas, B.A.J., Benaoudia, R.S.: Use of haptics to promote learning outcomes in serious games. Multimodal Technol. Interact. **1**(4), 31 (2017). https://doi.org/10.3390/mti1040031

17. Kanellos, T., et al.: FocusLocus: ADHD management gaming system for educational achievement and social inclusion. In: Proceedings of SPIE 10662, Smart Biomedical and Physiological Sensor Technology, vol. XV, p. 106620E (2018). https://doi.org/10.1117/12.230 7087

18. Aydin, M., Karal, H., Nabiyev, V.: Examination of adaptation components in serious games: a systematic review study. Educ. Inf. Technol. **28**, 6541–6562 (2023). https://doi.org/10.1007/s10639-022-11462-1

19. Vanbecelaere, S., Demedts, F.: The effectiveness of adaptive digital games for learning: calling for a broader view on assessment. In: Kiili, K., Antti, K., Muhterem, F.d.R. (ed.) Games and Learning Alliance: 11th International Conference, GALA 2022, Tampere, Finland, Proceedings, pp. 269–278. Springer International Publishing, Cham (2022). https://doi.org/10.1007/978-3-031-22124-8_26

20. Tran, H.Q., Wetterich, S.: Patterns of negative feedback in games. In: Proceedings of the Digital Games Research Association 2011 Conference: Think Design Play (2011)

Gamified Wearable EEG Technology to Support Controlling of Cognitive Load After Brain Injury

Sari Merilampi[1]([✉]) [ID], Taina Jyräkoski[1], Anja Poberznik[1], Nina Karttunen[1] [ID], Toni Seessalo[1], Johanna Virkki[2] [ID], and Tarmo Lipping[2] [ID]

[1] Satakunta University of Applied Sciences, Pori, Finland
`sari.merilampi@samk.fi`
[2] Faculty of Information Technology and Communication Sciences, Tampere University, Pori, Finland

Abstract. Traumatic brain injury (TBI) results from an injury to the head. Depending on the severity of the injury and the affected regions of the brain, consequences vary a lot. Apart from physical challenges, a person with TBI may have various cognitive deficits, which affect the cognitive load of the person in different situations. The paper presents an early paper prototype for a wearable cognitive load measurement device design using biomarkers from an electroencephalogram (EEG). The paper discusses how the rehabilitation and daily tasks could be adjusted and optimized for individuals' needs by using such a cognitive load measurement tool. Designing this kind of system requires skills from various disciplines. Thus, the early product design was created in a multidisciplinary workshop. As everyday EEG-based tools are still in their early development phase, it is very important to pay a lot of attention to technical development. However, in order to facilitate the implementation of such technology, it is also crucial to concentrate on easy-to-wear, user-friendly, and fashionable product design.

Keywords: EEG · cognitive load · traumatic brain injury · product design

1 Introduction

Developments in measurement technology, wireless communication, and signal analysis have enabled consumer-oriented EEG devices to the market. Common applications include monitoring of meditation sessions, brain-computer interfaces (BCIs) to control games or robotic devices, and assessment of sleep quality. In this study, we are creating a concept of using wireless consumer-oriented EEG devices for monitoring cognitive load and recovery from mental exercise. As the main target group, people suffering from TBI are considered. Persons with TBI often experience fatigue that restricts daily life and returning to school/work [1]. Therefore, it is important to have measurement tools for increasing self-assessment of fatigue and cognitive load to tailor goal-oriented and effective rehabilitation while heading back to as normal daily life as possible.

P. Dondio et al. (Eds.): GALA 2023, LNCS 14475, pp. 390–395, 2024.
https://doi.org/10.1007/978-3-031-49065-1_38

1.1 Traumatic Brain Injury (TBI) and Wearable EEG Measurements

TBI is a common condition worldwide. It results from an injury to the head, which causes sustained changes to brain activity. Depending on the severity and place of the injury, consequences vary a lot. Apart from physical challenges, TBI patients may have memory and learning difficulties, difficulties with paying attention and concentrating, following instructions, understanding others, difficulties completing complex tasks, word-finding difficulties, problems with organizing materials and many others [2]. Even simple tasks can increase the cognitive load, which is the stress put on our brain when learning new information or skills, and it is a consequence of the limitations of our short-term memory [3]. Cognitive load increases fatigue, which is another common symptom of TBI. Fatigue can significantly impact one's ability to participate in daily activities even years after a mild TBI [4].

When a person with a TBI returns to school or work, special arrangements might be needed. Recognition of fatigue and minimizing its effect are important parts of the arrangements as it is usually difficult for the person to recognize the signs of becoming tired. The ways of measuring fatigue are mainly subjective and patient-reported whereas objective tools are lacking. However, the ability to monitor cognitive load in real time would benefit the TBI patient, by allowing adjustments to be made to guarantee sufficient pauses and rest needed during cognitive tasks such as learning.

EEG is probably the most common objective indicator of TBI [5]. EEG measurements have also been successfully used to measure cognitive load in various contexts such as reading text of various complexity [6], undergoing intelligence tests [7], engaging in basic, logic and problem-solving tasks [8] and simple-to-multiple-choice tasks [8].

In a recent study [8] by the authors, EEG data was collected with ENOBIO® EEG recording system by Neuroelectrics® while test persons were playing an N-back memory game at different difficulty levels. The data was only acquired from the Fp1 and Fp2 electrodes, located on the forehead, to mimic the recordings with more easy-to-use EEG devices for real-life situations. Cognitive load variations were detected and EEG biomarkers for cognitive load developed. A classification accuracy of 81% was obtained when the data were categorized into segments of three levels of cognitive load. In a more recent, yet unpublished study even better classification accuracy was obtained by the authors using the MUSE® EEG consumer headband by InteraXion Inc. Recently, these kinds of wearable EEG devices have entered the consumer market. Common to all is a lower cost, lower number of electrodes, easier application, and no need for conductive gels as opposed to EEG devices in clinical applications.

1.2 Multidisciplinary Concept Creation and Product Design

The development of cognitive load measurement tools for everyday environments requires multidisciplinary skills and co-designing. Co-design refers to the collective creativity of a multidisciplinary group of people [9]. The users/user proxies play an important role in this process. The process starts with a pre-design phase, in which understanding of users and contexts of use is increased, and technological opportunities are explored. After this, the process follows the traditional design process, where the resulting ideas are developed into concepts and prototypes that are refined based on the feedback of the users. This study concentrates on the concept-level development and creation of an early product design. Jesse Garrets framework in UX design [10] is used as a guideline to support the product design process.

2   Concept Creation and Product Design Workshop

A co-design workshop was organized to design a wearable tool which utilizes developed EEG biomarkers for cognitive load recognition, introduced in the article [8]. People with versatile professional backgrounds (physiotherapy (1), nursing (1), research (1), automation (1) and radiography (1)) participated in the workshop.

Prior to the workshop, the participants listened to presentations about existing EEG devices, their possibilities and use applications as well as about detecting stress and cognitive load via EEG. The first part of the workshop aimed at a concept determining users and their needs (Garret's user needs layer [10]). The participants first created a user persona, specified the problem to be solved and created ideas to solve the problem. User profile, problem definition and idea canvas were used to help in the work. After producing ideas, the team voted on the best idea to be further developed.

The second part of the workshop focused on product design. The participants were guided by the question "How do the user's needs turn into a product?". In the product design phase, Jesse Garret's [10] Scope, Structure, Skeleton and Surface layers were taken into consideration. The aim was to provide a concept-level solution for the identified problem of the described person.

3   The Concept-Level Product and the Early Product Design

First, for the concept, the group defined the user as a young school-aged boy with a TBI. His rehabilitation was agreed upon to be at the stage where he could start attending school again. The most challenging symptom is fatigue and cognitive load during school days. It is difficult for him to analyze on his own whether he still has resources to continue studying or should he have a break. There is a personal assistant, a special education teacher and therapists (occupational and physiotherapist) beside the teacher in the multidisciplinary team that helps him in the rehabilitation process in studying. It is challenging also for them to recognize whether the boy has resources to study more.

Because most commercial EEG devices are very visible and sometimes uncomfortable, the visual design was ideated to be easily wearable and beautiful: a jewel or a tattoo-like plaster (Fig. 1). The electrode would for example look like a diamond and it would be placed on the forehead. Different models could be designed according to the user. This device would contain a wireless sticker electrode(s) and miniaturized readout electronics. Results of cognitive load would be seen through an app that is connected to the measurement device using a wireless connection such as Bluetooth.

A cognitive load app was created to increase engagement and to ease the interpretation of the data. The game elements of the prototype were chosen by the participants especially to provide a quick status check. The main screen sketch is presented in Fig. 1. From the main screen the user, therapist, or other stakeholder can quickly check the current status and the total cumulative cognitive load of the day, or navigate to see some more detailed statistics (trophies, progress, activities, cognitive load setting and status for different times of the day).

The health bar indicates how much resources for cognitive load the person still has for the day. The "max health" (maximum total cognitive load the person can experience in one day) is preset by the therapist according to the calibration discussed later. The current status is visualized as traffic lights which are easy to understand and fast to check. Green indicates normal cognitive load, yellow indicates that the cognitive load is increasing and red is a sign of alert in cognitive load. Also, these levels are calibrated for each individual. There are also optional additional functionalities to preset and check health bars for 6-12am, 12am-6pm and for the evening (6pm-sleeping time), in case the user needs help in dividing the load during different times of the day. There could also be preset activities whose cognitive load the app is measuring and visualizing. These can be enabled and adjusted in the app. The user receives trophies when achievements exceed the average goals set for a day. After the days that did not go that well, he receives feedback on the actions or periods when he should have decreased the load. This is discussed with the therapist. This prototype is only worn when awake and charged during the night. In the future versions, the device could also be further evolved to measure sleep and adjust the "health bar" according to the recovery during night and day.

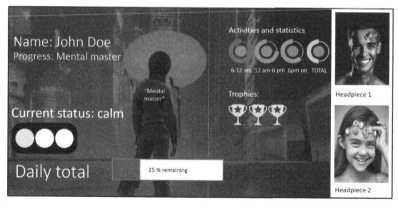

Fig. 1. A sketch of the app screen and headpiece designs (created with the help of [12] & [11]).

Since EEG and cognitive load are unique for everyone, a calibration must be done for each user. The calibration could be performed by measuring reference EEG data for an agreed time period during which the user performs the agreed activities in the agreed schedule while wearing the EEG device. In the first prototype, a data analyst could calculate the cognitive load which arose during the calibration period in different situations. In an advanced prototype, this could be automated and performed in the application. Based on the reference data, cognitive load settings would be then set up to the application by the therapist with know-how on the user's case and abilities. However, the rehabilitation process also includes constant interaction with the stakeholders and constant assessment for further adjusting the settings according to the user's progress.

4   Discussion

The purpose of the product design presented in this paper is to enhance the user's rehabilitation and education. The produced concept provides a tool for professionals such as the therapist as well as teachers to adjust the cognitive performance requirements according to the user's condition and state. It also teaches the user to control their own resources. However, the actual implementation of the prototype and the rehabilitation services needed in the use of the prototype should be further investigated and the processes modelled. The therapists and other stakeholders should be properly educated about the use and the purpose of the tool. The professionals should have an active, couch-like, role in setting the goals, observing the progress, and helping the user to recognize the signs of fatigue more easily using the app.

Although the prototype should be made enjoyable and easy to use, it is also highly important to implement gamified applications based on the needs and goals of the rehabilitee. The understanding of the symptoms and disabilities caused by TBI as well as tailored and goal-oriented rehabilitation is the key element when developing a device for supporting one's rehabilitation and coping in daily life.

Although the prototype is designed for a TBI patient, it can be easily modified for various other user groups. It could be used to adjust different kinds of activities of a person's everyday life according to personal goals and abilities. For the working-aged, it would offer a tool for supporting persons to achieve a more cognitively ergonomic working style. Additionally, it would serve various users with partial ability to work, to adjust the working conditions according to their situation. The tool could also benefit teachers in classrooms. It would allow them to more easily assess the need for breaks, and extra study support as well as apply adjustments in teaching while seeing the students' cognitive load status. This would contribute to optimizing the learners' capacity to make learning easier and more enjoyable. Such tools could promote the inclusion of all learners.

As everyday EEG-based tools are still in their early development phase, it is very important to pay attention to technical development. However, it is important to concentrate on easy-to-wear, user-friendly and fashionable product design. Since EEG is typically measured in clinical settings, there is still a lot of work in product designing for everyday environments. Our future work will focus on making the first functional prototype of the app with existing EEG measurement hardware as the development of new hardware requires long development and test phases and potentially fine-tuning the biomarkers. As the focus of this paper was on the user needs, further game design is also required. A well-known MDA framework [12] will be applied in the design process, as the "entertainment" element will play a crucial role in the next development steps.

5   Conclusions

Monitoring stress using physiological signals has recently achieved attention since cognitive load has a significant adverse influence on an individual's daily health and efficiency. In addition to technical development, the implementation of such technology requires a desirable design of the product. This paper concentrated on the product design of a wearable cognitive load measurement device using biomarkers from EEG. The development in this study focused on the product design of such a tool for the rehabilitation of a person with TBI. The aim of the tool is to enable adjustment of the rehabilitation and daily tasks according to the cognitive load experienced by the person. As this requires skills from various professionals, the concept was created in a multidisciplinary workshop. The next step is to focus on the technical development.

References

1. Mollayeva, T.: A systematic review of fatigue in patients with traumatic brain injury: The course, predictors and consequences. Neurosci. Biobehav. Rev. **47**, 684–716 (2014)
2. Traumatic brain injury support Homepage, https://www.braininjurysupport.org/living-with-a-traumatic-brain-injury/cognitive-consequences/, Accessed 1 June 2023
3. Lewis, P. J: Brain friendly teaching-reducing learner's cognitive Load. Acad Radiol. Jul; **23**(7):877–80 (2016)
4. Johansson, B.: Mental fatigue after mild traumatic brain injury in relation to cognitive tests and brain imaging methods. Int J Environ Res Public Health. Jun 2; **18**(11):5955 (2021)
5. Tenney, J., et al.: Practice guideline: use of quantitative EEG for the diagnosis of mild traumatic brain injury: report of the guideline Committee of the american clinical neurophysiology society. J. Clin. Neurophysiol. **38**(4), 287–292 (2021)
6. Mostow, J., Chang, K., Nelson, J., Toward Exploiting EEG Input in a Reading Tutor. In Proceedings of the 15th International Conference on Artificial Intelligence in Education. Berlin, Heidelberg: Springer, 230–237 (2011).
7. Friedman, N., Fekete, T., Gal K., Shriki O.: EEG-based prediction of cognitive load in intelligence tests. Front Hum Neurosci. Jun 11; 13:191 (2019)
8. Chaouachi, M., Frasson, C: Exploring the Relationship between Learner EEG Mental Engagement and Affect. In Proceedings of the 10th International Conference on Intelligent Tutoring Systems. Berlin, Heidelberg: Springer, 291–293 (2010).
9. Schapkin, S.A., Raggatz, J., Hillmert, M., Böckelmann, I.: EEG correlates of cognitive load in a multiple choice reaction task. Acta. Neurobiol. Exp. (Wars). **80**(1), 76–89 (2020)
10. Beiramvand, M., Lipping, T., Karttunen, N. & Koivula R.: Mental workload assessment using low-channel prefrontal EEG signals, 2023 IEEE Int. Symp. Med. Meas. Appl. (MeMeA). In press. (2023)
11. Sanders, E., Stappers, P.: Co-creation and the new landscapes of design. CoDesign **4**(1), 5–18 (2008)
12. Garret, J.J., The elements of user experience, New Riders, Berkeley, CA (2011)
13. https://deepai.org/, Accessed 28 June 2023
14. https://www.craiyon.com/, Accessed 28 June 2023
15. https://users.cs.northwestern.edu/~hunicke/MDA.pdf, Accessed 11 Sep 2023

Future Blocks: Sci-Fi Storytelling as a Serious Game for Leadership Development

Avo Schönbohm[(✉)] [iD] and Jan-Henrik Walter

Hochschule für Wirtschaft und Recht Berlin, Berlin, Germany
avo.schoenbohm@hwr-berlin.de, post@janhenrikwalter.de

Abstract. The short paper explores the integration of serious games and specu-lative fiction in leadership education. The serious game Future Blocks uses sci-fi narratives to foster strategic thinking, adaptability, and foresight in participants, essential skills in effective leadership. The preliminary research investigates the game's potential to stimulate critical thinking and creativity while enhancing com-municative skills through its engaging and interactive structure. It demonstrates the potential of serious gaming in leadership development pedagogy.

Keywords: Serious Game · Science Fiction · Leadership Development · Narrative Pedagogy

1 Educational Goals and Background of the Serious Game

In today's swiftly changing technological landscape, there is an imperative for leaders to possess a futuristic vision and a deep grasp of technological advancements [1–3]. Lead-ers' roles today are not only about overseeing operational activities but also navigating the complex interplay of societal and technological evolutions [4, 5]. Contemporary lead-ership demands a mindset attuned to the digital era, accentuating skills like storytelling [6] and negotiation [7].

Future Blocks is a board game designed to nurture these essential leadership attributes. Drawing from narrative pedagogy [2] and effective game design [9], the seri-ous game combines technological literacy with storytelling. In this competitive setting, players not only learn but actively discuss the interplay between technology and soci-ety. They're encouraged to envision future solutions, highlighting the power of group dialogue in shaping societal viewpoints.

In 2022, Future Blocks was trialled in an exploratory manner with 37 students at the Berlin School of Economics and Law, accentuating foundational business and entrepreneurial capacities [10]. Future Blocks supplements this groundwork, nurturing innovation and clarity in communicating intricate ideas.

Acknowledging that unconstrained spaces bolster creativity, Future Blocks provides an environment for free ideation [11, 12]. It diverges from the expert-only linear innova-tion model, advocating for a participatory approach to technological evolution [1, 13]. The game aims to democratise tech-centric narratives, inviting inclusive understanding and participation.

P. Dondio et al. (Eds.): GALA 2023, LNCS 14475, pp. 396–401, 2024.
https://doi.org/10.1007/978-3-031-49065-1_39

Distinctively, Future Blocks is not just a gamified educational experience but a serious board game that engages players in a process of learning and reflection. While the mechanics, dynamics, and aesthetics of the game are elucidated in subsequent sections, it is pertinent to mention here that players engage in timed sessions, accumulating scores based on their visionary propositions and decisions, with clearly defined end conditions. As we continue to refine and deploy Future Blocks, our future research will involve more structured evaluations, potentially including control groups, to rigorously assess its pedagogical impact.

2 Serious Games, Leadership and Storytelling

Serious games: Introduced by Abt [14], serious games denote an intentional blend of entertainment and pedagogy. Abt underlined the potential of games to serve purposes beyond mere amusement, particularly in education and training. Supporting this, subsequent research has demonstrated that the interactive and immersive aspects of gaming can augment learning experiences [15]. On the other hand, gamification, or the incorporation of game-like elements into traditionally non-game contexts, has shown promise in enhancing user engagement and productivity [16, 17]. Future Blocks resonates with the core tenets of serious games, striving for deep engagement and educational value, rather than merely gamifying an existing curriculum.

Modern leadership in a technological context: While traditional leadership models [18] focus on traits and behaviours, the digital revolution demands more versatile leaders. These modern leaders are not just decision-makers; they strive to become visionaries equipped to navigate technological and societal complexities [4, 19]. This evolving landscape necessitates contemporary and forward-thinking leadership development methodologies [20].

Storytelling's educational value: Storytelling, rooted in pedagogical literature, serves as a potent tool for facilitating comprehension, inspiring action, and fostering knowledge-sharing in organisational realms [21]. Its interactive nature, as posited by Armstrong & McCain [8], makes it an ideal approach for engaging learners.

3 The Game Mechanics: Finding the Right Technology to Evolve from the Prescribed Presence into an Envisioned Future

At its core, Future Blocks sets two players head-to-head, while the others act as the jury. The game mechanics are designed to foster creative thought and strategy, using a tripartite structure: players blend a present situation, a future scenario, and a technology card they have drawn. Its imaginative approach draws inspiration from Dixit, a card game centred around pictorial interpretation [22], and the Future Wheel, a brainstorming tool for forecasting diverse future scenarios [23]. The game stands on the foundational work of Rapp, Bruns, and Walter from Berlin University of the Arts, and is a progression from their game Future Shock [24]. This game equally allows for discussions of the repercussions of disruptive developments. Take the introduction of a space elevator as a primary development. Its secondary effect might be casting a vast shadow, leading to unforeseen social consequences (Fig. 1).

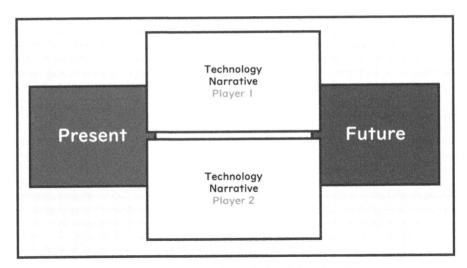

Fig. 1. The Future Blocks' Reduced Gameboard

Within the realm of Future Blocks, players find themselves delving into a hand that unfurls a random present (e.g., "power supply issues"), a whimsical future scenario (e.g., "elephants in urban parks"), and a set of three technology cards. Tasked with the challenge of selecting a single technology, players try to weave it seamlessly into a story that connects the present with the given future. Each round is an arena for two riveting narratives, making it an engaging exercise for the jury to adjudicate the victor. In Future Blocks, each juror has the discretion to award either one or two plastic chips to the narrative they find most compelling. The storyteller amassing the most chips at the end of a round emerges as the winner of that narrative face-off. Ultimately, the player who accumulates the most chips over the course of the game is declared the overall victor.

This jury, composed of the non-narrating players, is not merely a passive audience. They actively dissect each story, discussing its merits and pitfalls. Furthermore, they have the authority to query the narrators, ensuring that the story's underpinnings are robust. Furthermore, the dialogue is not unilateral. Narrators have the leeway to reward jurors with plastic chip tokens, a gesture recognising constructive feedback or keen insights. For instance, Player A is developing a tale where urban park elephants become the epicentre of biogas energy solutions amidst Germany's power woes. In contrast, Player B might pivot and narrate a world where these behemoths evolve into powerful, autonomous vehicles, navigating a landscape devoid of conventional electricity.

While deciding on a winning narrative, jurors employ a multi-faceted lens, evaluating tales based on their feasibility, allure, coherence, and gaps. Adding layers to their judgment process, jurors adopt specific personas, like the eco-conscious "environmentalist" or the ROI-focused "investor". These roles, determined by drawn cards, infuse the decision-making process with personal biases and unique perspectives. A strategic layer grafted onto this deliberation process allows jurors to place wagers on which openly displayed technology they surmise narrators will anchor their tales, amplifying the game's unpredictability quotient. They can bet up to two plastic chips on their prediction. If their foresight aligns with the narrator's choice, they double their bet. However, if their prediction falls short, they lose their wagered chips. At its heart, Future Blocks is designed to serve as a platform for players to craft and navigate socio-technological tales that resonate, challenge, and inspire, providing insights into potential futures and the technologies that might shape them.

4 Gameplay Feedback and Observations

Future Blocks underwent an evaluation involving 37 business students at the Berlin School of Economics and Law which serves as a preliminary study aimed at understanding the game's reception and potential areas of improvement. The mixed-method evaluation methodology included a custom survey with closed-ended questions, observations undertaken during gameplay sessions and subsequent two focus-group interviews with two play groups (n = 10) with open-ended questions by the authors. Our primary findings included:

Elevated technological curiosity: Post gameplay, the majority exhibited heightened curiosity about the technologies featured in the game. One participant remarked, "There are many technologies I was previously unaware of. Through the game, I gained insight into them." This sentiment was shared by a noteworthy 83% (31 out of 37) of participants.

Acknowledgement of technology's societal impact: A salient feature of the game was highlighting the pivotal role of technology in shaping society. This notion found resonance with 80% (30 out of 37) of participants. A staggering 98% (36 out of 37) recognised the imperative to understand these technologies given their prospective roles as economic decision-makers.

Skill augmentation: While opinions varied on whether the game offered a novel perspective on technologies, many believed it honed their storytelling and presentation capabilities. One student noted, "The game challenged me, enabling me to share stories I hadn't envisaged." Approximately 68% (25 out of 36) concurred with this observation. Furthermore, 92% (34 out of 37) expressed willingness to recommend Future Blocks to their peers.

Appreciation of game dynamics: Participants enjoyed the game's fusion of competitive and collaborative elements, necessitating astute thinking, persuasive presentation, and inventive storytelling. The diverse jury roles, like the environmentalist and mayor, were commended for adding layers of complexity and engagement. However, some found the betting process somewhat confusing.

Proclivity for proactive learning: Observational data revealed a trend where students proactively sourced online information about the game's technological components. While this highlighted a knowledge gap regarding certain technological trends (i.e., cloud computing, CRISPR-Cas, vertical farming) it underscored the game's ability to ignite curiosity, encourage knowledge assimilation, and advocate for self-driven learning, particularly concerning unfamiliar technological topics.

5   Implications for Teaching and Leadership Training

Based on our evaluation, participants exhibited heightened technological curiosity after engaging with Future Blocks and reported increased confidence in their creative and visionary thinking capabilities. Addressing potential "future shock", a term by Alvin Toffler from 1970, the Future Blocks might prepare players for the psychological strain of rapid societal changes [25]. Today's leaders need to be equipped to navigate fast-paced technological shifts. Immediate post-game insights suggest Future Blocks as a valuable educational tool that advances early leadership development. It fosters engagement with complex tech topics, supporting the case for serious games in shaping future leaders.

Beyond education, it could be suitable for corporate team-building, leadership training, and strategic development. By simulating future scenarios, players prepare for potential realities. Future Blocks serves as a multifaceted platform with the aim of strengthening leadership foresight and team collaboration, while also promoting critical thinking Additionally, organisations might harness its potential for innovative brainstorming and policy-makers can utilise it for informed technological forecasting.

As Future Blocks continues to evolve as a pedagogical instrument, there is room for improvement. Refinements in game mechanics can be introduced based on broader feedback and, over time, the use of validated scales. Adding contemporary scenarios and updating existing ones for relevance to specific audiences is also on the horizon. To further validate the game's educational impact, we are designing a subsequent study in a corporate environment that will incorporate a control group. Additionally, recognising the growing demand for remote learning tools, we are considering the development of an online version of Future Blocks.

Acknowledgement. The development and research of the game were facilitated by the Ludix Project, funded by the Institut für angewandte Forschung Berlin (IfaF Berlin), reflecting Berlin's dedication to pioneering educational strategies.

References

1. Bijker, W.E., Hughes, T.P., Pinch, T. (Hrsg.): The social construction of technological systems: new directions in the sociology and history of technology. Cambridge, Mass: MIT Press (2012)
2. Ylimaki, R.M.: Toward a new conceptualisation of vision in the work of educational leaders: cases of the visionary archetype. Educ. Adm. Q. **42**(4), 620–665 (2006)
3. Sugar, W., Holloman, H.: Technology leaders wanted: acknowledging the leadership role of a technology coordinator. TechTrends **53**(6), 66 (2009)
4. Day, D.V., Fleenor, J.W., Atwater, L.E., Sturm, R.E., McKee, R.A.: Advances in leader and leadership development: a review of 25 years of research and theory. Leadersh. Q. **25**(1), 63–82 (2014)
5. Pfeffer, J.: Building sustainable organisations: the human factor. Acad. Manage. Perspect. **24**(1), 34–45 (2010)
6. Harris, J., Barnes, B.K.: Leadership storytelling. Ind. Commercial Training **38**(7), 350–353 (2006)
7. Shmueli, D., Warfield, W., Kaufman, S.: Enhancing community leadership negotiation skills to build civic capacity. Negot. J. **25**(2), 249–266 (2009)

8. Armstrong, J.P., McCain, K.D.: Narrative pedagogy for leadership education: stories of leadership efficacy, self-identity, and leadership development. J. Leadersh. Stud. **14**(4), 60–70 (2021)
9. Deterding, S.: Situated motivational affordances of game elements: a conceptual model. In: Gamification: Using Game Design Elements in Non-Gaming Contexts, A Workshop at CHI, vol. 10, no. 1979742.1979575 (2011)
10. Kuratko, D.F.: The emergence of entrepreneurship education: development, trends, and challenges. Entrep. Theory Pract. **29**(5), 577–597 (2005)
11. Daniel, G.R.: Safe spaces for enabling the creative process in classrooms. Aust. J. Teach. Educ. **45**(8), 41–57 (2020)
12. Hüther, G. & Quarch, C.: Rettet das Spiel! München, btb (2018)
13. Greenhalgh, T., Robert, G., Macfarlane, F., Bate, P., Kyriakidou, O.: Diffusion of innovations in service organisations: systematic review and recommendations. Milbank Q. **82**(4), 581–629 (2004)
14. Abt, C.: Serious Games. University press of America (1970)
15. Michael, D.R., Chen, S.L.: Serious Games: Games That Educate, Train, and Inform. Muska & Lipman/Premier-Trade (2005)
16. Deterding, S., Dixon, D., Khaled, R., Nacke, L.: From game design elements to gamefulness: defining "gamification". MindTrek (2011)
17. Hamari, J., Koivisto, J., Sarsa, H.: Does gamification work? A literature review of empirical studies on gamification. In: 2014 47th Hawaii international conference on system sciences, pp. 3025–3034 (2014)
18. Blake, R.R., Mouton, J.S.: The Managerial Grid: Key Orientations for Achieving Production Through People Houston. Gulf Publishing Co., TX (1964)
19. Bennis, W., Nanus, B.: Leaders: The Strategies for Taking Charge. Harper & Row (1985)
20. Maheshwari, S.K., Yadav, J.: Leadership in the digital age: emerging paradigms and challenges. Int. J. Bus. Globalisation **26**(3), 220–238 (2020)
21. Kemp, A., Gravois, R., Syrdal, H., McDougal, E.: Storytelling is not just for marketing: cultivating a storytelling culture throughout the organisation. Bus. Horiz. **66**(3), 313–324 (2023)
22. Libellud. (n.d.). Stella - Dixit Universe. https://www.libellud.com/en/our-games/stella-dixit-universe/. Accessed 13 June 2023
23. Daffara, P.: Applying the futures wheel and macrohistory to the Covid19 global pandemic. J. Futures Stud. **25**(2), 35–48 (2020)
24. Walter, J.-H., Schönbohm, A.: Future Shocks: Sci-Fi-Storytelling für (angehende) Manager*Innen. In: A. Schönbohm & P. Celik (Eds.), Ludic Innovation Experiences – Führungskräfteentwicklung mit Spiel und System, pp. 170–177 (2023)
25. Toffler, A.: Future shock, random house (1970)

Astera, an Educational Game About the Evolution of Galaxies

Tobias Grubenmann[1(✉)] and Francesco Shankar[2]

[1] School of Computing, Engineering and the Built Environment, Edinburgh Napier University, Edinburgh, UK
t.grubenmann@napier.ac.uk
[2] School of Physics and Astronomy, University of Southampton, Highfield, Southampton SO17 1BJ, UK
f.shankar@soton.ac.uk

Abstract. The Universe at its largest scales remains still almost a mystery for most of the people not working in this field. With Astera, we present an educational video game that can teach about the cosmos whilst providing a thrilling and fun gaming experience. Astera allows the user to fly through the Universe up to the most distant galaxies, and "build" the Universe by growing and merging galaxies according to the most recent findings in astrophysics. As our results show, games like Astera can have a positive impact on players attitude towards galaxy evolution and science in general, and the player's willingness to follow up on related activities.

Keywords: Educational Games · Galaxy Evolution · STEM education

1 Introduction

Galaxies are some of the largest objects in the universe. Their size and age are almost incomprehensible to us humans. To give an example, our own galaxy, the Milky Way, has tens of billions (10^{10}) of stars and light originating from one edge of the Milky Way takes around one hundred thousand years to reach to other end [6]. However, galaxies do not look all the same. On the contrary, galaxies come in different shapes, colors, and sizes. Figure 1 shows a few examples of how different galaxies can be in their appearances.

Astera is an educational game that teaches the players the mechanisms responsible for determining the appearance of galaxies based on state-of-the-art research in Astrophysics. Astera has been developed at the Astronomy Group at the University of Southampton as part of a research project aimed at educating high school students, hobbyists, and the general public about the evolution of galaxies. Astera is based on the same-titled cosmological visualizer [4].

One of the reasons we developed Astera is that there is a lack of interactive material in general and games in particular which (i) capture the imagination of the public regarding the large-scale structure of our universe, (ii) make the

P. Dondio et al. (Eds.): GALA 2023, LNCS 14475, pp. 402–407, 2024.
https://doi.org/10.1007/978-3-031-49065-1_40

topic of galaxy evolution approachable and fun, and (iii) do not require any prior knowledge about astronomy or astrophysics. The closest games similar to Astera are Universe Sandbox [2], Space Engine [1], or At Play in the Cosmos [7]. However, none of the aforementioned games do cover the topic of galaxy evolution.

By playing Astera, our aim is that players not only learn about galaxy evolution, but also change their attitude towards scientific topics in general. As has been shown by previous research, educational games can be excellent tools for changing students' attitudes towards subjects like mathematics [5] or environmental sustainability [3].

2   A Primer on Galaxy Evolution

In this section, we want to give a brief overview of the main concepts of galaxy evolution and how these are mapped to Astera. All the topics covered in this section are also explained within Astera in the form of in-game tutorials.

To approach the topic of galaxy evolution, it is important to understand the main properties of galaxies that change over time. In Astera, one of the first concepts that a player is introduced to is the concept of the *mass* of a galaxy. Due to the massive scale, the mass of a galaxy is usually measured in *solar masses*, which is the mass of our sun. However, even in this massive unit of measurement, a galaxy can easily have a mass of billions or trillions solar masses.

One of the most striking differences between galaxies are their shape. Whereas there exist different classifications for the shape of a galaxy, in Astera, we focused on the most basic distinction of *spiral* and *elliptical* galaxies [6]. Within the game, we use different models for spiral galaxies and elliptical galaxies. Another difference in appearance is whether a galaxy is *active* or not [6]. Active galaxies often exhibit massive jets which extends to opposite directions from the center of the galaxy. Figure 1 shows in-game footage of different galaxies (top row) as well as their real-life counterparts (bottom row).

The final property of a galaxy covered by Astera is the number of *satellites* or *accompanying* galaxies. A satellite is a smaller galaxy that is gravitationally bound to a larger central galaxy. Due to dynamical friction—a force that slows down the satellite—the galaxies will eventually *merge* [6], a process which we will discuss next.

Galaxy mergers are the driving force between galaxy evolution and the main game element of Astera. The history of galaxy mergers define the properties of today's galaxies. A galaxy merger is the collision of two galaxies and their subsequent union into one bigger galaxy [6]. Before two galaxies merge together, they become gravitationally bound, starting a "cosmic dance" together through space. After a certain amount of time, the two galaxies will be so close together that they cannot be distinguished as two separate galaxies anymore. Subsequently, we combine the two galaxies into one bigger galaxy and add together their masses. In addition to combining the mass, mergers may change the shape of the galaxy or trigger an active state.

Fig. 1. Top left to right: In-game footage of: Sprial galaxy, elliptical galaxy, active spiral galaxy. Bottom left to right: NGC 6946: ESA/Hubble & NASA, A. Leroy, K.S. Long. IC 2006: ESA/Hubble & NASA, Image acknowledgement: Judy Schmidt and J. Blakeslee (Dominion Astrophysical Observatory). NGC 1300: NASA, ESA, and The Hubble Heritage Team (STScI/AURA).

3   Game-Play

In this section, we describe how the player experiences Astera and the unique challenges the player faces while playing.

Astera is organized into different *scenarios*. Figure 2 shows a screenshot of a player engaged in one of the scenarios. Each scenario requires the player to change the evolution of a galaxy according to some given objectives. An *objective* within a scenario is a set of constraints on the properties that a galaxy should currently have. For example, an objective might be to have a galaxy with a certain mass or a specific shape. During a scenario, the player is in charge of a given galaxy. Astera will spawn new galaxies within the vicinity of the player's galaxy, which will eventually merge together. Whereas some of these newly spawned galaxies have properties beneficial for the current objectives, others will be disruptive. The task of the player is to influence these newly spawned galaxies in order to be aligned with the objective as best as possible. To make Astera more exciting and to allow a player to play more strategically, objectives change during the scenario. The player will accumulate points during a scenario depending on how well she or he manages to align the property of the galaxy with the current objective.

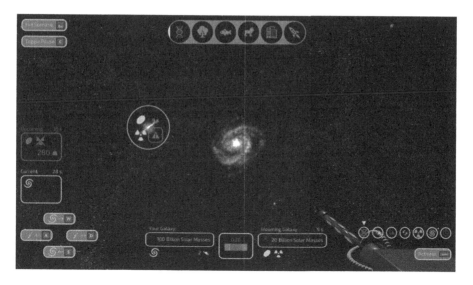

Fig. 2. Player playing a scenario in **Astera**. Galaxies are based upon: NGC 5194: S. Beckwith (STScI) Hubble Heritage Team, (STScI/AURA), ESA, NASA. IC 2006: ESA/Hubble & NASA, Image acknowledgement: Judy Schmidt and J. Blakeslee (Dominion Astrophysical Observatory).

As mentioned before, the player needs to ensure that the galaxy under their care is aligned with the current objective as best as possible. To do this, the player can influence the properties of the newly spawn galaxies which are soon to be merged with the player's galaxy. We call these newly spawn galaxies which the player can influence *incoming galaxies*.

The player has seven different abilities to influence an incoming galaxy. These are: removing the incoming galaxy, doubling the mass of the incoming galaxy, halving the mass of the incoming galaxy, changing the shape of the incoming galaxy, toggling galaxy activity of the incoming galaxy, delaying the incoming galaxy, and duplicating the incoming galaxy. To increase the difficulty of the game and to enforce strategic thinking, each ability has a cool-down period which disables any further use of the ability for a short amount of time after it has been used.

4   Mapping Educational Goals to Gameplay

In the following, we will describe how a player experience different challenges while playing **Astera** and how these correspond to our goal of teaching about galaxy evolution.

While playing different scenarios in **Astera**, the player encounters incoming galaxies that may alter the player's galaxy. For example, the player's galaxy might currently be a spiral galaxy, but the current objective asks the player to maintain an elliptical galaxy. An incoming galaxy poses an opportunity to exploit merger mechanics to change the player's galaxy from spherical to elliptical. From an educational point of view, we want the player to recall how the ratio between the masses of the two merging galaxies affect the shape of the resulting galaxy after the merger.

As mentioned before, the objectives in Astera do not stay the same. By changing the objectives throughout a scenario and letting the user know what the upcoming objective will be, we create an opportunity for the player to plan ahead. For example, assume that the current objective is to maintain an elliptical shape, but this objective will change towards maintaining a spherical shape. From an educational point of view, we want the player to learn that it takes time for two galaxies to merge together after they become gravitationally bound.

When playing Astera, a player might encounter situations where not all parts of an objective can be matched simultaneously. For example, assume that the player's galaxy is non-active, spiral, with a mass of 50 billion solar masses. However, the objective requires to have an active, elliptical galaxy, with a mass of 50 billion solar masses. As the player will realize, it is not possible in this situation to match all the aspects (activity, shape, and mass) of the given objective. The best strategy in this situation also depends on what upcoming objectives demand from the player and which abilities are currently unavailable because they are on cool-down. From an educational point of view, we want the player to realize how galaxy mergers affect multiple galaxy properties simultaneously.

5   Showcasing at a Public Event

We tested Astera during the Science and Engineering day at the University of Southampton in March 2023. At this event, people of all ages were invited to visit the university and participate in different activities related to the different areas of teaching and research done at the university. The visitors also had the chance to play Astera[1] and fill out a questionnaire at the end. In total, we got 46 responses during the event.

The overall enjoyment was between "It was OK" and "I liked it a lot" (average score 3.66 out of 5) indicating that games about very scientific topics like the evolution of galaxies can also be fun and entertaining. The average response when asked whether the participants would tell their family or friends about Astera fell between "Not sure" and "Likely" (average score 3.43 out of 5). Similarly, When asked about whether the participants would play Astera if it were released to the public, the answers again fell between "Not sure" and "Likely" (average score 3.55 out of 5), with almost 60% responded with either "Likely" or "Very Likely". This is very positive feedback and encourages us to release Astera to the public.

When asked whether playing Astera did change the participants excitement towards science and astronomy, 60% responded with either "Likely" or "Very Likely", with an average response between "Not sure" and "Likely" (average score 3.58 out of 5), which indicates a clear positive impact on Astera towards

---

[1] Codename: Astera Evolution, version 0.3.4.

making young people excited about science and astronomy. Finally, we asked the participants whether they were more likely to do any of the following activities: Read about astronomy or galaxies; Go to a talk or event about astronomy or galaxies; Watch videos about astronomy or galaxies; Sign up for a course about astronomy or galaxies; Take a science subject at a school/college/university. Most responses were about either reading or watching videos. However, we also got a lot of people saying that they would more likely take a science subject in a school, college, or university. Also, note that almost 70% of all participants ticked at least one of the available activities in the questionnaire. From this feedback, we conclude that educational games like Astera can not only educate people about the target subject but also encourage players to follow up on related activities.

6   Conclusions

We introduced Astera in this paper and presented the main game-play and relevant background. In addition, we showed how Astera has been perceived by the audience at the Science and Engineering day at the University of Southampton. As the results show, Astera has been received quite favorably by the audience and showed a positive impact on the players' attitudes towards topics like galaxies and science. This is in line with other research indicating that educational games can be excellent tools for changing students' attitudes towards STEM subjects like mathematics [5] or environmental sustainability [3]. Given this positive feedback, we are currently working on releasing Astera to the public. We believe that games such as Astera can have a significant impact on how students perceive and engage with complicated scientific topics.

Acknowledgments. The development of Astera has been supported by the STFC FoF grant ST/V002945/1.

References

1. Cosmographic Software. Space Engine [Computer Software]. Steam Version (Early Access) (2019)
2. Giant Army LLC. Universe Sandbox [Computer Software]. Steam Version (2015)
3. Janakiraman, S., Watson, S.L., Watson, W.R.: Using game-based learning to facilitate attitude change for environmental sustainability. J. Educ. Sustain. Dev. **12**(2), 176–185 (2018)
4. Marsden, C., Shankar, F.: Using unreal engine to visualize a cosmological volume. Universe **6**(10) (2020)
5. Mavridis, A., Katmada, A., Tsiatsos, T.: Impact of online flexible games on students' attitude towards mathematics. Educ. Tech. Res. Dev. **65**(6), 1451–1470 (2017)
6. Mo, H., van den Bosch, F., White, S.: Galaxy Formation and Evolution, 1st edn. Cambridge University Press (2010)
7. Squire, K.: At play in the cosmos. Int. J. Designs Learn. **12**(1), 1–15 (2021)

A Security-Focused Architecture for Gameplay Telemetry in Serious Games

Stefan Bodenschatz$^{(\boxtimes)}$, Tilo Mentler , and Christof Rezk-Salama

Trier University of Applied Sciences, Schneidershof, 54293 Trier, Germany
{S.Bodenschatz,T.Mentler,C.Rezk-Salama}@hochschule-trier.de

Abstract. Serious games are a promising approach for diagnostic and therapeutic as well as educational purposes. Capturing player performance and behavior along with details of gameplay directly from the game is a valuable data source for evaluating serious games and for their iterative refinement. In many serious games, the collected data can however be especially sensitive for privacy, as it may imply learning or health state progression, and thus should be strongly protected. In this paper, we specify goals for a security-enhanced game telemetry system, model a security architecture based on them, and present the design of such a system, which we implemented for evaluation of health games in our research group. The presented system is designed to be applicable for various types of serious games. It employs end-to-end encryption, signatures, and data separation to improve protection of collected data without the addition of usability burdens on players from these security measures.

Keywords: serious game telemetry · serious game analytics · privacy · data security · end-to-end encryption

1 Introduction

When evaluating serious games, gathering data about gameplay experience, player behavior and performance directly from the game can be one important means of analysis. Such techniques are known as game telemetry/analytics. Applying them to serious games, however, poses additional challenges related to privacy and data security [3,5], as learning outcomes, training progress, and treatment metrics might be recorded in various educational and health settings.

In the following sections, we will specify goals for improving data protection and base a security architecture on them (2). Building upon this, we propose the design for a security-enhanced telemetry system (3) and summarize implementation information with respect to the project *Senior Health Games* focusing on serious games supporting the treatment of ailments affecting elderly people (4).

2 Security Architecture

To protect collected data, we propose a system architecture of multi-layered security. General measures like a firewall, authentication, backups, and transport

© The Author(s), under exclusive license to Springer Nature Switzerland AG 2024
P. Dondio et al. (Eds.): GALA 2023, LNCS 14475, pp. 408–413, 2024.
https://doi.org/10.1007/978-3-031-49065-1_41

encryption form the fundamental layer. Recipient authentication requirements are upgraded to a key-pair-based scheme. Beyond that, we propose layers that meet the following general objectives for handling sensitive game telemetry data:

G1 Separate pseudonymous game data from potentially identifiable user data
G2 Protect data confidentiality even if a server is compromised
G3 Do not add usability burdens on players through the extra safeguards

2.1 Service and Data Compartmentalization

Data collected by a telemetry system can be divided into gameplay data and user registrations. The former is usually not personally identifiable on its own. However, it must be associated with a user id to allow linkage to user-specific data and to analyze a user's progress across multiple sessions. Hence, it is pseudonymous. The user registrations can hold associated data needed for the analysis, e.g. demographic data or identifiers for linking other evaluation participant data. Only recipients who need this data should have access to it (cf. goal G1).

To achieve goal G1 and contribute to goal G2 by an additional security layer, the backend of our system is compartmentalized into microservices. Each of these keeps its own database, including the authorized recipients. This facilitates, e.g. providing gameplay logs to game designers while restricting user data to researchers for evaluation. Optionally, the services can even be isolated onto separate servers. This happens transparently to the user, contributing to goal G3.

2.2 End-to-End Encryption

A key security feature of our system is end-to-end encryption of all collected data where reasonably possible, especially the full body of gameplay logs. For user registrations, there are two sets of game-specific key-value data, one is server-readable (for query criteria), the other is end-to-end encrypted.

End-to-end encrypted data is protected by a two-layer encryption scheme: The content of each data object is encrypted symmetrically on the client using a generated key, referred to as the *data key*. A copy of this key is asymmetrically encrypted for each authorized recipient using their respective public key. These encrypted data keys are then attached to and stored with the object's metadata. The original data key is discarded after encryption, thus only the encrypted per-recipient copies can be used to decrypt the content. For this, the corresponding private key, which must be kept secret by its owner, is needed to first decrypt the data key. As a result, no entity except the authorized recipients can read the data, not even a server that was compromised by an attacker (cf. goal G2). As the in-game client only generates one-time keys, this process is automatic and does not require player intervention or key management (cf. goal G3).

2.3 Signing of Authorized Recipient Public Keys

End-to-end encryption is the key factor in achieving goal G2, but on its own only does so for data collected before a successful attack. Since clients must obtain the list of authorized public keys from the server, attackers in control of the server could modify the list. To achieve goal G2 for data collected after a successful attack, another layer of protection is required: Each recipient public key in the authorized list must be properly signed using a different key pair, referred to as the *signer key pair*. The public key of this pair is built into the game app and the private key is not present on the server. Instead, it is kept by a trusted person in the project who only needs to use it for adding new recipients. Compromising the server would neither allow swapping the public signer key in the app, nor obtaining the private signer key. Therefore, a recipient key injected by an attacker would be rejected by the clients. As signature validation is automated and does not involve the player, this layer also satisfies goal G3.

3   System Design

An overview of the telemetry collection system, building upon the architecture presented above, is given in Fig. 1. It is explained subsequently.

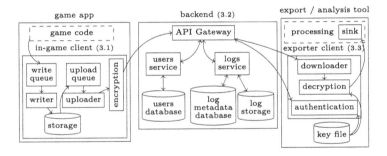

Fig. 1. A graphical overview for the structure of the system presented here

3.1   In-Game Client

Data collection begins with the in-game client library component (Fig. 1, left column), used to log game data streams. The game code interacts with it using a client object that provides easy-to-use methods for dispatching log entries, controlling log streams, and registering or authenticating the user. Each log entry either represents an event that happened during gameplay or a snapshot of some part of the game's state. Both entry types have a payload object where the game code can pass arbitrary JSON-serializable data associated with the event or describing the game state. All entries contain a high-resolution times-tamp of when they were recorded and also carry a logical channel string tag for categorization. Additionally, event entries indicate the type of event, e.g. some player action. Snapshot entries contain an object id to separate states of multiple objects.

Log content is encrypted on-the-fly during the upload, with key material generated immediately beforehand. The encrypted content and the metadata, including the encrypted recipient data keys, are sent in one multipart upload. Thus, either the transfer of both is successful and after confirmation by the server, the local file is removed, or if it fails, the local log data is kept for a later reattempt. Because the local files are not encrypted, their data keys only need to exist temporarily. This avoids the complexity and potential failure points of local key storage, such as when the file exists but the key is lost in a crash.

3.2 Backend

The backend infrastructure (Fig. 1, center column) is divided into containerized microservices, deployable on a single server or on separate servers for additional isolation. They are placed behind an API gateway, routing URI prefixes under a unified API endpoint to services. Both services can collect data for multiple game projects separately, which are registered in each service using a unique name and an API access token for the app itself. To facilitate separation of authorized recipient sets of game projects, these sets are also kept per game.

The users service stores user accounts, including hashed and salted user or device credentials, authenticates users, and issues session tokens. Optionally, game-specific user data can be stored as flexible key-value properties, split into unencrypted database-mapped ones and end-to-end encrypted ones.

The logs service stores encrypted log contents and associated metadata, consisting of the uploading user's id, id of the originating game app, timestamps of start and end of recording, as well as of uploading, the log content size, and the encryption schemes and required key material for the content. API access to the logs service is authenticated using session tokens issued by the users service.

3.3 Exporter Client

The path of collected data ends on the analysis side (Fig. 1, right column), where authorized recipients load and decrypt data. It is implemented as a library that can be integrated into analytical or exporter tools. The library expects user key files that contain two private keys: One is used for authenticating the client with the backend, the other corresponds with the recipient public key and is used to decrypt data keys for collected data. The decrypted data elements are passed to sink objects, provided by the tool, for processing, e.g. filtering and projecting them into columns of per-user CSV files, or exporting them as raw JSON files.

3.4 Authentication and Identity

Multiple credential options are supported for player authentication. To minimize collection of personal data, games can use device tokens, i.e. randomly generated credentials stored on the device. If users play on different devices, or if multiple users share an OS account on a device, the device token method is insufficient. For those cases, authentication by username and password is supported.

A third option is to couple the telemetry system with an existing authentication mechanism, e.g. of a multiplayer mode. Then, the game passes a token from that upstream system through the client to the telemetry backend, which verifies it with the upstream backend. Upon success, the upstream user id is mapped to the telemetry account and the telemetry backend issues a session token.

As recipient users need to have a key file with their private key for the decryption anyway, authentication for them is also based on public key cryptography, by using a signature challenge. To authenticate, the client sends an authentication request containing the user's key id. The server responds with a challenge, consisting of a random byte sequence, a unique challenge id, and the signature digest to use. The client signs a sequence consisting of the challenge data and responds with the signature. The server verifies this using the user's public key in the user database and upon success issues the session token.

4   Implementation

After discussing security-focused serious games telemetry concepts in general terms, we describe key aspects of our implementation, which we plan to release as open source at: https://github.com/TUAS-Serious-Games-Lab/SGL-Analytics

The symmetric encryption of data objects is performed using AES-256-CCM, as AES-256 is a broadly established standard for symmetric encryption [10] and CCM protects content integrity [2]. The asymmetric encryption of the data keys for each recipient supports two schemes: One using RSA encryption [11] with PKCS1 encoding [9] and one using elliptic-curve cryptography [8]. To encrypt a data key using the latter scheme, first an ephemeral elliptic-curve key pair is generated. Then, elliptic-curve Diffie-Hellman (ECDH) [1] is performed using the recipient's public key and the ephemeral private key to obtain a value from which a key is derived using KDF2 [6] with SHA256 [4]. Finally, the data key is encrypted using AES-256-CCM [2,10]. The public key of the ephemeral key pair is attached to the object's metadata and the private key is discarded. To decrypt the data key, the recipient also performs ECDH, but with their private key and the public key from the object's metadata, to obtain the same value as the sender, from which the same key that protects the data key is derived.

Public keys of recipients and exporter users on the server are stored as X.509 certificates [7] for the key, signed by the game's signer and encoded in the PEM format. These have key usage extensions [7] to indicate whether the key is intended for end-to-end encryption or authentication by signature challenge to prevent (accidental or malicious) key swapping. The signer's public key is baked into the game as a plain public key or as an X.509 certificate authority (CA) certificate, indicated using CA basic constraints and key usage extensions [7].

Components described in Sect. 3 are implemented on the .Net platform. Backend services are containerized ASP.Net Core Web APIs in a docker-compose project for ease of deployment. The clients are Nuget packages, with the in-game client also repackaged for UPM to easily target the Unity game engine. Porting the in-game client for C++-based engines could be done with reasonable effort.

5   Conclusion and Future Work

In-game telemetry data offers many potential insights, but privacy and security of collected data is vital, especially in health- or education-related serious games. Transport encryption alone offers no protection against a severe data breach through a compromised server. Therefore, we recommend hardening of serious game telemetry systems using end-to-end encryption, signatures, and data separation as described here to enhance protection of player data.

A possible extension is splitting the current log stream into multiple log files by data category and encrypting each file for a different category-associated list of authorized recipients to enforce an even finer-grained access control.

Acknowledgements. Our research project *Senior Health Games* is partially funded by the Carl Zeiss Foundation (CZS Transfer program).

References

1. Barker, E., Chen, L., Roginsky, A., Vassilev, A., Davis, R.: Recommendation for pair-wise key-establishment schemes using discrete logarithm cryptography. Technical report, SP 800–56A, NIST (2018). https://doi.org/10.6028/nist.sp.800-56ar3
2. Dworkin, M.J.: Recommendation for block cipher modes of operation: the CCM mode for authentication and confidentiality. Technical report, SP 800–38C, NIST (2007). https://doi.org/10.6028/nist.sp.800-38c
3. Freire, M., Serrano-Laguna, Á., Iglesias, B.M., Martínez-Ortiz, I., Moreno-Ger, P., Fernández-Manjón, B.: Game learning analytics: learning analytics for serious games. In: Spector, M.J., Lockee, B.B., Childress, M.D. (eds.) Learning, Design, and Technology, pp. 1–29. Springer, Cham (2016). https://doi.org/10.1007/978-3-319-17727-4_21-1
4. Hansen, T., Eastlake, 3rd, D.E.: US Secure Hash Algorithms (SHA and SHA-based HMAC and HKDF). RFC 6234 (2011). https://doi.org/10.17487/RFC6234
5. Heimo, O.I., et al.: Ethical gathering of exercise metrics from elderly: case jump-patikku. In: Kreps, D., Fletcher, G., Griffiths, M. (eds.) HCC 2016. IAICT, vol. 474, pp. 14–24. Springer, Cham (2016). https://doi.org/10.1007/978-3-319-44805-3_2
6. ISO/IEC JTC 1/SC 27: Information technology - Security techniques - Encryption algorithms - Part 2: Asymmetric ciphers. Standard ISO/IEC 18033–2:2006, ISO, Geneva, CH (2006)
7. ITU-T: Information technology - Open Systems Interconnection - The Directory: Public-key and attribute certificate frameworks. Standard ITU-T X.509 (10/2019) / ISO/IEC 9594–8, ITU (2019). https://handle.itu.int/11.1002/1000/14033
8. Koblitz, N.: Elliptic curve cryptosystems. Math. Comput. **48**(177), 203–209 (1987). https://doi.org/10.1090/s0025-5718-1987-0866109-5
9. Moriarty, K., Kaliski, B., Jonsson, J., Rusch, A.: PKCS #1: RSA Cryptography Specifications Version 2.2. RFC 8017 (2016). https://doi.org/10.17487/RFC8017
10. NIST: Advanced Encryption Standard (AES). Standard FIPS 197, NIST (2023). https://doi.org/10.6028/NIST.FIPS.197-upd1
11. Rivest, R.L., Shamir, A., Adleman, L.: A method for obtaining digital signatures and public-key cryptosystems. Commun. ACM **21**(2), 120–126 (1978). https://doi.org/10.1145/359340.359342

Game-Based Teaching Scenarios in Upper Secondary Mathematics Teaching – European User Experiences

Antti Koivisto[1], Sari Merilampi[1] , Darija Marković[2] , Johanna Virkki[3] ,
and Mirka Leino[1(✉)]

[1] RoboAI Research and Development Centre/Faculty of Technology, Satakunta University of
Applied Sciences, 28130 Pori, Finland
mirka.leino@samk.fi
[2] School of Applied Mathematics and Computer Science, Josip Juraj Strossmayer University of
Osijek, 31000 Osijek, Croatia
[3] Tampere Institute for Advanced Study/Faculty of Information Technology and
Communication Sciences, Tampere University, 33720 Tampere, Finland

Abstract. Research shows that digital games can engage students in mathematics
and enhance their performance. While mathematics teachers see "maths games"
as useful tools, their lack of knowledge about teaching with such games as well as
shortage of appropriate games for teaching upper secondary school mathematics
prevents the full potential of game-based teaching. This study presents GeomWiz, a
gamified geometry quiz, for learning geometry in upper secondary schools as well
as two teaching scenarios for using it in teaching. A student user experience study
was carried out in three European countries in which teachers piloted GeomWiz
and the teaching scenarios. Based on the results, game-based learning with game
contents that matches the learning objectives is suitable for geometry teaching in
upper secondary schools. Teaching scenarios assist the inclusion of the game into
teaching.

Keywords: Maths Game · Game-based Learning · Implementation · Teaching
Scenario · User Experience

1 Introduction

Mathematics is a fundamental educational requirement and continues throughout different levels of teaching. Research shows that digital games can engage students in
mathematics and enhance their performance [1–3]. Such "maths games" are not neutral tools but designed around teaching philosophies targeting specific outcomes [1].
Likewise, teachers are not neutral agents in game-based activities. In fact, how teachers
support students in use of a maths games affects its usefulness [1, 2]. Thus, training the
teachers on the use of maths games and instructional strategies are essen-tial points [2].

Several countries have highlighted the need for integrating technology into mathematics education [4]. There is, however, a major gap in game-based teaching and learning in maths: While maths games are used in elementary classes, they are not yet widely implemented in upper secondary school mathematics [3]. Research shows that while mathematics teachers see maths games as useful tools, their lack of knowledge about teaching with such digital games as well as shortage of appropriate games for teaching upper secondary school mathematics prevent them from using maths games for their full potential [3].

This study provides tools for the identified need by developing a gamified geometry quiz (GeomWiz) for learning geometry in upper secondary schools as well as two teaching scenarios for the implementation of the tool. Through these, it is possible for any mathematics teacher to use the GeomWiz tool as part of their teaching. A student user experience study was carried out in three European countries, in Finland, Croatia and Greece, where teachers piloted the GeomWiz with both teaching scenarios. The results of the student experiences are reported in this study.

2   GeomWiz in Game-Based Learning of Geometry

Successful implementation of game-based learning requires development of proper tools as well as processes for their use [5]. These tools and processes need to be developed by multidisciplinary groups consisting of experts in pedagogy, maths, as well as game design and programming [6]. In this paper, GeomWiz gamified geometry quiz and two scenarios for its use is discussed as an example of these.

Geomwiz is a single player gamified geometry quiz, for now on referred as game. GeomWiz is targeted for learning geometry in upper secondary schools. It was implemented as part of an international GAMMA (GAMe-based learning in MAthematics) project funded by Erasmus+. The game has six levels, each of which has its own geometry-related theme (shapes, angles of triangle, right angle, area of triangle, sine rule and cosine rule). The themes were determined by maths teachers according to the maths curriculum. GeomWiz is meant to be played with a mobile device, but it can also be played on PC. It was made with Unity game engine using isometric 2D elements as it makes the game look like 3D.

The game has a wizard character controlled with a virtual joystick. The wizard tries to collect as many points as possible by learning through multiple choice questions and given learning material. The game starts from the main menu from which the player selects a level (theme) to learn. After selecting a level, the game shows material through which the player learns the main points about the geometry topic of the level. The learning material can also be accessed later during the gameplay from an info icon (i).

Figure 1 illustrates the game screen. There is no time limit in the game. Each level consists of a different number of rooms, which the wizard must visit and complete. The difficulty level of the rooms will gradually increase as the game proceeds. Each room has four question boxes with difficulty levels from 1 to 4 concerning the same topic (marked with stars on the box). Each box will show the player one question, which is randomly selected from a question pool (made by maths teachers) from the database. The questions are multiple-choice tasks, in which one answer is correct, and four answers are incorrect.

The player may take all the question boxes (Fig. 1) of the room to earn more points. The number of points earned depends on the difficulty level of the box. This encourages the player to take also more difficult ones, although only one question from any of the boxes in the room needs to be answered correctly to open the next room. Additionally, if the player selects all boxes in the room but answers incorrectly to all questions, the next room will automatically open to enable the player to continue studying. The player can also take a hint for each question without affecting the points. After answering a question incorrectly for the 1st time, the game will automatically give a hint and a new try. The previous incorrect answer is removed from the answer options. When completing a level, the player earns a trophy and the game shows a summary window with the level statistics, including points, correct answers, incorrect answers and hints taken. There is also an exit button in the game if the player wants to quit playing. That will lead back to the main menu.

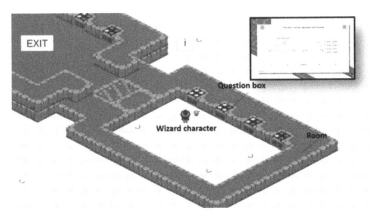

Fig. 1. Game screen of GeomWiz and example of multiple-choice question.

From the main menu, the player can also open a diploma that opens in a web browser, which shows all player's results from all times of playing the game. The statistics can be shared with a teacher by the player sharing a link to the player's statistics webpage. The statistics themselves do not contain any personal information. Thus, only the teacher (or the person to whom the link is shared) knows whose data that is. Sharing the results is a very important feature in the game to allow teachers to see the progress and the gaming activity of each student. Another important feature of the game from the teacher's perspective is the ability to modify the content (questions) in the database without any programming.

2.1 Teaching Scenarios for GeomWiz to Ease the Implementation

For the implementation of all the games of the GAMMA project in the classrooms, teaching scenarios were produced. With the help of the scenarios, it is possible for any mathematics teacher to implement the game as part of their teaching. The teaching scenario template was designed by the Croatian researchers and evaluated and modified by other researchers and teachers of the project. The teaching scenarios contain detailed information on subject, domain, and topic of the game, the learning objectives of the game, keywords, description & name of the game, summary of the scenario, age range of the students playing the game, prerequisite knowledge for students, prerequisite knowledge for teacher, preparation time, teaching time, needed resources (e.g., devices, paper and pencil, etc.), instructional setting (individual works, small groups, whole glass…), correlation with other subjects and/or cross-curricular topics, instructions for the activities (introduction, preparation, motivation, pregame info, playing the game, formative assessment), students' feedback about GBL, teacher's remarks, activities for students who wish to know more, suggestions for further activities and sources like literature and links to the game. The detailed scenarios are publicly available at http://www.project-gamma.eu/.

GeomWiz geometry game is extensive with its six levels, but the game was piloted for levels 4 (area of triangle) and 6 (cosine rule). The researchers carried out the game design and implementation, while the high school mathematics teachers produced the game's tasks and the teaching scenarios.

3   User Experience Study

In total n = 95 upper secondary students from Finland (n = 60) and Croatia (n = 35) participated in the lesson provided by maths teachers according to teaching scenario for GeomWiz at level 4 (L4). The corresponding number for level 6 (L6) was n = 111, from Finland (n = 18), Croatia (n = 70) and Greece (n = 23). After the scenario-based lessons, the students answered a questionnaire to evaluate the usefulness of the game & the scenario as part of mathematics education, and the attitude towards the game. The questionnaire contained 11 questions, of which 6 were compulsory and 5 optional. All optional questions were open type of questions. There were two Yes/No questions with an additional sub-question for a No answer, as well as a Likert scale question (with 5 sub-questions), where 1 = strongly disagree, 5 = strongly agree.

4   Results and Discussion

The first question students were asked about the game was: Is this digital game different from what you consider a game? 52% of the students who played L4 and 58% of the students who played L6 answered Yes. When asked about the differences, they referred to the educational aspect of the game, the need to think (in their own words "to use brain") and solve mathematical problems. There were some comments that it is more of a quiz than a game, while some pointed out the lack of a storyline.

The next question was about the comparison between regular mathematics lesson and lesson with GBL. The relative frequencies of the answers (1–5, Likert scale) to this question can be found in Fig. 2. A positive impact can be clearly seen in all aspects, with the exception of the aspect of engagement, especially for L6.

When asked about the positive aspects of the game, about 50% of the students said it made learning mathematics more fun. A few mentioned the possibility of answering a question twice and getting hints. Other positive aspects were learning at your own pace, learning through play, something different and more interesting than the usual maths lessons and the motivating aspect. Negative aspects mainly concerned some technical problems in the game, which were fixed after the pilot phase. Other negative aspects were the lack of storyline, game graphics, not knowing the correct answer when both guesses were wrong and the lack of additional explanations for formulas.

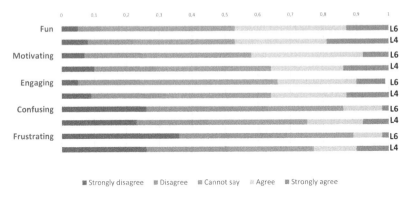

Fig. 2. Experiences of lesson with game compared to a regular mathematics lesson.

About 86% of students who played L4 and 81% who played L6 did not need any additional explanations during the game, but only 54% for both levels indicated in the self-assessment that they learned all or most of the predicted content. Students were mostly successful in perceiving the maths content included in the game and gave more precise answers in L6, while giving more general answers in L4.

The game still needs development especially when it comes to the engagement. As the focus of this paper was on the instructional design and implementation of a digital tool (GeomWiz) in teaching, further game design is required. Well-known MDA framework [7] will be applied in the design process, as the entertainment element will play a crucial role in the next steps for developing a full-scale math game, including evolving avatars, storytelling and reward mechanisms.

From the learning viewpoint it would be necessary to add a feature, which teaches the player the correct answer if the player is incorrectly answering the question after the hint is given. This could be linked to the tutorial material in which the topic is first introduced. The next steps in the game development also include further development of a teacher's dashboard for modifying questions and for analyzing the shared results. There could also be a chat to enhance and motivate and guide learning.

Our future research includes more detailed analysis of the students' and the teachers' feedback in different countries. Further research is also needed from the teachers to study the teaching scenarios & implementation and their thoughts of the long-term role the game would have in teaching. Using the game as a part of the assessment is also a future goal. The versatile tools for formative assessment could support the teacher's assessment work. Another interesting future research topic is to study how games development as such could be used as a tool for maths learning, as the development typically requires understanding of physics and maths.

To summarize the learning outcomes of this study, designing and implementing the game and producing all the tasks in the game was a huge job, even though it was done in a multidisciplinary team of researchers and teachers. The higher the level of expertise the game aims for, the more in-depth knowledge of the subject is required (in this case teaching and maths). This is why such games for the upper secondary schools are not yet widely available. Cultural aspects were also observed in this study, especially with regard to the production and publication of learning materials. Sharing the best practices between different countries is and will be an important tool in creating and implementing new ways of working in this subject area.

5   Conclusions

This paper presented the design, implementation, and user experiences of GeomWiz gamified geometry quiz and teaching scenarios for learning geometry in upper secondary schools. It can be concluded that game-based learning is suitable for geometry teaching in upper secondary schools. The game contents must match the learning objectives and it is useful to produce a teaching scenario for the help of the teachers. By following the scenario, the inclusion of the game as part of mathematics teaching is smooth. This requires multidisciplinary collaboration between researchers, teachers and game designers. From the teachers' point of view, important features included the player's possibility to share learning analytics with the teacher and that the tasks of the game are in the database, where they can be modified and supplemented without programming the game. Teaching scenarios were seen to be important in that a teacher can actually use the game as part of geometry teaching without much initial effort.

References

1. Kacmaz, G., Dubé, A.K.: Examining pedagogical approaches and types of mathematics knowledge in educational games: A meta-analysis and critical review. Educ. Res. Rev. **35**, 100428 (2022)
2. Fadda, D., Pellegrini, M., Vivanet, G., Zandonella Callegher, C.: Effects of digital games on student motivation in mathematics: a meta-analysis in K-12. J. Comput. Assist. Learn. **38**(1), 304–325 (2022)
3. Jukić Matić, L., Karavakou, M., Grizioti, M.: Is digital game-based learning possible in mathematics classrooms? A study of teachers' beliefs. Int. J. Game-Based Learn. **13**(1), 1–18 (2023)
4. Mullis, I.V.S., Martin, M.O., Loveless, T.: 20 years of TIMSS: International trends in mathematics and science achievement, curriculum, and instruction. TIMSS & PIRLS Inter-national Study Center, Lynch School of Education, Boston College and International Association for the Evaluation of Educational Achievement (IEA) (2016)
5. Pan, L., et al.: How to implement game-Based learning in a smart classroom? A model based on a systematic literature review and Delphi method. Front. Psychol. **12**, 749837 (2021)
6. Ibrahim, R., Jaafar, A.: Educational games (EG) design framework: combination of game design, pedagogy and content modeling. In: Alsurori, M., Salim, J. (eds.) 2009 International Conference on Electrical Engineering and Informatics. Selangor, Malaysia, vol. 1, pp. 293–298 (2009)
7. https://users.cs.northwestern.edu/~hunicke/MDA.pdf. Accessed 11 Aug 2023

Serious Escape Room Game for Personality Assessment

George Liapis[1]([⊠])(iD), Katerina Zacharia[2], Kejsi Rrasa[3],
and Ioannis Vlahavas[1](iD)

[1] Aristotle University of Thessaloniki, Thessaloniki, Greece
gliapisa@gapps.auth.gr
[2] Leiden University, Leiden, The Netherlands
[3] University of Padua, Padua, Italy

Abstract. Personality traits are essential parts of human behavior analysis and may be applied in scientific domains like job screening. Nowadays, organizations utilize self-assessment methodologies to evaluate people or groups to establish productive teams. Even though study has been done on questionnaires and other self-assessment techniques to profile a candidate or an employee, they are frequently mundane and repetitive. In this study, we present a serious 3D Escape Room game with the goal of analyzing behaviors based on the OCEAN Five Personality Traits model. This model encompasses an individual's behavior on five dimensions: openness, conscientiousness, extraversion, agreeableness, and neuroticism. We created corresponding rooms to monitor the player's gameplay style to develop customized models that assess personalities. These models use gameplay data generated by deep reinforcement learning agents that emulate human behavior, as a ground truth for each trait. Undergraduate and postgraduate students from Greece and Italy took part in our preliminary study and the game results are correlated with the baseline established by weighted questionnaires. The results show that there is indeed a correlation between the profiles from the questionnaires and the game.

Keywords: Personality Assessment · Serious Escape Room Game · OCEAN Five · Reinforcement Learning Agents

1 Introduction

Personality traits' importance lies in understanding a person's behaviors in both personal and professional relationships while also helping with decision-making, goal-setting, and identifying opportunities for personal improvement.

There are several models for evaluating personality however, the Five-factor Personality has gained prominence due to substantial research into it by psychologists since 1949 [6]. Openness, Conscientiousness, Extraversion, Agreeableness, and Neuroticism are abbreviated as OCEAN. Given the limitations and

P. Dondio et al. (Eds.): GALA 2023, LNCS 14475, pp. 420–425, 2024.
https://doi.org/10.1007/978-3-031-49065-1_43

drawbacks of self-reference [1], a virtual environment like a serious game, that objectively assesses behavior appears to be a new way of evaluating one's personality.

In this paper, we propose MindEscape, a serious digital Escape Room (ER) game that collects and analyzes each player's style and offers a novel, engaging, and effective approach to assessment based on the OCEAN five model. To identify the distinctive behaviors, however, a large amount of game data with a variety of player behaviors is necessary. To do this, we created Deep Reinforcement Learning agents that produce data through self-play while simulating personality characteristics from the OCEAN Five model based on the HiDAC mathematical formulas [3].

This paper's novelty and contribution are summarized as follows:

- An AI-based immersive game that assesses personality and behaviors.
- An agent-based system that emulates human behaviors in a dynamic gamified environment.
- A methodology for assessing personality through specific puzzles and events in custom-made digital escape rooms.

The structure of the paper is as follows. In section two, we discuss background-related work on topics like serious games and Reinforcement Learning (RL). Last, the system is analyzed, how the game was built and then the results are presented.

2   Background

2.1   Personality Model

An individual's personality represents their feelings, ideas, and behaviors. These characteristics are divided into positive and negative traits.

Each one of the OCEAN Five model is associated with distinct qualities and actions, although there are some commonalities as well, that govern how a person interacts with others and how he responds in certain situations. People with high Openness, for example, are open to broadening their horizons and are a valuable part of the team because they will seek to solve challenges without adopting a standard way of thinking.

These traits also have a significant impact on one's work performance efficiency, making this model an ideal option for profiling a candidate or an employee of a company.

2.2   Reinforcement Learning

Machine Learning (ML) is a subset of Artificial Intelligence (AI) that is used when computers do not need to go through a programming process but merely a training one, such as analyzing data to generate predictions or judgments. AI is the processing of human intellect by computer systems to tackle issues such as natural language processing, robots, healthcare, gaming, and so on.

RL Learning is a subfield of ML that involves teaching an agent to learn by exposing it to an unfamiliar environment. In general, by considering information from previous experiences, it balances the views of previous acts and therefore learns to pick the optimum action to maximize a reward function in a certain context. Each subsequent stage and hence all future rewards are also affected [4]. The main aspects are defined as a Markov Decision Process (MDP) described by the observation and action space, as well as the rewards.

3   Related Work

Modeling personality traits is a difficult undertaking, and earlier efforts relied on simulation and statistical approaches. The High-Density Autonomous Crowds (HiDAC) simulation system delivers individual distinctions by assigning distinctive psychological and physiological traits to each participant [3]. This study demonstrates the feasibility of modeling behavior in simulated environments or specific scenarios, and it serves as the foundation for our models.

Another example is a French website, S'cape [7], that provides a variety of games for elementary and secondary students to learn about biology, geology, arithmetic, physics, chemistry, history, geography, literature search, information, and media education, citizenship education, and foreign languages.

Furthermore, to the best of our knowledge, it is the first attempt to relate Escape Rooms and behavioral modeling. However, our previous work is related to the use of a gaming environment as a simulation for modeling behaviors. The paper [5] demonstrates how, in theory, an escape room may evaluate unique gaming data about a player's personality by employing specialized puzzles and riddles.

4   System

For the purpose of this paper, we showcase the room that assesses the Openness trait, while there are others following the same pattern for the other traits.

MindEscape is an immersive first-person game, where the player explores and interacts with the environment while being able to check information like the map, the tasks, hints, and the time, which plays a big role.

The game begins with a short narrative that introduces players to the story of each room. The player must solve three puzzles in the Openness room: finding the music sheet and playing the piano, then using the camera and finding the hidden key to unlock the bathroom door, and finally uncovering the pin code to open the exit door and escape.

Different data reflecting the player's gaming style were discovered, acquired, and reviewed for the assessment and final profile. Based on Durupinar's [3] study in HiDAC and the bibliographic research, we calculate each personality trait based on basic actions and behaviors, for example openness trait is tied with two behaviors, exploration and previous knowledge. Equations regarding the behaviors are used to calculate the personality trait variable based on the gameplay

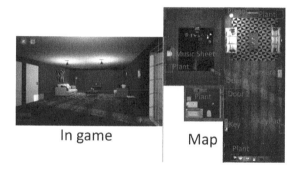

Fig. 1. Openness in-game screenshot and map with objectives

data we collected. So if the tutorial was played, there is +1 in the final Openness score, while the exploration behavior is based on the (number of actions/number of correct actions from solving the puzzles) * 10. So, at the end of each play-through, we calculate a score for the personality, based on these formulas using the collected players' data from their interactions with the room (Fig. 1).

4.1 Evaluation

To evaluate the mathematical models, we created Deep RL agents. They oper-ate and emulate specific behavioral templates, through self play to reduce the requirement for gaming data from human players. Our agents are built based on the Unity Machine Learning Agents package and trained using the Proximal Policy Optimization (PPO) algorithm.

The agent's action space included movement (forward, backward), rotation (left, right), and speed (slow, normal, fast). At the same time, the observations are made using Ray casts (function to detect a target with Boolean results). These include information regarding walls, doors, buttons, goals, decorations (e.g. table), his position, and the goals' positions. Some observations are vectors (such as locations), while others are the distance to items or the object tags.

The mathematical models, described before, are used as custom reward func-tions for the agents' actions to emulate the Openness behaviors based on their final gameplay style and they are given at the end of each episode.

Following the modeling of the Openness agent rewards, we trained it for 25 million steps in the ER environment, and the results are displayed in the Fig. 2. The training steps are mentioned on the horizontal axis, while the value of the rewards is represented on the vertical axis. We can see that the agent with the positive attribute has more consistent and high rewards.

For their assessment, behavioral baselines set by experimental results from Durupinar, are used for comparison purposes. The results of the training process show that the agents can indeed emulate human behaviors to some degree and that the mathematical models used can be employed for assessing personality through gameplay data.

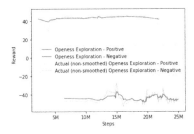

Fig. 2. Exploration results for Openness Agent.

4.2 Questionnaires and Results

We were granted permission to utilize the weighted psychometric instruments in the Greek language, the TPQue questionnaire [8] as well as the corresponding Italian Big Five Questionnaire-2 (BFQ-2) [2]. The rationale behind using different weighted/official questionnaires is to guarantee that the questions are contextually relevant and understandable to participants in each country, both linguistically and culturally.

In Greece and Italy, students were instructed to complete the corresponding questionnaires (TPQue and BFQ-2) and then play the MindEscape Openness room, with the final sample sizes being 116 and 28 respectively after some exclusions.

For a uniform analysis, the collected data were preprocessed, including normalization to 0–1, using min-max scaling, and then using SPSS to execute a bivariate correlation. The Cronbach alpha score in the TPQue questionnaire is .856, showing good internal consistency while in BFQ-2 is .643 for average consistency. According to the results, both Greece and Italy have statistically significant correlations (the p (sig) value is lower than .005) while a medium positive correlation is showcased in both countries (.323 and .462 regarding Pearson coefficient). That means that the game's results are linked to the questionnaire's findings; however, the size or the quality of our sample restricts a greater connection.

These results are very positive and promising for the mathematical models and the way the game is created since the results have a statistical correlation with two different kinds of questionnaires, from two different countries that are weighed in a different way and have varying questions.

5   Conclusion and Future Work

We introduced MindEscape, a serious game designed for personality assessment based on OCEAN five personality model. Deep Reinforcement Learning agents were used to evaluate our mathematical models. Moreover, we analyzed the results from weighed questionnaires in Greece and Italy to showcase similarities of our assessment with the established methods.

The drawbacks to this study include a small sample size, limiting the statistical power, though it is a good starting point for the proof of concept. Also, it is critical to recognize that other factors, such as past experience with escape rooms or digital games, may have impacted the outcomes. Our approach will be expanded for more personality types and rooms as well as a more varied sample size alongside more sophisticated agents.

To conclude, incorporating digital ERs into personality assessment might result in more reliable findings, thereby broadening the well-known applications of Escape Rooms in psychology.

Acknowledgements. We would like to thank Professor Tsaousis Ioannis from the Kapodistrian University for providing the TPQue questionnaire, associate Professor Panagiotis Gkorezis from the Aristotle University of Thessaloniki for assisting in data collection in Greece, and Professor Anna Spagnolli from the University of Padua for her help in data collection in Italy.

References

1. Mcdonald, J.: Measuring personality constructs: the advantages and disadvantages of self-reports, informant reports and behavioural assessments. Enquire **1** (2008). https://api.semanticscholar.org/CorpusID:13331990
2. Caprara, G.V., Barbaranelli, C., Borgogni, L., Perugini, M.: The big five questionnaire: a new questionnaire to assess the five factor model. Pers. Individ. Differ. **15**(3), 281–288 (1993). https://doi.org/10.1016/0191-8869(93)90218-R
3. Durupinar, F., Pelechano, N., Allbeck, J., Gudukbay, U., Badler, N.: How the ocean personality model affects the perception of crowds. IEEE Comput. Graphics Appl. **31**, 22–31 (2011). https://doi.org/10.1109/MCG.2009.105
4. Sutton, R.S., Barto, A.G.: Reinforcement Learning: An Introduction. Adaptive Computation and Machine Learning Series, 2nd edn. The MIT Press, Cambridge (2018)
5. Liapis, G., Zacharia, K., Rrasa, K., Liapi, A., Vlahavas, I.: Modelling core personality traits behaviours in a gamified escape room environment. In: European Conference on Games Based Learning, vol. 16, no. 11, pp. 723–731 (2022). https://doi.org/10.34190/ecgbl.16.1.602
6. McCrae, R.R., Costa Jr., P.T.: Personality trait structure as a human universal. Am. Psychol. **52**, 509–516 (1997). https://doi.org/10.1037/0003-066X.52.5.509
7. Nadam, P.: Patrice nadam (2017). https://scape.enepe.fr/_patrice-nadam_.html
8. Tsaousis, I.: The traits personality questionnaire (TPQue): a Greek measure for the five factor model. Pers. Individ. Differ. **26**(2), 271–283 (1998). https://doi.org/10.1016/S0191-8869(98)00131-7, https://www.sciencedirect.com/science/article/pii/S0191886998001317

Appling a Solution-Focused Approach (SFA) to Overcoming Barriers in Integrating Video Games into the Classroom

Elena Shliakhovchuk[1(✉)] and Miguel Chover Selles[2]

[1] The Polytechnic University of Valencia, Camino de Vera S/N, 46022 Valencia, Spain
olsh@upvnet.upv.es
[2] Jaume I University of Castellón, Vicent Sos Baynat, S/N, 12071 Castellón de La Plana, Spain

Abstract. Integration of video games in classroom instruction poses challenges for teachers, including the need for technical and financial resources, support from parents and administrators, concerns about toxic gaming culture, and uncertainty in teaching and evaluating using video games. These barriers hinder teachers' progress, diminish their motivation, and impede the transition toward game-based teaching. This article explores the valid barriers faced by teachers during video game integration into their classrooms and explores the application of the Solution-Focused Approach (SFA) instruments, namely SFA questions, as a possible means to address these barriers. The SFA questions facilitate a shift in focus from deficiencies to existing strengths and from an ineffective Problem Talk to an effective Solution Talk. Various SFA questions are provided to guide teachers toward fostering a healthier and more productive dialogue with themselves and others, allowing concentration on desired outcomes. Promising results of the SFA-based Education Professional Development Programme for Teachers are presented, and future directions are proposed to explore SFA application in this area.

Keywords: Solution-Focused Approach (SFA) · Video Games · Education Professional Development

1 Introduction

Over the last two decades, research has focused on teachers' perceptions of the use and value of video games, yielding a range of mixed findings. On the one hand, educators express a desire to serve the learning needs of today's digital learners to the best of their ability and have been experimenting with gaming environments to examine their place in the classroom for a while [1]. Only under 10% of them consider that video games have no place in schools [2]. On the other hand, studies continue to highlight valid concerns and reservations among teachers about the use of video games in the classroom [3, 4]. Addressing these concerns and providing teachers with training and support focused on game-based teaching can help them gain confidence to effectively integrate video games into their teaching practices.

P. Dondio et al. (Eds.): GALA 2023, LNCS 14475, pp. 426–431, 2024.
https://doi.org/10.1007/978-3-031-49065-1_44

1.1 Positive Attitudes Toward Video Games in the Classroom

A much-quoted survey of 1,704 teachers documented that teachers currently use games in the classroom and anticipate an increased role for them in the near future, recognizing their value in engaging and motivating students during learning [1]. Another study reported positive perceptions regarding the use of video games with educational features, with 83% of teachers expressing their intention to use these games in their future courses [2]. The Interactive Software Federation of Europe surveyed teachers in 27 different European countries and found that 80% expressed a genuine interest in learning about video games potential to make more use of them [5]. In addition, after talking to K-8 teachers in the United States, researchers reported that 74% bring video games into their classrooms at least monthly and more than half at least weekly with 71% believing that digital learning games help teach mathematics, and 42% teach science [6]. Another study involving teachers from 34 countries revealed that teachers believed that video games improve students' motivation to learn and facilitate their understanding of how concepts are applied in daily life [7]. Teachers also consider video games to promote verbal information learning, procedural learning, attitude, and e-learning [8]. Generally, video games are among four types of digital products popular among teachers, including supplementary applications or websites, free resources for educators, and Learning Management Systems [9].

1.2 Barriers to the Use of Video Games in the Classroom

As early as 2002, The British Education and Technology Agency surveyed UK teachers regarding their use of video games in the classroom and revealed challenges such as the need for extra time for game-related learning, technical issues, difficulties in measuring learning outcomes, and the presence of distracting or irrelevant content in many suitable games [4]. Similarly, the University of Michigan surveyed teachers across the United States and presented game costs, curriculum time constraints, limited technological resources, integration uncertainty, content-specific game discovery and standardized test pressures as critical barriers to video game use [3]. Consistent with the above mentioned, Korean teachers mentioned challenges in integrating games with the established curriculum, concerns regarding potential negative impacts of video games, variations in student computer literacy stemming from socioeconomic disparities, insufficient supplementary resources for incorporating video games, inflexible class timetables, and constrained budgets for hardware, software, and high-speed Internet connectivity [10]. Other barriers found by the researchers are fear of reprisal and condemnation from colleagues, social influences, including perceived social pressure to use or not use games, and general scepticism about the pedagogical value of video games [11]. Moreover, parents and caregivers of students are being critical online about using video games in the classroom [5].

In the 2020s, not much has changed. Recent findings indicate that lack of confidence, professional development and support, lack of proper equipment and time, followed by more recent concerns related to cyberbullying, hate speech, and cybersecurity continue to hinder technology adoption[3, 9, 12].

1.3 The Role of Professional Training Opportunities

Although many Ministries of Education support the use of games in education, there is a lack of adequate training for teachers and administrative support for innovation [13].

To begin with, three-quarters of pre-service teachers and the majority of in-service teachers are not being taught to use video games in the classroom [1]. Of the teachers who received these training opportunities, 48% of the teachers received less than 5 h, and only 4 out of 10 teachers considered it 'very' or 'extremely' effective [9]. Similarly, although two-thirds of educators believe adequate training is a funding priority, only 15% feel they receive adequate training and support. As a result, around 72% of teachers strive to innovate by using new educational technologies [14]. To be more specific, even after both a short and a prolonged training session on video game use, teachers maintained their scepticism toward teaching through video games [11]. Therefore, these poor results advocate for the search for new approaches to 21st-century training that would convert the favourable teachers' beliefs about video games into actual practices.

2 Solution-Focused Approach in Education

The Solution-Focused Approach (SFA) emerged in the late 1970s and early 1980s as a therapeutic approach developed by a team of therapists led by Steve de Shazer and Insoo Kim Berg at the Brief Family Therapy Centre in Milwaukee, Wisconsin. Instead of detailing the root of a problem (problem-focused approach), SFA assesses strengths and potentials and attempts to maximise and utilise them to solve problems [15].

In the decades since its inception, SFA has evolved and been applied to other fields outside of therapy, such as coaching, social work, supervision, management, and leadership, among others [16]. Research and practical experience strongly endorse the suitability of SFA in educational settings where it helps to empower students to envision desired outcomes and facilitate positive changes, while serves as a valuable tool for teachers seeking to focus on the preferred future for themselves and their students, what already works, their resources and signs of progress[17, 18].

2.1 Language of a Solution-Focused Talk

In the SFA, there is a noticeable shift in language from problem-focused to solution-focused. That is what a classical Problem Talk might look like:

"The problem is that I have neither the technical resources nor strong support to adopt video games in my teaching practice. Our educational establishment does not have a budget for the necessary hardware and software, and the Head is not really interested in including video games in the curriculum, labelling them as "harmful". Maybe I should wait for better times..."

Often, when there is a Problem Talk, the situation gets more clouded. In contrast to a Problem Talk, a Solution Talk doesn't detail the problem but encourages thinking of how the best outcome can be achieved. That is how a Solution Talk might sound:

"I'd like to have more technical resources and stronger support for the adoption of video games in our educational establishment. Let us see what is already there and what resources are available. And what else is needed? How can I build a wider support network? Which of my previous experiences of solving problems can be useful now?"

2.2 SFA Instruments to Eliminate Barriers to the Use of Video Games in the Classroom

To facilitate practical solutions to some specific barriers, SFA questions could help discover solutions in the present by picturing previous successful experiences, triggering the reflection, emphasising the impact of small, positive changes or envisioning a future without the problem. The spectrum of these questions could include:

Scaling questions help to locate where we are on the way to the desired on a scale from 1 to 10, explore what is already available and consider steps of further progress.

If I knew where to find suitable games that fit my curriculum, what is the probability that I would use them in my classroom? Mark on a scale from 0 to 10.

A Miracle and "first signs" questions suggest imagining a scenario in which the problem is miraculously solved overnight. They discuss the little signs of progress and the art of noticing.

Imagine that you have all the support from colleagues you need, how will you know they support you? What difference would it make to you? And for your students?

Questions to explore resources focus on what is going well.

What do I already know about cybersecurity?

Coping questions identify existing coping strategies and build on those strategies to overcome the barrier.

How can I co-operate with others to get access to the funding I need?

Focus on preferred future & benefits questions guide towards envisioning desired outcomes and exploring the positive impacts that those outcomes would bring.

What feedback from my students makes me confident that they learn effectively with video games?

Noticing progress questions highlight and acknowledge the progress and positive changes that individuals have made towards their desired outcomes.

What could be the first sign that parents are becoming more tolerant of video games in the classroom?

Small steps questions focus on breaking down larger goals or desired outcomes into smaller, manageable actions or changes that can be taken.

If I decide to do an experiment with teaching with video games, what could it be?

3 Tentative Results of SFA-Based Education Professional Development for Teachers

The SFA for education professionals was introduced in various professional development workshops, webinars and conferences online and offline for 2020–2022 years in Ukraine. Interested teaching and administrative staff working in different educational settings explored the basic principles and instruments of SFA and applied them to a variety of challenges they faced in their educational setting, ranging from disinterested learners to technology integration in the classroom. Written components, demonstration videos, case examples, and multiple individual and group practice exercises demonstrating how SFA instruments can be applied to a specific problem, challenge, or barriers provided teachers with sufficient knowledge and practice to try out them in their educational settings.

To assess the impact of one of the SFA professional development programme, a questionnaire was administered three weeks following the conclusion of a series of four 2-h workshops delivered to fifteen educational female professionals aged 25–55 from a medium-sized high school in Kyiv with no previous exposure to SFA interventions. 93.3% of the participants indicated that they understood the difference between Problem Talk and Solution Talk and 86.7% felt that they had acquired the skill of focusing on what is helpful after this SFA professional development programme. The participants admitted using SFA techniques to address challenges daily (26.7%), often (40%) and occasionally (33.3%). Generally, 71.4% of participants reported feeling better equipped to address challenges. Finally, the answers to the scaling question about the general usefulness of the SFA-based professional development programme, where 10 means that it was extremely useful and 1 means that it was useless, revealed that 13,3% marked 10 and 13,3% marked 9 stating that it was extremely useful, 20% marked 8 and 26,7% marked 7 demonstrating that it was very useful.

As a notable aspect, SFA places great importance on continuous support [15]. To address this, future plans include organising follow-up meetings, providing access to additional resources, and establishing mentoring opportunities for teachers who have previously attended SFA professional development workshops and seminars. This ongoing support aims to enable teachers to further enhance their knowledge and skills in SFA, as well as to overcome any new barriers that may arise. In addition, a specialised session will be offered to focus on technology integration, including video games, to provide targeted guidance in this area.

4   Conclusions

The introduction of new educational technology into the classroom can be a challenging process for teachers. The use of SFA instruments might help make this process more manageable and effective. The focus on strengths, collaboration, positive reinforcement, and continuous improvement often ensure that teachers are able to effectively incorporate games into their teaching and that all students have the opportunity to benefit from this innovative and engaging teaching approach. However, it is important to note that SFA questions may not address certain barriers and may not always work for every teacher or in every situation. Thus, it may be challenging to change established patterns and routines, individual or systemic barriers that prevent technology integration only with the use of the SFA instruments. Undoubtedly, future research with the collection of follow-up data is needed to learn more about the real effects of SFA instruments over time in this field of application.

Acknowledgements. The authors express their appreciation to the renown SFA expert Viktoria Spaschenko for sharing data, reviewing and providing feedback on the content of this article.

References

1. Ruggiero, D.: Video games in the classroom: the teacher point of view. In: Games for Learning workshop of the Foundations of Digital Games Conference (2013)

2. Can, G., Cagiltay, K.: Turkish prospective teachers' perceptions regarding the use of computer games with educational features. Educ. Technol. Soc. **9**, 1176–3647 (2006)
3. Cohen, L., Popoff, E.: 2022 State EdTech Trends Report (2022)
4. Kirriemuir, J., McFarlane A.: Use of computer and video games in the classroom. In: DiGRA 2003 - Proceedings of the 2003 DiGRA International Conference: Level Up (2003)
5. Wastiau, P., Kearney, C.: How Are Digital Games Used in Schools? (2009)
6. Takeuchi, L.M., Vaala, S.: LeveL up Learning: A National Survey on Teaching with Digital Games, New York (2014)
7. Rocha, M., Tangney, B., Dondio, P.: Play and learn: teachers' perceptions about classroom video games. In: 12th European Conference on Games Based Learning, Sophia Antipolis, France (2018)
8. Pozo, J.I., Cabellos, B., Sánchez, D.L.: Do teachers believe that video games can improve learning? Heliyon. **8**, e09798 (2022)
9. Vega, V., Robb, M.B.: The Common Sense Census: Inside The 21st-Century Classroom, San Francisco, CA (2019)
10. An, Y.-J., Haynes, L., D'Alba, A., Chumney, F.: Using educational computer games in the classroom: science teachers' experiences, attitudes, perceptions, concerns, and support needs. Contemp. Issues Technol. Teach. Educ. **16**, 415–433 (2016)
11. Gaudelli, W., Taylor, A.: Contemporary issues in technology and teacher education: CITE. Contemp. Issues Technol. Teach. Educ. **11**, 70–91 (2011)
12. Stankova, M., Tuparova, D., Tuparov, G., Mihova, P.: Barriers to the use of serious computer games in the practical work with children with educational difficulties. TEM J. **10**, 1175–1183 (2021)
13. Hébert, C., Jenson, J., Terzopoulos, T.: Access to technology is the major challenge: teacher perspectives on barriers to DGBL in K-12 classrooms. E-Learning Digi. Media **18**, 307–324 (2021)
14. The State of Technology in Education Report 2021/22 (2022)
15. De Shazer, S., Berg, I.K.: 'What works?' remarks on research aspects of solution-focused brief therapy. J. Fam. Ther. **19**, 121–124 (1997)
16. Kim, J., Jordan, S.S., Franklin, C., Froerer, A.: Is Solution-Focused Brief Therapy Evidence-Based? An Update 10 Years Later. Families Soc. **100**, 127–138 (2019)
17. Ajmal, Y., Ratner, H.: Solution focused practice in schools: 80 ideas and strategies. Routledge (2020)
18. Simmonds, S.: A critical review of teachers using solution-focused approaches supported by educational psychologists. Educ. Psychol. Res. Pract. **5**, 1–8 (2019)

BlendMaster: A Collaborative Board Game for Training Teachers in Blended Learning

Mariana Rocha[✉] and Paul Doyle

School of Computer Science, Technological University Dublin, Dublin, Ireland
`mariana.rocha@tudublin.ie`

Abstract. Blended learning (BL) combines face-to-face and computer-aided resources, promoting students' engagement and independence. However, teachers may struggle due to a lack of technological skills and pedagogical challenges. Serious games have proven to be an efficient tool for enhancing teachers' training, providing immersive and interactive learning experiences, and allowing teachers to develop classroom management strategies in a risk-free environment. We present the design and implementation of BlendMaster, a collaborative board game for training teachers in BL. The game challenges players to make decisions, addressing classroom challenges in both face-to-face and online settings. By exploring the game's mechanics, dynamics, and aesthetics, we foster reflection on BL while creating an engaging experience. Feedback from players during a training session shows BlendMaster is positively received by teachers and provides insights for further improvements and future directions for the game.

Keywords: teacher training · blended learning · board game

1 Introduction

This paper presents the design and implementation of BlendMaster, a board game that addresses teachers' training needs in blended learning (BL). Players are invited to navigate complex decision-making processes and address challenges that arise in both face-to-face and online settings. We explore possible strategies to foster reflection upon BL while attempting to create an engaging and enjoyable experience. Furthermore, we examine the feedback players provided during a training session, highlighting potential improvements and future directions for the game.

1.1 Blended Learning and the 21st-Century Education

Blended Learning can be defined as a learning process that combines face-to-face and computer-aided learning [1]. Previous research demonstrates that efficiently implementing BL techniques in the classroom can result in a constructivist learning experience, potentially increasing students' motivation [2]. A study conducted in an Australian university suggested BL can foster classroom engagement, leading students to spontaneously initiate discussions, besides offering more flexibility and interaction between

P. Dondio et al. (Eds.): GALA 2023, LNCS 14475, pp. 432–437, 2024.
https://doi.org/10.1007/978-3-031-49065-1_45

teachers and students [3]. However, the same study makes it clear there is a need for instructors to be flexible to adapt when technology fails, being able to provide a workaround solution. One of the main challenges behind blending a course is the lack of teachers' training. A systematic review of previous literature demonstrated that teachers face technological literacy and competency challenges [4], which can lead to a lack of self-confidence and avoidance of adopting BL techniques [5].

1.2 The Impact of Game-Based Learning on Teachers' Training

Previous literature suggests teachers have positive perceptions about game-based training, improving their confidence after playing [6]. Serious games offer a dynamic platform for educators to develop pedagogical skills and classroom management strategies in a risk-free environment, where trainees can replay teaching scenarios many times [7]. Pre-service teachers often struggle with limited practical experience. Games can serve as effective simulators, immersing them in scenarios requiring developing problem-solving skills and refining critical thinking abilities [8]. However, not all game designs are equally effective in facilitating teachers' learning process. Previous studies have focused on the effectiveness of serious games in business training contexts [9], often leveraging competitive mechanics inherent in many games. This approach may not be conducive to the educational environment [10]. The flexible nature of game design allows the implementation of collaborative gameplay, which would be more suitable and beneficial for teacher training. Teachers can actively participate in the learning process by emphasising collaboration and fostering a supportive and cooperative environment conducive to their professional growth.

2   The BLITT Project

The present study was carried out in the context of the BLITT (Blended Learning International Train the Trainer) project. BLITT is an initiative by organisations from five European countries designed to support educators with the necessary knowledge and skills to implement and facilitate BL classrooms [11]. The goal is to train educators to become BL champions capable of disseminating their knowledge to train and motivate other teachers. The project is developed in two phases. First, teachers access materials and courses on BL techniques to blend their courses and register the process as case-study documents. Second, teachers develop and implement their own BL training courses for other teachers. The current paper presents the design and testing of a prototype of Blend-Master, an educational game board used as part of teacher training in the first phase of the BLITT project.

3   BlendMaster Game Design

The BlendMaster is a collaborative board game where players team up to propose teaching solutions combined with technological tools to specific classroom challenges that emerge from the BLITT case studies. The goal is for teams to cooperate, make informed decisions, and progress through the game by effectively supporting other teachers to blend their classes. BlendMaster aims to enhance teachers' understanding of BL and stimulate critical thinking and problem-solving skills within a collaborative learning environment.

3.1 Components

A high-fidelity prototype was designed and implemented as an analogue board game to evaluate the potential of BlendMaster as a teacher training tool. The BlendMaster game is composed of:

- a six-sided dice
- a game board with a *Start* space (players' tokens are positioned here at the beginning of the game), a *Finish* space (when a team token reaches this space, the game is over), empty spaces (no action is expected from the player), *Blend it!* spaces (the team needs to draw a *Blend it!* card), an *Oh, no!* spaces (the player needs to draw an *Oh, no!* card)
- playing cards
- game coins
- miniatures representing each team

3.2 Mechanics

Players team up and decide who will start. The game is played on a physical board, where players move the miniatures representing each team across different spaces. At the beginning of the game, each team receives:

- 3 *Solution* cards: present possible solutions for the classroom problem faced in the game.
- 3 *Technology* cards: presents a BL technology and its definition.
- 2 *Empty* cards: players can use blank cards to suggest solutions or technologies not found in their *Solution* and *Technology* cards.
- 8 coins that can be used to buy new cards

Figure 1 shows the different cards present in the BlendMaster game.

Once the game begins, miniatures representing each team are positioned in the *Start* game board space. The first team rolls the dice and moves the miniature according to the result. If they land on an empty space, their turn is over, and the next team rolls the dice. If they land on a *Blend it!* space, they need to draw a *Blend it!* card that contains a short statement describing a situation faced by one of the personas created based on the BLITT real-life case studies. Once the playing team draws a *Blend it!* card, they read it out loud and take some time to discuss among the team members which of the three *Solution* cards in their deck could be used to solve that case and move the miniature one space forward. If they combine the chosen *Solution* card with a *Technology* card, they can move two spaces forward. They can also use their blank cards to create other solutions or technologies. After selecting the cards and elaborating on the strategy to solve the challenge, the team shares their idea with the other teams. However, this is not enough to move forward on the board as the other teams now have two choices: to accept the strategy proposed by the playing team or to suggest another solution based on their

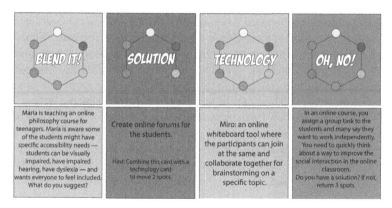

Fig. 1. Examples of the *Blend it*, Solution, *Technology*, and *Oh, no!* cards.

own deck of cards. If all teams agree that another team provided a better solution than the playing team, this other team takes the turn and rolls the dice. The playing team will not progress on the board.

Teams can also land on the *Oh, no!* spaces, where players must draw a card that describes teaching situations where a problem arises during the blending process. For example, it could describe an instructor teaching online and receiving an email from a student complaining about the lack of social interaction and saying they want to leave the course. Differently from the *Blend it!* card, teams must provide a solution to the *Oh, no!* cards, and the other teams must agree that it is suitable. In this case, the other teams cannot suggest a solution. If the playing team does not provide a suitable solution, they must return three spaces on the board. For both *Blend it!* and *Oh, no!* cards, players are allowed to use the coins they received at the beginning of the game to buy new cards in case they are unhappy with the ones they got. Each team should always have at least a deck of eight cards for every turn (three *Solution* cards, three *Technology* cards, and two blank cards). Rolling the dice in turns, drawing cards and proposing solutions continues until one team reaches the *Finish* space, winning the BlendMaster game.

3.3 Implementation

In the Spring of 2023, a gameplay test of the BlendMaster took place during the BLITT training week. 22 teachers attended the event and played the game in teams of five or six players. The participants came had a wide range of experience and came from various backgrounds: some teachers worked with primary and secondary school students, others with university students, and others on adult learning. The game board was placed in the centre of the room, and the teams were distributed around the board. A team representative approached the board to roll the dice and draw the cards. After the gameplay, an online survey was distributed and responded by 19 participants. The survey had two open questions: "Did the board game (BlendMaster) help you to reflect upon the challenges of blended learning?" and "Do you have suggestions to improve it?" The feedback was highly positive, and participants stated the game was an excellent tool for brainstorming and identifying unresolved issues related to BL. Participants proposed incorporating a faster version of the game focused solely on the cards, removing the board and implementing a timer, allowing for a more time-efficient gameplay experience. Some players suggested an app-based system where teams could anonymously propose solutions to the blending challenges, enabling virtual voting for the best solutions. One participant noted that certain solutions proposed in the game might not be applicable or preferred depending on the context. This concern was expected, considering the project includes educators from five countries. Participants expressed a desire for the game to be adaptable to educational contexts besides BL, such as vocational education and training. Regarding logistics, participants suggested creating more copies of the game to accommodate larger groups and allowing groups to keep written records if necessary. They also mentioned the importance of increasing engagement and involvement from the outset, possibly by modifying the game to be less teacher-controlled. Overall, the feedback highlighted the effectiveness and value of the BlendMaster board game in facilitating reflection on BL challenges. The suggestions provided valuable insights for improving the game, including enhancing its dynamics, adapting to different cultural contexts, and ensuring flexibility for various educational settings.

4   Conclusion and Future Work

BlendMaster encourages critical thinking and fosters engagement by providing a platform for teams to debate possible solutions from different perspectives. The competitive element, wherein teams can propose their solutions during their opponent's turn, motivates continuous reflection and discussion even when it is not their team's turn. The availability of multiple copies of the game is crucial to effectively disseminate the game and enable widespread implementation in teacher training. This ensures that all teachers can actively participate in the game-based learning experience. Concerning the game mechanics, implementing coins as an award for progressing in the game is considered for future iterations. To address this issue, future work should explore the possibility of launching a digital version of the game as a second-screen experience could be considered, leveraging technology to overcome logistical limitations and enabling a more scalable and accessible implementation in various training contexts. The digital version could also allow the trainer to input personalised challenges, solutions and technology cards, adapting the game to different contexts.

References

1. Lalima, D., Lata Dangwal, K.: Blended learning: an innovative approach. Univers. J. Educ. Res. **5**, 129–136 (2017). https://doi.org/10.13189/ujer.2017.050116
2. Zhang, R.: Exploring blended learning experiences through the community of inquiry framework. Lang. Learn. Technol. **24**, 38–53 (2020). http://hdl.handle.net/10125/44707
3. McKenzie, S., Hains-Wesson, R., Bangay, S., Bowtell, G.: A team-teaching approach for blended learning: an experiment. Stud. High. Educ. **47**, 860–874 (2022). https://doi.org/10.1080/03075079.2020.1817887
4. Ashraf, M.A., et al.: A systematic review of systematic reviews on blended learning: trends, gaps and future directions. Psychol. Res. Behav. Manag. **14**, 1525–1541 (2021). https://doi.org/10.2147/PRBM.S331741

5. Philipsen, B., Tondeur, J., Pareja Roblin, N., Vanslambrouck, S., Zhu, C.: Improving teacher professional development for online and blended learning: a systematic meta-aggregative review. Educ. Technol. Res. Dev. **67**(5), 1145–1174 (2019). https://doi.org/10.1007/s11423-019-09645-8

6. Ragni, B., Toto, G.A., di Furia, M., Lavanga, A., Limone, P.: The use of digital game-based learning (DGBL) in teachers' training: a scoping review. Front. Educ. **8** (2023). https://doi.org/10.3389/feduc.2023.1092022

7. Connolly, T., Tsvetkova, N., Hristova, P.: Gamifying teacher training: simulated practice learning for future and practising teachers interacting with vulnerable learners. In: Bradley, E. (ed.) Games and Simulations in Teacher Education, pp. 55–73 (2020). https://doi.org/10.1007/978-3-030-44526-3_13

8. Hixon, E., So, H., Hixon, E., So, H.: International forum of educational technology & society technology's role in field experiences for preservice teacher training published by: international forum of educational technology & society linked references are available on JSTOR for this artic. J. Educ. Technol. Soc. **12**, 294–304 (2009)

9. Mayer, I., van Dierendonck, D., van Ruijven, T., Wenzler, I.: Stealth assessment of teams in a digital game environment. In: De Gloria, A. (ed.) GALA 2013. LNCS, vol. 8605, pp. 224–235. Springer, Cham (2014). https://doi.org/10.1007/978-3-319-12157-4_18

10. Pozzi, F., Persico, D., Collazos, C., Dagnino, F.M., Munoz, J.L.J.: Gamifying teacher professional development: an experience with collaborative learning design. Interact. Des. Archit. **29**, 76–92 (2016). https://doi.org/10.55612/s-5002-029-004

11. Gordon, D., Doyle, P., Becevel, A., Baloh, T.: All things merge into one, and a river runs through it: exploring the dimensions of blended learning by developing a case study template for blended activities. Int. J. e-Learning Secur. **11**, 648–656 (2022). https://doi.org/10.20533/ijels.2046.4568.2022.0081

Oral Examinations Simulator – An Intelligent Tutoring Tool to Reduce Oral Exam Anxiety

Sören Aguirre Reid[1]([⊠]), Richard Lackes[2], Markus Siepermann[1], Georg Vetter[2], and Wladimir Wenner[2]

[1] Technische Hochschule Mittelhessen, 35390 Gießen, Germany
soeren.aguirre.reid@mni.thm.de
[2] Technische Universität Dortmund, 44221 Dortmund, Germany

Abstract. Exam anxiety is a wide spread phenomenon. Although a learner is knowledgeable and well prepared, s/he often fails in examinations due to severe panickiness. In particular oral examinations can be problematic as the testee is directly exposed to the examinant, answers are immediately evaluated, form a picture of the testee's knowledge and cannot be revised later on. This paper presents the concept and realisation of an online game that prepares learners for the situation of an oral examination. The game simulates the specific situation of an oral examination where questions of the examinant refer to the answers of the testee and try to find out what the testee's real knowledge is.

Keywords: Oral Exam Training · Exam Anxiety · Intelligent Tutoring Tool

1 Introduction

Exams are an integral part of every study program, but they often trigger nervousness and tension among students, known as exam anxiety. Generally, exam anxiety can be divided into two fundamental components: cognitive, characterized by self-doubt in problem-solving and test-taking abilities, and physiological, leading to physical symptoms such as nervousness, sweaty palms, and an increased heart rate [1, 2]. From a medical point of view, exam anxiety of affected students does not correspond to the conditions of the exam or exam preparation and is, therefore, clinically relevant [3]. Especially when exam anxiety leads to more severe life problems and obstruct students from showing their testing abilities and knowledge in examinations [4] as well as from finishing their studies [5]. In addition to impairments, exam anxiety can cause mental stress, leading to cognitive impairment, cardiovascular disease, hypertension, and depression [6]. In a recent survey, it was found that 53% of students reported experiencing exam anxiety. This marks a significant increase of 60% compared to 2006 [7]. Hence, students who suffer from exam anxiety need support to fight this severe problem.

Many universities now offer counseling services, which are crucial. However, counseling alone is just one aspect of support and should be complemented with additional services [3, 7]. Another approach is incorporating games or game-based learning [8]. Studies have demonstrated that integrating games into education can substantially decrease

P. Dondio et al. (Eds.): GALA 2023, LNCS 14475, pp. 438–443, 2024.
https://doi.org/10.1007/978-3-031-49065-1_46

exam anxiety and reduce dropout rates among students facing psychological challenges [9, 10].

Hence, this paper introduces a Game-Based Intelligent Tutoring Tool (GBITT) to prepare students for examinations puts students in the role of a testee. This allows students to experience the exam situation in advance, potentially averting severe consequences. The focus is on oral examinations, which can worsen the exam situation due to immediate question response, contrasting with written exams where questions can read several times and answers changed. In oral exams it is rather unusual that a question is repeated several times. Moreover, in oral examinations the testee has to answer a question immediately which instantaneously forms the examinant's impression of the testee's knowledge and abilities and directly influences the final mark. Hence, the GBITT aims to reduce exam anxiety by exposing the testee to oral examination scenarios, helping them become adept at handling oral questions [23].

With regard to the related literature, this paper significantly contributes to several streams of literature on game-based learning and exam anxiety reduction. Firstly, it contributes to the research on designing serious games incorporating an intelligent tutoring tool (ITT) to enhance learning performance. The ITT in this study is designed to provide personalized learning support by continuously assessing the learner's performance during the game and adjusting the content or difficulty accordingly [11]. It simulates the situation of an oral examination where the examinant is responsive to the answers of a testee, builds the questions on each other, and digs deeper into topics depending on the answers of the testee. To achieve this goal, the ITT automatically correct testee's submissions based on a provided reference solution by the teacher. This concept aligns with the idea of "stealth assessment," where the learner's skills and knowledge are assessed discreetly, and the content is adapted accordingly [12]. In our study the ITT is embedded in a game which simulates an oral examination. By altering the difficulty, the game aims to provide challenging content, which enhances the acquisition of knowledge and skills [13]. Typically tests have a pre-defined static structure. In our oral examination game, we present the learner questions depending on his previous answers. This approach promotes engagement by tailoring the content to the learner's needs and aligns with the flow theory, where learners are motivated by challenges that fall within their individual flow area [14]. Former research has focused on utilizing ITT to enhance students' learning performance [11, 15–18], with limited attention given to its application for mitigating exam anxiety. Therefore, this paper builds upon existing literature on ITT, emphasizing the importance of adaptive e-learning and personalized support to enhance learning outcomes [19–21].

Secondly, this paper contributes to the literature on exam anxiety reduction through games. It explores the use of a game simulation of an oral examination to reduce exam anxiety, drawing on the idea that repeated exposure to a simulated exam situation can alleviate anxiety [22]. While there is limited existing literature on this topic, some studies have shown that game-based assessments can significantly reduce test anxiety [8–10, 23]. However, these previous studies did not specifically address oral exam situations or incorporate an ITT into the simulation. The unique approach presented here aims to create a more realistic exam environment where examiners can adjust question difficulty and provide guidance, mirroring the dynamics of real oral exams.

The remainder of this paper is organised as follows. The next section explains the underlying concept of the GBITT in more detail while the third section shows the implementation of the system. The paper closes with a conclusion and future prospects.

2 Oral Examination Simulator (OES)

2.1 Examination Concept

Oral exams differ markedly from written ones. In addition to the more personal interaction between the testee and the examiner, the key distinction is the examiner's ability to dynamically respond to the testee's answers, general knowledge, and specific abilities. Unlike written exams with fixed, standardized assignments for all testee's, oral exams feature adaptable tasks tailored by the examiner to the testee's current performance. This adaption mostly concerns two points:

1. The last answer of the testee and
2. The testee's level of knowledge exhibited during the examination.

For correct answers, the examiner has two options and can either proceed to the next topic or ask a more specific question to assess knowledge further. With incorrect answers, the examiner has three options: s/he can provide a hint and rephrase the question, or ask further based on the wrong answer. If the examinant has already asked several questions in and can assess the testee's ability and knowledge, s/he proceeds to the next topic.

New topics are introduced with an initial difficulty level, which can be low to middle for a smooth start or adjusted based on the testee's demonstrated knowledge. Proficient testee's face more challenging questions, while weaker ones receive easier one. Thus, the difficulty level and assessment will continuously settle down so that the final grade can be determined. The Oral Examination Simulator (OES) is designed to emulate oral examination characteristics, incorporating assessment tools from previous literature [8–10] such as multiple-choice, fill-in-the-blank, and any other types as long as the graded from 0 to 100%. This simulator operates based on the following overarching concept. Each exercise is related to at least one topic and has a difficulty level. Except for true-false exercises, testee responses are not binary but instead graded incrementally from 0% to 100%. All responses and their correctness are recorded to calculate the final grade. Exercises can be linked in different ways, with subsequent exercises associated with distinct answer options when feasible. If no follow-up exercise is triggered, the exam continues with a randomly selected exercise matching the testee's chosen difficulty level and their current grade level. If the current grade is low, exercises of a maximum matching difficulty level are chosen; otherwise, more challenging exercises are considered to enhance the testee's final grade.

To illustrate exercise linking, consider the following example: Let exercise E1 have options EA and EB as wrong and EC and ED as correct answers which are not interchangeable but must be given both to obtain the maximum grade for the exercise. Then, combinatorially, 16 different cases can be distinguished. To simplify this process, we differentiate between correct and incorrect options: 1. EA **and** EB are chosen; 2. EA **or** EB is chosen; 3. EC **and** ED are chosen; 4. EC **or** ED is chosen. If the testee gives two wrong answers with option 1 or 2, subsequent exercises can dig deeper into the problem to find out what the testee misunderstood or to what extent his knowledge is limited. In case, the testee answered the question correctly (option 3), a subsequent, specialised exercise can be linked to that case. If the testee gives only one correct answer (option 4), a subsequent exercise can be linked to that case, giving either a hint or asking more precisely. If the testee answers cannot be distinguished and there is only the level of correctness known, subsequent exercises are based on different correctness bands: 90–100% triggers specialized questions, 70–90% requires no further exercises, 50–70% prompts additional knowledge-based questions, and 0–50% leads to straightforward comprehension questions, helping to limit the degradation of his grade level.

In the beginning, testee's can choose how difficult the exam they want to simulate should be select, and subsequent questions adapt based on their selection and answers given, considering exercise difficulty weights. For each exercise, the scale of correctness of the testee's answer is recorded so that two different grade levels can be calculated: the overall grade and a temporary one for recent exercises, influencing the choice of the next exercise to either challenge or support the testee's performance.

2.2 Game Concept

The OES, a web-based e-learning system, simulates oral examinations, providing teachers with a tool to create exam simulations that enhance learning and mitigate exam anxiety. Teachers can compose questions, offer reference solutions and hints, and select avatars for the simulation. Integrating audio output, the OES addresses the challenge of exam anxiety impairing concentration, allowing students to familiarize themselves with and manage this stress aspect [1, 2]. Students assume the role of a testee in the simulation, engaging with various question types (e.g., quizzes, text questions), and subsequent questions are tailored based on their answers, promoting motivation through challenges [3]. Testee's are also informed about difficulty levels and remaining examination time.

Fig. 1. Screenshot of the testee interface (left) and sequence of questions structured as a tree (right)

Teachers can employ the system in two ways: 1) by creating questions within it or 2) by linking external learning systems. When creating content within the OES, teachers design questions for different topics and difficulty levels.

They then establish a question sequence using a tree structure, illustrated in Fig. 1, where subsequent questions and levels are determined by the testee's answers. Correctness levels are indicated on the edges of the tree (e.g., 100% = correct), and if a wrong answer is given, the system provides hints and repeats the question, allowing for further exploration if one or two incorrect answers are provided.

If a teacher wants to link external exercises to the OES, every node of this tree is replaced by an external exercise. The OES tracks the level of correctness of the learner and reports it to the external system as long as they reflect a percentage value for evaluating the testee's answer.

2.3 Evaluation

The evaluation comprises multiple components. Firstly, we assess grade differences between two student groups: those who prepared for the oral exam without ITT and those who used it. Secondly, we use the State-Trait Anxiety Inventory scale in two surveys to measure its impact on reducing exam anxiety [10, 24], before and after the actual exam e.g., [10, 11].

3   Conclusion

This paper presents a fully implemented game-based learning system, simulating oral exams to reduce learner exam anxiety. Learners engage as testee's, responding to sequenced questions from an examiner. Utilizing audio output for added realism [1, 2] and drawing on prior research [8–10] for diverse question types, audio, and avatars. The GBITT approach from previous studies by providing personalized support for learners in their learning and exam preparation [8], offering a range of diverse exercise types. Future enhancements will provide exam preparation guidance, easy and fast contact to counselling offers of the related university [3, 7] and incorporate more game-based elements like a rewards system or leaderboard.

References

1. McDonald, A.S.: The prevalence and effects of test anxiety in school children. Educ. Psychol. **21**(1), 89–101 (2001)
2. Stefan, A., Berchtold, CM., Angstwurm, M.: Translation of a scale measuring cognitive test anxiety (G-CTAS) and its psychometric examination among medical students in Germany. GMS J. Med. Educ. **37**(5) (2020)
3. Sommer, K., Odenwald, M., Fehm, L.: Stabilität und Prädiktion von Prüfungsangst bei Studierenden Ergebnisse einer Längsschnitterhebung mit Erstsemestern. Z. Klin. Psychol. Psychother. **51**(2), 87–95 (2022)
4. Seipp, B.: Anxiety and academic performance: a meta-analysis of findings. Anxiety Res. **4**(1), 27–41 (1991)
5. Falkai, P., et al.: Diagnostisches und Statistisches Manual Psychischer Störungen DSM-5. APA (2007)
6. Castaldo, R., Xu, W., Melillo, P., Pecchia, L., Santamaria, L., James, C.: Detection of mental stress due to oral academic examination via ultra-short-term HRV analysis. Annu. Int. Conf. IEEE Eng. Med. Biol. Soc. (2016)
7. Deutsches Studierendenwerk. https://www.forschung-und-lehre.de/lehre/studierende-haben-hohen-beratungsbedarf-wegen-pruefungsangst-1617. Accessed 29 June 2022

8. Hung, C.M., Huang, I., Hwang, G.J.: Effects of digital game-based learning on students' self-efficacy, motivation, anxiety, and achievements in learning mathematics. J. Comput. Educ. **1**, 151–166 (2014)

9. Mavridis, A., Tsiatsos, T.: Game-based assessment - investigating the impact on test anxiety and exam performance. J. Comput. Assist. Learn. **33**, 137–150 (2017)

10. Smits, J., Charlier, N.: Game-based assessment and the effect on test anxiety - a case study. In: European Conference in Game Based Learning, pp. 562-XVIII (2011)

11. Hwang, G., Sung, H., Hung, C., Iwen H., Chin-Chung, T.: Development of a personalized educational computer game based on students' learning styles. In: 4th Educational Technology Research and Development, pp. 623–638 (2012)

12. Shute, V.J.: Stealth assessment in computer-based games to support learning. Comput. Games Instruct. **55**(2), 503–524 (2011)

13. Qian, M., Clark, R.: Game-based learning and 21st century skills - a review on recent research. Comput. Hum. Behav. **62**, 50–58 (2016)

14. Csikszentmihalyi, M.: Flow - The Psychology of Optimal Experience, 1st edn. Harper Perennial, New York (1990)

15. Wang, Y.H., Liao, H.C.: Adaptive learning for ESL based on computation. Br. J. Edu. Technol. **42**(1), 66–87 (2011)

16. Moreno-Ger, P., Burgos, D., Sierra, J., Manjón, B.: A game-based adaptive unit of learning with IMS learning design and <e-Adventure>. EC-TEL **4753**, 247–261 (2007)

17. Shute, V., Hansen, E., b Almond, R.: You can't fatten a hog by weighing it – or can you? - Evaluating an assessment for learning system called ACED. IJAIED **18**(4), 289–316 (2008)

18. Shute, V.J., Glaser, R.: Large-scale evaluation of an intelligent tutoring system - Smithtown. Interact. Learn. Environ. **1**, 51–76 (1990)

19. Shute, V.J., Towle, B.: Adaptive e-learning. Educ. Psychol. **38**(2), 105–114 (2003)

20. Brusilovsky, P.: The intelligent tutor, environment and manual for introductory programming. Educ. Technol. Train. Int. **29**(1), 26–34 (1992)

21. Siepermann, M.: Lecture accompanying e-learning exercises with automatic marking. In: Richards, G. (eds) Proceedings of E-Learn 2005, pp. 1750–1755 (2005)

22. Gee, J.P.: What video games have to teach us about learning and implications for opportunity to learn. In: Assessment, Equity, and Opportunity to Learn, pp. 200–221. Cambridge University Press, New York (2007)

23. Reitz, L., Sohny, A., Lochmann, G.: VR-based gamification of communication training and oral examination in a second language. Int. J. Game-Based Learn. **6**(2), 46–61 (2016)

24. Spielberger, C.D.: State-trait anxiety inventory for adults. PsycTESTS Dataset (1983)

The Digital Serious Games, a Specific Educational Resource: Analysing Teachers and Educational Engineer's Information Seeking Behaviour Using the Concept of Information Horizons

Mamoudou Ndiaye$^{(\boxtimes)}$ ⓘ, Fabrice Pirolli ⓘ, and Raphaëlle Crétin-Pirolli

Le Mans Université, Le Mans, France
{mamoudou.ndiaye,fabrice.pirolli,
raphaelle.pirolli}@univ-lemans.fr

Abstract. We present the first study that analyses and understands the information seeking behaviour of teachers and pedagogical engineers in the context of Serious Games. Although digital serious games are increasingly recognized as valuable educational resources, research into teachers and pedagogical engineers' information-seeking behaviour and needs in this area remains sparse. To fill this gap, we engaged with 31 teachers to examine how they find, use and orchestrate digital serious games for their everyday classrooms. We conducted two workshops with the participants and used an elicitation toolkit to gather: teachers information sources, needs and challenges.

Keywords: Serious Games · Information behaviour · Information literacy

1 Introduction

In today's rapidly evolving digital landscape, the utilization of digital Serious Games (SG) as educational resources is gaining considerable attention. These games, designed with an intention to combine entertainment with learning, offer unique opportunities for engaging students and facilitating the acquisition of complex concepts. Yet, for these digital resources to be effectively found and integrated into the educational process, understanding the information seeking behaviour of educators and educational engineers is crucial. This study examines the information seeking behaviour of teachers and educational engineers who use or intend to use digital serious games in their pedagogical practices or contribute to their use. *Information seeking behaviour refers to the actions an individual might take to source, access, and utilize information to fulfil a certain need* [1]. This behaviour forms a significant part of the overall process of incorporating new educational resources, such as digital SG, into teaching and learning contexts. The present research employs the concept of *Information Horizons*, a theoretical framework developed by Diane Sonenwald [2] and Reijo Savolainen [3]. This concept allows us to

P. Dondio et al. (Eds.): GALA 2023, LNCS 14475, pp. 444–450, 2024.
https://doi.org/10.1007/978-3-031-49065-1_47

map out the varied sources of information that individuals draw upon, offering insights into their information seeking behaviour. Through this lens, we investigate the distribution and significance of different information sources for our target group, yielding a comprehensive understanding of how these teachers and educational engineers navigate through the information environments. The results of this study not only contribute to our theoretical understanding of information seeking behaviour in the context of digital Serious Games but also hold practical implications for the design and development of these educational resources. In the following sections, we outline the literature grounding our study, describe our methodology, present our findings, and discuss their implications in both theoretical and practical terms.

2   Literature review

2.1   Digital Serious Games as Educational Resources

Over the past decade, digital SG have emerged as particularly impactful educational tools. Unlike traditional video games, SG are designed with the primary purpose of learning or training, rather than entertainment [4, 5]. Numerous studies have demonstrated the potential of serious games to facilitate learning outcomes, promote learner engagement, and support the acquisition of complex skills [7]. Although digital Serious Games show promise in education, their effective integration requires educators to navigate a complex information landscape. This includes locating suitable games, understanding their pedagogical implications, and keeping abreast of latest developments in the field. Therefore, the information seeking behaviours of teachers and pedagogical engineers becomes a key area of investigation.

2.2   Information Seeking Behaviour

Information seeking behaviour refers to the various practices, habits, and skills individuals deploy in finding, utilizing, and managing information. Notable studies in information sciences have examined online information search strategies and skills. Additionally, several studies have highlighted the importance of metacognition and information comprehension in improving the efficiency of information search.

In this study, we adopt Chaudiron and Ihadjadene's perspective of information behaviours, referring to how various *"tools, formal or informal, and cognitive skills are mobilized by individuals or groups in different situations of information production, research, organization, processing, usage, sharing, and communication information"* [8].

2.3   Information Horizon Methodology

Diane Sonnenwald introduced the "information horizon" concept in Information and Communication Sciences [2], emphasizing its shaping by decisions, search processes, preferences, and situational impacts. It encompasses human, digital, printed, and organizational resources. Through semi-structured interviews, Sonnenwald discovered 13 primary information resources, highlighting the internet, teachers, and friends as primary choices. Raijo Savolainen [9] expanded on this, linking information horizons to socio-phenomenology, stressing the importance of social interactions, cultural norms, and history. Savolainen visualized the horizon through relevance-based positioning of information resources. Isto Huvila perceived information horizons as community constructions tied to professions [10], while Tsai [11] explored the influence of perception and source quality on Taiwanese students. Greyson [12] developed "Information World Mapping" based on Sonnenwald's concept, allowing participants to craft personal social information maps. Joanne du Hommet [13] applied Savolainen's approach to examine Ubisoft employees' information horizons, pinpointing motivations and factors influencing their resource choices.

2.4 Information Horizon in the Context of Digital Serious Games

Despite the growing recognition of digital serious games as valuable educational resources, there is a scarcity of research exploring teacher's information seeking behaviour concerning these resources. The present study seeks to fill this gap by investigating the Information Horizons of teachers and educational engineers who incorporate digital serious games into their pedagogical practices.

3   Method

The data for this study was gathered from a workshop focusing on teachers' information horizons within the context of Serious Games. Participants were invited to identify and categorize their varying information sources related to SGs.

Participants jotted down their information sources on post-it notes, categorising them into five key groups: people, books/journals, websites, organizations/institutions, and other sources. These sources were then arranged into three concentric circles representing different information zones. *Zone 1* housed **primary sources**, *Zone 2* included **intermediate sources**, and *Zone 3* contained **peripheral sources** as illustrated in Fig. 1 above. Afterwards, participants discussed their specific information needs concerning Serious Games. To conclude the exercise, a group discussion took place where participants deliberated over their chosen information sources and elucidated the reasons underpinning their preferences.

3.1 Participants

The workshop comprised 31 participants who registered through WeezEvent, an event management platform. These participants were a mix of secondary and higher education teachers, as well as instructional engineers with prior familiarity with Serious Games. The workshop sessions, each lasting 1.5 h, were conducted as part of "EdTech day" an event dedicated to research projects involving digital tools for learning hosted at Computer Science Laboratory (LIUM) of Le Mans Université in France.

3.2 Data Collection and Analysis

Participants were asked to imagine a situation in which they are searching for a Serious Game to use in class or suggest to teachers. They were then tasked with identifying all the potential sources they would consult, and to position them within the three concentric circles based on their relevance. In addition, participants were asked to express their informational needs related to Serious Games.

For data analysis, we first organized the collected data by participant in an Excel spreadsheet according to the different categories. Subsequently, we analysed the data in accordance with Savolainen's categories by assigning scores to the different Zones.

4 Information Sources in the Context of Serious Games

The analysis of the data reveals that people and online resources are considered the most important sources of information, with average score of 2.48 and 2.19 respectively. This suggests that participants place great importance on personal interactions and networks, as well as online resources such as websites and databases.

4.1 Information Zones Composition

Zone 1 - Primary Sources. Human interactions and online resources were dominant, both making up 34.23% of the total. Organizational sources made up 12.61%, books and journals 10.81%, and other miscellaneous sources 8.11%.

Zone 2 - Intermediate Sources. Online resources remained top at 38.60%, followed by organizations at 18.42% and books and journals at 17.54%. Human sources decreased to 14.91%, with other sources at 10.53%.

Zone 3 - Peripheral Sources. Online resources led at 30.65%. Organizations rose to 25.81%, while books and journals accounted for 20.97%. Human sources further declined to 12.90%, and other sources made up 9.68%.

4.2 Cross analysis of Information Zones

In line with Savolainen's study, we assigned a score to each information Zone to determine the relevance of one zone over another. Zone $1 = 3$, Zone $2 = 2$, Zone $3 = 1$. The average score represents the relative importance of each source. The total score represents the product of the average score of each category of information sources. The "Total sources" represents the total number of sources for each category of information sources. For instance, Human sources: Total score of human sources: $(38 \times 3) + (17 \times 2) + (8 \times 1) = 156$ Average score of people sources: $156/63 = 2.48$.

Human sources are predominantly consulted in Zone 1 (34.23%) compared to Zones 2 (14.91%) and 3 (12.90%), signifying a preference for personal interactions. Although journals and books are less frequent in Zone 1 (10.81%) than in Zones 2 (17.54%) and 3 (20.97%), suggesting a potential underutilization of academic resources. Online resources remain dominant in all zones, peaking in Zone 2 (38.60%). Institutions and organizations see increased consultation from Zone 1 (12.61%) to Zone 3 (25.81%), indicating a possible lack of awareness about their relevance. Other sources remain relatively consistent across zones. Overall, educators mainly rely on human interactions for SG related information, with diverse sources surfacing in Zones 2 and 3 (Table 1).

Table 1. Type of sources according to Savolainen.

Type of sources according to Savolainen	Average score	Total score	Total sources	Zone 1	Zone 2	Zone 3	%
Human sources	2,48	156	63	38	17	8	22%
Printed sources	1,98	91	46	12	21	13	16%
Websites – Online resources	2,19	221	101	38	44	19	35%
Organisational sources	1,96	100	51	14	21	16	18%
Other sources	2,11	57	27	9	12	6	9%
Total			288	111	115	62	100%

Of the 288 sources mentioned by participants, Zone 1 had 111 sources, Zone 2 had 115, and Zone 3 had 62. "Human sources" scored the highest average (2.48), emphasizing the value participants place on personal interactions. Online resources, while having the highest total score (221), signify their extensive use. Journals and books scored an average of 1.98, making them less favored than human sources and online resources. Organizations and institutions averaged 1.96, suggesting a potential lack of awareness about their significance in the SG field. The "Other sources" category had an average score of 2.11, although its total score (57) and number (27) were low, indicating infrequent use. In summary, human sources and online resources are viewed as vital, while organizations/institutions are deemed least significant.

5   Teachers and Pedagogical Engineer's Information Needs

The participants, comprising teachers and pedagogical engineers, articulated various information needs in relation to Serious Games. A common desire was for a specialized search engine dedicated to Serious Games, with advanced filtering by discipline, learner level, and pedagogical objectives. They also expressed a considerable demand for professional development opportunities, such as workshops and training on the use of Serious Games, as well as platforms for exchanging practices. In addition, participants emphasized their interest in shared resources and experiences, including the use of serious games by colleagues, feedback, and modifiable resources like informational videos. They advocated for comprehensive directories and catalogues of Serious Games and shared resources, facilitating contact with game creators and finding relevant teaching resources. Finally, a prevalent need for broader access to specialized online information underscored the importance of comprehensive, accessible digital resources on serious games.

6   Discussion

The study underscores educators' evolving information horizons regarding serious games, revealing a preference for Human and online sources. A significant reliance on "Human sources", especially in Zone 1, highlights the value of interpersonal networks in Serious Games, offering context-rich, tailored information. However, this might also hint at a lack of awareness of formal sources. The popularity of online resources signals a shift towards digital learning tools, suggesting a demand for dependable online databases on serious games. Conversely, the underutilization of books, journals, and institutional resources points to potential unawareness of their benefits. The "Other sources" category, while rarely used, had notable weight, hinting at untapped niche sources. The study's limitations include potential biases from self-reported data and a limited participant scope, suggesting a need for broader research.

In conclusion, findings reveal opportunities for better resource distribution and the promotion of underused sources. Enhancing collaboration between teachers, game designers, and institutions could deepen understanding of serious games' educational aspects. To further understand these findings, we'll conduct semi-structured interviews with participants, enabling a deeper exploration of themes and more effective addressal of unmet needs.

References

1. Case, D.O., Given, L.M. (eds.): Information Needs, Motivations, and Use. Studies in Information, pp. 79–96. Emerald Group Publishing Limited (2016)
2. Sonnenwald, D.H., Wildemuth, B.M., Harmon, G.L.: A research method to investigate information seeking using the concept of information horizons: an example from a study of lower socio-economic students' information seeking behavior, **22** (2001)
3. Savolainen, R., Kari, J.: Placing the internet in information source horizons. a study of information seeking by internet users in the context of self-development. Libr. Inf. Sci. Res. **26**, 415–433 (2004). https://doi.org/10.1016/j.lisr.2004.04.004
4. Abt, C.C.: Serious Games. University Press of America (1987)
5. Michael, D., Chen, S.: Serious Games: Games That Educate, Train, and Inform. (2006)
6. Zhonggen, Y.: A meta-analysis of use of serious games in education over a decade. Int. J. Comput. Games Technol. **2019**, e4797032 (2019)
7. Ypsilanti, A., Vivas, A.B., Räisänen, T., Viitala, M., Ijäs, T., Ropes, D.: Are serious video games something more than a game? A review on the effectiveness of serious games to facilitate intergenerational learning. Educ. Inf. Technol. **19**, 515–529 (2014). https://doi.org/10.1007/s10639-014-9325-9
8. Chaudiron, S., Ihadjadene, M.: De la recherche de l'information aux pratiques informationnelles. Études de communication. langages, information, médiations. 13–30 (2010)
9. Savolainen, R.: Information source horizons and source preferences of environmental activists: a social phenomenological approach. J. Am. Soc. Inform. Sci. Technol. **58**, 1709–1719 (2007). https://doi.org/10.1002/asi.20644

10. Huvila, I.: Analytical information horizon maps. Libr. Inf. Sci. Res. **31**, 18–28 (2009). https://doi.org/10.1016/j.lisr.2008.06.005

11. Tsai, T.-I.: The social networks in the information horizons of college students: a pilot study: the social networks in the information horizons of college students: a pilot study. Proc. Am. Soc. Info. Sci. Tech. **47**, 1–3 (2010). https://doi.org/10.1002/meet.14504701347

12. Greyson, D., O'Brien, H., Shoveller, J.: Information world mapping: a participatory arts-based elicitation method for information behavior interviews. Libr. Inf. Sci. Res. **39**, 149–157 (2017). https://doi.org/10.1016/j.lisr.2017.03.003

13. Joanne du Hommet, J., Ihadjadene, M., Grivel, L.: Information practices in coopetition context: the case of a large video game company. https://informationr.net/ir/27-SpIssue/isic22/isic2232.html. Accessed 16 Mar 2023. https://doi.org/10.47989/irisic2232

What Can You Do with a Sword? Gender Biases in Text Game Affordances

Erik S. McGuire[✉][iD] and Noriko Tomuro[iD]

DePaul University, Chicago, IL 60604, USA
emcguir8@depaul.edu, tomuro@cs.depaul.edu

Abstract. Game mechanics can be viewed in terms of *affordances*: possible actions offered by the environment—depending on the agent (e.g., in a fantasy role-playing game, a sword can be wielded by a knight, but probably not by a dragon). Recently, text generated by large language models (LLMs) has been used to create open-ended text-based game content. However, LLMs have been shown to generate sexist text when trained on gender-biased data. If bias manifests in educational text game affordances it could harm goal achievement. We examine binary gender biases in LIGHT, an English-language persona-based dataset for researching language grounded in a fantasy adventure world, training LLMs on LIGHT and analyzing the diversity of affordances in quests. We find male characters have a more diverse space of affordances yet are less diverse in practice (e.g., mostly wielding a sword) in original and generated quests. To gauge impact on gameplay, we create games from LIGHT quests which can be played in the TextWorld research framework. Artificial agents trained only on male games significantly outperform female, suggesting an impact of affordance biases. These findings illustrate risks in AI- or data-driven generation of serious game content where gender is involved: overlooked biases in affordances can propagate, autonomously enforcing harmful, stereotypical behaviors.

Keywords: gender bias · generative ai · text games

1 Introduction

Educational serious games are often text-based [18], and recent work [2,19] has used LLMs trained on human text to generate—and play in—text game worlds. Games exercise player agency (i.e., the capacity for meaningful action) [6,13] by manipulating *affordances* [9]—behaviors an object's properties afford certain agents—which may play a critical role in creativity, enabling novel, meaningful learning [10,14]. Previously, the concept of affordances was implemented to help artificial agents select actions [1,7]. In this work, we analyze binary gender biases in crowdsourced LIGHT [3,16] quests (Table 1), measuring the diversity of objects and their afforded actions. We also train an LLM on LIGHT data for the task of quest generation [2], identifying biases in generated quests. TextWorld [4] is a sandbox learning environment which enables creating and playing text

© The Author(s), under exclusive license to Springer Nature Switzerland AG 2024
P. Dondio et al. (Eds.): GALA 2023, LNCS 14475, pp. 451–456, 2024.
https://doi.org/10.1007/978-3-031-49065-1_48

Table 1. Example from LIGHT dataset; given character, location, and motivation, the LLM learns to predict quests and then generate similar quests. The extracted game is completed if the dress is taken and worn, as indicated by the TextWorld Walkthrough.

Character:	The Queen (Female)	TextWorld
Location:	The Courtyard	Walkthrough
Short Motivation:	I want to drop the tulip on the central atrium	
Quest:	*wear* dress, *follow* cardinal, *go* courtyard,	open large closet,
	get central atrium, *get* tulip, *put* tulip in central atrium,	Take dress from large closet,
	follow cardinal, *go* temple	wear dress

games. For insight on how affordance biases impact gameplay, we train agents to play games created from LIGHT quests, where success relies on affordances, to determine if an agent trained only on one gender's data performs better or worse on unseen (not encountered during training) male and female games.

2   Methods

To analyze gender biases in affordances we use LIGHT gender annotations collected previously [5]: LIGHT was found to be the most gender-biased dataset studied, but affordances were not addressed. We study only binary examples, as the neutral gender annotations are not a deliberately curated class: neutral is a problematic default label applied when annotators could not judge examples as male or female—often when characters are non-human or conventionally binary.

Given the mean difference between observed male (M) and female (F) values (such as diversity measures), we test the null hypothesis that values were assigned to M or F samples at random by repeatedly swapping pairs of M/F values. An effect is significant when the chance p of an equal or more extreme mean difference (e.g., some positive number if M > F) is below a threshold α. To describe the strength of the effect, for diversity measures we report Common Language Effect Size (CLES) [17], which gives the chance a randomly selected M or F value will be larger than the other gender. For game results we employ Almost Stochastic Order (ASO) [15], similar to CLES but designed for comparing neural networks (e.g., LLMs). We report significant ASO confidence scores ($\epsilon_{min} < \tau$ with $\tau = 0.5$) with $\alpha = 0.05$ and 1000 bootstrap iterations.

2.1   Affordance Diversity

To characterize biases in quests, we first use an off-the-shelf tagger[1] to extract the direct objects of LIGHT's 15 unique action verbs. For each action (e.g., "wield") in a gender's quests, we take the number of its unique affordant objects (e.g., wieldable objects such as swords) as the *type* (class) count and the sum of those objects' occurrences (e.g., counts of "wield [rusty, etc.] sword") as the *token* count–we do likewise for the unique actions afforded by each object across its

---

[1] https://spacy.io/universe/project/spacy-transformers.

Table 2. Original and generated (test set) diversity. CLES where they are significant (w/ Bonferroni correction $p < \frac{\alpha}{m}$ for models, where $\alpha = 0.05$ and $m = 3$) for the hypothesis that M > F for RGD or M < F (†) for TTR and NE. OD, AD: object or action diversity. Subcolumns: generated datasets per seed. Dashes: non-significant.

Metric	Original	All			All (Subset)			M			M (Subset)			F		
RGD (OD)	0.91	0.80	0.84	0.84	0.79	0.84	0.81	0.78	0.79	0.83	0.76	0.84	0.77	0.72	0.68	–
TTR† (OD)	0.64	0.62	–	–	–	0.59	0.56	0.61	0.60	–	0.59	–	0.68	0.61	0.63	0.60
NE† (OD)	0.60	0.64	–	–	–	–	0.62	0.62	0.66	–	0.58	–	0.66	0.63	–	0.61
RGD (AD)	0.53	0.56	–	–	0.56	–	–	0.57	0.58	0.58	–	0.58	–	–	–	–
TTR† (AD)	0.55	0.58	0.59	0.58	0.58	0.58	0.62	0.59	0.57	0.58	0.59	–	0.64	0.60	0.64	0.58
NE† (AD)	0.55	–	–	–	0.66	–	0.63	–	–	0.69	0.61	–	0.61	0.70	–	–

occurrences. A higher ratio of types to tokens (type–token ratio or TTR) suggests greater variation. We also compute the ratio of types for a given gender vs. overall to describe the relative gender diversity (RGD). Lastly, we use normalized entropy (NE) [8] to describe the distributions of actions and objects.

To study whether and how affordance biases manifest in LLMs trained on LIGHT, we use BART[2] [11]: commonly used in previous LIGHT research, BART is an LLM developed by Meta AI, pretrained on web data. Given character, location and short motivation as context, BART learns to predict quest words or subwords and can thereby generate quests when prompted with persona contexts. To more fairly compare the influence of gender we combine female training and evaluation data into a single set of 570 examples, comparable to the male training data (650). For exact gender balance we also train models on subsets capped at the size of the female data (570). To account for sensitivity to randomness each model is run with 3 seeds[3], generating 3 different quest sets.

Results are shown in Table 2. Male data are significally more diverse for RGD and significantly less for TTR. Given some action or object, female characters have fewer unique objects and actions available to them than what the data offer overall (RGD): they interact with a much smaller space of objects in the game world, and these objects are less richly affordant for them. Yet female characters have greater diversity of objects applicable for each action and of actions afforded by each object (TTR): male characters engage a smaller selection. Higher NE (closer to 1.0) reflects a uniform, less predictable distribution of tokens; lower NE (closer to 0) suggests frequent use of fewer types of actions or objects—as we find for male quests. Generated quests often perpetuate these biases.

2.2   Gameplay Impact

To assess the impact of LIGHT biases in affordance diversity, we can compare performance where success depends on agents learning these patterns by trial-and-error. We use TextWorld to create games from the objects and actions of

---

[2] `huggingface.co/facebook/bart-base/`.
[3] Seeds are numbers used to initialize random number generators.

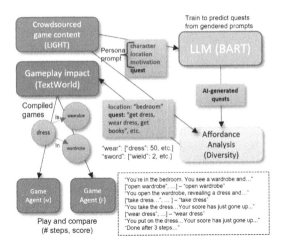

Fig. 1. Graphical overview of methodology: analysis of original and generated quests, game conversion and comparing male vs. female gameplay.

the parsed quests, a game from each quest (Table 1). TextWorld relies on formal rules and grammar to define the environment and possible actions. We limit focus to "wield" and "wear", which are stereotypically gendered and frequent. We only use quests containing those actions and preserve affordance distributions by assigning properties (e.g., wieldability) to objects based on their quest actions, using the most frequent (per gender) if a quest uses both actions with an object.

Every game occurs in a room organized by affordances via containers: wearable objects are randomly placed in a closet or wardrobe; wieldable objects in a chest or locker. Rewards are given when quest events are enacted—if a dress is worn in a quest: taking and wearing the dress are both rewarded (Fig. 1). Games are completed when all targets are enacted. To wield or wear an object, it must be taken from its container and carried by the agent. Agents are provided a list of available commands each turn. If a carried object has a wieldable or wearable property, the target command (e.g., "wield sword") appears as a candidate. To encourage affordance-based selection, we match target objects with a distractor—an object which, according to the gender's quests, does not afford the target action. The distractor is placed in the same container as the target and given the same affordance property so that it competes for all rewarded events (e.g., taking and wielding a dress vs. a sword). Distractors are unrewarded: they can increase the number of steps but not the score. To optimize results, agents therefore learn the target associations as dictated by each gender's affordances.

We use the neural agent architecture provided in the TextWorld documentation[4]. The agent receives current available commands, room description, inventory contents and feedback from previous commands at each timestep. Given 240 training games for each gender, agents play each game to completion (or until

---

[4] https://github.com/microsoft/TextWorld/blob/main/notebooks/.

max steps $= 100$ is reached) for 5 episodes (playthroughs). Each agent type is run with 10 random seeds. We evaluate trained agents on an equal combination of previously unseen male and female games (to assess their ability to generalize) and compare male (M) and female (F) agents for each game played for 10 episodes. Results (Table 3) show a strong ($\epsilon_{\min} < \tau$ with $\tau = 0.2$) significant superiority (higher scores achieved, fewer moves required) for male agents.

Table 3. Averaged results for 101 games from each evaluation set and significant ASO for the hypothesis that male-trained agent results are superior to female: higher for scores or fewer for steps ($\epsilon_{min} = 0.0$ expresses strongest confidence).

	Scores		Steps	
	Dev	*Test*	*Dev*	*Test*
Results M (overall)	0.994	0.995	17.36	16.45
Results F (overall)	0.948	0.951	30.85	29.22
ϵ_{min} (avg seeds)	0.0	0.0	0.014	0.015
ϵ_{min} (per seed)	0.0	0.002	0.006	0.028

3   Conclusions

We find gender biases in affordances in original and generated LIGHT quests, affecting the performance of agents trained on TextWorld–LIGHT games. Male characters' quests have a higher relative diversity of types (RGD)—a larger space of actions and objects, enabling a greater number of game behaviors. This richer experience may have increased male agents' robustness. Female characters are more fundamentally limited by the exclusion of objects and potential actions: in the universe of female quests, fewer types of acts can exist. Lower diversity in male quests (TTR, NE) might have helped male agents learn regular usage patterns. Artificial agents represent objects and actions by repeated association, their behavior shaped by biased observations. A related theory is that gender norms shape how humans automatically perceive objects in terms of their affordances, influencing us to reinforce biases by conforming to permissible behaviors [12]. This study shows how abstract biases can become concrete constraints. Curating environments (e.g., based on affordant object diversity) could mitigate bias. But affordances are relational, equally involving observers and environments: reexamining reliance on stereotypical roles offers another remedy.

References

1. Ahn, M., et al.: Do as I Can, Not as I Say: Grounding Language in Robotic Affordances. arXiv preprint arXiv:2204.01691 (2022)
2. Ammanabrolu, P., Jia, R., Riedl, M.: Situated dialogue learning through procedural environment generation. In: Proceedings of the 60th Annual Meeting of the Association for Computational Linguistics (2022)

3. Ammanabrolu, P., Urbanek, J., Li, M., Szlam, A., Rocktäschel, T., Weston, J.: How to motivate your dragon: teaching goal-driven agents to speak and act in fantasy worlds. In: Proceedings of the 2021 Conference of the North American Chapter of the Association for Computational Linguistics (2021)

4. Côté, M.A., et al.: TextWorld: A Learning Environment for Text-based Games. In: CGW@IJCAI (2018)

5. Dinan, E., Fan, A., Williams, A., Urbanek, J., Kiela, D., Weston, J.: Queens are powerful too: mitigating gender bias in dialogue generation. In: Proceedings of the 2020 Conference on Empirical Methods in Natural Language Processing (2020)

6. Fernández Galeote, D., et al.: The good, the bad, and the divergent in game-based learning: player experiences of a serious game for climate change engagement. In: Proceedings of the 25th International Academic Mindtrek Conference, pp. 256–267 (2022)

7. Fulda, N., Ricks, D., Murdoch, B., Wingate, D.: What can you do with a rock? Affordance extraction via word embeddings. In: Proceedings of the 26th International Joint Conference on Artificial Intelligence, pp. 1039–1045 (2017)

8. Garner, J.: The cross-sectional development of verb-noun collocations as constructions in L2 writing. Int. Rev. Appl. Linguist. Lang. Teach. **60**(3), 909–935 (2020)

9. Gibson, J.J.: The theory of affordances. Hilldale, USA **1**(2), 67–82 (1977)

10. Glăveanu, V.P.: A sociocultural theory of creativity: bridging the social, the material, and the psychological. Rev. Gen. Psychol. **24**(4), 335–354 (2020)

11. Lewis, M., et al.: BART: denoising sequence-to-sequence pre-training for natural language generation, translation, and comprehension. In: Proceedings of the 58th Annual Meeting of the Association for Computational Linguistics (2020)

12. McClelland, T., Sliwa, P.: Gendered affordance perception and unequal domestic labour. Philos. Phenomenological Res. **107**(20), 501–524 (2022)

13. Nguyen, C.T.: Games and the art of agency. Philos. Rev. **128**(4), 423–462 (2019)

14. Protopsaltis, A., Pannese, L., Hetzner, S., Pappa, D., de Freitas, S.: Creative learning with serious games. Int. J. Emerg. Technol. Learn. (iJET) **5**(2010), 4–6 (2010)

15. Ulmer, D., Hardmeier, C., Frellsen, J.: deep-significance - Easy and Meaningful Statistical Significance Testing in the Age of Neural Networks. arXiv preprint arXiv:2204.06815 (2022)

16. Urbanek, J., et al.: Learning to speak and act in a fantasy text adventure game. In: Proceedings of the 2019 Conference on Empirical Methods in Natural Language Processing and the 9th International Joint Conference on Natural Language Processing (2019)

17. Vargha, A., Delaney, H.D.: A critique and improvement of the "CL" common language effect size statistics of McGraw and Wong. J. Educ. Behav. Stat. **25**(2), 101–132 (2000)

18. Xinogalos, S., Satratzemi, M.: The use of educational games in programming assignments: SQL Island as a case study. Appl. Sci. **12**(13), 6563 (2022)

19. Yao, S., Rao, R., Hausknecht, M., Narasimhan, K.: Keep CALM and explore: language models for action generation in text-based games. In: Proceedings of the 2020 Conference on Empirical Methods in Natural Language Processing (2020)

Browser-Based Game Design for Cognitive Effort Aware Quality of Experience Evaluation

Pheobe Sun$^{(\boxtimes)}$ [ID], Flavia H. Santos [ID], and Andrew Hines [ID]

University College Dublin, Dublin, Ireland
wenyi.sun@ucdconnect.ie, {flavia.santos,andrew.hines}@ucd.ie

Abstract. Cognitive effort plays a crucial part in our multimedia consumption experience as it affects attention. However, traditional research in quality of experience (QoE) relies on the subjective ratings of a multimedia consumption experience under a lab-based environment without distractions. To make the collected QoE ratings closer to realistic usage scenarios we designed a browser-based game as an adapted QoE subjective test that can incorporate and quantify cognitive effort using a dual-task paradigm. Our pilot study results show that our proposed browser-based game is a viable protocol that can control for, and reflect, the cognitive effort via selected self-reported measures given an appropriate load range. Future work will further standardise and simplify the game protocol for robustness, repeatability and test duration.

Keywords: Quality of Experience (QoE) · Listening Effort · Cognitive Effort · Dual-task Paradigm

1 Introduction

1.1 QoE and Cognitive Effort

Quality of experience (QoE) is a paradigm that assesses multimedia consumption experience by mimicking human perceptual judgements. Although a new listening effort-informed QoE framework [15] is proposed, no existing test procedure has been established to investigate how cognitive effort affects perceived experience [17]. Inspired by the simulation games developed to measure cognitive load [10,14], we proposes and pilots a browser-based game as a QoE subjective test procedure to operationalise the effort-aware QoE framework.

1.2 Challenges of Measuring Cognitive Effort

There are three main categories of effort indicators: self-reported, behavioural, and physiological responses. In practice, at least two independent measures are recommended to use together to reduce structural interference when interpreting

© The Author(s), under exclusive license to Springer Nature Switzerland AG 2024
P. Dondio et al. (Eds.): GALA 2023, LNCS 14475, pp. 457–463, 2024.
https://doi.org/10.1007/978-3-031-49065-1_49

the occurrence of effort [8,13]. A *dual-task paradigm* is a practical way to measure cognitive effort by collecting both self-reported and behavioural responses. It is based on the cognitive capacity theory [8]. In a listening task, an increase in the listening effort will result in reduced performance of a concurrent task [4].

There are two practical challenges in dual-task implementation. First, cross-modal interference needs to happen. Early research [1] believes that dual-task only works on tasks recruiting the same modalities only while other research [6, 10] provide evidence that cross-modal interference exists. Second, an effective task load range needs to be calibrated [16]. Outside of the effective load range, no performance change can be observed [6] due to the 'ceiling's effect'.

This paper will first describe the game design according to the dual-task paradigm. Then we will address the dual-task desing challenges and evaluate the usability of implementing this browser-based game for QoE subjective test procedure based on the pilot study results.

2   Method

2.1   Game Design

Participants are asked to stay attentive to the listening material while performing a simple browser-based game that requires constant visual attention but minimal motor actions. Participants are asked to report their perceived effort as well as perceived quality of experience after each trail.

Listening Task. We ask the participants to prioritise the listening task in the dual-task. To ensure the participants stay attentive to the audio content at all times, inspired by [11], we ask the participants need to be able to repeat the last sentence whenever the audio stops. Further, varying number of sentences are used as the test audio to avoid anticipation of audio length,

Behavioural Task. The secondary task designed is the browser-based car aligning game. It is used to reflect the effect of cognitive effort from listening. The game is a simplified driving game where participants are asked to closely monitor the car's position and to use the left and the right arrow keys only to bring the deviated car back to the centreline. The car shifts sideways at random time points. The goal is to keep the car as central as possible at all times. A simple visual game ensures participants' constant recruitment of monitoring function [9,12]. Existing driving simulation games are not used to exclude the effect of the recruitment of complex executive functions such as decision-making and motor control.

2.2   Task Load Controls

Listening Task Load Control. The cognitive load resulting from the listening task can be controlled by many aspects of the listening material such as intelligibility, topic, sentence length etc. Therefore in our browser-based game design, content-neutral speech recording is used and the intelligibility of each test stimuli is controlled. We also used sentences consisting of 7–10 words to avoid extra cognitive load introduced by memorising a long sentence.

Behavioural Task Load Control. The behavioural task load is controlled by the car aligning game difficulty which is influenced by a) the speed that the car shifts, and b) the sensitivity of the car's response to keyboard control. The car's shift speed affects how promptly a player reacts to changes. The control sensitivity affects how easily and swiftly a player can correct the car's position. The game difficulty levels were generated using different combinations of the two parameters.

2.3   Measures

Both self-reported and behavioural responses are collected (see Table 1). The self-reported responses are collected after each trial whilst the behavioural responses are recorded during the game. The self-reported responses are selected and empirically tested based on the effort proxies from NASA-TLX [3] scales. Secondary task performance is measured by how well the user keeps the randomly-shifting car within the borders and aligned to the centreline. The indicators used include the car's border cross counts and the car's deviation from the centreline are used. We also collect the keypress counts hoping to find correlations with stress level.

3   Pilot Study

We incrementally conducted a few rounds of small-scale exploratory experiments to explore the browser-based game design. A total of 6 participants (3 native speakers) volunteered for the three exploratory experiments (Experiment 1–3 in Table 1). The experiments are done in a browser on the participants' own laptops. All participants use headphones for listening and the experiments are conducted in a quiet work environment. The experiments have been approved by the ethics committee at lab 1. We include the results from Experiment 4, a confirmatory experiment carried out in a controlled experiment room at lab 2, to show statistical results. More details about Experiment 4 will be published in the future.

The browser-based game is developed using three.js and jsPsych [2]. Non-repetitive speech recordings are used to motivate participants to allocate enough attention to the listening task in all trials. Varying the length of audio stimuli ensures participants stay attentive to the listening task at all times. The total duration of the audio stimuli is kept within 30 s to avoid listening fatigue [5]. Each track in Experiments 1–3 is generated using 3–5 Harvard sentences (9–14 s) from the TSP speech database [7]. The audio stimuli in Experiment 4 is generated using 1–3 sentences (4–17 s) from audio essays read by female and male Mandarin speakers.

Table 1. Summary of experiments and test conditions

Experiment	Participants	Game difficulty	Speech noise	Trials
1	1	1 - 10	N/A	70
2	3	3 - 10	N/A	24
3	2	4 - 7	N/A	40
4	30	3 & 6	0 & 5 dB SNR	4650

The audio stimuli used in Experiments 1–3 were generated from 6 English voices (3 male 3 female), and those tested in Experiment 4 were generated from 2 Chinese voices (1 male, 1 female).

The subjective ratings are collected using 100-step scales in Experiments 1–3. Within-subject min-max normalisation is applied before all participants' responses are aggregated. The behavioural measures including the car's border cross counts, the car's deviation from the centreline, and participants' keypress counts are normalised by the trial duration.

4   Results

4.1   Cross-Modality Interference

To check whether cross-modality interference happens in our designed test scenario, we compare participants' responses in the dual-task trials versus the responses in the single-task trials. If an additional task changes the behaviour or task performance, we regard that cross-modality interference exists in our test design, and thereafter the designed dual-task can be used to measure listening effort.

Figure 1 shows the aggregated response of five participants from Experiments 2 and 3 across eight different behavioural task load levels. The colour differentiates the responses collected in game-only versus dual-task trials. An obvious difference in the response mean and variance can be observed from both selected self-reported and behavioural response plots. Thus, we regard the cross-modal interference taking place when a concurrent task is added to a single task in our test scenario.

4.2   Effective Load

To explore the appropriate load range when implementing dual-task experiments, we analyse individuals' response change when task load changes. Figure 2 shows an individual's response across ten game difficulty levels in Experiment 1. The changes in both self-reported 'estimated durability' and the car's 'average deviation from the centre' are small between levels 1 and 2; The differences in the car's 'average deviation' are most obvious during levels 5–8. A similar trend can be observed in other individual response curves across eight difficulty levels in Experiments 2 and 3 (see Fig. 1). The individual response curves generally

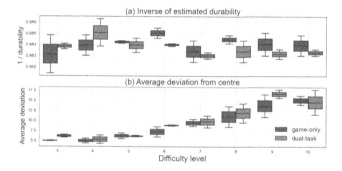

Fig. 1. Responses from two native speakers across eight difficulty levels

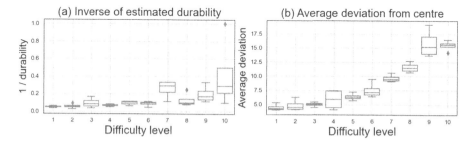

Fig. 2. Single person response across ten behavioural task load levels

conform to the effective load range theory and the 'ceiling's effect' in the litera-ture [6,16], indicating the effective load range for our subjective test procedure might lie between level 3–8.

4.3 Effort Observables

As 'effort' and 'cognitive load' are abstract ideas, we use a range of related aspects as effort observables. A dependent t-test is run on the data collected from 30 participants in Experiment 4 to evaluate the effectiveness of the selected effort observable when higher noise is added to the speech. The results in Table 2) show that all chosen self-reported effort-related aspects are responsive to a 5 dB SNR increase in the test speech when the behavioural task difficulty level is 3. The same pattern is found when the difficulty level is 6. However, our selected behavioural measures are less correlated with a 5 dB SNR noise level change. This analysis confirms that the self-reported measures are also effectively observable for perceived cognitive effort.

Table 2. Response change as a result of a change in noise level

Response type	Effort ovservables	p-value
Self-reported	Difficulty to concentrate	<0.0001
	Stress level	<0.0001
	Expected durability	<0.0001
Behavioural	Boundary cross frequency	0.043
	Deviation from centre	0.057
	Key press frequency	0.764

5   Conclusion

We proposed and piloted a browser-based game that can directly show the effect of cognitive effort using a dual-task paradigm. Our work provides a new test method for the recently proposed modified QoE framework [15] and confirms the plausibility of implementing the proposed browser-based game which allows for the control and the measure of cognitive effort in QoE subjective tests. This will broaden the applicability of QoE evaluation to more complex and realistic multimedia consumption scenarios. Future work will further standardise and simplify the game protocol for robustness, repeatability and test duration.

Acknowledgment. Special thanks to Fintan Costello, Markus Vaalgamaa and Xiaolin Mei for the continuous discussions on the experiment design, and David Baker and L-Miao Li for advices on statistical analysis.

References

1. Allport, D.A., Antonis, B., Reynolds, P.: On the division of attention: a disproof of the single channel hypothesis. Quart. J. Experiment. Psychol. **24**(2), 225–235 (5 1972). https://doi.org/10.1080/00335557243000102
2. Leeuw, J.R.: jsPsych: a JavaScript library for creating behavioral experiments in a Web browser. Behavior Research Methods **47**(1), 1–12 (2014). https://doi.org/10.3758/s13428-014-0458-y
3. Hart, S.G., Staveland, L.E.: Development of NASA-TLX (Task Load Index): Results of Empirical and Theoretical Research. Adv. Psychol. **52**(C), 139–183 (1988). https://doi.org/10.1016/S0166-4115(08)62386-9
4. Hunter, C.R.: Tracking cognitive spare capacity during speech perception with eeg/erp: effects of cognitive load and sentence predictability. Ear and Hearing, pp. 1144–1157 (2020). https://doi.org/10.1097/AUD.0000000000000856
5. ITU-T: P.800: Methods for subjective determination of transmission quality. Tech. rep., Int. Telecomm. Union (1996)
6. Johnsrude, I.S., Rodd, J.M.: Factors that increase processing demands when listening to speech. in: neurobiology of language, pp. 491–502. Elsevier Inc. (1 2015). https://doi.org/10.1016/B978-0-12-407794-2.00040-7
7. Kabal, P.: Tsp speech database. McGill University, Database Version **1**, 09–02 (2002)

8. Kahneman, D.: Attention and effort. Prentice-Hall, Inc. (1973)
9. Lavie, N.: Distracted and confused?: selective attention under load. Trends Cogn. Sci. **9**(2) (2005). https://doi.org/10.1016/j.tics.2004.12.004
10. Murphy, G., Greene, C.M.: Perceptual load induces inattentional blindness in drivers. Appl. Cogn. Psychol. **30**(3), 479–483 (2016). https://doi.org/10.1002/acp.3216
11. Murphy, G., Greene, C.M.: The elephant in the road: auditory perceptual load affects driver perception and awareness. Appl. Cogn. Psychol. **31**(2), 258–263 (2017). https://doi.org/10.1002/acp.3311
12. Peelle, J.E.: Listening effort: how the cognitive consequences of acoustic challenge are reflected in brain and behavior. Ear Hear. **39**(2), 204–214 (2018). https://doi.org/10.1097/AUD.0000000000000494
13. Pichora-Fuller, M.K., et al.: Hearing impairment and cognitive energy: the framework for understanding effortful listening (FUEL). Ear Hear. **37**, 5S-27S (2016). https://doi.org/10.1097/AUD.0000000000000312
14. Sevcenko, N., Ninaus, M., Wortha, F., Moeller, K., Gerjets, P.: Measuring cognitive load using in-game metrics of a serious simulation game. Front. Psychol. **12**, 572437 (2021)
15. Sun, P.W., Hines, A.: Listening effort informed quality of experience evaluation. Computational Neuroscience for Perceptual Quality Assessment (2022)
16. de Waard, D.: The Measurement of Drivers' Mental Workload. Ph.D. thesis, University of Groningen (1996). https://doi.org/10.1016/j.apergo.2003.11.009
17. Zacharov, N.: Sensory evaluation of sound. CRC Press (2018)

Design Gamification Strategies in a Digital Learning Environment: The Impact on Students

Francesco Floris[1] , Valeria Fradiante[1(✉)] , Marina Marchisio Conte[1] ,
and Sergio Rabellino[2]

[1] Dipartimento di Biotecnologie Molecolari e Scienze per la Salute, Università di Torino, Via Nizza, 52, 10126 Turin, TO, Italy
{francesco.floris,valeria.fradiante,marina.marchisio}@unito.it
[2] Dipartimento di Informatica, Università di Torino, Corso Svizzera, 185, 10149 Turin, TO, Italy
sergio.rabellino@unito.it

Abstract. Over the past few decades, gamification has become increasingly popular and widely used to motivate and engage learners in the digital age. Based on gamification strategies that have been shown to be useful in literature, we wondered how they can be developed in the Digital Learning Environment of the Digital Math Training project. To understand the impact and effectiveness of our implemented gamification strategies in the DLE, we considered the students' answers, from grade 9th to 13th, to initial and final questionnaire. The results show which of the strategies implemented were most appreciated by the DMT students and which were found to be effective in stimulating their motivation, especially for some categories of students.

Keywords: Gamification Design Principles · Gamification Strategies · Digital Learning Environment

1 Introduction and Framework

The development and diffusion of technological and IT tools, such as computers, smartphones, tablets or VR headset through which it is possible to play even from home, has contributed to the affirmation of the use of games or game mechanisms as new ways of interaction, learning and exploration [1]. Starting from gamification strategies that have been found to be useful in distance learning literature [2], we designed how to implement them in the Digital Learning Environment (DLE) of the Digital Math Training (DMT) project. In the "online training" phase of the DMT project, about 300 upper secondary students have to solve 8 contextualized problems within a DLE. The main goal is to support students in developing disciplinary competences in mathematics as well as problem-solving skills and competences in education for sustainable development. As the online training phase of the project had a relatively high dropout rate (around 50%) in the various editions, it was decided to reinforce the gamification strategies already in place in order to increase participant engagement without changing the difficulty of the path, as it is a course reserved for excellent students. Our research questions are: How can gamification strategies be developed using the tools available in a DLE? How are they perceived by the students?

P. Dondio et al. (Eds.): GALA 2023, LNCS 14475, pp. 464–469, 2024.
https://doi.org/10.1007/978-3-031-49065-1_50

To investigate the impact of our solutions in a DLE, we considered the answers to the initial and final questionnaires filled by the students involved in the online training.

1.1 Gamification in Education

Gamification refers to the use of the typical mechanisms of the game, such as the challenge, the use of points, levels and prizes, in a context that is essentially not a game [3]. It's been emphasized that gamification, when properly planned, stimulates and improves the learning process and teaching practice [4]. Many studies have shown how gamification can be successfully applied to distance learning to encourage interaction and engagement [5]. As Caponetto and colleagues highlighted in their literature review [6], the majority of gamification strategies were actually delivered through a Learning Management System (LMS) with features designed specifically to meet the needs of a gamified process. An important competence identified by DigiComp [7] is communication and collaboration. Gamification can also promote collaborative learning between students and for the achievement of certain common goals, for example by participating in a challenge that requires teamwork or by exchanging ideas and materials [8]. The DLE provides tools that support communication and collaboration between students and contributes to the development of a learning community [9].

1.2 Gamification Strategies

There are many strategies to implement gamification in education [10]. In their sequential exploratory research, Sümer and Aydın found that gamification contributes positively to students' motivation and engagement and they brought out some design criteria related to the most common gamification elements to consider when designing gamification strategies in distance learning [2]: use of points, challenge, rules, leaderboard, rewards, feedback. Although it is not essential to use storytelling as a means of gamification, it represents another important gamification strategy: telling a story, an event, a myth, a legend, or a mission is one of the most used ways to involve the user [11].

2 Research Context

The context of the research is the Digital Math Training (DMT) project funded by the Fondazione CRT within the Diderot Project and organized by the University of Turin. The core part of the project is the online training attended by the most skilled or motivated upper secondary school students selected by their teachers after the "in-presence training" phase. Those students are enrolled in the DLE of DMT project, which hosts several activities [12]. The technological component of the DLE includes a Moodle platform integrated with an Advanced Computing Environment, a tool designed for learning STEM disciplines [13]. Previous editions, like the ninth current one, were characterized by a challenge where students competed for about 25 final prizes [14]. In the current one we decided to intensify the gamified approach aiming to increase engagement and participation in the DMT online training and trying to reduce the dropout rate compared to previous editions, which had a fairly high dropout rate [13].

3   Method

3.1   Designing Gamification Strategies in the DLE of DMT Project

We have designed the possible applications of the gamification strategies to the DLE of DMT project. To help the implementation of the gamification within the DLE, we adopted the commercial Moodle plugin Level up XP+, which allows users to earn points and progress through the challenge by leveling up based on their scores gained from activities within the DLE. What we did to intensify gamification strategies was:

- Storytelling: in the 2022–23 DMT edition, on accessing the platform, each student found a Moodle resource that explains the mission they have to fulfil: as President, each student has been entrusted with the task of ensuring a fair society for its citizens by achieving as many of the Sustainable Development Goals (SDGs) of the 2030 Agenda as possible [15]. Viewing the mission is made mandatory by the settings to access all course activities and earn points. Previous editions did not contextualize the competition in a story.
- Use of points: the plugin allows to customize the points earned (e.g. coins, hearts, stars, etc.) as well as the levels. Special points have been used: the Digital Math Equos (DME), i.e. the currency used in the country where the mission is located. A new feature is that students accumulate DME directly in the plugin by participating in the activities offered in the course, i.e. forums, synchronous online meetings, submission of problems, initial and final questionnaires. In previous editions, the accumulation of points was within the Moodle gradebook.
- Progression is a novelty of 2022–23 edition: each level is associated with a SDG. Level 17 (linked to the last SDG) corresponds to the maximum scores achieved in the previous years, but an 18th level linked to the Super Sustainability goal has been introduced in case a student has exceeded this threshold.
- The challenge is not only to win the final prize, but also to get the most DME to Level up and achieve the greatest number of SDGs, Ensuring a fair society.
- The leaderboard is visible directly from the plugin rather than from the gradebook as past years. In this way, it is more personalized and motivating than the simple list that used to appear in the gradebook. In fact, it allows each user to see, in addition to his or her position, the first 5 students above and below him or her. In this way, the best students are rewarded, but the position of those who have reached low positions is only visible to those who are in the neighborhood. At the same time, students see how close they are to their opponents.
- The Level up plugin also tracks the progress of learners through a personal report that allows the teacher of the course to see how many points each user has earned, how they earned them and what level they have reached. Users receive a notification when they earn points, explaining the number of points and the activity for which they have been awarded. When users reach a higher level, a motivational message is displayed with the badge for that level.
- Students receive different types of feedback: weekly through the evaluation of problems, instantaneously through online tutoring or Level up, and daily through the forums where a tutor is available to answer students' doubts and questions.
- As in the past, the rules are specified in a Moodle page.

3.2   Evaluation of Gamification Strategies Implemented

Unfortunately, as in previous editions, the dropout rate was confirmed around 50%. The final questionnaire reveals that the main factors contributing to this phenomenon are both the difficulty of the problems encountered and the non-negligible extracurricular commitment required by the project. This leads us to conclude that the innovations in gamification strategies that we implemented were not enough on their own to reduce the dropout rate. However, we have tried to explore the students' perceptions of these strategies. To do this, we considered the students' answers to the final questionnaire related to an initial questionnaire, where we collected information about the students' self-assessed initial competency levels and their initial level of motivation at the time of enrolling in the online training. The final questionnaire aims to collect information about the students' self-assessed final competency levels and their perception of the gamification strategies implemented. From the initial questionnaire, we have that out of 302 students, only 6 were poorly motivated to finish the training and enrolled because they were forced to. 92 answered "More yes than no" and as many as 204 stated they were very motivated. A total of 142 students responded to the final questionnaire (the answer to which is optional). Looking only at students who responded to both questionnaires, 77% of respondents in the first questionnaire stated they were highly motivated to complete the online training, 21% stated they were moderately motivated and only 1% (2 students) said they were poorly motivated. Considering the dropout rate and the self-assessment of the level of motivation, we can conclude that students probably overestimated this value or underestimated the commitment required by the project at an early stage. This will require some improvements to be made to the initial questionnaire in future editions, in order to obtain more accurate and reliable data. Considering the low number of unmotivated students (2), we have decided to exclude these cases from the analysis and focus only on the 140 students, which we indicated with "moderately" and "highly motivated". The questions shown in Table 1 had a possible student response on a liking scale of 1 to 5, where 1 = not at all and 5 = very much. Table 1 shows that the accumulation of points, the chance to progress and the use of rewards detected by these questions had more positive results for the highly motivated students. The difference in perception is statistically significant for each question, with a pi value for t-test always less than 0.0001. Therefore, we can conclude that these strategies are useful for keeping students' motivation high in online DMT training, which is not obvious, given the effort required. Regarding the contextualization of the online training within the goals within the SDGs, the perception of the two groups is nearly the same, with an average value around 3 for the various questions, and there are no statistically significant differences. Similarly, regarding the effect of storytelling, the two related questions did not show statistically significant differences between the two groups, with the average of responses hovering around 2,5. But, on the other hand, 120 students said they liked the story and through it was suitable for online training, whereas 22 students would have preferred there to be no contextualization.

Table 1. Results of the final questionnaire for "highly" and "moderately motivated" students.

Questions	Highly motivated			Moderately motivated		
	1st Qu	Mean	3rd Qu	1st Qu	Mean	3rd Qu
Earning points with Level up involved me by making me actively take part in the online training	3	3,464	4	2	2,667	3
Collecting points with Level up stimulated in me the desire to improve my ranking position	3	3,445	4	2	2,767	4
Accumulating points with Level up made me want to beat the scores of my peers	3	3,418	4	2	2,667	3,750
The use of levels encouraged me to keep on solving problems and not give up at the first attempt	3	3,364	4	2	2,633	3
The use of more levels within the challenge pushed me to do more	3	3,245	4	2	2,633	3
The use of more levels got me more involved in the challenge	3	3,282	4	2	2,4	3

4   Conclusion, Future Developments, and Research

In this study, we analyzed the impact of gamification strategies already known in the literature, applied to the DLE of the DMT project, whose participants at the beginning are motivated students aiming to improve their skills, even if the dropout rate of online training is usually high. The results show that the sample consisting of the highly motivated upper secondary students appreciated the gamification strategies applied to the DLE more than the moderately motivated students. This finding helps us to understand how our gamification strategies in a DLE can work with upper secondary students who are already self-motivated, and whether it helps keep their motivation high. In particular, highly motivated students appreciated gamification strategies related to the use of a leaderboard, the setting of a multi-level challenge, the possibility to accumulate points and rewards. They also stated that these elements increased their involvement and engagement in the online training. The use of storytelling and the contextualization of the online training within the SDGs of the 2030 Agenda were equally appreciated by both categories of students (moderately and highly motivated). In order to reduce the dropout and stimulate even the least motivated students, it may be necessary to explore more targeted and personalized gamification strategies. For the next edition of the DMT project, we would like to create an initial questionnaire to understand the type of participants in the online training and propose targeted gamification strategies.

References

1. Gounaridou, A., Siamtanidou, E., Dimoulas, C.: A serious game for mediated education on traffic behavior and safety awareness. Educ. Sci. **11**(3), 127 (2021). https://doi.org/10.3390/educsci11030127
2. Sümer, M., Aydın, C.H.: Design principles for integrating gamification into distance learning programs in higher education: a mixed method study. Int. J. Serious Games **9**(2), 79–91 (2022)
3. Deterding, S., Dixon, D., Khaled, R., Nacke L.E.: gamification: toward a definition. In: CHI 2011 Gamification Workshop Proceedings, pp. 12–15, Vancouver (2011)
4. Behl, A., Choudrie, J., Giudice, M., Islam, N., Nirma, J., Vijay, P.: Gamification and e-learning for young learners: A systematic literature review, bibliometric analysis, and future research agenda. Technological Forecasting & Social Change **176**(C), (2022)
5. De la Peña, D., Lizcano, D., Martínez-Álvarez, I.: Learning through play: gamification model in university-level distance learning. Entertainment Comput. **39**(2), 1–24 (2021)
6. Caponetto, I., Earp, J., Ott, M.: gamification and education: a literature review. In: Busch, C. (ed.) 8th European Conference on Games Based Learning, vol. 1, pp. 50–57. Curran Associates, Inc., Red Hook (2014)
7. Commission, E.: The European Digital Competence Frameworks for Citizens. Publications Office of the European Union, Luxembourg (2016)
8. Azmi, S., Iahad, N.A., Ahmad, N.: Gamification in online collaborative learning for programming courses: a literature review. ARPN J. Eng. Appl. Sci. **10**(23), 1–3 (2015)
9. Barana, A., Marchisio, M., Rabellino, S.: Comunità di apprendimento con Moodle 3. MediaTouch 2000, Italia (2021)
10. Fissore, C., Fradiante, V., Marchisio, M., Pardini, C.: design didactic activities using gamification: the perspective of teachers. In: Nunes, M. B., Isaías, P., Issa, T., Issa, T. (eds.) Proceedings of E-Learning and Digital Learning, pp. 11–18. IADIS Press, Porto (2023)
11. Chorianopoulos, K., Giannakos, M.N.: Design principles for serious video games in mathematics education: from theory to practice. Int. J. Serious Games **1**(3), 51–59 (2014)
12. Fissore, C., Fradiante, V., Marchisio, M.: The generalization of the solution process in a mathematical problem- solving activity with an advanced computing environment. In: Jovanovic, J., Chounta, I. A., Uhomoibhi J., McLaren, B. (eds.) Proceedings of the 15th International Conference on Computer Supported Education, vol. 2, pp. 426–433. Scitepress, Prague (2023)
13. Fissore, C., Floris, F., Marchisio, M., Rabellino, S.: Learning analytics to monitor and predict student learning processes in problem solving activities during an online training. In: IEEE (ed.) Proceedings of 47th Annual Computers, Software, and Applications Conference, pp. 481–489. Turin (2023)
14. Barana, A., Marchisio, M.: From digital mate training experience to alternating school work activities. Mondo Digitale **15**(64), 63–82 (2016)
15. United Nations Website, https://sdgs.un.org/goals, Accessed 22 Sep 2023

Author Index

P. Dondio et al. (Eds.): GALA 2023, LNCS 14475, pp. 471–473, 2024.
https://doi.org/10.1007/978-3-031-49065-1

Printed in the United States
by Baker & Taylor Publisher Services